CAUSATION AND RESPONSIBILITY

Causation and Responsibility

An Essay in Law, Morals, and Metaphysics

MICHAEL S MOORE

OXFORD
UNIVERSITY PRESS

OXFORD
UNIVERSITY PRESS

Great Clarendon Street, Oxford OX2 6DP

Oxford University Press is a department of the University of Oxford.
It furthers the University's objective of excellence in research, scholarship,
and education by publishing worldwide in

Oxford New York

Auckland   Cape Town Dar es Salaam   Hong Kong   Karachi
Kuala Lumpur Madrid Melbourne Mexico City   Nairobi
New Delhi Shanghai   Taipei Toronto
With offices in
Argentina Austria Brazil Chile Czech Republic France Greece
Guatemala Hungary Italy Japan South Korea Poland Portugal
Singapore Switzerland Thailand Turkey Ukraine Vietnam

ISBN 978-0-19-959951-6

Printed and bound in Great Britain by
CPI Antony Rowe, Chippenham and Eastbourne

For my long-established circle of fellow 60-something friends and colleagues in criminal law theory.

Preface

This is a long book, so it may be worthwhile giving a road map as to where it is headed. The general conception is to relate two contexts in which causation figures, that of legal and moral responsibility on the one hand, and that of scientific explanation on the other. The central idea that organizes the book is that causation as a prerequisite to legal liability is intimately related to causation as a natural relation lying at the heart of scientific explanation. This central idea is based on two thoughts, one is metaethics and the other is legal theory. The metaethical postulate is that moral responsibility (like all moral properties) supervenes on natural properties like causation, intention, and the like. The postulate of legal theory is that legal liability in (torts and criminal law) falls only on those who are morally responsible.

This book defends neither of these postulates, that being a task undertaken elsewhere.[1] The book rather uses the central idea as its guiding hypothesis and seeks to show in detail how it plays out. Analytically, the book thus has two parts: one in legal and moral theory, and the other in the metaphysics of causation. As originally conceived, the book was literally to be so divided. The first half was to plumb both legal doctrine and the morality that underlay it for presuppositions of what causation must be like; the second half would examine the metaphysics of causation, seeking to extract a metaphysics that both matched the law's pre-suppositions and that was independently plausible. In the writing of the book it became evident that such complete separation of legal/moral discussions from metaphysical discussions would interrupt the natural flow of the argument. Thus, for example, metaphysics intrudes in Chapter 12, in the middle of the discussions of intervening causation and accomplice liability, because one cannot assess the viability of those legal doctrines without taking a position on metaphysical issues. As another example, the critique of the counterfactual and nomic sufficiency theories of the metaphysics of causation is interrupted by the moral/legal thesis of Chapter 18, which is that counterfactual dependency is a desert basis independent of causation.

Still, the book generally proceeds from legal and moral usages of 'cause' to those usages involved in ordinary and scientific explanations. Part I deals with legal and moral doctrines framed in causal terms. Chapter 1 of that part examines legal liability rules in tort and criminal law. The essential thesis of the chapter is that our liability scheme in both areas of law is causation-drenched, and that this is so irrespective of whether those liability doctrines use the word 'cause'

---

[1] See Michael Moore, *Objectivity in Law and Ethics* (Aldershot: Ashgate, 2004); Moore, *Placing Blame: A general theory of the criminal law* (Oxford: Clarendon Press, 1997).

explicitly or whether those doctrines use causally complex verbs of action like 'hit', 'kill' , and 'disfigure'. Chapter 2 leaves the law for the morality underlying it; the question is whether these areas of law should be so focused on causation. The thesis of the chapter is that moral blame depends in part on whether one caused the harm one intended, foresaw, or risked, and that therefore any legal doctrines depending on such degrees of moral blameworthiness rightly take causation into account in framing its liability rules.

Chapter 3 combines a legal with a moral thesis because the open-ended legal provisions on necessity and balance of evils simply reference whatever morality holds to be the correct balance here. The issue is when good consequences can (legally and morally) justify the violation of seemingly categorical norms, such as those norms prohibiting killing and torture. The thesis of the chapter is that causation plays a large role in drawing the line of permissible consequentialist justifications in morality and thus, in law.

Part II leaves off Part I's concern with the _role_ of causation in legal doctrines and moral norms, and turns to the presuppositions about the _nature_ of causation made by such doctrines and norms. Chapter 4 begins with an examination of the law's own explicit theory about those presuppositions. The aim of the chapter is largely taxonomical, aiming to arrive at a workable taxonomy of legal tests of causation. But by charting the heavy qualifications the law itself adds to what I describe as the standard legal tests about causation, I intend also to cast doubt on whether the law is committed to the concept of causation these tests _say_ it is committed to.

Chapters 5 and 6 leave the law's _explicit_ theorizing about causation in favor of teasing out the law's _implicit_ concept(s) of causation. Here I seek to draw out what the law must be committed to about causation implicitly, in light of what the law does with causation in its explicit legal doctrines. This is a matter of reconstructing a concept implicit in a body of practices, a matter always involving some interpretive choices. The thesis of these chapters is that the law's implicit concept of causation differs little from a concept of causation embedded in common sense explanations and evaluations of human behavior.

As Chapter 4 observes, there are three doctrinally dominant tests for proximate causation. These are the foreseeability, the harm-within-the-risk, and the direct-cause theories. Having said elsewhere my piece about foreseeability,[2] I in this book focus on the harm-within-the-risk and direct-cause theories. Parts III and IV are devoted, respectively, to each of these theories.

Part III deals with the risk theory. Chapter 7 lays out the history and essential tenets of the theory. I do this in some detail because the theory has been the standard educated view on proximate causation within the American legal

---

[2] In Moore, 'Foreseeing harm opaquely', in J Gardner, S Horder, and S Shute (eds), _Action and Value in Criminal Law_ (Oxford: Oxford University Press, 1993), reprinted in Moore, _Placing Blame_, Chapter 8.

academy for most of the last one hundred years. It was the favored approach of 'the best and the brightest' of tort theory in America in the 1920s, the dominant approach of the leading criminal-law theorists of the 1950s, and has returned as the dominant approach of those tort theorists in America responsible for the third iteration of the *Restatement of Torts*. After Chapter 7's largely historical introduction, Chapters 8, 9, and 10 then seek to critique this dominant theory. They do this by urging that as applied to crimes and torts of negligence, the harm-within-the-risk test in incoherent (Chapter 8); that as applied to crimes and torts of negligence, the test is morally undesirable (Chapter 9); and that as applied to any crimes or torts, the test does not address the issues that tests of proximate causation do and should address (Chapter 10).

Part IV deals with the direct cause theory. Chapter 11 lays out the doctrinal intricacies of the test, spending considerable time on the crucial idea of an intervening cause. Chapter 12 looks at the metaphysical possibilities for making sense of there being (literally) breakers of causal chains. The thesis of the chapter is that nothing in nature answers to the concept of an intervening cause. (A related subsidiary thesis of Chapter 13 is that no artificial construction of legal policy can do the justifying work needed doing, either.) The upshot is that the direct-cause test is not viable, except as a rule of thumb about substantiality of causation.

Chapter 13 then raises the question of what should become of the criminal law doctrines of accomplice liability once the supposition on which that doctrine is based—that of intervening causation—is discarded. The answer, unsurprisingly, is that the various doctrines of accomplice liability also should go, which is the bottom-line conclusion of the chapter.

The book then turns to the metaphysics of causation. There are two questions raised in such metaphysics: what is the nature of the things related by causation, and what is the nature of the relationship between those things? Parts V and VI deal with those two metaphysical questions.

Part V has two chapters. The first of these, Chapter 14, seeks to lay out a taxonomy of the sorts of things that may plausibly be thought to be related by causation, things like events, facts, states of affairs, objects, persons, properties, etc. Chapter 14 begins with the law's framing of this issue, both because there is wisdom in the law's simplified taxonomy of these possibilities and because the law is our ultimate interest here. The thesis of the chapter is that all plausible causal relata can be reduced either to coarse-grained things (events under the Davidsonian conception of them) or to relatively fine-grained things (either tropes, states of affairs, or facts).

Chapter 15 seeks some resolution about what causal relata might actually be, amongst these four possibilities. The metaphysical resolution is that one of the fine-grained things, states of affairs, is the true relata of the causal relation. The relation most desirable for use in law is different: (coarse-grained) events are the relata on which legal liability should turn, recognizing that such relata will be constructions based on the true relata of the causal relations, which are states of affairs.

Part VI examines three leading sorts of theories as to the nature of the causal relation, the counterfactual theory, generalist theories (including nomic sufficiency, probabalist, and Humean regularity theories), and singularist theories. The counterfactual theory receives the most attention. This is in part because of the dominance of such theory in both law and recent philosophy. But also, as I explore in Chapter 18, there is something roughly right about the theory as it pertains to responsibility assessments, and thus the theory would require such attention even if lawyers and philosophers were not so preoccupied with it.

Chapter 16 begins with an examination of counterfactual conditionals generally, without reference to using them as the reduction base for causation. The thesis of the chapter is that there are two analytically distinct and historically important conceptions of these conditionals. These are: (1) the older, law-related view; and (2) the newer, possible-worlds account. I focus on the latter in framing the discussion about causation, although my own long-term bets are on the former conception of counterfactuals.[3]

Chapter 17 examines the counterfactual theory of causation, applying the possible world conception of counterfactuals. For a variety of reasons I conclude that not only is causation not to be identified with counterfactual dependency, but such dependency is also not either a necessary or a sufficient condition for causation. Such dependency is thus unreliable as a test for when causation is present or absent.

Chapter 18 nonetheless defends counterfactual dependency as a desert determiner, independent of causation. Lawyers have not been wrong in looking for such dependency as the touchstone for liability for omissions, preventions, double preventions, and cases of de minimis causal contribution (they have only been mistaken in lumping such dependencies in as a kind of causation). The thesis of Chapter 18 is that in such cases counterfactual dependency determines moral responsibility and legal liability quite independently of causation.

Chapter 19 returns to the metaphysics of the causal relation proper. The chapter examines generalist theories of causation, theories that seek to reduce that relation to some law-based relation. Particular attention is paid to the one such generalist theory that has had a large influence in legal theory. This is the nomic sufficiency theory of John Stuart Mill and his intellectual descendents, Hart, Honore, Mackie, and Wright. The thesis of the chapter is that generalist theories founder on the same seven arguments that doom the counterfactual theory as well.

Chapter 20 concludes with an overview of singularist theories of the causal relation. A variety of singularist sorts of theories are distinguished and assessed for their relative plausibility. My own conclusion is that some such theory best survives the metaphysical tests for a good theory of causation. Some such theory is also the theory closest to the common-sense view of causation examined in Chapters 5 and 6, and, because of that, the theory is also closest to the legal

---

[3] For the kinds of reasons suggested in Richard Fumerton, 'Moore, causation, counterfactuals and responsibility', San Diego Law Review 40 (2003), 1274–7.

presuppositions of what causation must be like. I do not choose precisely which singularist theory will win the contemporary tournament of theories going on in modern metaphysics.

The book throughout focuses on causation as an element of responsibility for some harm in situations where one's obligations are not voluntarily undertaken by promise. This is the kind of moral responsibility that underlies the law of torts and of crimes. The book closes by dealing with responsibility for breach of promise-based obligations; thus, the Appendix deals with causation in the law of contract. The distinctive nature of promissory obligations, it is argued, places different demands on the concept of causation than those placed upon the concept by the law of crimes and torts. Nonetheless some common ground is found in the incorporation of causation's requirements by the explicit or implied terms in particular contracts. The point is given an extended illustration in the contract of insurance on the Twin Towers in New York City, which insured the leaseholder of the Towers against all risks up to the amount of approximately $3.6 billion 'per occurrence'. The crucial language, 'per occurrence', is standardly interpreted by a 'causal test' under New York insurance law, and the Appendix enquires into just what that means in the context.

Each of these chapters and the Appendix was written with an eye both to separate preliminary publication as a free standing article and to subsequent integration into this book. I have sought to rewrite each chapter to eliminate redundancies, supply cross-references and ease transitions. Hopefully the organization and state of the whole has not been hampered by the requirements of such separate, preliminary publication.

It may seem surprising that in a book on causation in the law little attention is given to formulating some precise test of causation to be given to legal fact-finders. There are a number of reasons for this. One lies in my own skepticism about the utility of giving detailed doctrinal tests to juries on issues where ordinary folk already have strong, common intuitions. Consider in this regard the example of the legal tests for insanity. Volumes have been written on how legal insanity should be defined, and the resulting variety of legal formula is considerable.[4] Despite this, many jurors who intuitively understand the general idea that insanity is a kind of loss of moral agency ignore the legal verbiage when they retire, asking only if the accused is mad or not.[5] Another example is that of

---

[4] See Moore, *Law and Psychiatry: Rethinking the relationship* (Cambridge: Cambridge University Press, 1984), Chapter 6.

[5] As the Royal Commission on Capital Punishment observed about the insanity tests prevailing in England: 'Howevermuch you charge a jury as to the M'Naghten Rules or any other test, the question they would put to themselves when they retire is—"Is this man mad or is he not?" (*Royal Commission on Capital Punishment 1949–53 Report* (London: Her Majesty's Stationary Office, 1953), 112) As the Commission observed, this is a matter of common sense prevailing over the stated tests for insanity: '[W]hen common sense says the verdict should be "guilty but insane" and the M'Naghten Rules say it should be "guilty", judges and juries usually recognize that common sense must prevail.' (Ibid)

intention. As Justice Holmes famously quipped, 'even a dog knows the difference between being stumbled over and being kicked',[6] in which event detailed instructions about intention in terms of, say, recent neuroscience would be unnecessary and unhelpful.

The same is true of causation. The view of the relation this book ultimately defends is singularist. Not necessarily a primitivist singularism, as that is described in Chapter 20, but perhaps instead a physically reductionist version of singularism. On the latter kind of theory, the ultimate truth about causation will often be unknown in those particular cases where the causal conclusion is not itself difficult to reach. Under either kind of singularist theory, the jurors' intuitive understanding of the relation may be a better heuristic than would attempts at speculating about the physics of the situation.

There are some things that should *not* be said about causation to legal fact-finders—indeed, most of the things the law now tells them. The law now tells them that: there are two distinct causal enquiries, that of cause-in-fact and that of proximate causation (rather than one enquiry about substantiality of causal contribution); that the cause-in-fact enquiry exhausts the scientific question of causation whereas the proximate cause enquiry is a matter for normative judgment as to how far liability should extend; that the scientific notion of causation is that of counterfactual dependency, or minimal sufficiency, or raises in the conditional probability of an effect, or of necessity of the effect having the probability it did in fact have; that effects counterfactually depend on events that accelerate, but not on events that delay, those effects; that particular harms were either foreseeable or unforeseeable to defendants at the time at which they acted, but not both; that there is *a* risk that makes one negligent so that in each case it should be asked whether the harm that happened was within that risk; that certain kinds of events, if they intervene between the defendant's action and some later harm, sever any causal connection between the two that otherwise might have existed; that at least some omissions are causes; that to prevent something is to cause that thing not to exist; etc.

These common legal sayings are all false, and because false, probably misleading to be told to legal fact-finders. One has to be careful here, because successful heuristics are where you find them, and it is possible that telling literally false statements can produce better decisions than would be obtained by telling nothing but the truth.[7] But usually we do better in giving instructions that say plainly what we think to be true, just as usually the best way to hit a target

---

[6] Oliver Wendell Holmes, Jr, *The Common Law* (Boston: Little, Brown, 1881), 7.

[7] In the context of insanity instructions, for example, Abraham Goldstein once urged that the so-called 'justly held responsible' definition of legal insanity might produce less accurate decisions by the jury, not because that test inaccurately defined insanity, but because it put too much pressure on jurors (by making painfully obvious their complete responsibility in deciding on an accused's future). Goldstein, *The Insanity Defense* (New Haven: Yale University Press, 1967), 82.

with an arrow is to aim straight at it. In which event telling jurors these and other falsehoods about causation, risk, and counterfactual dependency, is not helpful.

The main reason why the book gives only occasional attention to legal tests for causation stems from my interests in writing it, which are more theoretical than practical. Many legal theoreticians believe that it is not causation that is at the core of legal and moral prohibitions, it rather being proposed that some mysteriously irreducible human agency is the core natural property on which moral responsibility supervenes.[8] They believe, alternatively, that neither causing harm nor being an agent of harm adds to one's blameworthiness beyond the blameworthiness already earned by intending, trying, or risking that harm's occurrence.[9] They believe, alternatively, that the doctrine of doing and allowing 'is a mess', that the causal distinctions at the root of that doctrine are myriad, confused, empty, or otherwise without moral merit.

Moreover, many legal theorists not only doubt the relevance of causation to legal and moral judgments; they also doubt that there is any fact of the matter about causation itself. This skepticism then inclines them to accept some policy-based substitutes for causation, such as the foreseeability and the harm within the risk tests. Or they flee to some more direct policy calculus, be it economic or otherwise.

Such legal theorists also find the metaphysics of causation to be hard. They thus have some incentive to find it insoluable, arbitrary, irrelevant, or even undemocratic. They want to agree with Sir Frederick Pollock, who years ago proclaimed that 'the lawyer cannot afford to adventure himself with the philosopher on the metaphysics of causation'.[10] One basis for avoiding this adventure is to think that legal purposes justify the lawyer in creating his own notions of causation, one unique to the law and one immune to the challenges of metaphysical critiques.[11]

This book is mostly written to correct these errors of legal theory. That there are also practical, doctrinal pay-offs is nice but not essential. Law schools were once defined as the unholy mixture of Plato's Academy and the training ground

[8] Eg, John Gardner, 'Moore on complicity and causality', University of Pennsylvania Law Review PENNumbra 156 (2008), 432–3. I directly answer the 'mysterians' about human agency in Moore, 'The mysterious agency of the mysterians', forthcoming in JH Aguilar and AA Buckareff (eds), *Causing Human Action: New perspectives on the causal theory of action* (Cambridge, Mass: MIT Press, a Bradford book, 2009).
[9] Eg, Larry Alexander and Kimberly Kessler Ferzan, with contributions by Stephen Morse, *Crime and Culpability: A theory of criminal law* (Cambridge: Cambridge University Press, 2008).
[10] Sir Frederick Pollock, *Torts* (6th edn, New York: Banks Law Publishing Co, 1901), 36.
[11] Jane Stapleton, 'Choosing what we mean by "causation" in the law', Missouri Law Review (2008), 433–480, a shorter version appearing under the title, 'Causation in the law', in Helen Beebee, Peter Menzies and Chris Hitchcock (eds), *Oxford Handbook of Causation* (Oxford: Oxford University Press, 2008). Stapleton believes that 'causal language can be used to express information from a variety of interrogations into our world pursed for different purposes . . .'. From this (true enough) observation of ordinary language she concludes that the search for a unitary concept of causation—or worse, a unitary metaphysical nature—a real rather than a nominal essence—is a 'doomed project', that can only produce 'myths' for answers. Ibid, n 15.

for young Hessian mercenaries.[12] This book is on the Academy side of that line. I assume that it is worthwhile figuring out the function and nature of a property like causation, both in the law and out. There are practical benefits of achieving such understanding, but the reason for making the effort is, for me, mostly because it is there to be understood.

Writing this book has been a long-ongoing process and a large number of people have contributed to its completion. The students who have filled some of my seminars over the years communicated their insights and their enthusiasm, making this book a good deal more fun to write. This includes the law students in my Advanced Torts class at the University of Southern California who in 1989 opted to explore the legal literature on causation in extra sessions of that class; the philosophy students at the University of Pennsylvania who took my Philosophy of Action class and the Penn law students who took my moral luck classes; the law students in my seminar at the University of Virginia who worked through (what one of them accurately described as) the 'bone dry' literature in the history of causation in law; the philosophy students who filled my seminars on moral luck and on the metaphysics of causation at the University of Illinois Philosophy Department; finally, and most of all, the law students at the University of Illinois College of Law, who with interest and good humor worked through the present manuscript chapter by chapter in their seminar in the Fall of 2007. One of these students, Bill Houlihan, wrote his senior paper on causal apportionment, which was quite helpful to me in redrafting that section of Chapter 5.

A number of my colleagues in philosophy and in legal theory were kind enough to gather together in November 2006 to discuss the various topics raised in this book. This was at the Roundtable on Causation and Responsibility held at Timberline Lodge on Mt Hood, Oregon. I am indebted to the participants at that Roundtable—David Armstrong, Patrick Suppes, Peter Menzies, Dagfinn Follesdahl, Richard Fumerton, Michael Rota, Leo Katz, Claire Finkelstein, John Oberdiek, Laurie Paul, Jonathan Schaffer, Evan Fales, Phil Dowe, Doug Ehring—for lending their time and their energy to this project. I am particularly indebted to Richard Fumerton for his co-hosting of this event with me.

Also helpful to the project of this book were two earlier roundtables. One was the Roundtable on Causation and Probability, held in January 2004, at the Furnace Creek Inn in Death Valley, California, and jointly sponsored by the programs of Law and Philosophy, and Law and Economics, of the University of Illinois, together with the Institute for Law and Philosophy of the University of San Diego. The other was the Roundtable on The Law and the Metaphysics of Causation held at Druim Moir in Philadelphia in November, 1999, and sponsored by the Institute for Law and Philosophy of the University of Pennsylvania. The comments at these roundtables of Heidi Hurd, Simon Blackburn, Alvin

---

[12] Alan Stone, 'Legal education on the couch', *Harvard Law Review* 85 (1971), 392–411.

Goldman, Richard Fumerton, Chris Hitchcock, Richard Wright, and Ken Kress, stand out in memory as being particularly helpful to me.

As the Acknowledgements pages make plain, I have individually defended the chapters comprising this book in many venues. I am indebted to the audiences at these numerous gatherings for their many helpful comments and suggestions. The book is better because of them.

Particularly to be singled out are those who commented separately on various chapters of the book at or after these various presentations. These include Dana Nelkin and Kim Ferzan, each of whom separately commented on an earlier draft of Chapter 2; John Klenig, for his written comments on Chapters 1 and 2; Mitch Berman, for his written comments on Chapter 3; John Oberdiek, for his extended oral and written comments on Chapter 3; Richard Fumerton, for his oral commentary on Chapter 3 at the Mt Hood Conference, for his oral and written comments on Chapters 16 and 17 in San Diego, and for his written comments on Chapter 19; Jane Stapleton, Laurie Paul, and Peter Menzies for their detailed commentaries on Chapters 14–17 at the Centre for Law and Philosophy of the Australian National University; Peter Cane, who graciously arranged not only for the symposium at ANU at which these last commentaries were given, but also my visiting fellowships at ANU in 2002, 2004, and 2008, each of which made the writing of this book possible; Chris Kutz and Michael Corrado, for their separate written comments following the presentations of Chapters 14 and 15 at New York University; Stephen Perry, who commented on an earlier version of Chapters 5 and 6 at a workshop at the University of Pennsylvania Law School; Leo Katz, Alvin Goldman, Ken Abraham, Ellen Frankel-Paul, and Al Mele, who gave me helpful comments on Chapters 5 and 6 at the Center for Philosophy and Social Policy in Ohio; Chris Hitchcock and Sharon Lloyd, for their comments on Chapters 16 and 17 at the University of Southern California Philosophy Department; Jon Elster, for his commentary at Columbia University on Chapters 16 and 17, together with his co-sponsors of the Mellon Seminar at which these comments were given, Brian Barry and Akeel Bilgrami; Phil Dowe, for his probing questions at the presentation of Chapter 18 at the University of Queensland; Stephen Morse, for his detailed commentary on Chapters 11–12 at their presentation at the University of California, Berkeley; Chris Hitchcock, for his separate written comments on Chapters 11 and 12; Sandy Kadish and Meir Dan-Cohen, for their fruitful questions at my presentation of Chapter 13 at the University of California at Berkeley; John Gardner and Tony Duff, for their on-line commentaries on Chapter 13; Richard Epstein for some very early suggestions about the non-causal nature of preventions, made in his reply to my commentary on his work at the Center for Public Choice in Blacksburg, Virginia. All of these people, and many more besides, have had a causal impact on the content of this book. If there is praise to be had, I gladly share it with them. Blame too.

The research for this book, like all of my research these past six years, has been generously supported by the research funds attached to the Walgreen University Chair and to the Center for Advanced Study Professorship, both of which I hold at the University of Illinois. These two research funds supported the Mt Hood Conference; they also supported all three of my fellowships at the ANU in Canberra. The freedom such support makes possible is invaluable to a project such as the present one.

Finally, I feel a particular warmth in acknowledging the influence of my long-established circle of fellow 60-something (plus, in some cases) friends and colleagues in criminal-law theory. I mean Stephen Morse, Herbert Morris, Sandy Kadish, Richard Fumerton, Larry Alexander, Meir Dan-Cohen, Herbert Fingarette, Doug Husak, Michael Shapiro, Hans Oberdiek, George Fletcher, Kent Greenawalt, David AJ Richards, Paul Robinson, Jeffrie Murphy, Peter Westen, Phil Montague, Judy Thomson, Tony Duff, Joachim Hruschka, John Kleinig, and Leo Katz (an honorary 60-something, to be sure). We have been something of a wart hog going through the python of life together, an age-concentrated cohort of like-minded thinkers who have regarded the criminal law as a marvelous opportunity to combine abstract theory with practical concerns. Together with the now deceased Jean Hampton, John Kaplan, Herbert Hart, and Joel Feinberg, they have for me made the scholarship that would otherwise have been a solitary endeavor, an enjoyable social as well as intellectual enterprise. I feel fortunate in having had the encouragement and contributions of such companions.

Special thanks go to my assistant at the University of Illinois, Amy Fitzgerald. In addition to keeping some semblance of order in my professional life generally, she has input every word of this book, initially as separate articles, and then again as a book manuscript. Her transformation of my yellow pad scrawlings into the manuscript from which the following pages were printed was not only professionally exemplary, but also an act of personal friendship.

Lastly, my life-long partner in crime, Heidi Hurd has suffered through yet another set of conversations on topics that I know are of less than consuming interest to her philosophically. Of particularly fond memory is a lengthy (and apparently loud) debate between the two of us on the metaphysics of causation, had in 1987 at the El Tovar Bar on the South Rim of the Grand Canyon waiting for the weather to clear so we could take our annual 'rim to rim and back again' hike. We were so lost in disagreement on the fine points about counterfactuals as not to notice that the entire, crowded bar had ceased their own conversations to listen. But for such conversations, this book would never have been written. For sharing this, as well as many other things, I will always be grateful.

Michael Moore
Canberra, Australia
June, 2008

Acknowledgements

Chapter 1   The discussion of this chapter builds on portions of Chapter 8 of Michael S Moore, *Act and Crime: The Implications of the Philosophy of Action for the Criminal Law* (Oxford: Clarendon Press, 1993).

Chapter 2   The discussion of this chapter builds on the discussion of 'The Independent Moral Significance of Wrongdoing', given at the Conference on Culpability versus Harm at the Organizing Principle of the Criminal Law, University of San Diego, 1994, first published in Journal of Contemporary Legal Issues 5 (1994), 1–45, reprinted in Michael Moore, *Placing Blame: A general theory of the criminal law* (Oxford: Clarendon Press, 1997); this chapter itself was given at the Roundtable on Retributive Punishment, Institute for Law and Philosophy, University of San Diego, 2008, and has not been previously published.

Chapter 3   From 'Patrolling the borders of consequentialist justification', given as the 2005 Natural Law Lecture, Fordham University, to the Institute for Law and Philosophy, Rutgers University, 2005, to the University of Illinois Roundtable on Causation and Responsibility, Mt Hood, Oregon, November 2006, and to the Political Philosophy Forum of Cambridge University, Cambridge, England, November, 2007; first published in Law and Philosophy 27 (2008), 35–96.

Chapter 4   An extensive rewrite of 'Causation', first given at the Faculty of Law, University of Erlangen-Nurnberg, Germany, 2000, then at the University of San Diego, School of Law, 2000, then to the Department of Philosophy, University of California at San Diego, 2001; first published in Joshua Dressler (ed), *Encyclopedia of Crime and Justice* (2nd edn, New York: Macmillan, 2000).

Chapters 5   From 'Causation and responsibility', given at the Conference on
and 6   Responsibility, Center for Social Philosophy and Policy, Bowling Green State University, Bowling Green, Ohio, 1998, then to the Faculty Workshop, University of Pennsylvania Law School, Philadelphia, 1998, then to the Faculty of Law, Chiba University, Tokyo, Japan, 2003, then to the Faculty of Law, Kyoto University, Kyoto, Japan, 2003; first published in Social Philosophy and Policy 16 (1999), 1–51, reprinted in E Paul, F Miller and J Paul (eds), *Responsibility* (Cambridge: Cambridge University Press, 1999).

Chapters 7,   'Negligence in the air' (with H Hurd), first given at the Con-
8, 9, and 10   ference on Negligence in the Law, Faculty of Law, Tel Aviv
                   University, 2001, then to the Faculty Workshop Series, UCLA
                   School of Law, Los Angeles, 2001, and to the Faculty Collo-
                   quium, University of North Carolina Law School, Chapel Hill,
                   2001; first published in Theoretical Inquiries in Law 3 (2002),
                   333–411.

Chapters 11   From 'The metaphysics of causal intervention', first given at the
and 12   Symposium in Honor of Sanford Kadish, School of Law (Boalt
                   Hall), University of California, Berkeley, 1999; first published
                   in California Law Review 88 (2000), 827–77.

Chapter 13   First given at the Workshop of the Program in Criminal Law
                   and Procedure, University of Illinois, 2007, then to the Faculty
                   Colloquium, University of Pennsylvania Law School, 2007,
                   then to the General Aspects of Law Colloquium, University of
                   California at Berkeley, 2007, and then to the Faculty of Law,
                   Queen's University, Kingston, Ontario, as one of my Scholars
                   in Residence lectures; first published in the University of
                   Pennsylvania Law Review 156 (2007), 395–452.

Chapters 14   Given to the Ninth Annual Conference on Analytical Legal
and 15   Philosophy, New York University, New York City, 2004, and
                   to the Symposium, 'Moore on causation', Centre for Law and
                   Philosophy, Australian National University, June 2004; first
                   published in Sharon Byrd and JC Joerdan (eds), Philosophia
                   Practica Universalis: Festschrift for Joachim Hruschka, Annual
                   Review of Law and Ethics 13 (2005), 589–641.

Chapters 16   From 'For what must we pay? Causation and counterfactual
and 17   baselines', first given at the Conference on 'What Do Com-
                   pensatory Damages Compensate?', Institute for Law and Phil-
                   osophy of the University of San Diego, 2003, then to the
                   Philosophy Department Colloquium, University of Southern
                   California, 2003, then to the Symposium, 'Moore on caus-
                   ation', Centre for Law and Philosophy, Australian National
                   University, June 2004, then to the Mellon Seminar on
                   Responsibility, Columbia University, 2005; first published in
                   San Diego Law Review 40 (2003), 1181–272.

Chapter 18   First given at the Faculty Seminar, Department of Social and
                   Political Theory, Research School of Social Sciences, Australian
                   National University, Canberra, 2008, then to the Faculty
                   Workshop, Department of Philosophy, University of Queens-
                   land, Brisbane, 2008, and then as the keynote address, annual

meeting of the Australian Society of Legal Philosophy, Melbourne University, Melbourne, 2008; first published in the Australian Journal of Legal Philosophy, 2009.

Chapter 19   First given at the University of Illinois Conference on Criminal Law Theory, University Club of Chicago, 2008; first published in J Deigh and D Dolinko (eds), *Philosophy of Criminal Law* (Oxford: Oxford University Press, forthcoming, 2009).

Chapter 20   First written as the Introduction to the Symposium Issue on Singularist Theories of Causation, The Monist 91 (2008)(4).

Appendix   First given to the Faculty Workshop, University of Pennsylvania Law School, Philadelphia, 2002, then to the Faculty Workshop, Cardozo Law School of Yeshiva University, New York City, 2002, then to the Faculty Workshop, University of Illinois College of Law, 2002, then as a plenary paper at the annual meeting of the Australian Society of Legal Philosophy, Canberra, Australia, 2002, and then as a plenary paper at the annual meeting of the Royal Institute of Philosophy, New College of Oxford University, Oxford, England, 2002, and finally at the Law Faculty Workshop, Cornell University, 2005; first published in J Hyland and H Steward (eds), *Agency and Action* (Cambridge: Cambridge University Press, 2004).

Table of Contents

List of Cases

List of Statutes

PART I

THE ROLE OF CAUSATION IN MORAL AND LEGAL RESPONSIBILITY

1

The Embedding of Causation in Legal Liability Doctrines

Causation matters to legal liability. This is true in many areas of law, such as contract, property, and constitutional law. But the liability doctrines on which this book focuses are the doctrines of crimes and torts; this is because it is criminal law and the law of torts that are most directly reflective of an underlying moral responsibility. And it is the relationship between causation and moral responsibility that is the central concern of this book.

Many of the liability rules of both criminal law and torts are framed explicitly in terms of someone (usually the defendant) causing something (usually a harm). The Model Penal Code, for example defines homicide as the causing of the death of another human being.[1] Mayhem is often defined as the causing of disfigurement of another human being, child abuse, as the causing of abuse to a child, rape as the causing of penetration of a female, etc. Analogously, torts often defines battery as the causing of contact on the body of another, assault as the causing of apprehension of imminent contact, negligence as the causing of damage by the defendant's voluntary act, etc. In such doctrines, criminal law and tort law on their face seemingly predicate legal liability on causal responsibility, among other things.

It is of course possible that although the law uses the word 'cause', it does not refer to the causal relation. It is possible, in other words, that what these doctrines call causation has nothing to do with causation as a real relation in the world; rather, the possibility is that here as elsewhere the law uses a word in a technical, distinctively legal sense, even though the word already has an established meaning in non-legal English. This is certainly true with words like 'malice' (and even 'intention') in criminal law, and it is possibly so with regard to the law's usage of 'cause.'

Whether this is so depends on what sort of policies lie behind legal doctrines. Such policies can demand that ordinary words be given very non-ordinary meanings in legal contexts, or they can demand that legal usage conform to ordinary, non-legal meaning. If the policy behind tort and criminal law liability rules were, for example, to give incentives to desirable behavior by others in the

---

[1] American Law Institute, Model Penal Code, §210.1(1) (Proposed Official Draft, 1962).

future—a general deterrence rationale for such rules—then one might well legislate a very non-ordinary meaning to 'cause': one might well define 'cause' as some form of probability (because it is *ex ante* probabilities that rational actors can be given incentives to consider in making their choices, not *ex post* causation), even if probability in fact has nothing to do with causation.[2]

My own view, argued for at length elsewhere,[3] is that criminal law (and to a lesser extent, the law of torts) have as their dominant policies the achievement of retributive and corrective justice. If this is so, then criminal and tort liability must track moral responsibility, because justice is achieved only if the morally responsible are held liable to punishment or tort damages. If moral responsibility depends in part on causal responsibility—a point to be argued in the next two chapters—then 'cause' in law must mean what it means in morality.

It is sometimes suggested that 'cause' as it is used to ascribe moral responsibility still does not denote the natural relation in the world named when we use the word in scientific and common-sense explanations. The idea is that 'cause' used in moral discourse is but a misleading way of talking about moral responsibility itself. On this view, to say that Jones *caused* the damage is just to ascribe (perhaps prima facie) responsibility to him for the damage. In which case causation would be a way of stating the moral conclusion, but it would not be a ground for reaching it.[4]

Like many skeptical views, this old 'ascriptivist'[5] view of causation has an aura of realism and profundity. Yet to divorce 'cause', as used in ascribing moral responsibility, from 'cause' as used in explanations, and to equate the moral usage as a synonym for moral responsibility itself, leads to an embarrassing regress: if moral responsibility does not depend (in part) on causal responsibility—because causal responsibility is nothing different than moral responsibility—then on what natural property does the moral property (of responsibility) depend? Surely on

---

[2] Economists, for example, are usually concerned to recommend liability rules by their incentive effects. They accordingly define the causal elements of such liability rules in terms of probability. Guido Calabresi, 'Concerning cause and the law of torts: An essay for Harry Kalven Jr.', University of Chicago Law Review 43 (1975), 69–108; John Landes and Richard Posner, 'Causation in tort law: An economic approach', Journal of Legal Studies 12 (1983), 109–34; Steven Shavell, 'An analysis of causation and the scope of liability in the law of torts', Journal of Legal Studies 9 (1980), 463–503. For an overview, see generally Richard Wright, 'Actual causation vs. Probabilistic linkage: The bane of economic analysis', Journal of Legal Studies 14 (1985), 435–56.

[3] Michael S Moore, *Placing Blame: A general theory of the criminal law* (Oxford: Clarendon Press, 1997).

[4] For examples of three generations of skeptics about causation in legal theory, see Harry Edgarton, 'Legal cause', University of Pennsylvania Law Review 72 (1924), 211–44, 343–75; Wex Malone, 'Ruminations on cause-in-fact', Stanford Law Review 9 (1956), 60–99; Mark Kelman, 'The necessary myth of objective causation judgments in liberal political theory', Chicago-Kent Law Review 63 (1987), 579–637.

[5] I take the label, 'ascriptivist', from Herbert Hart's briefly held thesis that the function of causative verbs like, 'A hit B', was not to describe an event but to ascribe responsibility for it. HLA Hart, 'The ascription of rights and responsibilities', Proceedings of the Aristotelian Society 49 (1949), 171–94.

some; moral properties unrelated to natural properties would make for a very odd ontology, a 'non-naturalism' in ethics that many including myself find unacceptably counter to a scientific view of the world.[6]

It is better to think that 'cause' is univocal; it means the same thing in contexts of attributing responsibility as in contexts of explanation: it refers to a natural relation that holds between events or states of affairs. Because moral responsibility is tied to such a natural relation, and because the law is tied to morality, the law also is tied to this natural relation. In short, what criminal law and the law of torts mean by 'cause' is what we ordinarily mean by 'cause' as we explain the world, viz some kind of natural relation. It thus behooves us to enquire after the nature of such a relation.

Sometimes the liability rules of the criminal law and of torts do not use the word, 'cause.' Sometimes they use what linguists call 'causatives', those verbs that rather transparently seem to require that there be some causal relation even if they do not use the word, 'cause'. I refer to verbs like 'kill', 'hit', 'penetrate', 'disfigure', 'abuse', etc. Thus, liability doctrines that do not explicitly use the word 'cause' nonetheless define homicide (or wrongful death) as *killing*, not causing death; battery as *hitting*, not as causing contact; rape as *penetrating*, not as causing penetration; mayhem as *disfiguring*, not as causing disfigurement; child abuse as abusing a child, not as causing abuse; etc.

On the surface at least, the law of torts and of crimes treats this second form of liability doctrines as equivalent to the first. That is, 'killing' is treated as equivalent to 'causing death', 'hitting', with 'causing contact', etc. If this equivalence is true, then whenever the law uses causative verbs it is requiring causation as a prerequisite to liability fully as much as when it uses the word 'cause.'

The general form of the law's equivalence thesis is this: (1) for any causative verb 'v', X v-ed if and only if X did some act that caused a state of v-ing to exist. Sometimes the v-ing in this thesis will use the same root as the verb being tested, as in: 'X disfigured another if and only if X did some act that caused that other to be disfigured.' Sometimes the v-ing will use a different root, as in: 'X hit another if and only if X did some act that caused contact on the body of that other.' In either case, the thesis is the same; and it implies that causation is involved in all liability doctrines of criminal law and of torts.

Equivalences are of course bi-conditionals, that is, the conjunction of two conditionals. Thus, thesis (1) asserts both:

(2) If X v-ed, then X caused a v-ing to exist.

and

(3) If X caused a v-ing to exist, then X v-ed.

---

[6] On non-naturalism in ethics, philosophy of mind, and legal philosophy, see Michael Moore, 'Legal reality', Law and Philosophy 21 (2002), 657–64.

Thesis (2) is relatively uncontroversial within the philosophy of action. Surely, the thought is, you *kill* someone only if you cause their death. Only an infelicitous selection of states of affairs or events said to be caused by an act could tempt one to deny (2). Consider this example of Anthony Kenny's: 'Washing the dishes is bringing it about [ie causing] that the dishes are clean.'[7] One might well deny this on the ground that one can wash dishes so badly that one fails to get them clean—in which event it might seem that one v-ed without causing a v-ing to exist. Yet surely we need to match up the state of affairs caused more closely to the complex act description. Either: 'washing the dishes is to cause the dishes to be washed', or 'cleaning the dishes is to cause the dishes to be clean', will do. And these conditionals seem unproblematically true.

One might object here that the truth of (2) is being purchased at the price of triviality. That is, one might think that saying 'to wash the dishes is to cause them to be washed' is as trivial an implication as moving from an active voice to a passive one; as in moving from 'someone washed the dishes' to 'the dishes were washed by someone'.

True implications of the passive from the active are trivial. Both descriptions tell us the same thing, namely there was an act of washing the dishes done by someone. The verb 'wash' is univocal, no matter how it is voiced. Unnoticed, however, is that (2) is not trivial in this way because the verb is not used univocally. Change the example for a moment. It is not even tempting to think that 'death' names the same thing as 'killing'; 'death' names an event that can happen because of a human act causing it, but also in a myriad of other ways. Now see that the same is true about 'washed'. Dishes are washed whenever water runs over them, however that water is caused to do it. Dishes can be in a washed state by rainstorms and streams, even if that is not the usual ways in which they come to that state. To say 'X washed the dishes only if X caused the dishes to be washed' is thus as non-trivial as saying 'X killed another only if X caused the death of that other'.

What is missed about 'wash', 'penetrate', 'disfigure', etc, is the fundamental ambiguity in such English verbs (as in their nominalizations into nouns). The transitive sense of 'wash' is marked grammatically by its taking of an accusatory object (although 'Joe washed' is idiomatic, it is elliptical for 'Joe washed *himself*'). 'Washing' in this transitive sense refers to an action. 'Wash' in its intransitive sense has no such inference; it refers to something quite different, a state of affairs of (roughly) water moving over the thing washed. While it may seem obvious that to wash something is to cause that thing to be washed, it is not a tautalogical but a significant truth.[8]

The triviality objection has been pressed recently by John Gardner against my causal analysis of causative verbs.[9] Gardner complains that to analyze verbs like

---

[7] Anthony Kenny, *Action, Emotion, and Will* (London: Routledge, 1963), 177.

[8] Jennifer Hornsby, *Actions* (London: Routledge, 1980), 2–3.

[9] John Gardner, 'Moore on complicity and causality', University of Pennsylvania Law Review PENNumbra 156 (2008), 433–4.

'abuse' as the causing of abuse, is 'topsy-turvy'; such actions by some actor D 'do not consist in D's making any causal contribution c to any result r...This is because there is no independently specifiable result r, or no result r that consists of anything other than the action in question having been performed.'[10] To Gardner's ear, apparently, the state of being abused is not specifiable independently of an action of abusing; for Gardner, 'abuse' is an action of which the state is necessarily derivative. Yet notice that even if this is true about the accidents of English, nothing of interest follows about the conditional (2) above. Whether there is a state r of abuse—physical contacts of various kinds, for example—is not settled by our having or our lacking a word (or a sense of a word) with which to name it. This would be to reinvent the metaphysical naivety of ordinary language philosophy. Even if it were true that the only state of physical injury referred to by 'abuse' (as a noun) was a state caused by the agency of some person—a linguistic fact I doubt—that fact would go no distance towards showing that no such state exists, or that no causal relationship can exist with it as an effect.

Sub-thesis (2) is thus unproblematically true. Its only problem is that it is so obviously true that its significance is often overlooked. The conditional in (3) is much more controversial. This is the converse of (2), for now the claim is that to cause a v-ing is to v. If Jones causes the death of Smith, (3) asserts that necessarily, Jones killed Smith. Put more idiomatically, all there is to killing is causing death.

The truth of this conditional is not strictly needed here to show the prevalence of causal requirements in the liability rules of criminal law and torts. The truth of (2) is enough to show that. Yet (3) is not without interest for the larger project of this book. For if all there is to complex act descriptions like 'killing' is causing death, then whatever restrictions seem appropriate to the truth conditions of 'X killed Y' will also seem appropriate to causation. Theorists of causation have often been quite alive to this connection. Thus Hart and Honoré in their justly celebrated study of causation in the law subscribe to a version of (3) (insofar as they regard hittings, for example, to be the paradigm example of causings that give 'cause' its core or dominant sense).[11] Hart and Honoré are then able to use the restrictions on when one can truthfully assert, 'X hit Y', as restrictions on when one can truthfully say, 'X caused contact on Y.' At the other extreme, David Lewis (while refining his justly celebrated theory of causation) explicitly rejects (3);[12] this allows Lewis to disregard the limitations he too sees in the correct use of 'X hit Y' when Lewis is building a theory of causation to account for the truth conditions of 'X caused contact on Y'.

---

[10] Ibid, 434.

[11] HLA Hart and Tony Honoré, *Causation in the Law* (2nd edn, Oxford: Oxford University Press, 1985), 73.

[12] David Lewis, 'Postscripts to 'Causation', in *Philosophical Papers* II (Oxford: Oxford University Press, 1986), 184.

So like other theorists, we need to examine (3), and we might as well do so here. Does 'Jones caused the death of Smith' imply that Jones killed Smith? Most cases of causing-deaths-by-human-acts that come to mind are clearly killings so that this second entailment holds. Where Jones moves his finger on the trigger pointed at Smith's heart, causing the gun to discharge and thereby causing the death of Smith by the bullet lodged in Smith's heart, there is no doubt of the propriety of re-describing Jones's actions as 'killing Smith.' But there are a variety of related cases where we might think that Smith caused the death of Jones but that Smith did not *kill* Jones.

One such kind of case is where there is some spatial and temporal remoteness between Jones' act and the death. For example, Jones picks up a stone in a field and finding it too heavy, drops it on the side of a hill on his way home. During the course of a year normal weather patterns cause sufficient erosion that the stone rolls down the hill on to a path, and a year after that Smith's horse trips on the stone, throwing Smith on to it, which kills him. One might be tempted to say that Jones caused Smith's death but there seems to be little temptation to say that Jones killed Smith.[13]

A slightly different sort of case is presented where a death occurs as a result of some voluntary bodily movement, but that death comes about in a particularly freakish way. For example, Jones buys his wealthy uncle Smith an airplane ticket to a dangerous part of the world with the hope that something bad will happen to him so that Jones may accelerate his inheritance. Smith accepts Jones' gift of a free vacation with gratitude, and, as it happens, his plane crashes on its return to New York because of a once-in-a-lifetime wind-shear just off the runway at Kennedy Airport. Jones may have caused Smith's death, but did Jones kill Smith?[14]

Perhaps the most troublesome case for the thesis here considered is where another person's action is what Jones causes, and his/her action then causes the death of a third person. For example, Jones persuades X that Smith, having betrayed our organization, needs killing; or Jones orders X to kill Smith, X being Jones' military subordinate; or Jones threatens X with death of his family unless he kills Smith; or Jones knows that X intends to kill Smith if he can find him, and Jones tells X where Smith can be found; or Jones forces Smith at gunpoint to step outside knowing full well that X is waiting to kill him; or Jones tells X (truthfully or falsely) that Smith has been having an affair with X's wife, knowing full well X's explosive and uncontrollable temper and jealousy vis-á-vis his wife; and in all such cases, X shoots Smith dead. There may be some temptation in such cases to say that Jones caused Smith's death, but less temptation to say that Jones killed him—X did that.[15]

---

[13] The example is a variation of one found in Carl Ginet, *On Action* (Cambridge: Cambridge University Press, 1990), 5. See also Hornsby, *Actions*, 128.

[14] The example is from Kadish and Schulhofer (eds), *Criminal Law and Its Processes* (5th edn, Boston: Little, Brown, 1989), 228.

[15] See Judith Thomson, *Acts and Other Events* (Ithaca: Cornell University Press, 1997), 128.

There are of course two ways to deal with these cases so as to bring them into line with the equivalence thesis: either we can say that Jones did kill in each of these cases, or we can deny that Jones caused the various deaths. To start with, consider the first of these routes, that of stretching the extension of causative verbs to include all that causation itself includes. Leave 'killing' for the moment in favor of 'removing', an old example of Donald Davidson's. Davidson urged that 'The doctor's act caused the patient to have no appendix' does not imply the action description 'The doctor *removed* the patient's appendix'—for the doctor could cause the patient to have no appendix 'by running the patient down with his Lincoln Continental', in which case we would not say that 'the doctor removed the patient's appendix'.[16] Yet, we have to specify the effect caused with more precision than does Davidson here. We should compare 'The doctor re-moved$_T$ the patient's appendix' with 'The doctor's act caused the removal$_I$ of the patient's appendix.' The description 'removed$_T$ appendix' is not the same as the description 'having no appendix', in just the way that Davidson infers: the first description is more means-restrictive than is the second. So we should test the equivalence thesis with the first effect, not the second.

If we modify the example in this way, it is less plausible that a causing of a removal$_I$ would not be a removing$_T$. Suppose the doctor runs the patient down with his Lincoln Continental, hitting the patient in just the way that causes his appendix to fly out of his body. Has the doctor caused a removing$_I$ of the appendix? Suppose we concede *arguendo* that the answer to the second question is in the negative, that a removing$_T$ requires something like a surgical cutting as the means of getting the appendix out. Then I take such a means-restriction to be built into removing$_I$ too. Only something like a cutting (by something or someone) can be a removing$_I$. So the doctor did not cause a removing$_I$ of the appendix either. Alternatively, and more plausibly, if the doctor's 60s-style Lincoln has sharp edges that cut out the appendix with the deftness of a surgeon's scalpels, then the doctor did cause a removing$_I$ of the appendix. Of course, he also in such a case removed$_T$ the appendix, and the equivalence remains.

Jonathan Bennett, who is otherwise quite sympathetic to the equivalence thesis,[17] nonetheless thinks that some causally complex action verbs have individual names to them that are quite 'unmanageable'.[18] One of his examples: 'Suppose I contribute to a tree's falling by digging the earth away from its roots and burning them through; do I *fell* it? I am inclined to say no, but that seems to

[16] Davidson, *Essays on Actions and Events* (Oxford: Oxford University Press, 1980), 110–11.

[17] Jonathan Bennett, *Events and Their Names* (Indianapolis: Bobbs-Merrill, 1988), 221–9. According to Bennett, 'X killed Y' is equivalent to: (1) 'X (or X's movement) brought about Y's death' (ibid, 224); and (2) X's movement is pictured as being, in the circumstances, the sole input into Y's death (ibid, 224–6); and (3) no wholly intervening agency intervenes between X's movement and Y's death (ibid, 226–8). Bennett's restrictions (2) and (3) are his analogues to the proximate-cause limitations to be found in the law on when acts cause results, and to the same end: causally complex verbs can rather easily be given a casual analysis so long as causation is so restricted.

[18] Ibid, 230.

be partly because in communities with which I am familiar that is not a standard way of getting trees to fall.'[19] As a third example, consider a class of causally complex verbs to which Judy Thomson has drawn attention, verbs like 'kick', 'kiss', 'swallow', 'bite', 'slap', and 'punch'.[20] Such verbs seem to have quite explicit means-restrictions built into them. A kicking seems to require foot movement, for example, as a kissing requires lip movement, etc. The suggestion then is that 'X did some act that caused contact with Y's shin', does not entail 'X kicked Y's shin', for X might have caused such contact without moving his foot (ie without *kicking*). For example, 'If I start up a machine that a minute later thrusts my boot foot into your midriff, it need not ever be the case that I have kicked you.'[21]

My own view is that none of these examples does the work claimed for them. 'Remove', 'fell', and 'kick' do generate audience expectations about normal ways of removing appendixes, felling trees, or kicking others. These expectations get heightened and particularized when we are told that it was a doctor who did the removing, a lumberjack who did the tree-felling, or a little boy who did the kicking. Such expectations give us a kind of picture or stereotype of what such actions most commonly look like. Yet I see no reason to honor such stereotypical expectations with *semantic* dignity. Why should these individual nuances be part of the semantics of such verbs, rather than features of appropriate utterance on certain occasions? If one doctor tells another 'Remove the patient's appendix', he does not likely mean 'Use your sharp-edged Lincoln'; if a foreman tells a lumberjack to fell a tree, he does not mean 'Dig out its roots and burn them until the tree falls'; if one boy tells another 'Let's kick someone', he does not envision setting up a kicking machine. Yet the situations in which such utterances take place rule out these unusual removings, fellings, and kickings only because they are too unsafe, too time-consuming, or otherwise too impracticable. To my ear, each is nonetheless a literal removing, felling, or kicking. These situations are analogous to the situation in which one is told to 'pull up a chair' and join others for dinner—an easy chair is, semantically speaking, a perfectly good chair, but in the context of pulling it up to a dinner table it is a pragmatically deviant choice.

The 'kicking' class of verbs may seem to evade this response somewhat, for it may seem that 'kicking', 'kissing', etc involve specific body motions in the way that 'removing' and 'felling' do not.[22] Yet this is an illusion brought about by a failure to attend carefully to *what* must be caused in order for there to be a kicking, a kissing, etc. The actor's specific body parts are involved in such actions, but not

---

[19] Ibid, 229.
[20] Thomson, *Acts and Other Events*, 220–2. See also Bennett, *Events and Their Names*, 222–4.
[21] Bennett, *Events and Their Names*, 222.
[22] Thus, Thomson, *Acts and Other Events*, 220–1: 'Notice that you kick a thing only if you move something (you have to move your foot); you punch a thing only if you move something (your fist); you kiss something only if you move something (your lips); and so on . . . It seems very plausible that every event that is a kicking of something is a moving of a foot.'

as necessary means. Rather, some relation to such body parts is required as the state of affairs caused. The state of affairs involved in kissing is not just contact with the lips (or elsewhere) of another; it is contact between the lips of the actor and the lips or other body part of another. The state of affairs involved in kicking in the shins is not just contact with the shins of another; it is contact between the foot of the actor and the shins of another; etc. There is no requirement that the actor move his lips in order to kiss (it may well be a bad kiss if he does not move his lips, but a kiss nonetheless); the only requirement is that the actor move his body in some way so as to cause lip contact. There is similarly no requirement that an actor move his foot (as an act) in order to kick; granted, he will have to put the leg in motion by *some* act of his, but how he does this is irrelevant to his *kicking*.[23]

I conclude that there are no means-restrictions built into the meaning of causally complex verbs of action that make them more restrictive in their application than the corresponding causal idioms.

The verb, 'kill', does not have the implicit means-restrictions suggested by its idiomatic usage as does (perhaps) 'remove', 'fell', and 'kick'. So let us return to the three kinds of cases where 'X caused a v-ing' is not thought to entail, 'X v-ed', even for verbs like 'kill', namely cases where the causal link is attenuated, freakish, or involves an intervening third human agent. Let us for now put aside the first route to defending the equivalence thesis in the face of these examples. The second route may seem more promising. If we pursue this second route, we would deny that in any of these cases that Jones (or his acts) *caused* the deaths. This route demands, of course, that we employ some notion of 'cause' that is more restrictive than the counterfactual test lawyers regularly identify as 'causation-in-fact': but for my acts, would death have occured? By that minimalist notion of causation, Jones did cause the death of Smith in each of the above three examples.

Some linguists and philosophers despair of there being any more restrictive notion of causation available to rule out these apparent counter-examples to the equivalence thesis. Zeno Vendler, for example, sees the problem but refuses 'to trail off into the foggy regions in which causists and lawyers ply their trade'.[24] Jerry Fodor, who apparently has visited such regions, brings back the following report for his fellow philosophers and linguists:

'X caused Y to die' doesn't entail 'X killed Y'. Consider the case where X caused Y to die by getting someone else to kill him. It is usual to reply to this sort of objection by invoking a special relation of 'immediate causation' such that, by fiat, 'X immediately

---

[23] There may be other restrictions one wants to add to the kind of state of affairs caused in order to capture the meaning of verbs like 'kick'. Soft contacts on another's shins, for example, may not be the kind of contact required for a kick (as Thomson suggests, ibid, 222); but such refinements of the consequence that must be caused in order for there to be a kick cannot affect the causal analysis of 'kick'.

[24] Zeno Vendler, 'Agency and causation', *Midwest Studies in Philosophy* 9 (1984), 380.

caused Y to die' does entail 'X killed Y'. It is this relation of immediate causation that is said to figure in the definition of verbs like 'kill.' It is a mystery (apparently one which is to remain permanently unexplicated) what, precisely, this relation is. (In the most obvious sense of 'immediately cause' what immediately causes one's death isn't, usually, what kills one. If it were, we should all die of heart failure.)[25]

Fodor skeptically concludes that there is only one equivalence to be found here: 'of all the species of X causing Y to die, there is one and only one which is necessary and sufficient for making 'X killed Y' true: viz X's causing Y to die by killing Y.[26] In such an equivalence, of course, all the work of analyzing 'X killed Y' is done by the uselessly circular criterion 'killing Y'.

   Yet the law may not be the murky region that Vendler, Folor, Chomsky, and other linguists seem to think.[27] Take the first two classes of cases, those where the death is spatially or temporally remote or where it is any event freakishly brought about. Where it is too remote or too freakish, in law Jones did not (proximately) cause the death of Smith. Since Jones (on the hypothesis here pursued) did not kill him either, the two expressions remain equivalent. To be sure, there is great vagueness about 'too remote' or 'too freakish' limitations of proximity. Legal definitions, like that of the Model Penal Code, do not much reduce that vagueness: an act causes a result only if that result is 'not too remote or accidental in its occurrence to have a just bearing on the actor's liability'.[28] Yet the vagueness of 'causing' here may be a virtue, not a vice. After all, 'killed' is vague in its application too: the less remote or less freakish the death is from the act, the more likely that we should call the act a killing. If 'causing death' and 'killing' are indeed used equivalently, then one should expect a vagueness in the former if there is such vagueness in the latter.[29]

   The third kind of example is different, for we sense less uncertainty about 'killing' when we have other people doing the killing. If Jones persuades X to kill Smith, and X does it, seemingly Jones did not kill Smith—his agent did. Yet the crispness of this conclusion is matched by a like crispness about causation in the law: Jones's encouragement may have caused another to kill Smith, but it did not (proximately) cause Smith's death. The other's action was an intervening, voluntary act 'breaking the causal chain'. Legal doctrines mark a significant

---

[25] Jerry Fodor, *The Language of Thought* (Cambridge, Mass: MIT, 1975), 130–1 n 23.
[26] Ibid.
[27] While some linguists have long sought to analyze causally complex action verbs (what they call 'causatives') in terms of causing certain states of affairs, Noam Chomsky's skepticism about the possibility of such an analysis has prompted a large literature. See Noam Chomsky, *Studies on Semantics in Generative Grammar* (The Hague: Mouton, 1972), 72; JL Morgan, 'On arguing about semantics', Papers in Linguistics 1 (1969), 69–70; G. Lakoff, 'On generative semantics', in D Steinberg and L Jakobovits (eds), *Disciplinary Reader in Philosophy, Linguistics and Psychology* (Cambridge: Cambridge University Press, 1971); JD McCawley, 'Prelexical syntax', in PAM Seuren (ed), *Semantical Syntax* (London: Oxford University Press, 1974).
[28] Model Penal Code, §§2.03(2)(*b*), 2.03(3)(*b*).
[29] A point also made by Wilson, *The Intentionality of Human Action* (2nd edn, Stanford: Stanford University Press, 1989), 64, in his defence of this entailment.

difference between enabling conditions and full-fledged causes.[30] Jones's telling another where Smith may be found, convincing the other to do it, and the like, are only enabling conditions. The other's action was the cause of Smith's death just as surely as it was the killing of Smith.

Suppose, by way of contrast, that Smith died in the following way: Jones pushed another person from the top of an embankment on to Smith, who was standing below, and the impact killed Smith. Here there is no intervening voluntary act by the other, only the use of his body as the instrument for causing death by Jones. So here Jones clearly did cause Smith's death. With equal clarity, however, Jones also *killed* Smith.

There are of course many intermediate cases of lesser clarity. What if the intervening actor acted in killing Smith, say by shooting him, but that actor had a disability (insanity, uncontrollable temper, pressure of a threat, ignorance about Smith being still alive at the time he is shot, intoxication, youth) making his choice to kill Smith less deliberate or intentional. Where Jones utilizes the intermediary's known disability, he looks somewhat like the Jones who uses the intermediary's body as an instrument for the *causing* of the death of Smith; still, the intermediary in all such cases does act and (in some) even choose to kill. So there will be doubtful cases of intervention, rendering doubtful our judgment whether Jones (proximately) caused Smith's death. Yet are we not equally doubtful about whether Jones killed Smith? Do we not indicate such doubt with expressions of the form 'Jones as good as killed Smith himself?'[31] Again, if the vagueness of 'X caused Y's death' is matched by a vagueness of 'X killed Y' that is an argument in favor of the equivalence, not against it.

It is important not to confuse the proximate-causation criterion with our overall judgments about moral responsibility or about legal liability. When we say that Jones did not proximately cause Smith's death when Jones persuaded another to kill Smith, we have not said that Jones is not responsible, morally or legally, for Smith's death. He is—but not because he killed Smith. Jones persuaded another to kill, or aided the other to find the victim, so (under standard criminal law theory) he is an accomplice in that killing. Accomplice liability exists, as Sanford Kadish has shown in detail, precisely to make people like Jones liable for deaths that they do not (in law) cause.[32]

The same is true for those of our doubtful cases (where the act that intervenes is less than fully deliberate or intentional) where we may conclude that Jones did not cause Smith's death. We may well think Jones to be morally responsible for Smith's death, liable to punishment as a murderer, anyway. In law this gets reflected either in accomplice liability (where the disability of the intervening

---

[30] We shall examine these doctrines with a critical eye in Part IV.

[31] Wilson, *The Intentionality of Human Action*, 63.

[32] Sanford Kadish, *Blame and Punishment* (New York: Macmillan, 1987), Chapter 8. We shall have occasion later on (in Chapter 13, below) to question the law's non-causal conceptualization of accomplice liability.

actor does not excuse him) or in liability for causing an agent to cause death (where the disability does excuse the intervening agent, meaning that Jones cannot be held as the latter's accomplice).[33] In either case, we may hold people liable for deaths despite the fact that they neither (in law) caused them nor killed.[34]

I conclude that the equivalence thesis—at least when restricted to legal causation—looks much more plausible than many philosophers of action have thought. Despite this, many lawyers seek to evade the universality of causal requirements in tort and criminal law liability rules. They do this by denying that all of the verbs used in the *actus reus* prohibitions of the law of torts and crimes are *causative* verbs in English.

Leaving the law to the side momentarily and focusing on English semantics only, it is surely true that there are non-causative verbs in English. The existence of such complex descriptions of action that are not causally complex can be seen by starting with a basic description and adding to it only a circumstance. For example, 'X raised his arm' is usually a basic description, while 'X raised his arm while on a boat' is a complex description adding only a circumstance. The complex description of action as boat-situated-arm-raising is not causally complex, only circumstantially so.[35] If there are such non-causative verbs used in the law, then the equivalence thesis does not guarantee that causation is universally required for legal liability. It is thus semantically possible that the liability rules of the criminal law and the law of torts might not require causation in their act type descriptions. Let us see.

A rather orthodox view in criminal law theory has it that there are many crimes lacking any causation requirement in their *actus reus*. George Fletcher, for example, has often admonished his fellow teachers of substantive criminal law to end the traditional focus on homicide as the example of crime. Homicide prohibits the causally complex action of killing, which, Fletcher notes, assumes

---

[33] See eg Model Penal Code, §2.06(2)(*a*), which makes one liable for the conduct of others even when one is not an accomplice of those others. If one 'causes an innocent or irresponsible person to engage in such conduct', then one is as guilty as if one did it oneself.

[34] These different bases of legal liability complicate the *actus reus* requirements. Three ways to be guilty of homicide: (1) by soliciting or aiding another to kill, who does then kill; (2) by agreeing with another that a third should be killed, who is then killed by the other; (3) by causing an innocent or irresponsible agent to kill, who does then kill. In addition, some states eschew use of complex action verbs like 'kill', and 'prohibit': (4) causing the death of another human being (for example, Model Penal Code, §210.1(1)). The equivalence thesis we have been examining certainly holds for these alternative bases of liability. With the fourth possibility the equivalence is obvious, but with the first three it is equally so if we keep clear just what is the prohibited state of affairs that an actor must not cause. In (1), the effect is either understanding (Austinian 'uptake') of the person solicited, or aid being given to the killer; in (2), it is either the understanding required for agreeing or the conviction required for agreement; in (3), it is the killing by another agent. From what we have earlier said, these bases of liability are equivalently prohibited as 'No act that causes S'—so long as we remember that state (or event) S need not be the death of the victim.

[35] For further examples and analysis, see Irving Thalberg, Jr, *Perception, Emotion and Action: A component approach* (New Haven: Yale University Press, 1977), 96–7; Bennett, *Events and Their Names*, 219, 222, 231.

causation of a 'harmful event that is conceptually independent of human action',[36] namely, the victim's death. Fletcher categorizes crimes like killing to be part of a 'pattern of liability', namely, the 'pattern of harmful consequences'. Fletcher's admonition is based on the worry that 'one pattern of liability—often the pattern of harmful consequences—is taken as paradigmatic of the whole criminal law'.[37]

This is a legitimate worry only if there are other 'patterns of liability' using action verbs that do *not* assume causation of a 'harmful event that is conceptually independent of human action'. Fletcher assumes that there are such patterns, what he calls the 'pattern of manifest criminality' and what he calls the 'pattern of subjective criminality'. Theft (which commonly prohibits the taking of property of another with intent to deprive) for Fletcher is an example of the first, and attempt (which commonly prohibits attempting to do an act already made criminal by some other statute) is an example of the second. Fletcher thus must assume that the act descriptions 'taking' and 'attempting' do not have the structure of descriptions like 'killing', namely, that of a causing of some event that is 'conceptually independent' of the act that caused it. It is the thesis of this section that this assumption is false and that all complex descriptions of action used in the criminal law require at least a causing of some state of affairs.

Fletcher's assumption is a very common one amongst criminal-law academics. The leading American case-book in criminal law, for example, contemplates that there can be crimes that are 'defined without regard to any result of the defendant's conduct (for example, attempt, conspiracy, burglary) [where] there is no need to face the issue of causation'.[38] Many English criminal-law theorists also defend this thesis, urging that there are such crimes as 'conduct-crimes' where there are no result elements and thus no causation requirements.[39] Before I argue against this thesis, I first wish to clarify it.

First, what does Fletcher mean by an event that is 'conceptually independent' of the act itself? We can approach what Fletcher might mean by 'conceptual connection' easiest by seeing what he cannot mean. Suppose I cause my arm to rise, and thus perform the action of raising my arm. Is the description of the event, 'my arm rising', conceptually independent of the description of the act, 'raising my arm?' It might be thought that a reason for answering this question negatively is that the event description 'arm-rising' is related to the act description 'arm-raising', because a common root is involved. Yet even when the same word

---

[36] George Fletcher, *Rethinking Criminal Law* (Boston: Little, Brown, 1978), 388–9.
[37] Ibid, 390.
[38] Kadish and Schulhofer (eds), *Criminal Law and Its Processes*, 587. The assumption also pervades Stephen Schulhofer, 'Harm and punishment: A critique of emphasis on the results of conduct in the criminal law', University of Pennsylvania Law Review 122 (1974), 1497–607.
[39] See the discussion and citations in R Buxton, 'Circumstances, consequences, and attempted rape', Criminal Law Review (1984), 25–34, 28. John Gardner, as we have seen, also thinks that crimes such as child abuse and rape are conduct crimes because the actions of abuse and prevention cannot be given a causal analysis: Gardner, 'Moore on complicity and causation', 433–4.

is used, not just a common root, this is no reason to think that there is a conceptual connection here. The verbs of action, as we have seen, are systematically ambiguous between their transitive and their intransitive senses. 'He caused his arm to move' and 'He moved his arm' look quite similar, until we insert the subscript to mark the different senses of the word being employed. The first use of 'move' is intransitive, referring to the event of the arm moving$_I$; the second use is transitive, referring to the act of moving$_T$ the arm. There is no conceptual connection here between the moving$_I$ (or rising$_I$) and the moving$_T$ (or raising$_T$).

So in one sense the assumption of Fletcher and others is plainly false. If the volitional theory of action is true, all complex descriptions of actions require at least this much causation: a volition must cause a bodily movement$_I$. This weak causal thesis is not the thesis I wish here to defend, however, nor is its negation the assumption that Fletcher and most criminal-law academics have made. The weak thesis is no more than the volitional theory of action which I have defended elsewhere.[40] By contrast, the thesis that rebuts Fletcher et al is a much stronger thesis: all complex descriptions of actions used in the criminal law require that the volitionally caused bodily movement referred to by such descriptions itself cause some further event or state of affairs. The thesis is that all complex descriptions of actions share with 'killing' a built-in, *second* causal element: the bodily movement (that is caused by a volition) must itself cause some further, independent event to occur, like a death in the case of 'killing'. It is this second, stronger causal thesis that is at issue here.

The strong causal thesis is highly plausible for most of the complex descriptions of action used in criminal law. 'Killing' is only the most prominent example, but equally obvious are: 'disfiguring' as used in the crime of mayhem (causing the disfigurement of the body of another);[41] 'maiming' as used in the crime of mayhem (causing the loss of some body part);[42] 'hitting' as used in the law of battery (causing contact with the body of another);[43] 'abuse' as used in child abuse statutes (causing physical injury to a child);[44] 'rape' as used in the crimes of forcible and statutory rape (causing sexual penetration of the female);[45] 'confining' or 'detaining' as used in the crime of false imprisonment (causing another to be confined or detained against his will);[46] 'abducting' as used in the crime of kidnapping (causing the transportation of another and causing the false imprisonment of that other);[47] 'burning' as used in the crime of arson (causing any part of a building to be destroyed or damaged by fire);[48] etc.

---

[40] For a defense of the volitional theory of action, see Michael Moore, *Act and Crime: The philosophy of action and its implications for criminal law* (Oxford: Clarendon Press, 1993).
[41] See Roland Perkins and R Boyce, *Criminal Law* (3rd edn, Mineola: Foundation Press, 1982), 241.
[42] Ibid.   [43] Ibid, 152.   [44] See eg Annotated Code of Maryland, Art 27, §213.0(2).
[45] See eg Model Penal Code, §213.0(2).   [46] Perkins and Boyce, *Criminal Law*, 224.
[47] Ibid, 230.   [48] Ibid, 278.

This causal structure to complex descriptions exists also for verbs used in crimes that are part of what Fletcher calls the 'pattern of manifest criminality' and what English theorists call 'conduct crimes'. Consider larceny and burglary. Larceny requires the *taking* of property of another. One performs the action of taking only when one *causes* the movement of such property, and, by causing such movement, one *causes* oneself (or another) to come into possession of such property.[49] Similarly, burglary requires the actions of breaking and entering the dwelling house of another. One 'breaks' within the meaning of the burglary statutes only when one causes an opening of some part of the dwelling (door, window, etc);[50] one 'enters' only when one causes any part of one's body to be inside the dwelling.[51] While theft and burglary also require that many circumstances be true at the time of these acts, this in no way diminishes the fact that these crimes require that certain states of affairs be caused by some willed bodily movement.

The inchoate crimes of conspiracy, attempt, and solicitation are most often mentioned as *the* counter-examples to the thesis here examined. Fletcher most obviously has such crimes in mind as his 'subjective pattern of liability'. Since attempt and attempt-like crimes are the most frequently mentioned example, I shall focus on them alone.

Consider first the general category of attempt liability. As is well known, one is not guilty of an attempt (eg to murder) if one performed an act with the intent that it kill another. In addition, that act must cause a state of affairs to exist that is variously described as 'beyond mere preparation', 'in dangerous proximity to killing', a 'substantial step' towards killing, etc.[52] Attempt thus requires a causing of some further state of affairs beyond simply the moving of one's own body; that movement must itself cause enough other events to occur so as to satisfy these various descriptions of some further state of affairs.

---

[49] Perkins and Boyce, *Criminal Law*, 323, 302. For a close application of the requirement of 'asportation', see *State v Patton*, 364 Mo 1044, 271 SW 2d 560 (1954) (movement of concrete blocks by one other than the defendant held to be sufficient movement). Although the Model Penal Code (§ 223.2(1)) and the codes that follow its lead eliminate asportation as an element of theft, substituting 'exercise of unlawful control' by a defendant, this is only because the Code consciously merged attempted larceny with larceny. See American Law Institute, *Model Penal Code and Commentaries*, Comment to § 223.2(2), 164. One then still must ask (of those new larcenies that would have been attempted larcenies before) whether the actor's voluntary bodily movement has caused a proximity to movement and possession sufficient to be an attempt.

[50] Perkins and Boyce, *Criminal Law*, 248.   [51] Perkins and Boyce, *Criminal Law*, 253.

[52] The variously described states that must exist before attempt liability attaches are discussed in Kadish and Schulhofer (eds), *Criminal Law and Its Processes*, 633–55. For some of these tests of when an accused has gone far enough to cross over from 'mere preparation' into 'attempt', the line is not drawn in terms of actual proximity to the prohibited harms; rather, it is drawn in terms of how close to success was the actor if the facts were as he believed them to be. See, for example, Model Penal Code, § 5.01(1)(*c*). Here the causal question is a rather recherché one: did the defendant's acts cause enough other events to occur in the actual world so that in the possible world created by his mistaken beliefs those events would have been close enough to success so as to be an attempt? Recherché, but a causal test nonetheless.

One might think that the state of affairs (in some cases at least) will not be conceptually independent of the act that is its putative cause. Consider two variations on Squeaky Fromme's attempt to assassinate (then) President Ford. The first variation is close to the facts of the actual case: holding her pistol pointed at Ford she pressed her finger on the trigger with the intent of killing Ford; the trigger on the gun did not move because it was jammed.

Surely Fromme's movement took her beyond 'mere preparation' to the state called attempt, but not because the movement *caused* that state to exist—moving her finger caused nothing else (of relevance) to happen. Rather, the moving of her finger in these circumstances *constituted* the state of affairs referred to as an 'attempt', a 'substantial step', etc—or so the argument goes.

In this first variation, the way round the argument is easy: Fromme did many earlier acts that caused her to be in a position to pull the trigger of a gun pointed at President Ford. It is only because those acts *caused* various other events to occur that Fromme *attempted* to kill Ford. So make my hypothetical about Fromme harder (if much less realistic): she woke up finding that her hand had been wrapped round a loaded pistol that was pointed at Ford, decided for the first time at that moment to kill him, and moved her finger with that intent. As before, nothing else happened of relevance to Fromme's project of killing Ford, not even a contact of her finger on the trigger (she was stopped before her movement caused that contact to be made). Now the conclusion earlier advanced seems more plausible: the state of affairs that is referred to by 'dangerous proximity to killing Ford', or a 'substantial step towards it', or whatever, is constituted by the movement of her fingers in these circumstances.

Plausible, but false. If the only effect of Fromme's hypothesized finger movement$_T$ was that her fingers moved$_I$, *then* we should indeed conclude that the thesis here examined is false. For then the state of affairs caused is *part* of the action (volition-cause-movement$_I$) itself, so that Fromme's act (moving$_T$) could not *cause* Fromme's fingers moving. But Fromme's movement must have caused a further state than that in order to be an attempt. The state is one of dangerous proximity to (or a substantial step towards) Ford's death. Ford, to give an old phrase a new meaning, must have been caused to have had a 'near-death experience' by Fromme's moving$_T$ before that moving$_T$ can be called an attempt. True, Ford's *state* of being near death is not an event, like a trigger moving; it is a state of affairs, but it is no less an *effect* for that. And as a state, it is not identical to the state of Fromme's finger moving$_I$, once we properly individuate states.[53]

Consider an analogous example of Anthony Kenny's: 'when I learn French, I bring it about that I know French, ie that I have the capacity to speak French'.[54] On Kenny's analysis, what I cause when I do the complex action of teaching myself French is a state, namely, a capacity to speak French correctly. The

---

[53] On states of affairs, see Chapters 14–15, below.
[54] Anthony Kenny, *Action, Emotion, and Will*, 183.

capacity to speak French is a state I am in even if I never utter a word of French. Such dispositions and abilities are like a proximity to speaking French. Such a state is 'conceptually independent' from all the acts I did in order to acquire such an ability; such acts may thus be the *causes* of this proximity state to exist.

I have elsewhere defended the view that the *actus reus* requirements of conspiracy and solicitation also have causal requirements within them.[55] If such arguments succeed, then it is plausible to think that *all* liability doctrines in criminal law and torts require that a defendant's act cause something. To justify the enterprise this book undertakes, of course, nothing so strong needs to be true. If many or most liability rules require causation, that is reason enough for lawyers to ask after the nature of this requirement.

---

[55] Moore, *Act and Crime*, 220–5.

2

Causation and Moral Blameworthiness

As we saw in the last chapter, causation is a prerequisite of legal liability throughout both the law of torts and the law of crimes. That this *is* so is not of course to say that it *should be* so. That depends on the policies that both explain and justify the liability doctrines in tort and criminal law. On the view of those policies presupposed in this book—the corrective justice theory of torts and the retributive justice theory of criminal law—this question about liability devolves into a moral issue: does causation matter to moral responsibility?

Very broadly speaking, there are two ways in which causation could matter to moral responsibility. One has to do with causation's role in enhancing moral blameworthiness. That is the subject of the present chapter. The other has to do with causation's role in determining the permissibility of balancing evils so as to justify prima facie wrongful actions. That is the subject of the following chapter.

The topic of the present chapter is an ancient one.[1] It is an issue faced by all systems of criminal and civil liability. In criminal law the issue arises in the guise of the differential punishability of inchoate crimes. Inchoate crimes are crimes of attempt, attempt-like crimes of specific intent, and crimes of risk creation. The issue is whether attempts (such as attempted murder) should be punishable equally with completed crimes (eg, murder); whether attempt-like crimes of specific intent (such as assault with intent to rape) should be punished equally with crimes where the *actus reus* includes the object of the specific intent in question (eg, rape); and whether crimes of risk-creation (such as reckless endangerment) should be punished equally with crimes where the risk is realized (eg, manslaughter).

One can imagine criminal codes making causation sufficient for liability, in the sense that no guilty intent or other *mens rea* is necessary for punishment. One can also imagine codes making causation of harm necessary for liability, in the sense that there are no inchoate crimes but only crimes where the harm in question has been caused by the defendant. Either version or such codes would give a very prominent role to causation in assigning liability. Yet neither of these positions

---

[1] Plato, for example, was alive to the problem. *The Laws* IX, § 876, in *The Dialogues of Plato*, Vol 4, 445, trans B Jowett (1953). For a recent interpretation of Plato's views on the matter, see Peter Westen, 'Why criminal harms matter: Plato's abiding insight in the *Laws*', Criminal Law and Philosophy 1 (2007), 307–26.

reflects the tradition of Anglo-American criminal law. For centuries that criminal law has reflected a more nuanced role for causation.

The moral view reflected in the structure of Anglo-American criminal law makes causation of some harm neither sufficient nor necessary for moral responsibility. Rather, causation of a harm that some defendant either tried to bring about, or risked bringing about, increases the blameworthiness of an already blameworthy defendant. To cause a death that one intends to cause is morally worse than merely intending or trying to cause such a death; to cause a death that one has knowingly and/or unreasonably risked, is worse than merely knowingly and/or unreasonably risking such a death. How much worse? The common legal metric (for attempts) was by a factor of 2; it was believed to be twice as bad to kill, to rape, to hit, etc, as it was to try (unsuccessfully) to do any of these things, which resulted in punishments for these inchoate crimes being put at one-half the punishments of the completed crime analogues.[2]

This doctrinally dominant view has long been challenged within legal theory.[3] The dissenting view regards causation of harm as irrelevant in determining degrees of blameworthiness. On this dissenting view, a defendant's moral blameworthiness is fully determined by his intentions (either executed in action or not) and his risk-impositions. Whether one causes the harm one intends or risks is on this view irrelevant.

Tort law faces the same issue as does criminal law, although the doctrinal and theoretical setting for the issue differs somewhat. In torts the standard view is that a corrective-justice duty arises only for harms one causes.[4] Causation is thus a fully necessary condition for liability (unlike criminal law where causation is merely an enhancer of liability). There is even some doctrinal support for causation being sufficient for liability in certain isolated areas of tort,[5] and there is some theoretical support for making causation sufficient for liability throughout tort law.[6]

The challenge to this standard view raises the same issue as is raised in criminal law. In tort law, the challenge would supplant causation with risk. The motivating idea is (again) that to risk some harm is a complete basis for responsibility; causation

---

[2] Eg, California Penal Code, § 664.

[3] Stephen Schulhofer, 'Harm and punishment: A critique of the emphasis on results of conduct in the criminal law', University of Pennsylvania Law Review 122 (1974), 1497–607; Sanford Kadish, 'Forward: The criminal law and the luck of the draw', Journal of Criminal Law and Criminology 84 (1994), 2183–237; Kim Kessler, 'The role of luck in the criminal law', University of Pennsylvania Law Review 142 (1994), 2183–237; Stephen Morse, 'Reason, results, and criminal responsibility', Illinois Law Review (2004), 378–85; Larry Alexander, 'Crime and culpability', Journal of Contemporary Legal Issues 5 (1994), 1–30.

[4] This is usually called 'the fault principle' where culpability and causation are both necessary to liability. There are competing visions of corrective justice—in terms of unjust enrichment, risk alone, cause alone—but the fault principle states the dominant version.

[5] These are the pockets of strict liability for dangerous animals, ultra-hazardous activities and defective products.

[6] Richard Epstein, 'A theory of strict liability', Journal of Legal Studies 2 (1973), 151–204.

(on this view) adds nothing to the responsibility of the risking actor. What the actor controls are the actions imposing the risk; whether the risk is realized is irrelevant to his duties of repair because it is the world, not him, that controls such 'risk-realization' (ie causation).

Both dissenting views (in criminal law and torts) propose legal regimes quite different than the causation-drenched regimes we have in place. In criminal law, one would either redefine all crimes in terms of intent and risk alone, eliminating causation (and any use of causative verbs); or at least equalize the punishments between inchoate versus completed crimes, even if the distinction is not to be eliminated by redefining the latter crimes.[7] In tort law, one would redefine torts so that risking harms is sufficient for liability without causation; and then, if risks are not conceived to be harms requiring compensation, each individual risker contributes to a fund from which realized risk-bearers (ie those caused harm) can receive compensation (alternatively, if suffering a risk is regarded as a compensable harm, each risk-bearer recovers compensation from each risk-imposer).[8]

Whether these alternative legal regimes in tort and criminal law should be realized raises squarely the role of causation in assigning moral responsibility. If causation matters to serious moral blameworthiness, then the legal regimes we have are (at least roughly) the regimes we should have. If causation is irrelevant to the existence or the degree of an actor's moral blameworthiness, however, as the dissenting views in criminal law and tort theory hold, then the alternative legal regimes just sketched should be preferred. The moral relevance of causation is thus central, and it is to that issue that this chapter is devoted.

For the past 30 years philosophers have cast the crucial moral issue here as being one of 'moral luck'.[9] The label stems from the thought that moral responsibility, positive or negative, is *earned*; it is not generally a matter of luck because that would make morality unfair; yet with regard to whether one causes the harms one intends or risks, that is a matter of luck (in the sense that no one can control all the variables that make for successful execution of intentions or realizations of risks); and that therefore the law's position (that we are blamable for results) is best conceptualized as the view that there is a kind of moral luck under which we all suffer, despite our general revulsion to the idea.

---

[7] For a discussion of what criminal law would look like on the dissenting view, see Joel Feinberg, 'Equal Punishment for Failed Attempts: Some Bad But Instructive Arguments Against It,' Arizona Law Review 37 (1995), 119–21, reprinted in his *Problems at the Roots of Law* (Oxford: Oxford University Press, 2003).

[8] For a version of risk-based tort liability, see George Fletcher, 'Fairness and utility in tort theory', Harvard Law Review 85 (1972), 537–73.

[9] The modern discussion begun with Bernard Williams, 'Moral luck', Proceedings of the Aristotelean Society, (Supp) 50 (1976), 115–35, reprinted in his *Moral Luck* (Cambridge: Cambridge University Press, 1981), and Thomas Nagel, 'Moral luck', Proceedings of the Aristotelean Society, Supp 50 (1976), 137–52, reprinted in his *Mortal Questions* (Cambridge: Cambridge University Press, 1979).

My own sense has long been that the label 'moral luck' poorly casts the moral issue here. This is mostly because the 'moral luck' label presupposes a quite non-idiomatic idea of *luck*.[10] On this peculiar idea of *luck*, there is luck involved when someone dies because we put a gun at their head and pull the trigger intending to kill them. (There is luck involved, it is said, because we did not control whether a dud, lack of a bullet, or a sudden bird, prevented the death or not.) Our ordinary notion of 'luck' has no truck with such cases. Only if the death that occurred was unlikely, caused in some freakish way, unforeseeable and unpredictable, etc, would we ordinarily talk of there being any *luck* involved in the death.[11]

Secondarily, notice that 'moral luck' reverses the natural valence we ascribe to luck with respect to events like deaths. Normally we regard a *killer* as lucky if his bullet kills his intended victim (say, by a low-probability shot) because we judge the actor's luck as relative to his goals. *Moral* luck reverses the valence: the shooter who succeeds in killing is said to be morally *unlucky* because his blame has been increased (because of his success in causing what he was trying to cause). Such reversing of valence often confuses people and probably even more often clouds intuition.

The moral issue is thus better cast in terms other than 'luck.' The issue is better cast straightforwardly in terms of causation: does causation of harm increase moral blameworthiness, in the way in which existing criminal law supposes? Is causation of harm necessary to trigger a duty to repair, as existing schemes of tort law suppose? Those reform-minded theorists who answer both questions negatively can still put their arguments in terms of 'luck,' complaining that existing law supposes moral blame to attach to the 'morally unlucky.' But then such theorists have to argue for their (problematic) conceptualization of luck, and not have it handed to them in the very statement of the issue.

So, why does (or does not) causation matter to responsibility? Good arguments on either side of this issue are very hard to find, despite a voluminous literature in both legal theory and moral philosophy. Over a decade ago I surveyed the existing arguments on this issue, both pro and con, and concluded of all of them that they were not only bad—they were not even plausible.[12] Nothing in the literature since that survey has given me reason to change my mind.[13] Surveying these arguments

---

[10] See Moore, 'The independent moral significance of wrongdoing', Journal of Contemporary Legal Issues 5 (1994), 1–45, reprinted as Chapter 5 of Moore, *Placing Blame: A general theory of the criminal law* (Oxford: Oxford University Press, 1997), 211–18.

[11] Moore, 'The independent moral significance of wrongdoing', 213–216. See also Barbara Herman, 'Feinberg on luck and failed attempts', Arizona Law Review 37 (1995), 148 ('the domain of luck, good or bad, . . . [is] the unpredictable departures from the normal or expectable range of . . . effects').

[12] Moore, 'The independent moral significance of wrongdoing', 196–211. Joel Feinberg adopted this survey in reaching his conclusion that the numerous arguments advanced, although 'subtle and often ingenious', are so surprisingly bad. Feinberg, 'Equal punishment', 122.

[13] Dana Nelkin helpfully updates my survey in her 'Moral luck', *Stanford Encyclopedia of Philosophy*, 2004, available at <http://www.plato.stanford.edu>. See, eg, David Enoch and Andrei Marmor, 'The case against moral luck', Law and Philosophy 26 (2007), 405–36. See also 'Moral and Legal Luck', *Theoretical Enquiries in Law*, 9 (2008), Issue No.1.

reminded me of Bradley's old description of philosophers in ethics often 'inventing bad reasons for what they believe on instinct'.[14]

One striking fact did emerge from that survey of the extent arguments, however. This was that the dissenters—the reform-minded theorists who think causation to be irrelevant to responsibility—uniformly *think* that they have a respectable argument for their position. They think they can do better than rely on an exchange of 'naked intuitions' about paired hypothetical cases, the aspersion they regularly cast on their opponents' argumentation.[15]

The (supposedly) respectable argument such dissenters think they have is based on the notion of *control*.[16] The argument goes like this. First premise: moral blameworthiness would be unfair unless it attached only to things that we control. We have no control over the weather, for example, and so bad weather is something for which we are not responsible. For another example, when a diabetic goes into a hypoglycemic state without prior warning, where his body randomly flails and hits another, the hit is not his responsibility because he lacked control over the hitting. So, first premise of the argument here considered: there is moral responsibility for some factor x only if x is within the control of the subject.

Second premise: actors are not in control of the results of their actions. What happens in the world after we move our bodies depends on factors over which we have no control. We move our finger on the trigger of a gun pointed at our intended victim; yet whether that bullet *kills* (causes the death of) that victim depends on: whether someone unloaded our gun; whether a dud is in the gun's chamber; whether the trigger mechanism malfunctions; whether a large bird flies between our gun and our intended victim; etc, etc.

Conclusion: there is no (added) moral responsibility for the results of our actions. We do not control them, and therefore we are not (more) responsible because of them. We are only responsible for what we control, which is either our choice (intention) to kill, *or* our execution of that choice by willing the movement of our trigger finger, *or* the successful movement of our bodies. This is surely the core of the dissenters' certainty that they alone have arguments (as opposed to mere intuitions) on this issue.

And yet, just as surely, there is no even remotely plausible argument here, for the two premises trade on a glaring equivocation on the meaning of 'control'. The first premise gains its plausibility by using a compatibilist sense of 'control': we control something, such as a result, only where we have a reasonable chance of

---

[14] FH Bradley, *Appearance and Reality* (2nd edn, Oxford: Oxford University Press, 1897), xiv.

[15] This was driven home to me most recently by Jon Elster's sustained critique of my views at the Columbia University Seminar on Responsibility, January, 2005. Elster accused me of relying on naked intuitions in particular cases, contrasting with the argument from control that (supposedly) sustains the opposing view.

[16] See, eg, Nagel, 'Moral luck'; Feinberg, 'Equal punishment'; Morse, 'Reasons, results, and criminal responsibility'; Enoch and Marmor, 'The case against moral luck'.

bringing it about. We do not need to control every factor making this result possible; we only need a reasonable chance to have avoided the result, to have control in this compatibilist sense of the word.[17] The second premise abandons this compatibilist sense, for an *in*compatibilist sense of control; in this sense we control some result only when we can make causally efficacious choices about *every* factor that could cause or prevent this result. This shift in the sense of 'control' makes the dissenter's argument as valid as this one:

A foot has five toes.
Twelve inches is a foot.
Therefore, twelve inches has five toes.[18]

Of course, dissenting theorists plead they have no equivocation, that they intend only one of the other senses of 'control'. As a first option, consider a univocal use of the incompatibilist notion of control in the two premised argument above. Two points: first, the first premise then loses all plausibility. This is because it is self-defeating. None of us *control* (in the incompatibilist sense) the genetic and environmental factors that cause our choices; none of us control (in this sense) our intentions, our willings, our willed bodily movements, any more than the results of our actions. As I have argued in detail elsewhere,[19] it is an illusion to think that the surface of our skin marks any break in the degree of our control, that we lack control of what happens in the outside world while we have control of what goes on inside. In the incompatibilist sense of 'control', we control nothing. Therefore, control in this incompatibilist sense could not be what is meant in saying that the weather and our involuntary bodily movements are beyond our *control* and thus beyond our responsibility; for this would not be to contrast them with anything that we do control and which is therefore our responsibility.

Second, notice that the argument, using the incompatibilist meaning of 'control', differs not a whit from the older free-will debate in which compatibilist readings of 'ability', 'freedom', 'could have done otherwise', 'intention', 'voluntary', etc, compete with incompatibilist readings of those concepts.[20] There is nothing new going on in the badly labeled 'moral luck' debate not already going on (for centuries) in the free-will debate. See this clearly, and the implications are

---

[17] For the much more idiomatic, compatibilist notion of control, see, eg, John Bishop, *Natural Agency* (Cambridge: Cambridge University Press, 1989), 23; Moore, 'The independent moral significance of wrongdoing', 216–18; John Martin Fisher and Mark Ravizza, *Responsibility and Control* (Cambridge: Cambridge University Pres, 1998); Stephen Morse, 'Culpability and control', University of Pennsylvania Law Review 142 (1994), 1587–1660; DC Dennett, *Elbow Room: The varieties of free will worth wanting* (Cambridge, Mass: MIT Press, 1984), 51.

[18] With apologies to my former colleagues Bill Bishin and Chris Stone. See their *Law, Language and Ethics* (Mineola: Foundation Press, 1972), 526.

[19] Moore, 'The independent moral significance of wrongdoing', 233–46.

[20] For some of the debates, see Moore, 'Causation and the excuses', California Law Review 73 (1985), 1091–149, reprinted in Moore, *Placing Blame*, Chapter 12; see also Dennett, *Elbow Room*; Fischer and Ravizza, *Responsibility and Control*.

equally clear: for compatibilists like myself on the free-will issue,[21] the above argument is clearly fallacious (because of the equivocation on 'control'); for incompatibilists on the free-will issue, the above argument does not equivocate on control, but it is clearly irrelevant because no one is responsible for anything.[22] In either case, there is no argument about 'control' that is of interest to the debate about (enhanced) responsibility for results.

The only avenue along which the control argument can hold our interest is one which neither equivocates on the meaning of 'control' nor uses the (hopelessly useless) incompatibilist sense of 'control': in a compatibilist sense of 'control', could one show that we *control* our intentions and their executing volitions, in a way or to a degree that we do *not* control the results of our actions? A group of my friendly critics have attempted just such a showing, in response to the earlier published version of the argument just presented.[23]

Consider first this conclusion of one of those critics, Sandy Kadish. Recognizing that many factors over which we have no control may intervene to prevent us from choosing to do some evil (just as such factors may prevent us from causing a harm we have chosen to cause), Kadish concludes that 'fortuity prior to choice . . . may be accommodated to our notions of just desert; fortuity thereafter cannot'.[24] Why is that? Because 'the settled moral understanding is that what you deserve is a function of what you choose'.[25] Notice this is not an argument by Kadish relying on some control principle; Kadish already knows that choice matters, results do not, as desert bases—that is 'the settled moral understanding'— and therefore Kadish believes he can shrug off equivalent lack of control ('fortuity') as irrelevant.

All well and good, but the context of the argument here is different. Most people who hold the reformer's view on moral luck (including Kadish himself on other occasions) think some control argument establishes choice but not results as a desert basis. For such people, the question is not whether one can maintain some distinction between choices and results. That is too easy—of course there are lots of distinctions between these two quite different kinds of thing. The

---

[21] Moore, 'Causation and the excuses'.

[22] There is one way open to the incompatibilist to avoid the conclusion that we are responsible for nothing. This is explored by Michael Zimmerman, explicitly in response to me: if we assume (as does Zimmerman) that we are responsible for something (our choices, say), then one can use my point about the equal lack of control everywhere to conclude that we are responsible for all states of affairs that factors we did not control could have made happen differently. Thus, I am responsible for choices I did not make but would have made if I had had opportunities I did not have due to factors I did not control; and for the person I would have been, but am not, because of factors I did not control; etc: Zimmerman, 'Taking luck seriously', Journal of Philosophy 99 (2002), 553–76. I should have thought that Zimmerman's conclusions of an *increased* responsibility were as much a *reductio* as was my conclusion of a *decreased* responsibility. To reverse an old saying, one person's valid inference is another person's *reductio ad absurdum*.

[23] Moore, 'The independent moral significance of wrongdoing'.

[24] Kadish, 'Forward', at 17–18.   [25] Ibid.

question more precisely is: is there a distinction in terms of (compatibilist) control between the two?

Stephen Morse, Kim Kessler Ferzan, and Larry Alexander think so. Two of them, at least, are good, level-headed compatibilists on the free-will issue. Dragging the agnostic on this issue (Alexander) along, they seek to distinguish choice from results based on *control* in what they hope to be, univocally, the compatibilist sense of the word only. Yet I find what they say most puzzling. I quote the relevant passage from the forthcoming Alexander/Ferzan book at length:

> Michael Moore argues that 'result luck' is indistinguishable from 'constitutive luck' (luck involving the genetic and experiential fortuities that cause one to have the character that produces potentially harmful conduct) and various types of 'circumstantial luck', such as 'planning luck' (luck involving fortuities that may intervene to prevent one from forming plans to engage in potentially harmful conduct) and 'execution luck' (luck involving fortuities that prevent the execution of firmly formed intentions to perform potentially harmful conduct) . . . Moore convincingly argues that, in a deterministic world, variables over which the actor had no control exist at every stage, from character to execution . . . [I]n a deterministic universe, luck, understood in this way, 'goes all the way down' is correct as a matter of theoretical reason . . . [Yet] [l]uck may not provide a principled basis to draw the line between moral responsibility for action and moral responsibility for results, but perhaps another principle that does not lead to an unacceptable reductio will . . . The only form of control a responsible actor needs is the general capacity to be guided by reason, a capacity most adults possess in ample measure. Thus, compatibilists have good reason to 'draw the line' at human action because only action can be guided by reason, and not because action is free of the causal forces of the universe—of 'luck'. The potential for the law to guide people by reason is a good justification for holding people morally responsible for actions but not for results. For us, as for Moore, there is every reason to distinguish between 'result luck' and 'constitutive luck'.
>
> Ultimately, our position rests on the assumption that the control we have over our choices—our willings—is immune to luck and is thus qualitatively and morally different from our control or lack thereof over our heredity and environment, the situations in which we find ourselves, and the causal consequences of our choices. No matter our past history, the options we confront, or the causal forces that will combine with those we initiate, what we choose is up to us in a way these other factors are not. It is not just that we have *more* control over our choices than over our constitution, our circumstances, and what we cause. Our control over our choices is different in kind—total—not different in degree. Bad luck prior to choice and bad luck after choice is just bad luck; unlike choice, it cannot affect our culpability.[26]

As I understand this, Alexander and Ferzan concede that in the 'incompatibilist sense of "control"' we control nothing; if that kind of control is required for responsibility, we are responsible for nothing. However, they say, there is a compatibilist sense of control in terms of 'reason-responsiveness':[27] action and

---

[26] Larry Alexander and Kimberly Ferzan, with Stephen Morse, *Crime and Culpability* (Cambridge: Cambridge University Press, 2008), Chapter 5.
[27] Alexander and Ferzan, with Morse, *Crime and Culpability*.

choice can be guided by reason, but results cannot. This is apparently offered as a compatibilist conceptualization of 'control', one allowing it to be said that we control our choices but not the results of those choices.

In the situation where some defendant D intends to kill victim V, and where D carefully loads his gun, checking all bullets to be sure none are duds; tests the firing mechanism of the pistol; isolates V from all possible help or medical attention; screens off all birds or other objects that could interfere; puts the gun at V's head, pulls the trigger, and kills him—I would say that D *controlled* V's death. Apparently *not* in the Alexander/Ferzan sense of control, however; V's death does not respond to reason, whereas choosing to cause V's death, does.

I do not understand this. If D has control (in the compatibilist sense) over his choices, despite not having control over all the possible preventers or disrupters of those choices, does he also have control over *what* he chooses, viz that V die? His choice *is* reason-responsive; it is the product of his practical reasoning processes. But so are the bodily movements by which he executes that choice, and so is the intended effect of those bodily movements, viz V's death. It is D's reasoning processes that cause all three of them, D's choice, D's act of moving his finger, and V's death. All three of them are thus 'reason-responsive'.

Perhaps by 'reason-responsive' Alexander and Ferzan mean to include some criterion of direct causation. We do not usually do anything else as the means to making a choice; we just choose. Whereas we move our trigger finger by having first made the choice to do so, we kill V by moving the trigger finger. The suggestion might be that we *control* only that which we directly cause. Yet such directness of causation produces far too narrow a notion of control. For, in that sense, we do not even control those of our choices that we make only by doing something else first, such as getting up our courage by drink or otherwise, remembering how much we hate V, practicing such thoughts so as to make them routine, etc. Nor in that sense would we control anything we do by way of (non-mental) action in the world: not the movements of our bodies, what we wear, nor how, where, or who we kill.

'Reason-responsive' would be an inadequate notion of 'control' if it requires such directness of causation. That we cannot will a death with the directness with which we can will the choice to kill, is irrelevant to whether we control our choices to kill in a way different than the way in which we control whether we kill. When D has ruled out all the contingencies he can by the careful preparation mentioned earlier, and when he therefore succeeds in killing V by putting a gun at V's head and pulling the trigger, he has had *control* over V's death just as he has had *control* over whether he chose to kill V. In each case he controlled some but less than all possible preventers. That is enough for control in any reasonable, compatililist sense.

A better candidate for a compatibilist sense of 'control' is in terms of degrees of fortuity. Sometimes my friendly critics appear to rely on this preferable sense of control, to argue that there are different *degrees* of control over choice than over the real world effects of those choices. As Stephen Morse has written:

agents do not know the future when they act and cannot know if some intervention will prevent success, even in cases where success subjectively appears certain ... future success is never assured ... Events and other agents frequently intervene to prevent the occurrence of results that are entirely expectable ex ante ... At most, we know that our actions can guarantee only the possibility of a result occurring and not the result itself.[28]

Three points arise. First, notice that for Morse the implicit contrast case to results is not just choice but a choice executed by willed bodily movements. The claim has to be that results are more fortuitous than are either choices or the basic acts that execute choices. Second, the contingency and unknowability of results is surely overstated in cases like that of D putting a gun against V's head and pulling the trigger again and again until the gun is empty. The certainty that D will kill V is not much less than the certainty that she will be able to move her trigger finger if she tries, and not much less than the certainty that she will choose to kill V if that is what she most wants. Third, such differences in degree of probability vary more within each class (choices, bodily movements, results) than they do between such classes. Some bodily movements are high-probability events; others are quite low ones (try wiggling your ears simply by willing them to move). Some choices are highly probable, given the desires of the agent whose choices they will be, but other choices are highly improbable in light of conflicting desires, weakness of will, self-deception, and the like; some deaths are highly probable, like Bob's, while others are low-probability events. How could such a continuum of probability and predictability justify the bright-line distinction to which the reformers cling?

These would-be reformers of the criminal law and of torts think they have an argument for their position, an argument based on control. But in this they are entirely mistaken. Control does not distinguish choices from results.

Perhaps surprisingly, none of this goes any distance towards establishing that causation does matter to moral responsibility. All I have thus far been concerned to show is a parity (in poverty) of argumentation between both sides of the issue. The issue itself is untouched. Does causation matter to responsibility? That lack of control (in the incompatibilists' sense) is an irrelevant distraction, and that there is no lack of control (in any acceptable compatibilist sense), goes no distance towards establishing that causation of a harm does enhance our moral responsibility for trying to cause, or risking the causation of, that harm.

Plausible arguments here are hard to find, on either side. 'Causation matters' seems a pretty good candidate for a first principle of morality. *The* argument that convinced me in the past,[29] and convinces me still, is an experiential argument.

---

[28] Morse, 'Reason, results and criminal responsibility', 384.
[29] Moore, 'The independent moral significance of wrongdoing', 230–2.

There are two experiences of relevance here: a third-person experience when we judge other people's responsibility, and a first-person experience when we judge our own responsibility. As is my wont generally when testing responsibility issues, I think the first-person experience to be of primary importance.

That experience I have described before: we experience greater guilt when we have caused some harm that we either tried to cause, or unreasonably risked, than we experience when we have been equally culpable but we have not caused such a harm. My earlier example was driving intoxicated: if our intoxication leads us to hit and kill a child, we feel very differently about it than if we almost hit a child (to say nothing of the situation where although we are intoxicated and would have been unable to stop, no child is there to be hit). What we feel in the former situations is great guilt. To be sure, we may feel some guilt in the near-miss situation too, but the intensity is much greater when we have caused the harm we so unreasonably risked by driving drunk. It eats at us is a way that it does not in the cases of unrealized riskings.

What we typically feel in the cases of near misses is relief: we know we just escaped something, namely, being culpable killers of an innocent. No matter how culpable we may have been, if we did not in fact cause the harm the risk of which made us culpable, we feel relieved. Such relief can be tinged with some guilt although, even so, the guilt is not only of much lesser intensity but also of a rather different flavor than in cases of caused harms. For culpability alone, without causation, our guilt is self-focused: we should have been more careful, and for that *we* are blameworthy. In such cases our guilt is not other-focused. By contrast, when we have caused the harm we risked, we are other-focused: how could we have so unnecessarily caused another human being such suffering, injury, death?

The inference I drew (and draw) from this experience is that we *are* more blameworthy when we cause some evil, than if we merely try to cause it, or unreasonably risk it. The reason we *feel* so guilty in such cases is because we *are* so guilty. Some no doubt are troubled by the shortness of the inference chain here —although the longer one stays in philosophy the shorter seems to be the argument chains one finds acceptable. (I suppose at some point I will just have unsupported *views*.) Others no doubt reject *feelings* as a basis for moral argument, although I cannot see how to do moral philosophy if one puts aside the emotions. Some also might object to the use of *guilt* feelings as the basis of any inference even if they do not object to the relevance of feelings in general; these are the Nietzscheans and others who doubt that guilt (or other backward-looking emotions) is ever a decent response to anything.

But these objections I have dealt with before.[30] Anyone who wants to live the academic moral philosophy they write about, and who has felt the compelling

---

[30] On the shortness of argument chains, see Moore, *Placing Blame*, 165–82; on the relevance of virtuous emotions as heuristic guides to the truth of the judgments such emotions cause, ibid, 127–38; on the virtue of feeling guilt, ibid, 145–7.

power of deep guilt feelings for harms caused, will brush such arguments aside. More interesting are arguments that accept the experience and accept its relevance to moral insight, and yet seek to explain such experiences on grounds other than that of greater moral blameworthiness attaching to causation. Recently Susan Wolf has taken the argument from guilt feelings head-on and sought to explain it away.[31]

Wolf joins me in thinking that we feel—and rightly feel—worse when we have caused a harm than when we have only tried to cause it or risked causing it. Similar to my earlier example, she imagines a truck driver who negligently hits and kills a child. We would 'be appalled and condemning' of such a culpable harm-causer if he did not feel very badly, and we would find 'disturbing, indicative perhaps of a psychic imbalance', and 'positively eerie', anyone who did feel very badly who did *not* cause the harm but only risked it.[32] Yet Wolf seeks to re-describe the psychology, and then to draw an inference from it different than mine.

Wolf distinguishes guilt feelings, which involve our own judgment that we are blameworthy, from 'agent-regret', which carries no such judgment with it. As she defines this old notion originating with Bernard Williams, 'Agent-regret . . . is a special form of sadness or pain accompanying the wish that things had been otherwise with regard to something with which one's agency was somehow involved.'[33] We thus experience *regret* when we have caused some harm even though we were not at all culpable. It is when we are culpable that we experience guilt, not mere regret. And when we are both culpable and cause the harm the risk of which made us culpable, then, Wolf tells us, we tend to intermingle the wo feelings, confusing the regret mixed with guilt, as if it were a greater guilt alone.[34]

Wolf also argues that it is a virtue (what she calls a 'nameless virtue') to feel agent-regret when we have caused a harm. This is more than the impersonal regret we might all feel about some harm that has befallen a fellow human being. Rather, it is the more specific regret one should feel about his having a

---

[31] Susan Wolf, 'The moral of moral luck', Philosophical Exchange 31 (2000), 5–19. There are other debunking explanations for our apparent guilt reactions to causing harm. One of the oldest is that our guilt is really directed at *risking* the harm, the causing merely being evidential of there having been a risking. See, eg, Enoch and Marmor, 'The case against'. This is, as I have argued before, very implausible: Moore, 'The independent moral significance of wrongdoing', 208–9. Equally off the mark is Darren Domsky, 'There is no door: Finally solving the problem of moral luck', Journal of Philosophy 99 (2004), 445–64. Briefly, Domsky argues that we feel lesser guilt when we do paired hypotheticals like that involving a run-over child because of two biases: an optimistic bias, which is that *we* would be the lucky ones who failed to hit the child, and a selfish bias that would evade our true guilt by transferring on to the other, the guy who hit the child. Domsky, I believe, has never run over a child, or done anything else causing him any deep guilt feelings. In any case, what needs explaining is why we feel so guilty in such cases, and selfishness will hardly do (unless we are all masochists).

[32] Wolf, 'The moral of moral luck', 6.   [33] Ibid, 16.

[34] Ibid, 17.

connection to such a harm, a regret that such harm-causing is now part of his history, of his identity. This virtue should even lead us to *take* responsibility for more than we are in truth responsible for.[35]

Wolf's is the right kind of attack on my inference from differential guilt feelings. It takes the phenomenology seriously, and seeks to deflect that phenomenology's seeming implications for blameworthiness and causation. My disagreement with Wolf is twofold, however. First, at the level of psychology: regret is certainly a distinct psychological reaction from guilt, as both are yet distinct from other emotions such as shame.[36] And the regret of having one's agency involved, however innocently, is also a recognizable species of regret, felt on occasions of faultless causation of harm to others. The rub is in cases of culpable causation: it is not regret (even agent-regret) but guilt that so disturbs us. In such cases we blame ourselves, we judge ourselves to be blameworthy, and it is guilt, not regret, that is consistent with such self-judgments. Wolf says that we are confused about this, but where is any evidence of such confusion? We (or our friends) may try to isolate our guilt so as to attach it to our culpability alone; we may think 'others were just as negligent as we and didn't kill anyone'. Yet such attempts at palliation do not remove the guilt, and do not reveal it to really be something else like regret. The guilt remains, both in quantity and in its quality as guilt. It was our culpable carelessness that caused this, and for that combination we are truly guilty.

One can see this guilt-laden psychology at work clearly in the near-miss kind of cases. Such cases produce feelings of relief and judgments of the form 'there but for the Grace of God go I'. Wolf would have to account for such feelings and judgments as being about agent-regret and the 'nameless virtue' in feeling it: the near-misser just missed, not guilt, but the regret of having his agency involved in causing a bad state of affairs. He has escaped, not greater blameworthiness, but rather, a kind of 'dirty hands' that it would be his aretaic duty to regret. He thus feels relief. Surely this is inadequate as a description of what the near-misser both feels, and should feel. On its face, his feelings are those of relief that his culpable carelessness is much less blameworthy than it could have been had it caused the harm it merely risked. On its face he judges himself to be less guilty than he easily could have been, feeling grateful that he has been lucky enough to get a second chance to do better before his moral ledger is ruined forever.

Second, at the level of moral theory, Wolf gives us an incomplete taxonomy of the virtues here. There is virtue in feeling agent-regret in cases of non-culpable causation of injury to another, on pretty much the ground Wolf assigns: a non-culpable harm-causer should 'acknowledge that the consequences of his behavior have something specifically to do with him...we expect him to accept

---

[35] Wolf, 'The moral of moral luck', 12.

[36] The *locus classicus* for distinctions between such emotions remains Herbert Morris' lucid essays in his *On Guilt and Innocence* (Berkeley: University of California Press, 1976).

contingency in the determination and assessment of who he is'.[37] Just so, but *mutatis mutandis* for what we expect in the way of guilty feelings from a culpable harm causer: that he is the agent whose culpability has hurt someone and that this is now on his moral ledger forever, a part of his history and who he is. He too should accept the contingency of the moral fact. In neither case should he whine about factors outside his control also contributing to the harm; it cuts no more ice against the virtue of feeling guilt in the one case than it does against the virtue of feeling regret in the other.

As we have seen, those in Wolf's position—the anti-moral-luck camp—are primarily (if mistakenly) motivated by the thought that it would be unfair to blame people even in part based on factors (like results) that they do not fully control. Yet notice this worry evaporates for Wolf's nameless virtue: we *ought* to feel agent-regret whenever we have non-culpably caused harm, despite the 'contingency' involved in such causation. Analogously, however, we ought to feel guilt whenever we have culpably caused harm, despite again the 'contingency' involved in such causation. And from there it is but a short step to greater blameworthiness: if we do feel greater guilt at culpable harm-causing, and if it is virtuous to do so, that is good evidence that we are in fact more guilty in such cases.[38]

I conclude that Wolf has not explained away or more accurately interpreted our seeming feelings of greater guilt for causing harm. What we feel, and rightly feel, is that when our culpability causes serious injury to others, we are much more blameworthy than when it does not. Causation matters morally in this way. This means that on justice-oriented theories of criminal law and torts, causation also should matter to liability in these areas of law.

[37] Wolf, 'The moral of moral luck', 14.
[38] As I argue generally in Moore, *Placing Blame*, 127–38.

3

Causation and the Permissibility of Consequentialist Justification within Agent-Relative Morality and the Law

I. The Topic of this Chapter

In the last chapter we dealt with causation's role as an enhancer of moral desert, and thus, as an enhancer of justified legal sanctions. There our discussion was carried on without regard to the theory of ethics under which causing harm intended or risked made one more blameworthy. By contrast, in this chapter we shall examine causation's role within one kind of ethical theory, usually called 'deontological' or 'agent-relative'. Within such morality, causal distinctions have the apparent role of lessening or eliminating moral desert by licensing consequentialist justifications, even of actions like murder and torture that many regard as absolutely forbidden to us. To see the role causation plays within such morality, we must first understand the moral terrain from which it arises. This is the terrain of 'absolutist', 'categorical', 'deontological', 'agent-relative', or 'rights-protecting' morality. So let me step back from my immediate project and give some background material in ethics generally.

Aquinas told us that the first precept of deontological ethics is to do good and to avoid evil.[1] We obviously need to make that precept a bit more precise. More specifically, we need to understand the interplay between the good and bad states of affairs that our actions produce, on the one hand, and what we are obligated to do, on the other. Are our obligations simply a function of the harms/benefits that certain kinds of actions *cause*?

Consider the contemporary debate about whether torture can ever be justified when the stakes are high, as in the current 'war on terror.' Few disagree that

---

[1] More exactly: 'good is to be done and ensued, and evil is to be avoided', *Summa Theologica*, First Part of the Second Part, Q 94, Art 2.

torture is an evil and that morality prima facie forbids it.[2] Yet sometimes something like torture may nonetheless be justified by its good consequences. When such good consequences are in the offing, can we justify: sending terrorist suspects to other countries when we know the regimes of those countries will torture but we do no torture ourselves nor do we intend that they torture;[3] failing to save terrorists from torture when we could do so;[4] allowing nature to take its course in causing torture-like pain to terrorist suspects;[5] redirect torture from one suspect to others more likely possessed of life-saving information;[6] etc?

It is interesting that in the context of torture people often find these distinctions to the pretexts and evasions. Perhaps we are just used to being lied to in this context.[7] Yet even such evasions may be the proverbial compliments vice pays to virtue. The distinctions themselves may be more plausible than their use in this context.

In any event, such distinctions are central to the topic of this chapter. Such distinctions are of general interest in ethics for a variety of reasons. One such reason is that the question of whether the morality of our most stringent obligations can be free of conflict between such obligations seems to depend on how we draw the kinds of distinctions above alluded to. It may not be, as Kant famously proclaimed, that a conflict of such obligations is literally 'inconceivable'.[8] Yet it would be unfortunate for us in the extreme if morality often confronted us with choices where we will be 'damned if we do and damned if we don't'. The distinctions we shall examine hold out the possibility of so limiting

---

[2] On torture being evil, see David Sussman, 'What is wrong with torture?', Philosophy and Public Affairs 33 (2005), 1–33. On morality prima facie obligating us not to torture, see Moore, 'Torture and the balance of evils', Israel Law Review 23 (1989), 280–344, revised and reprinted as Chapter 17 of Moore, *Placing Blame: A general theory of the criminal law* (Oxford: Oxford University Press, 1997).

[3] The CIA's extraordinary renditions are described in some detail in Jane Mayer, 'Outsourcing torture', The New Yorker (14 February 2005), 106–23.

[4] Some of the pain used to extract information from terrorist suspects has been pain that interrogators have omitted to prevent, not pain that they have caused by torture. Al Qaeda's one-time chief of security, Abu Zubeida, for example, was wounded in the chest, thigh, and groin when captured by Pakistani forces; CIA interrogators withheld pain medication for some time to induce him to talk. Los Angeles Times, 6 March 2003.

[5] Sister Dianna Ortiz, a Catholic nun tortured in Guatemala, terms these techniques 'torture lite.' Adopted from British interrogative techniques used in the campaign against the IRA, they consist of sensory deprivation, sleep deprivation, distraction by loud lights and sounds, and the like. See the description of these techniques in Los Angeles Times, 3 March 2005, A-1.

[6] Arguably the extraordinary rendition of the Albanian Al Qaeda cell in 1998 was partly a redirection of Egyptian secret police from less knowledgeable to more knowledgeable members of the Egyptian Jihad. See the detailed story of this operation under President Clinton in The Wall Street Journal, 20 November 2001, A-1.

[7] See, for example, the plainly false statements by President Bush and his then Attorney General, John Ashcroft, that we did not even know that countries like Egypt were torturing the terrorist suspects we sent to them.

[8] Kant, *The Metaphysical Elements of Justice*, trans J Ladd (1965), 25.

our stringent obligations as to minimize or even eliminate such situations of moral conflict.[9]

Our interest in these distinctions is more particular. It lies in the seeming use of causal discriminations in making such moral distinctions. We can justify *allowing* torture, for example, even if we may not justify *doing* some torture ourselves. Our question will be: if these are morally valid distinctions licensing consequentialist justifications of otherwise forbidden actions, is it causation that is doing the heavy lifting here? Is a *doing* a kind of causing, whereas an *allowing* is something else?

One note about method. In this chapter I shall freely mix legal with moral examples. This is not because I think the connection between law and morality to be so tight that if something is legal it must also be moral. Rather, I find the law instructive in ethics because it contains examples we armchair-types would have trouble dreaming up. Moreover, the thought experiments these legal examples provide come with proposed resolutions by judges, who are both uncontaminated by acquaintance with the moral theories we wish to test, and whose resolutions are serious in the sense that real-world consequences turned on what they decided. I thus join JL Austin in thinking (for rather different reasons) that 'it is a perpetual and salutary surprise to discover how much is to be learned from the law' when one is doing ethics.[10]

II. Some General Considerations about Obligation and Justification in Ethics

A. The three-level analysis

Although the background we need to master is agent-relative obligation in ethics, many things I say will presuppose a certain view of even more general matters in ethics. So I shall begin by describing my general view of ethics briefly (which means with little argumentative support). Such baring of presuppositions will hopefully make things clear so that, if I am wrong later, I will at least be wrong clearly (which is not to say, clearly wrong).

1. Level one: The background of consequentialist reasons

I take consequentialism to be a true, general principle of practical rationality. I understand consequentialism to be the idea that we generally have reason to

---

[9] As many deontologists, beginning with Aquinas, have recognized. See the discussion in Anscombe, 'War and murder,' in Walter Stein (ed), *Nuclear Weapons: A Catholic response* (New York: Sheed and Ward, 1962), reprinted in PA Woodward (ed), *The Doctrine of Double Effect* (Notre Dame: University of Notre Dame Press, 2001). See particularly p 256 (in the reprinted version), where Anscombe finds some of these distinctions to be 'absolutely essential' to deontological ethics.

[10] JL Austin, 'A plea for excuses', Proceedings of the Aristotelian Society 57 (1957), 1–30.

maximize good states of affairs and minimize bad ones in our actions and institutions. Usually this idea is broken down into two parts. First, it presupposes some theory of the good. More precisely, we need a theory about what states of affairs are intrinsically good. Welfare of persons (in the form of pleasure, happiness, preference-satisfaction, etc) is one sort of answer, a utilitarian sort of answer if such welfare is the only intrinsic good thought to exist. But the keeping of moral duties, the non-violation of moral rights, the possession of moral virtue, the justness of an institution, are alternative theories of what is intrinsically good.

Second, consequentialism takes a position in the theory of the right: right action (or right institutions) consists of those actions (institutions) that maximally produce intrinsically good states of affairs. One can put this as a slogan: if something is good, surely more of it is better, and this 'betterness' gives us reason to do acts that produce it.

Surely many decisions in daily life are properly governed by consequentialist reasons. Many years ago a prominent law school was reconsidering the start date for that year's classes. Consequentialist arguments about shortened late summers versus earlier and longer holiday periods, summer employment opportunities for students versus faculty preferences, abounded. One well-known deontologist, however, spoke up: all these trade-offs between good states of affairs was by-the-by, he said, because by right he was entitled to the same start date as the school had when he began his employment. Needless to say, the argument did not carry the day. Is that not because none of us live by conformity to the stringent duties of deontology alone? Much of our reasoning is consequentialist, and rightly so.

I take consequentialism not only to provide a principle of practical rationality but also a principle of morality; maximizing the good, that is, not only gives us an objective reason so to act—it sometimes gives us that pressing kind of reason we call a moral obligation. That there are purely consequentialist obligations in morality is important to what follows, even though our interest here is agent-relative (or 'deontological') obligations. So consider one example by way of making plausible the idea. The proverbial baby is drowning face down in the puddle. You, eating your lunch on a park bench, could tip it over with your foot and thereby save it from drowning. But you munch away and the baby drowns.

Even though this is a stranger-rescue case—the baby is no relation to you—I am not so libertarian as to believe you lack an obligation to save the baby. And if you agree with me that you are so obligated, then also agree with me that your obligation is consequentialist through and through. You can appreciate this latter fact by imagining two other babies drowning in another puddle, and time being sufficiently short that you cannot save all three babies. In this variation, surely you can justify not saving the one baby in order to save the other two. In which case, notice, your obligation to save the first baby is gone the moment good consequences appear not to be maximized by doing what was obligatory. Obligations easily justified in such a consequentialist way are consequentalist obligations: it is because the act of saving a baby produces a good state of affairs that the act is obligatory.

2. *Level two: An overlay of agent-relative reasons*

My (true) story of the law-school start date was intended to show that no one can live by deontology alone. But the same is true of consequentialism. Two sorts of supplements are needed. First, we need agent-relative permissions not to be maximizing good consequences all the time. We might call this the good-dinner point: as you head into the restaurant for a fine (and expensive) meal, several street-people point out to you that the money you are about to spend on that meal could keep all five of them from being hungry for the next 24 hours and that (unless you have particularly gluttonous capacities) more good would be produced by you eating more modestly and giving them the rest of the money you are about to spend.[11] The familiar point is that we need relief from the saintly pressures of consequentialist reasons. We need permission on many occasions *not* to do acts maximizing of good consequences.

Second, we need agent-relative obligations that both *prohibit* actions even when those actions would produce the best outcomes, and *require* actions even when those actions would not produce the best outcomes. Intuitively, I may *not* torture one person even if my doing so will prevent the (equally awful) torture of two others by either me or someone else at some other time. Intuitively (at least to me), I *must* save my child from drowning even if that means I cannot save your two children nearby.

I, like many others, see these agent-relative permissions and obligations as a kind of overlay on a consequentialist background: we generally are governed by consequentialist reasons, save when we are permitted or obligated by agent-relative reasons.[12] This gets me to agent-relative obligations.

I shall focus on agent-relative obligations, and usually negative rather than positive versions of those. I shall not be directly concerned with agent-relative permissions (although I shall use them to contrast what I below call 'weak permissions'). With respect to such obligations, my concern is not what I take to be the major question about them, namely, their rationality. (Roughly: how can it be rational not to torture one person when that would minimize torture? If

---

[11] Not purely a hypothetical. Several blocks down from the University, on Telegraph Avenue in Berkeley, was at one time a fine restaurant. Often the entrance to it was lined (gauntlet-like) with Berkeley street people, some of them educated enough to make pretty good diminishing marginal utility arguments. Perhaps UC-Berkeley's Sam Scheffler ate there too. See his *The Rejection of Consequentialism* (Oxford: Oxford University Press, 1982), which argues for the existence of 'agent-centered prerogatives' to go have a good dinner once in a while. Tom Nagel's example of a similar point is his permission to satisfy his desire to climb Kilimanjaro in Africa. See his *The View from Nowhere* (New York: Oxford University Press, 1986), 166–75.

[12] For me, this way of thinking about these agent-relative reasons began with Robert Nozick's discussion of 'side constraints' in his *Anarchy, State and Utopia* (New York: Basic Books, 1974).

torture is so bad, why is not more of it even worse, and why does that not guide our action?)[13] My focus is more preliminary, more clarificatory: what sorts of things form the content of our agent-relative obligations? Are we forbidden to do the *action* of torturing; to *cause* torture to be done; to form the *intention* to torture; to *try* or attempt to torture; to torture intentionally; to even consider torture as a possible action? Each of these possible objects of our deontological obligations has had its proponents within ethics.[14] My question is, which is correct?

One way to argue for some position here is through what I shall call the front door. This is to give positive argument for why intentions to torture, for example, should be taken to be *what* we are obligated not to have or form.[15] I shall proceed in a more indirect, if time-honored way, however, through what might be called the back door. I shall ask about the proper use of consequentialist justifications vis-à-vis a variety of paired examples, hoping to tease out an answer to the question of what deontological obligations must prohibit, from considering when it is intuitively plausible to permit consequentialist justifications.

There is nothing mysterious about such a method. On the three-level view of ethics I have been describing, anything *not* governed by an agent-relative obligation or permission is governed by consequentialist reasons. (That is a consequence of the view of ethics as a consequentialist background with agent-relative overlays.) So if an omission, say, to rescue a stranger baby is something I am not deontologically obligated not to do, then I am permitted to justify such an omission on consequentialist grounds. One can thus seek the content of deontological obligation through the seeking of the range of permissible consequentialist justification.

One way to describe my topic thus is to call it the scope of permissible consequentialist justification of prima facie prohibited actions. Notice, however, that we are here referring to *weak* permissions: such permissions are simply the absence of deontological obligations. Such weak permissions do no more than land one back into the realm where consequentialism holds sway, so that one may yet be subject to consequentialist obligations. Contrast this with the strong, agent-relative permissions I mentioned earlier. These permit one to do some action A even if A does *not* maximize good consequences. Such strong permissions are thus not at all like weak permissions, which subject weakly permitted actions to the dictates of consequentialist reasons.

The distinction between weak and strong permissions is no mere technical distraction. On the contrary, it importantly bounds my topic. Consider the right of self-defense. Often in discussions of the kind I am about to begin, self-defense

---

[13] See the classic discussions of this topic collected in S Scheffler (ed), *Consequentialism and Its Critics* (Oxford: Oxford University Press, 1988).

[14] See the very nice survey of possibilities in Heidi Hurd, 'What in the world is wrong?', Journal of Contemporary Legal Issues 5 (1994), 157–216.

[15] See, eg, Christine Korsgaard, 'Acting for a reason' (Illinois Philosophy Dept paper, 2005).

examples are presented to make one point or another about the bounds of permissible consequentialist justification. Thomas Aquinas is an early sinner here, using self-defense cases to illustrate the doctrine of double effect.[16] Puzzles then get raised about how it can be correct for you to defend your life by killing any number of attackers—no matter what the discount placed on attackers lives, surely your (innocent) life at some point gets outweighed by their discounted but numerous lives?[17]

Such puzzles would be real if we were only weakly permitted to defend our lives with deadly force, for then our justification for self-defense would be consequentialist, and we'd have to defend the view that our life is a greater good than the lives of any number of culpable aggressors. Yet (on my view) we are strongly permitted to defend ourselves no matter what the consequentialist balance might say.[18] Culpable aggressor self-defense examples are thus out of place in the discussion to follow, focused as it is on agent-relative obligation (and thus, weak permissions) but not on agent-relative (or strong) permissions.

I similarly think (although here I am more tentative) that innocent aggressor self-defense cases are instances of strong permissions as well.[19] When two innocents threaten your life—they are children who do not understand the guns they are about to fire at you or they are two fat people falling on you through no fault of their own—I, like Nozick,[20] think you may kill them if necessary to save your own life. This 'may' is not the language of excuse: you are justified in killing them. Moreover, you are justified in killing them even though more good would be produced if you did not kill them and you died instead. You are, in other words, strongly permitted to kill them. If you agree with all of this, then you will agree with what I (in any event) intend to do for the remainder of this paper: I shall also put aside innocent-threat cases as not germane to my discussion.

3. Level three: The reappearance of consequentialist reasons over some threshold of moral horror

In this sketch of ethics so far we have an agent-relative overlay on a consequentialist background. Now I want to add a consequentialist override of the

---

[16] Aquinas, *Summa*, IIa, IIae, Q 64, Art 7.

[17] See, eg, the discussion of discounts and forfeitures in the self-defense context, in Judith Thomson, 'Self-defense and rights' (Lindley Lecture, University of Kansas, 1976).

[18] For reasons explored by Phil Montague, in his 'Self-defense and choosing between lives', Philosophical Studies 40 (1981), 207–17. As Montague recognizes (p 211), 'in a standard self-defense situation . . . one is not simply *permitted* to kill in self-defense, but one has a *right* to do so, and to kill as many aggressors as is necessary to save himself . . . '. In my language: self-defense is a strong permission not dependent upon achieving some net balance of good consequences.

[19] An early discussant of innocent-threat cases was George Fletcher. See his 'Proportionality and the psychotic aggressor: A vignette in comparative criminal theory', Israel Law Review 16 (1973), 367–90.

[20] Nozick, *Anarchy*.

agent-relative overlay. I confess it: I am only a threshold deontologist. This means that over some threshold of truly awful consequences, I will potentially do virtually anything to avert such consequences. If I can locate and defuse a nuclear device at 42nd Street only by torturing the innocent child of the terrorist who planted it there, I torture.

It would require a lengthy paper of its own to defend this (very un-Kantian) kind of deontology.[21] Other than a recent, detailed critique of my version of threshold deontology by Larry Alexander,[22] there is little *argument* in the ethics literature about this level. Assumptions and assertions abound, however, from Kant's not even, if 'the whole people should perish',[23] through Elizabeth Anscombe's 'it is immoral to even think about such examples',[24] through Bernard Williams' 'this is beyond morality',[25] to brief, undefended confessionals by other threshold deontologists such as Tom Nagel,[26] Charles Fried,[27] and many others.

But defending threshold deontology is not my present topic. Distinguishing its licensing of consequentialist justification, from the licensing of consequentialist justification given by weak permissions, is important to my topic, however. Examples of catastrophic consequences will not do to make any point about the scope of deontological obligations/weak permissions. If persuasive, such examples make a very different point, viz how and when deontological obligation can be overridden. My topic is what the content of those obligations may be in the first place.

B. Meta-ethical intrusions

One other glance at the forest before we start looking at the individual trees. I am not only a deontologist in my ethics, but (what some I know find peculiar to combine with that) I am also a naturalist-realist in my meta-ethics.[28] Many find it unsurprising to combine realism in meta-ethics with a deontological approach to ethics, but the naturalist version of realism is something else. Most naturalists are not realists to start with, and of those like Nick Sturgeon who are both,[29] they tend to be consequentialists (as is Sturgeon) in their substantive ethics.

---

[21] I make a few gestures in this direction in Moore, 'Torture and the balance of evils'.

[22] Larry Alexander, 'Deontology at the threshold', San Diego Law Review 37 (2000), 893–912.

[23] Kant, *The Metaphysical Elements of Justice*, 100.

[24] Heidi Hurd discusses Anscombe's (and Peter Geach's) refusal to discuss such cases in 'What in the world is wrong?', 170–4.

[25] Williams, 'A critique of utilitarianism,' in JJC Smart and B Williams, *Utilitarianism: For and against* (Cambridge: Cambridge University Press, 1973), 90–3, 118.

[26] Nagel, 'War and massacre,' in S Scheffler (ed), *Consequentialism and Its Critics*.

[27] Charles Fried, *Right and Wrong* (Cambridge, Mass: Harvard University Press, 1978), 10.

[28] See the essays in Part I of Moore, *Objectivity*.

[29] See the citation to Sturgeon and other contemporary naturalist—realists in Moore, *Objectivity* 105–6, n 27.

Naturalism, as I have defined it in ethics, is the view that moral properties supervene on natural properties. Supervenience means asymmetrical co-variance: any difference in moral properties must be underlain by a difference in natural properties, but not vice-versa. There can be alternative, multiple realizations (in natural properties) of one and the same moral property. This has the following implications for the present chapter: if there are moral differences between intending versus foreseeing, doing versus allowing, acting versus omitting, etc, then these moral differences must be underwritten by natural differences between these pairs. Put more simply, we need these distinctions to be based on real distinctions in psychology, in the nature of events, in the metaphysics of causation, etc. Giving an analysis of such distinctions in terms of further moral properties—omittings are failures to act where there was a *moral* duty to have acted, for example—will thus be unacceptably incomplete.

The worry here is not circularity. Sometimes there is, admittedly, that worry too, as when someone defines intending as that which one cannot justify consequentially, or defines allowing so that some very blameworthy omissions (such as Philippa Foot's starving of a beggar to death for his organs) are defined to be active killings on the ground that they are as blameworthy as truly active killings.[30] Rather, the worry is naturalism: for every moral difference, find a natural difference. Of course, one can be a *patient* naturalist: we do not need to reach *immediately* to natural properties, just so long as we eventually get there.

This suggests something important about doing this kind of ethics, which is that one cannot do it without simultaneously doing the philosophy of mind, the philosophy of action and of events, the metaphysics of causation, and the like. Such I have always thought in seeking to use metaphysics to moral advantage in my lifetime preoccupation with moral responsibility and blameworthiness.

As JL Austin used to say,[31] so much for the preliminary cackle. Now to the trees, considered one by one.

III. Intending versus Foreseeing: The Doctrine of Double Effect

A. Introduction

The oldest and the best known of the distinctions relevant here is that between intending a harm by one's action and merely foreseeing that a harm will be

---

[30] Philippa Foot, 'The problem of abortion and the doctrine of double effect', originally published in *The Oxford Review* (1967), reprinted in Woodward, *Double Effect*, 150. Foot reconsiders this in her 'Morality, action, and outcome', in T Henderich (ed), *Morality and Objectivity* (London: Routledge, 1985), reprinted in Woodward, *Double Effect*, 81–2, n 6.

[31] JL Austin, 'A plea for excuses'.

produced by one's action. The idea is that one may justify causing something bad with good enough consequences only if one did not intend to cause the bad thing when one acted. If one merely foresaw that one's act would produce the bad effect, then one is outside the agent-relative prohibition and may justify the action if it is productive of good enough consequences.

A standard example is bombing in war-time. Killing non-combatants is bad. Suppose an act of bombing causes a number of such deaths. Suppose further the bombing takes place during a just war so that the bomber's side winning such a war is a very good consequence, and that the bombing will produce just that consequence. Can the act that causes one bad thing (the killing of non-combatants) be justified by the fact that that act also causes a very good thing (the winning of a just war)? The doctrine of double effect ('DDE') holds that the bombing can be justified if the killing of the non-combatants was only foreseen as a side effect, not if it was intended as either a means or an end. So a bomber who is trying to hit military targets, but knows he will hit some civilians, is eligible to justify his bombing by its beneficial consequences. But the bomber who seeks to so dispirit the enemy by killing civilians that the enemy will surrender, and thus aims his bombs at civilian targets, is not eligible to justify his bombing by its good effects. He has intended the death of the civilians as a means to his end (winning the just war); he has not merely foreseen that the death of the civilians will be produced by the means he has chosen to end the war.

As with each of the distinctions we shall examine, there are two questions to ask here. First, what more precisely is the distinction marked by the DDE? What (ultimately natural) properties are being invoked when we distinguish intendings from foreseeings? Second, can this natural (psychological) distinction carry the moral freight with which the DDE loads it? How plausible is it that foreseen deaths can be justified by good consequences but that intended deaths cannot be justified by those very same good consequences? These two questions are not unrelated—we should adjust the natural distinction in any way that makes more plausible some moral significance for it. Still, like a pair of trousers, it helps to do one leg at a time.

B. The psychological distinction between intending and foreseeing

Start with the apparent psychological distinction. On the surface, the psychological distinction is clear enough. For over two thousand years the folk psychology we all share has posited the existence of three (or two, depending on who you like here)[32] separate kinds of representational states that figure in practical rationality: there are motivational states of desire or of ultimate intention; there

---

[32] I am thinking of the Davidson/Bratman debate about the independence of intention from both belief and desire. See the summary in Moore, *Act and Crime* (Oxford: Clarendon Press, 1993), Chapter 6.

are cognitive states of belief; and there are executory ('conational') states of mediate intending or willing. I want to be rich; I believe that the world is so arranged that if I work hard I will be rich; so I intend to work hard and, because of these desires, beliefs, and intentions, I do just that.

The DDE distinguishes cognitive states of belief from both motivational states of ultimate intention and from executory states of mediate intention.[33] The strategic bomber who only believes his bombings will kill civilians is to be distinguished both from the malicious bomber who is ultimately motivated by his desire to kill civilians and from the terror bomber who aims to kill civilians as his means to terrorizing the enemy into surrendering. The DDE allows the strategic bomber the chance to justify his acts; it does not allow the malicious or terror bomber this chance, no matter how good the consequences may be of their bombings.

So far so good. Belief, even predictive belief, is a distinct kind of mental state, different from both ultimate and mediate intentions. (Let us ignore Bentham's odd stipulation that such predictive beliefs are a kind of intention, which he dubbed 'oblique intention'.)[34] Things get sticky when we move from the *nature* of the mental states involved, to their *representational content*. When I was less of a fan of the DDE that I am now,[35] I presented the following kind of example as showing the doctrine's absurdity: Herod did not desire the death of John the Baptist for its own sake; he preferred that John live. Still, Herod did want to please Salome, and Salome wanted John's head on a plate. So Herod cut off John's head. Yet he did not intend John's death, not as a motivating end nor even as a means. He merely foresaw that John was going to have a hard time living without his head. So if pleasing Salome was a really good thing, Herod could justify cutting off John's head under the DDE. (Like examples were developed by Philippa Foot,[36] Warren Quinn,[37] Jonathan Bennett,[38] and others.)

A defender of the DDE cannot accept this kind of example. It is not that the psychology is bad, although it might be. Rather, it makes the DDE morally counter-intuitive. If the correct psychology makes individuation of the content of representational states as fine-grained as this example suggests, then few of us ever intend (as opposed to foresee) anything bad flowing from our actions. Bennett's example: the terror bomber does not intend the death of the civilians in order to

---

[33] 'Ultimate/mediate' are Bentham's terms: Bentham, *An Introduction to the Principles of Morals and Legislation* (Oxford: Basil Blackwell, 1948), 201–2.

[34] Bentham, *An Introduction to the Principles of Morals and Legislation*, 201–2.

[35] Moore, 'Intention and *mens rea*', in R Gavison (ed), *Issues in Contemporary Legal Philosophy* (Oxford: Oxford University Press, 1987), reprinted as Chapter 11 of Moore, *Placing Blame*.

[36] Foot, 'Abortion'.

[37] Quinn, 'Action, intentions, and consequences: The doctrine of double effect', Philosophy and Public Affairs 18 (1989) 334–51, reprinted in Woodward, *Double Effect*. This aspect of Quinn is critiqued in Fisher, Ravizza, and Copp, 'Quinn on double effect: The problem of "closeness"', Ethics 103 (1993), 707–25, reprinted in Woodward, *Double Effect*.

[38] Jonathan Bennett, *Morality and Consequences* (Salt Lake City: University of Utah Pres, 1981), 110–11.

dispirit the enemy and end the war; no, he sees he only needs the enemy to *believe* the civilians were killed, because it is that belief that does the dispiriting; so the terror bomber explodes the bomb over the civilians because that is what gives such an appearance that they are killed.[39] Of course, exploding it over them also kills them, but this further effect he only foresees; he strictly intended only to create the appearance of their deaths, not their actual deaths.

I shall not rehearse the various attempts of defenders of the DDE to get around this problem. (These include HLA Hart's idea of inevitable causal connection,[40] Foot's idea of 'closeness',[41] Quinn's idea of only intending the act that is aimed at the victim and which foreseeably directly causes his death,[42] the common idea that the 'by' relation is non-causal so that Herod could intend John's death as the means by which Herod gets what he does intend, John's head on a platter; or the suggestion of Lord Hailsham, that some intentions are morally equivalent even if not actually identical.)[43] I think the solution is close to several of these suggestions, but I will put it my own way.

Notice that the problem is *not* one of individuating numerically distinct intention-tokens, as I once thought.[44] Rather, the problem is a problem of classification that inevitably will have some slop in it, no matter how fine-grained may be the psychology of representational content.

To explain—the problem of individuating intention-tokens is this one: considering two differently described intention-tokens, are these putatively distinct things really one and the same thing? If Herod intended to kill John, and Herod intended to cut off John's head, are 'these' one intention or two? I still think what I thought over twenty years ago on this issue: these are two distinct representations, and as long as Herod has them both in his head (rather than an outside observer using these different descriptions to refer to Herod's intention(s)), then Herod has two distinct intention-tokens.[45]

Yet this is not dispositive of the issue at hand. Suppose morality (like the common law of mayhem) contains an agent-relative prohibition on maiming (disfiguring) another. Suppose the DDE is right: what is prohibited is not just maiming, but maiming while intending to maim. If D swings a stick intending to put out V's left eye, and (because V moves at the last second) D puts out V's right eye, has D violated the prohibition?

Stipulate (as is legally true) that putting out an eye is maiming (disfiguring); so the act-token done instantiates the type of action prohibited. Now focus on the intention: did he intend to maim, and did he intentionally maim? For more than one reason, these are two different questions. Take the second first. This asks

[39] Ibid.

[40] Hart, 'Intention and punishment', The Oxford Review 14 (1967), 5–22, reprinted in his *Punishment and Responsibility* (Oxford: Oxford University Press, 1968).

[41] Foot, 'Abortion'.   [42] Quinn, 'Double effect'.

[43] I explore Lord Hailsham's views in Moore, 'Intention and *mens rea*'.   [44] Ibid.

[45] Ibid.

whether there is a match between what defendant did and what he intended to do. What the defendant did was an act-token; 'he put out V's right eye' is one description of it. What the defendant intended to do is the representation of an act-type. We never intend or predictively believe about particular events—being in the future, it is hard to refer to them as particulars.[46] We always intend or predict the occurrence of some instance of a *type* of event. So the match question here is one of classification: is the act of putting out V's right eye an instance of the type of act that D intended? (If not, D is only an accidental maimer, not an intentional one.)

So what did D intend? Did he represent the type of event he was trying to bring about as a 'putting out of V's left eye', as a 'putting out of V's right eye', as a 'putting out of *an* eye of V's' (in the sense of any eye), as a 'putting out of *an* eye of V's' (in the sense of one particular eye), as a 'harming V', a 'disfiguring V', a 'maiming V', etc? My supposition is that *any* of these representations will suffice to match what D did to what he intended to do, to make D an intentional maimer, even though it is unlikely in the extreme he had more than one or two of them as the representation under which he acted. If so, notice how much slop there is in fixing what it was that D intended.

Now look at another classificatory question, one that is directly at issue with the DDE. Even though the intention D had takes a representation of a *type* as its content, the intention itself is a particular, an intention-token. To see whether V had the intention the norm against maiming prohibits, we need to see whether the intention-token D had instantiates the type of intention the norm prohibits. The norm prohibits (it is my hypo, so I can tell you authoritatively) intents to *disfigure* a person. Did D have such an intent? Suppose he represented what he was trying to do as 'put out V's left eye'—is this an intent to disfigure? Well, not in one literal sense; D did not use the representation 'disfigure' to refer to the type of thing he was trying to achieve. He used 'put out V's left eye'. But putting out an eye is within the extension of the act-type 'to disfigure', you say. Yes, but an intent to put out an eye is not necessarily within the extension of the relevant intention-type, 'an intent to disfigure'. As is well known, just because some particular act x is within the extension of some predicate F in the real world, is no guarantee that the intention to do x instantiates the type of intention, to do F.[47] The only intention-tokens that are clearly intentions to do F are those that have F as their intentional objects.

Since very few wrongdoers use representations exactly matching the act-type descriptions of moral norms, we have to get sloppy again; and we do. I am confident that D's intention-token will and should be taken to be an instance of

---

[46] Ibid n 27.

[47] Thus, on one occasion I might intend to ride a horse through the park, and on another occasion, intend to ride the city bus through the park. Knowing that a city ordinance prohibits riding a vehicle through the park, I might intend to ride a vehicle in the first case but not the second—despite the fact that the first is not within the extension of 'vehicle' while the second is.

the type of intention morality prohibits. D intended to disfigure V no matter which of the representations earlier mentioned he had in mind.

So let us reframe our question(s) about Herod's intention in these last directions. Did he intend John's death, conceding that he did intend John's head on the platter? Surely the answer to this classificatory question is yes, and yes, despite the slippage between what he intended and what is prohibited in the way of intentions.

If we reframe Philippa Foot's 'closeness' doctrine to be a doctrine about 'allowable slippage' in the dimension just described, then we can get out of the closeness doctrine what she sought, a relief of the DDE from moral absurdity; then if a terror bomber intends to explode a bomb right over a person, he intends that person's being blown to bits and thus that person's death; then a terrorist who places a bomb on a plane to explode it mid-air, in order to collect the insurance proceeds (having insured the plane and not the passengers), intends their death because he intends to destroy their only mid-air possibility of life; then the surgeon who crushes the skull of a wedged fetus intends the death of the fetus in intending to crush its skull; etc.

One way to view my answer to the closeness problem about the DDE, is as a version of the familiar 'broaden-the-discomfort' strategy. That general argumentative strategy goes like this: if there is a problem about some particular conclusion, show that that same problem infects some other conclusion that you or your audience holds dear. The strategy tends to motivate critics of the original conclusion to become interested in finding a solution to it in order to save the second conclusion from their own prior criticisms. As applied here, the problem of closeness is not just a problem for the DDE. It is also a problem for the use of intention as a marker of culpability generally. To distinguish an intended from a known harm, or to distinguish a known harm from a risked but unintended harm, one has to solve both of the classification problems adverted to earlier. One will need some doctrine of allowable slippage to do this. And the defender of the DDE needs no more. Moreover, no one wishes to give up the crucial distinction between intended harm and inadvertently caused harm. As Justice Holmes quipped, even a dog knows the difference between being stumbled over and being kicked,[48] as children early recognize with their accusation 'you did that on purpose'. So we need to solve the closeness problem generally and stop pointing fingers at the DDE particularly.

C. The moral force of the psychological distinction

There is undoubtedly a great deal more to be said here, but let me turn to the second query I raised about the DDE, that about the moral freight carried by the psychological distinction between intent and predictive belief. Assuming we *can*

---

[48] OW Holmes, Jr, *The Common Law* (Boston: Little, Brown, 1881), 3.

distinguish intended deaths from foreseen or risked deaths, *should* we do so in the context of permissible consequentialist justification?

One way to get at this moral questions was Herbert Hart's way.[49] He stripped the examples to be considered of their putative justifications and compared intent and foresight in terms of their relative culpability. His question was this one: if A intends to kill B, but C only foresees that the act he intends to do will certainly cause D's death, and both kill when neither killing produces any good consequences, is A more culpable than C? No, Hart thought, because both A and C knew that an innocent life would be lost if they acted and both *chose* to kill to get what they wanted. They both had control over the death of another, and chose to accept that death as an acceptable cost to getting what they wanted.

To put some meat on these abstract bones, suppose with Hart that C is seeking to break his mates out of prison, and that he intends to blow up the prison wall to accomplish this.[50] C knows that a guard is on the other side of the wall and that the explosion will certainly kill him; but the death of the guard is not necessary to anything C wants or needs. Is C less culpable than A, who intends the same end (escape of his mates) by the same means (blowing the prison wall), with this difference: A places the bomb at the point of the wall where the guard is stationed in order to kill the guard (who otherwise would prevent the break or identify the perpetrators)? Hart's answer was one of equivalent culpability.

It is common to respond to arguments like Hart's by noting that even if there is no difference in culpability in cases where justification is *not* in issue that does not show anything about cases where justification *is* in issue. This is the same kind of response as is made in act/omission cases, where people who find act/omission pairs equally blameworthy when no justification is in issue yet find one to be justifiable by good consequences and the other not when such justification is in issue. Logically, of course, this is a possibility. Yet if there is no difference in culpability (in the justification-less cases) between intent and foresight, is it not something of a puzzle *why* there should be such a marked difference in their potential for consequentialist justification?

I confess that I am one of those who thinks that there is a difference in culpability between intent and foresight in the no-justification-in-sight cases. Suppose that the death intended or foreseen does not occur; it was 'practically certain' to occur, but miraculously it did not. Is the foreseeing defendant—the one who does an act conscious that it will surely cause death—as blameworthy as the one who tries to kill, when in both cases death does not come about? One, after all, tried to kill, whereas the other only (strongly) risked death.

Grant me the conclusion I have argued for elsewhere, that the intender is more culpable.[51] Then it would not be surprising that the more culpable one

---

[49] Hart, 'Intention and punishment'.

[50] From the 19th-century case of *Regina v. Desmond, Barrett, and Others*, The Times, 28 April 1868.

[51] Moore, 'Prima facie moral culpability', Boston University Law Review 75 (1995), 319–33, reprinted in Moore, *Placing Blame*.

could not justify his act by its good consequences but that the less culpable killer could do so.

One might object to this line of reasoning by thinking that the *wrong* (killing an innocent) each killer does is the same, even if their culpability differs, and that it is degrees of wrongness that track permissible consequentialist justification, not degrees of culpability.[52] This objection sounds better than it is. To begin with, the objection rather begs the question. Why is wrongness limited to acts like killing? Why does the wrongness relevant here not include intentions as well as actions, intentional killings rather than killings as such? The objection pretty much stipulates its own answer here.[53] Second, the objection trades on the action-guiding nature of moral norms. In their (prospective) role of guiding our behavior, moral norms may omit to mention intentions. They may say 'do not kill' rather than 'do not murder' (ie, intentionally kill). But this is only because, in their acting-guiding role, mention of intention would be superfluous. 'Don't kill' could be telling us not to aim at killing, even though it does not mention intention; whereas, in their (retrospective) role, moral norms are used to judge behavior already done. When we judge our own or others behaviors, we do care about intentions; or at least, we could care even if the (prospective) version of the norm made no mention of them.

Putting aside culpability comparisons when justification is not in issue, we can test the DDE more directly. Is it intuitive that strategic bomber can justify his bombing (in a just war) in a way that neither terror bomber not malicious bomber can? In the Second World War the Americans engaged in daylight bombing so that they could see to aim at military targets. (They did this in part for strategic reasons, namely, they thought if they could destroy certain key German industries they could end the war more quickly; but they did it also for moral reasons.) By contrast, the British engaged in night-time bombing where no such aiming was possible; the aim was to dispirit the German people by destroying the civilian population of the cities. (A similar motivation lay behind the German bombing of Coventry, the Allied fire-bombing of Dresden, the American fire-bombing of Tokyo, and the nuclear bombings of Nagasaki and Hiroshima.) Were there real moral differences at stake here, or were the Americans simply deluded in thinking this, a delusion that cost them extraordinary losses in planes and men?

It seems to me that there is something to be said for the DDE in these cases. You may not aim at evil, but you may tolerate it for good enough results. This

---

[52] Joseph Raz voiced this objection to my reliance on intention in the joint seminar we taught in 1989 on consequentialism versus deontology.

[53] Although one could bolster the objection by bringing in other considerations making it important to confine wrongdoing to action, leaving intention to be distinguished as culpability. See, eg, Moore, *Placing Blame*, 192–3.

might suggest that intention does all the work in mapping out the content of deontological obligation, leaving no work for causation to do.

To test this, consider the following case. In 2003 in Frankfurt, Germany, the Chief of Police faced the following problem. He had in custody the probable perpetrator of a kidnapping-for-ransom of the 11-year-old son of a leading German industrialist. The Chief had reason to believe that the son might still be alive, but not for much longer, so to find out the victim's location he threatened the kidnapper with severe torture. (The threat was a colorful one—a specialist in torture was being flown in who knew how to inflict pain like no one else.) Moreover, the threat was not empty; the Chief intended to torture the kidnapper to reveal the child's location. As it turned out the threat to torture was enough, the child's location was disclosed, although tragically the child was already dead by suffocation.[54]

An implausibly strong version of the DDE would say that intending torture, by itself, is absolutely forbidden, even if no torturing is done. The Police Chief thus was unjustified in forming the intention to torture. I find this implausibly strong because suppose one could form the intention to torture knowing that it is very likely someone will stop you from executing your intention.[55] Surely that formation of an intention can be justified by good consequences. I think the Police Chief was justified in forming such an intention in the actual case, even without a belief that he would likely be prevented from torturing. The Chief was justified in forming the intention, even if one thinks that the Chief would not have been justified in actually torturing. (I am not one of those who thinks it rational to do what you intend when the balance of reasons for the one do not match the balance of reasons for the other, as in Kafka's well known toxin puzzle.[56])

So the objects of agent-relative obligation are not intentions *simpliciter*. They are intentions plus something, presumably something connected to the wrongful actions intentionally done. Yet even this may be too strong to be plausible, for it suggests that intending is *necessary* to agent-relative prohibition. Yet there seem to be cases where merely foreseen badness will be enough for prohibition, if that is combined with other things. Philippa Foot gives the example of a hospital in which you intend to manufacture a medicine for five patients, which will save their lives; unfortunately the only way to make the medicine in time is by use of a machine that will pump poisonous exhaust gas into another ward, killing one patient in that ward.[57] My sense is the same as Foot's: you may not justify saving the five by using the machine, even though you would only be foreseeing the one's death and not intending it as either an end or as a means. (This suggests

---

[54] Recounted in Richard Bernstein, 'Kidnapping has Germans debating police torture', New York Times, International, Thursday, 10 April 2003, A-3.

[55] An argument suggested in Hurd, 'What in the world is wrong?'.

[56] Greg Kafka, 'The toxin puzzle', Analysis 43 (1983), 33–6.   [57] Foot, 'Abortion', 152–3.

a structure that is more 'criteriological' than it is 'criterial' in the mode of combining these different factors.)[58]

One cannot take this elimination of intention too far, however. One cannot think that deontology could prohibit actions alone, with no intention *or* foresight requirement. This would be the view that, say, the act of killing is absolutely prohibited by itself, with no mental state qualifier. The problem with any such view is that we kill quite often, and think it to be unproblematically justified. We mine coal, build tall buildings, operate transportation systems, in ways that cause some deaths: eg, our driving an automobile sometimes kills children who jump out in front of us. Yet we justify such activities because in doing them we do not either intentionally or knowingly kill the individuals whom we do admittedly kill in such accidents. We do not think such accidental killings violate agent-relative prohibitions for if they did, how could we justify driving? We need *some* mental state to be attached to actions as the object of deontological prohibition.[59]

This pair of examples—the kidnap and the hospital—are together suggestive of the role of intention (vis-à-vis something else, such as causation) within the content of agent-relative obligation. Kidnap suggests that agent-relative obligation does not simply prohibit intentions, even intentions to torture; rather, it prohibits intentions when conjoined to something else, something like the action or causing of torturing. The hospital example suggests that if the something conjoined is too strong a form of the prohibited action—say a direct gassing of a patient to death—then intention is not needed; foresight conjoined with such action will form the content of the prohibition. Now both points together: something related to causation and action must be added to intention to give a plausible content to deontological prohibition, but add too much of that something and intention drops out as unnecessary to the content of the prohibition. We next need to enquire about the nature of that 'something else', which gets us to the role of causation in defining our deontological obligations.

IV. Doing versus Allowing I: Omissive Allowings

A. Introduction

We now need to pin down what the 'something else' is that is the object of deontological obligation besides intention. Generally speaking, the most obvious

---

[58] If the mode of combination of these factors were criterial, then we could say the presence of each such factor as intention was individually necessary, and only in combination with the other factors jointly sufficient, for deontological prohibition. If the mode of combination were criteriological in the sense of the later Wittgenstein, then each such factor was neither individually necessary nor sufficient, nor can one say clearly what combination of factors are jointly sufficient short of all of them. See Moore, 'The semantics of judging', Southern California Law Review 54 (1981), 151–294, 217–21.

[59] Hurd's conclusion in 'What in the world is wrong?'.

candidate is action. Causative act-types like killing, raping, torturing, maiming, etc are what we are categorically prohibited from doing (when we intend them). As opposed to what? Well, one suggestion: as opposed to all the other act-types that are morally okay, such as visiting a sick friend, teaching a class, etc. But these contrasting cases are uninteresting; they depend on the particular content of morality's prohibitions. Wanted is something more general. That more general candidate is usually called 'an allowing'. Killing is prohibited; letting someone die is not—more generally, *doing* something awful is prohibited, allowing that awful thing to occur is not. The general statement is often called the doctrine of doing and allowing (the 'DDA').[60]

To quote Frank Jackson at a recent seminar of mine: 'the doctrine of doing and allowing is a mess'.[61] Indeed. It will require the rest of this chapter to untangle its many strands. Let me start with a distinction of Philippa Foot's,[62] seconded explicitly by Warren Quinn[63] and implicitly by Frances Kamm.[64] There are two kinds of allowings, Foot tells us. There are omissive allowings, and there are enabling allowings. In the first, the 'actor' does nothing to prevent some mishap that is about to happen, from happening: eg, he watches the baby drown rather than prevent it from drowning. In the second the actor does something; he enables nature to take its course by removing what was preventing it from doing so: eg, he switches off the respirator, and the patient dies from lack of oxygen.

Finding both a solid metaphysical difference and some moral significance to exist between these two kinds of allowings, I shall consider them separately. Here I focus on omissive allowings. Unlike Foot,[65] I see no harm in calling these simply omission cases. The DDA in this context can be called the doctrine of acts and omissions, as it commonly is. As with the DDE, it will be helpful to separate the 'what is the difference?' question from the 'what difference does it make?' question. I shall again pursue the first question first.

B. The metaphysical distinction between acts and omissions

Just what precisely an omission is, and how it differs from action, is a surprisingly contentious issue. Like intentions, this is a topic I have visited before,[66] and

---

[60] Warren Quinn, 'Actions, intentions, and consequences: The doctrine of doing and allowing', Philosophical Review 98 (1989), 287–312.

[61] Colloquium on 'Moore on Causation', Research School of the Social Sciences, Australian National University, Canberra, May 2003.

[62] Foot, 'Morality, action, and outcome'.   [63] Quinn, 'Doctrine of doing and allowing'.

[64] Frances Kamm spends her time analyzing *acts* that remove defenses, but her examples accept omissions as kinds of allowings. See Kamm, 'Action, omission, and the stringency of duties', University of Pennsylvania Law Review 142 (1994), 1493–512. Kamm's detailed discussion of allowings is in her *Morality, Mortality*, Volume II (New York: Oxford University Press, 1996), Chapters 1–5.

[65] Foot, 'Morality, action, and outcome'.

[66] Moore, *Act and Crime*, 22–34, 54–9, 267–78: Moore, 'More on act and crime', University of Pennsylvania Law Review 142 (1994), 1749–840, reprinted in Moore, *Placing Blame*, 262–86.

rather than rehearse what has gone before I shall here simply pick up where I last left off with omissions. My conclusions were these.

First, generically, an omission is literally nothing at all. An omission to kill is not some ghostly kind of killing. It is like an absent elephant, which is no elephant at all. An omission to kill is an absent event of killing; not the absence of any particular event of killing—it is not an absent act-token—for there are no 'negative events'. There are negative propositions about events, such as 'James omitted to kill Smith' meaning 'it is not the case that James killed Smith'. Such negative statements are negative existentially quantified ones: if there is an omission to kill, then what is true is that it is not the case that some instance of the type of event, killing, existed.

Second, from this generic sense of omissions one can derive a more specific sense. Since omissions generically are absent actions, we make this derivation by plugging in our idea of what actions are. On my theory, defended elsewhere,[67] a killing is:

1. a willing (or volition) having as its object some bodily movement, when
2. that willing causes
3. the bodily movement willed, and
4. that bodily movement causes
5. death.

An omission to kill is the absence of any one or more of the above five items. Either the victim does not die (number 5) or, if he does, not because of my acts (number 4), or I do not move (number 3) or, if my body moves, it is not because I willed it to do so (number 2), or I do not even try to move my body (number 1). Notice that on this view I can omit to kill while I am quite busy dancing a jig, writing an article, or doing anything else. Nothing requires that if I am to omit to kill I must remain motionless. Remaining motionless is one way I can omit to kill, but it is not the only nor even the most common way.

Third, if we are to compare actions like killing with omissive allowings like letting die, we need to make sense of omissions to *save* from death, not omissions to cause death (ie, kill). The positive moral duties we plausibly have require us not to omit to *prevent* deaths, not not to omit to cause deaths. So we need to make sense of omissions to save, that is, to prevent something from happening. This requires us to understand preventions, because the omissions we care about are absent preventions.

A first temptation is to think that this is straightforward in that we can apply the above five-fold causal analysis of killing to preventing death. A saving of Smith would then be a willed bodily movement that causes the survival of Smith. Yet Smith's survival is just the absence of his dying. We must penetrate the seemingly positive language ('surviving', 'starving', 'keeping of the secret',

---

[67] Moore, *Act and Crime*.

'ignoring the pleas of the drowning man', etc) to the underlying reality: to survive is not to die.[68] Now the problem: an absence of Smith dying at some particular time is not a particular thing, a kind of ghostly dying (a 'near death experience?'). What makes the negative proposition ('Smith did not die') true is that there was no instance of the type (Smith dying) that occurred. If causation is a singular relation between either event-tokens or states of affairs as particulars, then how can there be causation of a nothing?[69]

Here my concern about the implications of meta-ethical naturalism for methodology intrudes. The late Warren Quinn once urged that ethical accounts like doing/allowing should be neutral between competing versions of causation, being framed so as to accommodate any plausible metaphysics of causation.[70] I, to the contrary, think there is no help but to do the metaphysics, see what you think causation is, and use your metaphysical conclusions in your ethical argumentation. The conclusion of the later chapters of this book on causation is that causation is a singular relation between token states of affairs.[71] On this view of causation, you cannot cause 'a nothing' any more than you can be caused by 'a nothing'. Absent events, or absent states of affairs,[72] can no more be effects than they can be causes. Causation does not relate absences.

Plug that metaphysical hog-choker in here and preventions become a puzzle. Why do they look causal if they are not causal in structure? My answer[73] (and Phil Dowe's[74]) is that preventings are intimately related to a causal structure even if they are not themselves such a structure. When Jones saves Smith from drowning and thereby prevents Smith from dying, Jones does do something. He volitionally moves his body and that bodily movement causes something. If Jones hauls Smith out of the water with a rope, Jones' movements cause Smith to exit the water. Since the water was the only place where Smith could have drowned right then, what Jones caused was a state of affairs incompatible with Smith drowning. Preventions are the causing of things incompatible with the occurrence of any instance of the type of thing prevented; and omissions are simply absent preventions.

Fourth, and following on the discussion on the third point above, omissions cause nothing. 'Nothing comes from nothing, and nothing ever can' is good

---

[68] It is important in general to reject the seeming indifference of our language at labeling what is really a presence versus what is really only an absence. This we shall explore a bit in Chapter 18, below.

[69] As we shall also explore in Chapter 18, below.

[70] Quinn, 'Doctrine of doing and allowing', 293–4.   [71] See Chapters 14–15, below.

[72] Cogniscenti in metaphysics may raise their eyebrows at this because on one reading of 'states of affairs' such things are propositional and may easily be negative. I intend the other reading of 'states of affairs', what Peter Menzies calls 'real situations', what David Mellor calls 'facta', and what David Armstrong calls simply 'states of affairs'. See Chapters 14–15, below. Incidentally, in the text of this chapter I shall use 'events' and 'states of affairs' interchangeably, because for these purposes I do not need the distinction between them.

[73] See Chapter 18, below.

[74] Dowe, *Physical Causation* (Cambridge: Cambridge University Press, 2000).

metaphysics, as well as catchy lyrics in musical productions.[75] Absent elephants grow no grass by their absence; absent savings cause nothing, and certainly not the deaths they fail to prevent.[76]

To sum up these tersely stated, and here undefended, conclusions with respect to one act-type killing: an omissive letting die is not a kind of killing. Such an omission contains no act, not even a mental act of willing, and the absence of any act is not itself an event or a state of affairs; an omission likewise is not a cause of the death it fails to prevent. To be held responsible for a failure to prevent Smith's death is thus very different from an act that causes Smith's death, that is, a killing. The difference lies in the existence of real states of affairs and of real causal relations for killings but not for lettings die.

C. The moral force of these metaphysical distinctions

We now need to address whether these significant metaphysical distinctions make any moral difference. Again, the difference we are interested in is the difference in consequentialist license: can we consequentially justify omissions by their good 'consequences' (read as, the states of affairs I cause by doing something else), whereas we cannot justify a paired action by its good consequences? Can I, for example, justify not throwing you the rope and thereby not saving you from drowning because I throw the rope to five others in the water and thereby save them from drowning? By contrast, presumably I cannot justify drowning you (to get you off the rope) in order to throw the rope you had to five others in the water (and thereby save them from drowning). I think the answer to the first question is very strongly yes. When it comes to saving the lives of strangers just about everybody I know thinks that you at least may omit to save one in order to save five. (I think in addition you *must* do so given the consequentialist background mentioned earlier.)

Consider a decision by Winston Churchill during the Second World War.[77] The British had broken the German coding device called Ultra, and learned that the Germans planned to bomb Coventry to dispirit the British populace. Churchill could have prevented the killings of the citizens of Coventry by alerting them; but this also would have tipped off the Germans that the British had obtained the German coding-device. Churchill justified his not saving the citizens of Coventry by his thereby saving many more British lives in a shorter, more successful war effort. A socialist War Cabinet colleague urged him not to 'play God' with people's lives. Yet given the consequences, was Churchill not right? However, if Churchill had had to kill the citizens of Coventry in order to

---

[75] Julie Andrews and Christopher Plummer, 'Something Good', in Rogers' and Hammerstein's *The Sound of Music*.
[76] Chapter 18, below.
[77] Churchill's decision is described by William Stevenson, *A Man Called Intrepid: The secret war* (New York: The Lyons Press, 1976). I owe this example to Peer Pedersen, who was kind enough to send me the book.

maintain the British advantage in intelligence—say some Coventry citizen was a spy who learned this but it was unknown which citizen it was—surely we would say he should not have done so in spite of achieving the same good consequence.

People often at least profess to find this moral difference puzzling. They point to cases where no justification is in sight and contrast killings with omissions to save from death, finding both to be equally blameworthy. Notice that this is to replicate Herbert Hart's assumption with respect to the DDE, where Hart assumed that justification-less culpability comparisons between intention and foresight were determinative of the truth of the DDE.[78]

The most famous example is probably that of James Rachels.[79] Two uncles are each bathing a baby who is their nephew; each wants the baby dead so that he can inherit the family wealth. One uncle is motivated by greed to drown the baby in the bathtub by holding its head underwater. The other is luckier: the baby slips under the water and cannot save itself. This uncle, for the same greedy motive, does nothing and the baby drowns. Rachel's own sense was that the two uncles are equally blameworthy, and this was taken to show the moral equivalence of acts and omissions.

There are three responses to Rachels' intuition here. One response is to deny the relevance of justification-less culpability comparisons to the question that interests us here, viz when putative consequentialist justifications *are* in the comparison cases, are such justifications available for omission but not for actions? A second response has been defended at length by Francis Kamm.[80] This response concedes the equivalent blameworthiness of the two uncles but refuses the general conclusion about acts and omissions. (This latter refusal is based on Kamm's very nice insight that acts and omissions have properties constituting them as acts or omissions and that those properties do make a moral difference; yet in particular cases some of such properties may be possessed by *both* of an act/omission pair, so that *that* pair of cases is morally equivalent.)

There is much to be said for both of these responses. The first response strikes many people as very intuitive: even conceding equivalent culpability between the two uncles when no justification is present, when justifications are present they are much more available to justify omissions to save than actions of killing. The second response also is developed by Frances Kamm with great ingenuity. Still, I shall only pursue a third response to Rachels: I do not share his intuition of equivalent blameworthiness.

To see why not, alter Rachels' case a bit. We need to rid the cases of relationships between the uncles and the babies. Suppose no familial relationship exists in either case, nor is either person in charge of the baby's bath. So: A and B are each having lunch on respective park benches. Each has an unattended

---

[78] Hart, 'Punishment and intention'.

[79] James Rachels, 'Active and passive euthanasia', New England Journal of Medicine 292 (1975), 78–80; Rachels, 'Killing and starving to death', Philosophy 54 (1979), 159–71.

[80] Kamm, *Morality, Mortality*, Volume II.

stranger baby toddle over to a puddle next to them. The baby next to A falls face-forward into the puddle and cannot get up. The noise it makes irritates A who therefore does nothing and watches it drown (this returns quiet to the park). The baby next to B is playing happily but noisily in the puddle. To return quiet to the park, B drowns it in the puddle by holding it face down in the water.

Surely we agree that A and B are both dreadful human beings. Our aretaic judgments of their character, as revealed in these choices, is extremely negative. Indeed, if we suppose (as did Rachels in his original case) that A would have drowned a noisy baby if by luck it was not already drowning, we should think A's and B's characters are equally awful. But these aretaic judgments mislead us about the deontic comparison we are supposed to be making: both are guilty of wrongful choices at a razor's point of time, but are they equally wrongful? One of them chose to kill, and killed, whereas the other chose not to save, and did not.

To be sure if one regards such deontic judgments to be elliptically expressed aretaic judgments—the character theory of responsibility of Hume and his intellectual descendents—then one will not accept my distinction. But I am not one of those.[81] Our responsibility for character is real enough, but it is a different form of responsibility from our choices and what those choices cause on particular occasions.

Those who persist in thinking that people like A and B are not just equivalently awful in their characters but are also equivalently wrong in their choices face a puzzle. Typically such people also share Churchill's intuition: we can justify failing to save people a lot more easily than we can justify killing them. If the not-saving were just as wrong as the killing, why is there such a difference in the justifiability between these two, supposedly equivalent wrongs?

So think again about the conclusion of equivalent wrongness. Perhaps it helps (as Kamm suggests) to consider what are our secondary duties of prevention with respect to acts versus omissions.[82] If we could prevent ourselves from killing versus prevent ourselves from failing to save, are such secondary duties to prevent equally stringent in both cases? There are two kinds of cases here, what Kamm calls pre- and post-effort cases.

a. Pre-effort
A has joined a gang. A comes to realize that if he stays in the gang some of their various activities will require him to kill a completely innocent person; A knows himself well enough to realise that when such occasions arise, he will yield to the group pressures by killing such innocents. B by contrast has joined a gang made up hard-hearted libertarians. B comes to realize that if he stays in the gang he will yield to the group pressures never to rescue anyone in peril. Supposing the

---

[81] See Moore, 'Choice character, and responsibility', *Social Policy and Philosophy* 7 (1990), 29–58, reprinted in Moore, *Placing Blame*.

[82] First used in her comment on Moore, *Act and Crime*, Kamm, 'The stringency of duties'; developed at length in Kamm, *Morality, Mortality*, Volume II.

probabilities (of the occasions arising in the future, and of A's and B's deadly responses to those occasions) to be equal, do A and B have equivalently stringent duties to quit the gangs? It seems to me much more obvious that A should quit his gang of killers than that B should quit his band of hard-hearted libertarians— but then it seems to me much more obvious that A should not kill than that B should not omit to save.[83]

b. Post-effort

At t_1 A starts a boulder down a hillside to kill V, his old enemy. The boulder will kill V unless A stops it, which he can do by rushing in front of the boulder at t_2 and diverting it. Such diversion will probably kill A, however, if that diversion is successful in saving V. B, by contrast, happens upon a boulder rolling down a mountain toward V. The boulder just happened to break loose through no act of B's. At t_1 B could have stopped the boulder early in its trajectory at no risk to himself; B did not do so, however, because V is his old enemy whom he wanted to die. At t_2 B has another chance to stop the boulder. He can stop it by rushing in front of the boulder and diverting it. Such diversion will probably kill B, however, if that diversion is successful in saving V. Does A have more of a duty to place his life on the line than B? My own sense is that he does—but then of course I think A was under a more stringent duty at t_1 not to kill than B was at t_1 to save.

It is difficult to argue for conclusions one finds intuitively obvious, and I must confess that I find the moral non-equivalence of acts and omissions to be obvious. So I shall cease beating (what for me is) a dead horse. We should clarify the intuitive conclusion, however. I am *not* reaching the libertarian conclusion that the only duties we have are negative duties not to cause harm by our actions. We do have consequentialist-based duties to prevent harm, even to strangers. I thus reject the idea that we have *strong* permissions to omit, across the board (the libertarian position). Rather, the conclusion I reach here is only that we have *weak* permissions to omit in many omission cases (not in all—we do have positive, deontological obligations to the near and dear). That is, in omission-to-rescue-strangers cases, we are not bound by agent-relative obligations and thus we are back in the land where consequentialist reasons hold sway.

I have thus eschewed arguments that illicitly trade on intuition about *strongly* permitted omissions. I refer to arguments based on the triggers of our positive duties to strangers. Such triggers consist in not only the danger facing some victim V from which we can save him, but also in the burden we must undertake if we are to save V. Look at Lord Macaulay's old example:[84] a surgeon need not take a train from Calcutta to Meerut in order to save someone not his patient,

---

[83] The qualifier has kept me from placing much weight on these arguments. See Moore, 'More on act and crime', 285–6 (in *Placing Blame*).

[84] Lord Macaulay, *Notes on the Indian Penal Code* (1837) reproduced in *The Works of Lord Macaulay*, Vol 7 (New York, 1897), 494.

even though unless the doctor takes the train that person will die. Whereas, if the doctor can prevent some act of his from becoming the cause of that person's death (so that the doctor would then have actively killed the person), then the doctor is obligated to take the train.

I am with Lord Macaulay: when the risk and even inconvenience are too great, the doctor is permitted not to take the train. And this is true even though that same level of inconvenience would hardly justify one is not completing a killing in which one is engaged. But notice the doctor is *strongly* permitted: the doctor does not have to justify his inaction on consequentialist grounds (nor can that inaction he so justified—if one is balancing inconvenience versus life in a consequentialist balance, life wins). Such strong permissions not to save of course negate the existence of *any* obligation to save (and thus *a fortiori* negate the existence of any *deontological* obligation to save); but this shows little about the shape of our deontological obligations from the availability of consequentialist justifications. Strong permissions negate deontological obligations on their own, not by virtue of the shape of those obligations.

V. Doing versus Allowing II: Non-omissive Allowings

A. Introduction

If it were plausible that the objects of our deontological obligations were executed intentions, then causation would have little role here other than its role in marking off omissions. Intending to kill, and then executing that intention in action would be enough, irrespective of success in causing the object of the prohibited intention to be realized. Yet notice that unsuccessfully executed intentions are no more plausible than intentions alone as marking the boundaries of permissible consequentialist justifications.[85] Revert to the example of the Frankfurt police chief and the kidnapper of the child: if the Chief knew that his attempt to torture the kidnapper would probably be thwarted, he might well be justified in trying to torture even if he would not have been justified in intentionally torturing.

The object of deontological prohibitions need to include whatever it is that makes something not only an act but an act of torture . . . or of killing, rape, mayhem, theft, etc. We thus need to add something beyond intention plus acting to capture what we are forbidden to do. If we examine the structure of the complex verbs naming the kinds of actions deontological morality seems to prohibit, there are a variety of features we must add.[86] As we saw in Chapter 1, however, one feature that is common to all act-types morality forbids is that of causation. The willed bodily movement (that is at the core of all actions) must

---

[85] See Hurd, 'What in the world is wrong?'.
[86] I explore these in Moore, *Act and Crime*, Chapter 8.

cause death (for killing), penetration (for rape), asportation (for theft), disfigurement (for mayhem), etc. This is the point we explored in Chapter 1, that
whatever else is required for an act to be, eg, a rape (such as lack of consent), also
required is causation of something.

The other connection between prohibited act-types like killing and causation
that we explained in Chapter 1 was the converse of the point just mentioned.
The point just mentioned was that if X kills Y, then X causes the death of Y.
Much more controversial is the converse: if X causes the death of Y, then X kills
Y. The reason that many philosophers disagree with this latter implication is
because they think causation to be a much less discriminating relation than I
think it to be. They thus think, for example, that if I suggest to you where to
find your victim, and you find him and kill him, then I have caused the victim's
death but I have not killed him—you did that; whereas (as we shall explore in
Chapter 13) I think that although you did not do much to kill the victim in such
a case you did not do much to cause his death either.

It will not ultimately matter much here whether one agrees with this second
point of Chapter 1. Whether one agrees does, however, make a difference to how
we should describe the distinctions I wish to draw shortly. I think they are all
causal distinctions, and will discuss them in those terms. Those with less discriminating notions of causation will have to reframe the same distinctions in
terms of the attributes of action verbs like 'killing' etc.[87] I think that such a
translation of the distinctions (and arguments for them) can be done, but not
being very ecumenically disposed towards other people's theories of causation,
that is not my concern.

I thus begin a discussion of the second kind of allowing distinguished earlier,
the enabling rather than the omissive kind. Consider the familiar example of
medically justified, passive euthanasia. P is hooked up to a respirator which is the
only thing keeping her alive. Her quality of life is very poor because she is in a
coma, her condition is incurable, and the machine she is on can save another,
higher quality, life. Under the doctrine of passive euthanasia, her doctor may
unhook her, *allowing* her to die. But in the exact same circumstances, giving
the exact same justification, her doctor may not give her a lethal injection.
That would be active, not passive euthanasia, forbidden by the deontological
prohibition against killing.

Notice in the passive-euthanasia kind of allowing, the doctor is not an omitter.
Turning off the respirator is an action. Although some courts have said that these
are omission cases,[88] they are surely stretching the concept of omission beyond
what it can tolerate. Some critics of these courts, however—such as my former

---

[87] Thus, David Lewis' extremely non-restrictive notion of causation (as counterfactual
dependence) does not track at all the limitations I explore; but then he rediscovers many such
limits in the semantics of causally complex verbs of action like 'kill'. See Chapter 17, n 24, below.

[88] *Barber v. Superior Court*, 147 Cal App 3d 1006, 195 Cal Rptr 484 (1983); *Airedale NHS Trust v.
Bland* [1993] All ER 821.

self—were wrong to think that such passive euthanasia cases, being act and not omission cases, must simply be strong permission cases.[89] Both I and the courts I was criticizing overlooked the possibility we need here to explore: that these are neither omissions nor active causings requiring justification, but are non-omissive allowings. I shall begin with the most intuitive kind of non-omissive allowings, a kind illustrated by the passive euthanasia example above.

B. Non-omissive allowings 1: Removing a defense one was entitled not to have provided

1. Introduction

There are seemingly many other well-known examples of non-omissive allowings besides passive euthanasia. Judith Thomson's violinist is one.[90] In the course of defending the right to abortion, Thomson imagined that you go to the symphony and fall asleep. You awake to find the lead violinist hooked up to you in a life support system that only you could provide. After nine months he can be unhooked, but if he is removed before then he will die. May you unhook him? Thomson intends that you agree with her in saying yes.

As well known are the Chris Boorse/Roy Sorenson tales of ducking.[91] Take the one of the grizzly bear, a tale that has descended to the level of cocktail-party conversation: you and I are camping in the woods. A ferocious and hungry grizzly bear charges out of the woods towards both of us, although I am closer to him. I jump into my running shoes. You shout at me, 'fool, you can't outrun a grizzly'. I shout back as I take off, 'I only have to outrun you'. May I 'duck' by outrunning you, even though that means the grizzly will kill you? Most people I know agree with me in saying yes.

The violinist and ducking cases share a common structure with the passive euthanasia cases. It is a two-part structure. First, the acts are all done against the backdrop of an imminent threat to the victim: a death from disease or grizzly bear. All I do by my action is enable that threat to be realized by removing the victim's defense to it: I remove the respirator, remove myself as a life-support system, or remove myself from between you and the bear. Second, the defense you had was one I was providing. The doctor (or her surrogate) hooked up the respirator to start with; your body is the only defense the violinist has; my body is your only defense against the bear. Call this the baseline point: by doing what he did the actor was only returning the victim to the state she would have been in had the defense never been provided to start with.

---

[89] See Moore, *Act and Crime*, 27. I repeat the mistake in Moore, 'More on act and crime', 276 (in Moore, *Placing Blame*).

[90] Judith Jarvis Thomson, 'A defense of abortion', Philosophy and Public Affairs 1 (1971), 47–66.

[91] Christopher Boorse and Roy Sorensen, 'Ducking harm', Journal of Philosophy 115 (1988), 115–34.

Yet despite this common structure I will focus on the passive euthanasia cases alone; this, because the doing/(non-omissive) allowing distinction operates too strongly in the violinist and ducking cases. In the latter cases, if you agree with the intended resolutions, that will be because the actors are *strongly* permitted to unhook or to run. They are not merely weakly permitted, meaning they must have good consequentialist reasons to do what they do. My sense is that they are entitled not to balance the consequences in preserving their freedom or their lives. If I am correct in this last conclusion, then these cases are not apt ones with which to test the line of permissible consequentialist justification, the line which marks the borders of our deontological obligations.

Focusing on passive euthanasia-like cases only, I shall again proceed by first asking after the natural properties involved in this kind of doing/allowing, and then asking after the moral significance of those properties.

2. The metaphysics of 'removing a defense to a death' while not causing that death

We saw earlier that preventings are not themselves causal; a saving someone from death is not the causing of a non-death. Similarly, I argued that omissions are not causal; an omission to save someone from death is not a causing of death (even when a death occurs that the saving omitted would have prevented). Here we need one more piece of the puzzle. When the doctor does something like pull the plug on the respirator, the moral philosophers call this a 'removing of a defense'. The metaphysicians call this a 'double-prevention'.[92] What the doctor literally does is prevent something (the respirator) from doing what it was doing, namely, preventing the patient's death. The doctor prevented a prevention of death. Thus the label.

Double-preventions cannot be causal if preventions and omissions are not causal.[93] Consider an old example of mine:[94] DP sees his old enemy V drowning in the ocean, which makes DP happy. Then DP spies a lifeguard, L, getting ready to save V. So DP ties up the lifeguard, and V drowns. DP has prevented the preventer, L, from preventing V's death. But DP has not caused V's death. What DP caused was L to be tied up, which was incompatible with L rescuing V. L therefore omitted to save V. If L's omission is not a cause of V's death, how can DP's act be a cause of that death? DP only caused something incompatible with L saving V; but DP no more caused an absence of saving by L than L caused the death of V by his omission to save.

---

[92] See, eg, John Collins, 'Preemptive prevention', Journal of Philosophy 97 (2000), 223–34; Michael McDermott, 'Redundant causation', British Journal of the Philosophy of Science 46 (1995), 523–44; Ned Hall, 'Causation and the price of transitivity', Journal of Philosophy 97 (2000), 198–222; Phil Dowe, *Physical Causation*.
[93] See Chapter 18, below.   [94] Moore, *Act and Crime*, 278, n 42.

One can see this even more straightforwardly if preventions were causal but omissions were not. Then we could say, DP caused L's omission to save; but since L's omission to save cannot be a cause of V's death, and since there is no other way DP caused V's death but through L's omission, then DP did not cause V's death.

Many people find this troubling because they perceive, correctly, that DP is morally responsible for V's death. Indeed, in criminal law DP is plainly guilty of murder. But we do not want this moral conclusion to drive the metaphysics here. Perhaps there are non-causal bases for responsibility, and unjustified double-preventions is one of them. After all, it is true that V's death counterfactually depended upon DP's act, and perhaps this is enough for a kind of moral responsibility for V's death.[95]

Recall also that the lifeguard scenario lacks the second requirement for an allowing of this type. The defense V had against drowning was L, and that defense was *not* one DP had been providing. Suppose L was not a lifeguard but just a private citizen with excellent life-saving skills in the water. He is initially disposed to save V and even takes a few steps towards the water with that intention. But he suddenly realizes that saving V would clearly violate the code of the Hard-Hearted Libertarian Gang of which he is a member, so L ties himself up to prevent his yielding to any more warm and fuzzy temptations. Make the defense one L himself is providing, as immediately above, and his removal of that defense—his preventing himself from preventing—now looks no more causal than a simple omission.

Indeed, this kind of double-prevention looks very much like an omission (because of the shortness of time during which the preventer—a person disposed to rescue—existed). So repair to the example of the doctor turning off the respirator. His act of turning it off looks not at all like an omission because his earlier act of turning on the machine was complete—the machine was preventing the patient's death and would continue to do so until he turned it off. Still, the doctor merely allowed the patient to die because his act simply let nature take the course it would have taken had not he, the doctor, temporarily prevented it from doing so. The patient simply died (pretty much) the death she would have died had not the doctor intervened to start with.

There is obviously a large counterfactual element at work in this second requirement for this kind of an allowing: is the harm allowed similar to the harm the victim would have suffered had no defense been supplied initially? Yet also at work is a moral element here, about the moral acceptability of the baseline to which return is made. If the good consequences justifying turning off the respirator at t_2 had been present and known to be present at t_1 when the respirator was turned on, would the doctor have been justified in not turning on the

---

[95] Argued for in Chapters 13 and 18, below.

respirator? If the answer to this question is yes, then that baseline (when the patient was dying) is an appropriate one to which to return.

One sees the moral element clearly in the violinist and the ducking cases as well. It is because I have a strong right to bodily integrity (that was violated by the hooking up of the violinist to me) that makes it so appropriate that the baseline to which return is made be the violinist unhooked (rather than hooked) up to me. It is because I have a strong privilege to defend myself against bears and other deadly perils that I may remove my body even though it is your only defense against the bear. (Notice it is because the baselines here are so strong— I am strongly permitted not to hook up to needy violinists or to be eaten by bears—that my returning to these baselines is also strongly permitted.)

The appropriateness of the baseline is of course a moral question. Yet a patient naturalism will not be offended by this. We will need to give some naturalist account of why there is no duty to provide a respirator to permanently comatose, incurable patients when other patients with better life prospects are in need of that respirator. But this we can give, in pretty straightforward consequentialist terms. And the same is true for our rights to bodily integrity.

3. The moral significance of removing defenses

So allowings metaphysically are double-preventions when the preventer prevented was something the actor provided but was (in retrospect) entitled not to provide. Such allowers do not cause the harm that they prevented something (they supplied) from preventing; why should this make a moral difference? Specifically, are such allowings eligible for consequentialist justification whereas causings of those same harms are not?

Plainly the moral appropriateness of the baseline, together with the counterfactual judgment that that is where we are returning to, does a lot of the work here. We can see this by recalling how responsible was DP in tying up the lifeguard so that V drowns. That is a true double-prevention case too, where DP does *not* cause V's death. Yet DP was not returning V to an appropriate baseline; DP had not provided the lifeguard and so was not entitled to tie him up. The appropriate baseline was thus *not* V drowning with no lifeguard rescue in sight.

Does the causal/double-prevention distinction do *any* moral work here? Suppose the only way the doctor could unhook the respirator or that Thomson could unhook herself from the violinist was to directly cause death, by lethal injection, knife through the heart, or whatever. Would such killings-that-return-to-the-baseline also be justified? Your answer may be yes, as I believe it is for Frances Kamm,[96] but is it so easily or obviously yes? Does the addition of such strong, direct causation of death not make us hesitate here?[97] There is something morally relevant about the difference between causing death, and allowing nature

---

[96] Kamm, *Morality, Mortality*, Volume II.   [97] See Chapter 18, below.

to cause death by double-prevention. Consider the 'stress and duress' techniques used by the British during interrogations of IRA suspects in Northern Ireland, techniques adopted by US interrogators post-9/11 in Afghanistan. These are largely double-prevention techniques—eg, sleep deprivation, where the interrogator prevents one from sleeping. We know (from no less an authority than Shakespeare) that sleep is what 'knits up the raveled sleeve of care' and that without such knitting we fall apart and eventually die.[98] These techniques make no pretense of returning the detainee to some baseline that is morally appropriate (if the interrogator was the one making sleep possible to start with, then this might be such a baseline). Nonetheless, such techniques are regarded as 'torture lite' rather than true torture in part because of the role of nature in making things unpleasant for the detainee.

In any event, both elements together give us one place where consequentialist justifications are appropriate: we can justify acting in such a way as to prevent something from preventing some harm, so long as we supplied the thing preventing the harm and we were entitled (in light of what we now know) not to have done so. We now need to see what else might be included as allowings of the non-omissive kind.

C. Non-omissive allowings 2: Accelerating a death about to happen anyway

Once one sees the distinctive part played by each of the two elements of a removal-of-defense-allowing, it is tempting to pry the two elements apart to see what we get. First I shall eliminate the double-prevention/cause distinction. So we will consider clear causing-death cases. But we will retain the second element above, the counterfactual judgment about returning the victim to pretty close to where he would have been had we not intervened to start with.

A narrow interpretation of this second element would yield the following kind of case. I heroically saved you a year ago; it was so risky, what I did, that I had no obligation to do it under anyone's view of positive duties. But I did it and now I need your organs to save a number of my relatives. Can I now kill you and take them? Surely not. That I gave you life when I did not have to does not free me from my deontological obligation not to kill you a year later.

So this narrow interpretation of the second element is not what is wanted here. Broaden the interpretation of that second element: what is really doing the work is the counterfactual judgment. When I remove a defense I was providing I return you to where you would have been without me, which is dead. True, the death you die when I remove the defense is not literally the death you would have died had I not provided the defense to begin with. (Recognizing that trans-world identity claims are notoriously difficult, this one seems true.) But the difference may seem immaterial.

---

[98] Ernest L Hartmann, *The Function of Sleep* (New Haven: Yale University Press, 1973).

All I did really was delay your death (by providing you a defense against it), but not by as much as I could have delayed it (because I later removed that defense).

What if we reverse this somewhat sloppy identification of deaths. Suppose what I do *accelerates* slightly the death you were about to come to anyway? Could that too be chalked up to the nature that was killing you (even though I finished the job for nature)? It is clearly widely intuitive to give an affirmative answer to this question.

In the lifeboat cases, where all will die unless some are thrown out, we should throw some out because they are about to die anyway.[99] Or, when all in the lifeboat will soon starve to death unless one is killed and eaten, one should be killed and eaten since the one killed would soon die anyway.[100] Or in the mountain-climbing cases, where all on a rope will be pulled to their deaths unless the rope is cut, the rope should be cut—those dangling down-rope are dead no matter what.[101] In the wedged fetus cases, if both mother and fetus will die unless the fetus' skull is crushed and the fetus is removed (saving the mother but not of course the fetus), we should kill the fetus.[102] Or in *Sophie's Choice*-like situations, when the Nazis will kill all of a group unless you choose one to be the example, better to choose the one rather than have that one killed anyway along with all the others.[103] I call these the 'almost dead' cases, because the one we kill is almost dead anyway at the hands of someone else or of nature.

Billy Crystal tells us in the film *The Princess Bride* that there is a big difference 'between being almost dead and being all dead'. Well, not here Billy. Although it is far from uncontroversial, I find it very intuitive that killing is justified in all of the above cases. What is guiding that judgment is not a causal distinction. All of these are cases of pre-emptive over-determination. You remember: two fires are approaching victim's house, each sufficient to burn it to the ground. Yet fire number 1 reaches the house first, burning it to the ground; fire number 2 gets there later and does not burn the house, although fire number 2 would have

---

[99] *United States v. Holmes*, 26 Fed Cas 360 (Cir Ct F D Pa 1842). The permissibility of jettisoning some from the lifeboat to save the rest was *dictum* for the court, inasmuch as in the court's view one needed to have a lottery or other fair procedure to select who would be sacrificed, and this was not done. Justice Cardozo's intuition about *Holmes* was that even if a fair procedure had been adopted to select those who must die, no one could throw them overboard although they could jump in themselves and they would be supererogatory to do so: Benjamin N Cardozo, *Law and Literature: And other essays and addresses* (New York: Harcourt, Brace and Company, 1931), 110–114.

[100] *Regina v. Dudley and Stephens*, 14 QBD 273 (1884). I obviously disagree with the court's holding in *Dudley and Stephens*, as did Glanville Williams: *Criminal Law: The general part* (2nd edn, London: Stevens and Sons, 1961), 741–5.

[101] This is one of the Model Penal Code examples of when it is permissible to kill. *Commentaries to the Model Penal Code* (Philadelphia: American Law Institute, 1985). For a real-life example, see the well-told tale (recently made into a film) by Joe Simpson, *Touching the Void* (New York: Harper Collins, 1988).

[102] The example of 1950s Catholic theology. See Hart, 'Punishment and intention', 122–25.

[103] Aside from the film *Sophie's Choice*, see Bernard Williams, 'A critique of utilitarianism', where Williams' famous example of 'Jim' having to choose who in a group of villagers should be shot (else all will be), is another example of this sort.

burned it to the ground had the house still existed to be burnt. In no sense of the word does fire number 2 *cause* the destruction of the house; in a full sense of the word fire number 1 *causes* the destruction of the house.

Mutatis mutandis for all of the above examples. We kill in each of them.[104] The other factors would have killed but we did not give them a chance.

So what guides our judgment here is purely the counterfactual judgment: if we did not do what we did, the victim would soon have died anyway. We thus accelerated his death a little, just as in the removal of defense cases we delayed it a little. But we did not in either case change the world very much from where it was heading without our help.

These are not of course true allowing cases, except by honorific designation. These are killing cases. Yet what we have done is export (Kamm's term)[105] a property of true allowings (of the defense removal kind) to killings. Such a property can be possessed by both true allowings and by true killings. Not surprisingly, that property makes almost as much moral difference for killings as it did for allowings. We are justified in killing by the good consequences of doing so in these cases.

How one accommodates this clear, weak permission into one's description of the objects of categorical obligation is a puzzle. We cannot do what we did to delayings (removal of a defense allowings): there we fastened onto the double-prevention versus cause distinction to say one was not really killing in those cases. But in the acceleration of death cases we are clearly causing death, and clearly killing. I once opined that we should accommodate accelerations as exceptions to categorical norms, like self-defense, defense of others, etc.[106] Perhaps that is right, although such exceptions tend to be strong permissions whereas this one seems clearly consequentialist in character.

More tempting is to liken these 'almost dead' cases to the 'mostly dead' cases. Part of what is at work with permanently comatose patients in passive euthanasia cases is that they have already lost a large part of what makes a member of the human species into a person (just as fetuses are not yet fully persons). By contrast with such 'mostly dead' cases, the 'almost dead' typically are not physically deteriorated to the point that rationality, autonomy, emotionally, and the other attributes of personhood are lost.[107] So the 'almost dead' are not literally the

---

[104] I thus reject Baruch Brody's conclusion that in acceleration cases (such as knifing a patient who is about to die anyway), 'the cause of the earlier death of the patient remains the patient's underlying disease condition'. Brody, 'Withdrawal of treatment versus Killing of patients' in Tom Beauchamp (ed), *Intending Death: The ethics of assisted suicide* (Upper Saddle River: Prentice Hall, 1996), 99. Brody's conclusion is supported by his faulty inference that the later death the patient would have suffered, and the earlier death he did suffer, are literally the same event (so that the causes of each must be the same). Ibid, 101–2. For why this does not work, see Chapter 15 (on states of affairs as causal relata) and Chapter 17 (on David Lewis' 'fragile events' approach to over-determination cases).

[105] Kamm, *Morality, Mortality*, Volume II.

[106] Moore, 'Causation and counterfactual baselines', 1266–7, 1267, n 205.

[107] I explore many attributes of personhood in Moore, *Law and Psychiatry: Rethinking the relationship* (Cambridge: Cambridge University Press, 1984), Chapter 2.

'mostly dead'. Nonetheless, what the 'almost dead' have is a lot less than the rest of us have. That is why in tort law when we kill one of the almost dead—we for example, electrocute a boy who is already falling to his death[108]—his life is valued at a fraction of the life of one with a normal life expectancy. In light of this, we might think that our categorical obligation not to kill a person is not very clearly violated when we (clearly enough) kill what is in reality but a thin time-slice of a person.

D. Non-omissive allowings 3: Aiding another person to cause

Now let me turn to the other of the two elements in the allowings of the removal of a defense kind, which is the purely causal/double-prevention point. Again, a narrow interpretation of this element produces cases like that we have seen before, such as tying up the lifeguard. The intuition of serious responsibility is quite strong in such cases, until we add in the other element (of having ourselves provided the defense removed when we did not have to).

Contrast the lifeguard case with this one.[109] Judge Tally heard that the Skelton boys were riding to another town to kill one Ross because Ross had seduced the Skeltons' sister. The Judge also wanted Ross dead but heard that a warning telegram had been sent to Ross's town to alert Ross to the Skeltons' imminent threat. Tally sent a countermanding telegram to Ross' town, instructing the telegraph operator not to deliver the warning telegram. He did not; the Skeltons caught up with Ross and killed him. How should we adjudge Tally's responsibility for Ross' death?

This is a double-prevention case: Tally by his act prevented the warning telegram from preventing Ross' killing by the Skeltons. So Tally did not *cause* Ross' death. Yet since Tally is not the one who sent the warning telegram, he is not a mere allower in the removal-of-a-defense sense and he seems thus quite responsible for Ross' death. Yet compare his responsibility to that of Ross' actual killers, the Skeltons. Is Tally *as much* to blame as those who shot Ross to death?

This is a familiar issue to students of the criminal law, because what is at issue is the degree of blameworthiness properly attaching to accomplice liability. Are accomplices who do no killing themselves as blameworthy as the principals who do? Despite the formal doctrines of modern Anglo-American criminal law equating accomplices to principals, I think the general answer is yes.[110] Absent special facts about psychological domination or manipulation by the accomplice, accomplices like Tally are less blameworthy than those whom they aid.

---

[108] *Dillon v. Twin State Gas and Electric Co*, 85 NH 449, 163 A 11 (1932).
[109] *State ex rel Attorney General v. Tally* 102 Ala 25, 15 So 722 (1894). We discuss the Tally case at length in Chapter 13, below.
[110] Chris Kutz reaches a similar conclusion about accomplices. See Chris Kutz, *Complicity* (Cambridge: Cambridge University Press, 2000).

Does this difference in blameworthiness when justification is not in sight make the kind of difference in which we are interested here, viz the licensing of consequentialist justifications for accomplices but not the principals they aid? Consider in this regard the British duress cases. In *Lynch*[111] the defendant drove the IRA gunmen to where they could kill a British policeman, and they did so. Lynch was not an IRA member or sympathizer; had he not driven the gunman they would have shot his family to death. The British courts had held that such threats could not justify actual killings; had Lynch himself shot the policeman, he would have had no defense. But merely aiding the killing (by driving) was eligible to be justified by the threats of greater harm to Lynch's family if he did not drive the IRA to its target. The lesser wrongness of aiding a killing was outside the categorical prohibition of killing and so could be consequentially justified.

My own sense is that this is correct. But why this should be right requires investigation. Contrast the actual Tally case with this variation of it: there is no warning telegram to be countermanded but Tally helps the Skeltons in a different way. He throws extra ammunition bags on their horses in case they have a prolonged shoot-out with Ross. As it turns out they did not need the extra ammo, but they could have. Notice that this hypothetical Judge Tally is not a double-preventionist. He helps to kill Ross but not by removing a defense Ross had against an impending death. Still, the hypothetical Tally is still incrementally less blameworthy than the Skeltons. It remains true that they killed Ross and Tally only helped them.

Notice that this is also true of Lynch. Lynch also did not remove a defense the British policeman had against an impending death (unless distance is a 'defense', but then anything is). Lynch simply made it easier for the IRA to kill the policeman by supplying transportation. Yet Lynch too does less wrong than those who kill, in his case allowing him the benefit of consequentialist justification for his action.

My conclusion is that the double-prevention/cause distinction is morally idle here. Some other factor is making the difference between direct causers of death and those who aid them. Those who aid have a lesser responsibility, irrespective of whether their aid takes the form of a double-prevention or not. My long-held hypothesis is that the factor that is doing the work here is what lawyers for centuries have called intervening causation.[112] The IRA and the Skeltons in the cases just discussed were 'free, informed, voluntary actors' whose actions both directly caused death and intervened between Tally's and Lynch's efforts in that regard. As the lawyers say, such intervening causes 'break the causal chains' that seem to exist between Lynch's and Tally's efforts, and the deaths. In law, neither Lynch nor Tally proximately caused those deaths.

---

[111] *Director of Public Prosecutions for Northern Ireland v. Lynch* [1975] AC 653.
[112] So argued in Moore, 'Torture and the balance of evils'.

I will later restate the law's intervening cause doctrine in detail[113] and will only give the briefest sketch here. Hart and Honoré devoted a long and masterful book to the topic,[114] showing how the legal notion of intervening causation has deep roots in common, everyday usage of causal idioms outside of the law. Sufficient for our purposes is to note that in law and everyday thought, when one party sets a chain of events in motion that increase the probability of some harm but another party intervenes by intentionally causing the harm the first party was trying to cause or risked causing, we conclude that only the later party caused the harm. The first party may have enabled the second to kill, may have aided the killing, may have made the killing easier or even possible at all—but only the later party caused the death, only the later party killed.

If this ordinary and legal notion of causation tracks the causal relation in reality, then we have what we need to make sense of the moral difference between accomplices and perpetrators: only the latter *cause* death, whereas the former *enable* it. We then have a metaphysical distinction with which to ground the perceived moral difference. I had long been hopeful that one could make out such a metaphysical distinction. But after a diligent exploration of the possibilities here—things like a libertarian metaphysics that makes persons' free choices literal uncaused causers and thus fresh causal starts—my conclusion is that both law and ordinary thought are wrong here.[115] In any acceptably literal sense of the words, there is often some kind of *causal relationship* between the act of an accomplice and the harm his principal (also) causes.[116] So there is no *crisp* metaphysical distinction here, between causers and aiders.

There is, however, a vague by degree distinction here that may be serviceable. This is suggested by our willingness to say that Lynch and my imagined Tally 'causally contributed' to the deaths, were a 'causal factor' in the deaths, or even were 'a cause' of the deaths; while being at the same time uncomfortable with saying that Lynch and Tally 'caused' the deaths, or that they were 'the cause' of the respective deaths, or that they 'killed' those people. What I think these linguistic intuitions are capturing is the ultimately *de minimus* size of Tally's and Lynch's causal contributions. Compared to the causal contributions of the Skeltons or the IRA, Tally and Lynch were small potatoes.

The suggestion is that what the law and ordinary thought have sought to capture with their seemingly sharp-edged bivalent notion of intervening causation, is in fact a rule of thumb about the degree of causal contribution: when there is a much larger cause of the harm that succeeds in time the accused's act, then that relegates the accused's act to a sufficiently small causal role that we

---

[113] See Chapter 11, below.

[114] HLA Hart and Tony Honoré, *Causation in the Law* (2nd edn, Oxford: Oxford University Press, 1985).

[115] See Chapter 12, below.

[116] There are both causal and non-causal accomplices, as well as three or four different varieties of the latter, as I explore in Chapter 13, below.

think of it as not a cause at all. It of course really is a cause, but size matters here, so that moral blameworthiness is diminished as the degree of causal contribution is diminished.

Such a suggestion has to answer two rather big questions. The first is a metaphysical question: are causal relations scalar; that is, a matter of degree? Not everything is. Being 'a little bit pregnant' is usually thought to be only a joke; not being 'much of a father' is not to be taken biologically, for in biology one either is or is not the father. And causation could be like these relations, not like being middle-aged. Second, there is a moral question: does moral responsibility diminish as the degree of causal contribution diminishes?

I shall argue shortly that causation is a scaler relation,[117] so let me here assume that that leg of the trousers is nicely on and move to the other leg. Does it matter morally to be a small cause as opposed to a big cause of some harm? Is it less wrong to be a small contributor to a death rather than a big one, holding all else equal? There are two kinds of test cases.

First, consider the 'at-a-time' cases, where the accused's causal contribution occurs at the same time as other factors that also contribute to a single, indivisible harm. Suppose first the causal contribution of each of the factors is equal: joint fire, joint noise, joint flood, joint pollution cases, for example. Is there more moral blameworthiness if you are one of three producers of some polluting harm, as opposed to one of a hundred? Does it matter to your conclusion here whether: (a) each polluter's contribution was necessary for the harm to occur, so that all together were only jointly sufficient; or (b) each polluter's contribution was sufficient by itself, so that all together were only jointly necessary; or (most commonly) (c) no polluter's contribution was either necessary or sufficient, since there was more pollution than was needed to produce the harm?[118]

My sense of these equal contribution cases is that it matters when you increase the numbers (and thus decrease the size of each contribution). Consider an example of Alvin Goldman's concerning the voter's paradox.[119] Why is it rational to vote, when the chance of your single vote making any difference in an election is virtually nil? Goldman's answer: since causal relations can exist even when the cause is not a necessary condition for the outcome (surely right), each voter has some causal responsibility for the outcome of the election. Yet are we not reluctant to think that this solves the voter's paradox, even if it is correct in its causal metaphysics? Elections have too many voters equally contributing to their outcome to think that my one vote contributes very much. I thus do not deserve much praise or blame for the election's outcome, given my *de minimus* (even if not zero) causal contribution to that outcome.

---

[117] Chapters 5–6, below.

[118] What I call 'garden-variety concurrent causes', 'over-determination concurrent cause', and 'mixed concurrent cause' cases respectively. See Chapter 17, below.

[119] Alvin Goldman, 'Why citizens should vote: A causal responsibility approach', Social Policy and Philosophy 16 (1999), 201–17.

Now vary the assumption of equal contribution. Suppose one cause is very much bigger than another in jointly producing an indivisible harm, eg Agatha Christie's *Murder on the Orient Express*, where the drugged victim dies of loss of blood from thirteen stab wounds, each of different intensity and each done by a different defendant. Did the slight stabbers do less wrong than the big stabbers? One can agree with the California Supreme Court when it got this kind of a case—that 'drop by drop' the life-blood flowed out of the victim 'from both wounds' and thus that each wounder is a causer of death[120]—and yet think that when there is more blood lost there is larger causal contribution, and when there is a larger causal contribution there is greater wrongdoing.

American tort law apportions liability for harms caused by more than one defendant in proportion to degrees of causal contribution by that defendant,[121] and to the extent that tort law is based on moral fault that is some evidence that degrees of fault follow degrees of causation. In theory Anglo-American criminal law goes the other way here, holding each wounder fully liable for murder without regard to the degrees of causal contribution. Yet criminal law's official theory here is no more to be credited than it is in postulating equal blame-worthiness between accomplices and perpetrators. My suspicion is that the 'law-in-action' (as opposed to the 'law-in-books') is quite different: more of a cause, more to blame.

If causation itself matters to overall responsibility—the topic of the previous chapter as well as this one—and if causation does come in degrees, then why would more of it not be worse or less of it better? Since causing more harm is worse, why is more causing of the same harm not also worse?

If we turn to the more directly relevant 'over-time' cases, we only need one assumption to apply here the results of what we did in the 'at-a-time' cases. That assumption is that spatio-temporal distance is a pretty good proxy for degree of causal contribution. The closer some event c is to some event e where c causes e, the more causal contribution c makes to e. The assumption is supported by the thought that any event e is the product of numerous causes, and that each of them in turn are the products of numerous causes, and so on. Causation is then pictured as an inverted cone, not as a simple chain. The further up the cone from e is some c, the less causal contribution it makes to e (because it is joined by so many other causes). Thus later is usually greater, when it comes to degrees of causation.[122]

So I assume that accomplices like Lynch or my imagined Tally are small causes compared to perpetrators like the IRA or the Skeltons, and it is just this that explains diminishment of wrongdoing by the former to the point where conse-quentialist justifications are available. It bears stressing that this vague-by-degree difference cannot be the crisp distinction the legal doctrines of intervening

---

[120] *People v. Lewis*, 124 Cal 551, 57 P 470 (1899).   [121] As I discuss in Chapter 5, below.
[122] Discussed in Chapter 5, below.

causation and accomplice liability pretend it to be. Nor are those doctrines unerring in their capture of major versus minor causal contributions. Consider in this regard another of the British duress cases, *Abbott*.[123] Abbott claimed the same justification for what he did in aiding a killing as had Lynch, namely Abbott's family was threatened with death unless he participated. But what Abbott did was more: he held the victim while she was stabbed to death by the perpetrator (who had to take several stabs at it because he kept hitting bone with his saber). One might well think (as did the court), that the technical classification of Abbott as an accomplice is not what should govern the availability of duress as a defense, but rather, how much he helped. Abbott was too big a cause of the victim's death to avail himself of consequentialist justifications, no matter that he was not the actual killer but only the accomplice.

Consider likewise the current practice of American intelligence agencies to do 'extraordinary renditions' when it comes to the torture of terrorist suspects possessing life-saving information. 'Extraordinary rendition' is a euphemism for transporting suspected terrorists to countries such as Egypt which are less restrictive in their interrogative techniques than are we. In 1998, for example, the CIA flew five members of the al Qaeda from Tirania, Albania, to Cairo for interrogation.[124] Assuming *arguendo* that good consequences could be obtained by such measures, are they eligible for consequentialist justification because the CIA only enables torture but does not itself torture? From what has been said, that depends on the degree of causal involvement of the CIA in torture. If mere transportation is provided, it looks like *Lynch*; if in-room suggestions are made during torture (as Sister Dianna Ortiz has said was true of the CIA involvement in her torture in Guatemala), then it looks more like *Abbott*. In principle, however, such extraordinary renditions could be eligible for consequentialist justifications (again, assuming there are such).

I know that this conclusion troubles many people. Partly that is due to their reflecting on cases where no good consequentialist justification is in sight. And of course, if no justification is around, you are not free to give would-be killers ammunition, countermand warnings to their victims, drive the killers to their victim, or fly the victims to their killers. You are seriously blamable for such enablings of evil. The only point is that you are less blamable than those who do evil, enough so that you can justify helping someone else do an act that you could not justify doing yourself. Think of the Greek islanders in John Fowles' novel *The Magus*, who had to reveal the location of three Greek partisans in order to save their 50 children from being killed by the Nazis. I think that it is easier to justify telling the Nazis where three partisans are hiding than it is to justify shooting the three partisans themselves.

---

[123] *R v. Abbott* [1976] 3 All ER 140. [124] See n 6, above.

E. Non-omissive allowings 4: Being a minor cause of harm vis-à-vis nature

If one takes the line I do about accomplices—that although they often do cause the harm they enable they do not do so strongly enough to rule out consequentialist justifications—then in general any truly *minor* causal contribution should also be eligible for consequentialist justification. In the last subsection I considered other persons as the big cause in comparison to which your contribution is minor. Now consider cases in which nature plays the role of big cause. I shall consider two possibilities. The first is where the big natural cause intervenes between the accused's act and the harm; the second is where the big natural cause precedes the act of the accused in time, and thus is already a 'force in motion' which he redirects.

1. Extraordinary natural events as big causes

Again the legal doctrine of intervening causation is instructive. In law, a freakish hailstorm, an unprecedented wind, a bolt out of the blue, etc will 'break causal chains' almost as surely as will the intervening free, informed, voluntary act of another wrongdoer.[125] There is even less metaphysical grounding for this bit of legal doctrine than there was for the intervening actor doctrine—nobody thinks storms have free will, for example.[126] So here it is even clearer we are simply making big cause/little cause comparisons when we say that some actor did not *cause* some harm because an intervening act of nature did.

The law does not quite have the courage of its convictions here. If the original actor intentionally uses the intervening storm as the means to a harm he wants to bring about, then the storm does not 'break the causal chain' so the actor is the cause of the harm after all. As I shall argue shortly,[127] this discrimination cannot be a causal one—the storm either is big enough to be an intervening cause or it is not, irrespective of the accused's intentions. Those intentions are not causal aphrodisiacs: they cannot make the accused's causal contribution bigger, nor the storm's smaller, all by themselves. So the reality is that if the accused's causal contribution (vis-à-vis some intervening storm) was small when the harm was not intended, that contribution is small when the harm is intended. If there is to be liability, it should be for aiding the storm, just as it is in the case of intervening human causers.[128]

If we can justify our small causal roles in the case of human intervenors, presumably we can do the same here. If I can justify telling the Nazis the location of the three partisans to save the 50 children, presumably I can order the three partisans to set out from the island in a storm that will surely kill them, if that is the only way to spare the 50 children from Nazi execution on the island.

---

[125] See Chapter 11, below. [126] See Chapter 12, below. [127] Chapters 5–6, below.
[128] See Chapters 5 and 6, below.

2. Redirecting presently existing threats

Now reverse the temporal order of the examples: the big natural cause is already in play, and all you do is make a 'minor course correction' for that natural cause. Philippa Foot's well-worn example was that of a runaway trolly:[129] it is headed towards five workman who cannot get off the track. You cannot stop it but you can redirect to another track where there is only one workman trapped. May you turn the trolley if you are its driver? May you turn it if you are merely a bystander at the switch?[130]

Real-world examples of such trolley-switching abound. You are a pilot in the Air National Guard. Your jet fighter has just had a flame out and is going down, headed right at a crowded school. May you redirect it onto an occupied single-family home instead? Or you sit beside a dike with dynamite. A flash flood is approaching in the river that the dike holds, and the flood will shortly inundate an entire town, killing all of its residents. May you blow the dike, sending the flood waters onto a single family farm, killing all of the farm's inhabitants but saving those of the village?[131] Or you and others are back in the woods with that charging grizzly. This time I do not 'duck' by removing myself as your defence against the bear. Rather, I do a little bit more: I throw fresh meat in your direction so that the bear that was headed towards five others is now headed towards you. Is this also permissible?

Like many people, I think the answer to these questions to be a pretty clear 'yes'. You may (and I would add, must) redirect the trolley, plane, flood, and bear from where it will kill many to where it will kill few. My favorite example of this kind is from the Second World War. The V-1 and V-2 rockets were targeted by burn time; this meant that the shots had to be called in by German spies in England so that the burn times could be adjusted. British counterintelligence had penetrated the German spy network calling in the targeting. The choice presented to Churchill: should British counterintelligence feed misinformation to the Germans, which would move the mean point of impact two miles per week to the east of central London? This killed a few people in Kent and Essex rather than a lot of people in central London. According to William Stevenson's recollections:

'War is an evil thing', Churchill said in a Secret War Cabinet session. 'Do you wish us to surrender, Mr Morrison?' Morrison shook his head angrily. 'Then I greatly fear, sir, that in order to live', replied Churchill, lowering his head, 'we must play God.'[132]

I think Churchill got it right, here as at Coventry.

---

[129] Foot, 'Abortion'.

[130] Thomson's variation. Judith Jarvis Thomson, 'The trolley problem', Yale Law Journal 94 (1985), 1395–415.

[131] This is another example used by the drafters of the Model Penal Code to illustrate when killing could be justified by its good consequences. See *Commentaries*.

[132] William Stevenson, *A Man Called Intrepid*, 414.

Many philosophers who have examined these redirection cases find the conclusions compelling but the rationale puzzling. Some wish to fictionalize the threats, pretending that all are threatened,[133] when in plain truth only some are (this is to mistakenly liken redirection cases to the 'almost dead' cases). Others wish to rely on the DDE, saying that I only foresee the death of the few even though I intend to redirect deadly things into them.[134] Still others, such as Judith Thomson, who has examined these cases more than anyone else, is just puzzled why redirection as such makes such killings justifiable by their good consequences.[135]

To me, redirecting cases seem plainly causal in their rationale. It is only a rule of thumb that later is usually greater when it comes to degrees of causal contribution. But rules of thumb are only rules of thumb because sometimes they prove to be bad heuristics, as here. Even though the trolley, plane, flood, bear, and rockets are all in motion when you act, your later act is a small contribution compared to theirs. You have limited decisional space, and you do not do much. You make, as I said, only minor course corrections. Make your causal contributions bigger—by starting any of these things yourself—and you may not justify your actions. So if a terrorist will kill many hostages unless you: start up a trolley to run down a few; steal a plane to crash it into a house; start a flood to flood a farm; attract a bear so that it kills someone; etc—you may not do these things even to produce good consequences, because such acts make a larger causal contribution to the deaths they cause. But keep the degree of causal involvement small, as in the redirection cases, then responsibility is lessened to the point that consequentialist justifications become available.

VI. Conclusion

It is time we again step back from the trees and look at the whole forest. From such a vantage point we can see four variables that have made a difference to the availability of consequentialist justifications: (1) acting, (2) intending, (3) causing, and (4) counterfactual dependence. When we *act* (rather than omit) because we *intend* to achieve something bad (rather foresee it or risk it), and when our act *strongly causes* that bad state of affairs to come about (rather than not cause it at all, or only weakly cause it), and when that bad state of affairs strongly depended

---

[133] James Montmarquet, 'Doing good: The right way and the wrong way', Journal of Philosophy 79 (1982), 439–55.

[134] Michael Costa, 'The trolley problem revisited', and 'Another trip on the trolley', in John Martin Fischer and Mark Ravizza (eds), *Ethics: Problems and principles* (New York: Harcourt, Brace, 1992).

[135] Thus Thomson confesses that she does 'not find it clear why there should be an exemption for, and only for, making a burden which is descending onto five descend, instead, onto one . . . on the other hand, the exemption seems to allow those acts which intuition tells us are clearly permissible . . .': 'Trolley problem', 1408.

for its existence upon the act done (rather than weakly so depended, either because that state of affairs would have occurred slightly earlier or later anyway in possible worlds very close to the actual world); then we may not justify what we do by its good consequences. Whereas when we only fail to prevent some bad state of affairs, or only foresee or risk that our acts will produce such a state of affairs, or our act only weakly causes (or prevents a preventer from preventing) that state of affairs, or that state of affairs could have rightly been brought about by us earlier, or it would have come about slightly later anyway, then we may justify our choices and behavior by their good consequences.

If we are strongly permitted to justify these choices and behaviors, then, while we are outside of our deontological obligations, we are so by virtue of an exception to these norms of obligation. But if we are only weakly permitted to justify these choices and behaviors, that shows something about the kinds of things that form the content of these obligations, namely that they are not directed toward our weakly permitted choices and behaviors. I have tried to limit the examples to those illustrating only weak permissions. If I have succeeded, then the shape of our deontological obligations is as I just described: we are obligated not to act so as to strongly cause something that was not about to happen later anyway, if such act is motivated by our intention to cause that thing. Even when we plug in all the 'somethings' like deaths, disfigurements, etc in this formula, we will not have exhausted our obligations. But we will have exhausted our *deontological* obligations, leaving us free to navigate by our consequentialist lights alone.

Causation is thus one of four ingredients in giving content to our deontological obligations. But it is the big dog in this pack of four. It is causation that patrols the borders of our consequentialist justifications—and thus the border of our deontological obligations—in the redirection cases, in the natural intervening-cause cases, in the human-agent intervening-cause cases (ie, the aiding cases), and in the removing-defense kind of allowing cases. Causation is also at work in the omission cases, although this is arguable, depending on whether it is causation or notions of general ontology that rule out negative relata (such as negative events, negative states of affairs, or negative properties). All the variations of the doctrine of doing and allowing, save the acceleration cases, thus involve causation. Causation is thus a major desert-determiner within deontological morality, just as it is more generally (as we saw in the previous chapter). Causation's role here is even more dramatic: here absence of causation *eliminates* responsibility (by licensing consequentialist justifications), rather than merely reducing it (when justifications are not in issue).

PART II

PRESUPPOSITIONS ABOUT THE NATURE OF CAUSATION BY LEGAL DOCTRINES

4

The Law's Own Characterizations of its Causal Requirements

I. Introduction

The special part of the substantive criminal law in all mature legal systems consists of several thousand prohibitions and requirements. Criminal codes typically *prohibit* citizens form doing certain types of action and sometimes (but less frequently) *require* citizens to do certain types of actions. As we saw in Chapter 1, causation enters into both the prohibitions and the requirements of a typical criminal code, for such statutes either prohibit citizens from causing certain results or require them to cause certain results. In either case causation is central to criminal liability.

The same is true for the liability rules of tort law. In the torts of negligence and of strict liability, causation of damage to the plaintiff is an explicit element. In intentional torts such as battery, assault, trespass, trespass to chattels, conversion, false imprisonment, the intentional infliction of emotional distress, etc, causation is also an implicit element (for the same reason as in criminal law, viz the *actus reus* requirements of both areas of law use causative verbs).

It was the thrust of Chapters 2 and 3 that the law's emphasis on causation is not misplaced, because the moral responsibility on which the law is based is itself concerned with causation. If causation determines both the degree of prima facie wrongfulness and the permissibility of consequentialist justification of otherwise wrongful actions in morality, then a justice-oriented tort and criminal law is justifiably focused on causation.

It is now time we leave discussion of the *role* of causation in ascriptions of legal and moral responsibility, to focus on the *nature* of this element of liability. Unsurprisingly, the law has its own theories about the nature of causation, theories put in terms of a variety of general tests of causation proposed for use throughout the law of torts and of crimes. It is the burden of Part II of this book to explore the parameters of the law's own theory about this central element of liability.

I shall proceed as follows. In this chapter, I shall briefly taxonomize and describe the various theories about causation adopted or proposed for adoption throughout the law of torts and crimes. The discussion of this chapter stays pretty much at the surface, having the modest ambition of organizing the diversity of views within law and legal theory as to what the causation requirements of the law are. In the next two chapters, Chapters 5 and 6, I seek greater depth. There, I seek to prune away legal doctrines so as to reveal a more or less coherent view of causation presupposed by the legal doctrines that are left. The principles of pruning are initially to discard those legal tests of 'causation' that on their face have nothing to do with causation. Such doctrines have nothing to do with causation because such doctrines explicitly aim at some other policy (such as measuring culpability of mental state), even though those doctrines carry on under the false colors of 'causation'. Second, the law is sometimes inconsistent. How it treats omissions, both as causes and yet not as causes, is an example. Some pruning is done to reveal what I take to be the better choice for the law in such circumstances. Third, and mainly, I seek to eliminate those doctrines presupposing an implausible metaphysics, either about causation itself or (more typically) about other items such as free will or telekenesis. The supposed causal potency of either moral qualities or mental states, when neither works through any act of the actor who is culpable or who has the mental state in question, is an example.

By the end of these prunings, I arrive at a quite common-sense notion of causation that I argue our (carefully pruned) law presupposes. The claim of this part will not be that this is the correct theory of causation, only that it is the most coherent theory of causation that can be extracted from all the things legal doctrines *say* about causation, considered as a whole.

II. The Dominant Analysis of Causation in the Law

Given the prolixity of liability doctrines having causation as an element in tort but even more in criminal law, one might think there would be as many tests of causation as there were causal requirements in such prolix doctrines. Yet what is commonly called the 'general part' of both criminal law and the law of torts is built on a contrary insight, viz that the elements of liability in each area of law do *not* vary with each different rule in which they appear. There are general notions of intention, voluntariness, excuse, and the like, and the law seeks a similarly general notion of causation. These are *general* in the sense that these notions apply to give a uniform meaning to each doctrinal requirement framed in terms of these concepts.[1] It is these doctrines of causation in the general parts of

---

[1] On the general part of the criminal law, see Michael Moore, 'A theory of criminal law theories', Tel Aviv University Studies in Law 10 (1990), 115–85, reprinted as Chapter 1 of Michael Moore, *Placing Blame: A general theory of the criminal law* (Oxford: Clarendon Press, 1997). Peter Cane develops an analogous notion of a general part to tort law in his 'The general/special distinction in criminal law, tort law and legal theory', Law and Philosophy 26 (2007), 465–500.

criminal law and torts that I refer to as the law's own theory about the nature of causation.

That, at least, is the promise held out by the doctrines of the general parts of criminal law and torts. This promise is blunted somewhat by the fact that there are different doctrines of the general parts competing for dominance within both tort and criminal law. The present taxonomic chapter is necessary just to give some order to this tournament field of competing doctrines, each of which purports to be *the* theory of causation of the general parts of both criminal law and torts.

In what follows I will often focus more on tort-law theories of causation than criminal law. This is because many of the leading cases on causation, most of the causal doctrines finding some acceptance in the law, and most of the theorizing about causation, originate in the law of tort and not in the criminal law. The reasons for this are not hard to discern. Unlike the thousands of specific actions prohibited or required by the criminal law, a large part of tort law consists of but one injunction: do not unreasonably act so as to cause harm to another. Such an injunction pretty obviously places great weight on causation. It leaves open a full range of causal questions, much more than do injunctions of criminal law, such as 'do not intentionally hit another'.

Criminal law thus has been a borrower from torts on the issue of causation. Such borrowing has not been uniform or without reservations. Aside from the greater demands of directness of causation implicit in specific criminal prohibitions, the criminal sanction of punishment is sometimes said to demand greater stringency of causation than is demanded by the less severe tort sanction of compensation. Still, the usual form such reservations take is for criminal law to modify causation doctrines in tort by a matter of degree only.[2] Foreseeability, for example, is a test of causation in both fields, but what must be foreseeable, and the degree with which it must be foreseeable, is sometimes thought to be greater in criminal law than in torts. Such variation by degree but not in kind has allowed causation in criminal law and in torts to be discussed via the same tests, which I shall now do.

The conventional wisdom about the causation requirement in both criminal law and torts is that in reality it consists of two very different requirements. The first requirement is that of 'cause-in-fact'. This is said to be the truly *causal* component of the law's two requirements framed in causal terms, because this doctrine adopts what is thought of as the 'scientific' notion of causation. Whether cigarette smoking causes cancer, or whether the presence of hydrogen or helium caused an explosion, are factual questions to be resolved by the best science the courts can muster. By contrast, the second requirement, that of 'proximate' or 'legal' cause, is said to be an evaluative issue, to be resolved by arguments of policy and not arguments of scientific fact. Suppose a defendant knifes his victim who

---

[2] Moore, *Placing Blame*, 363, n 1.

then dies because her religious convictions are such that she refuses medical treatment.[3] Has such a defendant (legally) caused her death? The answer to such questions, it is said, depends on the policies behind liability, not on any factual issues; factually, it is thought, the knifing surely caused her death.

By far the dominant test for cause-in-fact is the common law and Model Penal Code *sine qua non*, or 'but for' test.[4] Such a test asks a counterfactual question: 'but for the defendant's action, would the victim have been harmed in the way the criminal law prohibits?' This test is also sometimes called the necessary-condition test, because it requires that the defendant's action have been necessary to the victim's harm. The appeal of this test stems from this fact. The test seems to isolate something we seem to care a lot about, both in explaining events and in assessing responsibility for them: namely, did the defendant's act make a difference? Insofar as we increase moral blameworthiness and legal punishment for actors who *cause* bad results (and not just try to), we seemingly should care whether a particular bad result would have happened anyway, even without the defendant.

There is no equivalently dominant test of legal or proximate cause. There are in fact seven distinguishable sorts of tests having some authority within the legal literature. I shall defer description of these until after I have described the variations in the dominant legal test for cause-in-fact.

III. Problems with the Dominant Analysis of Cause-in-Fact Motivating Modified Cause-in-Fact Tests

The best way to approach the various tests for cause-in-fact in law is by examining problems for the dominant, counterfactual test; for it is these problems that motivate alternative tests of cause-in-fact. Very generally there are four sorts of problems with the counterfactual test for causation-in-fact that are raised in the legal literature. One set of these problems has to do with proof and evidence. As an element of the prima facie case, causation-in-fact must be proven by the party with the burden of proof. In criminal cases that is the prosecution, who must prove what would have happened absent the defendant's act beyond a reasonable doubt; in tort cases, that is the victim, who must prove what would have happened by a preponderance of the evidence. In either case counterfactuals by their nature are difficult to prove with any degree of certainty, for they require the fact-finder to speculate what would have happened if the defendant had not done what he did. Suppose a defendant culpably destroys a life-preserver on a sea-going tug.[5] When a crewman falls overboard and drowns, was a necessary condition of

---

[3] As in *R v. Blaue* [1975] 3 All ER 446 (Ct App 1975).
[4] American Law Institute, Model Penal Code § 2.03(1) (Proposed Official Draft, 1962).
[5] A variation on the facts of *New York Central RR v. Grimstad* 264 F 2d 334 (2d Cir 1920).

his death the act of the defendant in destroying the life-preserver? If the life-preserver had been there, would anyone have thought to use it; thrown it in time; thrown it far enough; have gotten near enough to the victim that the victim would have reached it? We often lack the kind of precise information that could verify whether the culpable act of the defendant made any difference in this way.[6]

A second set of problems stems from an indeterminacy of meaning in the test, not from difficulties of factual verification. There is a great vagueness in counterfactual judgments. The vagueness lies in specifying the possible world in which we are to test the counterfactual.[7] When we say 'but for the defendant's act of destroying the life-preserver' what world are we imagining? We know we are to eliminate the defendant's act, but what are we to replace it with: a life-preserver that was alternatively destroyed by the heavy seas; a defendant who did not destroy the life-preserver because he had already pushed the victim overboard when no one else was around to throw the life-preserver to the victim; etc, etc? To make the counterfactual test determinate enough to yield one answer rather than another, we have to assume that we share an ability to specify some definite possible world that is 'similar' to our actual world, and that it is in *this* possible world that we ask our counterfactual question.

The third and fourth sets of problems stem from the inability of the counterfactual test to match what for most of us are firm causal intuitions. The third set of problems arise because the counterfactual test seems too lenient in what it counts as a cause. The criticism is that the test is thus over-inclusive. The fourth set of problems arise because the counterfactual test seems too stringent in what it counts as a cause. The criticism here is that the test is under-inclusive.

The over-inclusiveness of the test is mostly raised by legal theoreticians in cases of coincidence. Suppose a defendant culpably delays his train at t_1; much, much later at t_2, and much further down the track, the train is hit by a flood.[8] Since but for the delay at t_1, there would have been no damage or loss of life at t_2, the counterfactual test yields the unwelcome result that the defendant's delaying caused the harm. While such cases of overt coincidences are rare, they are the tip of the iceberg here. Innumerable remote conditions are necessary to the production of any event. Oxygen in the air over England, timber in Scotland, Henry the VIII's obesity, and Drake's perpescuity, were all probably necessary for the defeat of the Spanish Amanda;[9] but we should be loath to say that each of these was a cause of the defeat. The problem is greatly exacerbated by the admission of omissions as causes: the Spanish Armanda was also defeated because the Martian

---

[6] Eric Johnson nicely details how courts often impose liability in both torts and criminal law by simply sweeping under the rug these uncertainties in verifying counterfactuals: Johnson, 'Lost chance in criminal cases', Iowa Law Review 91 (2005), 66–71.

[7] I explored this problem in Moore, *Placing Blame*, 345–47, and in Chapter 16, below, relying on the philosophical literature on counterfactuals. In the legal literature this indeterminancy was earliest explored in Robert Cole, 'Windfall and probability: A study of "Cause" in negligence law', California Law Review 52 (1964), 459–512, 764–821.

[8] *Denny v. NY Central RR* 13 Gray (Mass) 481 (1859).   [9] Moore, *Placing Blame*, 268–9.

space-ships did not show up to help them, and that, because there are no Martians.

The fourth set of problems for the counterfactual test has to do with the test's under-inclusiveness. Such under-inclusiveness is mostly exhibited in legal theory in the well-known overdetermination cases,[10] where each of two events c_1 and c_2 is independently sufficient for some third event e; logically, this entails that neither c_1 nor c_2 is necessary for e, and thus, on the counterfactual analysis of causation, neither can be the cause of e. Just about everybody rejects this conclusion, and so such cases pose a real problem for the counterfactual analysis of causation.

Legal theorists have long distinguished two distinct kinds of overdetermination cases. The first are the concurrent cause cases: two fires, two shotgun blasts, two noisy motorcycles, are each sufficient to burn, kill, or scare some victim. The defendant is responsible for only one fire, shot, or motorcycle. Yet his fire, shot, or noise joins the other one, and both simultaneously cause their various harms. On the counterfactual analysis the defendant's fire, shot, or noise was not the cause of any harm because it was not necessary to the production of the harms— after all, the other fire, shot, or noise was by itself *sufficient*. Yet the same can be said about the second fire, shot, or noise. So, on the 'but for' test, neither was the cause! And this is absurd.

The pre-emptive kind of overdetermination cases are different. Here the two putative causes are not simultaneous but are temporally ordered. The defendant's fire arrives first and burns down the victim's building; the second fire arrives shortly thereafter, and would have been sufficient to have burned down the building, only there was no building to burn down. Here our intuitions are just as clear as in the concurrent overdetermination cases but they are different: the defendant's fire did cause the harm, and the second fire did not. Yet the counterfactual analysis again yields the counterintuitive implication that neither fire caused the harm because neither fire was necessary (each being sufficient) for the harm.

Situated rather nicely between these two sorts of overdetermination cases is what I have called the asymmetrical overdetermination cases.[11] Suppose the defendant non-mortally stabs the victim at the same time as another defendant mortally stabs the same victim; the victim dies of loss of blood, most of the blood gushing out of the mortal wound. Has the non-mortally wounding defendant caused the death of the victim? Not according to the counterfactual analysis: given the sufficiency of the mortal would, the non-mortal wound was not necessary for, and thus not a cause of, death. This conclusion is contrary to common intuition as well as some legal authority.[12]

---

[10] Richard Wright, 'Causation in tort law', California Law Review 73 (1985), 1775–98.
[11] See Chapters 5 and 17, below.
[12] *People v. Lewis*, 124 Cal 551, 57 P 470 (1899).

Defenders of the counterfactual analysis are not bereft of replies to these objections, and we shall consider these later.[13] For present purposes we need to use these problems as stated to see how other tests have been substituted for the counterfactual test as a means of doing an end run on these problems. With regard to the problem posed by the overdetermination cases, the best known alternative is to propose an 'INUS' or 'NESS' test: an event *c* causes an event *e* if and only if *c* is a necessary element in a set of conditions sufficient for *e*.[14] It is the stress on *sufficiency* that is supposed to end run the overdetermination problems. In the concurrent-cause cases, where the two fires join to burn the victim's house, each fire is said to be a necessary element of its own sufficient set, so each fire is a cause. In the pre-emptive case, where the fires do not join and one arrives first, the first fire is a necessary element of a sufficient set, and so is the cause; but the second fire is not because it is not part of a sufficient set (absent from its set is the existence of a house to be burned).

Other modifications of the counterfactual test have also been adopted. One of these is the 'fine-grained effect' approach of the Commentary to the Model Penal Code.[15] On this test, one does not ask whether *the harm* would have occurred but for the defendant's act; rather, one asks whether a more particularly described harm would have happened without the defendant's act. So in the concurrent cause case of the two independently sufficient fires that join to burn down the victim's house, we do not ask, was the defendant's fire necessary to *destruction* of plaintiff's house; rather, we ask, was the defendant's act necessary to the destruction of the victim's house where, when, and in the manner that it was destroyed. It is much more likely that the defendant's fire *was* necessary to the destruction of the victim's house in just the way it was destroyed, so the counterfactual test seems to do better in the concurrent overdetermination cases with this fine-grained approach.[16]

For the pre-emptive overdetermination cases the problem is easier for the counterfactual test. Here one introduces a stipulation about the time of the event: if the defendant's act was necessary to the house destruction being earlier than it otherwise would have been, then he was the cause, but if his act was only necessary to the house destruction happening at some time or other (including later), his act is not necessarily the cause. As the cases put this point,[17] causes must *accelerate* their effects; if they fail to accelerate them (either by making no change or by retarding them), then such factors are not causes even though necessary to

---

[13] Chapter 17, below.

[14] JL Mackie, *The Cement of the Universe* (Oxford: Oxford University Press, 1980); Wright, 'Causation in tort law'. I have paraphrased Wright's shortened version of Mackie's longer stated test.

[15] American Law Institute, *Commentaries on the Model Penal Code*, § 2.03(1) (1985).

[16] That it only seems to do better is argued persuasively in Wright, 'Causation in tort law', 1777–80.

[17] *Oxendine v. State* 528 A 2d 870, 872–3 (Del 1987).

when the putative effect happened. This helps with the pre-emptive-cause cases because a pre-empting fire is necessary to a house's destruction at t_1, even if (given a pre-empted fire right behind it at t_2) that first fire is not necessary either to a house destruction later (at t_2), or to a house destruction sometime (t_1 or t_2). Let us call this stipulation regarding temporally asymmetrical necessity the third modification of the law's counterfactual test.

The coincidence objection to the counterfactual test yields a fourth modification to that test. In cases like that of the negligently speeding train that, because of its speed, arrives at just the place that a falling tree hits it,[18] one should not ask, 'but for the act of driving would the train have been hit?'; rather, one should isolate that aspect of the act that made it negligent. Thus: 'but for the fact that the driving was over the speed limit, would the train have been hit?' To this modified counterfactual question, the answer is yes. If the train had been going even faster it would not have been hit either (just as if it had been going slower).[19] So the fact that the act was one of *speeding* was not necessary to the harm, even if the act (which was an act of speeding, among other things) was necessary to the harm. This in law is called the 'aspect cause' version of the counterfactual test.[20]

A fifth modification to the counterfactual test of cause-in-fact is more by way of substitution than of amendment. This is the First and Second *Restatement of Torts* 'substantial factor' test.[21] Motivated mostly by worries about overdetermination cases, the American Law Institute in both of its first two *Restatements* urged that a 'substantial factor' test be substituted for *sine qua non* as the test of cause-in-fact in torts. The test asks only whether a defendant's action was a substantial factor in the production of the harm complained of. This admittedly circular and vague test was thought to help in overdetermination cases like that of the joint fires, because so long as each fire was quite substantial (in comparison to the other fire) each was a cause of the harm, even though neither fire was a necessary condition of the harm.

Notice that the substantial factor test 'solves' the overdetermination problem mostly because it does not say enough to get itself into trouble in the overdetermination cases. It thus allows our clear causal intuitions full play in these cases. The ad hoc nature of this solution is evident when one sees how the first two *Restatements of Torts* manage to salvage what they can of the *sine qua non* test: if a putative causal factor is a necessary condition of some harm, then (under the *Restatements*) it is per se substantial.[22] Necessary condition-hood, in other

---

[18] *Berry v. Borough of Sugar Notch* 43 A 240 (Pa 1899).
[19] As the Pennsylvania court noted, ibid.   [20] Wright, 'Causation in tort law'.
[21] American Law Institute, *Restatement of Torts*, §§ 431–5 (1934); *Restatement (Second) of Torts*, §§ 431–3 (1965).
[22] The *Restatements* hold that a but for factor is a cause-in-fact of a harm. *Restatement of Torts*, §§ 431–3 (1934).

words, is sufficient for cause-in-fact. But necessary condition-hood is not necessary for causation, so that a factor can be substantial even if it is not a necessary condition. This amounts to saying that one should use the necessary-condition test when it works, but when it yields counterintuitive results (as in the overdetermination cases) one should not use it but rely on naked causal intuition.

The sixth and final modification of the counterfactual test of cause-in-fact is motivated by the proof problem. Particularly in criminal cases (where one has to prove causation 'beyond a reasonable doubt') it is often impossible to prove that the harm would not have happened but for the defendant's act. What courts in effect adopt is a 'lost chance' approach to counterfactuals.[23] On this modified test, one does not ask whether the act was necessary to the harm actually occurring; rather, one asks only whether the act was necessary to the harm having the chance of occurring that it did. This is a 'necessary to chance (of harm)' sort of test, not a 'necessary to harm' test.[24]

As we shall see in later chapters, what courts and legal theorists have often done in modifying the counterfactual test in these six ways is to propose quite different theories about the nature of causation. The INUS and NESS tests are what we shall later call nomic sufficiency tests, a version of a general theory of singular causation that reduces it to general causal laws and does not make essential use of counterfactuals.[25] The substantial-factor test is really the law's version of a primitivist approach to singular causation, a version of singularist theories we shall examine later.[26] The necessary-to-chance modification is in reality the substitution of a probabilistic theory of causation for a purely counterfactual theory.[27] It is thus a mistake to think that the law's dominant statement of what is its test for cause-in-fact—*sine qua non*—in fact evidences any deep commitment of the law to a truly counterfactual theory of causation.

IV. Skeptical Approaches to the Cause-in-fact Requirement

Legal theory, like philosophy, has had its share of skeptics about causation. Most of such legally located skepticism has been directed at the proximate cause half of the dominant analysis of causation in the law. Such skepticism there considers 'proximate *cause*' to be a misnomer and reinterprets the proximate cause requirement in non-causal, policy terms (as we shall see later in this chapter). More radical is the skepticism here considered. Some legal theorists are skeptical

---

[23] Eric Johnson, 'Criminal liability for loss of a chance'.
[24] 'Necessary to chance' is explored in Chapters 13 and 20, below.   [25] Chapter 19, below.
[26] Chapter 20, below.   [27] Chapter 19, below.

of there being any natural relation in the world named by 'causation'. This includes what the law names 'cause-in-fact' as well as 'proximate cause.'

Before we describe such skepticisms in legal theory, we would do well to be sure we have a firm grasp on what skepticism about causation is. Take David Hume, often listed as a skeptic about causation.[28] As we shall explore in Chapter 19, Hume famously identified singular causal relations as spatio-temporally located instances of causal laws, and he identified causal laws as no more than uniformity in sequence between types of events. Hume was thus doubly a reductionist about the causal relation, reducing it ultimately to regular concurrence. In this he is commonly said to be a skeptic.

Because Hume's analysis takes 'the glue' out of the causal relation—a cause does not *make* its effect occur, it is only regularly followed by its effect—it is commonly classified as skeptical. And in a sense it is, if one treats the making-things-happen 'glue' to be essential to any relation properly called 'causal'. But Hume's views are not radical enough to count as skeptical in the sense intended by legal theoreticians. For Hume gives what Saul Kripke calls a 'skeptical solution'[29] to the problem of causation: he does not deny that causation exists, but rather, reduces it to something less ontologically queer than 'glue'.

A better model of the radical skepticism here considered is the once-held 'ascriptivist' views (since repudiated) of Herbert Hart.[30] In a famous analysis of causative verbs such as 'A hit B', Hart urged that we *describe* no natural relations (such as, A caused there to be contact on B's body); rather, we *ascribe* responsibility to A for the contact on B's body. If this bit of pre-Austin speech-act analysis were true, then causatives (and analogously, words of causation) would only be the labels used to express conclusions about responsibility. Such words would not name real relations that could be the justifying grounds for attributing responsibility to someone.

Such are the views of the legal skeptics here considered. Such skeptics appear to deny that causation exists as any kind of natural relation, whether 'glue-like',

---

[28] I am unconcerned with whether the regularity theory sketched below was really believed by Hume. On this see, eg, Barry Stroud, *Hume* (London: Routledge and Kegan Paul, 1977), Chapters 3 and 4; and Galen Strawson, *The Secret Connexion* (Oxford: Clarendon Press, 1989). The Humean theory is an interesting and an influential one even if it turns out that Hume never held it.

[29] Saul Kripke, *Wittgenstein on Rules and Private Language* (Cambridge, Mass: Harvard University Press, 1982), 66–8.

[30] HLA Hart, 'The ascription of responsibility and rights', Proceedings of the Aristotelian Society 49 (1949), 171–94. A like skepticism is directed specifically at causation in Meir Dan-Cohen, 'Causation', in S Kadish (ed), *Encyclopedia of Crime and Justice* I (New York: MacMillan, 1983) 165–6: 'the question of causation (namely, "Is there a causal relation between A's conduct and B's death?") amounts to asking whether punishing A is necessary . . .'. Citing Peter Geach's damning criticism in Geach's 'Ascriptivism', Philosophical Review 69 (1960), 221–5, Hart came to reject the speech-act semantics that lead him to his ascriptivism about causative verbs: HLA Hart, *Punishment and Responsibility* (Oxford: Oxford University Press, 1968), v.

regular concurrence in nature, or something else. Because it is easiest to approach such skepticism historically, I shall begin with the American Legal Realists (with whom almost all of the skepticisms about proximate causation also originated).

Most of Harry Edgarton's influential article in 1924 details his skepticism about proximate causation.[31] Some of it, however, reveals him to have been a skeptic about the cause-in-fact requirement as well. He notes, for example, that the symmetrically concurrent overdetermination cases[32] were divided into two camps by the cause-in-fact doctrines of his day: where there were two culpable actors starting fires (where the fires joined to produce a larger fire burning down plaintiff's house), either actor was a cause of the destruction; but when only one of the fires was of culpable origin, the other being either natural or of *innocent* human origin, then the culpable actor was not a cause of the destruction.[33] From such examples Edgarton suggested that the cause-in-fact requirement was (like the proximate cause requirement) all a matter of policy, a matter, that is, depending on 'our free and independent sense of justice and—perhaps—the interests of society'.[34]

A late blooming of this Legal Realist conclusion was the well-known work of Wex Malone.[35] Malone largely focused on an issue that preoccupied philosophers in the 1950s,[36] the pragmatic features by which we pick out *the* cause of some event; Malone found, unsurprisingly, only context-specific, practical interests guiding such locutions of causal emphasis, and skeptically concluded that that was all there was to causation. To be said to be 'the cause' of some harm was just another way of saying one was responsible for the harm.

The skepticism of American Legal Realism has had two intellectual descendents in legal theory. One of these are the self-styled 'critical' theorists, the 'Critical Legal Studies' movement whose hey-days were in the 1970s and 1980s

---

[31] Henry Edgarton, 'Legal cause', University of Pennsylvania Law Review 72 (1924), 211–44, 343–75.

[32] Explored in Chapters 17 and 18, below.   [33] Edgarton, 'Legal Cause'.

[34] Edgarton, 'Legal cause', 347. See also Leon Green, 'Are there dependable rules of causation?', University of Pennsylvania Law Review 77 (1929), 604–6: 'The inquiry while stated in what seems to be in terms of *cause* is in fact whether the defendant should be held responsible.'

[35] Wex Malone, 'Ruminations on cause-in-fact', Stanford Law Review 9 (1956), 60–99.

[36] Joel Feinberg nicely summarized much of this literature of 1950s philosophy (such as Morton White and RG Collingwood) in his 'Action and responsibility', in Feinberg, *Doing and Deserving* (Princeton: Princeton University Press, 1970), 143–7. The usual response of contemporary philosophy to this older literature is the same as the proper response to Malone: concede that '*the* cause' designations depend on a host of pragmatic factors, some of them evaluative, but deny that this affects the objectivity of causation judgments generally. See, eg, David Lewis, 'Causation', Journal of Philosophy 70 (1973), 556–67, reprinted in Ernest Sosa and Michael Tooley (eds), *Causation* (Oxford: Oxford University Press, 1993), 195–6. Richard Wright does a good job of demolishing Malone on this point. Wright, 'Causation in tort law', 1743–5.

in America.[37] Much of CLS skepticism is simply warmed-over post-modernism, a passing fashion in many disciplines besides law.[38] Much more interesting intellectually were criticisms not based on post-modernist platitudes but which were specific to causation.

Mark Kelman's skepticism was of this latter kind.[39] Kelman urged that all causal requirements in the law were part of the 'liberal myth' of objective criteria for liability, but rather than reciting (yet again) the platitude of the historically situated knower, Kelman actually directs arguments against the law's cause-in-fact tests mirroring anything in natural fact. Kelman accurately perceived that the counterfactual theory (in one of its several variations above explored) was 'the' dominant test of cause-in-fact in law, and produced some of the criticisms we ourselves shall later examine in Chapter 17. From the perceived failure of the counterfactual theory, Kelman concluded that cause-in-fact in law cannot be a matter of fact. (Whether this is correct, of course, depends on whether there are other metaphysical theories of causation that fit the demands of a cause-in-fact requirement in the law.)[40]

The general, positive prescription that is supposed to flow from the skepticisms of the Legal Realists and the 'Crits' is not so clear. One gathers that once skepticism (about causation being a matter of objective fact) has removed the blinders, we can see that it is only interests and policies that lead us to conclusions about moral responsibility and legal liability. Presumably then the positive prescription is for us to do this openly, balancing all relevant considerations, in arriving at our conclusions of what was the cause of what.

The other intellectual descendent to the American Legal Realists on causation is the Law and Economics movement in contemporary legal theory. These are theorists seeking to show that legal rules and institutions either are or should be *efficient*, in the post-Pareto sense of that word.

Like the Crits, legal economists tend to be radical skeptics about causation. The leading early papers on causation[41] all express skepticism about 'causation'

[37] See generally Mark Kelman, *A Guide to Critical Legal Studies* (Cambridge, Mass: Harvard University Press, 1987).

[38] Explored by me in Moore, 'The interpretive turn in modern theory: A turn for the worse?', Stanford Law Review 41 (1989), 871–957, reprinted as Chapter 10 of Moore, *Educating Oneself in Public: Critical essays in jurisprudence* (Oxford: Oxford University Press, 2000).

[39] Mark Kelman, 'The necessary myth of objective causation judgments in liberal political theory', Chicago-Kent Law Review 63 (1987), 579–637.

[40] As I noted in my response to Kelman; see Moore, 'Thompson's preliminaries about causation and rights', Chicago-Kent Law Review 63 (1987), 497–521, reprinted as Chapter 7 of Moore, *Placing Blame*.

[41] See, eg, Guido Calabresi, 'Concerning cause and the law of torts: An essay for Harry Kalven, Jr', University of Chicago Law Review 43 (1975), 69–108; Steven Shavell, 'An analysis of causation and the scope of liability in the law of torts', Journal of Legal Studies 9 (1980), 463–503; and William Landes and Richard Posner, 'Causation in tort law: An economic approach', Journal of Legal Studies 12 (1983), 109–34.

picking out any real relation in the world.[42] Lawyers are just doing intuitive economics or some other policy balancing in their use of causal idioms, because that is all they *can be* doing. Shavell, Landes, and Posner explicitly rely on Edgarton,[43] picking up precisely where Edgarton began his skepticism, in the liability rules for symmetrically concurrent overdetermination cases.

The positive, reconstructive prescriptions of the law and economics types differ from those of the Crits and the Realists in that the policy favored is much more specific: liability (including the supposedly causal requirements for liability) should give incentives for efficient behavior. Yet unnoticed by the economists was that this monistic policy focus on efficiency made their causal skepticism unnecessary and beside the point.

This is because if efficiency is the normative pole-star for both tort and criminal law, then there is a non-skeptical basis for denying the relevance of the metaphysics of causation to the interpretation of legal usages of 'cause'. Such a basis begins with the quite correct insight that legal texts are to be interpreted in light of the purposes (values, functions, 'spirit', 'mischief,' etc) such texts serve.[44] Often such purposes will justify an interpreter in holding the legal meaning of a term to be quite different from the ordinary meaning of the term in non-legal English. 'Malice', for example, means roughly 'recklessness' in Anglo-American criminal law, whereas it means spiteful or otherwise bad motive in ordinary English.[45]

[42] The influence of the American Legal Realists, Malone, Edgerton, and Green, is quite evident in the law and economics literature on causation. Thus, Guido Calabresi concludes to his satisfaction that 'in the law "cause-in-fact" . . . is in the end a functional concept designed to achieve human goals': Calabresi, 'Concerning cause and the law of torts', 107. There, he reached this conclusion on just the grounds Malone used in reaching a like conclusion. See ibid, 105–6. Similarly skeptical of causation are Landes and Posner: 'Causation in tort law: An economic approach'. Landes and Posner, in their rush to replace causation with probability theory, feel entitled to deride the philosophical attempt to define causation as 'fruitless', totally context-dependent in its meaning, and in any event irrelevant to the purposes for which tort law should use the concept: ibid, 109–11, 119. Steve Shavell explicitly adopts Edgerton's and Calabresi's 'instrumentalist' approach to causation, defining the concept so as to serve 'well-specified social goals': Shavell, 'An analysis of causation and the scope of liability in the law of torts', 502. Shavell recognizes that there exists a common-sense notion of cause that antedates the law, but in such a common-sense concept 'questions about causation are to an important extent resolved by resort to intuitions about the justness of applying a rule of liability': ibid. Calibresi, Landes, Posner, and Shavell are not fully aware of how truly skeptical they are about causation, because often they seek to rescue the concept by giving it a probabilistic definition. If they clearly saw the difference between *ex ante* probability theory, which deals with *types* of acts, and *ex post* causation theory, which deals with particular actions ('act-tokens'), they would see that they are not in any sense analyzing causation but are replacing it with something else. On this, see Richard Wright, 'Actual causation vs. Probabilistic linkage: The bane of economic analysis', Journal of Legal Studies 14 (1985), 435–56.

[43] See Shavell, 'An analysis of causation and the scope of liability in the law of torts', 495; and Landes and Posner, 'Causation in tort law: An economic approach', 110.

[44] On purposive interpretation of legal texts, see Michael S Moore, 'The semantics of judging', Southern California Law Review 54 (1981), 279–81; and Moore, 'A natural law theory of interpretation', Southern California Law Review 58 (1985), 383–8.

[45] On the criminal-law meaning of 'malice' in the law of homicide, see Moore, 'Natural law theory on interpretation', 332–6.

It is certainly possible that 'cause' is like 'malice' in this regard. Whether this is so depends on what one takes to be the purpose of those legal texts that use 'cause'. Consider American tort law by way of example. Following the welfare economics of AC Pigou, it was for a time fashionable to think that the purpose of liability rules in tort law was to force each enterprise or activity within an economy to pay its 'true costs'.[46] Those costs included damage caused to others by the activity as much as they included traditional items of cost like labor, raw materials, capital, etc. The thought was that only if each enterprise paid its true costs would the goods or services produced by that enterprise be correctly priced, and only if such correct pricing occurred would markets achieve an efficient allocation of resources. This came to be known as 'enterprise liability' in the tort-law theory of 1950s America.

If the point of tort law were to achieve an efficient allocation of resources, and if such efficiency could be achieved only by discovering the 'true costs' of each activity in terms of that activity's harmful effects, then 'cause' as used in tort liability rules should mean whatever the metaphysics of causation tells us the word means. For on this theory it is the harmful effects that an activity really cause that are the true costs for that activity; and this rationale thus demands a robust use of some metaphysical view about causation.

Contrast this Pigouvian view of tort law with the post-1960 view of Ronald Coase: tort law indeed exists in order to achieve an efficient allocation of resources, yet such efficiency will be achieved whether tort liability tracks causal responsibility or not.[47] Coase's essential insight was that opportunity costs are real costs too to economically rational actors, so that a foregone opportunity to accept a payment in lieu of causing another person some harm already forces the harm-causer to 'internalize' all costs of his activities. Such harm-causer need not be liable for such harms in order to have him pay for the 'true costs' of his activity; he already 'pays' by foregoing the opportunity to be bought-off by the sufferer of the harm. As each harm-causer and harm-sufferer decides on the desired level of his activity, he will thus take into account all effects of his interaction without tort liability forcing him to do so.[48]

On this Coasean analysis of tort law, there is simply no need for liability to turn on causation. Rather, either tort liability is irrelevant to efficient resource allocation (in a world of low transaction costs), or tort liability should be placed on the cheapest cost-avoider (in a world where transaction costs are high) in order

---

[46] A late expression of this view of tort law is to be found in Guido Calabresi, 'Some thoughts on risk distribution and the law of torts', Yale Law Journal 70 (1961), 499–553.

[47] Ronald Coase, 'The problem of social cost', Journal of Law and Economics 3 (1960), 1–44.

[48] I thus put aside those who interpret Coase to be a causal skeptic. (See, eg, Richard Epstein, 'A theory of strict liability', Journal of Legal Studies 2 (1973), 164–5, for an interpretation of Coase according to which the Coasean insight was that we cannot say what is the cause of what.) Although Coase, like other economists does evince some skepticism about causation, he made a much better point than this 'interactive effects' interpretation gives him credit for: it is that causation does not matter for the efficient allocation of resources.

to induce that person to take the cost-effective precautions. In either case, legal liability should not track causal responsibility, for even when there are high transaction costs the causer need not be the cheapest cost-avoider.

The irrelevance of causation to efficiency has left economists struggling to make sense of the cause-in-fact requirement of American tort liability rules. Since no metaphysical reading of 'cause' is appropriate to the goal of efficiency, some policy calculus is given as the legal meaning of 'cause'. Such policy calculus typically generates a probabilistic interpretation of 'cause' in tort law, so that any activity that raises the conditional probability of some harm that has occurred is said to have 'caused' that harm.[49] For any theory seeking to use tort law to give incentives to efficient behavior in a world of high transaction costs, this probabilistic interpretation is seemingly just what is required. To criticize such probabilistic interpretation of legal cause on the ground that probability is a poor metaphysical account of what causation is, would thus be beside the point—if efficiency is the point of tort law.[50]

My own view, undefended here, is that it is not. On my view, the best goal for tort law to serve is that of corrective justice. Such a corrective-justice view of tort law asserts that we all have primary moral duties not to hurt others; when we culpably violate such primary moral duties, we then have a secondary moral duty to correct the injustice we have caused. Tort liability rules are no more than the enforcement of these antecedently existing moral duties of corrective justice.

This corrective-justice view of tort law demands a robustly metaphysical interpretation of cause. For legal liability tracks moral responsibility on this view, and moral responsibility is for those harms we *cause*. 'Cause' has to mean what we mean when we assign moral responsibility *for* some harm, and what we mean in morality is to name a causal relation that is natural and *not* of the law's creation.

This is even more clearly true of criminal law. If the point of criminal law were the utilitarian point of deterring crime, then a constructed idea of legal cause perhaps could be justified; such a functional definition would take into account the incentive effects of various liability rules. But the function of criminal law is not utilitarian; it is retributive. Criminal law serves the exclusive function of achieving retributive justice.[51] This requires that its liability rules track closely the moral criteria for blameworthiness. As we saw in Chapters 2 and 3, one of those criteria is causation of morally prohibited states of affairs. Thus, again, 'cause' as

---

[49] Calibresi, 'Concerning cause and the law of torts'; Shavell, 'An analysis of causation and the scope of liability in the law of torts'; Landes and Posner, 'Causation in tort law: An economic approach'.

[50] For a good discussion of the economists' misuse of 'cause' to name an increase in conditional probability, see Richard Wright, 'Actual causation versus probabilistic linkage: The bane of economic analysis'; and Wright, 'The efficiency theory of causation and responsibility: Unscientific formalism and false semantics', Chicago-Kent Law Review 63 (1987), 553–78.

[51] Or so I argue in Moore, *Placing Blame*, Chapters 2–4.

used in criminal law must mean what is means in morality, and what it means in morality is to name a relation that is natural and *not* of the law's creation.

For those with non-justice-oriented theories of torts or criminal law, it remains true that the cause-in-fact requirement of both areas of law will have a probabilistic or other policy-based interpretation. Such an interpretation is also motivated by skepticism about there being any natural relation properly labeled 'causal', but as we have seen, such skepticism is but icing on the cake for non-justice oriented views of these areas of law.

V. Taxonomizing the Various Tests of Proximate Causation

It was useful in taxonomizing the seven variations of the counterfactual test to show how such variations were produced in response to problems perceived to exist for the first variation, the pure, unmodified counterfactual test. While there is no test of proximate causation that is comparably dominant (even in lip service only) to the counterfactual test of cause-in-fact, it is nonetheless useful to display the various proximate cause tests as they react to problems in other tests of proximate causation. I thus include some discussions of standard problems with each version of the tests within legal theory as I describe what motivates others of the tests.

The basic taxonomizing principle here is to separate tests that do not view proximate causation as having anything to do with real causal relations (the conventional view within legal theory), and tests that are motivated by the contrary thought. I shall begin with the former of these kinds of proximate-cause test, what I shall call policy-based proximate-cause tests. Policy-based proximate-cause tests are themselves usefully divided into two camps. Some tests are general-policy tests. These are tests justified by their service of a wide range of policies—indeed as wide as the policies that justify liability at all in torts or criminal law. By contrast, other tests are in the service of only one policy: the measurement of the culpability of the actor in terms of the mental state he had or should have had as he acted.

Beginning with the general policy-based proximate cause tests, the first of these are what we may call 'ad hoc policy tests'.[52] The idea is that courts balance a range of policies in each case that they adjudicate where a defendant has been found to have caused-in-fact a legally prohibited harm. They may balance certain 'social interests', like the need for deterrence, with certain 'individual interests', like the unfairness of surprising a defendant with liability. Courts then decide wherever such balance leads. Whatever decision is reached on such case-by-case policy balancing is then cast in terms of 'proximate' or 'legal' cause. Such labels

---

[52] The most influential example of ad hoc policy tests is Henry Edgarton, 'Legal cause'.

are simply the conclusions of policy balances; the labels have nothing to do with causation in any ordinary or scientific sense.

The second sort of test here is one that adopts general rules of legal causation. Such rules are adopted for various policy reasons also having nothing to do with causation, but this test differs from the last by its eschewal of case-by-case balancing; rather, per se rules of legal causation are adopted for policy reasons. Thus, the common-law rule for homicide was that death must occur within a year and a day of the defendant's harmful action, else the defendant could not be said to have legally caused the death.[53] Analogously, the 'last wrongdoer rule' held that when a single victim is mortally wounded by two or more assailants, acting not in concert and acting seriatim over time, only the last wrongdoer could be said to be the legal cause of the death.[54] Such sorts of test also found a temporary home in tort law with its 'first-house rule', according to which a railroad whose negligently emitted sparks burned an entire town was only liable for the house or houses directly ignited by its sparks, not for other houses ignited by the burning of those first burnt houses.[55] There is no pretense in such rules of making truly causal discriminations; rather, such rules were adopted for explicit reasons of legal policy. The first-house rule, for example, was said to be justified by the policy of subsidizing the then developing railroad industry.

The main problem with both ad hoc and the rule-based policy tests is that they seek to maximize the wrong policies. The general 'functionalist' approach[56] of such tests to legal concepts is correct: we should always ask after the purpose of the rule or institution in which the concept figures in order to ascertain its legal meaning. Yet the dominant purpose of the criminal law's concept of causation is to grade punishment proportionately to moral blameworthiness.[57] One who intentionally or recklessly causes a harm that another only tries to cause or risks causing, is more blameworthy, as I argued in Chapter 2. Proximate-cause tests thus should serve the function of grading offenders between the more blameworthy causers of harm, and the less blameworthy riskers or intenders of such harm. Analogously, in tort law the function of proximate-cause doctrines is to serve corrective justice. That justice demands that one pay for all and only the harms one has caused.[58] Tests of proximate causation thus must separate the true

[53] Joshua Dressler, *Understanding Criminal Law* (2nd edn, New York: Matthew-Bender, 1995), 466–7.

[54] Jeremiah Smith, 'Legal cause in actions in tort', Harvard Law Review 25 (1911–12), 111. See also Lawrence Eldredge, 'Culpable intervention as superseding cause', University of Pennsylvania Law Review 86 (1938), 121–35.

[55] *Ryan v. New York Central RR* 35 NY 210, 91 Am Dec 49 (1866).

[56] Felix Cohen, 'Transcendental nonsense and the functional approach', Columbia Law Review 35 (1935), 809–49; Cohen, 'The problems of a functional jurisprudence', Modern Law Review 1 (1937), 5–26.

[57] Moore, *Placing Blame*, Chapter 5.

[58] This is to reject risk-based corrective justice schemes, for the reasons to be exposed in Chapter 7, below.

causers who are obligated to compensate, from the non-causers who have no such obligation.

We must thus not seek the meaning of causation in extrinsic policies; rather, the legal concept of causation will serve its functions in tort and criminal law only if the concept names some factual state of affairs that both determines degrees of moral blameworthiness and grounds duties of compensation. By ignoring these dominant functions of causation in tort and criminal law, the Legal Realists' explicit policy tests constructed an artificial concept of legal cause unusable in any just punishment or compensation scheme.

This problem does not infect the next two policy-based proximate cause tests, foreseeability and harm-within-the-risk tests. For those tests do seek to describe a factual state of affairs that plausibly determines both moral blameworthiness and duties to compensate, and that plausibility connects a defendant's culpability to particular harms. They are thus serving the dominant policies that must be served by the concept of causation in justice-oriented theories of criminal law and the law of torts. Their novelty lies in their relocation of the locus of blame. On these theories, 'legal cause' is not a refinement of an admitted desert-determiner, true causation; it is rather a refinement of another admitted desert-determiner, namely, *mens rea* (or 'culpability' in the narrow sense with which I use that term).

Consider first the well-known foreseeability test.[59] Unlike the rule-based policy tests, here there is no multiplicity of rules for specific situations (like homicide, intervening wrongdoers, railroad fires, etc). Rather, there is one rule universally applicable to all criminal and tort cases: was the harm that the defendant's act in fact caused, foreseeable to him at the time he acted? This purportedly universal test for legal causation is usually justified by one of two policies: either the unfairness of punishing (or extracting compensation from) someone for harms that they could not foresee; or the inability to gain any deterrence by sanctioning such actors (since the threat value of tort or criminal law sanctions is non-existent for unforeseeable violations of liability rules).

Some jurisdictions restrict the foreseeability test to one kind of situation. When some human action or natural event intervenes between the defendant's action and the harm, the restricted test asks, not whether the harm was foreseeable, but rather, whether that intervening action or event was foreseeable to the defendant when he acted.[60] This restricted foreseeability test is like the restricted rules we saw before and is unlike the universal test of legal causation the foreseeability test usually purports to be.

Precisely because it is a culpability test, the foreseeability test becomes subject to its own policy-based objection, that of redundancy. Why should we ask *two* culpability questions in determining either blameworthiness or duties to

---

[59] Moore, *Placing Blame*, 363–99.
[60] Ibid, 363, n 1. This 'foreseeability' add-on is discussed in Chapter 11, below.

compensate? After we have satisfied ourselves that a defendant is culpable—either because she intended or foresaw some harm, or because she was unreasonable in not foreseeing some harm (the unreasonableness being judged in light of the degree of that harm's seriousness, the magnitude of its risk, and the lack of justification for taking such a risk), the foreseeability test bids us to ask 'was the harm foreseeable'? This is redundant, because any harm intended or foreseen is foreseeable, and any harm foreseeable enough to render an actor unreasonable for not foreseeing it, is also foreseeable.

The only way the foreseeability test avoids redundancy is by moving towards the other alternative here, the harm-within-the-risk test. That is, in situations where the defendant was culpable in intending, foreseeing, or risking some harm type H, but what his act in fact caused was an instance of harm type J, the foreseeability test of legal cause becomes non-redundant the moment one restricts it to asking whether J was foreseeable, a different question than the one asked and answered as a matter of *mens rea* about H. Yet this is to do the work of the harm-within-the-risk test, namely, the work of solving what I shall shortly call the 'fit problem' of *mens rea*. Moreover, it is to do such work badly. Foreseeability is not the right question to ask in order to fit the harm in fact caused by a defendant to the type of harm he either intended to achieve, or foresaw that he would cause, or risked. If the foreseeability test is to be restricted to this non-redundant work it is better abandoned for the harm-within-the-risk test.

Let us then examine this fourth policy-based proximate cause test, the rather badly labeled 'harm-within-the-risk' test.[61] Like the foreseeability test, this test purports to be a test of legal cause universally applicable to all tort and criminal cases. This test too is justified on policy grounds and does not pretend to have anything to do with factual or scientific causation. Doctrinally, however, the test differs from a simple foreseeability test.

Consider first the arena from which the test takes its name, crimes or torts of risk creation. If the defendant is charged with negligent homicide (or wrongful death in torts), for example, this test requires that the death of the victim be within the risk that made the actor's action negligent. If it was negligent to drop a can of nitroglycerine because it might explode and kill the victim, but instead it kills the victim by causing him to bleed to death, then the harm that happened (bleeding) was not within the risk of harm (explosion) that made it negligent to drop the can. Similarly, if the charge is manslaughter (for which consciousness of the risk is required in some jurisdictions), this test requires that the death of the victim be within the risk the awareness of which made the defendant's action reckless.

Extension of this test to non-risk creation crimes or torts requires some modification. For crimes or torts of strict liability, where no *mens rea* is required, the test requires that the harm that happened be one of the types of harms the

---

[61] Explored in detail in Chapters 7–10, below.

risk of which motivated the lawmaker to prohibit the behavior. For torts or crimes requiring knowledge (or 'general intention') for their *mens rea*, the test asks whether the harm that happened was an instance of the type of harm foreseen by the defendant as he acted. For torts or crimes requiring purpose (or 'specific intent') for their *mens rea*, the test asks whether the harm that happened was an instance of the type of harm the defendant intended to achieve by his action.

What motivates all of these variations of the harm-within-the-risk test is the following insight: when assessing culpable *mens rea*, there is always a 'fit problem'.[62] Suppose a defendant intends to hit his victim in the face with a stick; suppose further he intends the hit to put out the victim's left eye. As it happens, the victim turns suddenly as he is being hit, and loses his right ear to the blow. Whether the harm that happened is an instance of the type of harm intended is what I call the fit problem. Fact-finders have to fit the mental state the defendant had to the actual result he achieved and ask whether it is close enough for him to be punished for a crime of intent like mayhem. (If it is not close enough, then he may yet be found guilty of some lesser tort or crime of battery or reckless endangerment.)

The essential claim behind the harm-within-the-risk test is that 'legal cause' is the label lawyers should put on a problem of culpability, the problem I call the fit problem. Proponents of this test urge that legal cause, properly understood, is really a *mens rea* doctrine, not a doctrine of causation at all.

The main problem for the harm-within-the-risk test itself does not lie in any of the directions we have just explored with respect to foreseeability as a test. The harm-within-the-risk test is in the service of a justice-oriented policy in its seeking of a true desert-determiner, and the test does not ask a redundant question. To grade culpability by the mental states of intention, foresight, and risk we have to solve the fit problem above described. The real question for the harm-within-the-risk test is whether this grading by culpable mental states is all that is or should be going on under the rubric of 'legal cause'.

Consider in this regard two well-known sorts of legal cause cases. It is a time-honored maxim of criminal and tort law that 'you take your victim as you find him'[63]—standard translation: no matter how abnormal may be the victim's susceptibilities to injury, and no matter how unforeseeable such injuries may therefore be, a defendant is held to legally cause such injuries. Hit the proverbial thin-skulled man or cut the proverbial hemophiliac, and you have legally caused their deaths if they die. This is hard to square with the harm-within-the-risk test. A defendant who intends to hit or to cut does not necessarily (or even usually) intend to kill. A defendant who foresees that his acts will cause the victim to be

---

[62] Moore, *Placing Blame*, 469–76. See also Chapter 3, above, in the discussion of the doctrine of double effect.
[63] See Chapter 11, below.

struck or cut, does not necessarily (or even usually) foresee that the victim will die. A defendant who negligently risks that his acts will cause a victim to be struck or cut is not necessarily (or even usually) negligent because he also risked death.

The second sort of case involves what are often called 'intervening' or 'superseding' causes.[64] Suppose the defendant sets explosives next to a prison wall intending to blow the wall and to get certain inmates out. He foresees to a practical certainty that the explosion will kill the guard on the other side of the wall. He lights the fuse to the bomb and leaves. As it happens, the fuse goes out. However: a stranger passes by the wall, sees the bomb, and relights the fuse for the pleasure of seeing an explosion; or, a thief comes by, sees the bomb and tries to steal it, dropping it in the process and thereby exploding it; or, lightning hits the fuse, reigniting it, and setting off the bomb; etc. In all variations, the guard on the other side of the wall is killed by the blast. Standard doctrines of intervening causation holds that the defendant did not legally cause the death of the guard.[65] Yet this is hard to square with the harm-within-the-risk test. After all, did not the defendant foresee just the type of harm an instance of which did occur? Because the harm-within-the-risk question asks a simple type-to-token question—was the particular harm that happened an instance of the type of harm whose foresight by the defendant made him culpable—the test is blind to freakishness of causal route.[66]

The American Law Institute's Model Penal Code modifies its adoption of the harm-within-the-risk test in section 2.03 by denying liability for a harm-within-the-risk that is 'too remote or accidental in its occurrence to have a [just] bearing on the actor's liability or on the gravity of his offense'.[67] Such a caveat is an explicit recognition of the inability of the harm-within-the-risk test to accommodate the issues commonly adjudicated as intervening-cause issues.

Such a recognition is not nearly broad enough to cover the inadequacy of the harm-within-the-risk approach. The basic problem with the test is that it ignores *all* of the issues traditionally adjudicated under the concept of legal cause. The test is blind not only to freakishness of causal route in the intervening-cause situations, not only blind to the distinction between antecedent versus after-arising abnormalities so crucial to resolution of the thin-skulled man kind of issue, but the test also ignores all those issues of remoteness sought to be captured by Sir Francis Bacon's coinage, 'proximate causation'.[68] Even where there is no

---

[64] Explored in detail in Chapter 11, below.   [65] See Chapter 11, below.

[66] As we explore in Chapter 10, above.

[67] American Law Institute, Model Penal Code, § 2.03(2)(b) (Proposed Official Draft, 1962).

[68] Bacon's first maxim was, 'Injura non remota causa sed proxima spectator': Bacon, 'Maxims of the law', in Bacon, *The Elements of the Common Law of England* (London: Assigns of I Moore, 1630), 1. See the discussion of Bacon's causa proxima in Joseph Beale, 'The proximate consequences of an act', Harvard Law Review 33 (1920), 633–58. Beale (unsurprisingly, since this was also Beale's own view) concludes that 'Bacon's idea of the remote cause . . . was a purely physical idea . . .': ibid, 634, n 4.

sudden 'break' in the chain of causation as in the intervening-cause cases, there is a strong sense that causation peters out over space and time. Caesar's crossing the Rubicon may well be a necessary condition for my writing this chapter, but so many other events have also contributed that Caesar's causal responsibility has long since petered out. The logical relationship at the heart of the harm-within-the-risk test—'was the particular harm that happened an instance of the type of harm whose risk, foresight, or intention made the defendant culpable?'—is incapable of capturing this sensitivity to remoteness. As such, the harm-within-the-risk test is blind to the basic issue adjudicated under 'legal cause'. The harm-within-the-risk test asks a good question, but it asks it in the wrong place.[69]

I turn now from the policy-based tests of proximate causation to those tests based on the view that proximate causation, like cause-in-fact, has to do with real causal relations in the world. The oldest of these tests is that suggested by Sir Francis Bacon's coinage, *causa proxima*. The simple idea behind such a remoteness test is that causation is a scalar relation—a more or less sort of thing, not an all-or-nothing sort of thing—and that it peters out over time.

A criticism of the remoteness test, often voiced in the legal literature,[70] is that distance in space and remoteness in time are irrelevant to degrees of causal contribution. Examples like *People v. Botkin*,[71] where poisoned candy went a great distance (from California to the victim in New Jersey), or an undetonated bomb left buried for many years before it explodes and injures a victim, are trotted out in support of the criticism.[72] Justice Cardozo rejoined that such criticism surely ran counter to strong community sentiment that spatio-temporal distance does matter to degrees of causal contribution,[73] but I shall later hope to do better than that. I shall urge in Chapter 5 that spatio-temporal distance is a proxy for the number of events or states of affairs through which a cause exerts its influence on its effects, and that the number of events is relevant to the degree of causal contribution. This is the metaphysical view that causation 'tires' through its links.

A second and quite distinct kind of cause-based proximate cause test is the 'direct cause' test. Despite the name, this test does *not* require that there be no event or state of affairs intervening between a cause and its effect for that cause to be legally 'proximate'. Not even the ancient direct/indirect distinction between the writs of trespass and trespass-on-the-case were this stringent in their

---

[69] The place to ask and answer these questions of fit is with respect to mental states, not causation. With respect to negligence, which is not a mental sate, I shall urge (in Chapters 8–9, below) that we should not ask the fit question at all, anywhere.

[70] See, eg, Beale, 'Proximate consequences of an act', 642–3.

[71] *People v. Botkin* 132 Cal 231, 64 P 286 (1901).

[72] Beale, 'Proximate consequences of an act', 642.

[73] 'There is no use in arguing that distance ought not to count, if life and experience tells us that it does.' *Bird v. St Paul F and Minneapolis Ins Co* 224 NY 47, 120 NE 86 (1918). See also Edgarton, 'Legal cause', 367–72.

requirement of directness (for trespass).[74] On the contrary, chains can be sufficiently *direct* for the direct cause test even though they are quite long chains extending over considerable space and time. It is only if a special kind of event—an 'intervening' (aka, 'superseding', 'extraneous') cause—intervenes that the chain is insufficiently direct. The heart of the direct cause test is thus the idea of these chain-breaking, intervening causes.

Beginning in a series of articles in the 1950s,[75] and culminating in their massive book, *Causation in the Law* in 1959,[76] Herbert Hart and Tony Honoré sought to describe the idea of intervening causation that they saw as implicit both in the law and in everyday causal idioms. One can see their concept most easily in three steps. First, presuppose some version of the counterfactual analysis: a cause is at least a necessary condition for its effect (or perhaps a NESS condition, as it was for Hart and Honoré).[77] Second, a cause is not *any* necessary condition; rather, out of the plethora of conditions necessary for the happening of any event, only two sorts are eligible to be causes. Free, informed, voluntary human actions, and those abnormal conjunctions of natural events we colloquially refer to as 'coincidences', are the two kinds of necessary conditions we find salient and honor as 'causes' (versus mere 'background conditions'). Third, such voluntary human action and abnormal natural events cause a given effect only if some other voluntary human action or abnormal natural event does not intervene between the first such event and its putative effect. Such salient events, in other words, are breakers of causal chains ('intervening causes') as much as they are initiators of causal chains, so that if they do intervene they relegate all earlier such events to the status of mere background conditions.

Hart and Honoré built on considerable case-law support for their two candidates for intervening causes.[78] Indeed, it is arguable that the basic distinction between principal and accomplice liability in criminal law depends in large part

---

[74] Despite Bacon telling us that the law 'contenteth it selfe with the immediate cause and judgeth of acts by that, without looking to any further degree' (Bacon, 'Maxims', 1), even the ancient distinction between the writ of trespass (for directly caused harms) and trespass on the case (for indirectly caused harms) was not so strict about directness. A famous example is the 'squib case', *Scott v. Shepard* 96 Eng Rep 525 (KB 1773), in which a lighted squib containing gunpowder was thrown by the defendant near one person, who threw it near another, who threw it near the victim, where the squib exploded. The court held that 'the injury is the direct and immediate act of the defendant', so that the writ of trespass was appropriate.

[75] HLA Hart and AM Honoré, 'Causation in the law', Law Quarterly Review 72 (1956), 58–90, 260–81, 398–417.

[76] HLA Hart and AM Honoré, *Causation in the Law* (Oxford: Clarendon Press, 1959).

[77] HLA Hart and Tony Honoré, *Causation in the Law* (2nd edn, Oxford: Clarendon Press, 1985). The second edition works a number of changes, almost all of them at the behest of Tony Honoré. One might doubt whether Herbert Hart ever fully shared the NESS view. Honoré certainly did. See Honoré, 'Necessary and sufficient conditions in tort law', in David Owen (ed), *Philosophical Foundations of Tort Law* (Oxford: Oxford University Press, 1995).

[78] The early case law is summarized in Charles Carpenter, 'Workable rules for determining proximate cause', California Law Review 20 (1932), 229–59, 396–419, 471–539. Even more exhaustive is Carpenter, 'Proximate cause', Southern California Law Review 14 (1940), 1–34, 115–53, 416–51; 15 (1942), 187–213, 304–21, 427–68; 16 (1943), 1–23, 61–92, 275–313.

on this conceptualization of causation, as does the tort law distinction between 'in concert' versus 'concurrent causer' kinds of joint tortfeasors.[79] One worry for this view of causation, nonetheless, is the worry that it is incomplete with respect to the remoteness range of issues usually dealt with under the rubric of 'legal cause' in the law. Causation in the law fades out gradually as much it breaks off suddenly, and the direct cause analysis ignores this.

VI. Unified Approaches to Causation in the Law

The problems with the conventional analysis of causation—in terms of a bifurcation into cause-in-fact and proximate causation—have tempted some legal theorists to abandon the conventional analysis, root and branch. This generates a search for a unitary notion of causation that is much more discriminating (in what it allows as a cause) than the hopelessly promiscuous counterfactual cause-in-fact test of the conventional analysis. Indeed, the search is for a unitary concept of causation that is so discriminating that it can do the work that on the conventional analysis is done by both cause-in-fact and proximate cause doctrines. It is far from obvious that causation is in fact a sufficiently discriminating relation that it can do this much work in assigning responsibility. Nonetheless, there are three such proposals in the legal literature, each having some doctrinal support in the law.

One we have seen already. This was the fourth variation in the counterfactual test for cause-in-fact. If one does not ask whether the defendant's act was necessary for the occurrence of the harm—if one instead asks whether that aspect of the defendant's act that made him negligent or otherwise culpable caused the harm—then one has a causal test almost as discriminating as the simple counterfactual test coupled with a harm-within-the-risk version of the proximate cause test.[80] This is not surprising, because both tests rule ineligible any aspects of the defendant's act that does *not* make him culpable. For the aspect-causation view, such culpability-irrelevant aspects of the defendant's action are not (relevantly) the cause of the harm; for the harm-within-the-risk test, such culpability-irrelevant aspects of the defendant's action do not fit the culpable mental states of the defendant. Whether one puts it as causation (the aspect-cause view), or as culpability (the harm-within-the-risk view), the discriminating power is roughly the same.

A second unified view of causation in the law is the oldest of these kind of proposals. It conceives of causation as a metaphysical primitive. Causation is not reducible to any other sort of thing or things, and thus there is little by way of an

---

[79] Explored in detail in Chapter 13, below.
[80] The fit is not perfect. For some counterexamples, see Carpenter, 'Workable rules for determining proximate cause', 408; see also Wright, 'Causation in tort law', 1759–66.

analysis that one can say about it. However, the one thing we can say is that the causal relation is a scalar relation, which is to say, a matter of degree. One thing can be *more* of a cause of a certain event than another thing. Given the scalarity of causation, all the law need do is draw the line for liability somewhere on the scale of causal contribution. On matters that vary on a smooth continuum, it is notoriously arbitrary to pick a precise break-point; where is the line between middle age and old age, red and pink, bald and not-bald, or caused and not-caused? This approach thus picks an *appropriately* vague line below which one's causal contribution to a given harm will be ignored for purposes of assessing responsibility. Let the defendant be responsible and liable for some harm only when the degree of his causal contribution to that harm has reached some non-*de minimus*, or 'substantial', magnitude. This is the original 'substantial factor' test, as articulated by Jeremiah Smith in 1911.[81] To the common objection that the test tells us little, its defenders reply that that is a virtue, not a vice, for there is little to be said about causation. It, like hard-core pornography, is something we can 'know when we see it',[82] without need of general definitions and tests.

The third and last of these unified notions of causation is physicalist in its ambitions. Some theorists have thought that we can say more about the nature of the causal relation than that it is scalar and that a substantial amount of it is required for responsibility. On this third view the nature of causation is to be found in the mechanistic concepts of physics: matter in motion, energy, force.[83] This test is similar to the substantial factor view in its conceiving the causal relation to be scalar, but it differs in its reductionist ambitions: causation is not a primitive, but can be reduced to some kind of physical forces.

This view handles easily the overdetermination cases that are such a problem for the conventional analysis. When two fires join, two bullets strike simultaneously, two motorcycles scare the same horse, each is a cause of the harm because each is doing its physical work. When one non-mortal wound is inflicted together with a larger, mortal wound, the victim dying of loss of blood, each is a cause of death because each did some of the physical work (loss of blood) leading to death.

Such a mechanistic conception of causation is mostly a suggestion in the legal literature because of the elusive and seemingly mysterious use of 'energy' and 'force' by legal theorists. One suspects some such view is often applied by jurors, but unless theorists can spell out the general nature of the relation being intuitively applied by jurors this test tends to collapse to the metaphysically sparer substantial factor test.

The law, as we have seen, has a bafflingly complicated number of legal tests for causation. There is no univocal theory in the general part of the law of torts and

[81] Smith, 'Legal cause in actions of tort'.
[82] Justice Potter Stewart's famous 'test', in *Jacobellis v. Ohio*, 378 US 184, 197 (1961).
[83] Beale, 'The proximate consequences of an act'; Beale, 'Recovery for consequences of an act', Harvard Law Review 9 (1895), 80–9; Epstein, 'A theory of strict liability'.

crimes. We have thousands of separate usages of 'cause' in the thousands of liability rules in these areas of law; and we have nine variations of cause-in-fact tests, seven varieties of proximate cause tests and three proposals supposing that a unified test should supplant any of the 63 possible combinations of the bifurcated tests. Despite this prolixity and disagreement in the law, in the next two chapters I shall seek to extract *a* concept of causation presupposed by the law of torts and crimes. Obviously, I am going to prune away a lot of legal doctrines in order to do this.

Legal Tests of Causation

I. Bifurcated Tests

A. Cause-in-fact Tests

1. Simple counterfactual test (The legal test of '*sine qua non*')
2. Modified counterfactual tests in law
   a. Necessary element of a sufficient set
   b. Necessary to the time, place, and manner of an effect's occurrence
   c. Asymmetrically temporal test: necessary to accelerations (but not retardings) as cause
   d. The necessity of negligent aspects of acts (versus acts that are negligent) as causes
   e. Necessity as a usually present and always sufficient criterion of 'substantial factor' causation
   f. Causation as necessity to chance
3. Tests regarding cause-in-fact to be a matter of policy
   a. Ad hoc balancing of all policies
   b. Incentive-based policies and probabalistic tests

B. Proximate Cause Tests

1. Tests Regarding Proximate Causation to be a Matter of Policy
   a. Tests based on a wide range of policies
      i.   Ad hoc policy balancing test
      ii. Rule-based policy tests
         (1) Year and a day rule
         (2) First house rule
         (3) Last wrongdoer rule
   b. Tests based on the policy of gauging culpability (mental state) of the actor
      i.   Foreseeability
      ii. Harm-within-the-risk
2. Tests regarding proximate causation to be a matter of fact (about real causal relations)
   a. Space/time proximity tests and the sheer number events in the chain between cause and effect
   b. Direct cause tests
3. Tests regarding proximate causation to be partly causal and partly policy: direct cause with foreseeability (of the intervening cause)

II. Unified Tests

A. Aspects Cause Revisited (See I.A. 2.d. above)

B. Cause as a Scalar Primitive: the original substantial factor test

C. Physically Reductionist Tests: cause as physical force

5

The Prima Facie Demands of the Law
on the Concept of Causation

We now leave what the (general part of) the law explicitly *says* its theories of causation are, for the concept of causation implicit in the myriad of legal doctrines making up the substantive law of torts and crimes. Both this chapter and the next seek to tease out a concept of causation implicit in legal usages.

As I mentioned at the beginning of Chapter 4, there are some prunings to be done if we are to have a chance of extracting any coherent concept of causation from the thousands of its usages in the law. The first pruning should be done now. This is to prune away (meaning, to ignore) the legal literature on causation that is skeptical in nature. After all, the three generations of legal skeptics that we examined briefly in Chapter 4 hold the view that the law has no coherent concept of causation. Causal requirements, on their view, are empty of any real content. 'Cause' is merely the honorific label lawyers place on conclusions about responsibility, conclusions that have been reached on other grounds. It would be a bootless enterprise to seek to extract a coherent concept of causation from views explicitly denying that such a concept exists.[1]

It is true enough that some of such legal skeptics about causation have proposed positive analyses of the law's causal requirements. For example, the Legal Realists proposed general policy balances, either case-by-case or rule-based, and the legal economists have proposed probabilistic interpretations of the law's causal requirements. At least to the legal skeptics proposing them (as well as to anyone accepting their policy orientation), these interpretations are neither senseless nor incoherent. Yet as I argued before, at least for torts and for criminal law these interpretations are in the service of the wrong policies. Deterrence-oriented and efficiency-based policy reinterpretations of 'cause' in law are fine if

---

[1] One can imagine a kind of skepticism where such an enterprise would not be bootless. In other areas of philosophy, such as ethics, there are skeptics who are cognitivists about the discourse in question but skeptics ontologically. That is, they think that talk of moral rights is meaningful and capable of having a truth value; but also think that there is nothing in the world answering to the phrase, 'moral right,' so the truth value of such moral statements is always 'false'. One can extract a concept from such skeptics' beliefs. But the legal skeptics we examined in Chapter 4, above, deny not only that there is a causal relation in nature, but even more deny that the law has any coherent conception of causation. They are, in other words, both non-cognitivist and ontological skeptics.

the law is broadly utilitarian in its justification, for then its liability rules should be interpreted so as to incentivize efficient or other optimal behavior. But on justice-oriented theories of torts or criminal law—and even on mixed theories that have a justice component—such constructed notions of causation will have no place. If causation matters to moral fault—the thesis of Chapters 2 and 3—and if moral fault matters to legal liability, then causation cannot be the artificial construct that the Legal Realists and the legal economists have plumped for.

In what follows I shall thus ignore doctrines and proposed doctrines having their basis in non-justice-oriented theories of tort or criminal law. More significantly, I also will ignore the two policy-justified tests of proximate causation that were proposed by the Legal Realists and that did *not* assume non-justice-oriented theories of torts and crimes. I refer to the foreseeability and harm-within-the-risk tests mentioned in Chapter 4. Putting these tests aside requires some justification other than that they serve non-justice oriented theories of torts or crimes, since they do not.

Part III of this book, Chapters 7–10, is devoted to showing why we should reject the harm-within-the-risk test as a test of causation (the argument of Part III was summarized briefly in the last chapter). The conclusion of Part III is that the question asked by the harm-within-the-risk test must be answered by any justice-oriented theory of torts or crimes, at least with respect to crimes or torts of intent, knowledge, or recklessness; but that such culpability enquiry cannot supplant a true causal requirement for moral blameworthiness and attendant legal liability.

With regard to the foreseeability test, I have not included a similar, sustained critique in this book. This, because I think the redundancy objection I summarized in Chapter 4 to be conclusive against foreseeability as a test; and because I have argued elsewhere in detail[2] that foreseeability is literally an empty concept, one that thus masks a variety of intuitions under the always available (and *equally* available) labels, 'foreseeable' and 'unforeseeable'.

Having eliminated a large chunk of the legal literature and legal doctrines from the start, it is perhaps surprising how much remains to form the data for this chapter and the next. My question is this: when lawyers have at least tried to use 'cause' as the label for a natural relation that must exist for liability to be found, what notion of 'cause' is implicit in their usage? Many years ago Sir Frederick Pollock advised us that 'The lawyer cannot afford to adventure himself with philosophers in the logical and metaphysical controversies that beset the idea of cause.'[3] Yet adventure themselves they have, because (on a justice-oriented view of the law) they must, and our question here is: with what result?

---

[2] Michael Moore, 'Foreseeing harm opaquely', in John Gardner, Jeremy Harder, and Stephen Shute (eds), *Action and Value in Criminal Law* (Oxford: Oxford University Press, 1993), reprinted in Moore, *Placing Blame: A general theory of the criminal law* (Oxford: Oxford University Press, 1997).

[3] Sir Frederick Pollock, *Torts* (6th edn, New York: Banks Law Publishing Co, 1901), 36.

During the heyday of ordinary-language philosophy, Peter Strawson urged a task he termed 'descriptive metaphysics'.[4] The idea was that instead of asking how things are, we could ask how a given body of discourse presupposed how things are. In other words, we can tease out the metaphysical presuppositions of a body of practices without ourselves committing to the metaphysics of such practices.

This is the task I set for myself in this chapter and the next succeeding. Without (here) taking a position on what metaphysics of causation is correct, I attempt to describe what the liability doctrines we have in the law presuppose causation to be like. I save for the later parts of the book the question of whether this metaphysical view of causation is true.

I shall approach the law's presuppositions about causation in two steps. In this chapter I shall take at face value the usages of 'cause' by various legal doctrines, here assuming that all such doctrines are what they purport to be, doctrines of cause-based liability. In the next chapter, Chapter 6, I shall be more critical, throwing out some doctrines on the grounds that they cannot be doctrines of cause-based liability, whatever may have been the beliefs of their proponents. This second step allows us to narrow the concept of cause employed by the law to a point where there might be some chance of discovering an answering concept of cause in some plausible metaphysics.

I. Distinguishing Causation from Mere Correlation

Juries are routinely instructed that they must not confuse mere temporal succession (between the defendant's act and some harm), with causation between the two. For example, the defendant's negligently maintained transom hit the plaintiff at a certain place on his head; the plaintiff subsequently developed cancer at that spot. Not only is such temporal succession not identical to causation, but such succession is not even very good evidence of causation. Evidence of such succession, without something more, is not enough evidence of causation to get a jury.[5]

What if the plaintiff introduces evidence that such trauma on heads is *always* followed by such cancers? This may well be enough evidence of causation to get to the jury, but it is still not to be identified as causation. Juries are still instructed that even invariant succession does not inevitably betoken causation.[6] After all, it

---

[4] PF Strawson, *Individuals* (London: Methuen, 1959). Ordinary-language philosophy (eg, at Oxford University from 1945 to 1965) went further than I go in the text. Such ordinary-language philosophers as Gilbert Ryle, Ludwig Wittgenstein, and JL Austin thought that the *only* metaphysics one can do is the descriptive metaphysics described in the text. For a critique, see Michael Moore, 'The interpretive turn: A turn for the worse?', Stanford Law Review 41 (1989), 927–34, reprinted in Moore, *Educating Oneself in Public: Critical essays in jurisprudence* (Oxford: Oxford University Press, 2000).

[5] See, eg, *Kramer Service, Inc v. Wilkins* 184 Miss 483, 186 So 625 (1939).

[6] Although *invariant* succession is admissible as good evidence of causation.

might be true that there have been and will be only five such head traumas ever, that all five are followed by cancers, and yet, that there is no causal connection between any of these head traumas and cancer. It is universally true that all clumps of gold that ever have existed and that ever will exist are less then a cubic mile in size; yet there is no causal relationship between the fact that some clump is gold and the fact that such clump is less than a cubic mile in size.

Seemingly missing in examples such as the last is any *necessitation* of the second fact by the first. Missing is the kind of necessity seemingly present between the fact that a clump is uranium and the fact that a clump is less than a cubic mile in size. A clump of uranium *cannot* be a cubic mile in size (because it would exceed critical mass); that necessity backs up and explains why, in fact, there never has been a cubic mile of uranium. No such necessity backs up and explains why there never has been a cubic mile of gold.[7]

Thus, universal correlation cannot be identified as causation (even if the former is good evidence of the latter). Needed is some kind of necessity explaining why there is a universal correlation between two types of events such as head traumas and cancers.

Surprisingly, perhaps, such universal correlation backed up by some kind of necessity is still not to be identified as causation. For yet to be ruled out is the problem of epiphenomenal correlations.[8] In the case of the head trauma and the cancer, suppose it were true that the kind of cancer involved is caused by, and can only be caused by, the kind of blow the defendant inflicted. Suppose further that the contusion on the victim's skin is not only caused by such a blow, but also it can only be caused by such a blow. Since the cancer takes longer to develop than the contusion, the cancer *of necessity* always succeeds the contusion, and thus one might think that the contusion caused the cancer. Yet we know this is false: the blow caused the cancer (it is my hypothetical) as well as the contusion, but the contusion is merely epiphenomenal to the cancer—in which case a universally true correlation, and one which is backed by a kind of necessity, is still not to be equated with causation.

All of this, of course, is quite commonsensical and not peculiar to the law's use of 'cause'.[9] Yet in its requirements that a jury be attuned to the possibility that a

---

[7] The example is David Armstrong's in his argument that accidentally true generalizations must be distinguished from true causal laws. See Armstrong, *What Is a Law of Nature?* (Cambridge: Cambridge University Press, 1983).

[8] For discussions of the epiphenomena problem, Wesley Salmon, 'Probabilistic causality', Pacific Philosophical Quarterly 61 (1980), 50–74; David Lewis, 'Causation', Journal of Philosophy 70 (1973), 556–67; and Jaegwon Kim, 'Epiphenomenal and supervenient causation', in Peter French, Theodore Vehling, and Howard Wettstein (eds), *Midwest Studies in Philosophy IX: Causation and Causal Theories* (Minneapolis: University of Minnesota Press, 1984).

[9] For a discussion of how laws, morals, common sense, and science all converge to distinguish correlation from causation, see Moritz Schlick, 'Cauasality in everyday life and in recent science', University of California Publications in Philosophy 15 (1932), 99–125.

temporal sequence (no matter how universal and necessary) may not be a causal sequence, the law adopts common sense without change.

II. Distinguishing between Equally Indispensable Conditions: The Cause/Condition Distinction

The law, like common sense, assumes that causes necessitate their effects, as we have seen. They, in that sense, 'make' such effects happen. The law also joins common sense in thinking that usually causes make a difference. This is expressed by the law in its widely used *sine qua non* doctrine, a doctrine which requires a jury to ask, 'But for the defendant's acts, would the harm have happened?'

An immediately obvious problem (for the idea that a cause is that which makes the difference for the happening of some effect) is that there are so many such conditions.[10] Sir Francis Drake could not have defeated the Spanish Armada without ships, without the lumber with which to build such ships, without oxygen in the air in England, without a Queen with some backbone, etc, etc. If all such conditions necessary to the happening of some event *x* are causes of *x*, then every case of causation is a case of *multiple* causation. (Such garden-variety multiple cause cases are to be distinguished from the overdetermination kind of cases discussed in the next section.)

John Stuart Mill, with whom this problem is most famously associated, took exactly this view.[11] Each temporally present necessary condition had equal claim with every other such condition to be called the cause of some happening, in any suitably scientific sense of 'cause'. Mill relegated the discrimination we do make in ordinary speech, between 'the cause' and 'a mere background condition', to pragmatic features of the contexts in which such things were said. If we are doctors, we pick out the factors that we can treat; if we are moralists, those that are blamable; if we are historians, those that have appeal to normal human interest, as 'the cause'.[12] In reality, Mill held, all such conditions together constituted the cause.

It is often said that the law is much more discriminating than science in its usages of 'cause'.[13] This is easy to show with regard to temporally successive chains of conditions; as I shall explore later, the law's concept of cause presupposes that causation both tapers off over time and breaks off suddenly at certain points in time.

---

[10] See Moore, *Act and Crime: The implications of the philosophy of action for the criminal law* (Oxford: Clarendon Press, 1993), 267–76.

[11] John Stuart Mill, *A System of Logic* (8th edn, London: Longman, 1872), Book III, Chapter V, section 3.

[12] For a discussion of these pragmatic features in various contexts, see Joel Feinberg, *Doing and Deserving* (Princeton: Princeton University Press, 1970).

[13] Jeremiah Smith, 'Legal cause in actions of tort', Harvard Law Review 25 (1911–12), 104.

It is rare, however, that the law actually discriminates between *temporally co-present*, equally necessary conditions—what I am calling the ordinary, garden-variety multiple-cause situations. It is only with its occasional 'sole cause' doctrines that the law discriminates between equally necessary conditions, honoring one but not others as 'the cause'. Thus, one version of the irresistible-impulse test of insanity asks whether 'the alleged crime was so connected with such mental disease, in the relation of cause and effect, as to have been the product of it *solely*'.[14] Likewise, gross negligence that intervenes between a defendant's action and some harm such as a death is sometimes said to break causal chains only 'when it is the sole cause of death'.[15] Similarly, one version of the abuse-of-process tort imposes liability only if the improper ('abusing') motive was the *sole* reason motivating the defendant's use of court process. Since there are always other co-temporal conditions necessary for the actions at issue in these cases, and yet liability is imposed despite this multiplicity, the law presupposes some criterion for distinguishing causes from merely necessary conditions.

III. Preserving the Possibility of Over-determining Causes

A well-known conundrum in the law concerns what are often called the over-determination cases.[16] These are what might be called the exotic variety of multiple cause cases, in contrast to the garden-variety multiple cause cases discussed in the previous subsection. These are cases where there is more than one set of conditions sufficient to bring about the harm, in which case neither set is necessary to the occurrence of the harm. The law rather crisply assumes: (a) that we can distinguish concurrent overdetermination cases from pre-empting overdetermination cases; (b) that for the concurrent type cases, each set of sufficient conditions is regarded as the cause of the entire harm; (c) that in the pre-emptive type cases, we can distinguish pre-empting causes from pre-empted factors; and (d) that pre-empted sets of sufficient conditions are not causes of the harm and that preempting conditions are causes of the harm.[17]

---

[14] *Parsons v. State* 81 Ala 577, 597, 5 So 854, 866–7 (1887).

[15] *State v. Shabazz* 719 A2d 440, 445 (Conn 1998).

[16] The best contemporary legal discussion of these cases is to be found in Richard Wright, 'Causation in tort law', California Law Review 73 (1985), 1775–98. Overdetermination cases are to be distinguished from garden-variety multiple cause cases. In the latter, no one event or state is sufficient to produce the harm, because more than one event is individually necessary to produce the harm. Such sets of individually necessary, only jointly sufficient conditions, are very frequent and may well be the most frequent kind of case. Wright mentions (ibid, 1793) a kind of case intermediate between regular multiple cause cases and the overdetermination variety. If there are three fires, no one of which is sufficient, but any two of which are sufficient, to burn the plaintiff's structure, then no fire is individually necessary to produce the harm. Although I do not here separately treat these (but see Chapter 17, below), we should consider these too to be overdetermination cases.

[17] See Wright, 'Causation in tort law'.

Thus, in the much-discussed two-fire cases, where each fire is sufficient to destroy the building that has burned to the ground: (a) we should distinguish concurrent cases where the two fires join, and the larger fire resulting from this then burns down the structure,[18] from pre-emptive cases where one fire arrives first and burns down the structure, leaving nothing to be burnt by the second fire when it arrives; (b) when the fires join (the concurrent case), each fire is the cause of the destruction of the building; (c) where the fires do not join (the pre-emptive case), the first fire pre-empts the ability of the second fire to cause the building's destruction; and (d) therefore, in the latter case, only the first fire is the cause of the harm, and the second fire is not a cause of the harm.

With regard to (a) above, there is some ambiguity as to how we are to classify what I shall call *asymmetrical* overdetermination cases. That is, suppose the fire set by the defendant is much smaller than the second fire; the two join as before and the resultant fire destroys the structure. The second fire would have been sufficient by itself to have destroyed the structure, but the defendant's smaller fire would not have been, since it would have been extinguished by the available equipment before it could have destroyed the structure. There is some authority for the proposition that the larger fire is a pre-emptive cause, not a concurrent cause, and that therefore the defendant's fire is pre-empted as a cause of the harm.[19] Preferable, I think, is Richard Wright's view: these are concurrent causation cases, making both fire-starters liable for the whole damage.[20] Each fire was still doing its burning (unless of course it could be shown that the large fire literally extinguished the defendant's fire by taking its oxygen or fuel), and each was a cause of the building's destruction.

With regard to (b) above, there is some authority for the proposition that it matters to the causal question exactly how each fire was started. Where (i) each fire is the result of culpable action by a different individual, each individual's culpable act in starting his fire is the cause of the harm. But where only one fire is the result of the defendant's culpable action, and the other fire is the result of (ii) another person's innocent action, (iii) a natural event, or (iv) the victim's own culpable action, then the defendant's fire is not a cause of the building's destruction.[21]

This pattern of liability repeats itself for all kinds of physically caused injuries. Thus, where two defendants independently stab or shoot the victim, who dies of

---

[18] These are the facts of *Anderson v. Minneapolis St Paul and S St Marie RR Co* 179 NW 45 (Minn, 1920), and *Kingston v. Chicago NW Ry* 191 Wis 610, 211 NW 913 (1927).

[19] Cf *City of Piqua v. Morris* 98 Ohio St 42, 120 NE 300 (1918) (negligent maintenance of drainage wickets held not a cause of plaintiff's injury from overflowing reservoir, because the flood would have overflowed the reservoir even if the wickets were not clogged).

[20] Wright, 'Causation in tort law', 1794, 1800.

[21] *Cook v. Minneapolis St Paul and S St Marie Ry* 98 Wis 624, 74 NW 451 (1898). Peter Cane regards this as a majority view in the UK, although it is not in the United States: Peter Cane, *Responsibility in Law and Morality* (Oxford: Hart Publishing Co, 2002), 121–2.

loss of blood, each is a cause of the victim's death.[22] However, where the first defendant inflicts a stab wound on the victim that would prove fatal given enough time, but the second defendant kills the victim instantly by shooting him, the shooting pre-empts the stabbing as the exclusive cause of death (so long as the shooting is 'independent' of the stabbing in the sense that the latter in no way causes the former, as where a stabbing motivates the shooter to put the victim out of his misery).[23] Likewise, where two defendants shoot the victim through the head, but one of the bullets kills the victim before the second arrives, only the first shooter is said to have caused the death of the victim.[24] Where at the same time two defendants each ride their motorcycles by the victim's horse, which is startled and injures the victim, each caused the injury despite the sufficiency of the noise form each motorcycle to have done the job;[25] but it is otherwise if one motorcycle arrives first, scaring the horse before the second arrives.

This pattern of liability is also extended beyond physically caused injuries to overdetermined reasons cases. It is only occasionally that the law concerns itself with the reasons for which an action was done. Treason sometimes, for example, is defined in such a way that one must act 'with the intent to help the enemy'.[26] If one acts for 'mixed motives'—where a sufficient reason motivating the action was to help the enemy, but where another, also sufficient reason motivating the action was to help a friend—this suffices for conviction. Concurrent, overdetermined reasons are each causally operative. By contrast, if one wanted to help the enemy, stood ready to do so, but was then threatened with death if one did not do the act in question, this second sufficient reason pre-empts the first and is the exclusive cause of one's action.

The overdetermination cases with regard to omissions, preventions, and double-preventions do not follow this pattern (it is arguable that they do not follow much of any pattern). Consider first the overdetermined omission cases. Suppose that each of two individuals has the legal duty to input her part of a code in order to prevent a rocket launch, and that it takes both parts of the code being separately but simultaneously inputted to prevent the launch. Suppose that Betty and Susan each culpably omit to input their part of the code. Each of their omissions is sufficient under these facts not to prevent the launch—for if Betty had input her part, but Susan had not, the rocket would launch, and vice-versa.

---

[22] Agatha Christie, *Murder on the Orient Express* (New York: Pocket Books, 1960). See also *People v. Lewis* 124 Cal 551, 57 P 470 (1899) (initial gunshot and later knife would both caused victim's death because 'drop by drop his life current welled out from both wounds and at the very instant of death the gunshot wound was contributing to the event').

[23] See generally HLA Hart and Tony Honoré, *Causation in the Law* (2nd edn, Oxford: Clarendon Press, 1985), 124, 239.

[24] *People v. Dlugash* 41 NY 2d 725, 363 NE 2d 1155, 395 NYS 2d 419 (1977).

[25] *Corey v. Havener* 182 Mass 250, 65 NE 69 (1902).

[26] The less seriously punished treason statute in force in England during the Second World War. See *Rex v. Stean* [1947] KB 997, 32 Crim Ap Rep 61, [1947] 1 All ER 813.

Arguably the weight of authority in the United States is that neither Betty nor Susan can be liable for the harm the launch causes, because neither is a cause of the launch.[27]

My own view is that the overdetermination prevention and double-prevention cases, like the overdetermination omission cases, do not follow the pattern of liability described earlier. An overdetermination prevention case would be where some benefit will come to some victim V unless prevented by some act. As it happens, two or more individuals independently (ie, without prior concert) do acts that are individually sufficient to present V from receiving the benefit. Whether simultaneous or successive, such preventative acts should not be construed to have caused V the harm of losing the benefit.[28]

An overdetermination double-prevention case is where two or more actors each independently do an action that is individually sufficient to prevent something from preventing a harm, when without any of such acts that thing would have prevented the harm. For example, suppose that a very large man, V, is drowning in the ocean, that it takes two lifeguards to save him, and that the two lifeguards are about to do that from their respective lifeguard stands when each is prevented from doing so by an enemy of the drowning man. Each of these enemies of V ties up one of the necessary lifeguards. When the man drowns, if the two enemies of V do not act in concert, neither should be held to have caused the victim's death, for neither's preventative act was necessary for that death. A different case, it is thought, is a slight revision of JA McLaughlin's famous hypothetical:[29] A and B each independently intend to kill V, who is headed into the desert. A drains V's water keg, replacing the water with salt; B steals the keg full of salt, which B believes is full of water; V dies of thirst in the desert. This is commonly said to be a case of pre-emptive overdetermination, not concurrent overdetermination, yet there is no agreement on who is doing the pre-empting, A or B. Some legal commentators hold A to be the pre-emptive cause of V's death;[30] others hold B;[31] and some even think that neither caused V's death because each pre-empted the other.[32]

---

[27] David Fischer, 'Causation in fact in omission cases', Utah Law Review (1993), 1349–60. It might be otherwise if Betty's and Susan's omissions succeed on another in time, where there is some authority that the later pre-empts the earlier (and so only the later pre-empts the earlier and so only the later causes the harm): Ibid. See also Richard Wright, 'Causation in tort law,' 1787. I discuss this case in Chapter 18, below.

[28] Argued for in Chapter 18, below.

[29] JA McLaughlin, 'Proximate cause', Harvard Law Review 39 (1925), 155, n 25.

[30] This is Richard Wright's conclusion. See Wright, 'Causation in tort law', 1802.

[31] This is Wright's conclusion on a slightly varied version of the hypothetical: Wright, 'Causation in tort law'. See also JL Mackie, *The Cement of the Universe* (Oxford: Oxford University Press, 1980), 45–6.

[32] This is Hart's and Honoré's conclusion in *Causation in the Law*, 239–40. Jane Stapleton surveys the variety of responses in the legal literature to this hypothetical in Stapleton, 'Perspectives on causation', in Jeremy Horder (ed), *Oxford Essays in Jurisprudence* Fourth Series (Oxford: Oxford University Press, 2000).

The overdetermination cases present a complex set of distinctions drawn by the law. We must simplify this pattern if we are to extract any coherent conception of causation presupposed by the law. In particular, we need to examine whether omissions can be causes, whether acts which create dangerous conditions by removing safety features can be causes, and whether culpability can affect causation. I shall thus defer commenting on what conclusions we should infer from the overdetermination cases until we have done some pruning in these directions.

IV. The Scalar Nature of Legal Causation

Some qualities and relations are two-valued, all or nothing, like being the natural parent of someone else, being pregnant, or being dead. Others are matters of continuous variation, like color or age. In various places, the law assumes that the causal relation is in the latter category, so that there can be more or less of a causal relation, not just its total presence or total absence.

The clearest doctrinal home for this presupposition is in the idea of causal apportionment.[33] Casual apportionment would apportion liability in tort by degrees of causal contribution. This is in marked contrast to comparative fault, which (at least formally) apportions liability based on comparisons of culpability, not of causal contribution.[34] Comparative fault schemes make use of causal notions, but the use they make is only to require the fault to be causally relevant; the phrase 'causal fault', as it is commonly used in comparative negligence statutes, thus refers to fault that is causally relevant, and the phrase is not an invitation to apportion damage based on degrees of fault *and* on degrees of causal contribution.

That at least is the formally stated law of torts on explicit causal apportionment. Only in the product-misuse area of strict liability has explicit comparative causation gained much of a foothold.[35] Still, the Anglo-American case law is in fact more sympathetic to causal apportionment than this would indicate. Courts smuggle in notions of causal apportionment even in negligence cases through two open doors. One is through the idea of divisible harms. In 1965 the American

---

[33] On the idea of causal apportionment, see Mario Rizzo and Frank Arnold, 'Causal apportionment in the law of torts: An economic approach', Columbia Law Review 80 (1980), 1399–429; Kaye and Aicken, 'A comment on causal apportionment', Journal of Legal Studies 13 (1984), 191–208; and Mario Rizzo and Frank Arnold, 'Causal apportionment: Reply to the critics', Journal of Legal Studies 20 (1986), 219–26.

[34] In its original opinion creating comparative fault in California (*Li v. Yellow Cab Co of California*, 532 P 2d, 1226 (Cal Sup Ct 1975)), the California Supreme Court held that one should apportion tort liability 'in direct proportion to the extent of the parties' causal responsibility' (119 Cal Rptr 858 footnote 6a [1975] [advance sheets only]). Prior to final publication, the court recognized its error, proportioning liability to degrees of fault, not to degrees of causation.

[35] See the citations in Rizzo and Arnold, 'Causal apportionment', 1402.

Law Institute invited courts to divide damages based on causation on the basis of *Restatement of Torts (Second)*, section 433A, which provided that 'damages are to be apportioned among two or more causes where (a) there are distinct harms, or (b) there is a reasonable basis for determining the contribution of each cause to a single harm'. The American Law Institute successor section 26(b) of the *Restatement (Third) of Torts* more narrowly provides that 'damages can be divided by causation when the evidence provides a reasonable basis for the fact-finder to determine: (1) that any legally culpable conduct . . . was a legal cause of less than the entire damages . . . and (2) the amount of damages separately caused by that conduct'.

The doctrine of divisible harm was not thought by the American Law Institute to be equivalent to causal apportionment. Rather, a harm is divisible on causal grounds where one or more defendants made *no* causal contribution to some part of the victim's injury; in such cases, the injury is divided into its indivisible parts, and such defendants have no liability to any part to which their conduct made no causal contribution. Nonetheless, despite this intent, the case law sometimes treats divisibility as an invitation to do true causal apportionment, where each defendant is assigned a percentage of causal contribution to some *in*divisible harm to which all contributed.[36]

The second open door to causal apportionment in negligence cases in torts lies in the elision of causal apportionment into comparative fault. As stated earlier, comparative fault (or 'comparative responsibility,' as the American Law Institute now labels it) is supposed to divide liability up on the basis of degrees of negligence or other fault, not on the basis of degrees of causation. This is made explicit by comment a to section 8 of the *Restatement (Third) of Torts: Apportionment of Liability*: 'Assigning shares of 'causation' wrongly suggests that indivisible injuries jointly caused by two or more actors can be divided on the basis of causation.' Despite this clear rejection of causal apportionment in negligence cases, American tort cases continue to smuggle in consideration of degrees of causal contribution to their calculations of comparative negligence.[37]

---

[36] Thus, in *Kolland v. North American Van Lines* 716 F 2d 570 (9th Cir 1983), the trial court separately calculated degrees of causal contribution and degrees of negligence in a multi-vehicle collision case (reversed on this by the Ninth Circuit Court of Appeals). In *Moore v. Johns-Manville Sales Corp* 781 F 2d 1061 (5th Cir 1986) the Fifth Circuit Court of Appeals rejected a pro rata recovery against each of several defendants in a product liability case, apportioning liability rather than 'the degree of relative causation' (ibid, 1062). Justice Russell of the Minnesota Supreme Court in a recent dissent stated his causal apportionment reading of the *Restatement (Second) of Torts*, § 433A: 'the touchstone of apportionment is reliance on the contribution that causes the ultimate harm and not to some actual division of the harm itself', *Morlock v. St Paul Guardian Ins Co* 650 NW 2d 154, 164 (Minn 2002).

[37] This is certainly true of jury verdicts, where the mixing of causal with fault judgments can go undetected; but it is also true in some appellate opinions. See the cases cited earlier footnote 36. Of *Moore v. John-Manville Sales Corp*, for example, the Reporter's Note to § 26 of *Restatement (Third) of Torts* says this: the court 'muddled through' by 'using comparative-responsibility percentages to make what appears to be an apportionment based on causation'.

The second set of legal doctrines laying bare this presupposition is the 'substantial factor' test first proposed by Jeremiah Smith[38] and adopted by both the *Restatement of Torts* and the *Restatement (Second) of Torts*.[39] Smith's idea was that we can judge whether a factor was a legal cause of that injury, by asking whether it was a 'substantial' cause (or factor) of the injury. Clearly a quantitative measure is intended here, presupposing that causation can be a matter of degree.

Another doctrinal home for this scalar idea about causation is to be found in the causal licenses for consequentialist justifications in criminal law and in torts that we examined in Chapter 3. Recall the cause/aiding distinction as it is drawn in homicide cases. According to the common law, acting under the threat of another can never be a defense to murder—murder is so awful that one is supposed to 'just say no' to the threatener.[40] For a time, however, English law distinguished the accomplice who only drove the car from the trigger man who did the killing, in that the former could avail himself of the defense of duress even though the latter could not.[41] This I take to be a causal discrimination: even though the accomplice contributes to the victim's death in the sense that he makes it possible, his causal contribution is nowhere near that of the actual killer. On the view that a lesser causal responsibility is necessarily a lesser moral responsibility, the lesser wrong done by the accomplice could thus be eligible to be justified/excused by the existence of a sufficiently serious threat.

The English courts eventually abandoned the distinction, but why they did so is also instructive: as they saw, there can be a great deal of difference between the causal contributions of accomplices. Recall the facts of *Abbott*:[42] the defendant held the victim while she was being skewered by a saber, it taking several thrusts because the sword kept hitting bone, In such a case, the court properly concluded that the causal contribution of the accomplice (the holder) was not so much less than that of the principal (the skewer) and refused the defense of duress to either.

Similarly, in interpreting the general justification defense ('balance-of-evils', or 'necessity') in criminal law and in torts, it is generally agreed that one is not justified in doing a normally criminal or tortious act—that is, an act causing bad consequences—simply because the act will also cause more good consequences. Rather, as we saw in Chapter 3, the act must cause its bad consequences in the right way in order to be eligible for justification by its good consequences. Thus, we may not stab to death one person in order to harvest his organs, which are needed by five other, near-death patients. Yet we may (a) allow one person to die in passive euthanasia, in order to assure the survival of others; (b) pick one for someone else to kill, as where we send out one of our own in exchange for four hostages held by another when we know that the one will be killed in lieu of the four hostages who

---

[38] See Smith, 'Legal cause.'
[39] *Restatement of Torts*, §§ 431–5 (1934); *Restatement (Second) of Torts*, §§ 431–3 (1965).
[40] *R v. Howe* [1987] 1 All ER 771.
[41] *Director of Public Prosecutions for Northern Ireland v. Lynch* [1975] AC 653.
[42] *Abbott v. R* [1976] 3 All ER 140.

are released; (c) redirect an already moving force (such as a flood, an avalanche, or a runaway trolley) so that instead of killing five people it only kills one; and (d) omit to save one person in order to save five other equally in peril.

As I argued in Chapter 3, all of these are causal discriminations. Put crudely, when we are not much of a cause of the evil the law normally prohibits, we may act so as to prevent greater evils; but when we are substantially the cause of the first evil, we may not act even though such action would prevent greater evils. Put this way, one sees the presupposition of causal scalarity clearly in these licenses for consequentialist justification.

V. The Limited Transitivity of the Causal Relation

A relation (R) is transitive when, if R(x, y) and R(y, z) then R (x, z). The causal relation would be transitive if one could trace causal chains through time in this way. If my lighting a match causes rum to ignite, and the ignition of the rum causes the entire ship to burn,[43] and the burning of the ship causes a large loss at Lloyd's of London, and the large loss at Lloyd's causes a certain insurance executive to take his own life—and if the causal relationship were transitive— then my lighting a match caused the death of the insurance executive (together with yet further consequences like the loss of support for his widow, etc).

Although sometimes legal theoreticians have thought that the only truly causal notion used in the law is fully transitive in this way,[44] in fact no area of law traces causal responsibility indefinitely. One of the long recognized deficiencies with the necessary-condition test of factual causation is that, used alone, it would generate an unlimited liability into the future.[45] Our liability doctrines thus presuppose that causation is the kind of relation that can 'peter out'. The metaphorical picture is of the ripples emanating from a stone dropped into a quiet pond: gradually they diminish to nothing the further the ripples travel from their source. This attribute of legal causation presupposes that the relation is scalar, because only a more-or-less sort of relation can gradually peter out. Yet this attribute is a specific use of such scalarity, for it asserts a proportionality between proximity and more causation, between distance and less causation.

Early writers from Sir Francis Bacon[46] (who coined the Latin *causa proxima*) on, held that spatio-temporal proximity of cause to effect was that on which such

---

[43] These are the facts of *R v. Faulkner* 13 Cox CC 550 (Ireland, Court of Crown Cases Reserved, 1877).

[44] See the *Restatement (Second) of Torts*, § 431, comment a (1965), which proclaims that in law, 'cause' is used 'in the popular sense, in which there always lurks the idea of responsibility, rather than in the so-called "philosophical sense" which includes every one of the great number of events without which any happening would not have occurred'.

[45] See, eg, Smith, 'Legal cause', 109.

[46] Sir Francis Bacon, 'Maxims of the law', in Bacon, *The Elements of the Common Law of England* (London: Assigns of I Moore, 1630), 1.

strength of causation depended. Plausibility is lent to this Baconian view by the 'spatio-temporal coincidence' cases that we looked at in Chapter 4. Consider the case of the streetcar motorman who recklessly speeds early on his route in one part of the city.[47] No one is injured while he is speeding, and when he catches up to his schedule he resumes his normal, non-reckless speed. Nonetheless, because he sped early on his route, he arrives at the last part of his route just in time to have a tree fall on his car, injuring a passenger. One may think that it is the simple fact of spatio-temporal distance (between the motorman's negligent act and the harm) that accounts for non-liability here.[48]

Yet simple spatial or temporal distance does not seem to be what diminishes or 'tires' causation. Poisoned candy sent from California to Delaware, or from the moon, is still the cause of the victim's death if she eats it and is poisoned;[49] poisoned candy left in a place and in a state where it will be found and eaten a generation later, still causes death at that much-later time. Spatio-temporal proximity thus seems a proxy for something else.

One possibility is to look for those free, informed, voluntary human choices, or those abnormal conjunctions of natural events amounting to a coincidence, intervening between the defendant's act and the harm. Spatio-temporal distance might be a proxy for these kinds of 'intervening causes'. Yet intervening causes are not what is wanted here (although they may account for the streetcar coincidence case above). Such causes are abrupt (see the next section) in the way they break causal chains, whereas what is wanted is something that allows causation to diminish gradually in its strength. My own suggestion is that what the law uses here is simply sheer numbers of events that intervene between the defendant's act and the harm. None of these events need itself be an intervening cause as the law defines that phrase; rather, when there are too many event-links in the causal chain, it becomes too attenuated to support judgments of transitivity.[50]

The particular scalarity the law presupposes causation to have is thus a diminishment in the strength of causation in proportion to the number of events

---

[47] *Berry v. Borough of Sugar Notch* 191 Pa 345, 43 Atl 240 (1899). For another coincidence case, see *Denny v. NY Central RR* 13 Gray (Mass) 481 (1859) (railroad's negligence in delaying at one section of track, and its subsequent arrival at a flood plain just when a flood sweeps down and destroys goods on the train, held not to be a cause of the damage to the goods).

[48] Cf *Bird v. St Paul F and Minneapolis Ins Co* 224 NY 47, 120 NE 86 (1918) ('There is no use in arguing that distance ought not to count, if life and experience tell us that it does'); and Henry Edgarton, 'Legal cause', 369–70.

[49] *People v. Botkin* 132 Cal 231, 64 Pac 286 (1901).

[50] A refinement may be necessary here. If the causal relation is transmitted over many events that are of the same *type*, then the diminishment of causation often seems to be less. See, eg, *Scott v. Shepherd* 96 All ER 525 (KB 1773) (liability for causing injury to plaintiff by explosion of a lighted squib that was thrown into a crowded marketplace by defendant, and then re-thrown by each subsequent possessor of it so as to rid himself of the danger). The analogy here is to a long row of dominos; the falling of each is plausibly individuated as one event, but their ability to transmit causal force seems unrelated to the number of such events. A colorful example offered by Alfred Mele is a variation of *People v. Botkin*: Would it matter if the poisoned candy was sent from California to Delaware by Pony Express (with numerous handoffs) rather than by train?

through which it is transmitted. Where all causal relata are events, if t causes w, w causes x, x causes y, and y causes z, t may well cause y but not z. That is what I mean by the limited transitivity of the causal relation as it is presupposed by our proximate-cause doctrines.

VI. The Sudden Breaking of Causal Chains by (Apparently) Fresh Causal Starts

In addition to the gradual petering out of causation over sheer numbers of intervening events, the law assumes that the causal relation can be ended suddenly by the intervention of one of those special kinds of intervening events which the law designates an intervening (or superseding) cause. Such intervening causes may interrupt the causal contribution of an otherwise potent cause (in which case we have an instance of pre-emptive overdetermination); or such intervening causes may build on the causal contribution of the defendant's action.[51] In either case the intervention of such causes between the defendant's act and the harm relieves the defendant of any causal responsibility for that harm.

In *Causation in the Law*, HLA Hart and Tony Honoré nicely detailed how the law recognizes two sorts of intervening causes.[52] One involves the free, informed, voluntary act of a third party that intervenes between the defendant's act and the victim's injury. Thus, a defendant company negligently spills gasoline from its railroad tanker car into a city street, yet what ignites the gasoline and burns down the town is the intentional lighting of the gasoline by a cigar-throwing arsonist.[53] Even though the defendant's negligent spilling of the gasoline was quite necessary to the town's destruction, the arsonist's choice to use the results of the railroad's negligence to his own ends relieves the railroad of causal responsibility for the town's destruction. The choice by the arsonist operates as a fresh causal intervention breaking any causal chain that might otherwise have existed between the spilling of the gasoline and the destruction of the town.

Only free, informed, voluntary actions by a third-party intervenor will break causal chains in this way. As Hart and Honoré describe the cases, if:

(i) the bodily movement of the arsonist was *involuntary*, in the sense that the cigar slipped from the hand and was not dropped or thrown;

---

[51] This line is much more difficult to draw than is recognized in any of the legal literature, yet it is a necessary line to draw in that pre-emptive intervening causes do not have to meet the criteria below articulated for an intervening cause.

[52] Hart and Honoré, *Causation in the Law*. Although the clarity and the non-legal analogues of the idea of an intervening cause were new with Hart and Honoré, they built on a solid body of case law. This case law is detailed in Charles Carpenter, 'Workable rules for determining proximate cause', California Law Review 20 (1932), 229–59, 396–419, 471–539. Hart's and Honoré's detailing of the case law is in *Causation in the Law*, 133–85, 325–62.

[53] *Watson v. Kentucky and Indiana Bridge and Ry Co* 137 Ky 619, 126 SW 146 (1910).

(ii) the act of throwing the cigar *was not intentional* with respect to the burning of the gasoline, because the cigar-thrower was ignorant of the presence of the gasoline in the street;

(iii) the act of throwing the cigar was done under the duress of dire threats, and so was in that sense *involuntary*;

(iv) the act of throwing the cigar was done under the limited opportunities for choice created by natural necessity, as where the cigar would otherwise painfully burn its holder;

(v) the cigar-thrower was so young, so crazy, or so intoxicated as to be adjudged irresponsible;

then the cigar-throwing act does not break the causal chain and the defendant's initial act of spilling the gasoline causes the destruction of the town.[54]

The second kind of intervening cause involves natural events, not deliberate human intervenors. Suppose that the defendant is negligent in its installation and maintenance of the roof bolts holding a multi-ton warehouse roof in place. If the roof bolts fail so that the roof falls on and injures workmen below, the defendant's negligent actions will be said to have caused the injuries to the workmen. This will be true even if a stiff (but not unusual) breeze contributed to the injuries, in the sense that without the pressures on the roof created by the breeze the roof would not have fallen when it did. If, however, the breeze is that kind of extraordinary event we call 'an act of God', so that the roof does not simply fall but flies over one hundred feet before it injures its victims, then such a gale will be an intervening cause relieving the defendant of causal responsibility for the injury.[55]

Hart and Honoré call such cases acts of 'coincidence'.[56] They analyze such intervening causes as satisfying five requirements. First, there must be an *abnormal conjunction* of natural events. Only winds extraordinary for this time and place qualify as abnormal; breezes normal for this time and place do not qualify. Second, the event in question must have *causal significance*. Merely co-present abnormalities do not qualify. Third, the wind must be *causally independent* of the defendant's actions. If the defendant's design for the building so focused the winds' strength as to make them abnormally high, the winds are not intervening causes. Fourth, the coincidence must be *uncontrived* by the defendant. If the defendant sent out the workmen to work where he hoped the forthcoming storm would blow off the roof, then he has used the storm for his own ends and it is not an intervening cause. Fifth, the intervening natural event must be *subsequent* to the defendant's action. Pre-existing conditions, no matter

---

[54] Hart and Honoré, *Causation in the Law*, 74–7. I explore these items in greater detail in Chapter 11, below.

[55] These are roughly the facts of *Kimble v. Mackintosh Hemphill Co* 359 Pa 461, 59 A 2d 68 (1948).

[56] Hart and Honoré, *Causation in the Law*, 77–81.

how abnormal or coincidental they may be, do not eliminate the causal connection between the defendant's act and the harm.[57]

There is an odd lacuna in both the case law and academic discussions of causation raised by the fourth criterion for a coincidence. One would have thought that the purposeful exploitation of a natural-event coincidence would give rise to a kind of non-causal liability, strictly analogous to the kind of 'aiding of human intervenors' liability shortly to be discussed. Yet Hart and Honoré are correct that the cases treat contrived coincidences on strictly causal grounds. Thus, in the case of the extraordinary winds carrying the heavy roof to where it injured a workman, if the defendant had foreseen such a wind and the possibility of such resultant roof movement and had sent the workman to the spot in order to injure him, such 'contrived coincidence' is treated as no coincidence at all. The wind then does not operate as an intervening cause; rather, the defendant is held liable for causing the injury.[58]

The law could have developed differently. It might have eschewed causal talk in such cases, just as it has in the analogous human intervenor cases. It might have said that all that need be shown in either case is that the defendant made it somewhat easier for either natural circumstances or human intervenors to do their causal work, in order to place a non-causal 'aiding' liability on defendants. We shall pursue this neglected possibility when we seek to economize the law's metaphysical presuppositions in the next chapter.

The law's notion of intervening cause is actually somewhat broader than the two criteria described by Hart and Honoré. Particularly with non-deliberate human intervenors, there are many cases in which, if the intervention is freakish or dramatic enough, the intervention is held to break the causal connection between the defendant's act and the harm. The more freakish of these cases can no doubt be explained by applying the Hart and Honoré criteria for natural coincidence, to human interventions.[59] That is, suppose that in the spilled-gasoline scenario a good Samaritan sees the gasoline, decides to drain it off the street, slips and falls in it, rushes to a house to dry off, instead ignites himself by running into a cigar-smoker, seeks to put out the fire on his body by jumping into a pool, which has unbeknownst to him become filled with the same gasoline, and sets off the entire town. Even though this case involves a human intervention, if we apply the criteria for a coincidence we may well find this to be one.

Also accounting for some of these merely negligent human intervenor cases are the factors at work in our judgment of preemptive overdetermination cases. If one defendant has intentionally poisoned the victim, who is gradually dying of

---

[57] I rework these five conditions a bit in my own restatement of the intervening-cause doctrines in Chapter 11, below.
[58] See cases cited, and discussion, in Hart and Honoré, *Causation in the Law*, 170–1.
[59] This is something which Hart and Honoré suggest in *Causation in the Law*, 136, 182–5.

the poison, but another defendant inadvertently (innocently or negligently) shoots the victim dead instantly, the second defendant's shooting is a preemptive cause.[60] It is a kind of intervening cause, no matter how unintentional or how lacking in culpability in any way it may have been. The shooting's status as an intervening cause also does not depend on any freakishness of the kind that makes one think of coincidence. We simply know that the victim died of the gunshot, not of the poison.

With these qualifications for some merely negligent intervenors breaking causal chains, Hart and Honoré accurately describe the law as regarding a free, informed, voluntary act of a human intervenor as breaking causal chains. Despite this, Hart and Honoré rather inelegantly excepted the giving of reasons and the provision of opportunity from their thesis.[61] That is, if the defendant suggested, offered, encouraged, threatened, or otherwise induced another into causing a harm, then such reason-giving behavior was a cause of that harm despite the intervening choice of the person to whom the defendant gave such reasons. Analogously, if the defendant's culpability consisted in providing an opportunity to another to cause harm—say by leaving the key in the ignition of a bulldozer that some vandals then run down a hill into a house[62]—then such opportunity-providing acts are the cause of the harm despite the intentional acts of those who seize the opportunity.

The legal fact that Hart and Honoré were trying to accommodate is the fact that there is liability for such reason-giving or opportunity-providing actions in both torts and criminal law. Oddly overlooked, however, was the fact that the law largely deals with the reason-giving half of this phenomenon in noncausal terms. That is, the liability of one who solicits, offers, suggests, or procures another to cause a harm is not for causing the harm; rather, the former is liable for the harm on the criminal-law theory of accomplice liability[63] and on the tort-law theory of a joint tortfeasor by virtue of acting in concert. The principal in such a theory must cause the harm in question to be held liable, but it is well established that the procurer need not cause the harm; his soliciting, offering, suggesting, or

---

[60] Eg, *State v. Scates* 50 NC 409 (1858) (defendant who burned child not liable for the child's death if an intervening blow on the head by a third party killed the dying child).

[61] In the original edition of their book, Hart and Honoré simply except such situations from the normal rule about intentional intervening agents. See HLA Hart and AM Honoré, *Causation in the Law* (Oxford: Clarendon Press, 1959). As Joel Feinberg noted, these were ad hoc, unexplained, and seemingly unlimited as exceptions. See Feinberg, 'Causing voluntary actions', in Feinberg, *Doing and Deserving*. In the second edition of *Causation in the Law*, Chapters VII and XIII now deal extensively with the provision of opportunities and the giving of reason as 'non-central' kinds of causings.

[62] *Richardson v. Ham* 44 Cal 2d 772, 285 P 2d 269 (1955).

[63] Particularly clear and systematic about this is Sanford Kadish, 'A theory of complicity', in R Gavison (ed), *Issues in Contemporary Legal Philosophy: The influence of HLA Hart* (Oxford: Oxford University Press, 1987); and Kadish, 'Causation and complicity: A study in the interpretation of doctrine', California Law Review 73 (1985), 323–410, reprinted in Kadish, *Blame and Punishment* (New York: MacMillan, 1987).

procuring is enough for accomplice liability (or joint-and-several tort liability) without need of any causal relationship to the harm itself.[64]

The only catch here is that the procurer who induces the principal to cause the harm must do his inducing with the purpose (or 'specific intent') that he induce the principal to cause the harm. If one gives reasons to another to cause a harm, but does so innocently, negligently, recklessly, or merely knowingly, this lesser culpability is insufficient for liability. In such cases the reason-giving procurer must be liable on causal grounds if he is to be liable at all; but the intervening choice of the one who causes the harm eliminates (in law) any causal responsibility here. The upshot is that a less-than-purposeful inducer is not liable for either aiding or causing.

The procurer who threatens another and in that way induces another to cause harm is distinguished from other types of procurers. The threatening procurer places the harm-causer under duress, making his choice to cause the harm not sufficiently voluntary to be an intervening cause. Thus, the threatener is liable for causing the harm he induces another to cause by his threats, and this causal liability does not require the high level of culpability (purpose) with which other types of procurers must do their procuring in order to be liable on an accomplice theory.

The existence of these two different bases for holding someone liable in both criminal law and tort law has generated considerable confusion. Suppose that a more-culpable procurer or other aider induces or otherwise aids a less-culpable principal to cause some harm. For example, A tells B, falsely, that B's wife is having an affair with C. A tells B this with the intent that B (who is very jealous, has a nasty temper, and is prone to violence) will kill C. B does so in a fit of jealous rage, making B guilty in many jurisdictions of voluntary manslaughter. A, the theory goes, is guilty of aiding B in the voluntary-manslaughter killing of C, but A is not a voluntary-manslaughter killer of C himself because A did not cause C's death. But A is also guilty of causing C's death by his use of a partly innocent agent, B; since A was not provoked, his causing of C's death is murder. A both is and is not the cause of C's death because B's act both is not and is an intervening cause of C's death![65]

Things are somewhat different where liability is predicated on the provision of opportunities to another to cause harm. There is a form of accomplice liability here in criminal law, as there is a form of joint tortfeasor liability here for one not acting in concert. One can be liable in tort law or criminal law for aiding another to cause harm, when the aid is not of the reason-giving kind but is, rather, of a kind that makes it easier for the principal to cause the harm even when he does not know of the aid he has been given. I may intercept a warning telegram that

[64] See the two essays by Kadish cited immediately above. We shall have occasion to re-examine the allegedly non-causal status of accomplices in Chapter 13, below.
[65] See Glanville Williams, *Criminal Law: The general part* (2nd edn, London: B Henworths, 1961), 391.

otherwise would have warned the victim that a murderer is looking for him; I have no agreement with the murderer, we are not 'acting in concert', and he does not know that I exist or that he has been aided. Yet such aid is sufficient for liability here, and the liability is by law regarded as non-causal.[66] I am held liable for making it easier for the harm to be caused; I am not liable for causing the harm, because intervening between my act of aiding and the harm is the free choice of the murderer.

So far, this is very much the same as it was for the reason-giving kind of aiding. And what was true of the latter is also true here: such not-in-concert aiders must act with the highly culpable mental state of *purpose* to be liable as accomplices. Merely negligent, reckless, or even knowing aid is insufficient for accomplice liability. Unlike the reason-giving situation, however, when an actor provides opportunities to another to cause harm, and the first actor is negligent precisely because of the risk of such causing of harm by another, there is a causal liability placed on the first actor, at least in tort law. Thus, where a defendant railroad negligently carries a passenger beyond her destination and then leaves the passenger on a dark and dangerous stretch of track, and the risk that makes this negligent is realized—the passenger is raped by a third party—the railroad is liable in tort for the rape.[67] Similarly, when a construction company leaves keys in a bulldozer after the close of work, and the risk that makes this negligent is realized—vandals start up the bulldozer and run it down-hill from the construction site into the plaintiff's house—the construction company is liable in tort for the damage.[68] In such a case, the free, informed, voluntary choice of the primary wrongdoer is *not* considered to be an intervening cause.

Putting aside, for now, this last exception (about tort liability for negligently providing opportunities to wrongdoers), the existence of a non-causal, accomplice basis for liability allows one to alleviate the apparent tension between saying *both* that free, informed, voluntary acts break causal chains *and* that the provision of reasons or of opportunities that a third party then freely chooses to exploit nonetheless causes the harm such a third party brings about. Rather, one can more consistently maintain that such third-party choices always break causal chains and yet maintain that sometimes noncausal liability is placed upon the original actor anyway.

This accommodating strategy works as well as it does because accomplice liability is designed to pick up behind the intervening-cause doctrine (of the free, informed, voluntary actor).[69] That is, if the would-be principal does not have the kind of free, informed, voluntary choice that breaks causal chains, then the

---

[66] *State ex rel. Att'y Gen'l v. Tally* 102 Ala 25, 15 So 722 (1894).

[67] *Hines v. Garrett*, 131 Va 125, 108 SE 690 (1921).

[68] *Richardson v. Ham* 44 Cal 2d 772, 285 P 2d 269 (1955).

[69] See the two essays by Kadish, 'A theory of complicity' and 'Causation and complicity: A study in the interpretation of doctrine'.

would-be accomplice is liable for the harm on causal grounds, not on accomplice grounds. Suppose A threatens P with serious injury unless P causes a certain harm. If P causes the harm, P has an excuse of duress, and P's choice is not an intervening cause, so that A is liable for causing the harm. Similarly, if A knows that P is ignorant, crazy, intoxicated, under the duress of another or of natural circumstance, and A exploits this weakness by getting P to cause some harm, A again is liable on causal, not accomplice, grounds. It is only when P meets the conditions for being an intervening cause, so that A cannot be held on causal grounds, that the law makes use of accomplice liability.

VII. The Limited Liability for Omissions

The law has always had difficulty in dealing with omissions. It helps to be clear at the start about what omissions are: they are literally no things at all.[70] Suppose A stands on the dock and watches V drown, when A could have saved V with little risk or even inconvenience to himself. A has omitted to save V. What this means is that A did nothing to save V. More technically: there was no act-token of A's that had the properties needed for it to be an instance of the type of action, saving V. The omission to save V is literally the absence of any action of saving V by A.

By and-large the law adopts this conceptualization of omissions, at least implicitly. The Model Penal Code, for example, defines acts or actions as bodily movements,[71] defines *voluntary* acts or actions as bodily movements caused by the 'effort or determination' of the actor,[72] and defines omissions as the absence of such actions.[73] One thus omits to kill, on this conceptualization, when there is no bodily movement willed by the actor that has the causal property, causing death of another. Sometimes, however, the law adopts a very different conceptualization of omissions. In the passive euthanasia cases in particular—cases where the feeding tube is removed, or the respirator is turned off—there plainly is a willed bodily movement that was necessary to the patient's death. Yet courts nonetheless call these *omission* cases,[74] which they plainly are not by the law's own general conception of omissions. What is insufficiently recognized is that these specially conceptualized 'omission' cases are cases of non-omissive allowings that we analyzed in Chapter 3. Insofar as the law opposes 'causing' to 'omitting' (which we shall shortly discuss), the law is actually opposing two things, not one, with 'causing.'

---

[70] Michael Moore, *Act and Crime*, 28–9; Moore, 'More on act and crime', University of Pennsylvania Law Review 142 (1994): 1788.
[71] Model Penal Code, § 1.13(2).   [72] Ibid, § 2.01(2)(d).
[73] Ibid, § 1.13(4).
[74] Eg, *Barber v. Superior Court* 147 Cal App 3d 1006, 195 Cal Rptr 484 (1983); *Airedale NHS Trust v. Bland* [1993] All ER 821.

Focusing on the law's dominant sense of 'omission'—as absent actions—Anglo-American law of torts and crimes rarely imposes liability for such omissions. The cases of liability are generally limited to cases: (1) where A is the parent or other close relation of V, A is liable; (2) where A culpably causes V's condition of peril, A is liable; (3) where A innocently causes V's condition of peril, A is liable; (4) where A undertakes to rescue, but either abandons his undertaking, or performs it culpably, A is liable.[75]

There are two standard routes that attempt to account for these legal facts on causal grounds, The first rests on the premise that all omissions are causes, so that A's omission to save V is a kind of *killing* of V.[76] What distinguishes the usual case (where there is no liability) from the exceptional cases (where there is liability) is a non-causal notion of legal duty. Strangers owe no legal duty not to kill by omission (although they do have a duty not to kill by commission); close relatives, causers-of-the-condition of peril, and rescue-undertakers do have a legal duty not to kill by omission as well as by commission.

The second route begins with the opposite premise: almost all omissions are not causes of the harms they omit to prevent. In the exceptional cases, however, such omissions are causes. One might think this (rather crazily, to be sure) on the ground that the bare fact of legal duty can give causal potency to omissions that are otherwise without it.[77] More plausibly, this route looks behind the legal conclusion about duty to the facts that give rise to the various legal duties not to omit. Each of these facts, so goes the argument, represents a kind of causal involvement in the victim's situation.[78] By causing the condition of peril, by undertaking to rescue, or by entering into an intimate relation with the victim, A has so entered into the genesis of the victim's harm as to be its cause.

VIII. A Lesser Liability for Preventions

The omissions the law cares about are almost always not omissions to cause something, like a death; rather, they are omissions to prevent events like deaths. So to understand omissions, we need to understand preventions. We need to examine preventions anyway, for in their own right they present us with another example of where the law regards what it often calls 'causal' as less fully so than standard cases of causation. A prevention generally is where some act of a

[75] Joshua Dressler, *Understanding Criminal Law* (New York: Mathew Bender, 1987), 83.

[76] See, eg, George Fletcher, 'On the moral irrelevance of bodily movements', University of Pennsylvania Law Review 142 (1994), 1443–53.

[77] This is Joseph Beale's apparent view, in Beale, 'The proximate consequences of an act', Harvard Law Review 33 (1920), 637.

[78] See Richard Epstein, 'A theory of strict liability', Journal of Legal Studies 2 (1973), 192; and Eric Mack, 'Bad Samaritanism and the causation of harm', Philosophy and Public Affairs 9 (1980), 240–1, 242–3.

defendant is said to 'cause' an absence of some benefit the victim would otherwise have received. Suppose some property owner O builds a tall building on his own land. Neighbor N heats the building on his adjacent property by both fireplaces with chimneys and solar panels. Suppose O's new building both shades N's solar panels and blocks the prevailing breezes so that N's fireplaces no longer draw properly.[79] O has *prevented* the light from reaching N's solar panels, O has *prevented* the wind from drawing across the tops of N's fireplaces, and because of this, O has *prevented* the heating of N's premises.

The history of Anglo-American tort law with regard to such cases is revealing. For the older tort of trespass there would have been no liability—for O has not *invaded* N's land.[80] Stopping something (such as light and air) from coming onto one's land was and is not an invasion, whereas causing something (such as smoke or air molecules) to go onto someone else's land was and is an invasion. (This I believe remained true after the writ of trespass on the case allowed recovery for *indirectly*—as opposed to directly—caused injuries; stopping drafts and blocking light were not a *causing* of injury at all).[81]

The more recent tort of private nuisance replaces the requirement of an invasion with the requirement of an interference. Preventions such as the stoppage/blockage by O could constitute an interference with N's use and enjoyment of his land so that it would be an actionable nuisance (if the other elements of nuisance were met).[82]

American constitutional law reflects this distinction as well. The Fifth Amendment of the US Constitution requires that compensation be paid when private property is taken for a public purpose. The clearest exemplars of such *takings* are trespassory invasions.[83] If the government causes TV reception equipment to be affixed to one's real property, that is a taking irrespective of the amount of diminution of value.[84] Whereas if the government only prevents one from certain beneficial uses of one's property, that is not a taking, unless a very substantial diminution of beneficial use is prevented.[85]

In such a way tort and constitutional law reflect a distinction between two levels of responsibility. The primary mode of being responsible for some unhappy state of affairs is by causing it. Alternatively, however, a more occasional and lesser form of responsibility for some such state exists even without causation, and that is for failing to prevent the receipt of some benefit. If I prevent a benefit otherwise headed your way, I may not have caused you a harm but I have

---

[79] I owe these examples to conversations with Richard Epstein many years ago. On Epstein's singularist, physicalist theory of causation, these are not causings of harm.
[80] William Prosser, *Torts* (4th edn, St Paul: West Pub Co, 1964), 63.
[81] Prosser, *Torts*, 65–6.   [82] Ibid, 573.
[83] Frank Michelman, 'Property, utility, and fairness: Comments on the ethical foundations of "just compensation" law', Harvard Law Review 80 (1967), 1184–5.
[84] *Loretto v. Teleprompter Manhattan CATV Corp* 458 US 419 (1982).
[85] *Lucas v. South Carolina Coastal Council* 505 US 1003 (1992).

deprived you of something of value that you would otherwise have had. I may well be morally responsibility for that unhappy state of affairs, although not as frequently or as seriously as I would be if I had made you that much worse off by causing you harm equal in value to your loss of benefit.

IX. Preserving the Extensionality of Causal Statements while Accommodating the Distinction between 'An Act that is Negligent Causing' and 'The Negligence Causing'

Imagine a case where unlabeled rat poison is placed with food near a stove in a kitchen.[86] A person in the kitchen is injured when the rat poison explodes because of the heat of the stove. A court focusing on the danger that such unlabeled rat poison might mistakenly be consumed might well say both (1) that the act of placing the rat poison in the kitchen caused the injury; and (2) that the act of placing *unlabeled* rat poison in the kitchen did not cause the injury. Since the second is the description of the act that describes it in the way which reveals the act to be negligent, the second description is the basis for the causal judgment, relieving the defendant of liability.

It is not clear how the law can make both of these statements, at least on the most plausible view of event individuation. There was only one act of placing rat poison, even though there are many descriptions of that act differing from one another by their mentioning of differing properties possessed by that act.[87] It was 'the first act the defendant did that morning'; it was 'the stupidest act he did that day'; it was 'the placing of unlabeled rat poison with the food in the kitchen'; and it was 'the placing of combustible items near the stove'.

Yet if this is but one act with many different descriptions, then it seems the law is guilty of violating Leibniz's principle that identicals are indiscernible in all of their properties.[88] That is, if 'x' is one description of the act, and 'y' is another, and $x = y$ because there is but one numerically distinct act, then anything that can be truthfully said of x can also be truthfully said of y, and vice versa. Formalized, the principle is: $(x)(y)[(x = y) \supset (Fx \equiv Fy)]$. This is sometimes called the principle of substitutability *salva veritate*, because if x and y are one and the same thing, we can everywhere substitute one description for the other without changing the truth value of the overall expression in which they appear.

---

[86] This is the famous hypothetical used by Robert Keeton, *Legal Cause in the Law of Torts* (Columbus: Ohio State University Press, 1963), 3. The hypothetical is based on the facts of *Larrimore v. American National Insurance Co* 184 Okla 614, 89 P 2d 340 (1939).

[87] For a defense of the view that there is only one act here, although there are many different descriptions of it, see Moore, *Act and Crime*, Chapter 11. As I label this in Chapter 14, below, I adopt the Davidsonian view of events.

[88] For a discussion of Leibniz's principle in a legal context, see Michael Moore, 'Foreseeing harm opaquely'.

The legal example given seems to violate this principle. If 'placing the rat poison' and 'placing the unlabeled rat poison' are just two different descriptions of the same act, then any property of one must also be a property of the other. Yet the relational property, being the cause of the injury, is said to be true of the act described as 'placing the rat poison', and false of the act described as 'placing the unlabeled rat poison'.

If one is a radical skeptic about law, one might celebrate this lack of extensionality to statements of legal causation.[89] For such statements' dependence upon description for a truth value is just what is wanted by the skeptic in order to deny sense to these statements. Anything can be the legal cause of anything else, or not, depending on which descriptions of the events are arbitrarily selected.

Such skepticism gives up on there being any relation in the world named by 'cause'. If we want to look for a concept of cause that the law uses and that makes sense, then we have to see what can be done to alleviate this problem, not celebrate its existence. The most obvious way to accommodate the pair of legal statements with which we began is to change what, quite literally, the statements are about.[90] Specifically, the idea is that the second statement is not about the *act* of placing the rat poison in the kitchen; rather, the statement's subject is really the *fact* that that act had a certain property, being the placement of a poison that was both near food and unlabeled.[91] So translated, the second statement really says that the fact that the act was one of placing *unlabeled* rat poison in the kitchen had no causal relevance to the fact that the injury took place.

Now there is no incompatibility between the two statements with which we began. It can be true that the *act* of placing the rat poison caused the injury, and yet also true that the *fact* that the injury occurred was not caused by the *fact* that the rat poison placed in the kitchen was unlabeled. The event that is the action is not the same as the fact that that event had a certain property, so both of these statements can be true without violating Leibniz's principle.

The law thus presupposes that there are such things as facts about events, as well as the events themselves. Such facts about events are sometimes conceptualized as tropes, or abstract particulars, or concrete universals.[92] The general idea is that the possession of a property by an event is a thing in its own right, in

---

[89] This is what Mark Kelman does, albeit with an imperfect grasp of just what extensionality is. See Kelman, 'The necessary myth of objective causation judgments in liberal political theory', Chicago-Kent Law Review 63 (1987), 604–6.

[90] For a discussion of this reference-shifting strategy, see Moore, 'Foreseeing harm'.

[91] For an excellent discussion of the difference between facts and events, see Jonathan Bennett, *Events and Their Names* (Indianapolis: Bobbs-Merrill, 1988). Chapters 14 and 15, below, go into this distinction in some detail.

[92] See Keith Campbell, *Abstract Particulars* (Cambridge, Mass: Blackwell, 1990). It is not uncontroversial whether facts are tropes, or whether they consist instead of a complex of substance-particulars and universals. See 'Introduction', in PH Mellor and Alex Oliver (eds), *Properties* (Oxford: Oxford University Press, 1997), 18–20. I shall try to sort out the possibilities here in Chapter 14, below.

addition to both the particular thing (the event) and the universal thing (the property). Such having-of-a-property things can then be both causes and effects, as both the law and common sense recognize in their discourses.

The law could be committed to such tropist metaphysics in one of two ways.[93] In the moderate form, the law could assert that both events, and facts about events, can be causes and effects. The law would then have to spell out when events are to be used as causal relata, and when facts are to be used instead, because, as we have seen, events and facts give quite different answers to causal questions. The law would also have to make sense of two such different things standing in the causal relation. Alternatively, the law could be more extreme in its tropist metaphysical commitments: it could hold that the only true causal relata are tropes, that its usage of events is not to be taken seriously, and that the latter event-talk can be paraphrased away when it becomes troublesome.[94] In either the moderate or the extreme form, the law must make sense of there being such tropes and of tropes being the kinds of things that can stand in the causal relation.

X. The Causal Relation Must Be Temporally Asymmetrical

The law joins common sense in presupposing that the causal relation is asymmetrical: if x causes y, then it is not the case that y causes x. Further, the law assumes that this asymmetry exists in only one direction in time: if x causes y, then y cannot precede x in time. Apparent counter-examples—such as when we attribute the solid hit on a golf ball to a golfer's follow-through on his swing[95]—are to be paraphrased away. A more accurate rendering is that the golfer's focus on his follow-through at or just before contact with the ball is what causes a square hit with the ball; since the mental focus precedes the hit, no violation of the temporal asymmetry of the causal relation is to be found in such examples.

The law's presupposition that causality is temporally asymmetrical is to be found in the law's liability doctrines. If A sets off his dynamite and scares B's minks into killing their young,[96] A may be liable for B's loss of minks; B is not liable for A's loss of his dynamite, because in no sense did the killing of their young by B's minks cause A's dynamite to be destroyed.

---

[93] These two kinds of commitments to tropes are distinguished in Chris Daly, 'Tropes', *Proceedings of the Aristotelian Society* 94 (1994), 253–61; rewritten and reprinted in Mellor and Oliver (eds), *Properties*.

[94] See JL Mackie's position on facts versus events as causal relata, in *The Cement of the Universe*.

[95] Jennifer Hornsby, *Actions* (London: Routledge, 1980), 76, n 1.

[96] These are the facts of *Foster v. Preston Mill Co* 44 Wash 2d 440, 268 P 2d 645 (1954).

XI. The Greater the Culpability with which an Act Is Done, the Greater the Causal Power of that Act

There is a tendency, noted by many of the earlier commentators on causation in the law,[97] for courts to find a highly culpable actor to have caused a harm when a less culpable actor would not have been said to have caused such a harm. Culpability might increase because of the grossness of the negligence of the defendant; because his act was not only tortious but criminal; because his act was not merely negligent, but reckless or intentional; or because his motives were particularly bad.[98] In any case, such increased culpability has been treated as a kind of aphrodisiac to causation, enhancing the latter's reach and power.

Such a relationship between culpability and causation is distinct from the relationship discussed in connection with 'contrived coincidence'. In the latter cases, the defendant not only intends the type of harm that actually occurs—he also utilizes the quirks of nature as his intended means to bring about the harm. The cases presently considered make a cruder judgment: just because the defendant has greater culpability in virtually any dimension, he can be held liable for causing the harm even when the causal relationship between his act and the harm is quite attenuated.

---

[97] See, eg, Smith 'Legal cause in actions of tort', 230–2.
[98] All of these cases are detailed in Edgarton, 'Legal cause', 356–60.

6

Pruning the Law's Demands on a Concept of Causation

A common fault of the legal literature on causation has been its credulity with regard to the law's demands on the concept of causation. Typically, legal theorists have taken legal usages of 'cause' at face value in the sense that, without questioning such usages, they have thought that their theory of legal causation had to fit all of them. For theorists with ambitions to account for legal causation in terms of a metaphysics of causation, this credulity and conservatism has made their task impossible. The law has mixed too many extraneous elements into what it calls 'causation' for there to be much hope for any metaphysical translation. In this chapter, I shall, accordingly, seek to prune back these legal usages of causation so that the demands made on the concept are not obviously impossible ones for any metaphysics to meet.

I. Eliminating any Supposed Aphrodisiac Effect of Culpability on Causal Potency

I shall begin with the demand last discussed in the previous chapter, that causation be a relation affected by the degree of culpability with which the act (that is the putative cause) was done. As skeptics about causation in the law have often pointed out,[1] there is no metaphysical account of causation that could meet this demand. For to meet this demand would require the (metaphysically) strange view that the mental state of the actor itself had a causal influence on the injury, independent of its influence through the act that executes such mental state. If the defendant intends some harm H, and he acts in a way such that H comes about, albeit in a rather freakish way, then on this view the intent literally adds causal power to the act of the defendant's that executed his intention. The only way the intention could do this is by itself causing H, in addition to the causing of H done by the intention through the defendant's action. Absent some

---

[1] See, eg, Henry Edgarton, 'Legal cause', University of Pennsylvania Law Review 72 (1924), 356–60.

stronger evidence than we have about the telekinetic powers of our minds, this is surely impossible. Intending H by itself does not make H occur, and even clicking your heels three times will not help.

Now consider the role of gross negligence as a causal extender (as compared to ordinary negligence). To be grossly negligent, one need have no attitudinal difference vis-à-vis the person who is only ordinarily negligent; to be grossly negligent, it is enough that one does some objectively stupid act, namely, one where the harms risked far exceed any possible gains. (In the colorful language of the late Judge MacGruder, the difference between being merely negligent and being grossly negligent is the difference between being a fool and being a damned fool.) In such cases of gross negligence, we do not even have a mental state of the actor to do the magically extra causal work. Rather, the moral quality of culpability (in the form of gross negligence) would have to pull the extra load here. Even to those moral realists like myself who are sympathetic to the causal power of moral qualities,[2] this seems a strange causal power to attribute to such qualities. The normal sorts of things moral qualities are said to cause are behaviors and beliefs of persons; this view would require us to think that moral qualities like culpability can also causally contribute—again, directly and without mediation by the acts of the individual who is culpable—to earthquakes and train wrecks.

If one finds the needed metaphysics to be too implausible to be even seriously considered, then one should reject those cases (and the doctrines they announce) that would impose this demand on legal causation. Such cases should be considered to be a kind of understandable mistake—understandable because often we cloud our judgment on one issue by our fervor on another, but a mistake because we have no need to double-count our culpability judgments. We should adjust our overall judgments of moral responsibility and legal liability by giving culpability its proper due, no more, no less; having done this, we have no reason to gerrymander other components of responsibility, such as causation, so as to give even more weight to culpability. If we are clear-headed about this, we will simply get rid of such doctrines, not try to accommodate them in our construction of the law's presupposed concept of causation.

The doctrines that we need to prune back here are four in number. First and foremost, we should eliminate the entire family of doctrines that allow the comparatively greater culpability of a defendant to extend the causal power of his actions through space and time. I refer to the proximate-cause doctrines alluded to at the end of Chapter 5, above, doctrines holding that 'no harm is too remote if it is intended', etc.[3]

---

[2] Michael Moore, 'Moral reality', Wisconsin Law Review (1982), 1061–156; Moore, 'Moral reality revisited', Michigan Law Review 90 (1992), 2424–533, both reprinted in Moore, *Objectivity in Law and Ethics* (London: Ashgate, 2004).

[3] Chapter 5, § XI, above.

The second place in which culpability is given magical causal powers is in the overdetermination cases of the concurrent type. Our earlier example was the two fires, independently set and each sufficient to burn the structure, that join to burn the structure.[4] The doctrinal suggestion was that it matters to a culpable defendant's status as a cause of the destruction whether the other fire was also culpably set, or whether it was either innocently set or was a fire of natural origin. For reasons similar to those just discussed, there is no metaphysics that can make sense of this distinction. If the only difference between the second fire in the range of cases we are considering is the culpable intention, culpable negligence, or moral agency of the second fire's source, that can make no difference in the defendant's causal responsibility. The suggestion that it does should be rejected, and the law should be treated (as it mostly is anyway) as finding the defendant causally responsible for the destruction in all variations of these concurrent overdetermination cases. This does not necessarily mean that the defendant will be liable in all of these cases, for there may be some non-causal doctrines that save certain causally responsible defendants from liability. Where the concurrent overdetermining cause is the *victim's* own culpable fire-starting (in the two-fires-that-join sort of example), then the non-causal doctrines of 'contributory negligence' and 'assumption of the risk' will relieve the culpable fire-starting defendant of liability in tort (although not in criminal law).

The third doctrine to be eliminated here is the doctrine of contrived coincidences. As we have seen, contrived coincidences are not said to break causal chains. The factory owner who hopes that this workers will get hit by the roof being carried by an extraordinary wind, and sends them out for that reason, cannot escape a cause-based liability for their deaths despite the intervening act of God.

Here again, we have to alter doctrine if we are to have any hope of finding a coherent conception of cause presupposed by the law. For it cannot be the case that the very same storm is an intervening cause, or is not, depending on the state of mind of the defendant; it cannot be the case that the very same acts and omissions of the defendant are the cause of the workmen's deaths, or not, depending on the state of mind of that defendant. Again, our minds do not have these kinds of telekinetic powers.

The law ought to say that the criteria for an intervening cause do not include contrivance by the defendant. This means that irrespective of whether the defendant intended the storm to kill the workmen, the defendant did not cause their deaths if the storm is otherwise an intervening cause.

As I have suggested in Chapter 5, this negative conclusion about cause-based liability does not preclude a non-causal liability. Perhaps liability in such cases should be predicated on a kind of accomplice liability. Just as one who purposely aids an intervening human agent to cause a harm is liable as an accomplice for

---

[4] Chapter 5, § III, above.

that harm, so one who purposely aids an intervening act of God to cause a harm should be liable as an accomplice for that harm ('God's little helper?'). One has made it easier, and perhaps one has even made it possible, for the storm to cause its harm, and one has done so with the specific intent that this happen. That should be enough for liability, just as it is in the human-intervenor situation. And in both situations, no resort need be had to any cause-based liability. One has only aided, not caused, the bringing about of the harm.[5]

Here, as in the case of human intervenors, one might well worry that such a non-causal basis of liability could be extended to the lesser forms of culpability of negligence, recklessness, and knowledge. If such extensions were made, then the intervening-cause doctrine would, again, not be rendered senseless, but it would be rendered pointless. However, here as well as in the provision-of-opportunity cases, such extensions cut against the central idea that animates accomplice liability: we can relax our normal causation requirement (from causing to mere aiding) only because of the high level of culpability with which the aider acts. Accomplice liability is like attempt liability in this regard. In both cases, one substitutes a lesser causal requirement[6] (respectively, of aid, or of proximity to success) because the actor is motivated by the wrong to be done to another. Such alternative, non-causal liabilities are less justifiable if one also relaxes culpability below this highest level.

The fourth doctrine requiring modification (on the ground that culpability judgments must be separated from causal judgments) deals with what I earlier called the negligent-provision-of-opportunity cases. In such cases, as we have seen, the foreseeability (to the defendant) of the intervention by a third party changes the causal status of both that intervention and the act of the defendant. Such alteration is inconsistent with a metaphysical reading of causation, on the same grounds as we have just seen. Nonetheless, I shall defer discussion of this fourth doctrine until we have examined omission liability (for reasons that will become apparent later).

II. Eliminating the Demand that Omissions Be Treated as Causes

We should abandon both of the previously described strategies which seek to account on causal grounds for the limited liability for omissions in tort and criminal law. The first regards all omissions as causes, distinguishing the few for

---

[5] Of course, such liability will be non-causal (in the case of both human and non-human intervenors) only if we can sustain this causing/aiding distinction. As we saw preliminarily in Chapter 3, that is problematic. See Chapters 12 and 13, below.

[6] We explored the lesser (but not nonexistent) causal requirement for attempt liability in Chapter 1, above.

which liability is imposed from the many where it is not on noncausal grounds of legal duty.

There are metaphysical theories of causation that seemingly have the ability to explain how omissions can be causes. Counterfactual theories of causation (discussed in Chapters 16 and 17, below) in particular, look promising in this regard. The problem with the first strategy, then, is not its metaphysical impossibility; rather, the problem is moral.[7] In the first place, if we literally can kill, rob, rape, maim, etc, by omission as well as by commission, then how can we explain the usual absence of legal or moral duties not to kill, etc, by omission? Our obligations apply to causally complex act-types like killing, and if omissions cause deaths and are thus killings, why do we not have a general legal duty not to omit to save? Second, where we *do* have a moral and a legal duty not to omit to prevent harm, why are our failures to do so regarded as so much less blameworthy than are our failures to refrain from killing, etc, by commission? Our negative duties not to kill by commission are so much stronger than are our positive duties not to kill by omission (that is, not to omit to save). Yet if these omissions truly are a breach of our obligation not to cause death—that is, not to kill—why should this distinction be drawn at all, and with such force?

We have a moral distinction we want to draw here. It is the distinction between our responsibility for making the world worse and our responsibility for making it better. The easiest, most intuitive way to draw this distinction is by using causation to mark the difference.[8] We violate our negative duties when we cause harm, but not when we fail to prevent harm; when there are less stringent positive duties, we breach them by failing to prevent harm, not by causing that harm.

Regarding omissions as causes is thus a mistake. Avoiding that mistake does not require us to change our doctrines of liability. Rather, it allows us to make better moral sense of the doctrines we have. Not making this mistake also has the added benefit of relieving us from causal perplexities about the overdetermination omission cases mentioned in the previous chapter. We need not puzzle over cases like the omission to repair the brakes followed by the omission to use the brakes (which would not work if they were used). We lack intuitions about whether these cases are concurrent or preemptive kinds of cases, and, if they are preemptive, which omission preempts which. We lack any such intuitions because these are not causal issues at all, so we *should* be at a loss as to how to apply these causal distinctions.

---

[7] Or mostly moral. As Phil Dowe notes in *Physical Causation* (Cambridge: Cambridge University Press, 2000), 217–8, we do have a strong 'intuition of difference' between causing and failing to prevent in metaphysics even when moral blame is not in the offing.

[8] Although as we shall see in Chapter 18, causation needs to be supplemented by both counterfactual dependance and the act/omission distinction in order to draw the boundaries of positive versus negative duties.

The second strategy for explaining omission liability avoids the mistake of thinking of all omissions as causes. Yet this strategy reintroduces the mistake in its attempt to explain liability in the exceptional cases where we do owe positive duties to others. The crudest form of the mistake here is to think that the bare fact of legal duty can turn an omission from a non-cause into a cause:

[W]hereas an actor may always rightly be held to answer for the consequences of his act, since he has taken it upon himself to change the course of events, it is otherwise with a non-actor; he should be held responsible only if his failure to act was in itself a legal wrong, that is, if he had a duty to act. The non-action of one who has no legal duty to act is nothing. It does not alter the course of human events, and therefore it has no consequences. It is true that an omission of a legal duty also does not alter the course of events; but the non-actor, having been obliged by law to change events, is rightly held responsible for the consequences of not doing so.[9]

Surely the bare fact of legal duty cannot transform an omission from a nothing that can cause nothing, to a nothing that can have 'consequences', ie that can cause something!

A more plausible approach is to take the existence of a legal duty not to omit to be a proxy for some other, more plausible causal discrimination. Thus, as Eric Mack[10] and Richard Epstein[11] argue, if we examine the four bases for a duty not to omit that we described in Chapter 5, we will discover a plausible causal responsibility in each case. The grain of truth in this argument lies in there being some kind of causal involvement by the defendant with the victim in the exceptional cases of duties not to omit. Yet what is crucial to see is that the liability of the defendants in these cases is not for any such causal involvement. When we hold an omitter liable because he had a duty not to omit to rescue one whose rescue he has undertaken, we are not holding him liable on the ground that his acts of undertaking the rescue caused the victim's death. Rather, our liability doctrines explicitly and correctly hold the failed rescuer liable for his omission to rescue, even though his duty not to omit rescue arose from those acts of undertaking rescue. Those acts need not have worsened the victim's peril, nor need they have been done with a culpable *mens rea*, in order to give rise to the duty not to omit; by contrast, if such acts were an independent basis of liability on causal grounds, both these things would have to be proven about the acts of undertaking rescue.[12]

The upshot is that in the four situations earlier described, we hold omitters responsible for their omissions, not for any earlier acts of theirs that gave rise to

---

[9] Beale, 'Proximate consequences of an act', Harvard Law Review 33 (1920), 637.
[10] Mack, 'Bad Samaritanism and the causation of harm', Philosophy and Public Affairs 9 (1980), 240–1, 242–3.
[11] Epstein, 'A theory of strict liability', Journal of Legal Studies 2 (1973), 192.
[12] This latter point is argued more extensively in Michael Moore, *Act and Crime: The implications of the philosophy of action for the criminal law* (Oxford: Oxford University Press, 1993), 31–4.

their duty not to omit. This means that in these cases we are imposing a non-causal liability, and we should be upfront about it. We are liable in such cases because we failed to prevent harm, not because we caused harm. Accordingly, no theory of causation in the law need accommodate such liability.

Of course, shelving omission liability under 'non-causal' will not relieve us from all problems about omissions. In particular, we may still worry about the kinds of capacities (to have prevented a given harm) defendants must have had in order to be fairly held liable for failing to prevent that harm. And those capacity judgments may get quite tricky, as when we deal with what I earlier called the 'overdetermination omission' cases; for in such cases each person's failure in his positive obligations seems to take away the other's capacity not to fail in his own obligations. Still, these problems are not problems that a theory of legal causation need resolve, for they make no demands on the concept of causation needed by the law.[13]

III. Eliminating the Demand that Allowings Be Conceptualized as Omissions

As we saw in Chapter 5, in the passive euthanasia class of cases courts have classified acts that remove defenses against harms as omissions. Thus, the *act* of turning off the respirator (that the doctor had earlier attached) is said to be an omission, and thus, passive, not active euthanasia. Yet when someone else does the exact same type of act—say an intruder bent on killing the patient—the act is treated as what it is, an act, not an omission, and liability follows. The very same kind of act cannot both be, and not be, an omission. Moreover, by the law's generic notion of an omission—as an absent action—passive euthanasia cases are not cases of omission. For both of these reasons, we should put aside as not serious the cases that classify acts of passive euthanasia as omissions.

If one agrees with the law's bottom-line conclusion that passive euthanasia is not blameworthy, one then has two remaining routes by which to reach this conclusion. One would be to admit that in cases of passive euthanasia doctors kill their patients; but then urge that these killings can be justified (by the good consequences of, say, redirecting the victim's medical equipment to more fruitful uses, or by the ending of a painful existence, etc). But to go this route would be to lose a distinction many wish to preserve, that between active and passive euthanasia. After all, if pulling out the feeding tubes, turning off the respirator,

---

[13] My sense of these 'overdetermined omission' cases is that so long as the two or more defendants do not act in concert (where *collectively* they would have had the ability to have prevented the harm), each omitter pre-empts the other from having that ability (to prevent the harm) necessary for liability for the harm. Each omitter's breach of his positive duty is thus limited to the inchoate crimes and torts of risk creation and attempt, if any such exist. I argue for this conclusion in Chapter 18, below.

and the like is a causing of death, then it differs in no relevant respect from instances of active euthanasia, such as legal injections, knife through the heart, etc.

The law should thus be construed to demand the concept of a true or full allowing that we explored in Chapter 3. Because the law accepts passive euthanasia while rejecting active euthanasia, and because passive euthanasia is not typically an omission, the law supposes there to be the kind of cause/allowing distinction we explored in morality in Chapter 3. What makes for an *allowing* of death, again, is: (1) defendant's action prevents some preventer from preventing the victim's death; and (2) dying that death is morally appropriate because (a) the patient would have died a similar death at about the same time had the doctor not initiated the preventative treatment to begin with, and (b) the doctor would have been justified in not initiating the treatment initially if what was true now was true then.

Given the self-cancelling nature of the pairs of actions involved in cases of full allowing—the doctor unhooks the very device that he attached to start with— such cases have much the same role within morality as do omissions. The metaphysical differences between omissions and allowings, in other words, makes for little moral difference. Allowings, like omissions, are more rarely the subjects of moral duties than are the corresponding causings; when there is such a duty not to allow some harm to happen breach of that duty is less serious than breach of the corresponding duty not to cause such a harm; and when good consequences of breach are in the offing, it is permissible to justify an allowing with such good consequences more easily and more often than one could do for the corresponding causing. Given this moral equivalence, the law's temptation to classify full allowings as omissions is thus understandable. Yet it is a mistake, one which if made bedevils the law's conceptualization of omissions more generally.

The law thus needs another category of responsibility for harm, in addition to causing and failing to prevent. It needs to recognize a category of allowing a harm to happen (it needs this to make sense of its own distinction between active and passive euthanasia, as well as related distinctions in ducking and like cases). To have such a category of non-causal responsibility, the law needs in turn to recognize that double-preventions (such as removing a respirator that would have prevented death) are non-causal. The latter recognition, of course, will extend more than just to the allowing cases. It will extend as well to cases of what I called (in Chapter 3) cases of partial allowings as well. True enough, legal doctrines presently treat such double-preventions that are not full allowings as causal.[14]

---

[14] The law here is more complicated than that. The hypothetical defendant in Chapter 3, above who ties up the lifeguard who was about to save a drowning victim would be classified as a causer of death when the victim drowns. Yet the defendant who sends a countermanding telegram to prevent a warning telegram from preventing the killing by others of some victim would be held responsible on a non-causal basis as an accomplice. Even though the law's conclusion in the latter case is in line with my proposed interpretation of the law in double-prevention cases, as I argue in Chapter 13 the law's correct conclusion here is for the wrong reason and thus is only weakly supportive of the interpretation argued for here.

But like omissions, the law cannot have it both ways. If double-preventions are causal, then so are that sub-class of double-preventions that are allowings. Moreover if double-preventions are causal, then there would be no basis not to so classify omissions. So there is an interpretive choice to be made here, as there was for omissions. I think the best sense to be made of the law we have is to construe it as treating omissions, allowings, and double-preventions that are not full allowings, as non-causal.

As with omissions, classifying double-preventions as non-causal will mean that we need not seek *causal* intuitions about how to solve overdetermination variants of double-prevention cases. As we saw in the previous chapter, legal theorists are all over the map in their proposed resolution of cases such as MacLaughlin's dead prospector who dies in the desert because of the individually sufficient, double-preventative acts of two of his enemies.[15] No wonder there is such confusion, if such cases present no real issues of causation. Still, as with omissions, shelving such cases under the category 'non-causal' will not at the end of the day relieve us from resolving how such cases should come out under a *non*-causal, counterfactual basis. This is a task I undertake in Chapter 18.

IV. Making Sense of the Legal Distinction Between Trespasses and Interferences

As we saw in Chapter 5, tort criminal, and constitutional law impose different duties on trespassers than they do on interferers. Those doctrines impose more stringent duties on each of us not to trespass on someone else's land (trespass proper), personal property (trespass to chattels), or person (battery), than they do with respect to interfering with the beneficial use of our persons or property (as in the torts of nuisance, negligence, and loss of prospective advantage). The duties of non-interference require a showing of severely diminished value, their breach is less severely regarded, and their prima facie violation more easily justified, than the corresponding duties not to trespass. If (as I argued in Chapter 3, above) morality also recognizes some such distinction in duties then some metaphysical difference must underlie this moral/legal difference. A natural basis that suggests itself is the difference between causing a harm to someone and preventing someone from receiving a benefit of equivalent value. The idea would be that preventions are yet another non-causal basis for responsibility that our law presupposes.

If a cause/prevention distinction is drawn, then clearly counterfactual dependency will be the basis of liability for preventions: one would have to show that but for the act of the defendant the victim would have received the benefit in question. This is of course precisely what our law requires. To be sure, it does so

[15] McLaughlin, 'Proximate cause', Harvard Law Review 39 (1925), 155, n 25.

in the guise of 'causation'. Yet this is only because of the law's identification of cause-in-fact with counterfactual dependency, as I noted in Chapter 4. Show such an identification to be unsustainable (as I try to do in Chapter 17), and a non-causal analysis of preventions becomes possible. Such a reclassifying of preventions as non-causal has the benefit of explaining the differential stringency of legal duties mentioned above (trespass vis-à-vis interference).

Again, as with omissions and double-preventions, classifying responsibility for preventions as non-causal relieves us of seeking *causal* resolutions of the over-determination variants of prevention cases. Still, shelving prevention liability as non-causal will not relieve us of saying how such cases should come out on a counterfactual basis. This is a task I undertake in Chapter 18.

V. A Temporary Clean-up of the Doctrines of Intervening Causation

One of the most troublesome areas of legal doctrine about causation is that having to do with the sudden breaking of causal chains by fresh causal starts. Indeed, making sense of this idea—either as a matter of metaphysics or as a matter of legal policy—is so troublesome that in Part IV, below, I ultimately recommend discarding the idea entirely. On the recognition that such radical revision of these doctrines might not be done, my aim here is more modest. Can we at least make the doctrines as internally consistent as possible, and as plausible as possible (even if at the end of the day these more minor amendments do not make the doctrines either coherent enough or plausible enough to warrant their retention)? The more modest pruning of these doctrines is all I seek to do here.

As we have seen, such fresh (or 'intervening', or 'superseding') causal starts are of three kinds: deliberate third-party intervention; extraordinary natural events amounting to a coincidence (or an 'Act of God'); and subsequent but pre-empting causes. I have pruned all I intend to prune with respect to the second of these three kinds of intervening causes. Eliminating the defendant's intention (to make use of some extraordinary natural event) as a criterion for when an extraordinary natural event should not amount to a coincidence (and, thus, not an intervening cause) is the major reform needed here. Yet notice that accomplice liability can be extended to place liability on just those defendants on whom the doctrine of contrived coincidence placed it. One who purposefully utilizes extraordinary natural events to produce harm to others should be liable on an 'aiding-of-nature' ground.

Such will be my general strategy in pruning the doctrines about the first kind of intervening cause. Often I shall urge that a non-causal basis for liability should be established to preserve the liability of one who is presently but erroneously held liable on causal grounds. In light of the earlier concluded discussion of omissions, we can now add omission liability to accomplice liability as a second, non-causal[16] means for preserving existing legal results while economizing on the law's demands on causation.

I shall begin with the intervening human-agent doctrines. Here there are two categories of troublesome cases, one having to do with supposedly cause-based liability for negligently providing another person with the opportunity to do some harm, and the other having to do with supposedly cause-based liability for negligently providing another person with reasons for doing some harm. I begin with the provision-of-opportunity cases.

A. The negligent-provision-of-opportunity cases: Non-causal but omissive liability

As we have seen, in cases like that of the railroad that drops its passenger off into a dangerous situation and the construction company that leaves its bulldozer (with the keys in it) perched above a house, the negligent provision of opportunity makes the defendant liable despite the intervening use of the opportunity by a free, informed, voluntary wrongdoer. Such liability is a puzzle for law that generally proclaims such free, informed voluntary wrongdoers to be intervening causes. Negligence is insufficient *mens rea* for accomplice liability, which requires purposeful aiding of the wrongdoer. Yet this seemingly forces us to concede an ad hoc exception to the intervening human agency doctrine.

Hart's and Honoré's original reaction to these cases was simply to carve out an ad hoc exception and leave it at that.[17] In the second edition of their *Causation in the Law*, however, they sought to explain such liability in terms of a newly discovered, second kind of causal relation. On this new view, such cases represent a weaker form of causation called 'occasioning', 'enabling', or 'inclining' causation. Such a special kind of causal relation is peripheral or penumbral to the 'central case' of causation, where intervening intentional actors break causal chains; for such a weaker relation, its weakness paradoxically proves to be a kind of strength, for intervening intentional actors do not break these 'weaker-linked' causal chains.[18]

This is pretty obviously hopeless as a reconciliation of the intervening human-agency doctrine with the negligent-provision-of-opportunity cases. The original ad hoc solution is no solution at all, because it makes causation depend on

---

[16] As we shall see in Chapter 13, below, much of what is currently *said* by the law to be non-causal (because accomplice) liability is in fact a kind of causal liability.

[17] See Chapter 5, above, n 61.

[18] Hart and Honoré, *Causation in the Law* (2nd edn, Oxford: Oxford University Press, 1985), 186:

The main feature that unifies 'inducing wrongful acts' and 'occasioning harm' is that these two types of 'causal connection' (to use the expression in the wide sense commonly found in legal writings) are not negatived by the factors that negative the simpler type of causal connection... for both... may be traced through an intervening voluntary action and the second form may also be traced through an intervening coincidence.

whether the harm that happened was one within the risk that make it negligent to act—and this, on Hart's and Honoré's own showing,[19] is a non-causal notion. Causation cannot be a real relationship in the world and be influenced by this kind of culpability ('harm within the risk') analysis. Likewise, the invention of non-central notions of causation is of no help. Not only are such postulated special senses of concepts always suspicious, postulated as they are to save a theory that is otherwise in trouble; but left unexplained is why this second kind of causal relationship is not generally sufficient for liability if it is sufficient in the negligent-provision-of-opportunity cases. Why, for example, is the railroad which negligently spilled its gasoline throughout a town not liable when an intentional arsonist torches it off? Because, you say, the risk of the arsonist is not the risk that made it negligent to spill the gasoline. Yet that is, again, to resort to the non-causal criterion of harm-within-the-risk. The relation between the *action* of the railroad and the burning of the town seems in all relevant respects similar to the relation between the *action* of the railroad and the rape of its bounced passenger: each such action made possible (provided the 'opportunity' for) the causing of harm by a third party. It is only a culpability discrimination (harm-within-the-risk) that distinguishes these cases, and this kind of discrimination should be irrelevant to causation (as I argue in Part III, below).

We could invent a negligence kind of accomplice liability for the provision-of-opportunity cases. Yet if we did this, we would face a problem analogous to that faced by Hart and Honoré: why is anyone who negligently acts in a way that makes possible the intervening intentional wrong of another not liable on this ground? Such extensive accomplice liability does not make a hash out of our causal notions, as do Hart's and Honoré's solutions; but such liability would render pointless the law's insistence that intervening intentional actors break causal chains.

Preferable to any of these solutions would be to decide that the provision-of-opportunity cases in torts are wrongly decided. Criminal law does not hold railroads or construction companies liable for negligently allowing others to rape, or to destroy buildings. (At most, criminal law creates separable crimes of leaving keys in the ignition, leaving vehicles unlocked, serving too much liquor to known drivers, inchoate crimes of reckless endangerment, etc.) One could preferably urge that tort law doctrine is simply mistaken in imposing liabilities for harms when only an opportunity was negligently provided to another to cause such harms.

My own sense is that tort law is not mistaken here, however. Liability is proper in the negligent-provision-of-opportunity cases. However, the liability is not cause-based liability (nor is it liability for purposefully aiding another to cause). Rather, these are cases of true omission liability. When the railroad is held liable for the rape of its passenger, it is not liable because it caused the rape by a third

<hr />

[19] Hart and Honoré, *Causation in the Law*, lxii–lxv, 286–90.

party; rather, it could be held liable for failing to prevent the rape when it could so easily have done so by carrying the passenger to a place of safety. Likewise, a construction company is not liable because it caused the destruction of the house by leaving the keys in the ignition of its bulldozer; it is liable because it failed to prevent such damage when it could so easily have done so by removing the keys.

The duty not to omit in these cases arises because of the 'culpable causing of the condition of peril' exception discussed in Chapter 5.[20] The defendants in these cases have caused the victim to be placed in peril, and have culpably caused this because the peril presented by intervening third-party actors was so foreseeable. Their omission to correct a situation they have caused is the true basis for their liability here.

Such a non-causal omission rationale explains why negligent provision of opportunity generally (which opportunity is utilized by a third-party wrongdoer) is not enough for liability. Rather, the opportunity must be provided to a wrongdoer the risk of whose intervention was a large part of what made the original actor negligent to start with. It is only prevention of the realization of *this* peril that is the first actor's duty; that other actors may come along and utilize the opportunity provided is not enough. Thus, when the railroad's negligence consists in the spilling of gasoline, that negligence does not consist (in the main) in the foreseeable intervention of an arsonist.[21] Such arson is not the main peril for whose creation the railroad was responsible, and thus for whose correction it has a duty. Likewise, when a railroad's negligence consists in carrying a passenger too far, but it does not drop her off in a place of danger but in a reputable hotel, where she is raped, the railroad has no liability because that was not the peril that made it negligent to carry her beyond her destination.[22]

One way to test whether we hold defendants liable in these cases for their omissions (when the duty not to omit arises from their having caused the peril), or whether we hold them liable for the culpable action causing the harm, is to eliminate culpability at the earlier time. Suppose the railroad is not at all negligent in carrying a passenger beyond her destination to some end-of-the-line, deserted freight yards; she was also not at fault, let us suppose, but overslept due to involuntary intoxication. If the railroad which has innocently caused her condition of peril—being at an isolated, dark, and dangerous location—were to fail to carry her further (when it could do so easily because another train is heading there anyway), and she is raped, then I take the railroad to be liable. It is liable because it omitted to prevent her rape when it could have done so at little cost or inconvenience to itself. It is not liable for having caused her rape by its action of carrying her to the end of the line, because that action was not culpable in any way.

---

[20] Chapter 5, § VII, above.

[21] *Watson v. Kentucky and Indiana Bride and Ry Co*, 137 Ky 619, 126 SW 146 (1910).

[22] This is a variation of the facts in *Central of Georgia Ry Co v. Price*, 106 Ga 176, 32 SE 77 (1898).

Another way to test whether the proper basis for liability here is causal or omissive, is to imagine a scenario where there is no fair opportunity for the railroad to prevent the injury. Suppose, as in the actual case, the railroad negligently carries her beyond her destination to a dangerous place. However, this time the railroad arranges transportation back for her as soon as it can, and places her in the safest position possible in the interim. If she is still raped in that interim period, I take it that there would be no liability. Yet if the basis of liability in the actual case was the negligent action of carrying the passenger beyond her destination, there should be liability here. The reason there is not is because without any capacity to have prevented the rape, the railroad cannot be held liable for any omission to prevent it. Thus, it is omission that is the true basis for liability here.

It may seem that criminal law is remiss in not imposing punishment in these provision-of-opportunity cases. For criminal law, like tort law, provides that there is a duty not to omit when one has innocently or culpably caused the victim's condition of peril, and thus it might seem that there should be criminal omission liability wherever there is omission liability in tort law. Yet most of these provision-of-opportunity cases are negligence cases and, by and large, criminal law does not punish negligence. Where criminal law does punish negligence, as in negligent homicide, there should be criminal liability in this class of cases—not for causing death, but for negligently failing to prevent someone else from causing death. And in those cases where the defendant is more than negligent—he knows to a practical certainty that vandals will use his bulldozer to ram another's house if he leaves the keys in the ignition—he should be convictable of any crime on property destruction requiring a *mens rea* of knowingly or recklessly failing to prevent someone else from causing such destruction. Criminal law thus does parallel tort law here, if one looks closely.

The upshot is that we do not need to modify the notion of an intervening cause to accommodate liability in the provision-of-opportunity cases. There is liability in such cases, but such liability can be non-causal: one can be liable for purposefully aiding, or for knowing, reckless, or negligent omitting. This allows the law to say clearly and without exception that a free, informed, voluntary third party's intervention between the defendant's act and the victim's harm does indeed break the causal chain between that act and that harm.

B. The giving-of-reasons cases revisited: The playoff of causal versus accomplice liability

If we now turn from the provision-of-opportunity to the giving-of-reasons cases, we also can sharpen the law's commitment to the status of a free, informed, voluntary act constituting an intervening cause. Such clarification is desperately needed, because the law otherwise seems committed to a flat contradiction here.

The contradiction is to be found in the partly innocent agent cases. As mentioned in Chapter 5,[23] the official rationale for punishing the reason-giving procurer for a more serious crime, and the one procured (who committed the crime) for a less serious crime, is that the procurer is an accomplice as to the less serious crime but he is a principal as to the more serious crime. Take my earlier example of the intentional use of a provokable individual to have another person killed; the procurer tells the hot-tempered and jealous man that his wife is having an affair with the intended victim of the homicide. The procurer is said to have aided and abetted the voluntary manslaughter (provoked intentional killing) committed by the hot-tempered, jealous man; the procurer is also said to have caused the death of the victim himself through the use of a comparatively innocent agent, and therefore is guilty of murder as a principal. The contradiction lies in saying *both* that the choice to kill by the hot-tempered husband is, and that it is not, an intervening cause—and, thus, that the procurer's telling of the falsehood both did not, and did, cause the death of the victim.

This contradiction is easily eliminated if we but seize one horn of the dilemma or the other in any given case. That is, sometimes the one who is induced to commit a crime is so distressed, ignorant, or compelled as not to be an intervening cause on the ordinary criteria for that concept. If the killer is misled about whether he is killing, or misled about facts that would justify the killing, then his choice to act is not intentional with respect to material facts. If the killer is threatened, or placed in a hard choice situation, or rendered not in control of his faculties, his choice also does not constitute an intervening cause on the ordinary criteria of that concept. In these cases, the one who induces the killer to kill, himself causes death. Whether the inducer's culpability is greater (or lesser, for that matter) than that of the one he uses is irrelevant, for it is his own culpability that is used to measure the degree of blame appropriate for his having caused the harm.

The only reservation one might have about this conclusion lies in the linguistic features of causative verbs that we examined in Chapter 1. One may experience some reluctance in saying that the inducer *kills*, Indeed, this sense of linguistic oddity may increase for other verbs, like 'rape', 'hit', 'maim', and 'take'. Surely, one might think, it is the person who is induced to do these things who does them; the inducer of rape does not rape, the inducer of a hitting does not himself hit, etc.

Yet this linguistic discomfort should be momentary. If one looks at the acts prohibited by the criminal law, all of them are described by causally loaded verbs. Just as one kills by causing death, so one rapes by causing penetration, one hits by causing contact, one maims by causing disfigurement, and one takes by causing movement of the object taken. It is true that we often have a stereotype of how these causings are done—we picture the actor using his own body as the means.

---

[23] Chapter 5, § VI, above.

Yet these stereotypes do not give the meaning of these verbs. Those who induce others to use their bodies to cause the states of affairs which the law prohibits violate our pragmatic (in the linguists' sense) expectations of the typical way these states of affairs are brought about; such unusual routes no more relieve one from being considered a cause of such a state of affairs than would the use of any other unusual means. Inducers quite literally rape, hit, maim, and take, and are properly held liable for doing so.[24]

Furthermore, if one is uncomfortable with this linguistic conclusion, then one should urge adoption of language similar to that of the American Law Institute's Model Penal Code, section 2.06(2)(a). My rewording of that subsection would make one liable for the conduct of another person when, acting with the culpability sufficient for commission of the offense, he causes an agent who lacks the voluntariness, intention, or capacities sufficient for the status of an inter-vening cause, to engage in such conduct. If there is a linguistic problem here, one can simply stipulate it away. Where there is a causal relation between the inducer's reason-giving action and the harm, there should be liability as prin-cipal, whatever the etymological accidents of language are construed to require.

Alternatively, sometimes the one who wields the knife meets the ordinary criterion for an intervening cause. The hot-tempered, jealous husband is, to my mind, such a person. He intentionally killed; his only ignorance was immaterial, since believing your wife to have had an affair is not a justification for homicide, not even in Texas anymore. His only 'involuntariness' is due to his own emo-tional impulses, which, despite the partial defense of provocation, do not compel one to kill.[25] Easier cases are those where the inducer tells another where his intended victim may be found; when the victim is found and shot, the shooter's action is an intervening cause, making the teller's liability only that of an accomplice.

The conundrum in the law of accomplice liability with which we began this subsection, is also present in certain of these cases. If the provider of false information in my main example can only be guilty as an accomplice and not as a principal, then under standard doctrine he may be held liable for no greater degree of homicide than can be proved of his principal. Since the principal here is the hot-tempered man who may only be convicted of heat-of-passion manslaughter, this would limit the inducer to liability for aiding and abetting manslaughter. Yet the inducer's culpability is greater, since he intended to kill and was not provoked. If one finds this reasoning to be compelling, then the standardly stated rule should be discarded: an accomplice may be held liable for a higher degree of crime than the principal of whom he is the accomplice. One

[24] One of the routes to preserving the equivalence thesis discussed in Chapter 1, above.
[25] Moore, *Placing Blame*, Chapter 13.

should make this reform directly, and not attempt to warp causal doctrines to accommodate it.[26]

VI. Conclusion

My 'pruned' concept of causation presupposed by the law will have the following characteristics:

(1) Mere correlation is not causation. Some particular event x is not a cause of another particular event y just because x is an instance of some type of event X, y is an instance of some type of event Y, and Y regularly follows X. Something more is required. When the correlation is a weak, probabilistic one, so that an event of type X raises the conditional probability of an event of type Y, one has to 'screen off' spurious causes from real ones by asking more complicated probability questions. Something more is required even when the correlation is a stronger, universal one, where events of type Y always follow events of type X. Such correlations are modes of proving that a causal relation exists between x and y; they are not themselves constitutive of such a causal relation. As a special case of this last point, the correlation that exists between epiphenomena is not a causal relation. If x causes y and z, and y always occurs prior to z, y does not cause z. My jogging in the morning both scares my dog and makes me tired; my dog's fright does not make me tired.

(2) For x to be a cause of y, it is not necessary that x be a sufficient condition for y's occurrence. In ordinary, garden-variety concurrent-cause cases, other conditions may also be necessary for y to occur, meaning that x by itself is not sufficient even though it is a cause of y. In short, it is not necessary that a cause be sufficient.

(3) Not every condition necessary for the happening of some harm y is a cause of y. When the law enquires after the 'sole cause' of some event, the existence of many such necessary conditions does not rule out some other

---

[26] Sandy Kadish argues that in these cases we should retain the rule limiting accomplices to the crimes actually committed by their principals. A well-known example is provided in Isabel Richards: *R v. Richards* [1974] QB 776. There the defendant tried to get two thugs to beat her husband quite severely (rather than the minor beating they in fact gave him). Kadish likens Richards to attemptors: like an attemptor who does not succeed in causing the harm he tried to cause, the appropriate punishment for anything beyond being an accomplice (to a non-severe beating) must be for culpability alone: Kadish, 'Causation and complicity', California Law Review 73 (1985), 323–410. The argument is persuasive on Kadish's assumptions, viz that accomplices do not *causally contribute* to the harm their principals cause, because the acts of the latter are intervening causes. In Chapters 12 and 13, below, I give grounds for rejecting that assumption, in which case so-called 'accomplices' should be punished like everyone else, in proportion to the culpability they individually possessed in *causing* some legally prohibited state of affairs.

event x being designated the sole cause. In short, even amongst those events or states present at the time of some harm for which they are necessary, it is not sufficient for causation that some condition be necessary.

(4) The causal relation may exist between an act x and a harm y even if x is not a necessary condition for the occurrence of y because some other condition z is sufficient for the occurrence of y; such causal relation will exist where x and z are concurrent overdeterminers, and it will also exist when x pre-empts z as a cause of y. In short, for x to cause y, it is not necessary that x be a necessary condition for y.

(5) The causal relation may sometimes not exist between an act x and a harm y even though x is a sufficient condition for the happening of y. This will be true in the pre-emptive overdetermination cases where another condition z sufficient for y pre-empts x from causing y. In short, for x to cause y, it is not sufficient that x be a sufficient condition for y.

(6) Causation is a scalar property. An act x may be *more* of a cause of a harm y than some other event z, even though z too is a cause of y.

(7) Causation diminishes over the number of events through which it is transmitted. This makes the causal relation one of only limited transitivity. Being an earlier necessary condition for some harm is thus not sufficient for being a cause of that harm.

(8) Causal chains may be sharply broken and not merely gradually diminished. The intervening causes responsible for such breaks may be of three kinds: deliberate human interventions, freakishly abnormal natural events, and subsequent pre-emptive causes. Although there may be liability for failing to prevent certain such interventions, or of aiding such interventions in doing their causal work, there is no causal relationship across such intervening events at the basis of such liability.

(9) Omissions, being no things at all, do no causal work. While there is a counterfactual question to ask about omissions when they are the basis for liability—namely, the 'capacity' question of whether the omitter could have prevented the harm—this is not a causal question.

(10) True allowings are not omissions; they are actions. Such allowings are nonetheless non-causal: they are a subclass of double-preventions, that is, acts that prevent those events that, if they had occurred, would have prevented some harm.

(11) Preventing someone from receiving some benefit is not to be analyzed as causing an absence of such benefit. Rather, if one is liable for such prevention, it is on the counterfactual basis that had the preventer not so acted the victim would have received such benefit.

(12) The causal relationship is asymmetrical, so that if x causes y, then y does not cause x. Moreover, the asymmetry is temporal, in that if x causes y, then x must not be preceded temporally by y.

(13) Both whole events and aspects of whole events are the relata of the causal relation. Causal contexts are extensional, and this extensionality can be preserved only by allowing both whole events and their aspects to be causal relata.

The question for the latter part of this book is whether there is any metaphysical theory of causation that can endow causation with these thirteen characteristics.

PART III

THE FIRST BLIND ALLEY: THE ATTEMPT TO REPLACE PROXIMATE CAUSATION WITH CULPABILITY AS A PREREQUISITE FOR LEGAL LIABILITY

7

'Negligence in the Air Will not Do'

I. Introduction

As we saw in Chapter 4, legal skeptics about causation come in a variety of flavors. One of the most influential of those is the view examined in Part III. This is a skepticism directed specifically at the proximate cause half of the law's causal requirements. Such skepticism has sought to replace a causal requirement for liability with a culpability requirement. Historically, the culpability for negligence was the central focus of the view here examined, so I shall begin there.

'Negligence in the air, so to speak, will not do.' This old maxim from Pollock's *Torts*,[1] much quoted by Benjamin Cardozo in *Palsgraf v. Long Island RR*[2] and elsewhere,[3] is the battle cry for one side of one of the most famous debates in Anglo-American tort law and criminal law. This is the debate about the essence of negligence: Is negligence a relational concept, so that it is properly used only in relation to a person and a harm? Or is negligence non-relational, in the sense that it makes good sense to speak of a person being negligent, full stop, without any isolation of any particular person or harm?

Those who repeat the maxim take the relational view. On their version of the relational view, an actor is liable for negligence only when: (1) the harm caused to another is an instance of the type of harm the risk of which made the actor negligent; and (2) the person suffering the harm is a member of the class of persons the risk to whom made the actor negligent. These two requirements of negligence are sometimes collapsed into the following question: 'Was the defendant negligent as regards the victim's damage?'[4] Such an inquiry invites what is usually described as a 'harm-within-the-risk' (hereinafter 'HWR') analysis. The latter label comes from this formulation of the negligence liability question: Was the harm that happened to this plaintiff within the risk that made it negligent for the defendant to have acted as he did?[5]

---

[1] Sir Frederick Pollock, *The Law of Torts* (11th edn, London: Stevens 1920), 455.

[2] *Palsgraf v. Long Island RR*, 162 NE 99, 102 (NY 1928).

[3] Cardozo also employs the quotation in his most famous per se negligence opinion, *Martin v. Herzog*, 126 NE 814, 816 (NY 1920).

[4] Glanville Williams, 'The risk principle', Law Quarterly Review 77 (1961), 179.

[5] For a classic, short, clear statement in unqualified form of the harm within the risk formulation, see Warren Seavey, 'Mr Justice Cardozo and the law of torts', Harvard Law Review 52 (1939), 372–407.

Despite their unitary labels, it is both historically common and analytically helpful to separate the harm-relative from the person-relative aspects of negligence. Formally, one should represent the non-relational view of negligence as using a one-place predicate for negligence, as in: 'x is negligent', or Nx. The relational view then comes in two flavors. A person-relative conception of negligence construes negligence as a two-place predicate, as in: 'x is negligent to y', or Nxy, where x and y range over persons. A person-and-harm-relative conception of negligence construes negligence as a three-place predicate, as in: 'x is negligent to y with respect to z', or $Nxyz$, where x and y range over persons and z ranges over harms. Let us henceforth call these the non-relational, the partially relational, and the fully relational conceptions of negligence, respectively.

When put formally (in terms of two- and three-place predicates), one might well wonder how tort and criminal law got embroiled in this debate over how negligence is best conceptualized. What moved courts and scholars to adopt one of these views of negligence and to defend it vigorously against the others? There are two ways of getting at this motivational question.

The first stems from some ideas about culpability generally (including but not limited to the culpability of negligence). As is well known, Anglo-American tort law and criminal law both grade the culpability with which an act was done by the mental state of the actor. Roughly, we distinguish intentional wrongdoing from reckless wrongdoing, and both of these from merely negligent wrongdoing. Culpability increases as we move up this list and more severe legal sanctions (such as greater punishments in criminal law and punitive damages in tort law) are attached to the more serious levels of culpability. Such a classification scheme demands that we be able to identify an intentional wrong, distinguish it from a reckless one, and distinguish both of these sorts of wrongs from a merely negligent wrong.

In drawing these distinctions, it is not enough to define each of these terms; that is, it is not enough to unpack 'intentional' in terms of purpose or knowledge to a practical certainty, 'reckless' in terms of conscious appreciation of an unjustifiable risk, and negligence in terms of an unreasonable risk not adverted to by the actor. It is not enough because every human action is accompanied by some intention and some predictive beliefs. No event can be a human action unless it is both intended and done knowingly with respect to some aspects of it. Such 'voluntariness' is built into the very concept of human action. To distinguish intentional actions from reckless ones, and reckless actions from negligent ones, we thus have to answer relational questions in addition to defining the nature of these different requirements. For intention: if the defendant intended some type of harm H, was the particular harm h that he in fact caused by his action an instance of H? If so, he intentionally caused h; if not, while he caused h, and while he did so with some intention, he did not cause h intentionally. We have, in other words, to fit the particular thing done to the type of thing intended to see whether a defendant acted with the culpability of an *intentional* wrongdoer.[6]

The same is true of knowledge and recklessness. To be adjudged a knowing or reckless causer of some harm *h*, it is not enough to be found to have consciously believed that one's act certainly would cause, or risk, some type of harm *H*; in addition, it also must be true that the harm that one's act caused, *h*, be an instance of the type of harm foreseen or risked, *H*. The harm that occurred, in other words, has to be 'within the foresight' that makes one culpable or 'within the risk' the conscious appreciation of which makes one reckless.

Our familiar culpability gradations—in terms of purpose (intent), knowledge (foresight), and recklessness—thus require us to do two things, not merely one. First, we must define the *nature* of each of these mental states, in such a way that they are distinct from one another. Second, we must fix the *object* (or representational content) of each mental state making one culpable so that we can classify acts as either fitting such objects or not.

At first glance, the same would seem to be true of negligence. It would seem that we must do more than define 'negligence' as any act that imposes an unjustified risk of some type of harm *H* on some class of persons *Y*. In addition, it would seem that the harm an act causes, *h*, must be an instance of the type of harm *H*, and the person one injures, *y*, must be within the class of persons *Y*. It would seem, in other words, that the harm that occurs must be 'within the risk' that made the action negligent to perform.

We may summarize this motive for adopting the HWR (or fully relational) view of negligence by saying that culpability assessments in general are incomplete until the content of the mental state that makes an actor culpable is compared to the actual results of his actions. Culpability, one might say, is inherently relational in this way, making one think that negligence must be so too.

The second motive for getting interested in the relational nature of negligence stems from certain frustrations with the concept of proximate causation. It is well known that the tests for proximate causation in Anglo-American tort law and criminal law are elusive, multiple, and often conflicting in their implications for cases.[7] The interest in the relational view of negligence partly stems from the promise it holds of bypassing the thorny questions of proximate causation. The temptation is to think that perhaps the more tractable question of culpability— how an act does or does not fit the object of some culpable mental state—could be substituted for the vagaries of proximate causation. Perhaps instead of asking

---

[6] The fitting of the objects of intentions to the actions done is explored in Michael S Moore, 'Intention and mens rea', in Ruth Gavison (ed), *Issues in Contemporary Legal Philosophy* (Oxford: Oxford University Press, 1987), reprinted in Michael S Moore, *Placing Blame: A general theory of the criminal law* (Oxford: Clarendon Press, 1997), 449–77. We also explored this issue briefly in discussing the doctrine of double effect in Chapter 3, above.

[7] As we explored in Chapter 4, above.

whether a defendant's act proximately caused some harm *h*, one could ask the seemingly more tractable question of whether *h* was within the risk that made it negligent for the defendant to do the act.

Apart from these skeptical views about the consistency, determinancy, or coherence of the proximate-cause tests, there is also the thought that these tests ask the wrong question. On this view the central problem the proximate-cause tests really address (whatever their pretensions) is the problem of lack of fit between what defendant intended, foresaw, or risked, on the one hand, and what defendant caused in fact, on the other. The defendant intends to hit one person with a rock, but, in fact, hits the window belonging to another with the rock; the defendant risked an injury to a passenger attempting to alight a moving train, but caused a different sort of injury to someone else. If such cases are illustrative of the central problem addressed by the proximate-cause tests, then those tests are cast in the wrong terms. The supposed 'proximate cause' issue, on this view, has nothing to do with causation but, rather, with culpability.

Both of these suspicions about the proximate-cause tests motivate HWR theorists to seek to substitute the HWR test for the proximate-cause tests.[8] A strong version of this motivation is the hope that an HWR analysis can wholly supplant the proximate-cause tests. A weaker version is expressed by the hope that an HWR analysis can at least take some of the pressure off the proximate-cause tests by excising at least these culpability questions (of mismatch between harm intended and harm done, for example) from the domain of proximate causation. An HWR test on this weaker version, supplements, but does not entirely supplant, the tests for proximate causation.

These two considerations—optimism about culpability and skepticism about proximate causation—converge to produce an idea of considerable interest, namely, relational negligence, or the view that negligence cannot be assessed without doing an HWR analysis. Not only does it seem that we must ask relational questions in order to complete an analysis of culpability, but it also seems that asking such questions helps us to cut the Gordian knot of proximate causation at the same time. These are reasons enough to induce many legal theorists, not just to become interested in, but to adopt, some version of an HWR analysis.[9]

---

[8] For an expression of such a hope, see, eg, Seavey, 'Mr Justice Cardozo'. For a contemporary expression of the second of these ideas—that proximate-cause problems are in reality problems of mismatch 'between the actual result and the result intended or risked'—see Sanford Kadish and Steven Schulhofer (eds), *Criminal Law and Its Processes* (7th edn, Boston: Aspen Publishers, 2001), 517. The three problems we introduce in Chapter 10, below—the problems of intervening causes, of pre-existing conditions, and of spatio-temporal remoteness—are intended to dispute this latter point.

[9] See Seavey, 'Mr Justice Cardozo'; Warren Seavey, 'Principles of tort', Harvard Law Review 56 (1943), 72–98; Fleming James and Robert Parry, 'Legal cause', Yale Law Journal 60 (1951), 761–811; Williams, 'The risk principle'; Robert Keeton, *Legal Cause in the Law of Torts* (Columbus: Ohio State University Press, (1963); Wayne Thode, 'A reply to the defense of the use of the hypothetical case to resolve the causation issue', Texas Law Review 47 (1969), 1344–58.

From the above discussions one can see that there are several varieties of HWR analyses. The fully relational, strong version of an HWR test holds that negligence is relative to both persons and harms and that the question of such fully relational negligence supplants entirely the traditional proximate cause enquiries. This strong, fully relational version of the HWR test will be the principal stalking horse for Part III. Also of interest, however, are the weaker types of HWR analyses. Largely because of the accidents of history, American tort law has tended to adopt only a weaker, partially relational HWR analysis. We shall thus want to examine the weaker and the only partially relational versions of an HWR test as well.

I shall proceed as follows. In this chapter, I will further introduce the notion of an HWR test by sketching briefly its history in Anglo-American tort law and criminal law. This will not only situate the idea within legal theory, but it will also allow us to further refine the idea of an HWR analysis by winnowing out certain historical variations. In Chapter 8, I will begin the task of critique by examining the concept of negligence generally. I will develop and defend a holistic view of negligence according to which all risks are taken into account in judging negligence. I will then examine two conceptual problems that exist for any version of an HWR analysis, weak or strong, full or partial. One of these problems stems from the holistic account of negligence.

In Chapter 9, I will then put aside problems for HWR stemming from the concepts of negligence and of risk and will discuss instead normative reasons why HWR is not a good test for liability. (Here I shall concede *arguendo* that the test is conceptually coherent, a point disputed in Chapter 8.) Finally, in Chapter 10, I will focus on the strong version of an HWR test, the version that would supplant entirely the proximate cause question with an HWR analysis. In this chapter, I will raise problems specific to this strong thesis, problems having to do with the inability of HWR to duplicate the results currently reached under proximate cause doctrines.

II. The Doctrinal Development of the Harm-within-the-Risk Test

The idea that there must be some relation between the type of harm intended or foreseen and the token of harm that some wrongdoer causes is as old as the ideas of intention and foresight. One cannot blame people for intentionally, knowingly, or recklessly causing a certain result, without asking and answering this relational question, however implicitly. The analogous relational question for negligence was a later development (as was the idea of negligence itself).

Often Baron Pollock is given credit for proposing an HWR analysis of negligence in his opinions in 1850.[10] Indeed, Pollock expressed the idea that the

[10] *Greenland v. Chaplin*, 155 Eng Rep 104 (1850); *Rigby v. Intewitt*, 155 Eng Rep 103 (1850).

extent of liability for negligence should be no greater than the *basis* for liability; whatever risks, in other words, made one negligent should also be the only risks for which one should have to pay if they have materialized in actual harm. This thought came to be associated with a rather different proposal, however, for usually Baron Pollock is interpreted as laying down the foreseeability test of proximate causation. The leading work of Baron Pollock's grandson, (Frederick) *Pollock on Torts*, so construes these cases,[11] as do current hornbooks such as *Prosser and Keeton on Torts*.[12]

Foreseeability tends to be a different test than is the HWR test.[13] This is because the foreseeability question is usually asked on a stand-alone basis, that is, a basis not limited to negligence. 'Was the harm foreseeable to the defendant when he acted?' or 'Was the intervening action of some third party foreseeable to the defendant when she acted?' are the typical formulations of the foreseeability test. These questions do not call for an HWR analysis. They do not ask whether a type of harm, in light of its gravity and the justification for running it, was *sufficiently* foreseeable that its risk was unreasonable—the negligence question; and they do not ask whether the harm that was caused by the defendant's action was an instance of this sufficiently foreseeable type of harm—the HWR, or relational, question.

For this reason it is more accurate to trace the origins of an HWR analysis to the cases of the mid-19th century that use criminal statutes to set the duty of care in negligence cases in torts. The usual citation is to *Gorris v. Scott*,[14] decided in 1874. In *Gorris*, the defendant shipowner violated the Contagious Disease (Animals) Act of 1869, which required carriers by water to provide separate pens for transported animals. The plaintiff's unpenned sheep were washed overboard by a storm, when arguably they would not have been had they been properly penned. In denying recovery to the plaintiff, the English Court of Exchequer held that the statute was aimed at preventing the spread of contagious diseases among animals, not at preventing their loss at sea, and that accordingly the harm

---

[11] Frederick Pollock, *The Law of Torts* (1st American edn, 3rd English edn, St Louis: Thomas Law Book Co 1894), 45.

[12] W Page Keeton et al, *Prosser and Keeton on Torts* (5th edn, St Paul: West Publishing Co, 1984), 281.

[13] See, eg, Kenneth Abraham, *The Forms and Functions of Tort Law* (2nd edn, New York: Foundation Press, 2002), 119–22. Occasionally the foreseeability test is not asked on a stand-alone basis, but is rather asked in a way duplicating the full calculus of risk for negligence. In *Wagon Mound No 2*, for example, the Privy Council asked whether the ignition of the furnace oil was *sufficiently* foreseeable, given the gravity of the harm threatened and the ease of the elimination of the risk: *Overseas Tankship (UK) Ltd v. Miller Steamship Co (Wagon Mound No 2)* [1967] 1 AC 617 (PC 1966) (appeal taken from New South Wales). This way of framing the foreseeability test does make it equivalent to the HWR test. For that reason most commentators hew to the simple formulation of foreseeability, which is distinguishable from the HWR test. See, eg, Leon Green, 'The Wagon Mound No. 2: Foreseeability revisited', Utah Law Review (1967), 197–206.

[14] 9 LR Ex 125 (1874).

the plaintiff had suffered was not within the risk the danger of which motivated the passage of the statute.

Gorris was translated early on into two questions: (1) is the harm the plaintiff suffered within the type of harm the risk of which motivated the legislature to prohibit the defendant's conduct; and (2) is the plaintiff within the class of persons the legislature intended to protect when it prohibited the defendant's conduct?[15] These two questions, staples of current American tort law,[16] are of course nothing other than the two questions that make up a fully relational HWR test, with the *caveat* that they are restricted to cases of negligence based on violations of criminal statutes.

In 1901 Francis Bohlen urged that the second of these questions—the one relating to classes of persons, not to types of harms—should be asked generally as part of the negligence issue in negligence tort cases.[17] Bohlen made no reference to the use of criminal statutes to set the duty of care, but rather regarded the negligence question generally. Bohlen urged that late-19th-century American cases already made negligence relational with respect to persons risked, so that a risk to *this plaintiff* must be shown before the defendant could be liable in tort to such a plaintiff. Bohlen did not think this risk-to-this-plaintiff question, categorized as duty, supplanted the proximate-cause questions; quite the contrary. Bohlen gave both a general test of proximate causation—in terms of natural laws[18]—and a test specific to the intervening-cause issue.[19]

It was only eight years later, in 1909, that the HWR analysis was presented at full flower. In 1909 Joseph Bingham proposed the expansion of a fully relational HWR test beyond cases of negligence based on statutory violations.[20] Without limiting himself to statutory violation cases, Bingham wrote a two-part article in which he distinguished two questions: (1) Bohlen's question, whether the plaintiff is within the class of persons owed a legal duty by the defendant; and (2) if the plaintiff is owed some duty by the defendant, is the harm suffered by the plaintiff within the scope of that duty owed to the plaintiff by the defendant? These duty questions in turn were translated into risk questions. This was because, Bingham asserted, all legal duties are imposed for a reason. In torts, that reason is the prevention/compensation of certain sorts of harms to certain sorts of

[15] Eg, *Osborne v. McMasters*, 41 NW 543 (Minn 1889). For a history of the development of the per se negligence doctrine in the 19th century, see Patrick Kelley, 'Who decides? Community safety conventions at the heart of tort liability', Cleveland State Law Review 38 (1991), 358–9.

[16] Eg, Keeton et al, *Prosser and Keeton on Torts*, 222–7.

[17] Francis Bohlen, 'The probable or the natural consequences as the test of liability in negligence, (Part 1)', American Law Register 49 (1901), 79–88; Francis Bohlen, 'The probable or the natural consequences as the test of liability in negligence (Part 2)', American Law Register 49 (1901), 148–64. The person-relative nature of negligence is rather incidental to Bohlen's main purposes in the article. Bohlen, 'Probable or natural consequences (Part 2)', 151–2.

[18] Bohlen, 'Probable or natural consequences (Part 2)', *passim*.   [19] Ibid, 162–4.

[20] Joseph Bingham, 'Some suggestions concerning "legal cause" at common law (Part 1)', Columbia Law Review 9 (1909), 16–37; Joseph Bingham, 'Some suggestions concerning "legal cause" at common law (Part 2)', Columbia Law Review 9 (1909), 136–59.

persons. (This, for Bingham, was as true of common-law duties as of duties founded on criminal statutes.) Accordingly, to ascertain the scope of a defendant's duties (both with respect to persons and harms) is to ascertain which risks it was culpable of the defendant to take. To answer whether a particular plaintiff and a particular harm are within the scope of a defendant's duty is to ask whether this plaintiff's harm is within the risk that made the defendant negligent.

Bingham proposed a strong version of this fully relational view of negligence. That is, unlike Bohlen, Bingham saw an HWR analysis as fully supplanting the proximate cause enquiry. According to Bingham, proximate-cause language only produces 'a great deal of confusion'.[21] The question is whether the defendant breached his duty, and this question is to be framed in terms of whether 'the specific consequence comes within the limits of defendant's responsibility for his wrong'.[22] To answer such a question, 'we have to deal with no question of cause or consequences'.[23]

Bingham's fully relational version of an HWR test was endorsed by Leon Green in 1923,[24] Warren Seavey shortly thereafter, and, eventually, Francis Bohlen[25] when he became Reporter for the American Law Institute's *Restatement of the Law of Torts*. Bohlen had drafted a section of the *Restatement* adopting Bingham's expansion of Bohlen's earlier views, and Justice Benjamin Cardozo joined Bohlen, Green, and Seavey for discussion of this draft in 1926 in New York.[26] (Cardozo, Green, and Seavey were Advisors to Bohlen as Reporter for the *Restatement of the Law of Torts*.)

Such background facts make very clear what Cardozo was up to in his majority opinion in *Palsgraf v. Long Island RR* in 1928.[27] Cardozo was attempting to write Bingham's strong version of a fully relational view of HWR into law. Unfortunately for Cardozo's purposes, the facts of *Palsgraf* (as Cardozo saw them) only allowed a partially relational view to emerge as the holding of the case. In that case, the defendant's employee negligently assisted a passenger to board a moving train. Mrs Palsgraf, the plaintiff, was standing so far down the platform that it was highly unlikely that the employee's negligence would cause her any harm. The facts allowed Cardozo to write Bingham's first duty question into law: to recover, Mrs Palsgraf had to show that she was within the class of persons foreseeably injured by the defendant's negligence. Negligence, Cardozo intoned, was at least person-relative. In Cardozo's famous words, 'The risk reasonably to

---

[21] Bingham, 'Suggestions (Part 1)', 25.   [22] Ibid.   [23] Ibid.

[24] Leon Green, 'Are negligence and "proximate cause" determinable by the same test?', Texas Law Review 1 (1923), 243–60, 423–45.

[25] Bohlen's early views were not those of a fully relational HWR. See his once very influential article 'The probable or the natural consequences as the test of liablity in negligence (Parts 1 and 2)'. As Prosser tells the tale, Bohlen became convinced by the mid-1920s that the risk-duty approach of a fully relational HWR was preferable to the alternative proximate cause approach to these issues: William Prosser, 'Palsgraf revisited', Michigan Law Review 52 (1953), 4.

[26] See Robert Keeton, 'A Palsgraf anecdote', Texas Law Review 56 (1978), 513–18.

[27] *Palsgraf v. Long Island RR*, 162 NE 99 (NY, 1928).

be perceived defines the duty to be obeyed, and risk imports relation; it is risk to another or to others within the range of apprehension.'[28]

In *dicta*, Cardozo sought to write the rest of an HWR analysis into law as well. Thus, he opined:

There is room for argument that a distinction is to be drawn according to the diversity of interests invaded by the act, as where conduct negligent in that it threatens an insignificant invasion of an interest in property results in an unforeseeable invasion of an interest of another order, as eg, one of bodily security.[29]

This is Cardozo anticipating the second of Bingham's two duty questions. Where the plaintiff is owed some duty (because the risk to her is one of the risks that makes a defendant negligent), there remains Bingham's second question about the scope of that duty, viz was the harm that happened of a type the risk of which made defendant negligent?

And if a fully relational HWR test were in place, Cardozo could also adopt the strong version of it that supplants entirely the proximate cause question. As he says, 'The law of causation, remote or proximate, is thus foreign to the case before us. . . . We may assume, without deciding, that negligence, not at large or in the abstract, but in relation to the plaintiff, would entail liability for any and all consequences, however novel or extraordinary.'[30]

Cardozo's fully relational HWR analysis found immediate acceptance in the *Restatement of the Law of Torts*, section 281(b) (which is hardly a surprise given the influence that Bohlen's draft of that section had on Cardozo's *Palsgraf* opinion). Section 281(b) adopted not only the holding of *Palsgraf* but also its *dicta*: 'The actor is liable for an invasion of an interest of another, if . . . (b) the conduct of the actor is negligent with respect to such interest.'[31] As the Comments make plain,[32] this abbreviated language was meant to capture both the risk-to-the-class-of-persons question and the risk-of-the-type-of-harm question (although the latter question is further subdivided between types of harm and types of interests harmed). With regard to the latter question, the Comments gave what was to be an often-cited example of an HWR analysis: If defendant negligently gives a loaded revolver to a youngster to carry, and the youngster drops it, both crushing the foot of B, a bystander, and firing the revolver so as to wound A, defendant is liable to A, but not to B.[33] Only A's harm is within the risk that made it negligent to entrust the revolver to the youth; the risk of injuring someone by crushing is too slight to make the act negligent.

---

[28] *Palsgraf*, 162 NE at 100 (citing Warren Seavey, 'Negligence, subjective or objective', Harvard Law Review 41 (1927), 6.
[29] Ibid, 101.   [30] Ibid, 101.
[31] *Restatement of the Law on Torts: Negligence*, 2 (1934), 734.   [32] Ibid, 735–8.
[33] Ibid, 736.

As Warren Seavey noted in his well-known retrospective on Cardozo and the law of torts,[34] the *Restatement* did not adopt a strong HWR test. Rather, it merely confused things (in Seavey's description) by still requiring a finding of 'legal cause' in addition to asking HWR questions,[35] and it pretty much threw in the kitchen sink in its sections on legal cause.[36] (This, of course, was consistent with Bohlen's endorsement 33 years earlier of only the weak version of HWR.[37])

The American Law Institute retrenched even further in the version of the HWR analysis that emerged in the *Restatement (Second) of the Law of Torts* in 1965.[38] Like the first *Restatement*, the current section 281(b) rejects a strong version of the HWR analysis, but unlike the first *Restatement*, section 281(b) now only requires a partly relational HWR analysis.[39] It adopts, in other words, the holding, but not the dicta, of *Palsgraf*, so that the plaintiff must be within the class the risk to whom made the defendant's action negligent, but the harms caused to the plaintiff by the defendant need not be among those that prompt the court to find him negligent.

Here American tort law has rested, roughly in the position outlined by Bohlen 100 years ago.[40] The older chorus of scholars called for a strong version of a fully relational HWR test, starting with Seavey and continuing on with Fleming James, Roger Parry, Wayne Thode, and others.[41] Given the only partial endorsement of *Palsgraf* by the *Restatement (Second)* and by the case law, however, these proposals are more in the way of normative recommendations than restatements of the law. The one area of tort law in which this is not true is the area in which an HWR analysis started, namely, in cases in which criminal statutes are used to set the standard of care. Here the fully relational, strong version of an HWR analysis dominates. Here courts still ask both of Bingham's questions, about harms risked as well as about persons risked. Here there is no proximate cause inquiry to pursue once a court has decided the HWR questions, for the legislature is held to have determined that there is proximate causation as a matter of law if the harm that occurs is within the risk that motivated the enactment of the statute.

Current tort theorists seem content with the *Restatement (Second)*'s acceptance of only a partially relational, weak version of HWR. In a recent symposium on the late Gary Schwartz's discussion draft of *Restatement (Third) of Torts: General*

---

[34] Seavey, 'Mr Justice Cardozo'.
[35] *Restatement of the Law of Torts: Negligence*, 2 (1934), § 281(c).   [36] Ibid, §§ 430–62.
[37] Bohlen, 'Probable or natural consequences (Parts 1 and 2)'.
[38] *Restatement (Second) of the Law of Torts* (1965), § 281(b).
[39] Since William Prosser was the Reporter for the *Restatement (Second) of the Law of Torts* this is not surprising. Prosser claimed to be unable to find any case support for Cardozo's *dictum* in *Palsgraf*: William Prosser, *Torts* (4th edn, St Paul: West Publishing Co, 1971), 259. Yet Prosser was not looking in the right places, for he did not see that Cardozo was simply adverting to a fully relational harm within the risk test.
[40] Bohlen, 'Probable or Natural Consequences (Parts 1, 2)'.
[41] See n 9, above. See also Henry Foster et al, 'The risk theory and proximate cause: A comparative study', Nebraska Law Review 32 (1952), 72–102.

principles,[42] such contemporary torts scholars as Benjamin Zipursky,[43] John Goldberg,[44] Ernest Weinrib,[45] Robert Rabin,[46] David Owen,[47] Patrick Kelley,[48] and Richard Wright[49] unanimously criticize the proposed *Restatement (Third)* for its seeming overruling of *Palsgraf*'s holding. Although none of such scholars (save perhaps Richard Wright and Patrick Kelley) plumps for the fully relational, strong version of HWR that moved two earlier generations of torts scholars,[50] all defend at least the partially relational, weak version of HWR that constitutes the *Palsgraf* holding.

Rather remarkably, the current doctrinal home for any *general*, strong, fully relational HWR test is in American criminal law. In 1962, the American Law Institute adopted section 2.03 of its proposed Model Penal Code. This section is the exclusive section defining proximate causation in the Code, and it replaces a proximate cause analysis with an HWR analysis. The Model Penal Code, section 2.03(1) provides that 'conduct is a cause of a result when: (a) it is an antecedent but for which the result in question would not have occurred; and (b) the relationship between the conduct and result satisfies any additional causal requirements of the Code'. The only other 'additional causal requirements' are those of the succeeding subsections of section 2.03, all of which (with certain qualifications that we shall examine later) are framed in terms of culpability requirements, not proximate cause requirements. With respect to negligence, section 2.03(3) provides that 'when . . . negligently causing a particular result is an element of the offense, the element is established if the actual result is not within the risk of which the actor . . . should be aware'. Section 2.03 has been adopted in about a dozen of the American state criminal codes, but the cases decided under it give room to doubt how many judges and scholars really

---

[42] *Restatement (Third) of Torts: General Principles* (Discussion Draft, 5 April 1999).

[43] Benjamin Zipursky, 'Rights, wrongs, and recourse in the law of torts', Vanderbilt Law Review 51 (1998), 1–100.

[44] John Goldberg and Benjamin Zipursky, 'The Restatement (Third) and the place of duty in negligence law', Vanderbilt Law Review 54 (2001), 709–12.

[45] Ernest Weinrib, 'The passing of Palsgraf', Vanderbilt Law Review 54 (2001), 807–11.

[46] Robert Rabin, 'The Duty Concept in Negligence Law: A Comment', Vanderbilt Law Review 54 (2001), 798, n 50.

[47] David Owen, 'Duty rules', Vanderbilt Law Review 54 (2001), 778.

[48] Patrick Kelley, 'Restating duty, breach and proximate cause in negligence law', Vanderbilt Law Review 54 (2001), 1061–2.

[49] Richard Wright, 'Once more into the bramble bush: Duty, causal contribution, and the extent of legal responsibility', Vanderbilt Law Review 54 (2001), 1092–6.

[50] By my lights, the first generation of HWR theorists holding the fully relational and strong version of HWR consisted of Green, Bingham, Seavey, and Cardozo. The second generation consisted of Glanville Williams, Robert Keeton, Fleming James and Roger Parry. Of the present generation of torts theorists represented above (see nn 46–52 above), only Patrick Kelley could clearly be classified as a strong, fully relational HWR theorist. See Patrick Kelley, 'Proximate cause in negligence law: History, theory and the present darkness', Washington University Law Quarterly, 69 (1991), 49–105. I would also classify Richard Wright as a strong, fully relational HWR theorist—even though that classification requires one to overcome Wright's own protestations that his aspect-causation theory is no kind of HWR analysis.

understand the HWR test that the Code adopts. Meir Dan-Cohen, for example, discusses the Model Penal Code test in his encyclopedia article on causation in criminal law and treats the Code as if it uses a 'justly attachable cause' test rather than a fully relational HWR test.[51]

It remains to be seen whether the American Law Institute will eventually move its version of proximate cause in tort law closer to its version of proximate cause in criminal law. The most recent draft of *Restatement (Third) of the Law of Torts* unqualifiedly adopts the fully relational, strong version of the HWR analysis.[52] The draft thus goes further towards adopting Cardozo's full view (holding and *dicta*) in *Palsgraf* than did even the first *Restatement* in tort law that Cardozo so directly influenced. As of the date of this book's preparation, the full membership of the Institute is not scheduled to vote on these provisions until the entire *Restatement (Third)* is completed.

III. The Historical Argument for the Harm-within-the-Risk Test Based on the Concept of Negligence as Undue Risk

The early proponents of the HWR test certainly sought to justify the test on normative grounds, roughly those of Baron Pollack earlier quoted: in torts, liability must be limited, and what better limit to liability but the extent of the risk that is the ground of that liability? This normative argument shall be examined in Chapter 9. But early HWR analysts also thought the test to be justified on conceptual grounds, namely, that if one understands the concept of negligence, one is driven to adopt an HWR test. It is this historically important argument that we shall here examine, because to do so will help sharpen just what the relational view of negligence amounts to.

In his *Palsgraf* exposition of an HWR test of duty, Cardozo appears to have believed that an HWR analysis is as conceptually necessary as it was normatively desirable. It is this claim of conceptually necessity that is my focus here. As Cardozo opined:

Negligence, like risk, is a term of relation. Negligence in the abstract, apart from things related, is not a tort, if indeed it is understandable at all. Negligence is not a tort unless it

---

[51] Meir Dan-Cohen, 'Causation', in Sanford Kadish (ed), *Encyclopedia of Crime and Justice* 1 (New York: Macmillan, 1983), 162. For a similar confusion in the case law see, eg, *People v. Acosta*, 284 Cal Rptr 117, 126 n 19 (1991). What misleads courts and commentators here is the language of the Model Penal Code providing for no liability in cases where the harm caused is an instance of the type of harm the risk of which made the actor negligent yet the harm is intuitively regarded as 'too remote or accidental in its occurrence to have a [just] bearing on the actor's liability...'. Model Penal Code, § 2.03(3)(b). As I discuss Chapter 10, below, this qualifying language is not to be taken as a stand-alone test of proximate causation but is rather an invitation to courts to qualify the HWR test when confronted with cases of intervening causes or spatio-temporal remoteness.

[52] *Restatement of the Law of Torts (Third)*, tentative draft No 3 (Philadelphia: American Law Institute, 2003) 29.

results in the commission of a wrong, and the commission of a wrong imports the violation of a right.... But [such rights are] protected, not against all forms of interference or aggression, but only against some.... [One] must show that the act as to him had possibilities of danger so many and apparent as to entitle him to be protected against the doing of it though the harm was unintended.... The victim... sues for breach of duty owing to himself.[53]

If we summarize Cardozo's chain of inferences, it goes like this: negligence *implies* (in the sense of presupposes) wrongdoing; wrongdoing *implies* a rights-violation; a rights-violation occurs only when the rights-holder is unreasonably risked, not when the rights-holder is caused harm. This latter is true because a victim's rights (with respect to non-intentional interference) are rights against being placed at risk of harm. A victim whose rights are not violated has not suffered a wrong that entitles him to compensation. This, because only those who are themselves wronged (by having their rights violated) are the beneficiaries of the wrongdoer's duty to correct the injustice his actions have produced.

We should separate two distinct strands of Cardozo's argument. One is what might be called the object-of-the-duty strand; the other, the relational strand. With regard to the object-of-the-duty strand, Cardozo's insight is that the concepts of wrongdoing, rights-violation, and duty-violation all are ambiguous between two views of their objects. One view is that our rights are rights against being *caused* harms of certain kinds; the correlative duties of others are thus duties not to *cause* such harms, and wrongdoing consists of such (rights-violating and duty-violating) *causings* of harms. The second view is that our rights are rights against having others *intend or risk* harms of certain kinds; the correlative duties of others are thus duties not to *intend or risk* such harms, and wrongdoing consists in forming intentions or creating risks of such harms. Having isolated such an ambiguity, Cardozo then plumps for the second view with respect to negligent wrongdoing. That is, whatever may be the case for intentional wrongdoing (which Cardozo puts aside), in the case of negligence, the wrong is not the causing of harm, but, rather, the risking of harm. Our duties are not with regard to harms caused, but with regard to harms risked.

Cardozo completes his chain of inferences with what I will call the relational strand of the argument. The relational strand asserts that wrongs are always wrongs to somebody, that duties are always duties to some particular person(s), that duties and wrongs (duty-violations) are owed or done only to those who hold the correlative rights—in a phrase, that 'negligence in the air, so to speak, will not do'.

The two strands together produce Cardozo's intended conclusion: if duties are owed to particular people and if those people are those risked harm rather than those caused harm, then only those who are within the orbit of unreasonably imposed risk can sue for negligently imposed injury. I shall examine these two strands separately.

---

[53] *Palsgraf*, 162 NE at 101.

A. The object of duty argument

Andrews, in dissent, disputes the object-of-the-duty strand of Cardozo's argument. Conceding (at least *arguendo*) the second point we shall discuss shortly—that negligence 'does involve a relationship between man and his fellows'[54]—Andrews argues that the relevant relationship is 'not merely a relationship between man and those whom he might reasonably expect his act would injure'.[55] Rather, Andrews plumps for the first view: rights, duties, and wrongs presuppose rather 'a relationship between him and those whom he does in fact injure'.[56]

It is doubtful that either Cardozo or Andrews were aware of the longstanding debate in moral philosophy on precisely this question.[57] About the categorical duties of morality, there is a long-standing debate concerning their proper objects: are we categorically obligated not to *kill* (ie, cause death)? Or are we categorically obligated not to intend to kill or to risk killing? More generally, are our moral duties not to cause harm of certain kinds (described by causally complex action verbs like 'killing')? Or are we obligated not to intend or risk such harms? Are our moral wrongs complete only when we cause harm, because that is when we violate our moral duties? Or are our moral wrongs complete when we form intentions to harm others or when we do actions intending or risking such harms?

One of the conclusions of Chapter 3 was that the objects of our moral duties are causings and not either intendings or riskings.[58] This conclusion is largely supported by showing how the categorical force of moral duties cannot plausibly be accommodated by the alternative views. The way to test whether we regard a norm as having categorical force is to see whether it is plausible that good enough consequences can justify a violation of the norm. Consequential justifications seem very plausible for intending and for risking in a way that they do not for actual causings of harm. We can justify risking another's death (by building highrise buildings or setting higher speed limits, for example) in a way that we cannot justify intentionally causing it. Therefore, it seems implausible that the categorical norm against killing prohibits risking death instead of causing death.

To the extent that *legal* rights, duties, and wrongs are simply moral rights, duties, and wrongs written down in appropriate legal texts, legal duties will share the categorical force of moral duties. Leo Katz has argued persuasively that the prohibitions of the criminal law (at least for *malum in se* crimes) track the categorical obligations of morality in this way.[59] But, of course, the criminal law

---

[54] *Palsgraf*, 162 NE at 102.   [55] Ibid.   [56] Ibid.
[57] See the full treatment of this debate in Heidi Hurd, 'What in the world is wrong?', Journal of Contemporary Legal Issues 6 (1994), 157–216. This was of course also the subject of Chapter 3, above.
[58] See also Hurd, 'What in the world is wrong?'.
[59] Leo Katz, *Ill-Gotten Gains* (Chicago: University of Chicago Press, 1996).

by and large deals with intentional wrongdoing. The central concept of torts, by contrast, is negligent wrongdoing. Cardozo's insight was that the wrongs that are merely negligent do not correspond with the categorical obligations of morality. Actions like that of the defendant's servant in *Palsgraf*—helping a passenger with a package board a moving train—are not wrong in themselves in the way that killing, maiming, hitting, etc, are wrong. Such actions are wrong, Cardozo seems to say, only because, and only when, they *risk* injury to others.

Yet even if Cardozo were right about this difference between negligent wrongdoing and intentional wrongdoing, we still should not concede his conclusion. It is plausible that legal duties like that of the defendant in *Palsgraf* do not correspond with *categorical* moral duties (although they may well correspond to non-categorical, or 'consequentialist', moral duties). Even so, such duties concern themselves with harms caused, not harms risked.

One can grasp this by seeing how Cardozo's views of legal duties, legal rights, and legal wrongdoing have played out in two more recent proposals. One is George Fletcher's view that the legal wrongdoing targeted by tort law is asymmetrical risk-imposition; on such a view, one actor legally wrongs another (violates the victim's rights and his own duties) when he risks that other in a way that the other does not risk him.[60] Our rights, according to Fletcher, are rights not to be risked harms (in excess of the risks we impose on others), and those rights are violated by excessive risking, not by the causing, of harms. The second proposal is that of David Lewis in criminal law.[61] On Lewis' view, we should punish criminals by a 'penal lottery', ie, a device that matches the risk of harm they impose on their victims with an equal risk of equivalent harm being imposed on them. Because the risking of harm to others is the wrong, defendants deserve punishment (on Lewis' view) because of, and in proportion to, such risking; because getting hit with a risk of painful consequences is itself a harm, such criminals are appropriately punished by being forced to participate in a penal lottery, a lottery in which they are exposed to a risk of painful consequences. To Lewis, such criminals are appropriately punished by being exposed to such a risk, irrespective of whether such criminals actually suffer real punishment or not (and irrespective of whether their 'victims' ever suffered any real losses).

Simply to state these proposals is pretty much to refute them. As Charles Fried once confessed, he had not seen the incoherence of his own, once-held, similar views (about risk-pooling) until Fletcher drove it home by making it so concrete.[62] The problem is this: it makes no sense to speak of risks as wrongs, or to

---

[60] George Fletcher, 'Fairness and utility in tort theory', Harvard Law Review 85 (1972), 537–73.

[61] David Lewis, 'The punishment that leaves something to chance', Philosophy and Public Affairs 18 (1989), 53–67.

[62] Charles Fried, 'Right and wrong: Preliminary considerations', Journal of Legal Studies 5 (1976), 177, n 31. Fried's similar idea of 'risk-pooling' may be found in Charles Fried, *An Anatomy of Value* (Cambridge, Mass: Harvard University Press, 1970), Chapter 11.

regard getting 'hit' with a risk as being itself a harm or a punishment. Likewise, it makes no sense to speak of risks being reciprocal or non-reciprocal, or of risks being equal or proportional. These locutions make no sense because they trade illicitly on the ambiguity between objective versus subjective notions of risk.[63] Such notions require an objective idea of risk to make sense, yet all of their plausibility draws on using 'risk' in its subjective sense. Risk in its subjective sense is an epistemic notion, wholly dependant on some particular person's epistemic location. Put another way, what is risky is wholly dependant on what the person making the assessment knows. In a deterministic world, nothing is really risky in this sense. Thus, whether one 'non-reciprocally risks' another, or whether one's risk of punishment 'is equal to' the risk of harm one imposed on another, wholly depends on specifying the epistemic vantage points from which the respective risks are assessed.

Two points follow from this. One is that there is no epistemic vantage point that can make sense of reciprocity or equality of risk. It makes no sense to assess the plaintiff-victim's risk-impositions from the defendant's epistemic situation, but neither does it make sense to assess the defendant's risk-imposition from the plaintiff-victim's epistemic situation. We could assess each from their respective epistemic situations, but then we would be comparing apples to oranges when assessing reciprocity/equality of risk imposition. Finally, we could posit an idealized epistemic situation from which to measure both risk-impositions, but what would be the normative relevance of that if such situations were not that of either victim or injurer?

Second, and more fundamentally, to see that risk (in its subjective probability interpretation) is an epistemic notion is to see its ineligibility to serve as the touchstone of wrongdoing, duty-violation, or rights-violation. Epistemic failure by persons is the locus of their culpability, not of their wrongdoing. Since to 'hit another with a risk' is literally to hit the other with nothing at all, we cannot regard risks as harms or risking as wrongdoing. There is blame to unreasonable risk-taking, but it is the blame of being culpable, not the blame of rights-violation or wrongdoing.

The result is that the law cannot make risking into a violation of some victim's rights. Our legal rights are not rights against being hit by some risk; they are rights against actually being caused harm. They are rights only against risks that materialize, in other words. It is true that criminal law could punish risk-taking alone (although it typically does not). If it were to do so, it would not be punishing a moral wrong—ie, a violation of the defendant's duty or a violation of some victim's rights. Rather, such *inchoate* liability (ie, liability in the absence of actual wrongdoing) would be punishing culpability alone. It is also true that we do both punish and impose duties of compensation for *apprehended* risk, such

---

[63] We shall explore subjective versus objective interpretations of probability briefly in Chapter 19, below.

as assault. But a risk that is apprehended by its victim is itself a kind of harm (for fear and apprehension impede upon life projects). To say this, however, is not to treat the risk itself as a harm or its imposition as a wrong.

The upshot is that there is no sustainable notion of risk as a kind of wrong, not in morality and not in law, even if law were to diverge from its moral base. Perhaps, however, we can reconstruct the Bingham–Cardozo argument so as to wean it of any dependence on an illicit notion of risk. Perhaps the argument can be made using an avowedly epistemic notion of risk. Such an argument starts with Bingham's thought that legal 'rights and duties are always concrete'.[64] Bingham was here echoing the view of Holmes[65] and John Chipman Gray,[66] to the effect that law properly so-called consists of those singular propositions that decide concrete cases. Singular propositions of law are those that assign legal relations to particular people in particular situations. 'The Long Island Railroad owed Mrs Palsgraf a duty not to assist another passenger onto a moving train' and 'The Long Island Railroad owed Mrs Palsgraf no duty not to assist another passenger onto a moving train' would both be examples of singular propositions of law, propositions decisive of *Palsgraf* one way or the other.

One way that Bingham and Cardozo could have argued from here—although there is no evidence that they did—was to assume: (1) that all concrete legal duties must exist at the time that the actor (whose duties they are) committed the act that violated (or conformed to) those duties; and (2) that such concrete legal duties must not only have existed, but must also have been knowable by the actor as he acted, otherwise he cannot fairly be held liable for violating them. With these assumptions, Bingham and Cardozo could then have argued that only risk-based abstract legal duties could have existed or could have been knowable by the Long Island Railroad's employee when he assisted the fireworks-carrying passenger onto the moving train. Because the action of assisting such a passenger is not wrong in itself, the action could only be wrong, and the defendant could only have known that the action is wrong, if there existed a general risk-oriented duty, viz a duty not to unreasonably *risk* harm.

The duty not to *cause* Mrs Palsgraf injury by assisting another passenger, by contrast, either did not exist at all at the time the Railroad's servant acted or, if such a duty existed, the Railroad's servant could not have known he had violated that duty until he had actually caused Mrs Palsgraf injury. On Andrews' view that our duties are not to cause injuries to others, it is a future fact that either brings the concrete duty into existence or at least makes the concrete duty knowable; and this cannot be squared with assumptions (1) and (2) above. Therefore, the abstract legal duty cannot be cause-based, but, rather, must be risk-based.

---

[64] Bingham, 'Suggestions (Pt 1)', 17.

[65] Oliver Wendell Holmes, 'The path of the law', Harvard Law Review 10 (1897), 457–78.

[66] John Chipman Gray, *The Nature and Sources of Law* (New York: Columbia University Press, 1909).

The problem for this reconstructed argument does not lie in its assumptions, but, instead, in their supposed implications. We can assume with Bingham that *singular* legal propositions (about *concrete* legal duties) are needed to decide particular cases. We can further assume that such duties must exist at the time the actor acted, so that new law is not being retroactively applied to actors.[67] Such assumptions do not rule out Andrews' view of legal duty. Even though it is a future effect (Mrs Palsgraf's injury) that makes the Railroad's action wrong, that such an effect would be caused by the Railroad's action was a present fact at the time the Railroad acted. It was wrong—a violation of existing legal duty—for the Railroad's servant to assist the passenger, even though the event that made it wrong did not occur until some time after the servant's action. Unless one adopts Aristotle's peculiar view that facts about future events like sea fights are not real facts,[68] there is no problem in conceiving of legal duties in these terms. Indeed, the very view of legal duty that Bingham adopts—that of Holmes—presupposes that Aristotle was wrong about the reality of future facts.[69]

We can also assume (at least for negligence cases)[70] that concrete legal duties must not only exist but be knowable to those whose duties they are when they act. An abstract legal duty not to cause harm can generate notice of the concrete legal duty not to assist the other passenger as easily as can an abstract legal duty not to risk harm; this, because the calculation (from abstract to concrete duty) is the same. It is of course the risk that gives the notice, but it is a risk of *causing harm*. If the abstract legal duty is framed in terms of causing harm, one who is applying that abstract duty to a concrete action like assisting a passenger of course has to assess the likelihood that his act will, in the future, cause harm. But so does one applying an abstract legal duty not to risk the causing of harm. The calculations required of the non-negligent actor are identical, and the supposed advantages in knowability of the risk-based view are illusory.

B. The relational argument

Let us now turn to the other strand of Cardozo's argument, what I earlier called the relational strand. This is the aspect of the argument where Cardozo seeks to show that the objects of legal duties are not just risks as such, but risks *of* certain sorts of harms *to* particular classes of people. This strand, too, Andrews denies in

---

[67] The existence of legal duties and legal rights at the time an actor acts is a formal postulate of our practice of law. See Ronald Dworkin, *Taking Rights Seriously* (Cambridge, Mass: Harvard University Press, 1978), Chapters 2–4.

[68] Aristotle, 'On Interpretation', *Aristotle's Categories and De Interpretatione, translated with Notes*, trans John Lloyd Ackrill (Oxford: Clarendon Press 1962), 43.

[69] As is well known, Holmes sought to reduce legal duty to predictions of judicial behavior. Such predictive theory of law would make the present existence of all legal duties depend on future facts.

[70] The parenthetical restriction to negligence cases, because in other cases one might well think that legal duties exist even though only superhuman judges could know that they exist. These are 'hard cases' of complex law.

his dissent in *Palsgraf*: 'Every one owes to the world at large the duty of refraining from those acts that may unreasonably threaten the safety of others.'[71] Since, on Andrews' view, a duty is owed to every other person in the world, when one such person is injured, 'her claim is for a breach of duty to herself'.[72]

Cardozo's argument against Andrews here seems wholly dependent on the first strand of argument rejected above. Namely, because Cardozo thought that the object of the duty is risking, not causing, he also thought that the duty has to be relational: risks are risks *of* certain types of harm *to* certain people. This corollary he derived because risk is an object-taking concept. Risk as such is incomplete, just as intention by itself is incomplete. It makes no sense to say 'I intend' or 'I risk'. Intentions and risks both take objects in the sense that one intends *that* a certain harm be caused to someone and one risks *that* a certain harm will befall someone. In Cardozo's abbreviated epigram, 'Risk imports relation'.[73]

If we reject the first strand of Cardozo's argument, as we did above, that will be to reject his basis for sustaining the relational strand. But perhaps we can find another basis for the relational strand of the argument, one that does not depend on the view that risks are wrongs. If we repair to Cardozo's intellectual antecedent here—Joseph Bingham's article that preceded *Palsgraf* by over 20 years[74]—we can discern a seemingly independent basis for the relational view.

Bingham prefaced his detailed exposition of a fully relational HWR test with this discursus on legal rights and duties generally:

Rights and duties are always concrete. A right presupposes possible opposition. A duty is owed to some person or persons. Therefore, before one or the other is defined completely, we must know against whom the right exists or to whom the duty is owed, and what concrete 'thing' is demanded. These are elementary facts of the greatest importance to a proper comprehension of our common law system of jurisprudence.[75]

Notice that Bingham is not discussing legal rights and duties in negligence, nor does he restrict his thesis even to tort law more generally. Rather, he makes a set of perfectly general points about all legal rights and duties. It is this very general relational view of rights and duties that allows him to slip so easily to the more particularly relational view of the duties of negligence.

It is a curious bit of intellectual history why Bingham did not acknowledge the influence of his colleague on the Stanford faculty of 1909, Wesley Hohfeld, for Hohfeld's then-developing views are unmistakable in Bingham's views about legal duties just quoted. Hohfeld believed: that the content of legal rights proper (what he came to call 'claim-rights') are never actions of the right-holder, but, rather, the actions of others; that rights proper are fully correlative with duties on the part of others, and vice versa; that legal relations such as rights and duties are always two-person affairs, so that a complete description of a right requires one to

---

[71] *Palsgraf*, 162 NE at 103.   [72] Ibid.   [73] Ibid, 100.
[74] Bingham, 'Suggestions (Pt 1)'.   [75] Ibid, 17.

specify not only the action one has a right to and who holds the right, but also against whom one holds the right; that a complete description of a duty requires one to specify not only the action there is a duty to do and who holds the duty, but also to whom the duty is owed; that any so called 'right against the world', like a right *in rem*, is in reality a collection of discrete rights against discrete people of similar content; that more complex legal relations like the rights of ownership are in reality bundles of more discrete rights.[76]

Hohfeld's reasons for adopting the two-person view of legal duties are complex; they have to do with the elegant system of inferences made possible if we conceptualize legal relations in this way. It is tied up with: Hohfeld's insights about the content of claim-rights (which are always the actions of others) versus the content of liberty-rights (which are always actions of the right-holder); the correlativity of claim-rights and duties and the correlativity of liberty-rights and the absence of claim-rights; and the need always to be able to translate abstract legal rights and duties into the concrete legal rights and duties that decide actual cases.

Hohfeld's scheme is as well known in moral philosophy as in law, for the scheme seems as accurate of moral rights and duties as of their legal analogues. This should not be surprising for those of us who view legal rights and duties to be kinds of moral rights and duties. Indeed, I have elsewhere argued that there are substantively moral reasons to adopt Hohfeld's two-person view of moral rights and duties.[77]

Bingham was thus on quite defensible ground in thinking that *all* legal duties are relational in Hohfeld's sense: a duty is always a duty to some particular person, the one who holds the correlative right. Yet this Hohfeldian view of legal duties generally is insufficient to generate Bingham's (and Cardozo's) conclusion that the content of our duties to others is with respect to *risking* them. As Andrews saw clearly in dissent in *Palsgraf*,[78] one can fully adopt Hohfeld's view that all duties are owed to particular people and still conclude that the Long Island Railroad owed just such a duty to Mrs Palsgraf, ie a duty not to cause harm to her. It was a 'multital duty' (Hohfeld's term) in that a duty of similar content was owed by the Railroad to every person in the world; but such a duty was also owed to Mrs Palsgraf personally. It is a mistake to equate the HWR approach with a relational view of negligence. HWR is one way negligence may

---

[76] Wesley Hohfeld, 'Some fundamental legal conceptions as applied in judicial reasoning', Yale Law Journal 23 (1913), 16–59; Wesley Hohfeld, 'Fundamental legal conceptions as applied in judicial reasoning', Yale Law Journal 26 (1917), 710–70. These essays were collected in Wesley Hohfeld, *Fundamental Legal Conceptions* (New Haven: Yale University Press, 1919).

[77] In Michael S Moore, *Act and Crime: The implications of the philosohy of action for the criminal law* (Oxford: Oxford University Press, 1993), 356–65, I argue that the counting-of-moral-wrongs problem (involved in double-jeopardy determinations in criminal law) is solved by the Hohfeldian view of duties as two-person relational.

[78] *Palsgraf*, 162 NE at 102–3.

be relational, but it is not the only way. Andrews' cause-based view of duty is as relational to persons and to harms as Cardozo's risk-based view of duty.

What this shows is that it was a misnomer to label HWR the relational view of negligence. One can appreciate the rhetorical gains to proponents of HWR by this labeling—for negligence *is* necessarily relational, and it then can seem that HWR is also conceptually necessary to negligence. Once this mislabeling is eliminated, one can see that HWR has to be argued for on normative grounds. That sort of argument we shall examine in Chapter 9. For now, it is worth emphasizing this final preliminary clarification of HWR: it is not *the* relational view of negligence; it is only one relational view among others, the one relating the defendant's negligent act to the plaintiff's harm by relations of risk rather than by relations of cause.

8

Conceptual Problems in Applying the Harm-within-the-Risk Test to Crimes/Torts of Negligence

In this and the succeeding chapter I shall focus on the harm-within-the-risk (HWR) test as it applies to torts or crimes having negligence as their *mens rea*. The limited focus of these two chapters is motivated by the thought that negligence is special in this context, in two ways. First, negligence does not involve a state of mind, as does intention, foresight, or recklessness. Negligence is simply unreasonable behavior. To be sure, a defendant has to have certain capacities (and a fair opportunity to use them) to be blamable for negligence, but such capacities are not particular states of mind as are involved in the law's requirements of intention and belief. This means that for crimes/torts of negligence, there is no actual psychological state whose content can then be used to ask whether the act done is 'within the risk' (or within the foresight, or intent, as the case may be). This makes HWR applications to negligence much more problematic conceptually, as we shall see in this chapter.

Second, negligence in the law of both crimes and torts is the lowest step in the graduations of culpability used in both fields of law. This difference makes a difference to the normative justifiability of the HWR analysis, as we shall see in Chapter 9. Both of these reasons thus justify the focus of these two chapters on applications of the test to crimes and torts of negligence. Only in Chapter 10 shall I return to criticisms applicable to all uses of the HWR analysis.

I. Negligence as Unreasonable Risk Imposition

We should start with the notion of negligence in general. We can then ask more particularly about the viability of an HWR test as part of the negligence analysis. Anglo-American torts casebooks and treatises, and the law professors who teach from them, regularly give not one but two definitions of negligence.[1] One is in

---

[1] See, eg, Richard Epstein, *Cases and Materials on Torts* (6th edn, Boston: Aspen Pub, 1995), Chapter 3.

terms of a 'calculus of risk', by which negligent actions are defined as those whose justifications are outweighed by the harms that they risk. The other is in terms of an epistemic idealization, by which negligent actions are defined as those that would not be done by a 'reasonable person'. A rational legal system, of course, would not simultaneously embrace two different notions of negligence capable of generating two different results in any given case, so the assumption is made that these two definitions are synonymous (or at least extensionally equivalent in the cases they decide).

Although the calculus of risk formulation is my principal focus in this chapter, it is worth pausing to ask why tort and criminal law contains the alternative conceptualization of negligence in terms of a hypothetical reasonable person. One possibility is that the reasonable-person test is merely a heuristic that helps some fact-finders do better in their calculations of risk than they would otherwise do. Some people claim to be helped in their ability to reach justified conclusions by asking what some epistemically idealized person would do or think. Adam Smith imagined an 'ideal observer' to be consulted for truth in ethical matters,[2] and John Rawls closer to our own times imagined a rational contractor in an 'original position' for the same purpose.[3] Similarly, Plowden recommended to judges that they imagine themselves in the shoes of an ideal legislator when interpreting statutes,[4] and Richard Posner has recently echoed Plowden in this regard.[5] Tort law's reasonable person, on this view, joins these other heuristic devices. Viewed as a mere heuristic, the reasonable-person test does not deviate from the calculus of risk test at all,[6] but rather, it supposedly makes the calculus more tractable by allowing thought experiments about what the fact-finder (who no doubt regards himself as reasonable) would have done had he been in the defendant's situation.

A second explanation for the law's reasonable person conceptualization stems from the fact that risk as it is used in law is commonly thought to be an essentially epistemic notion.[7] For God in a deterministic universe, the thought is,

[2] Adam Smith, *A Theory of Moral Sentiments* (London: Printed for A Millar, and A Kincaid and J Bell, 1759).

[3] John Rawls, A *Theory of Justice* (Cambridge, Mass, Harvard University Press, 1971).

[4] *Eyston v. Studd*, 75 Eng Rep 688 (1574); *Heydon's Case*, 76 Eng Rep 637 (Exch 1584). See generally Warren Lehman, 'How to interpret a difficult statute', Wisconsin Law Review (1979), 489–507.

[5] Richard A. Posner, 'Statutory Interpretation—in the Classroom and in the Courtroom,' University of Chicago Law Review 50 (1983), 800–822.

[6] This is the view taken in a draft of *Restatement (Third) of Torts: General Principles* (Discussion Draft, Apr. 5, 1999).

[7] *See generally* Heidi M. Hurd, 'Correcting Injustice to Corrective Justice,' Notre Dame Law Review 67 (1991), 73, 51–96; Hurd, 'The Deontology of Negligence,' Boston University Law Review 76 (1996), 249–72; Hurd, 'Justifiably Punishing the Justified,' Michigan Law Review 90 (1992), 2203–324.

there are no risks; there are only certainties—that is, 'risks' with a probability of 0 or 1. Indeterministic microphysics to the side, there is on this view no such thing as an objective risk of a particular event occurring,[8] there are only risks to be perceived from certain epistemic vantage points. A risk-based legal standard thus must specify the epistemic vantage point from which a risk is to be assessed. Arguably, the reasonable-person test is tort law's way of specifying this epistemic vantage point. A fact-finder starts with his own information base and inferential abilities to ask what he would have done in a defendant's situation; he then uses the reasonable-person standard to assess just how accurate the defendant's calculus of the risk had to be to be non-negligent. In emergencies, for example, it is often held under Anglo-American law that a defendant is allowed greater leeway in misjudging whether a risk is justified.[9] Likewise for certain characteristics of a defendant that make it more difficult for him to calculate risks (such as youth).[10] Sometimes we use the reasonable-person formulation to adjust the acceptable accuracy of the calculus of risk upwards rather than downwards. One who enters a profession, for example, is held to the higher standard of a reasonable professional. This means that a medical doctor must do *better* in calculating the benefits and risks of various procedures than legal fact-finders could do, even with the benefit of hindsight.[11]

A third explanation for the reasonable-person test of negligence is that it allows for true divergence from the demands of the calculus of risk.[12] On this view, the calculus of risk is too utilitarian (or at least too consequentialist) to be of universal application. On a deontological view of morality, our moral duties and permissions are not measured exclusively by whether they produce cost-justified risks. The reasonable-person test may exist, on this view, to deviate from the strictly consequentialist calculus of risk in two ways: (1) actors may be permitted to do some activities that are not cost-justified under the calculus of risk; and (2) actors may be obligated to refrain from some activities that are cost-justified under the calculus of risk. On this view, the reasonable person may be the (deontologically) moral person, not the one who correctly sums the consequentialist balance of benefits versus risks.

Whatever view one takes of the reasonable-person test of negligence, I intend in this chapter to put it aside. I shall assume, for purposes of this discussion, that the idea of negligence is captured by the calculus of risk, and thus, it shall be on that conceptualization that we shall focus.

---

[8] This view need not deny that there is such a thing as objective probability in the sense of relative frequency, since that notion deals with *types* of events, and does not easily assign probability values to particular events.

[9] *Restatement (Second) of the Law of Torts*, § 296 (Philadelphia: American Law Institute, 1965).

[10] Ibid, § 283A.   [11] Ibid, § 299A.

[12] See Hurd, 'Deontology of negligence', 254–5.

II. The Hand Formula for Measuring Unreasonable Risk

For reasons having little to do with the historical importance of the case or the originality of its insight[13] and more to do with the accidents of converging academic attention, Learned Hand's opinion in *United States v. Carroll Towing*[14] has become the *locus classicus* of the calculus of risk conceptualization of negligence. I shall also defer to academic convention and begin with *Carroll Towing*.

The question Hand addressed in *Carroll Towing* was whether the plaintiff barge-owner had been (contributorily) negligent in not having a bargee aboard his barge. This barge had broken away from the line of barges that the defendant's tug had been towing, had struck a tanker's propeller, and had sunk. Had a bargee been aboard, he probably could have saved the barge. Hand held that the barge owner's duty not to be negligent was:

a function of three variables: (1) the probability that she will break away; (2) the gravity of the resulting injury, if she does; and (3) the burden of adequate precautions . . . to state it in algebraic terms: if the probability be called P; the injury, L; and the burden, B; liability depends upon whether B is less than L multiplied by P: ie, whether B [is less than P x L].[15]

This deceptively simple formula is surely incomplete as a risk-based conception of negligence. The easiest way to see this is to do an eight-fold expansion of the Hand formula into what I shall call the 'expanded Hand formula for negligence'.

A. The burden of adequate precautions

When assessing the burden of having a bargee aboard, Hand seemingly focused only on the out-of-pocket cost to the employer-plaintiff and the cost in liberty to the employee of remaining on a barge. Yet surely the burden of taking that precaution includes as well the benefits of not having a bargee aboard the barge, for those benefits would be lost if the precaution were taken. Those benefits prominently include the absence of harms bargees can cause—sabotage, accidental death or injury to bargees, injury to rescuers of bargees in trouble, accidental injury to barges because of drunken or careless bargees, etc. Not suffering these harms is surely a benefit to be taken into account in assessing how 'burdensome'—ie, desirable—it is to have a bargee aboard.[16] These benefits can also include all the beneficial things a barge owner can do with the wages he would

---

[13] More original was Henry Terry's five-factored calculus of risk laid out in Henry Terry, 'Negligence', Harvard Law Review 29 (1915), 42–3.

[14] 159 F 2d 169 (2d Cir 1947).   [15] *Carroll Towing*, 159 F 2d, at 173.

[16] See, eg, *Cooley v. Pub Serv Co*, 10 A 2d 673 (NH 1940) (in assessing burden of precautions against risk of excessive noise transmitted by telephone lines one must weigh risk of electrocution of others if the precaution is taken). See generally the *Restatement (Third) of Torts: General Principles*, § 4 (Discussion Draft, 5 April 1999), which recognizes that the burden of adequate precautions 'can take a wide variety of forms' including all the 'advantages' gained if the precaution is not taken.

otherwise pay a bargee and all the beneficial things a bargee could do with his time if he were not stuck on a barge all day. The burden of this precaution, in other words, includes its opportunity costs and not just its out-of-pocket costs.

B. The probabilities involved in assessing the burdens of adequate precautions

Focusing on out-of-pocket costs hides a risk calculation inherent in Hand's formula, for the probability of incurring such out-of-pocket costs, such as the labor costs by having a bargee aboard, approaches 1, and this makes it easy to ignore any probabilistic calculation. Yet this is not true of the other items making up the 'burden of adequate precautions'. It is far from certain that a bargee will turn out to be a saboteur, will get killed or injured, will need rescue, will get drunk and himself damage the barge, etc. It is far from certain that a bargee would, in fact, find better employment than as a bargee. These benefits and opportunity costs must surely be discounted by the improbability of their occurrence.[17]

The result is thus doubly a calculus of risk. On the downside, one discounts the gravity of the harm if no bargee is aboard by the improbability that that harm will occur, and on the upside, one discounts the value of the benefits obtained if no bargee is aboard by the improbability of those benefits being achieved. A precaution is negligently foregone only if the discounted value of the harm risked exceeds the discounted value of the justification for taking the risk, viz all the benefits obtainable if the precaution is not taken.

C. All harms risked

Once we expand the upside benefit calculation if a bargee is not aboard, we also should expand the downside detriment calculation if a bargee is not aboard. After all, just as it is the case that many good things have some chance of occurring if a bargee is not aboard, so it is the case that there are many bad things that could occur if a bargee is not aboard. It is a mistake to focus just on the one bad thing that *did* happen in thinking about the downside risks.[18] One risk was that the

---

[17] See *Restatement (Second) of the Law of Torts*, § 292(b).

[18] See, eg, *Marshall v. Nugent*, 222 F 2d 604 (1st Cir 1955). In applying the HWR test: 'one should contemplate a variety of risks ... [Such a] bundle of risks' is what determines negligence. See also Warren Seavey, 'Mr Justice Cardozo and the law of torts', Harvard Law Review 52 (1939), 92–3: '[W]here one shoots a gun in a crowded thoroughfare, it is not merely the risk to the person struck by the bullet which is considered; the risk to the entire group of persons endangered is considered in determining whether the act is negligent.'; Joseph Bingham, 'Some suggestions concerning "legal cause" at common law', Columbia Law Review 9 (1909), 153: 'Conduct may be wrongful in more than one aspect and as regards the rights of more than one person.'; W Page Keeton et al, *Prosser and Keeton on Torts* (5th edn, St Paul: West Publishing Co, 1984), 298: 'the risk of harm itself, when the defendant is found to be negligent, is usually an aggregate risk of many possibilities'; *Restatement (Third) of Torts*, § 4 Comment g.

barge could have been damaged or sunk by going adrift and hitting another ship. But surely many other bad things were risked by the unattended barge: with no bargee aboard to help lookout for crossing traffic and to cut the tow line if need be, there could have been a collision with another moving ship; life could have been lost by a loose barge, or by one not loosed when it needed to be; the barge could have wedged under a wharf, flooding upstream users; etc. In assessing the reasonableness of not having a bargee aboard, one must include all downside detriments as much as all upside potentials, discounted by their respective risks of non-occurrence.

D. Levels of the precaution

It is, of course, a mistake to think that the decision to take any given precaution is a two-valued decision, viz to have a bargee or not to have a bargee.[19] Hand recognizes as much when he distinguishes full-time bargees, who live aboard the barge, from part-time bargees, who are aboard only during daylight working hours.[20] Full-time bargees doubtless give greater protection against loss of the barge than do part-time bargees; presumably two full-time bargees do even better. The dual calculus of total risks against total benefits if no given precaution is taken surely must be run for each *level* of that precaution, for that precaution is reasonable at certain levels but unreasonable at others.

E. Alternative precautions

Once one sees the *level* of precaution point, one will also see the *kind* of precaution point: surely bargees are not the only means of preventing barges from getting loose, nor are they necessarily the most effective or cheapest means. Television monitors, other automatic sensing devices, more secure lines or cleats, etc, may be more effective than bargees at preventing the range of harms barges cause, or they may be as effective at lesser cost. The non-negligent barge owner thus must run the full calculus of risk not just for every level of the bargee precaution, but also for every level of all other precautionary actions he might alternatively take to lessen the total risks of his activity.[21]

F. Level of activity

Even if one correctly calculates the optimal precautions to take in operating a barge, it is still quite likely that some harm will result from the barge's operation.

---

[19] See Epstein, *Cases and Materials on Torts*, 203, n 3; Kenneth Simon, 'The Hand formula in the Draft Restatement (Third) of Torts: Encompassing fairness as well as efficiency values', Vanderbilt Law Review 54 (2001), 904, n 12.
[20] *Carroll Towing*, 159 F 2d at 173.   [21] *Restatement (Second) of the Law of Torts*, § 292(c).

'Shit happens', as a popular bumper sticker of the 90s had it. A reasonable barge-owner thus will assess the benefits of barging versus these costs, even when the barging is done with an optimal level of precautions against all possible harms. He will do this because at some point, it is possible that it is unreasonable to be engaged in so much barging activity.[22]

G. Kinds of activities

The benefits of barging presumably include all the benefits that derive from local transportation of high bulk items. Potentially these benefits could be obtained, with lesser downside risks, by other kinds of activities: trucks, trains, self-propelled boats, etc. A non-negligent barge owner would also assess the possibility that barging is altogether too dangerous, given the other, less risky ways of achieving the benefits of barging that have developed.[23] He will calculate not just whether he would do well to reduce the level of barging activity in which he is engaged, but whether he ought to go out of the barging business altogether.

H. Information/calculation costs

At some point, a reasonable barge owner will cease calculating items A–G above. That is, he will run the expanded Hand calculation on the upside and downside risks of continuing to run the expanded Hand calculation! He will only calculate as far as this second-order calculation tells him, so that if he fails to optimize somewhere in A–G, his actions may still be reasonable (because it would have been unreasonable to calculate further in order to find the optimal action).[24]

The expanded Hand formula presents a very different picture of negligence than is suggested by Hand's own simplistic algebraic formula. Hand presents negligence as if it were a matter of balancing *a* risk of *a* certain kind of harm (the one that happened) against the cost of taking *a* precaution to eliminate that risk. This is understandable as a matter of litigating any single case. In a typical case, *a*

---

[22] For a contrary assumption about negligence, see Steven Shavell, 'Strict liability versus negligence', Journal of Legal Studies 9 (1980), 1–25. Shavell assumes without argument that 'by definition' negligence does not extend to the level or kind of activity questions and thus favors strict liability for such questions. In this he appears to be joined by Richard Posner: *Ind Harbor Belt RR Co v. Am Cyanamid Co*, 916 F 2d 1174 (7th Cir 1990). Yet one need not flee to strict liability to judge the reasonableness of either kinds or levels of given activities. For activities inherently risky to others but with little social utility to engage in them at all may be adjudged negligent under the expanded Hand formula. See, eg, *Bolton v. Stone* [1951] AC 850 ('If cricket cannot be played on a ground without creating a substantial risk, then it should not be played there *at all.*'); *Restatement (Third) of Torts*, § 4 Comment i.

[23] Just as perhaps one should not be playing cricket at all in *Bolton v. Stone.*

[24] The law's most explicit recognition of this point is in the 'emergency doctrine'. *See Restatement (Second) of the Law of Torts*, § 296. The emergency doctrine is more in the nature of an excuse, not of a justification for not calculating further. *Restatement (Third) of Torts*, § 4 Comment f, contains a more clearly justificatory version of such second-order calculations.

harm has been suffered by *a* plaintiff. This gives the illusion of fixing *a* risk to be considered. In addition, the adversary system tends to produce one precaution upon which parties focus and to litigate whether *it* should have been taken by the defendant.[25]

Yet this heuristic shortcut, understandable in the actual litigation of a negligence case, should not be confused with the nature of negligence itself. On its own terms, Hand's calculus of risk demands expansion in the eight directions indicated. It requires one to weigh the total harms risked versus the total benefits risked if a given precaution is not taken, considered for each level of each kind of precautionary action possible, for all levels and kinds of activities in which the defendant might be engaged. An action is negligent, on this holistic view, 'if its disadvantages exceed its advantages'.[26] This holistic view of negligence makes it challenging to isolate *a* risk that makes a defendant negligent, a seeming prerequisite to finding a given harm to be within or outside of such *a* risk. This I shall explore shortly in this chapter.

The HWR analysis in fact appears to invite two quite damning conceptual challenges. First, once one appreciates that *all* risks created by a defendant count in an assessment of his negligence, it would appear that *any* and *all* harms that materialize from the defendant's conduct are within the category of risks that make such conduct negligent. If this is true, then of course the test fails as a test of anything; for it fails to provide any means of distinguishing harms for which the defendant ought not to be held responsible from harms for which he ought to be liable. I shall refer to this as the 'all-inclusiveness problem'. Second, it would appear that the test suffers from a fatal 'description problem', for how one describes the risk(s) that make(s) the defendant's conduct negligent does all the work to place the harm(s) in question either within or outside of the stated risk(s). In the succeeding sections of Part III, I shall take up these two general conceptual challenges to any attempt to insert an HWR analysis into the prima facie elements of a negligence cause of action (be it at the level of assessing the defendant's duty to the plaintiff, his breach of that duty, or his proximacy to the harm caused to the plaintiff).

III. The All-inclusiveness Problem

The first problem, then, with any HWR inquiry is that it would appear that *all* harms are within the risks that make a defendant's conduct negligent. As we saw a moment ago, *all* risks enter into the calculus that determines the justifiability of a defendant's conduct. If a harm materializes from a defendant's conduct, then

---

[25] Mark Grady so argues in Mark Grady, 'Untaken precautions', Journal of Legal Studies 18 (1989), 139–56.

[26] *Restatement (Third) of Torts*, § 4 Comment k.

necessarily there was some risk of it so doing, and that risk was on the list of risks created by the defendant's conduct, the cumulative total of which make the defendant's conduct unjustified. While the harm in question may not have been among the most likely harms to have materialized from the defendant's conduct, the earlier discussion makes clear that the concept of negligence demands that one include *all* harms risked by the defendant's conduct in the calculus of the benefits and burdens of the defendant's conduct. But if *all* harms, discounted by their probability, are to be included in the calculus of risk, then it would appear that any harm that happens as a result of a defendant's unjustified conduct is within the risks that make the defendant's conduct unjustified. In short, once one understands the concept of negligence as analyzed earlier, one must conclude that an HWR test is impotent to test anything—be it duty, breach, or proximate causation. Properly applied, it yields the conclusion that all defendants are responsible for all harms that they cause to all persons. Inasmuch as its purpose is to sort between harms for which defendants should be held responsible and harms for which they should not be responsible, that purpose is thwarted by its own formulation.

In response to this seemingly quite damning indictment, defenders of HWR have to rebut the idea that *all* risks are considered when judging an action to be negligent. Needed is thus some principled distinction between the risks that go into the calculus of risk of the expanded Hand formula and those that are excluded from that calculus. Below, I consider five possible distinctions.

A. Risks that are individually sufficient for negligence

Advocates of an HWR analysis might be inclined to argue as follows: the calculus of risk should include only risks that are *individually sufficient* to make a defendant's conduct negligent. That is, in assessing the gravity of the harms imposed by a defendant's conduct, discounted by their probability, we should concern ourselves only with harms that individually outweigh, by themselves, the cumulative benefits that accrue from the defendant's conduct (and, therefore, the burden of forgoing the activity or of adopting further precautions). For example, consider the well known case of *Gorris v. Scott*,[27] discussed in the last chapter. Advocates of the HWR analysis might argue that if the discounted value of the loss of livestock due to drowning was, by itself, less than the cost of the pens that would have been required to prevent such drownings, then the risk of the livestock drowning did not make it negligent on the part of the shipowner to refuse to pen the sheep. The fact that the shipowner should have penned the sheep as a means of preventing disease—because the discounted value of the loss of livestock due to disease was, by itself, *greater* than the cost of the pens—is neither here nor there on this view. The spread of disease among the sheep was a

---

[27] *Gorris v. Scott*, 9 LR-Ex 125 (1874).

risk sufficient to declare the shipowner negligent for failing to pen the sheep; their drowning at sea was not. While the sheep would not have drowned had they been penned and while they should have been penned to prevent them from contracting diseases, the shipowner should not be held responsible for their deaths, because the risk of the sheep drowning was insufficient, by itself, to justify the precaution of penning them.

On this view, it is possible that a defendant's conduct may engender numerous risks that are individually sufficient to declare that conduct negligent; hence, there will be multiple harms that, if they materialize, will be within the risks that make it negligent for the defendant to act as he did. But the list of these individually sufficient risks will not be as long as the list of *all* risks created by the defendant's conduct—a list that will include many risks that are not, by themselves, sufficiently grave to declare the precautions taken by the defendant vis-à-vis those risks to be inadequate. On this view, a defendant can properly be held liable for all harms that materialize from risks that are individually sufficient for negligence. And when a defendant's negligence is 'overdetermined' by the fact that there is more than one risk that is sufficiently grave to make the defendant's conduct unjustified, a defendant can properly be held liable for the materialization of more than one type of harm. But, on this account, the HWR analysis will not make him liable for many harms, much less all of the harms, that he causes.

As a means of assessing the plausibility of limiting the calculus of risk to risks that are individually sufficient to declare a defendant negligent, let us consider a second kind of case—a case in which a defendant creates multiple risks, no one of which is sufficient, by itself, to declare the defendant negligent. If we have good reasons to think that a defendant who creates such risks can be negligent, then we have good reasons to believe that the view advanced in this subsection on behalf of the HWR test is indefensible.

Imagine a case in which the risks created by a defendant's conduct are individually necessary and only jointly sufficient for a finding of negligence. No harm risked is, by itself, greater in discounted value than the cost of precautions that would be necessary to avert that harm. But the summed value of all harms risked, discounted by their improbability, exceeds the costs of precautions available to eliminate those risks. Under these circumstances, is it not plausible to say that the defendant is negligent in acting in a manner that imposes these risks, the cumulative value of which exceeds the benefits of his conduct?

Imagine the carpool mother who, at 65 miles an hour, repeatedly diverts her gaze from the highway so as to shuffle through a collection of children's cassette tapes, select one, and pop it in the tape recorder. The increased risk to the children in the back seat is relatively small; the increased risk to other drivers is relatively small; the increased risk to hitchhikers along the highway is relatively small; and the increased risk to animals who might be crossing the road is relatively small. And yet, these small risks, when cumulatively considered, appear to outweigh the burden to her of pulling over long enough to change tapes in complete safety. And had any one of these small risks in fact materialized—had she rear-ended a car that suddenly put on its brakes in front of her during the moment she was searching for the volume control—it would seem entirely plausible to conclude that she was, at the time, driving negligently, even though the particular risk of a rear-end collision was insufficiently high, by itself, to merit the precaution of stopping.

Indeed, in a great number of run-of-the-mill negligence cases, it would seem that the risk that materialized in the harm caused by the defendant was not, itself, a risk sufficient to merit precautions, but was instead a member of a set of risks only jointly sufficient to justify a charge of negligence. *Carroll Towing*[28] is itself a good example. The risk that a barge would break free of a line of barges (being moved through the New York harbor by the defendant's tugboat), and thereby sustain hull damage as a result of striking a tanker's propeller, had to be of reasonably low probability; by itself, such a harm would seemingly not merit the employment of a bargee. But add to the risk of *this* harm the multitude of other risks created by not having a bargee aboard the barge (eg, that fire would break out and destroy the barge; that rats would eat away at the cargo; that vandals would pirate the contents) and it becomes entirely plausible to conclude, as Learned Hand did, that the plaintiff was contributorily negligent for failing to have a bargee aboard, at least during daylight hours in the full tide of war activity.[29]

In light of the fact that many cases of negligence appear to be cases in which the risks that make defendants' acts negligent are only jointly sufficient to do so, it would appear difficult for advocates of the HWR test to sustain the thesis here examined—the thesis that the calculus of risk should sum only risks that are themselves individually sufficient to make a defendant's conduct negligent. It would appear that they would have to expand their view so as to make relevant to the negligent assessment not only all risks that are *individually sufficient* for a finding of negligence, but all risks that are *individually necessary and only*

---

[28] *United States v. Carroll Towing*, 159 F 2d 169 (2d Cir 1947).

[29] Ken Abraham similarly argues that the only means of making sense of the court's conclusion in the textbook case of *Wagner v. International Railway Co*, 133 NE 437 (1921), is to attribute to the court the view that a defendant is negligent with regard to all risks that are individually necessary and only jointly sufficient to outweigh the burden of precautions available to avert those risks. In *Wagner*, the plaintiff sought to rescue his cousin after his cousin was thrown from a train because its door had been left unfastened by negligent railroad employees. As Abraham explains, the court held that the defendant Railroad was liable for the plaintiff's injuries, because while those injuries were not *themselves* the principal harms risked by leaving a train door ajar:

one of the risks that makes it negligent to risk harm to another ... is the risk that a different individual will be injured while attempting to rescue him from the consequences of the defendant's actions. ...; therefore harm to the rescuer is within the cluster of risks that makes the defendant's actions negligent—or so a jury may find.

(Kenneth Abraham, *The Forms and Functions of Tort* Law (New York: Foundation Press, 1997), 121.)

jointly sufficient for a finding of negligence. They would then have to admit that any harm whose discounted value could not be subtracted from the sum of risks created by the defendant's conduct without affecting the judgment that the defendant's conduct was negligent is within the risks that made the defendant negligent—even if its probability and gravity were of little consequence by itself.

B. Risks that are individually necessary for negligence

In light of the plausibility of liability in the many cases of risks that are individually necessary and only jointly sufficient for negligence, it might be tempting to an HWR theorist to restrict the risks eligible for the HWR test to those that are at least necessary to an actor being negligent. Yet a moment's reflection will show that this restriction is hopeless. Consider the overdetermined risk cases mentioned before, where each of two or more risks is individually sufficient for an actor to be negligent. When one of such risks materializes into the harm risked, surely no proponent of HWR would wish to deny liability (for the overdetermined risk cases are cases of severe negligence, the actor in such cases doing an act posing a number of risks any one of which it would be negligent to take). But that is precisely the result this suggested limitation would reach; for if risk one, risk two, and risk three are each individually sufficient for negligence, then as a matter of logic no one of them can be necessary for negligence.

C. Risks that are either individually necessary or individually sufficient for negligence

The obvious way to remedy the problems for the last two tests is to combine them in a disjunctive way: if a risk is either sufficient for negligence, or at least necessary for negligence, then that risk leads to liability if it materializes in the harm risked under the HWR test. To test this third suggested restriction, imagine a case in which a defendant's conduct risks numerous harms, all of which are of identical discounted value. Suppose that the sum of any two of these is sufficient to make it negligent to fail to take precautions against their realization. In such a case, the risks created by the defendant's conduct are neither individually sufficient for, nor individually necessary to, a determination of his negligence. Two risks are jointly sufficient to find the defendant negligent, but inasmuch as any two will do, none of the multiple risks created by his conduct is necessary to that finding.

In such a case it would seem that one must consider the defendant's conduct negligent, notwithstanding the fact that the risk that materialized was neither individually sufficient, nor individually necessary, for a finding of negligence. To say otherwise would invite absurd counter-examples. Suppose, for instance, that a defendant releases a slingshot containing several stones in the direction of a crowd of persons.[30] The risk that any given person will be hit by a flying stone is presumably small. But the risk that *someone* will be hit is predictably large. When someone is in fact hit, one's ability to declare the defendant negligent in causing the injury turns on one's willingness to countenance findings of negligence in mixed concurrent risk cases. On pain of inviting absurdity by exonerating defendants whenever their conduct risks many people, but none in particular, it would seem that one must indeed include in the calculus of risk all risks irrespective of whether they are individually necessary or sufficient to a finding of negligence.

D. 'INUS' risks: Risks that are individually insufficient but necessary to a set of risks being sufficient, although the set may be unnecessary

Modeled on the late John Mackie's INUS conditions as an analysis of caus-ation,[31] the HWR proponent might restrict risks the way Mackie restricted putative causal factors. On this view, a risk may well be insufficient by itself for negligence, yet it may be a necessary element of a set of risks that are jointly sufficient; such a sufficient set may be itself unnecessary to the finding of neg-ligence, because there may be more than one such sufficient set. Such a restriction seems to take care of the three kinds of counter-examples hitherto found troublesome. There would be liability in: (1) the concurrent risk cases, where no one risk is sufficient, but the risk realized is necessary to negligence; (2) the overdetermined risk cases, where two or more risks are individually sufficient for negligence, although none of such risks can be individually necessary for negligence; and (3) the mixed concurrent/overdetermined risk cases, where no one risk is either necessary or sufficient, but subsets of such risks are sufficient for negligence.

Notice how close this brings the advocate of an HWR test towards having to concede the general *reductio ad absurdum* that prompted this inquiry—the challenge that *all* risks will ultimately be within the class of risks that make a defendant's conduct negligent on any proper application of an HWR analysis. For now, all risks created by a defendant that *could* be conjoined with one another in a manner that would cumulatively dictate the taking of available precautions are properly among the risks that make the defendant negligent when he fails to take such precautions. It is not obvious that *any* risk could not be conjoined with some other risks to form a set of risks sufficient for negligence, and the risk thus conjoined could be necessary to the negligence of the set.

---

[30] Warren Seavey's kind of example, in Seavey, 'Principles of torts', Harvard Law Review 56 (1943), 92–3.

[31] John L Mackie, 'Causes and conditions', American Philosophical Quarterly 2 (1965), 245–64.

Advocates of an HWR analysis might respond by arguing that there remains a significant class of cases in which small risks are displaced by large ones, so that the small risks cannot be conjoined with other risks as necessary elements of a set of risks sufficient for negligence. The cases they might have in mind can be called 'asymmetrical overdetermination risk cases'. In such cases, the defendant creates both a single large risk, the discounted value of which is sufficient by itself to justify a finding of negligence, and a host of small risks, the discounted values of which are either (a) jointly sufficient to justify a finding of negligence or (b) are jointly insufficient, without the addition of the discounted value of the large risk also created by the defendant's conduct, to justify a finding of negligence.

Consider Warren Seavey's famous discussion of cases that may seem to be of this sort:

[T]he owner of a dog, known to be vicious, who would be liable without fault if it should bite a person after escaping, is not . . . liable to a person whom the dog clumsily knocks down, since the risk created by the dog was only that of being bit. I would assume that a court . . . would not hold liable the possessor of a pile of boxed explosives if . . . the boxes were to fall upon and crush the foot of a privileged visitor. . . . The risk is one of explosion and not of crushing.[32]

As his examples illustrate, Seavey took the view that large risks altogether eliminate small ones from the calculus of risk.

We can extract at least two variants of this view. Seavey wrote as if he literally believed that in many cases, there are only large risks, ie, that dogs pose literally no risk of harm other than by biting. Despite his language, however, it would surely be uncharitable to assign such a view to him, for he must have contemplated harms from dogs that are much less probable and much less grave. On a second interpretation, then, Seavey recognized that most conduct creates both large and small risks, but he thought that as a moral matter, the large risks swamp the small risks, rendering them irrelevant to the assessment of a defendant's culpability. That is, risks that are individually sufficient to support a finding of negligence displace small risks that, when cumulated, might otherwise themselves demand the taking of precautions. On this more plausible interpretation of Seavey's view, it remains meaningful to inquire whether the harm brought about by a defendant was within the risk(s) that made the defendant negligent, for many risks imposed by the defendant were displaced by, rather than added to, the risk(s) that made him negligent, and if any of *those* small risks had, in fact, materialized, they would not have been risks as to which the defendant is negligent—or so would go Seavey's argument.

While many theorists who champion an HWR analysis talk as Seavey did and thus lend support to the view that at least in asymmetrical overdetermination risk

---

[32] Warren Seavey, 'Mr Justice Cardozo and the law of torts', Harvard Law Review 52 (1939), 387.

cases, there is a multitude of risks that do not enter into the calculus of the defendant's negligence, they must ultimately admit that this class of cases is not special. Indeed, all of the cases in this category can ultimately be collapsed back into one of the three sorts of cases already discussed; as such, the conclusions drawn above will apply to them as well. If the cumulative value of the small risks created by a defendant in an asymmetrical overdetermination case is sufficient to justify a finding of negligence, then the defendant's case will constitute a hybrid of the first and second sorts of cases discussed above—the overdetermination risk cases and the concurrent risk cases. Inasmuch as we concluded that HWR advocates would have to admit that the risks in such cases *all* enter into the calculus of negligence, it would appear that in cases in which defendants create individually sufficient risks together with a multitude of otherwise individually necessary and only jointly sufficient risks, *all* such risks would also enter into the determination of these defendants' negligence. And were any one of these risks to materialize in harm, be it the large risk (ie, a dog bite) or a small risk (ie, a dog bump), such a risk would be within the class of risks that make it negligent for the defendant to act as he did (ie, to refuse to restrain his dog).

If, on the other hand, the small risks created by the defendant are jointly *insufficient* to justify a finding of negligence absent the addition of the large risk, then the defendant's case will be, in all morally relevant respects, akin to the mixed concurrent risk cases. To appreciate this fact, juxtapose two cases. The first is a true mixed concurrent risk case: the defendant creates 15 equally-valued small risks and one risk that is five times as great as any of the 15. No risk is individually sufficient to justify a finding of negligence, but the larger risk combined with any one of the smaller risks or, alternatively, any six of the smaller risks are jointly sufficient to justify a finding of negligence on the part of the defendant. In the second case, the defendant creates five small risks and one significant risk that is three times as large as the five small risks combined. In this case, the large risk is individually sufficient to declare the defendant's conduct negligent, but the small risks, even when combined, are insufficient, absent the addition of the large risk, to justify a finding of negligence.

While it might tempt HWR defenders like Seavey to declare that the small risks in the first case are relevant to the negligence determination, while the small risks in the second case are irrelevant, such a claim should be embarrassing: In both cases the total risk creation by the defendant is the same. Why should it matter how that package of risks is apportioned? What could possibly be the moral relevance of finding that one package is divided into one very large and a multitude of very small risks, while another is divided into many small risks with one slightly larger risk? Why should a defendant who creates a multitude of small risks that are only jointly sufficient to justify a finding of negligence be liable if one of those small risks materializes, while another defendant, who creates the same total level of risk and who causes the same small risk to materialize to a similarly situated plaintiff, walks away scot-free because he had the good fortune to also create a very great risk (that did not materialize), which, by itself, would have been sufficient to justify a finding of negligence had it materialized? Indeed, does not such a conclusion get the culpability judgments in these cases exactly backwards?

It thus appears that if advocates of the HWR test are prepared to grant that in mixed concurrent risk cases, *all* risks enter into the negligence calculus, then they should be prepared to grant that in the asymmetrical overdetermination cases that we have been talking about, *all* risks similarly are within the class of risks that determines the defendant's negligence. But with this admission, they have seemingly been driven to the wall; for advocates of an HWR analysis have now been forced to concede that every risk created by a defendant in every kind of case enters into the calculus that determines the justifiability of the defendant's conduct. Hence, if a defendant's conduct is deemed negligent, any harm it causes is within the set of harms the risk of which make the defendant's conduct negligent. The HWR analysis is thus impotent to sort between cases in which defendants should bear plaintiffs' losses and be criminally liable for victims' harms, and cases in which plaintiffs should bear their own losses and in which defendants are not criminally liable.

E. Risks exceeding some threshold of *de minimus* risk imposition

At this point, the proponent of HWR analyses might give up specifying the role a given risk must have in justifying a finding of negligence. He might, that is, eschew all talk of risks necessary or sufficient for negligence. Instead, he might propose a kind of threshold limitation: any risk that is below a certain threshold is to be regarded as *de minimus*, so that if (miraculously) it does materialize in harm, that harm falls outside the risks considered in the HWR test.

Presumably such a threshold is to be set probabalistically. If the harm that some defendant's action caused was extremely unlikely, as judged from what a person in the defendant's situation could be expected to know, then such a harm is outside the risk and the defendant is not liable under the HWR test.

Such a proposed limitation to the risks eligible to serve in the HWR test, of course, collapses the HWR test into a simple foreseeability test. Once one eliminates the relation a risk must have to the finding of negligence and substitutes a threshold of probability below which a risk does not count for purposes of the HWR test, then one is really only asking the general foreseeability question with the HWR test: Was the harm caused in fact by the defendant's act foreseeable to him at the time that he acted?

The problem with any such absolute threshold of probability ('foreseeability') has been stated many times. To the classic HWR proponent, such a threshold test is not stringent enough: it allows liability where an isolated risk of small magnitude—one that neither by itself nor in conjunction with any other risks makes the defendant negligent—is created by the defendant's action. Equally damningly, such a threshold test is too stringent: it bars liability when a very low probability risk is created, but that risk is of harm of very great magnitude and that risk is run without any justification. The foreseeability test is also subject to the description of the risk problem, to be discussed shortly.[33]

I conclude that there is no way to specify a limitation on the risks eligible to be used in the HWR test. Yet without some such limitation, every harm that is in fact caused by some defendant's action had some *ex ante* risk of being caused by that action. Every harm that some defendant's act causes, then, is within the risk, and the test is without effect.

IV. The Description Problem

There is a level-of-risk problem that is (seemingly, at least) distinct from the all-inclusiveness problem just discussed. To even state the problem of describing the level of risk requires that we make some assumption about how the HWR advocate solves the all-inclusiveness problem. It does not matter to the description problem *how* the HWR theorist solves the all-inclusiveness problem, but some solution must be stipulated so that we can even state the description-of-risk problem. In the discussion that follows let us assume the sufficiency version of HWR. That is, assume a risk must be sufficient by itself to adjudge an actor negligent for it to be *the* risk (or risks, in the risk-overdetermination kind of cases) within which the harm caused must be if there is to be liability.

The description problem is this: how one describes the risk(s) that make(s) the defendant negligent—in terms of types of harm and classes of persons—determines whether the harm that happened is within the risk(s) (so described). *And*, crucially, there is no right answer to the question of how one ought to describe the types of harm risked. Inasmuch as any given harm instantiates any number of types of harm, all levels of description of the harm risked can be equally accurate; it would thus appear that any choice of a description is inherently arbitrary. And this makes the HWR test inherently arbitrary.

Suppose the defendant is adjudged negligent in that he winds the plaintiff's antique clock too tight, and suppose that *the* risk that makes the action negligent is the risk that the plaintiff's clock would be broken. What happens is that a third party drives by the plaintiff's house and is so distracted by seeing (through the window) the defendant winding the plaintiff's clock too tight that the third party runs into the plaintiff's car.

It is easy to imagine quite different descriptions of the risk sufficient to make the defendant's action negligent. From most general to most particular, the

---

[33] This general problem has been explored before with respect to the foreseeability test. See Michael S Moore, *Placing Blame: A general theory of the criminal law* (Oxford: Oxford University Press, 1997), Chapter 8.

defendant risked: harm to someone; harm to the plaintiff; damage to the plaintiff's property; damage to the plaintiff's clock; a broken spring in the plaintiff's clock. These are all equally accurate descriptions of the types of harms risked, and each seems to be a risk sufficient for negligence. Yet under the first three descriptions, the harm that happened—the damage to plaintiff's car—is within the risk, while under the latter two descriptions, such damage is not within the risk.

As a second illustration, suppose a case where the defendant is negligently speeding in an automobile, hits the pedestrian plaintiff, and injures her. If we describe the risk that makes it negligent for the defendant to act as he did as a risk that he would bring about: 'harm to someone', 'harm to pedestrians', or 'personal injury to pedestrians', then the harm is within the risk that makes the defendant's conduct negligent. On the other hand, if we describe the type of harm risked by the defendant as 'a perforated lung, resulting from a stake impaling the plaintiff after being catapulted through the air at 37 mph by the impact of a speeding blue Ford 1997 Taurus which had swerved to avoid a nine-year-old', then surely the risk that an instance of that type of harm would occur was so low that such risk was not sufficient to make the act negligent, so that the harm caused will not be within the risk. Since it is equally accurate to describe the type of injury risked both as 'a harm to someone' and as 'an impaling by a stake launched at 37mph by a blue Ford 1997 Taurus which had swerved to avoid a nine-year-old child', the harm that happened was both within and not within the risk.

If there are no right answers as to how we ought to describe the risks that defendants impose, then it would appear that the HWR test is entirely vacuous. Where would the needed answers (as to the correct *type* of harm about which to do a risk assessment) come from? We cannot flee to some notion of objective probability in terms of relative frequencies, because the relative frequency interpretation of probability first requires us to fix on a type of event and only then seek the probability of its instances—whereas our quandary here is precisely what type of event we should fix on.

Perhaps human psychology could provide us with a 'natural' typing, one that does not correspond to any objectively natural sizing of types but that is none-theless one that human beings do in fact agree on in their psychology.

If persons were asked to predict the consequences, say, of leaving a dog unrestrained, it is possible they would converge upon a set of common predic-tions in the sense that the classes of events they would foresee would overlap. Could we not use the average response, or the response that enjoys the broadest consensus, to fix the description of the risk(s) of the defendant's conduct? Suppose such average description of the case were, 'a dog bite'. We would then describe the risk created by the defendant as the risk of 'a dog bite', and if the harm caused by the defendant's dog were 'a dog bite', we could then conclude under the HWR test that the harm caused by the defendant is within the risk that makes the defendant negligent.

There is, of course, a real doubt whether there are such average or most popular descriptions on which a populace converges. But even if there are such average descriptions, there is also the question of how a court could ever be confident about how average persons would describe the risks of a defendant's conduct. One can only imagine just how much judicial projection would occur were we to license courts to unpack the HWR test in terms of their armchair assumptions about the descriptive generalizations of ordinary folks.

But set aside the empirical problems that this solution to the description problem poses for advocates of the HWR test. Is not the real problem with this appeal to ordinary psychology the fact that it is without obvious moral motivation? Why, as a moral matter, should we fix the content of the HWR test by appealing to the descriptions of the risks and harms generated by a defendant that would predictably be provided by ordinary persons? One answer might come from those who hold a 'majoritarian theory' of negligence.[34] This was the understanding of negligence that was at work in *Osborne v. Montgomery*,[35] when the Wisconsin Supreme Court declared:

We apply the standards which guide the great mass of mankind in determining what is proper conduct of an individual. . . . Such a standard is usually spoken of as 'ordinary care', being that degree of care which under the same or similar circumstances the great mass of mankind would ordinarily exercise.

As Robert Rabin argues, it is this majoritarian view of negligence that best captures early torts theorists' conception of negligence, for they conceived of reasonableness as conformity with statistically prevalent norms of conduct, rather than as the exercise of rationality.[36] Yet on most contemporary accounts, what is reasonable and what are ordinary are two quite different things. As Learned Hand famously wrote: '[I]n most cases reasonable prudence is in fact common prudence; but strictly it is never its measure; a whole calling may have unduly lagged in the adoption of new and available devices. . . . [T]here are precautions so imperative that even their universal disregard will not excuse their omission.'[37] If what ordinary persons ordinarily *do* may still be negligent (eg, smoking, speeding, failing to use seatbelts), then what ordinary persons *say* about what other ordinary persons do is of questionable moral consequence. Inasmuch as we think that such persons can be wrong about what is reasonable, we can hardly regard their descriptions of the risks attendant upon an defendant's conduct as *constitutive* of the risks to be compared by an HWR analysis. But if the average is

---

[34] For an extended discussion of majoritarian theories of negligence, see Hurd, 'Deontology of negligence', 269–70.

[35] 234 NW 372 (Wis 1931).

[36] Robert L Rabin, 'The historical development of the fault principle: A reinterpretation', Georgia Law Review 15 (1981), 931, n 25.

[37] *The TJ Hooper*, 60 F 2d 737 (2d Cir 1932). As Clarence Morris put it, 'Those who follow bad examples may still be at fault even though their models are respectable and numerous'. Clarence Morris, 'Custom and negligence', Columbia Law Review 42 (1942), 149.

not constitutive of the ideal, what can justify employing it to fix the content of the HWR test?

I conclude that those who advocate HWR inquiries are without a means of answering the description problem, which thus renders their inquiries vacuous. Absent a source of determinate answers concerning how the risks generated by a defendant's conduct ought to be described, the question of whether the harm caused by a defendant is within the risk(s) that make(s) the defendant negligent is an empty one.

V. The Two Problems Combined

Each of the two conceptual problems that we have now discussed is individually sufficient to declare any HWR analysis quite literally incoherent as applied to negligence. Indeed, after one fully appreciates each of them, it is extremely hard to continue talking about an HWR test as if it were capturing a meaningful question—even when one wants to do so in order to exhaust the difficulties that separately confront such a test. This difficulty presumably became apparent simply in the transition from the discussion of the first conceptual problem (the all-inclusiveness problem) to the discussion of the second conceptual problem (the description problem); and it would surely confront one if one were to review these problems in reverse. Having demonstrated in the first section that, as a conceptual matter, *all* harms must be thought to be within the risks that make a defendant's conduct negligent, it is then hard to get a grip on the question posed by the description problem of how one could and should describe *a risk* so as to determine whether the harm that the defendant caused is within *the* risk, as required by an HWR test. Conversely, once one appreciates the fact that how one describes the risks generated by a defendant determines whether the harms that occurred are within the risks that make the defendant negligent, it is hard to get a grip on how one would individuate risks so as to even make meaningful the question that the all-inclusiveness problem addresses—namely, whether there is some subset of risks that alone make a defendant negligent.

In any case, whether there is one problem here or two, HWR is conceptually bankrupt as applied to negligence. Because two arguments are better than one, I shall nonetheless turn in the next chapter to the normative desirability of the HWR analysis, concluding that it is as undesirable as it is conceptually suspect.

9

Normative Problems in Applying the Harm-within-the-Risk Test to Crimes/Torts of Negligence

I. Generally

As was mentioned in the historical treatment of the HWR test in Chapter 7, early advocates of an HWR analysis defended the test on normative as well as on conceptual grounds. It is now time to address those normative grounds. What motivated early proponents of an HWR analysis to limit the defendants' obligations of corrective justice to harms that materialize from the big or obvious risks attendant upon the defendants' actions?

The answer to this question must be this: inasmuch as negligence is a doctrine of culpability, the risks that go into its assessment should include only those that it was culpable for a defendant to ignore. While there might be an infinitesimal chance that by sitting in a chair, one will put enough pressure on the floor below to cause it to give way so as to drop through the floor onto a person standing in the room below, no one should be required to imagine, deliberate about, or guard against such an infinitesimal risk; hence, such a risk should not be added to the calculus that measures a defendant's culpability. Rather, the negligence calculus should be limited to those risks that reasonable persons, subject to common cognitive constraints and limited research possibilities, would anticipate and deliberate about in the time available to them. Inasmuch as persons typically find themselves in circumstances that permit the contemplation of only a handful of possible harms prior to action—most naturally, the two or three of greatest discounted value—the calculus that determines the justifiability of persons' conduct should be limited to the risks of these harms alone. In short, the calculus should include only those risks that would have been *subjectively* appreciated by reasonable persons at the time of a defendant's action; it should not measure all risks that *ex post facto* are believed to have been attendant upon the defendant's conduct, most of which would only have been subjectively appreciated at the time by God. When a risk materializes from a defendant's conduct in a manner that would surprise a reasonable person, it is flatly unfair to exact compensation for it from the defendant.

This argument on behalf of an HWR analysis is least persuasive in the over-determination and asymmetrical overdetermination risk cases that we discussed in Chapter 8. Recall that in these sorts of cases, defendants' conduct imposes at least one risk that is, by itself, sufficient to justify a finding of negligence: its discounted cost, by itself, exceeds the burden of precautions required for its elimination. In such cases, defendants patently know or should know that they have no business doing what they are doing. They are on moral notice, if you will, that their conduct is unjustified. When different, less significant risks in fact materialize from their conduct, they can hardly claim that it is unfair to impose upon them the costs of those harms. On the contrary, the fact that their conduct could also cause other harms beyond those that were obvious and sufficient for finding them negligent is grounds for thinking them all the more blameworthy. Thus, for example, while the fact that an unrestrained dog might bury a neighbor's Ming vase is not something a defendant might spend time contemplating, it can hardly be unfair to hold the defendant liable for the loss of the vase, since the significant possibility that his dog would cause *other* harms (by biting, digging, trampling, etc) put him on moral notice that his dog should be restrained. As Judge Friendly wrote when deciding *Petition of Kinsman Transit Co*[1] (arguably an asymmetrical overdetermination case in which a poorly tied ship was knocked loose of its dock by cakes of ice, dislodging another ship downstream and, with that other ship, jamming a drawbridge, in a manner that caused flooding for miles):

We see no reason why an actor engaging in conduct which entails a large risk of small damage and a small risk of other and greater damage, of the same general sort, from the same forces, and to the same class of persons, should be relieved of responsibility for the latter simply because the chance of its occurrence, if viewed alone, may not have been large enough to require the exercise of care. By hypothesis, the risk of the lesser harm was sufficient to render his disregard of it actionable; the existence of a less likely additional risk that the very forces against whose action he was required to guard would produce other and greater damage than could have been reasonably anticipated *should inculpate him further* rather than limit his liability.[2]

A slightly different way of making essentially the same point is to deny that there ever really are asymmetrical overdetermination risk cases. For notice that, in a case like *Kinsman Transit*, the untaken precaution (securing the ship properly) would have prevented both the large risk and the smaller risk; since the very same conduct was required to eliminate both risks and since the larger risk already outweighed the burden of taking the adequate precaution, *there was no justification (or 'burden') whatsoever for taking the smaller risk*—in which event, even a very, very slight risk is sufficient for negligence itself. Really, therefore, supposed asymmetrical overdetermination risk cases are a kind of overdetermination risk

---

[1] *Petition of Kinsman Transit Co*, 338 F 2d 708 (2d Cir 1964).
[2] Ibid, 724–5.

case where the tiny risk that materializes is sufficient for negligence because the larger risk (that does not materialize) is by itself sufficient for negligence.

The normative argument for limiting the negligence calculus to those risks that would be appreciated by reasonable persons is perhaps more compelling in pure or mixed cases of concurrent risks in which all of the risks that attach to the defendants' actions are individually trivial, but in which all of them together (the pure case), or some subset of them together (the mixed case), are sufficient to make the defendants' conduct negligent. In a case of this sort, advocates of the HWR test might insist that it would be grossly unfair to hold a defendant responsible for the materialization of one of these trivial risks *just because* a multitude of other trivial risks that *did not* materialize might otherwise have done so. Imagine, for example, that all of the risks associated with a defendant's driving are small—but that there are a great many such risks attendant upon this activity: a tire might blow out and cause the defendant to lose control of the vehicle; a seagull might bounce off the car's roof and hit an old lady; a sudden bee sting might cause the defendant to go into anaphylactic shock and careen off the road; a sonic boom might frighten the defendant into swerving toward oncoming traffic; the defendant, while in no way predisposed to a heart-attack or a stroke, might have one; etc. If the benefits of driving are, ultimately, out-weighed by the sum of the discounted harms risked by that activity, then on the earlier analysis, the defendant would properly be held liable for the materialization of any of these risks. But, advocates of an HWR analysis might argue, why should the defendant pay for the injuries sustained by an old lady who is hit by a seagull that ricocheted off his car roof *because* while driving, he might have experienced a bee sting, or a heart attack, or a stroke, or a tire blow out, or a distracting sonic boom—all of which are wildly improbable happenings to which no reasonable person would give a thought? Inasmuch as the defendant had no *single* good reason, and even no obvious *set* of reasons, to fear that he would cause any harm at all, given the individually trivial nature of all of the harms associated with his activity, how can he fairly be held liable when a harm of enormously low probability materializes, just because other, equally low-probability harms might have occurred?

While this argument has superficial bite, it is crucial to remember just what it means to say that a defendant's conduct risked harms. In this context it is to say that from the epistemic situation of the defendant, it was possible to predict, with a certain degree of confidence, that the conduct would cause a harm. Risks in the present context are only epistemic constructs that help us to compensate for our inability to know whether particular harms resulting from particular conduct have an objective probability of one or zero. As such, there is no 'Monday-morning-quarterbacking' going on here. When applying the negligence calculus, the risks ascribed to a defendant's Saturday conduct must be those that could have been assessed on Saturday, not those only knowable on Monday. Inasmuch as the negligence calculus must accurately measure a defendant's *culpability*, the conventional view is the right view: that risks only made apparent as a result of, or after, the defendant's conduct do not belong in the calculus.

But once these reminders are issued, it should be clear that there are only two possible things to say in a case in which a defendant creates thousands of small risks, no one of which, and even no subset of which, is sufficient to make him negligent: either the total sum of those risks never exceeds the total sum of the benefits associated with the defendant's activity—in which case the defendant is not negligent for behaving in a way that imposes thousands of risks—or else those risks indeed cumulatively outstrip the benefits of his conduct—in which case, *because they are knowable to him* (given the epistemic reading of risk), it is fully appropriate for them to weigh in an assessment of his conduct and fully appropriate for us to hold him liable for the materialization of any one of them.

Those who would persist in arguing otherwise must be assuming one of two things, namely that there are risks that are not knowable to reasonable persons at the time of a defendant's actions; or that risks that can be appreciated by reasonable persons only after a defendant's actions can properly be included in the calculus that determines the defendant's negligence. But one should not subscribe to either of these claims. To believe that there can be risks independent of a reasonable person's ability to know them is to believe that risks possess the ontological status of tables, chairs, and protons. While perhaps propensity versions of an objective interpretation of probability can say this, the epistemic notion of risk we use in assessing human conduct cannot. I thus eschew such a view in favor of the claim that risks as used in the culpability assessment of negligence constitute probabilistic calculations about future events that a reasonable person would make if he were in the defendant's situation. On this epistemic interpretation of risk, if a defendant risks a harm, it is knowable that he does so; for what it means to risk a harm is simply to have access to evidence acquired from past experience (one's own and others') from which it is possible to predict a causal connection between one's own act and a future harm.

Similarly, there should be no temptation to judge the defendant's decision to act based on evidence that only became available after the defendant's action. Culpability is a function of a defendant's epistemic state at the time of action. A defendant is culpable for an unjustified harm if he positively intended to cause the harm, knew that it would happen, was consciously aware of a risk that it would happen, or should have been consciously aware of a risk that it would happen. On the 'ought implies can' principle, to say that a defendant risked a harm, one must mean that evidence was available to the defendant at the time of action from which he could have inferred that he would cause a harm.

In the end, then, there can be no normative objection to holding a defendant liable for all risks apparent at the time of action that materialize in harm and that were individually sufficient, individually necessary, or members of sets that were sufficient to justify a finding of negligence on the part of the defendant. *Ex hypothesi*, all such risks were knowable to the defendant, and *ex hypothesi*, all such risks could be summed by the defendant so as to determine their collective justifiability, relative to the anticipated benefits of acting. That people often do not consciously calculate the myriad risks created by their conduct is no argument that they should not or could not calculate such risks.

Indeed, it is precisely because people appreciate that they could and should calculate many more risks than they generally do that they adopt heuristics or proxies in concurrent and mixed concurrent-risk cases. For example, when one is driving on the freeway during rush-hour traffic and one's cellular telephone rings, one only needs to conjure up an image of rear-ending the car in front of one's own in order to generate an effective proxy for all of the risks that one knows are attendant upon the act of answering the phone while driving. While the risk of a rear-end collision is probably insufficient by itself, and even in tandem with other such risks, to make answering the cell-phone negligent, one appreciates the fact that rear-ending someone is but one example of the many sorts of risks one could avert, and as such, its prospect puts one on moral notice of the riskiness of driving one-handed while trying to concentrate on sustaining an unbroken conversation with another person. That we use such proxies regularly as a means of overcoming the difficulty of assessing risks in concurrent and mixed concurrent risk cases suggests not that such risks are irrelevant to the justifiability of our actions, but, rather, that they are constitutive of it. By arguing that only some risks—ie, the most easily knowable—enter into the negligence calculus, proponents of an HWR analysis are likely confusing obvious proxies for the lengthy list of risks to which they are proxies. In the end, however, inasmuch as all risks are knowable and inasmuch as many risks serve as useful proxies for others, defendants cannot complain of unfairness when they are held liable for harms that are not among the risks to which a reasonable person would consciously avert; and adjudicators should not be misled into thinking that it is unfair to hold defendants liable for anything other than harms that materialize from the most obvious risks associated with their activities.

I conclude that there is no unfairness in holding defendants liable for 'harms *outside* the risk'. The idea of negligence as *knowable* risk(s) prevents any such charge being leveled at the more extended liability. It remains to enquire, however, whether there are any positive reasons for extending such liability. Consider this question first in torts, then in criminal law.

In torts, the argument for liability is pretty straightforward. Indeed, the kernal of the argument is contained in the quotation from Judge Friendly given earlier. In the cases we are supposing, some defendant is at fault because he did not take some cost-justified precaution against a risk (or a bundle of risks) of which he should have been aware. Further, in such cases the act that he did, without the precaution, caused the victim injury. Friendly's question is rhetorical: why should it matter (to the defendant's tort liability) that the risk(s) that made the defendant's act negligent were not realized, when other and lesser risks imposed by his action were realized, causing the victim's injury? The defendant did something he should not have been doing, and the victim (who did nothing wrong) was hurt as a result.

Negligent harm-causing is the lowest rung on the ladder by which we grade culpability in torts. Thus there is no ability in torts to match harm caused to harm(s) risked, and thus deny liability for negligence, while yet leaving open the possibility of some lesser form of liability. There is no lesser form of liability, so our choice is a stark one: the innocent victim suffers the harm uncompensated, or the culpable defendant pays for the harm he caused. Even though (by hypothesis) that harm was not an instance of the type of harm the risk of which made him negligent, that fine-grained question seems inappropriate as a basis to deny liability entirely. My choice would be with Friendly: make the negligent defendant pay for the harm he caused, irrespective of the lack of match between that harm and the type(s) of harm the risk of which made him negligent.

The argument for liability (for harms 'outside the risk') has to be different in the law of crimes, for in criminal law we seemingly do not face the same all-or-nothing starkness that marked the choice in torts. In criminal law there is a fall back form of lesser liability in the cases we are supposing, and that is inchoate liability. Defendants who cause harms 'outside the risk' that made them negligent could be punished for negligent risking, not for negligent causing, of some harm.

This possibility raises squarely the normative relevance of the 'match' question in negligence cases. Does the lack of match (between harm caused and type of harms risked) make for lesser blameworthiness, much as the lack of causation itself does? This is a difficult question for me to get a handle on, because: (1) I am in general loath to punish for negligence at all,[3] and (2) I do not believe there are any cases of harm truly 'outside the risk' (for the two conceptual reasons given in Chapter 8). Still, this chapter purports to be making an argument alternative to those offered in Chapter 8. So, assuming, *arguendo*, that there are cases of punishably negligent defendants who cause harms that are 'outside the risk' that made them negligent, how stands their level of blameworthiness?

If we are in the business of punishing for negligence at all, a merely inchoate liability punishes outside-the-risk harm-causers too lightly. Shift focus momentarily to intent-based crimes; in cases where the harm caused in execution of some culpable intention does not match the type of harm intended, we do not merely punish for the inchoate crime of attempting to cause the type of harm intended. We also punish for the completed crime of (knowingly, recklessly, or negligently) causing the harm that actually occurred. This latter possibility does not exist for crimes of negligence; here, causing harms not matching the risk that made the defendant negligent precludes conviction for any completed crime. This is too little punishment, in light of the admitted fact that the defendant did cause the legally prohibited harm.

---

[3] For reasons given in Michael Moore, *Placing Blame: A general theory of the criminal law* (Oxford: Clarendon Press, 1997), 588–92.

Although the issue is closer, I conclude that criminal law too has good reason not to require a match between harm caused and type of harm risked—again, assuming (contrary to Chapter 8) that that is a coherent question.

II. The Alleged Analogy to Transferred Intent

There is a particular normative argument made on behalf of an HWR test that merits separate treatment. This is an argument by analogy to the doctrine of transferred intent in torts and in criminal law. As made by *opponents* of an HWR analysis,[4] the argument is that we do 'transfer intent'—in the sense that we hold a defendant liable for intending a type of harm H to a person x even though that defendant intended a type of harm J to person y—so that equality demands that we similarly transfer negligence. As made by *proponents* of an HWR analysis,[5] the argument is that we by and large do *not* transfer intent, so equality demands that we likewise should not transfer negligence, ie, that we should adopt an HWR test of negligence. Obviously, the first question to be settled here is just what is the doctrine of transferred intent; then we will be in a position to assess how compelling is the analogy to it by the critics and proponents of an HWR analysis.

Transferred intent began as a criminal law doctrine.[6] Very generally speaking, the doctrine is that intent is to be transferred across persons, but not across harms. Let us consider persons first. If x intended to hit y, but hit z instead, x is guilty of criminal battery; his intent to hit y is treated as an intent to hit z, so his battery of z is deemed intentional and not merely negligent. With regard to harms, suppose again that x intended to hit y with a rock; instead, x missed y, but hit and broke z's shop window. In such a case, x's intent to hit y is not transferred to z's window, because the crime of malicious destruction of property involves a different harm than does the crime of assault intended by x.[7] Each crime must 'rest on its own bottom' (in the metaphor of the courts), in the sense that the *mens rea* sufficient for one crime (that the defendant did not do) will not be treated as *mens rea* sufficient for the crime the defendant did do.

The latter branch of the doctrine is limited in criminal law by two other doctrines. One is the doctrine of felony-murder. Under this doctrine an intent to do one criminal act, such as theft, is treated as an intent to do another, murder, so long as a killing takes place during the theft.[8] The second is the legal wrong

---

[4] See Keeton et al, *Prosser and Keeton on Torts* (St Paul: West Pub Co, 1984), 284.

[5] Glanville Williams treats transferred intent as a doctrine so limited that one could admit an analogous doctrine of transferred negligence that 'would operate as a strictly limited exception to the risk principle . . . used only in a comparatively narrow class of cases to prevent he risk theory giving results some might regard as absurd'. Williams, 'The Risk Principle', Law Quarterly Review 77 (1961), 179, 187.

[6] *R v. Salisbury*, 75 Eng Rep 158 (1553); *R v. Saunders and Archer*, 75 Eng Rep 706 (1576).

[7] *R v. Pembliton*, 12 Cox Crim Cas 607 (Ct Crim App 1874).

[8] See generally Joshua Dressler, *Understanding Criminal Law* (2nd edn, New York: Mathew-Bender, 1995).

doctrine, according to which types of harm will be substituted so long as the substitution is merely between harms that mark different grades of the same offense.[9] Thus, if *x* intends to break and enter a building that he believes to be unoccupied, but in fact he breaks into a dwelling house, *x* will be held for first-degree burglary and not some lesser degree of burglary, because his intent to break into an unoccupied building (second- or third-degree burglary, typically) is treated as an intent to break into a dwelling house (first-degree burglary).[10]

Transferred intent was extended to torts when the writ of trespass still was used to invoke the intentional torts[11] (whereas the writ of trespass on the case was later used to invoke the tort of negligence). Transferred intent in torts is still influenced by this history in that the doctrine is limited to those intentional torts that could have been brought under the old writ of trespass.[12] These included assault, battery, trespass, trespass to chattels, conversion, false imprisonment, but not newer intentional torts such as the intentional infliction of emotional distress.[13]

The classic application of transferred intent in torts is the same as in criminal law; it transfers across persons but not across harms. If *x* intends to hit *y* by throwing a glass ashtray but hits *z* instead, the intent is 'transferred' so that *x* is guilty of the intentional tort of battery to *z*. On the other hand, intent does not usually transfer between types of harm. If *x* intends to hit *y* but instead destroys *z*'s property, one does not transfer *x*'s intention to make him guilty of the intentional tort of conversion.[14] As in criminal law, tort law has some exceptions to this latter doctrine: for example, between the closely related torts of assault and battery, we do transfer intentions between the different types of harm (contact versus apprehension of contact).[15] If *x* intends to scare *y*, but hits her, he is guilty of battery; if *x* intends to hit *y*, but in missing *y* scares her, *x* is guilty of assault.

Notice that within types of harm, there is sometimes no need for a doctrine of transferred intent in either criminal law or torts. For example, suppose that the defendant intends to put out *an eye* of *v*'s with a blow to *v*'s head. If the blow was headed for *v*'s left eye, but *v* moved her head at the last moment so that it was her

---

[9] See eg, *R v. Prince*, 2 CCR 154 (1875) (Judge Brett).

[10] The American Law Institute's Model Penal Code, § 2.04(2) (Proposed Official Draft 1962), modifies the common law legal wrong doctrine by convicting the mistaken defendant of the less serious grade of crime he thought he was doing rather than on the more serious grade of crime he was in fact doing.

[11] Prosser's thesis. William L Prosser, 'Transferred intent', Texas Law Review 45 (1967), 650–62.

[12] Ibid.   [13] Ibid, 650–62.

[14] In the property-protecting torts of trespass, trespass to chattels, and conversion, the non-transfer of intention is easily missed because the question of whose property it is is held not to be material for purposes of these intentional torts. Thus, I am liable if I intend to enter land I believe belongs to you but in fact belongs to Jones; such liability does not depend on any transfer of intention.

[15] See, eg, *Restatement (Second) of the Law of Torts*, §§ 16, 20 (Philadelphia: American Law Institute, 1965).

right eye that was damaged, defendant will be held liable for intentionally disfiguring v (mayhem), but this will not be because of any 'transfer' of intention. The defendant intended to put out some eye, the putting out of v's right eye is an instance of this type of harm, so that no transfer of intent is needed to match the harm caused to the type of harm intended.

The same is true within classes of persons in the comparatively rare cases where the defendant intends to harm 'someone', not in the sense of some particular person, but in the sense of anyone. In what English criminal lawyers called the 'implied malice' cases, defendant shoots into a crowd or bombs a building full of people; in doing so, defendant intends to kill someone, but not anyone in particular. If defendant succeeds in killing someone, v, then the harm he has caused is an instance of the harm he intended. The defendant is thus appropriately held for intentionally killing someone, and this result obtains with no need to 'transfer' any intentions.[16] The cause of this mistake is to confuse two different questions. One is the question of match or 'concurrence' on which we have been focusing: Is the harm caused an instance of the type of harm intended? Different is the question asked by those making this mistake: Was the intent of the defendant (say, to hit y) an instance of the type of intention (to hit someone) the law requires for conviction of intentional battery? In the classic transferred-intent cases, the answer to the second question is plainly yes, for defendant's intention to hit y is an instance of the type of intention required; yet the answer to the first question is plainly no, for the hitting of z is not an instance of the type of act intended, a hitting of y. The doctrine of transferred intent thus cannot be dispensed with if there is to be liability for intentional wrongdoing in the classic transferred intent cases.[17]

In light of the complexities in the doctrines of transferred intent in both criminal law and torts, it is easy to see why legal scholars have drawn analogies both ways with respect to negligence. On the one hand, opponents of an HWR analysis can certainly argue that prima facie, the *Palsgraf* holding is inconsistent with transferred intent—for if we transfer intentions across persons, as we do, then why not similarly transfer negligence across persons? On the other hand, proponents of an HWR an analysis can certainly argue that, prima facie, the *Palsgraf dicta* is consistent with transferred intent—for if we do not transfer intentions across types of harms, as by and large we do not, neither should we transfer negligence from harms risked to harms caused.

---

[16] It is common to think that one can dispense altogether with the doctrine of transferred intent on this basis and yet still hold defendants liable for intentional wrongdoing in the classic 'transferred intent' cases. See, eg, Joshua Dressler, *Understanding Criminal Law*, 109. Yet when x intends to hit y, but hits z instead, what x has done in fact does not match what he intended to do. The hit on z is not an instance of the type of wrong intended, a hitting of y, whereas in the cases supposed in the text, the harm done is literally an instance of the type of harm intended.

[17] See generally Moore, 'Intention and mens rea', in Ruth Gavison (ed), *Issues in Contemporary Legal Philosophy* (Oxford: Oxford University Press, 1987).

In fact, the analogy is unpersuasive in both directions. This is partly because the transferred intent doctrine is fractured in an irrational way: Why should there be transfers across persons when there are such limited transfers across types of harms? This makes as little sense as the *Restatement (Second) of Torts'* fracturing of *Palsgraf,*[18] so as to allow negligence to be transferred across types of harms but not across persons. Both of these doctrines ought to go one way or the other rather than residing in these untenable halfway houses.

Moreover, the direction to go from the halfway house of current transferred intent doctrine is towards abolition of transferred intent, not towards expansion. Transferred intent may well have made good sense when the doctrine originated in the 16th century, for there were then no crimes or torts of negligence. The choice was thus to transfer defendants' intention in the cases put above or to exonerate defendants entirely. Now, however, we distinguish intentional torts and crimes from negligent torts and crimes, attaching more severe sanctions to the former vis-à-vis the latter. Now we can afford to be more discriminating as to when a defendant should be held to the more serious sanctions attached to intentional torts and intentional crimes. Where x throws an ashtray at y but hits z, we should hold x liable for his negligence in hitting z. We might also hold x for both criminal assault (attempted battery) of y and tortious assault (causing apprehension of contact) on y. We have no reason to get sloppy in our culpability judgments by pretending that x is guilty of the one thing he is not guilty of, an intentional battery on z.

The best thing to do with the doctrine of transferred intent is thus to get rid of it entirely.[19] However, abolition of transferred intent across persons suffering intended harms does not need to eliminate a kind of transferred intent across harms that has always gone on in both torts and criminal law. Suppose the defendant strikes v intending specifically to put out v's left eye, but v turns her head and the blow puts out v's right eye. The defendant's intent is clearly an instance of the type of intention the law requires for conviction of mayhem, for the intent to put out v's left eye is of the type—an intent to disfigure a human being.[20] Yet the harm the defendant caused—putting out v's right eye—is not literally an instance of the type of harm the defendant intended—a putting out of v's left eye. In such a case, I nonetheless would hold the defendant liable for mayhem, as does present law. This, in effect, is a limited transfer of intention, one that operates *within* the type of harm the law prohibits (disfigurement in

---

[18] See discussion in Chapter 7, above.

[19] In recommending the abolition of the doctrine of transferred intent, we do not, of course, recommend results different from those obtaining in implied malice and like cases discussed earlier in the text. If a defendant intends some disfigurement to some person (but he does not care what kind of disfigurement or which person), then when he causes the loss of Jones' right eye, he is guilty of intentional disfigurement (mayhem). Such results, as we noted earlier, in no way depend on some doctrine of 'transferred intent.'

[20] Actually, the intent often required for mayhem is only an intent to hit. *State v. Hartley*, 384 Pzd 252 (NW 1963).

mayhem, for example). The defendant in the case imagined is close enough to success in achieving what he set out to do that he should be held liable for an intentional crime and not merely some lesser crime of recklessness or negligence. Lest this seems to leave open the door for the proponent of an HWR analysis, let me be explicit about why this is not so.

Negligence now occupies the lowest rung on the ladder by which we grade culpability. If there were any cases in which the harm that was caused by a defendant's action lies outside the risk that makes that action negligent—a point that the two conceptual arguments made in Chapter 8 deny—then such cases would present us with the 'transfer-culpability-or-exonerate entirely' choice that was faced by the originators of the transferred intent doctrines in the 16th century. In the situation imagined, my choice would be the same as theirs: a culpable defendant who causes harm to an innocent victim should both pay for doing so and be punished, rather than be exonerated entirely, which is the only other alternative. The normative argument made above as to why negligent riskers should pay for harms caused that were not among the obvious risks created by the action have no application to higher forms of culpability, where the whole idea is to be more discriminating in our culpability assessments.

III. Reduction to Absurdity?

One way to argue against a position is to demonstrate that it proves too much. Proponents of an HWR analysis of negligence may insist that the conceptual and normative arguments that have been directed against their project ultimately generate *reductio ad absurdums* suggesting that I have proved too much. In particular, it may seem that these same arguments are of equal force against two legal tests that are similar to general HWR tests: (1) the requirement that harm caused be an instance of the type of harm intended, foreseen, or knowingly risked for that harm to be intentionally, knowingly, or recklessly caused; and (2) the requirement that a harm be an instance of the type of harm that motivated the legislature to pass a criminal statute before that statute may set the standard of care in torts. The thought is that if the arguments of this and the preceding chapter condemn these very well-established doctrines in the same breath as they condemn HWR tests, then there must be something wrong with the arguments. I shall examine each of these challenges in the subsections that follow.

A. Intent, foresight, and recklessness

As was mentioned in Chapter 7, it is well established in the law of torts and crimes that we must match harms caused to harms intended, foreseen, or consciously risked before we can hold the defendant to the culpabilities of intent, knowledge, or recklessness. Moreover, as a matter of morality, such matchings seem essential if we are to grade culpabilities by the mental states of intent and belief. Thus, it would be troublesome indeed if the arguments of this and the preceding chapter (directed against HWR as applied to negligence) were to challenge these matching tests.

Fortunately they do not. For in these cases of more serious culpability, there is a canonical description of some type of harm intended, foreseen, or consciously risked. This is the description that the actor had in his head at the time that he acted.[21] If the defendant intended to start a *fire*, or predicted that his act would cause a *fire*, or knew that his act might start a *fire*, then fire is the type of harm an instance of which the defendant must cause in order to be an intentional, knowing, or reckless arsonist. There thus seems to be no description problem for these true mental states, for unlike negligence (which is not a state of mind), the type of harm is fixed by the defendant's state of mind.

It is true that there are approaches to cognitive psychology and the philosophy of mind that would deny that the objects of intentions or beliefs can yield canonical descriptions of certain types of events. These are holistic, pragmatic, or hermeneutic approaches to the question of the content of propositional attitudes like intentions or beliefs. These are not approaches to the nature of mind to which I subscribe. On my view, intentions and beliefs are aptly named by Russell's label—'propositional attitudes'—because they are attitudes necessarily representing the world under certain descriptions.[22] Such fixed descriptions of the objects of intentions and beliefs means there is no 'description of the risk' problem as there is for negligence.

Given that there is a description of the type of harm intended, foreseen, or consciously risked, there also does not seem to be an 'all-inclusiveness problem'. That is, one cannot reduce intent, foresight, and recklessness to absurdity by showing that all harms caused were necessarily intended, foreseen, or consciously risked, as we did for negligence. This is because legal fact-finders privilege the type of harm intended, foreseen, or consciously risked and ask whether the harm caused is or is not an instance of this type of harm only.

It is not that other risks of other harms do not enter into the culpability judgments of intent, foresight, and recklessness. Such other risks are part of these culpability judgments because of their relevance to the justification considerations that are built into these culpability judgments. That is, to judge whether an actor has recklessly caused a harm, it is not enough to find that he was

---

[21] The relevant description does *not* come from the law, such as a criminal statute prohibiting an act if done with a certain intention. As set forth earlier, see text at nn 16–17, above, the matching or concurrence question is to be distinguished from the question of whether the intention of a particular defendant is an instance of the type of intention prohibited by some statute. To answer this latter question of classification, one would use the statutory description. To answer the matching question, however, one uses the type of action defendant intended to see if the act done is an instance of this type or not.

[22] For one such realist view of content, see Jerry Fodor, *The Language of Thought* (Cambridge, Mass: MIT Press, 1975); Jerry Fodor, *Psychosemantics* (Cambridge, Mass: MIT Press, 1987).

consciously aware of the risk of some type of harm occurring of which this harm is an instance; in addition, the risk must be unjustified in the sense of the expanded Hand formula—all the benefits of taking this risk need to be factored in, balanced against the detriments of taking this risk (which includes all other harms risked in addition to the one that was caused).[23] Similarly, to hold an actor for intentionally or knowingly causing a certain harm, it is not enough to find that he intended or foresaw some type of harm of which the harm caused was an instance; in addition, one must find the causing of such a harm to be unjustified in the sense of the expanded Hand formula: all the benefits likely to be brought about by causing this harm need to be factored in, balanced against *all* the detriments risked by the action (not just the detriment that is this harm).[24]

Thus the question of a defendant's justification imports holistic-risk questions into the culpability determinations for intentional, knowing, and reckless wrongdoing, just as for negligence. Still, there is no problem analogous to the all-inclusiveness problem for negligence; this, for the obvious reason that *a* type of harm is risked, foreseen, or intended, even though other types of harm also are risked and even though these other risks must also be considered. There are thus many cases where a harm that is caused is outside the risk(s) of which the actor was aware or outside the type(s) of harm that he foresaw or intended, even though such harms are within *some* risk that entered into the calculation of whether his action was unjustified.

There are thus no conceptual obstacles (to doing the matching between mental states and harms required for the more serious culpability determinations) that are at all analogous to the conceptual problems I raised for negligence in the last chapter. Nor are there normative problems analogous to those I raised for negligence in this chapter. As I alluded to when discussing transferred intent, negligence is the lowest rung on the culpability ladder. We do not try to distinguish negligence from some other state of even lesser culpability. Thus, a defendant who causes a harm outside the risk(s) that make(s) him negligent must be either exonerated or held liable. As argued earlier, I would opt for liability. But that is not the choice in cases that involve intention, foresight, or recklessness. For these higher forms of culpability, the whole idea is to match the harm caused to the type of harm intended, foreseen, or risked so that one can distinguish the intentional wrongdoer from the merely reckless wrongdoer and both from the merely negligent wrongdoer.

---

[23] See, eg, Model Penal Code, § 2.02(2)(c): 'A person acts recklessly with respect to a material element of an offense when he consciously disregards a substantial and *unjustifiable* risk...' (emphasis added).

[24] I ignore the fact that, in both torts and criminal law, lack of justification is separated out from intent and knowledge, so that general justification (or 'necessity') becomes a defense and not part of the *mens rea*.

B. Negligence per se

The second *reductio* with which one must deal in defending the so-called non-relational view of negligence is this: if one rejects the view that negligence is relational by relations of risk—if one denies, that is, that negligence is properly applied by an HWR analysis—then one cannot make sense of tort law's traditional negligence per se doctrine. For the two-pronged doctrinal test of negligence per se is a special sort of HWR test; so if HWR tests are both conceptually and morally indefensible, then the tort law doctrine of negligence per se must be both conceptually and morally indefensible as well. Since this is absurd, goes the argument, the non-relational theory of negligence that yields such a conclusion must be false.

In tort law, a defendant is deemed negligent per se when his conduct violates a criminal statute and both (1) harms a person who is within the class of persons sought to be protected by that statute and (2) causes a harm that is within the type of harms sought to be prevented by that statute. Consider, for example, the textbook case of *Martin v. Herzog*,[25] in which the plaintiff's husband, who was killed when his buggy was struck by the defendant's car, was deemed to be contributorily negligent per se in driving the buggy at night without lights, in violation of a statute. Cardozo held that inasmuch as the statute requiring buggies to have lights was 'intended for the protection of travelers on the highway' (a class of persons within which both the defendant and the decedent were members) and inasmuch as the collision that occurred and the harm that ensued from that collision were instances of the types of harms intended to be prevented by the statute, the plaintiff's omission constituted 'negligence in itself'.[26]

In describing the plaintiff's omission in this way, Cardozo is often thought to have articulated the majority rule concerning the legal relevance of a statutory violation that satisfies the two-pronged test articulated above. On this dominant view, such a statutory violation is *conclusive* evidence of a defendant's negligence (or a plaintiff's contributory negligence). To establish the violation is to exhaust the inquiry into the reasonableness of the defendant's conduct. As Cardozo maintained:

By the very terms of the hypothesis, to omit, willfully or heedlessly, the safeguards prescribed by law for the benefit of another that he may be preserved in life or limb, is to fall short of the standard of diligence to which those who live in organized society are under a duty to conform.[27]

The rule that statutory violations constitute, by themselves, conclusive evidence of negligence can usefully be juxtaposed to four other, progressively less stringent, rules concerning the possible relevance of a statutory violation to the question of a defendant's negligence.

[25] 126 NE 814 (NY 1920).   [26] Ibid, 815.   [27] Ibid, 815.

The first alternative rule would be that a statutory violation constitutes *practically conclusive* evidence of negligence—evidence sufficient to obtain a summary judgment or a directed verdict for the plaintiff unless rebutted by the defendant. The second alternative rule would be that a statutory violation constitutes prima facie evidence of negligence—evidence sufficient to withstand a motion for summary judgment, or a motion for a directed verdict, by the defendant. On alternative interpretations of *Martin v. Herzog*, Cardozo was articulating one of these alternative rules, for after describing the plaintiff's conduct as 'negligence in itself', he went on to state that '[t]he jury should have been told that the omission of the lights was *prima facie* evidence of contributory negligence, ie, that it was sufficient in itself unless its probative force was overcome'.[28] Inasmuch as he maintained that the plaintiff's 'omission of these lights was a wrong, and being wholly unexcused was also a negligent wrong',[29] Cardozo seemingly contemplated the possibility that a party might be able to defend against a charge of negligence by advancing some excuse for his statutory violation—in which case, his violation would not constitute *conclusive* evidence of negligence.

The third alternative rule governing the relevance of statutory violations to negligence determinations constitutes the clear minority rule in American jurisdictions—the rule that such violations are simply *some* evidence of negligence. This was the view adopted by the trial court in *Martin v. Herzog*, which instructed members of the jury that they could 'consider the default as lightly or gravely' as they chose.[30] Under this rule, the fact that the defendant violated the criminal law is probative of the question of whether he breached his duty of reasonableness in tort law, but it does not exhaust the question, nor does it even provide sufficient evidence of negligence to withstand a defendant's motion for summary judgment. One is hard pressed to describe this as a negligence per se rule, since it does not take statutory violations to be proxies for findings of negligence under either the reasonable-person test or Learned Hand's more exacting calculus of risk. For present purposes, however, I shall proceed by treating any and all rules that require at least some deference to legislative judgments when setting the standard of care in tort law to be negligence per se doctrines, recognizing that in most instances, true negligence per se is typically thought to be captured only by the conclusive-evidence view articulated above.

Before courts can assign weight to statutory violations, be it some weight or conclusive weight, they are bound to find first that the harm caused by the defendant's statutory violation is within the class of harms sought to be prevented by the legislature and that the person who was so harmed is within the class of persons sought to be protected by the legislature. Each of these doctrinal requirements patently demand an analysis that bears a disturbing similarity to an HWR test. A court must satisfy itself that the harm caused by the defendant is

---

[28] 126 NE at 816.   [29] Ibid, 815.   [30] Ibid.

within the risk that made the legislature criminally prohibit the defendant's conduct to begin with; and it must establish that the plaintiff is within the class of persons to whom the legislature found a duty, the breach of which it deemed serious enough to merit criminal penalties. Inasmuch as these doctrinal hurdles demand analyses that are just the strong version of a fully relational HWR analysis, it would seem that they must stand or fall together with the general HWR tests. If a general HWR analysis invites fatal conceptual problems and is otherwise morally unmotivated, then it would seem that the requirements for finding a defendant to be negligent per se would suffer similar fatal difficulties.

Can negligence per se, in any of its variations, be saved from the difficulties above articulated for HWR inquiries? Consider, first, whether the description problem bedevils the doctrine of negligence per se. One might plausibly deny that it does, for one might argue that the risk within which the harm caused by the defendant must fall is given a determinate description by the legislation (as is the class of persons sought to be protected). But of course, that description nowhere figures in the legislature's enacted language. In order to determine whom the legislature sought to protect and what harms the legislature sought to prevent by enacting a statute that requires buggies to travel by night with lights, one cannot merely read the statute—for its language simply requires the use of lights at night, on pain of criminal penalty. One must, instead, look to the legislature's intent, as reflected, presumably most reliably, in legislative history. If one can extract from that history an unconflicted intent to prevent one or more discrete types of harm to a determinate class of persons, then one can presumably solve the description problem. If, for example, expressions of legislative intent reveal that by requiring lights on buggies at night, the legislature sought only to prevent 'highway collisions' (but not 'espionage by foreign spies' or 'an over-population of flying insects'), the harm caused by the defendant must be an instance of a 'a highway collision'. If it is not an instance of this type of harm, then it cannot be thought to be within the harm sought to be prevented by the legislature.

If the description problem can be solved, then one might think that so too can the all-inclusiveness problem. For once one can identify a determinate class of harms sought to be prevented by the legislature and a determinate set of persons sought to be protected by the legislature, not all harms to all persons will be among those targeted by the statute. The two-pronged test of when a statutory violation makes a defendant negligent per se thus would have real bite. It would clearly sort, in a non-arbitrary, non-question-begging fashion, those whose allegedly tortious behavior is, in fact, also criminal from those whose allegedly tortious behavior is not. If we have sound reasons to think that criminal conduct is very often (and perhaps always) tortious conduct when the two-pronged test is satisfied, it would appear that we can continue to infer the one from the other without fear that the problems that beset a general HWR analysis make such an inference arbitrary.

This solution (saving the negligence per se doctrine from the two conceptual problems that beset the HWR analysis) is of course wholly hostage to there being something properly called the intention of the legislature. For it is only by likening legislatures to individual persons that one can assume they too have canonically described texts forming the content of their intentions. I have else-where argued at some length that there is no reason to be optimistic about there being any such determinate notion of legislative intent.[31]

In the face of difficulties in ascribing determinate intentions to legislatures, it seems unlikely that it is even possible to detect whether legislators shared a single, identical description of the harms and persons with which each was concerned when enacting a criminal prohibition. One strongly suspects that when courts and commentators make reference to legislative intentions concerning particular statutory enactments, they are not discovering facts of shared psychology, but, rather, moral facts about the good; that is, they are articulating a purpose that makes the best moral sense of the particular statute within the larger corpus of statutory and common-law rules, and they are then asking whether application of the statute to the facts of a given case well serves that good. But, of course, how one describes the purpose of a statute, once one no longer means by 'purpose' a fixed intention singularly shared by a legislature, is open to multiple levels of abstraction. And hence, whether a defendant's conduct offends that purpose will be a function of its description and the description of that purpose. A leash law can be equally described as serving the purpose of 'preventing harms to others' and 'preventing persons from being bitten'. If a person's Ming vase is buried by her neighbor's rottweiler, the neighbor's conduct in failing to leash his dog will be negligent per se under the first description, and not under the second. Inasmuch as we can expect that courts will craft their descriptions of the purposes of criminal statutes in accordance with their antecedently formed judgments about whether a defendant should be held to be negligent per se, we can expect that their negligence per se analyses will be as vacuous as are general HWR analyses.

In addition to this conceptual worry with using legislative intention to solve the description problem, there is a second, normative obstacle in the way of such a solution. In order to appreciate this obstacle, consider again the case of *Gorris v. Scott*,[32] in which the plaintiff's sheep were washed overboard in a storm after the defendant shipowner failed to pen them as required by the Contagious Disease (Animals) Act of 1869. As the court held:

[I]f we could see that it was the object, or among the objects of this Act, that the owners of sheep and cattle coming from a foreign port should be protected by the means

---

[31] See Michael S Moore, 'A natural law theory of interpretation', Southern California Law Review 58 (1985), 338–58; Michael S Moore, 'The semantics of judging', Southern California Law Review 54 (1981), 246–70.

[32] 9 LR Ex 125 (1874).

described against the danger of their property being washing overboard, or lost by the perils of the sea, the present action would be within the principle.

But looking at the Act, it is perfectly clear that its provisions were all enacted with a totally different view; there was no purpose, direct or indirect, to protect against such damage; but, as is recited in the preamble, the Act is directed against the possibility of sheep or cattle being exposed to disease on their way to this country.... [T]he damage complained of here is something totally apart from the object of the Act of Parliament, and it is in accordance with all the authorities to say that the action is not maintainable.[33]

Why have courts like this one consistently refused to declare a defendant negligent per se when that defendant's criminal violation has brought about a harm outside of the type of harms sought to be prevented by the legislature or when the harm has befallen someone outside the class of persons sought to be protected by the legislature? The answer must be that with regard to such harms and such persons, criminal legislation is poor evidence of negligence. That is, criminal prohibitions are assumed to be a product of extensive legislative fact-finding and deliberation concerning how efficiently to prevent particular harms to particular persons. They thus provide good evidence—perhaps the best evidence possible—of the conclusions generated by Learned Hand's calculus of risk if that calculus is limited to the harms, persons, and precautions contemplated by the legislature. As the *Gorris* court assumed, in enacting the Contagious Disease (Animals) Act, Parliament had presumably researched the probability and gravity of harm resulting from the arrival in England of diseased livestock and had concluded that penning animals during trans-oceanic shipments constitutes a cost-efficient means of eliminating that risk. But, as the court further assumed, that legislative conclusion is no evidence that the risk of drowning is cost-efficiently eliminated by penning animals, because the legislature was not gathering facts and deliberating about the probability and gravity of losing animals to drowning.

Yet once one appreciates that an assessment of a defendant's negligence requires one to consider *all* of the risks attendant on his conduct (as was argued in Chapter 8) and once one accepts that a defendant can fairly be held liable for *any* risk that materializes from negligent conduct (as was also argued also in Chapter 8)—even when that risk is not, by itself, sufficient to make the defendant's conduct negligent (as is true in concurrent risk cases), and even when it might not have been strictly necessary to finding the defendant's negligent (as is true in mixed concurrent risk cases)—then one of two conclusions must follow. Either statutory violations are not good heuristics by which to assess the reasonableness of a defendant's conduct, because in crafting them, the legislature did not comply with the full demands of the calculus of negligence by considering *all* of the risks, *all* of the benefits, and *all* of the precautions that might maximize benefits and minimize risks. (If this is the case, then statutory violations should hardly be accorded conclusive, practically conclusive, or even prima facie weight.) Or

---

[33] 9 LR Ex 125 (1874) at 129.

statutory violations are good evidence that the defendant created certain risks that were individually or jointly sufficient to make his conduct negligent (eg, the risk of contagious disease). On this second alternative, the two limitations on finding a defendant negligent per se are themselves confused because the fact that a defendant realizes a risk different from those that are themselves sufficient to make his conduct negligent is morally irrelevant.[34]

It follows from this analysis that even if negligence per se can escape the description problem that threatens to render it as incoherent as the more general HWR analyses to which it is akin, it cannot be preserved intact. Either courts must refuse to treat statutory violations as anything more than *some* evidence that a defendant created sufficient risks to be found negligent—evidence that jurors may weight 'as lightly or as gravely' as they see fit—or they must lift the limitations on the negligence per se doctrine so as to permit rebuttal by defendants who, by virtue of their criminal violations, are found (with conclusive, or practically conclusive, or prima facie certainty) to have created risks individually or jointly sufficient to make their conduct negligent (even when risks other than those in fact materialize from their conduct).

My conclusions about the general HWR analysis thus do not entail that the concept of negligence per se be altogether abandoned, but it certainly reveals: (1) that a negligence per se analysis very often asks unanswerable questions (in the same way that general HWR analyses asks unanswerable questions); and (2), that even when its questions are answerable, they are not questions that yield morally relevant, or morally consistent, answers. If a defendant's criminal violation, by itself, entails that the defendant has generated a risk to someone sufficient to make him negligent, it matters not that some other risk to some other person materializes—he still should be liable for that risk and to that person. And if a defendant's criminal violation does not, by itself, entail such a conclusion, then it should not be treated as most jurisdictions currently treat it—namely, as conclusive proof that the defendant acted unreasonably.

---

[34] As was argued at the beginning of the chapter.

10

The Descriptive Inaccuracy of the Harm-within-the-Risk Analysis as Measuring Proximate Causation

If the analysis of the last two chapters is correct, then with regard to negligence as a basis for culpability the HWR test is both a conceptually suspect and a normatively undesirable criterion of liability in torts and criminal law. Yet neither of these conclusions bedevil the HWR analysis when it is applied to crimes or torts whose culpability requirements are those of purpose, knowledge, or recklessness. For such torts or crimes, making an HWR inquiry is a proper part of the culpability determination for civil liability and criminal liability. Still, even for such torts or crimes, the question remains whether an HWR analysis can supplant entirely the need for any proximate cause requirement. Proponents of a strong version of HWR analysis assert that it can, and it is this assertion that I shall examine here.

Sometimes the fully relational HWR analysis is said to be compatible with the decisions courts have made on proximate-cause grounds, in the sense that an HWR analysis decides those cases the same way as they were decided under proximate-cause tests. At other times, an HWR analysis is presented as working a change in the proximate cause decisions. Under the latter scenario, proponents of an HWR analysis are advancing a normative proposition: the law of proximate causation should be changed to conform to an HWR test because such a test is so normatively attractive. In the former scenario, proponents of an HWR analysis are advancing a descriptive proposition: the law that we have is really an expression of an HWR test, although the courts and some commentators have mistakenly thought that the grounds for their decisions lie elsewhere. We shall thus want to probe the strong version of an HWR analysis both for its descriptive accuracy with respect to proximate cause decisions and for its normative superiority over proximate cause rationales for those decisions.

There are three sorts of proximate-cause cases and doctrines that are prima facie incompatible with an HWR analysis. These are the intervening-cause cases, the take-your-victim-as-you-find-her cases, and the remoteness cases. I shall consider each in turn.

I. Harm-within-the-Risk and Intervening Causation

As we shall explore in some detail in Chapter 11, below, standard intervening-cause doctrines in American tort law and criminal law hold that the intervention of a subsequent, independent event, when that event is either a pre-emptive cause, an extraordinary ('abnormal') event, or a third party's action intentionally exploiting the situation created by the defendant, 'breaks the causal chain' between a defendant's act and his victim's harm. Thus, if a defendant poisons v's water when v is headed into the desert, but another drains the water in an attempt to kill v, the second party's pre-emptive intervention relieves the first defendant of causal responsibility for v's death in the desert.[1] If a defendant's negligence causes a fire to ignite, but an unprecedented gale happens along so as to fan the fire and spread it to v's house miles away, the intervention of the extraordinary storm relieves the defendant of causal responsibility for the loss of v's house.[2] If a defendant negligently derails a tanker car and spills its gasoline throughout the streets of a town, but a third party intentionally ignites the gasoline that destroys the town, the arsonist's intervention relieves the defendant of causal responsibility for the town's destruction.[3]

Descriptively, an HWR analysis has a difficult time accommodating these cases. A HWR test, in its pure form, only asks after a logical relation between a type of harm (the one the defendant intended, foresaw, or the risk of which made the defendant negligent) and a token of harm (the harm that actually happened). If the token is an instance of the type, then the harm was 'within the risk'. This logical relation takes no notice of the freakishness of the route by which the defendant's act caused the harm. It makes no difference what the means, instrumentality, or causal route may have been; if death was the type of harm risked by the defendant and a death occurred, the harm was within the risk that made the defendant negligent.

Some proponents of an HWR test embrace this conclusion. Glanville Williams celebrates that with an HWR analysis 'we shall be spared ... "the never-ending and insoluble problems of causation", together with the subtleties of *novus actus interveniens*'.[4] Williams is right about an HWR analysis in its pure form. The question remains whether this fact about HWR is something to be celebrated or regretted. And that depends on what one thinks of the intervening-cause cases and their doctrines.

There are two issues here. One is what the tort and criminal law doctrines we now have say about intervening causation. The commentary to the proposed

---

[1] James McLaughlin's famous hypothetical, in James McLaughlin, 'Proximate cause', *Harvard Law Review* 39 (1925), 155, n 25.

[2] *Kimble v. Mackintosh Hemphill Co*, 59 A 2d 68 (Pa 1948).

[3] *Watson v. K & Ind Bridge Co*, 126 SW 146 (Ky 1910).

[4] Glanville Williams, 'The risk principle', *Law Quarterly Review* 77 (1961), 179.

Restatement (Third) of the Law of Torts accurately enough notes 'the waning influence of superseding-cause jurisprudence'[5] in the sense that some courts now hold tortfeasors liable despite the intervention of third-party intentional wrongdoers.[6] Yet: (1) there are many courts that do not, explicitly on intervening-cause grounds;[7] (2) many courts do not on HWR or foreseeability grounds, exploiting the vacuousness of the HWR and foreseeability doctrines to reach intervening-cause results on these other bases;[8] (3) many of the cases imposing liability despite intervening, intentional wrongdoers do so in the provision of opportunity cases, which we saw in Chapter 6 to be omission liability cases, not cause cases, anyway;[9] and (4) the doctrine of intervening causation seems to retain its full vigor in criminal law, where the distinction between principals and accomplices is built around this doctrine.[10]

The second issue is whether the continued vitality of the intervening-cause doctrines is justified. It is true that, as Herbert Hart and Tony Honoré charted in great detail,[11] the intervening-cause distinctions are supported by many common intuitions about both causation and responsibility. Glanville Williams responded that whatever the common-sense credentials of the doctrine, 'no satisfactory reason is suggested for drawing [the distinctions of intervening causation]' and that the intervening-cause cases 'must often have the most arbitrary results'.[12] As we shall explore in Chapters 12 and 13, some of the intervening-cause cases are difficult to justify either as a matter of policy or as a matter of the metaphysics of causation. Particularly puzzling is the intentional intervening-wrongdoers doctrine, which makes the question of whether an action is an intervening cause turn on the mental state of the intervener. Other intervening-cause doctrines, such as the pre-emptive-cause and extraordinary natural-events doctrines, are more easily explained on causal grounds. At the end of the day, I shall conclude that the most that can be said for the intervening-cause doctrine is that it serves as a rough proxy for something that is both

[5] *Restatement (Third) of the Law of Torts: Liability for Physical Harm (Basic Principles)* (Philadelphia, American Law Institute, 2003, Tentative Draft No. 3), Chapter 6, § 34, Comment a.

[6] See ibid, 'Reporter's Notes', 110–16.

[7] *Restatement (Third) of the Law of Torts: Liability for Physical Harm (Basic Principles)*, 'Reporter's Notes', 116–19.

[8] Ibid, 122–3.   [9] Ibid, 109–12.

[10] See, eg, *People v. Kevorkian*, 447 Mich 436, 527 NW 2d 714 (1994), where the Michigan Supreme Court reaffirmed that Kevorkian's acts were not the legal cause of his patients' deaths whenever such patients did the last act causing death.

[11] HLA Hart and Tony Honoré, *Causation in the Law* (2nd edn, Oxford: Oxford University Press, 1985).

[12] Williams, 'The risk principle', 181. For Williams' extended disenchantment with intervening-cause doctrines, see his review of the first edition of Hart and Honoré, Glanville Williams, 'Causation in the law', Cambridge Law Journal (1961), 62–85. But see Glanville Williams, 'Finis for novus actus?', Cambridge Law Journal 48 (1989), 391–416, where Williams expresses apparent agreement with intervening-cause doctrines so long as they are clothed as moral (not causal) limits on responsibility.

metaphysically respectable and morally relevant, viz degrees of causal contribution. Often enough, intervening causes reduce or eliminate the degree of causal contribution made by some earlier actor's act.

Yet even this the pure HWR analysis cannot accommodate. The pure HWR analysis simply asks a question of logical relationship: was the harm in fact caused by some defendant's act an instance of the type of harm he either intended, foresaw, or risked? There is no room for degrees of causal contribution in answering this logical question of instantiation; a death of some victim instantiates the type (death of a person) no matter how diminished may be the defendant's causal contribution to that death.

The more typical response to the intervening-cause cases by proponents of a strong HWR analysis is to abandon a pure HWR analysis and to modify that HWR analysis. One way to do this is to go the route of the first *Restatement of Torts*, which abandoned a strong version of an HWR test for a weak version. Rather inelegantly, Bohlen's first *Restatement* let the HWR analysis do the work of proximate causation until an intervening-cause problem was encountered; then the prolix rules of intervening causation took over.[13]

The American Law Institute's much later Model Penal Code follows the lead of the first *Restatement of Torts* in this regard. Section 2.03 qualifies its HWR test by denying liability for a harm within the risk that made an actor negligent if that harm is 'too ... accidental in its occurrence to have a [just] bearing on the actor's liability or on the gravity of his offense'.[14] This is an open-ended invitation to judges to allow traditional intervening-cause doctrines to decide cases without regard to the results of an HWR analysis. Unlike the first *Restatement of Torts*, however, the Code does not spell out what those intervening-cause doctrines might be.

A second, seemingly less ad hoc way of modifying an HWR analysis so as to accommodate the intervening-cause cases is to exploit the vagaries in the description of the risk, adverted to in Chapter 8. Here, the game is to build into the description of the risk that makes a defendant culpable not only a type of harm, but also a type of means by which such a type of harm comes about. As Warren Seavey baldly stated this strategy, 'The fact that the harm is directly caused by an intervening act of a stranger induced by the defendant's negligent conduct prevents the supposition of liability upon the first wrongdoer only if the type of intervention was not within the risk.'[15] For example, where a defendant

[13] Warren Seavey's critical analysis of what Bohlen had done. Seavey, 'Mr Justice Cardozo and the law of torts', Harvard Law Review 52 (1939), 390–1.
[14] Model Penal Code, § 2.03 (Proposed Official Draft 1962). The Code Commentary makes clear that this language is an invitation to courts and juries 'to deal with intervening or concurrent causes, natural or human...'. Ibid, 133.
[15] Seavey, 'Mr Justice Cardozo', 387.

negligently leaves an unprotected bulkhead next to a slippery sidewalk, he is liable to the plaintiff when the plaintiff slips and falls into the bulkhead and when the plaintiff is negligently jostled towards the bulkhead by a crowd of rowdies; but the defendant is not liable when the plaintiff is intentionally pushed towards the bulkhead by an old enemy. 'The risk was that a traveler might slip or be inadvertently pushed in, and not that he might be thrown in.'[16]

Well . . . does anyone really believe this? The slipperiness of a sidewalk next to an unprotected bulkhead risks just the *kind of injury* the victim suffers under any of the three scenarios Seavey imagined. The type of injury risked is identical no matter how the victim is propelled—by her own motion, the inadvertent jostling of rowdies, or the intentional shove of an enemy. What Seavey's unprincipled willingness to alter the risk-description reveals is that he too wished to supplement his HWR analysis with intervening-cause doctrines. The only difference between Seavey's arguments and the rule articulated by Bohlen's *Restatement of Torts* is the honesty with which each abandons a strong version of an HWR analysis. What the *Restatement* did openly, Seavey did with smoke and mirrors.

The honest response of the HWR proponent is the earlier one. One should keep the HWR analysis pure, so that the relevant risks are of types of harms, not including the routes or instrumentalities by which such harms are produced. Such purity does not accommodate the intervening-cause cases, but admitting this then allows issue to be joined as to whether those cases are rightly decided.[17]

II. Harm-within-the-Risk and the Take-Your-Victim-as-You-Find-Her Maxim

One of the essential prerequisites for an intervening cause is that it *intervenes* between the defendant's culpable act and the victim's harm.[18] Pre-existing conditions, no matter how extraordinary or abnormal, do not occur subsequent to a defendant's act and so are ineligible to serve as breakers of causal chains. There is thus liability in such cases, no matter how extraordinary or unforeseeable may have been the harm. This legal result is encapsulated most famously in the common-law maxim that a defendant must 'take his victim as he finds her'. If the

---

[16] Seavey, 'Mr Justice Cardozo', 387–8.

[17] One can almost accuse the proposed *Restatement (Third) of Torts* of such honesty. Unlike the Model Penal Code, § 2.03, with its qualifying language earlier quoted, *Restatement (Third) of Torts*, § 29 unqualifiedly states that 'an actor is not liable for harm different from the harms whose risks made the actor's conduct tortious'. Yet as the Comments to § 34 make plain, even the *Restatement (Third)* drafters are willing to allow jurors to do Seavey-like adjustments to the description of the risk so as to allow intervening causes to break causal chains. See ibid, 106, Illustrations 4 and 5.

[18] See Chapter 11, below.

victim is particularly susceptible to injury because she has a proverbially thin skull (hemophilia, a psychiatric condition, religious scruples against transfusions, etc), the defendant is liable for the full extent of the victim's harm, no matter how unforeseeable.

This maxim, embraced by both tort law and criminal law, is not easy to square with an HWR analysis. Again, there are two basic stances an HWR theorist might take when faced with these cases. The first is to deny that these cases are correctly decided. As Glanville Williams concluded, 'It seems obvious that, if the risk principle is not to be seriously undermined, the thin-skull rule must either be denied or carefully restricted.'[19] Yet this again frames a difficult normative issue for the HWR theorist. Is not the common law of torts and crimes compelling? After all, defendants in these cases have culpably caused (in often the most direct of ways) serious injury to their victims. Such culpability exists even though the kind of injuries caused may have seemed freakishly impossible to defendants who were ignorant of their victim's peculiar susceptibilities. Why should an innocent victim, whose susceptibilities to injury are not her fault, bear such an uncompensated loss when harmed by a culpable harm-causer? Why should such a culpable harm-causer be let off the hook for all the harms he has clearly caused? Consider, for example, the facts of *Koehler v. Waukesha Milk Co*,[20] where a defendant milk vendor negligently left a chipped milk bottle on a victim's stoop. The victim cut her hand on the bottle and, because of a rare blood condition, contracted blood poisoning and died. In torts, the defendant is liable not only for the cut but also for the death. And is this not the right result?[21]

If the thin-skulled victim rule is properly retained, the other response of the HWR theorist is to attempt to accommodate thin-skulled victims within the risk analysis. Consider again Warren Seavey on this solution. Seavey illustrates both of the variations of this kind of response that we saw before with respect to intervening causes. He at one point appears to abandon the strong version of an HWR analysis for the weak version. This is where Seavey concedes, with respect to the take-your-victim-as-you-find-her maxim, that:

[t]he theory of risk is only partially invoked in determining the extent of liability for an admittedly negligent completed tort. There may be liability for consequences which were not within the risks as they existed immediately before the impact.[22]

---

[19] Williams, 'The risk principle', 195.
[20] 208 NW 901 (Wisc 1926).
[21] Admittedly, criminal law differs, for the defendant must have culpable *mens rea* with respect to every material element of homicide, including death, and the defendant seems not even negligent with respect to that element.
[22] Seavey, 'Principles of tort', Harvard Law Review 56 (1943), 91.

Yet this again seems an ad hoc concession for a true believer in the power of the HWR analysis.[23]

At another point, Seavey appears to try the other tack. He excludes from the risk that makes one negligent the extent of the harm, including in the description of the risk only the type of the harm.[24] Yet this type-of-injury versus extent-of-injury distinction, familiar from Pollock's writings,[25] is seemingly unprincipled. If, as Seavey said, the basic idea behind an HWR analysis is that 'the reasons for creating liability should limit it',[26] prima facie liability for death should follow only on a risk of death sufficiently serious that it makes leaving a chipped milk bottle negligent. Yet in cases of abnormally susceptible victims, liability is imposed for serious injuries even though the basis for that liability—an unreasonable risk of serious injury—was not present.

Because the type/extent distinction is unprincipled, it is also hard to draw. Was the victim's death by blood poisoning the same type of injury as the cutting of her finger, only to a greater extent? Or was the death a different type of injury from the cutting?

Again, the honest response of the HWR proponent is to concede that an HWR analysis does not decide the thin-skulled cases consistent with current law, but to dispute the correctness of the thin-skulled victim rule. This, of course, concedes that an HWR analysis does not absorb all of the proximate cause doctrines. It also commits proponents to the uphill normative argument discussed in Chapter 9.

III. Harm-within-the-Risk and the Remoteness Rules

As is suggested by Sir Francis Bacon's phrase '*causa proxima*', an act is not the proximate cause of some harm if that harm is too remote from that act. Remoteness is not a product of intervening causes; those are separate doctrines in

---

[23] Equally ad hoc and unprincipled is the proposed *Restatement (Third) of Torts*, § 31, which provides that 'when an actor's tortious conduct causes harm to a person that, because of the person's pre-existing physical or mental condition or other characteristic, is of greater magnitude or different type than might reasonably be expected, the actor is nonetheless subject to liability for all such harm to the person'. As the Comments to this section recognize, there will be liability in the thin-skulled man cases 'even in those cases in which the harm may be found to be beyond the risk . . .': Ibid, 71, Comment b. Yet such liability flatly contradicts the mandates of the HWR analysis. A defender of HWR might be conceding these cases on the ground of unanimous legal authority: 'Every United States jurisdiction adheres to the thin-skull rule . . . extensive research has failed to identify a single United States case disavowing the rule.': Ibid, 74. But such unanimous legal authority does not seem to be in error; there *should be* liability in such cases, contrary to the plain import to the contrary of an HWR analysis.

[24] Seavey, 'Mr Justice Cardozo', 385. See also *Restatement (Third) of Torts*, following Seavey in the hope that many of the thin-skulled cases can be treated as extent or manner of injury cases, not type of injury cases. Ibid, 71, Comment b.

[25] Frederick Pollock, 'Liability for consequences', Law Quarterly Review 38 (1922), 167.

[26] Seavey, 'Mr Justice Cardozo', 386.

the law. Rather, remoteness is simply a matter of spatio-temporal remove, a remove that need not involve the intervention of pre-emptive causes, extraordinary natural events, or deliberate third-party actions. These simplest of proximate-cause cases are also difficult to square with an HWR analysis. For again, in its pure form, a finding that a harm is within the risk that made a defendant culpable is a logical relation between a type of harm intended, foreseen, or risked and a token of harm caused. Such a logical relation is blind to spatio-temporal location of events, and it is blind to the length of the causal route between events, be it short or long.

Again, the HWR theorist can have one of two responses to these remoteness doctrines of proximate causation. The first is to deny that they are correct. As Seavey wrote, 'The fact that there is a long space of time or series of events intervening between the negligent act and the harm does not prevent liability.'[27] This seems to be an assertion by Seavey that our present law does not contain simple remoteness doctrines. Yet Seavey's much admired Cardozo thought differently: 'There is no use in arguing that distance ought not to count, if life and experience tell us that it does.'[28]

So proponents of a strong HWR analysis are forced to deny the correctness of remoteness doctrines on normative grounds. They are forced to argue that spatio-temporal remove ought not to make a difference for responsibility. Yet as Cardozo noted, this is not only contrary to the decided cases and the common sense on which the law is built, it is also contrary to a plausible metaphysics of causation. On a plausible theory of causation, causal relations peter out gradually by transmission through events. This is because causation is a scalar relation (a more-or-less affair) and because the degree of causal contribution by some act to some harm becomes less and less as successively larger groups of other events join the act in causing the harm. Spatio-temporal proximity, on this view, is a rough but good proxy for this progressive diminishment in causal contribution.[29]

The second response available to proponents of a strong HWR analysis is to concede the correctness of the remoteness cases, but to modify their HWR analysis to accommodate those cases. There are, again, two varieties of this response, just as there are in intervening cause and thin-skulled victim cases. The first is to abandon the strong version of an HWR test for a weak version. This is the Model Penal Code's tack, for the Code makes an exception for any harm that is 'too remote . . . to have a [just] bearing on the actor's liability or on the gravity of his offence', even if that harm is fully within the intent, foresight, or risk that makes the actor culpable.[30] This is yet another ad hoc concession that any true believer in an HWR analysis should be loath to make.

[27] Seavey, 'Principles of tort', 91–2.
[28] *Bird v. St Paul F & Minn Ins Co*, 120 NE 86 (NY 1918).
[29] As I argued in Chapter 5, above.   [30] Model Penal Code, §§ 2.03(2), 2.03(3).

Alternatively, the HWR theorist might further gerrymander her description of the risks that make the actor negligent so as to include not just types of harms but also the causal routes by which those harms occur. Thus a death brought about by a remote act of a defendant would not be within the risk that makes defendant negligent, because that risk was only of a death brought about by a *short* causal route. The arbitrariness of this tack should by now be apparent.

IV. Conclusion

The upshot is that an HWR analysis cannot fully replace proximate-causation doctrines. An ungerrymandered HWR test decides the intervening-cause cases, thin-skulled cases, and remoteness cases both differently than do existing proximate-cause doctrines, and wrongly. A gerrymandered HWR test arrives at the results of the proximate cause tests only because it in fact employs, rather than replaces, those tests.

Rather than reviving this old proposal as does the proposed *Restatement (Third) of Torts*, we should abandon the harm-within-the-risk analysis, root and branch. Introduced over a century ago as the enlightened alternative to the hoary doctrines of proximate causation, it turns out on careful inspection to be no real alternative at all. As applied in negligence cases, the analysis is both conceptually incoherent and normatively undesirable. As applied to all cases, intent and foresight as well as negligence, HWR gives an inaccurate description of the decided cases and it leaves out the crucial issues of (proximate) causation properly adjudicated by those cases. Each of these is reason enough to abandon the analysis, despite its distinguished lineage. Taken together, the case for such abandonment should be conclusive.

PART IV

THE LEGAL PRESUPPOSITION OF THERE BEING 'INTERVENING CAUSES'

11

The Legal Doctrines of
Intervening Causation

I. Introduction

Part III was largely a blind alley. The promise held out by the risk theory was to replace proximate causation with risk as the relevant desert-determiner in morality and as the relevant trigger of legal liability. For the reasons given, that hope is not to be realized. That leaves us with the thorny questions of proximate causation, avoidance of which partly motivated the HWR analysis.

In Part IV we shall explore what will largely turn out to be another blind alley. This is the law's supposition, raised in Chapters 5 and 6, that causation breaks off suddenly upon the occurrence of an 'intervening cause'. Unlike the risk analysis of Part III, the intervening-cause doctrines have not been proposed or enacted into law by skeptics about causation. Quite the contrary, the lawyers and theorists who for centuries have applied these doctrines have, by and large, regarded the law on this topic to be expressing factual *truths* about the causal relation in nature. Ultimately putting such doctrines aside (as I shall do by the end of Part IV) thus involves us in the metaphysics of causation as much as in the intricacies of legal doctrines and in the moral distinctions that lie behind them.

I shall proceed as follows. Because considerable exegetical work is required to derive the intervening-cause notion cleanly from the law we have, I shall spend the present chapter in doctrinal exegesis. Some of this exegetical work we already did in Chapters 5 and 6. There we reallocated liability for omissions, for provision of opportunities to third-party wrongdoers, for aiding and encouraging third-party wrongdoers, for aiding forces of nature, away from their supposed causal bases, into non-causal forms of liability. Having spent considerable time doing this part of the exegetical work, I shall not repeat or even summarize here the reasons for such reallocation. Rather, I shall here assume such reallocations to be justified so that the law we wish to examine can say simply and without exception: 'Certain interventions by third-party actors or by nature break the causal chains that would otherwise have existed between some defendant's action and some harm to another.'

The overall inquiry of this and the next chapter is to see what metaphysical sense we can make of this intervening-cause doctrine of the law. How can causation be a relation that breaks off suddenly with the intervention of some new force or agency, rather than petering out gradually over space and time? I say 'metaphysical sense' advisedly, because my inquiry is not into the policy reasons that may or may not support the *construction* of a legal doctrine of intervening causation. At one time, for example, lawyers constructed a notion of intervening causation in the form of the last-wrongdoer rule.[1] The doctrine stated that the wrongdoer closest in time to the harm was alone liable for having caused that harm; the policy justification was that neither tort plaintiffs nor the state (in criminal prosecutions) needed more than one guilty party per wrong. All prior wrongs were thus 'cut off' by the intervention of the last wrongdoer in law, even if not in fact. Such a construction makes no bones about its fictional, constructed character; such intervening-cause doctrine seeks no support from any underlying metaphysics of causation.

By contrast, my inquiry in Chapter 12 will be avowedly metaphysical. The question is whether the intervening-cause notions of the law can be based on a pre-legal notion of causation, one that provides a solid grounding for the sharp breaks in causal chains so marked by the law. In such a case, the doctrines of intervening causation would not be bereft of policy justification—for all law, on my view of it, must be based on 'policy': that is, on good reasons. But on the metaphysical view of intervening-causation doctrines, the policy justification would be two steps removed. The policy would be to attach legal liability (in the form of tort damages and criminal punishments) to morally blameworthy actions. It is morality, not legal policy, that tells us that actions that cause harm are more blameworthy than those that merely attempt or risk such harm.[2] It is metaphysics, not legal policy, that tells us when an action *causes* a certain harm. Such a desert-oriented policy behind the law of torts and the law of crimes thus justifies not looking to policy in seeking the meaning of causation in general and of intervening causation in particular. A legal doctrine of intervening causation is justified—on this corrective justice view of torts and retributive justice view of crimes—if it corresponds to a pre-legal, metaphysical notion of intervening causation.

I realize that to many post-Legal Realist legal academicians the foregoing description of my enterprise makes them wonder whether or not they have landed on Mars; for the Legal Realists achieved some of their most resounding victories over their enemies, the 'formalists', on the battlegrounds of intervening causation.[3] They convinced subsequent generations of legal scholars that all proximate-cause doctrines, including those of intervening causation, were merely misleading metaphors for underlying policies, and that such policies were better brought into

---

[1] The last-wrongdoer rule is discussed in Laurence Eldredge, 'Culpable intervention as superseding cause', University of Pennsylvania Law Review 86 (1938), 121–35.

[2] The thesis of Chapters 2 and 3 above.

[3] See, eg, Henry W Edgarton, 'Legal cause', University of Pennsylvania Law Review 72 (1924), 211–44, 343–75; Leon Green, 'Are there dependable rules of causation?', University of Pennsylvania Law Review 77 (1929), 601–28.

the light of day instead of being obscured in mysterious but ultimately empty metaphors of forces being spent, causes intervening, and the like.[4]

Yet the intellectual forebears of the inquiry of Part IV are not simply those pre-Legal Realist scholars of causation, such as Joseph Beale,[5] Francis Bohlen,[6] Jeremiah Smith,[7] Henry Terry,[8] James McLaughlin,[9] and others.[10] Most notably, I have been anticipated in my post-Legal Realist rescue project by the significant work on intervening causation done by Herbert Hart and Tony Honoré between 1956 and 1995.[11] For they too sought to rediscover a pre-legal notion of causation that made metaphysical sense of the law's doctrines of proximate (and intervening) causation. In my explication of those doctrines in the rest of this chapter, I shall thus rely heavily on their work as well as that of the pre-Legal Realist scholars.

The other intellectual forebear here is Sandy Kadish.[12] For Dean Kadish too felt the appeal of the Hart and Honoré rescue project for causation in the law and has added his own considerable talents to furthering that project. In particular, Kadish saw more clearly than Hart and Honoré how embedded in criminal-law

---

[4] The present draft of the proposed *Restatement (Third) of Torts* (Philadelphia: American Law Institute, Tentative Draft No 3, 7 April 2003), §§ 29–36, is a prominent example of such intellectual descendents. See ibid, § 34, Comment a, which pooh-poohs the 'formalism' of thinking that proximate causation could be based on a 'logical and objective inquiry', (or on a 'neutral scientific inquiry'). The proposed *Restatement (Third)* thus adopts the straight Legal Realist line that 'proximate *causation*' is a misnomer because the policy-based limits on liability going under that name have nothing to do with causation.

[5] Joseph Beale, 'Recovery for consequence of an act', Harvard Law Review 9 (1895), 80–9; Joseph Beale, 'The proximate consequence of an act', Harvard Law Review 33 (1920), 633–58.

[6] Francis H. Bohlen, 'The probable or the natural consequence as the test of liability in negligence', American Law Register 49 (1901), 78–88, 148–64.

[7] Jeremiah Smith, 'Legal cause in actions of torts, Harvard Law Review 25 (1911), 103–28, 223–52, 303–27.

[8] Henry T Terry, 'Proximate consequences in the law of torts', Harvard Law Review 28 (1914), 10–33.

[9] James Angell McLaughlin, 'Proximate cause', Harvard Law Review 39 (1925), 149–99.

[10] See Norris J. Burke, 'Rules of legal cause in negligence cases', California Law Review 15 (1926), 1–18; Charles E Carpenter, 'Proximate cause' (Pts 1–3), Southern California Law Review 14 (1940), 1–34, 115–53, 416–51; Southern California Law Review 15 (1941), 187–213, 304–21, 427–68; Southern California Law Review 16 (1943), 1–23, 61–92, 275–313; Charles E Carpenter, 'Workable rules for determining proximate cause', California Law Review 20 (1932) 229–59, 396–419, 471–539; Eldredge, 'Culpable intervention as superseding cause'; Albert Levitt, 'Cause, legal cause and proximate cause', Michigan Law Review 21 (1922), 34–62, 160–73; Andrew C McIntosh, 'Intervening criminal act as breaking causal chain', Law Notes, September (1931), 109; Victor I Minahan, 'The doctrine of intervening cause in the law of negligence', Marquette Law Review 4 (1919–1920), 75–80.

[11] HLA Hart and AM Honoré, 'Causation in the law', Law Quarterly Review 72 (1956), 58–90, 260–81, 398–417. Hart and Honoré, *Causation in the Law* (Oxford: Clarendon Press, 1959); Hart and Honoré, *Causation in the Law* (2nd edn, Oxford: Oxford University Press, 1985); Tony Honoré, 'Necessary and sufficient conditions in tort law', in David Owen (ed), *Philosophical Foundations of Tort Law* (Oxford: Oxford University Press, 1995).

[12] Sanford Kadish, 'Causation and complicity: A study in the interpretation of doctrine', California Law Review 73 (1985), 323–410; Kadish, 'A theory of complicity', in Ruth Gavison (ed), *Issues in Contemporary Legal Philosophy* (Oxford: Oxford University Press, 1987).

doctrine is the notion of intervening causation. As Kadish has pointed out in great detail, the doctrine forms a watershed divide in criminal law, separating liability as a principal from liability as an accomplice. Indeed, as Kadish saw, it is precisely because of the nature of our intervening-cause doctrine that we impose a secondary liability for those actors whose wrongful conduct makes possible the later wrong-doings of others. Accomplice liability fits like soft clay around the contours of principal liability, contours set by the doctrines of intervening causation.

Kadish took this doctrinal insight in two directions. First, he sought to ground the doctrines of intervening causation in metaphysics, specifically, in a libertarian metaphysics of free will. Although he himself did not endorse or reject such metaphysics, he sought to show how such a metaphysical view was plausible, accepted by many, and made metaphysical sense of the doctrines of intervening causation. Second, Kadish sought to ameliorate the Model Penal Code's glossing over of intervening causation, by adding language to section 2.03 of that Code explicitly putting the concept back in.[13] Although California did not adopt Kadish's proposed language, other states have done so.[14]

II. The Role of Intervening Cause within the Causal Requirements of the Law

In this chapter, I undertake the description of what it is that needs justification in metaphysics, namely, the legal doctrines of intervening causation. Mostly I shall describe the content of such doctrines. Preliminarily, however, we need to assay the place of such doctrines in the larger scheme of things.

Least controversially, intervening-cause problems are a subset of the larger problems of proximate causation.[15] On this view, causation in tort and criminal law is divided into two separate requirements, causation-in-fact and proximate causation. Intervening-cause doctrines are assigned exclusively to the second of

---

[13] Model Penal Code, § 2.03(2)(b) and (3)(b) qualify its general harm within the risk test by requiring that a harm not be 'too remote or accidental in its occurrence to have a [just] bearing on the actor's liability or on the gravity of his offense'. Kadish's proposed revision of this language was to add 'or dependent on another's volitional act' after 'occurrence': California Legislature Joint Comm for the Revision of the Penal Code, *Penal Code Revision Project*, § 408(i)(a)(ii) (Tentative Draft No 2, 1968). California did not adopt this language because, as the late John Kaplan used to jest, Kaplan and Kadish had also liberalized the Penal Code's marijuana provisions.

[14] See the citations in Sanford H Kadish and Stephen J Schulhofer (eds), *Criminal Law and Its Processes* (6th edn, Boston: Aspen Pub, 1995), 581, n 2.

[15] This is the view of Sandy Kadish, among others. See particularly his proposed revision of Model Penal Code, § 2.03 (n 13 above), which makes intervening causation only a kind of per se rule about freakishness of consequences. For other examples, see Meir Dan-Cohen, 'Causation', in Sanford Kadish (ed), *Encyclopedia of Crime and Justice* 1 (New York: Macmillan, 1983), 163, who regards intervening-cause tests as supplements to more general tests of proximity and foreseeability. See also Bohlen, 'Probable or natural consequences'; Carpenter, 'Proximate cause'; Carpenter, 'Workable Rules'.

these requirements. They are something of a sideshow even here. The main show has to do with remoteness issues, couched in terms of spatio-temporal proximity, substantiality of causal contribution, foreseeability, and the like. Intervening-cause doctrines are needed only in that subset of cases where something unusual intervenes between defendant's action and his victim's harm. In all other cases, proximate-cause issues are adjudicated without reference to such doctrines.

A more controversial role for intervening-cause doctrines is to see them as occupying the entire logical space of proximate causation.[16] A proximate cause is a 'direct cause', and a direct cause is any cause-in-fact of the harm where no intervening cause has intervened. Such a direct-cause test of proximate causation relies on the notion of intervening cause to fill out entirely the legal requirement of proximate cause. On this view, simple remoteness is irrelevant; what counts is the intervention of those special events we call intervening causes.

The most expansive view of intervening causation is one fairly attributable to Hart and Honoré.[17] On this view, the concepts involved in elucidating the notion of intervening cause are the very same concepts that give the meaning of causation generally. This view of intervening causation thus has the idea occupying the entire field of causation, not just some separable part of it such as proximate causation. The criteria by which one ascertains what is or is not an intervening cause are the very same criteria by which one decides what a cause is at all. There is thus no separable, preliminary step of isolating 'causes-in-fact'. Rather, we use certain paradigms to ascertain what is the cause of a certain event, albeit we use them twice: what is a cause must both fit such paradigms and not be succeeded in time by some other event that also fits such paradigms.

For our present purposes we need not determine initially which of these roles for intervening causation requirements is correct. Such a role falls out naturally enough from the content of the doctrines of intervening causation and from the metaphysical rationale behind such content. We should thus turn to that content itself.

III. The Content of the Intervening-cause Doctrines

It has been customary in the literature of intervening causation to divide intervening causes into two kinds, those consisting of extraordinary natural events and those consisting of wrongful human actions.[18] Although there are good reasons to

---

[16] This is the view of Terry, see Terry, 'Proximate consequences', and (implicitly, as McLaughlin argues), of Beale. See Beale, 'Recovery'; Beale, 'Proximate consequence'.

[17] Jointly authored works always pose some special problems of interpretation. I am more confident that the view in the text was that of Herbert Hart than I am that it was fully shared by Tony Honoré. As I explore below, Hart believed in paradigms as a mode of giving the meaning of expressions in natural languages, whereas Honoré perhaps always held the view that one could define a separate notion of cause-in-fact in terms of necessary and sufficient conditions.

[18] See, eg, Beale, 'Recovery', 87; Smith, 'Legal cause', 321–7; and Hart and Honoré, *Causation in the Law*.

honor this traditional division, and I shall do so later, initially it is helpful to regard intervening causes as a unitary phenomenon and to seek the general properties shared (or thought to be shared) by all species of the genus. I consider several such general properties below.

A. The causal condition: Intervening causes must be causally significant in the production of the harm

Not surprisingly, intervening causes must themselves be causes of the ultimate harm complained of.[19] Intervening causes, in other words, are not only barriers through which causal influence cannot be traced; they are at the same time initiators of new causal chains. Only initiators of causal chains can be breakers of causal chains, according to the law on intervening causation.

That of course leads one naturally to the question, what is a cause (or causal contribution, causal significance, causal initiator, etc)? Whether the intervening-cause doctrine gives an answer to this question depends on the level of ambition with which the doctrine is framed. In what I called the most expansive role assigned to intervening cause in Part II of this chapter, causes in general share the nature of intervening cause; that nature is given by the paradigms of abnormal natural events or free, voluntary human choices. Less ambitious roles for intervening cause do not purport to analyze causation itself; in its less ambitious versions, intervening-cause doctrines presuppose some more basic notion of causation. This much can be said generally, however: intervening causes must be causes first before they can be barriers to the influence of other causes.

B. The temporal condition: Intervening causes must intervene between the defendant's act and the harm

The second, most basic feature of an intervening cause is that it must *intervene.* This will obviously eliminate events occurring after the victim's harm from the category of intervening causes (or, indeed, causes of any kind, causation not working backwards through time). Less obviously, this rule also precludes events that predate the defendant's action and states that are in existence at the time the defendant acts, from being intervening causes.[20] Thus, the *event* that is the placement of gas vapors in a ship's hold and the *state* of its presence at the time of the ship's explosion do not intervene between the defendant's negligent act (dropping a plank) and the explosion caused by the sparks generated by the

---

[19] Hart and Honoré, *Causation in the Law.*

[20] See the case citations and discussions in Hart and Honoré, *Causation in the Law* (2nd edn), 79–80, 172–6; Beale, 'Proximate consequence', 641; Bohlen, 'Probable or natural consequences', 162; Carpenter, 'Workable rules', 473–4, 476–84; and McLaughlin, 'Proximate cause', 159–64.

plank.[21] Contrast that scenario with one in which the gas vapor had been introduced after the defendant had negligently lit his pipe (which was still burning when the vapors were introduced); in this variation, the introduction of the gas vapors would have intervened between defendant's negligent act and the explosion.

This well-entrenched, temporal distinction often takes the form of the maxim 'You take your victim as you find him.'[22] No matter how abnormally or unforeseeably a person may be thin-skulled, a bleeder, an epileptic, a religiously scrupled person,[23] or otherwise predisposed to injury, a defendant will be held to have caused the extensive injuries resulting from his normally harmless actions. The onset of the peculiar vulnerabilities of the victim, and the existence of those vulnerabilities at the time of the defendant's action, do not intervene between defendant's action and the harm.

This temporal limitation of intervening causes brings with it an ontological limitation as well. There is an old debate about what sorts of things can stand in the causal relation; that is, what sorts of things can be 'causal relata'.[24] One subdebate here is between those who urge that only events can be causal relata and those who urge that states can also be causal relata.[25] However one comes out in this more general debate, *for intervening causes* one must restrict causal relata to events. As Hart and Honoré put it: 'If a contingency is ... to negative causal connection it must be an *event* [;] ... *a state of the person or thing affected* existing at the time of the wrongful act ... does not negative causal connection.'[26] This is not only a temporal distinction, but an ontological one as well: 'The distinction [is] between an existing state of affairs and an intervening event.'[27]

One can see why the ontological requirement is a corollary of the temporal requirement by returning to the facts of *In re Polemis*. There was in fact an interval of time between defendant's act, dropping the plank, and the harm, the explosion of the ship.[28] During that interval, the state of gas-vapor-being-in-the-hold did exist. One thus disqualifies such a state from being an intervening cause

[21] *In re Polemis*, 3 KB 560 (CA 1921).

[22] Hart and Honoré, *Causation in the Law* (2nd edn), 173, 343.

[23] *See R v. Blaue* 3 All ER 446 (CA [1975]) (holding liable a defendant who stabbed a victim who subsequently died at the hospital because she refused blood transfusion in accordance with her preexisting Jehovah's Witness faith).

[24] To my knowledge, Jaegwon Kim has done the most to reintroduce this issue into modern discussions of causation. See Jaegwon Kim, 'Causes and events: Mackie on causation', Journal of Philosophy 68 (1971), 426–41.

[25] The states/events debate is discussed briefly in Michael Moore, *Placing Blame: A General Theory of the Criminal Law* (Oxford: Oxford University Press, 1997), 344–5. I shall discuss the general issue of states, events, states of affairs, facts, etc, as causal relata, in Chapters 14 and 15, below.

[26] Hart and Honoré, *Causation in the Law* (2nd edn), 172 (original emphasis).   [27] Ibid.

[28] Temporally locating acts and other events is itself a tricky metaphysical issue. I elsewhere defend at length the view that the defendant's act in a case like *In re Polemis* ends with that movement of his body that caused the plank to drop. See Michael S Moore, *Act and Crime: The philosophy of action and its implications for criminal law* (Oxford: Clarendon Press, 1993).

on the ontological ground that it is a state, not an event, whereas, in my contrasting hypothetical, the introduction of the gas vapor is an event and thus is eligible to serve as an intervening cause. This is to use an ontological distinction as well as the temporal distinction to make out intervening causation.

It is natural that those who favor a foreseeability approach to proximate causation will find the temporal/ontological distinction problematic.[29] After all, whether an extraordinarily unlikely thing occurs before or after a defendant's act, and whether that thing is an event or a state, makes no difference to the foreseeability of the harm that such a state or event makes possible; defendant can reasonably be ignorant of such a thing no matter what it is or when it comes into existence. The proper conclusion to draw from this, however, is that foreseeability has nothing to do with intervening causation. If we are restricting ourselves to a causal inquiry, not a culpability inquiry, we properly focus on what intervenes between defendant's act and the harm. All that went before has nothing to do with defendant's causal responsibility in bringing about some harm. Whether a world is extraordinary or dull, monotonous or uniform, is all one for the causal inquiry. Whichever it is, it is the stage on which defendant begins his causal contribution.[30]

C. The independence condition: Intervening causes must not themselves be caused by the defendant's action

Another strand of the idea of 'intervention' is the newness of that which intervenes. This strand is well captured by the English label, 'extraneous cause'. To intervene between defendant's act and his victim's harm, an event must not itself be the product of defendant's act. If it is such a product, then the event is merely part of the mechanism or means by which defendant's act caused the harm; it is not an intervention preventing such causation by defendant.

Hart and Honoré give this example: a defendant who culpably pushes his victim to the ground is not liable for that victim's death when the victim is killed on the ground by a falling tree.[31] The falling tree, in such a case, intervenes between defendant's push and the victim's death. By contrast, if the defendant's push caused the victim to stagger into a rotten tree, and the impact caused the tree to fall and kill the victim, the defendant is held to have caused the death. While the tree's falling was subsequent to the defendant's act of pushing, it was not causally independent of the push and so does not constitute an intervening cause.

---

[29] As does Glanville Williams, for example. See Glanville Williams, 'Causation in the law', Cambridge Law Journal (1961), 81–3.
[30] See Hart and Honoré, *Causation in the Law* (2nd edn), 172, 179–80.
[31] Ibid, 77–9.

There is considerable case law support for the independence criterion of intervening cause.[32] Consider the example of *Bunting v. Hogsett*.[33] The defendant's culpable act consisted of operating a railroad engine at too great a speed. To avoid a collision with the plaintiff, the defendant reversed throttle, shut off the steam, and jumped. The collision occurred anyway, but did not injure the plaintiff. The collision, however, opened the engine's throttle, and the engineer-less train backed with increasing velocity around its track (which met the plaintiff's road a second time), again hitting the plaintiff and this time injuring him. None of these rather extraordinary events was causally independent of defendant's culpable act, and so none of such events was held to constitute an intervening cause. As the Pennsylvania Supreme Court described its rationale:

[N]o intermediate cause, disconnected from the primary fault and self-operating, exist[ed] in this case, to affect the question of the defendant's liability; it was the engineer's negligence that caused the first collision, and what occurred in consequence of this collision was not broken by the intervention of any independent agent, whatever. The first collision . . . opened the throttle, and turned loose the destructive agency which inflicted the injuries complained of.[34]

Presumably, had the engine's throttle been set in reverse and opened up by a child at play, a bolt of lightning, or virtually anything else with a genesis independent of the first collision, the court would have deemed such events intervening causes.

The older literature on intervening cause regarded causal independence as an unproblematically universal requirement for intervening causes.[35] Yet as McLaughlin,[36] Carpenter,[37] and Hart and Honoré[38] came to see, with regard to certain kinds of intervening causes, some qualifications have to be made. Consider first intervening voluntary actions by human agents exploiting the situation created by defendant's culpable action. As Hart and Honoré recognize:

[A] voluntary act which negatives connection will always be found to be in some sense dependent on [defendant's original wrongdoing], eg, it will be motivated by the fact that

---

[32] See ibid, 176–8, 347; see also the case-law summaries in Beale, 'Proximate consequence', 646; Bohlen, 'Probable and natural consequences', 157–8, 162–3; Carpenter, 'Workable rules', 484–5; Terry, 'Proximate consequences', 20.

[33] 21 A 31 (Pa 1891). The case is relied on by the *Restatement (Second) of Torts*, § 435, cmt a (Philadelphia: American Law Institute, 1965); by Hart and Honoré, *Causation in the Law* (2nd edn), 176–7; and by Bohlen, 'Probable and natural consequences', 157–8.

[34] 21 A at 32.

[35] See the extended discussion in Levitt, 'Cause, legal cause, and proximate cause', 55–60; see also Bohlen, 'Probable and natural consequences', 162–3; Terry, 'Proximate consequences', 20.

[36] McLaughlin 173–5.

[37] Carpenter, 'Workable rules', 526–39.

[38] Hart and Honoré, *Causation in the Law* (2nd edn), 136, 181–5.

the wrongful act has occurred or by the belief that it may occur. It will be done in response to or in anticipation of some untoward situation.[39]

As an example of this last point, consider the facts of *Watson v. Kentucky & Indiana Bridge & Railroad Co.*[40] The defendant negligently spilled its gasoline throughout the town. The subsequent fire, however, was caused by the intervention of a third party; such person either dropped his cigar negligently into the petrol or intentionally threw it in to ignite a blaze. The court held that if it was the latter situation, the act of throwing the cigar would constitute an intervening cause and relieve the defendant of liability for the fire. In such a case, Hart and Honoré would point out, the intervenor's act in some sense is not causally independent of the defendant's act, for the intervenor's act is made possible by the act of the defendant and in that sense is done in response to the defendant's act.

While all of this is quite in accordance with case law and common-sense notions of causation, unnoticed by Hart and Honoré is the continued power of the independence criterion, even in the cases of intervening voluntary human action. Consider first intentional third-party intervenors, such as the second factual possibility in *Watson* above. As McLaughlin,[41] and before him Beale,[42] observed, it is generally true that 'stimulated voluntary action'[43] by a third-party intervenor will not constitute an intervening cause. That is, if the defendant coercively supplies the motive for the intervenor's behavior, then that behavior does not break the causal chain between defendant's action and the harm. Whereas, as Bohlen put it long ago, if the intervening voluntary act 'divert[s] the natural results of the wrong to some new and different end',[44] then there is an intervening cause. In *Watson* itself, the intervenor threw his cigar for his own, independent reasons. His motivation was in no way dependent on defendant, even if his action was made possible by defendant's negligence.

Hart and Honoré do not so much disagree with this analysis as they reclassify it. Rather than talk of independence of motivation, they smuggle the same requirement into their concept of 'voluntariness'. Where the defendant threatens or pressures the intervenor into doing what he does, they, like McLaughlin and Beale before them, recognize that such 'stimulated action' does not constitute an intervening cause. This is one of Hart and Honoré's categories of 'non-voluntary' action, as we shall see.[45] The intervenor choosing on his own to exploit the

---

[39] Ibid, 136.   [40] 126 SW 146 (Ky 1910).
[41] McLaughlin, 'Proximate cause', 173.
[42] Beale, 'Proximate consequence', 646–9.
[43] The phrase is McLaughlin's: McLaughlin, 'Proximate cause', 173.
[44] Bohlen, 'Probable and natural consequences', 163.
[45] Hart and Honoré, *Causation in the Law* (2nd edn), 144–5.

situation created by the defendant's wrongdoing is their paradigm case of voluntary action constituting an intervening cause.[46]

Consider, second, intervening voluntary acts in which the intervenor does not intentionally bring about the harm. In *Watson,* this is the negligent thrower of the cigar, one who does not know the gasoline to be present (although he should). With considerable support in the case law,[47] Hart and Honoré observe that negligent action by an intervenor merely reactive to defendant's wrongdoing does not constitute an intervening cause.[48] Hart and Honoré cast this again as a non-voluntary/voluntary distinction, but it is easy to see the causal independence criterion at work here as well.

Hart and Honoré also except animal behavior and involuntary human conduct from the independence requirement. That is, according to their theory, while an independent event of these kinds will always qualify as an intervening cause (if other requirements are met), sometimes a dependent event will also qualify if it is of one of these two kinds. For animals, if the intervening behavior of the animal is not in accordance with the nature of an animal of the kind in question, then that behavior, though causally dependent upon defendant's wrongdoing, may still constitute an intervening cause.[49]

Examples of such dependent animal behavior that nonetheless negative causal connection are hard to come by. Most cases are like *City of Waco v. Branch.*[50] The defendant city negligently released its sheep from their pens located on municipal park land. A dog chased the sheep onto the roadway in front of plaintiff's car. Plaintiff wrecked his car and injured himself in avoiding the sheep. Carpenter concluded that the city should properly be held liable, partly because of the dog's intervention supposedly depended upon the defendant's wrong. As Carpenter

---

[46] Ibid, 136–7. The intermediate cases are those in which the defendant supplies the motivation for the intervenor, but does so by way of offers, encouragements, requests, and the like, rather than by threats or pressure. Hart and Honoré rightly observe that there is liability in such cases, and on 'causal or quasi-causal grounds', so one could easily account for these cases on the independence criterion: since the intervenor's motive was supplied by the defendant, there is no motivational independence and therefore no break in causation. As we saw in Chapter 6, above, however, in such cases the law as presently constituted has no need for a causal basis for liability; rather, in torts and in criminal law, defendants are held as an accomplice (or as a joint tortfeasor by virtue of actions in concert, rather than joint causation). If one takes this seriously, the independence test here is thus trickier. Still, the difference between an offer and a threat lies precisely in what the recipient of the offer brings to his decision to accept: In the case of true offers (as opposed to 'offers one cannot refuse'), the recipient who accepts finds reasons sufficient for his choice within himself, whereas in yielding to a threat the recipient has his motivation supplied by the coercive consequences threatened.
[47] See Carpenter, 'Workable rules', 526–39 (dealing with acts done to avert threatened harm to the inventor, to rescue others from threatened harm, to mitigate or repair damage done by defendant';s act, to prevent deprivation of rights, and to defend from attack).
[48] Hart and Honoré, *Causation in the Law* (2nd edn), 152; see also Burke, 'Rules of legal cause', 11: 'Courts often will not relieve a defendant where the intervening act , even though negligent, was motivated by a desire to prevent defendant's act . . . from causing some apparent damage.'
[49] Hart and Honoré, *Causation in the Law* (2nd edn), 182, 348.
[50] 8 SW 2d 271 (Tex Civ App 1928).

put it, 'The defendant's wrong in leaving the sheep in the park was a cause-in-fact of the dog's chasing them.'[51]

Causal independence is a better theory to apply to such cases than is Carpenter's 'foreseeability' or Hart and Honoré's 'in the nature of the beast' criteria. One has to get away from 'but for' causation in assessing the causal independence of the intervention from the defendant's wrong. I would say, in the *City of Waco* situation, that the dog's intervention was causally *independent* of the defendant's act. The defendant's wrong in unpenning the sheep provided the opportunity for the dog's intervention, and in that anemic sense it made possible (was a necessary condition of) the dog's act. But the defendant's wrongful act gave no impetus to the dog to chase the sheep—no more so than the provision of opportunity to voluntary human intervenors, who when they exploit the situation presented by the defendant's wrong do so for their own reasons. Contrast such a case with the facts in *Isham v. Estate of Dow*,[52] where defendant's wrong of shooting a dog sent the dog scurrying for cover in plaintiff's house, knocking plaintiff down and injuring him. There, the dog's behavior is truly causally dependent on defendant's wrong and was properly held not to be an intervening cause.

According to Hart and Honoré, the cases also except certain intervening, involuntary human acts from the causal independence requirement. On their reading of the cases, even a causally dependent involuntary act may 'negative causal connection if not in accordance with human nature'.[53] There is very little authority cited for this proposition, however. In *Commonwealth v. Root*,[54] for example, one of the cases cited by Hart and Honoré,[55] the court held that the defendant's act of starting an auto-speed contest was not the proximate cause of a subsequent crash because the victim (who was the other racer) recklessly swerved into oncoming traffic during the race; there is no mention of human nature in the court's opinion, nor is it obvious that such recklessness is not pretty natural for road racing. Hart and Honoré's more general formula for dealing with intervening recklessness and negligence seems more apt;[56] if the reckless or negligent intervening action was done to escape or thwart the danger created by defendant's wrong, then it is not an intervening cause, whereas if the intervening act is independently motivated (as it was in *Root*), then it can constitute an intervening cause.

Construing causal independence in this motivational manner for intervening human and animal actions allows us to retain the uniform requirement that a subsequent event must be independent of the defendant's wrong if it is to negative a causal connection between that wrong and some harm. The earlier writers on intervening causes were thus closer to the truth than they knew.

---

[51] Carpenter, 'Proximate cause' (Pt 3), 16.　　[52] 41 A 585 (Vt 1898).

[53] Hart and Honoré, *Causation in the Law* (2nd edn), 183, 350.

[54] 170 A2d 310 (Pa 1961).

[55] Hart and Honoré, *Causation in the Law* (2nd edn), 183, 350.　　[56] Ibid, 152, 335–6.

D. The core of the doctrine of intervening causation: Three kinds of chain-breakers

1. *Voluntary human actions*

The guts of the intervening-cause doctrine lie in what (subsequent, causally independent) events qualify as intervening causes. Most theorists have focused their attention on voluntary interventions by third-party wrongdoers. Some of our clearest intuitions of causal chains being broken lie here; judges, too, have shared these intuitions in building a considerable body of case law.

The *Watson* case discussed earlier provides an example.[57] If Duerr, the cigar smoker, intentionally threw his cigar onto the gasoline that the defendant railroad had negligently spilled into the city streets, and he did so in order to ignite the gasoline, then his action would constitute an intervening cause. Even though it was defendant's negligently spilled gasoline that soaked the town, Duerr's voluntary intervention was a fresh causal start making him alone causally responsible for the fire damage.

'Voluntary' is given quite an extended meaning in intervening causation doctrine. It includes principally: (1) voluntariness of action in the law's more usual sense, (2) accompanied by an intention to bring about the harm or, sometimes, foresight or even negligence, (3) which intention is formed in the absence of coercive pressure making the choice difficult, (4) by one sufficiently possessed of his faculties as to be a generally responsible agent. Let us consider these briefly one at a time.[58]

a. Voluntariness of action in the law's usual sense

To be an action at all, behavior must be voluntary in the sense used in criminal law and torts when assessing the defendant's (not the intervenor's) conduct.[59] In *Watson,* if Duerr had dropped his cigar by reflex reaction, done so while asleep, unconscious, or under hypnosis, had the cigar knocked from his hand by another, a gust of wind, or a passing trolley, he would not have acted; in such cases, his cigar would have dropped from his hand as the leaves drop from trees, which is to say he did nothing causing it to drop. At a minimum, for Duerr's behavior to be an intervening cause, such behavior cannot consist of involuntary bodily movement.

When assessing the defendant's conduct, usually it is said that omissions to prevent some harm do not constitute a voluntary act unless the defendant was in one of the exceptional situations where he had a positive legal duty to prevent such harm. For the intervening actor, fortunately, the situation is not clouded

---

[57] See n 40, above.

[58] For an overview (although not in my four categories in the text), see Hart and Honoré, *Causation in the Law* (2nd edn), 41–4, 74–7, 136–62, 326–40.

[59] For a discussion of the meaning of 'voluntary' in the criminal law's voluntary act requirement, see Michael Moore, *Act and Crime*, 6–8, 17–59, 245–79.

with distinctions based on legal duties. Rather, omissions are not voluntary acts even where the intervening actor was under a legal duty not to omit.[60] Omissions, on the best conceptualization of them, are literally no things at all; they are the absence of certain events.[61] It is difficult to see how they could intervene as a new cause when they cannot constitute any kind of cause at all.[62]

b. The intervenor's state of mind

The second aspect of 'voluntariness' for these purposes has to do with the intervenor's state of mind. In the clearest cases of intervening causation, the intervening actor intends to exploit the opportunity left by defendant's wrongdoing, and he intends by his intervening act to accomplish the very harm for which the defendant is charged. In *Watson,* if Duerr threw his cigar intending to torch the village, his act would constitute an intervening cause relieving the defendant railroad of liability because of its negligently spilled gasoline. Such an intent (when motivating an action that is subsequent and causally independent) is thus almost always sufficient to break the causal chain and relieve defendant of liability.[63] But is such intent necessary for a human act to be an intervening cause?

---

[60] See *Restatement of Torts*, § 452 (Philadelphia: American Law Institute, 1934): 'Failure of a third person to perform a duty owing to another to protect him from harm threatened by the actor's negligent conduct is not a superseding cause of the other's harm.'; see also Carpenter, 'Workable rules', 485–90: '[I]n nearly every case when the question has arisen an omission has been held not to constitute an intervening cause.' Hart and Honoré are extremely unsympathetic to this doctrine, but this seems mostly due to their extreme lack of sympathy with there being any distinction between acts and omissions worth marking. See Hart and Honoré, *Causation in the Law* (2nd edn), 138–41.

[61] See Moore, *Act and Crime*, 22–34; Moore, *Placing Blame*, 262–72.

[62] On the inability of omissions to be any kind of cause, intervening or otherwise, see Moore, *Act and Crime*, 267–76; Moore, *Placing Blame*, 273–4; Paul K Ryu, 'Causation in criminal law', University of Pennsylvania Law Review 106 (1958), 779: 'One of the basic axioms in natural science is that "nothing" cannot produce "something." ' Julie Andrews probably said it best in Rodgers and Hammerstein's *The Sound of Music*: 'Nothing comes from nothing, and nothing ever could.'

[63] Two large qualifications are in order here. One has to do with foreseeability. Many cases have said that even a fully intentional causing of the harm by a third-party intervenor will not relieve a defendant of liability if the intervention was *foreseeable* to the defendant at the time that he acted. As I discuss below, foreseeability has no place in the doctrines of intervening causation. Plus, the concept is so fully manipulable (see Moore, *Placing Blame*, 363–99) that what courts *do* in fact (as opposed to what they may *say* they are doing) is to treat intervening intentional wrongdoing as per se unforeseeable, even when we know that it is not.

A second complicating factor lies in the kind of cases Hart and Honoré categorize as 'provision of opportunity' cases. See Hart and Honoré, *Causation in the Law* (2nd edn), 59–61, 81–2, 194–204, 374–7. In those cases the intervention by a third-party wrongdoer is not merely foreseeable to the defendant; rather, it is precisely the likelihood of some such intervention that makes defendant negligent to start with. Leaving ignition keys in automobiles, for example, is negligent precisely because wrongdoers may steal them. Hart and Honoré seek to except out such cases from the general rule stated in the text. By contrast, I argued in Chapter 6 that the rule stated in the text makes no exception for such cases; there often is liability in such cases, but it is a non-causal liability (for failing to prevent such intervening wrongdoing.)

In their article[64] and in the first edition of their book,[65] Hart and Honoré thought so. By the second edition, however, they realized that they had to account for those numerous cases where the intervening actor is held to be an intervening cause despite the lack of any intention to cause the victim harm. Their revised description of the doctrine is that a 'deliberate, informed' act 'intended to exploit the situation created by defendant' is sufficient to constitute an intervening cause.[66] Their example is of an intervenor who decides to rob a victim rendered unconscious by defendant's negligence; if the intervenor accidentally injures the victim, defendant will not be responsible for such injury. 'This is because the decision to exploit the situation by stealing from the pedestrian has intervened . . . even though, in executing it, the thief has brought about a consequence which he did not intend.'[67]

In examples like these, it is inevitable to attribute some degree of culpability to the intervenor: if not intention, then foresight, recklessness, or negligence with respect to the harm suffered by the victim. This is the grain of truth in the older maxim that criminal conduct by an intervenor is sufficient to constitute an intervening cause.[68] Yet this maxim suffered from serious overbreadth. Not any reckless or negligent act will suffice to create an intervening act. As Hart and Honoré recognize, 'every merely negligent act is non-voluntary in our sense, since by hypothesis the actor did not intend to exploit the situation' created by the defendant's wrong.[69] The actor must have enough knowledge of the circumstances created by the defendant's wrong that his decision to go ahead is properly viewed as a decision to take advantage of those circumstances. Such a decision may be merely reckless or negligent and still constitute an intervening cause,[70] but negligence or even recklessness by the intervening actor in failing to learn of such circumstances is not enough.

The only caveat to this is when the behavior of the intervening actor is so extraordinary that, although only negligent, it nonetheless fits the criterion (described below) of 'abnormal natural events'. If the defendant's negligence has left the victim unconscious and with a broken arm, yet a doctor treats the patient with kerosene-soaked rags for fever, not noticing the broken arm, and the patient is severely sickened, the defendant should not be liable for the more severe sickening; the doctor's negligence would doubtlessly be categorized as gross

---

[64] Hart and Honoré, 'Causation in the law', 267.

[65] Hart and Honoré, *Causation in the Law* (1st edn).

[66] Hart and Honoré, *Causation in the Law* (2nd edn), 136. In a review of the first edition of their book, Luke Cooperrider had gently protested that the cases rather often allowed merely negligent intervening actions by third parties to break causal chains. Luke Cooperrider, 'Causation in the law', Michigan Law Review 58 (1960), 954–5. See generally Eldredge, 'Culpable intervention as superseding cause', for many such negligence cases.

[67] Hart and Honoré, *Causation in the Law* (2nd edn), 151.

[68] See Beale, 'Proximate consequence', 657.

[69] Hart and Honoré, *Causation in the Law* (2nd edn), 138.   [70] Ibid, 141–2, 153–3.

negligence for the purpose of a suit against her but (more to the point in this context) such extraordinarily negligent behavior may well constitute an intervening cause by reason of its abnormality.[71]

c. Absence of coercion

The third feature making an intervening choice fully voluntary in the relevant sense is suggested by the adjective 'free'.[72] Hart and Honoré define 'free' in the compatibilist manner familiar from Herbert Hart's earlier writings:[73] a human agent is 'most free when he is placed in circumstances which give him a fair opportunity to exercise normal mental and physical powers and he does exercise them without pressure from others'.[74] I call this a compatibilist sense of 'free' because it does not rely on any contra-causal kind of freedom; an act may be fully caused and yet 'free' (in this compatibilist sense) in that the actor was possessed of adequate capacity to decide what to do and was given a fair opportunity to exercise that capacity.[75]

The factors that can erode adequate capacity or fair opportunity for free, unpressured choice are numerous. A threat of serious bodily harm, or of damage to property, or a threat of economic injury, can so reduce the intervenor's options as to render his choice to intervene non-voluntary. 'Threats' by natural circumstance can similarly reduce opportunities; if one's choice is reduced to burning to death or jumping to one's likely injury, the jump is involuntary and does not constitute an intervening cause. Likewise, strong emotions, such as fear, provoked anger, addictive cravings, and the like may so incapacitate an intervenor as to render his choice non-voluntary.[76] It is important to see that such threats, natural necessities, or emotional reactions need not originate with the defendant in order to make an intervening choice non-voluntary. As we saw earlier, if such items did originate with the defendant, then the intervenor's choice lacks causal independence and cannot be an intervening cause on that ground alone. It is where such items originate other than with the defendant that such non-voluntariness disqualifies a choice on its own hook. It is defects in the intervenor's choice itself, not a causal connection of that choice to the defendant's action, that is doing the work here. Non-voluntary choices are incapable of breaking the causal chains that may be broken by fully voluntary human decisions.

---

[71] Hart and Honoré, *Causation in the Law* (2nd edn), 184.   [72] Ibid, 136.

[73] HLA Hart, 'Legal responsibility and excuses', in Sidney Hook (ed), *Determinism and Freedom in the Age of Modern Science* (New York: NYU Press, 1958), 81, reprinted in HLA Hart, *Punishment and Responsibility* (Oxford: Oxford University Press, 1968), 28.

[74] Hart and Honoré, *Causation in the Law* (2nd edn), 138.

[75] I elaborate on Hart's adequate capacity/fair opportunity sense of freedom in Moore, *Placing Blame*, 481–592.

[76] All such cases are discussed in Hart and Honoré, *Causation in the Law* (2nd edn), 144–9, 155–7, 330–5. See also Carpenter, 'Proximate cause (Pt 3)', 72–86.

d. Capacity necessary for voluntariness

Fourth, if the intervenor's general capacity to make choices is eroded, such intervening choices as he does make do not constitute intervening causes. The insane, those diminished in mental capacity due to mental disease, drugs, or alcohol, and the very young all lack the kinds of capacity that would enable their choices to qualify as intervening causes.[77] These are not compelled choices or ignorant choices so much as they are defectively reasoned choices. Only the chosen actions of sane, sober, adults can constitute intervening causes (unless insane or immature choices are so abnormal as to qualify as intervening causes on that distinct ground).

If one considers these four conditions of non-voluntariness together, we can see the descriptive power of the old last-wrongdoer rule. For the voluntary act, *mens rea*, absence of coercion, and general capacity requirements pretty much constitute the conditions we use to assess culpable wrongdoing generally. As Hart and Honoré recognize, 'the various circumstances [of voluntariness for intervening-cause purposes] correspond with the factors which diminish moral and legal responsibility'.[78] Even so, not all culpable wrongdoing constitutes an intervening cause when it intervenes temporally between defendant's act and some harm, and not even all causally independent wrongdoing so qualifies. Holmes's old view is the right one here: while 'the general tendency has been to look no further back than the last wrongdoer',[79] the tendency is shot so full of qualifications that it cannot be elevated into the hard and fast rule the last-wrongdoer rule purported to be.

2. Abnormal natural events

Even if a subsequently arising, causally independent event does not qualify as a fully voluntary human act, that event may yet qualify as an intervening cause if it is in some sense 'extraordinary'. Such extraordinary events may be natural events, like floods, storms, and earthquakes, or they may be human actions. In either case, 'acts of God' or 'coincidences' may break causal chains as surely as the most deliberate intervention by a third-party wrongdoer.

Hart and Honoré helpfully subdivide these cases into two kinds: events that are abnormal in almost any context, and events that are abnormal in conjunction with certain other events.[80] Meteorites, unprecedented winds or rains,[81] tidal waves, extraordinary floods, and the like are examples of the first kind, usually called *vis major* or 'acts of God'. Trees falling just where and when some victim

---

[77] See Hart and Honoré, *Causation in the Law* (2nd edn), 153–6.   [78] Ibid, 138.
[79] *Clifford v. Atlantic Cotton Mills*, 15 NE 84, 87 (Mass 1888).
[80] Hart and Honoré, *Causation in the Law* (2nd edn), 163.
[81] *Kimble v. Mackintosh Hemphill Co*, 59 A 2d 68 (Pa 1948).

has been placed by defendant's wrongdoing[82] and lightning igniting explosive dust negligently spilled by defendant into his warehouse[83] are examples of the second kind, aptly termed 'coincidences'. It is not unusual for trees to fall or lightning to strike; what is extraordinary is that such events should have happened just where and when they did, which was the only time and place at which they could have caused injury to a victim made susceptible to such injury by defendant's wrongful act.[84]

Hart and Honoré nicely distinguish three rather glaring indeterminacies in the use of this abnormality criterion.[85] Most obvious is the indeterminacy stemming from the degree-vagueness of 'abnormal': Just how extraordinary must an event (or conjunction of events) be in order to qualify as abnormal?[86] Light winds ordinary in the evenings for a given place are obviously not abnormal, while winds of unprecedented force are abnormal; in between these extremes, one can only say, 'highly unlikely',[87] 'extremely unlikely',[88] or 'very unlikely'.[89]

The second indeterminacy is a bit less obvious. It stems from the fact that when assessing probabilities at the macro level, we almost never assess the probability of a particular event.[90] Rather, we assess the probability of *some* event occurring that instantiates the type of event in which we are interested. Although idiomatic English misleads us here, when we ask, 'What was the probability of that storm?' we actually mean, 'What was the probability of some storm occurring where and when this one did?' Hence, indeterminacy number two: it is indeterminate what types we mean to use when we assign degrees of likelihood. Do we mean, for example, some instance of the type, rainstorm; long rainstorm; long, one-inch-per-hour rainstorm? Since probabilities differ considerably by the type one has in mind, the indeterminacy in assessing degrees of abnormality is a significant issue.[91] Hart and Honoré attribute to the law what they call the plain man's view: 'It will in general be enough to take the description of the events

---

[82] This is Hart and Honoré's example. See Hart and Honoré, *Causation in the Law* (2nd edn), 78; cf *Berry v. Borough of Sugar Notch*, 43 A 240 (Pa 1899) (holding irrelevant the plaintiff's much earlier negligent speeding, even though that speeding placed him just where a tree happened to fall on him).

[83] This is the hypothetical framed by the court in *People v. Warner-Lambert Co*, 414 NE 2d 660 (NY 1980).

[84] I ignore a distinction Hart and Honoré draw within the coincidence cases; they separate out coincidences of time and place on the ground that in such cases, it does not matter how unlikely the conjunction might be, such coincidence still intervenes. See Hart and Honoré, *Causation in the Law* (1st edn), 157; *Causation in the Law* (2nd edn), xxxix, 168–70. I ignore the distinction because the time/place cases are some of the best examples of coincidences precisely because of the unlikelihood of such conjunctions.

[85] Hart and Honoré, *Causation in the Law* (2nd edn), 165–8.   [86] Ibid, 168.

[87] William L Prosser, *Handbook of the Law of Torts* (4th edn, St Paul: West Pub Co, 1971), 276.

[88] Hart and Honoré, *Causation in the Law* (2nd edn), 400.

[89] Ibid, 168.   [90] See Moore, *Placing Blame*, 382–9.

[91] Ibid, 389–95.

which would ordinarily be given.'[92] As they recognize, this does not uniquely determine types, but perhaps it restricts the range of variation somewhat.

The third indeterminacy is the uncertainty about the epistemic vantage point from which the assessment of likelihood is to be made. As Hart and Honoré recognize, 'like the cognate idea of what is "foreseeable", "probable", or "within the risk", the idea of coincidence is essentially a function of limited knowledge of the events concerned'.[93] That is, from an omniscient epistemic vantage point, the likelihood of some instance of some type of event occurring during a given interval of time is either 0 or 1 (assuming a deterministic universe). For all of us less-than-omniscient mortals, the subjective probability depends on what we know.

One could assess the likelihood of a given conjunction of events from the epistemic vantage point of the defendant: given what the defendant knew or should have known, what likelihood would he have assigned if he were reasonable? This collapses abnormality into foreseeability. Preferable for these purposes is to repair again to the ordinary person's view. From the epistemic vantage point of most of us, the observers, what would we (in retrospect) judge the probability to have been? Although abnormality is like foreseeability in that both are probabilistic notions, the epistemic vantage point from which subjective probability is to be assessed differs.

3. Intervening pre-emptive causes

In the older literature on intervening causation it is often suggested that an event will be an intervening cause if it is 'sufficient' by itself to have caused the harm. As the US Supreme Court once opined:

One of the most valuable of the criteria furnished us by these authorities is to ascertain whether any new cause has intervened between the fact accomplished and the alleged cause. If a new force or power has intervened of itself sufficient to stand as the cause of the misfortune, the other must be considered as too remote.[94]

Terry and others were unable to find any clear meaning to 'sufficient' in such cases.[95] My own interpretation of this criterion would be as follows.[96]

---

[92] Hart and Honoré, *Causation in the Law* (2nd edn), 166.   [93] Ibid, 165.

[94] *Insurance Co v. Tweed*, 74 US (7 Wall) 44, 52 (1868); see also *Milwaukee & St Paul Ry v. Kellogg*, 94 US 469, 475 (1876): 'We do not say that even the natural and probable consequences of a wrongful act or omission are in all cases chargeable to the misfeasance or nonfeasance. They are not when there is a sufficient and independent cause operating between the wrong and the injury. In such a case the resort of the sufferer must be to the originator of the original cause.'

[95] See Terry, 'Proximate consequences', 21; Smith, 'Legal cause', 326–7.

[96] After the article from which this chapter was published, *Restatement (Third) of Torts* in its Reporter's Notes to § 34 on Superseding Causes also sees the interpretation of 'sufficiency' I give in this context. See ibid, 126: 'Only when the actor's tortious conduct and the intervening act were overdetermined causes . . . would the sufficient-to-cause-the-harm element be satisfied.' However, in its rush to get rid of intervening-cause doctrine, the *Restatement (Third)* finds that 'this standard for superseding causes cannot be helpful to courts confronted with the issue'. Ibid.

It is well known that overdetermination cases pose thorny problems for many theories of causation.[97] A case is one of 'overdetermination' when two independent events are each sufficient to produce a single, indivisible harm. For example, two individuals, not in concert, each negligently start a fire; each fire is sufficient to destroy the victim's house; as it happens, the fires join and the resultant fire destroys the house. Each is held to be a cause of the destruction.[98]

More relevant for our purposes are a subclass of the overdetermination cases, those often dubbed 'pre-emptive' (as opposed to concurrent) overdetermination cases.[99] For example, the two negligently set fires do not join; the defendant's fire reaches the victim's house first and destroys it; the other fire then arrives sufficient to have destroyed the house if it were still standing, but there is no house left to destroy. The defendant's fire is said to have pre-empted the other fire as the cause of the destruction.

Often a pre-emptive cause does its work after the factor pre-empted has begun to do its work. Examples: the defendant poisons the victim, but as the victim is dying of the poison another comes along and shoots the victim dead;[100] the defendant's negligently constructed bridge allows the victim to fall to what would be a certain death, but, as he is falling, the victim is electrocuted by uninsulated wires;[101] the defendant pushes the victim from a tall building but half-way down the victim is shot and killed instantly by another;[102] the defendant seeks to kill the victim by poisoning water needed by the victim to cross a desert, but before the victim drinks any poison another drains the poison from the keg and the victim dies of thirst;[103] the defendant mortally burns the victim but before the victim dies of the burns another kills the victim instantly by a blow to the head;[104] the defendant's fire has begun to burn victim's property but before it can destroy much of the property a flood extinguishes the fire and destroys victim's property.[105]

---

[97] The best contemporary discussion of these cases in the purely legal literature is Richard W Wright, 'Causation in tort law', California Law Review 73 (1985), 1775–98.

[98] *Anderson v. Minneapolis, St Paul & Sault Ste Marie Ry*, 179 NW 45 (Minn 1920); *Kingston v. Chicago & NW Ry*, 211 NW 913 (Wis 1927).

[99] See Honoré, 'Necessary and sufficient conditions', 374–80; Wright, 'Causation in tort law', 1775.

[100] Wright, 'Causation in tort law', 1798.

[101] *Dillon v. Twin State Gas & Elec Co*, 163 A 111 (NH 1932).

[102] Jerome Hall, *General Principles for Criminal Law* (1st edn, Indianapolis: Bobbs-Merrill, 1947), 262.

[103] This is a variation of McLaughlin's famous hypothetical. See McLaughlin, 'Proximate cause', 155, n 25. The standard view of who killed the victim in the desert is that the intervenor did so, given that the victim died of thirst rather than poison. JL Mackie, *The Cement of the Universe: A study of causation* (Oxford: Oxford University Press, 1974), 45–6; Wright, 'Causation in tort law', 1802; Hart's and Honoré's long-held view was that neither defendant nor intervenor caused the victim's death because each was pre-emptive of the other (but each should be liable on some unspecified, non-causal basis). Hart and Honoré, *Causation in the Law* (2nd edn), 239–40. Tony Honoré has recently recanted and joined the standard view here: Honoré, 'Necessary and sufficient conditions', 378.

[104] *State v. Scates*, 50 NC 409 (NC 1858).

[105] Hart and Honoré give this example. Hart and Honoré, *Causation in the Law* (2nd edn), 239.

In all such cases the second factor that intervenes after defendant's action has taken place pre-empts the ability of defendant's action to cause the harm it was normally sufficient to cause. I call such subsequently arising, causally independent pre-emptive-cause cases a third kind of intervening cause. For notice that the electrocution, the shots, the draining of the poisoned water, the blow to the head, and the flood in such cases may or may not qualify as intervening voluntary action or intervening abnormal natural events. Yet irrespective of their meeting either of these other two criteria, it is clear that such intervening events break the causal chain that would have existed between defendant's action and the harm. Thus, although it is uncommon so to classify them, I include such pre-emptive-cause cases as a third kind of intervening cause, distinct from and in addition to voluntary human acts and abnormal natural events. It is such a preemptive variety of intervening causes that is the best interpretation of 'sufficient' in the older doctrine of intervening causation.

E. An absence-of-culpability condition: The defendant may not intend, foresee, or have foreseeable to him an intervening cause

There is a considerable body of case law and commentary that purports to attach a fifth general condition to intervening causation. I call it an absence-of-culpability condition because it demands that a defendant not intend, foresee, or have foreseeable to him—that is, that he not be culpable with respect to—the putative intervening cause. I shall urge that this case law and commentary is entirely mistaken in presuming that the culpability of the defendant can affect the causal status of his action. If the legal doctrine of intervening causation has any claim to correspond to some underlying metaphysics of causation, it better not have any such culpability condition attached to it.[106]

1. Where the defendant either intends the harm, or intends the intervening cause that is that harm's means

It is a sweeping maxim of the common law that no harm intended by the defendant can be too remote for liability to attach. As Terry stated the maxim, 'Any intended consequence of an act is proximate.'[107] This proposition is surely too broad. A defendant may intend to kill his victim by burns or by poison, yet if another intervenes, killing the victim by shots or blows to the head, the defendant has not caused the death of the victim, as we saw immediately above. More generally, when the harm intended by the defendant only comes about

---

[106] As I suggested in Chapter 6, above.
[107] Terry, 'Proximate consequences', 17. Disappointingly, the proposed *Restatement (Third) of Torts*, § 33 adopts a version of this common law maxim, treating intentionality as the kind of supposed causal aphrodisiac diagnosed in Chapter 6, above.

through the intervention of a causally independent cause of any of the three kinds just explored, the defendant is not liable for causing the harm[108] (although he may be liable for attempt in criminal law).

Hart and Honoré sought to breathe new life into this old maxim by narrowing it. In their hands, the maxim became a fifth condition for intervening causation: If the defendant knows that a hurricane will hit victim's house, or knows that the victim's enemy will try to murder the victim at his house, and defendant acts so as to cause victim to be in his house at the time, then no matter how abnormal the hurricane or voluntary the murderer, defendant has still caused victim's death.[109] We must exclude the possibility of 'contrived coincidences' or of 'contrived voluntary actions' if such items are eligible to be intervening causes, on their view.

Admittedly, the cases better support this narrower use of intention, for there is liability of defendants in the cases cited by Hart and Honoré. Overlooked by Hart and Honoré, however, is the possibility that there is only non-causal liability in such cases.[110] In the case of voluntary intervention by human agents, defendants are liable but only as accomplices (in criminal law) or as non-causal joint tortfeasors (in torts). Defendants who persuade a victim to sleep in a house which defendants know will be firebombed by another,[111] or who wrongfully eject victim from their bar knowing that assailants are waiting outside,[112] may be liable for the resulting injuries if they specifically intend such assaults to take place; yet this liability is for aiding another to cause such injuries, not for causing such injuries themselves.[113]

The same should be true for the contrived coincidence cases. The defendant who uses a foreseeable hurricane as his intended means to spread a fire he intentionally sets is liable for the whole damage; the proper grounds for such liability, however, is in aiding and not in causing. The hurricane remains an intervening cause breaking the causal chain between defendant's act and the harm, despite defendant's intention, but the possibility of a non-causal liability remains nonetheless.

I thus conclude that absence of intention by the defendant is not a proper criterion for determining the presence of an intervening cause. Whether the defendants intend the harm, or in addition intend the intervening action or other event as the means to cause such harm, is irrelevant to intervening causation. Such intentional use of another is the precise target of non-causal accomplice liability, and such intentional use of the freaks of nature should be the target of an analogous non-causal liability for aiding nature.

---

[108] *Restatement (Second) of Torts*, § 435 A.
[109] Hart and Honoré, *Causation in the Law* (2nd edn), 170–1.
[110] I explored this in Chapters 5 and 6, above.
[111] This is Hart's and Honoré's example. Hart and Honoré, *Causation in the Law* (2nd edn), 171.
[112] Ibid.
[113] For the causing/aiding distinction under present law, see Kadish, 'Causation and complicity'; Kadish, 'Theory of complicity'. For the reasons hinted at in Chapter 3, above, and developed in detail in Chapters 12 and 13, below, present law should change so as to eliminate this distinction.

2. Where the defendant foresees the intervening event even if he does not intend it

Suppose one foresees the above-hypothesized hurricane or murderer intervening after one's acts, but is indifferent to the harm it will cause. In such cases one does not adopt the intervening events as intended means to the harm one intends. In criminal law at least, this absence of a specific intent to aid another by one's acts eliminates accomplice liability.[114] So, if there is liability in such cases, it cannot be on that non-causal basis.

Despite this, Francis Bohlen argued that a defendant's knowledge of such matters as predicted hurricanes or murderous intentions should exclude the events predicted or intended from the category of intervening causes.[115] Thus, where defendant's negligence consisted in not removing his boats from blocking the victim's access to locks in a river that the defendant predicted would flood suddenly, the flood that did ensue and that did sweep the victim's boat over a dam could not constitute an intervening cause because the result was foreseen by the defendant.[116]

I have elsewhere argued that liability may be proper in cases such as these, but it is again a non-causal liability. In such 'provision of opportunity' cases, the defendant is liable for failing to prevent the injury that he clearly foresaw. The positive duty to prevent, in such cases, arises because the defendant has caused something (even if not the injury), namely, he has caused the victim's peril. One who culpably or innocently bumps another into the water has a duty of rescue, a duty not shared by those free of causal responsibility for the victim's peril.[117] Similarly, one who places his boats so as to imperil plaintiff's boats has a duty to remove them. Failure in such positive duties, however, does not make one a cause of the harm. One is liable for failing to prevent it, but not for causing it. Liability in such cases is thus non-causal, and we do not need to tinker with the concept of intervening causation in order to accommodate liability in such cases.

3. Where the intervening event is foreseeable to the defendant

The commentary on the foreseeability of intervening causes is extensive and uniform. Nearly all of the early commentators were agreed that the foreseeability of an intervening event was relevant to that event's status as an intervening cause.[118] More specifically, the orthodox view was (and is) that unforeseeability of the intervention is a necessary condition for that intervention to be an

---

[114] Model Penal Code, § 2.06 (Philadelphia: American Law Institute, 1962).
[115] See Bohlen, 'Probable and natural consequences', 162.
[116] *Scott v. Hunter*, 46 Pa 192 (1863).
[117] See Joshua Dressler, *Understanding Criminal Law* (New York: Matthew Bender, 1987), 83.
[118] As Charles Carpenter summarized his predecessors in this regard, 'where causes intervene, the practically universal view is that if they are foreseeable proximate cause exists': Carpenter, 'Proximate cause (Pt 3)', 312. See generally ibid, 275–313.

intervening cause.[119] On this view, we should add unforeseeability to the other main criteria for intervening causes.

Hart's and Honoré's contrary view came as a welcome dissent to this notion. Part of their disagreement stemmed from a different reading of the cases: 'When ... the intervening act is voluntary and is done with the deliberate intention of causing harm, it is at least doubtful, on the cases, whether the fact that the intervention was foreseeable is sufficient to render the wrongdoer liable for the ultimate harm.'[120] Courts that have indulged the fiction that deliberate causing of harm is per se unforeseeable[121] give support to Hart's and Honoré's view, despite the lip service given in such cases to the unforeseeability requirement of intervening causation.

Another facet of Hart's and Honoré's dissent was the easy slippage that exists between foreseeability and abnormality.[122] It is easy to slip from a judgment of improbability from an idealized epistemic vantage point ('abnormality') to a judgment of improbability from the epistemic vantage point of the defendant ('unforeseeability'). Hart and Honoré correctly observed that many decisions couched in terms of unforeseeability are in reality decisions based on intervening abnormal natural events.

Hart's and Honoré's major move to reconcile their view to the decided cases consists of their reallocation of the basis of liability in what they call the 'provision of opportunity' cases. They recognize that there is and should be liability in those (common enough) cases where the defendant's negligence consists precisely in her failure to anticipate some foreseeably intervening, harm-causing, voluntary human action or abnormal natural event. Where the defendant is negligent in leaving the ignition keys in another's car precisely because he should reasonably anticipate loss of the car through theft, the defendant is and should be liable to the owner for the loss of the car, despite the intervening voluntary act of the thief. Such liability, Hart and Honoré argue, is only 'quasi-causal'.[123] The-defendant has only 'enabled' or 'occasioned' the harm in such cases; he has not *caused* the harm, by the central meaning of that concept.

This is almost right, but the liability that does properly exist in the provision-of-opportunity cases is not even 'quasi-causal' or 'non-centrally causal'; it is not caused-based liability in any sense. As in the case of foreseen harm, here the liability is entirely omission-based (as I argued in Chapter 6). The defendant who fails to remove the keys is liable for failing to prevent the loss of the car, not for causing its loss. The duty to prevent the loss stems from earlier acts of the defendant, which placed the victim's car in peril, namely, parking where and when he did, and leaving the car with the keys in the ignition. These acts gave

---

[119] *Restatement of Torts*, §§ 447, 448 (1934); Prosser, *Handbook of the Law of Torts*, 266, 272, 276.

[120] Hart and Honoré, *Causation in the Law* (2nd edn), 280.

[121] *Watson v. Kentucky & Indiana Bridge & RR Co*, 126 SW 146 (Ky 1910).

[122] See Hart and Honoré, *Causation in the Law* (2nd edn), 278.   [123] Ibid, 194–204.

rise to the positive duty, failure in which is the true basis for liability here. Properly construed, liability in such cases thus places no demands on the concept of intervening causation. Liability not based on causation at all is irrelevant to intervening causation.

It is probably true that some cases using foreseeability of the intervention as a basis for liability cannot be explained away in one of these three ways. So let me add a fourth: foreseeability is such a manipulatable concept[124] that any result that is intuitive on the basis of intervening-cause doctrines without the concept is also reachable with the concept.

To the extent that there are cases that are not explainable in one of these four ways, the intervening-cause doctrine should simply regard such cases as mistakes. That allows the law on intervening causation to say clearly that intervening cause in no way depends on foreseeability or on any other matter having to do with defendant's culpability.

---

[124] Moore, *Placing Blame*, 306–8.

12

The Lack of any Metaphysical Basis for the Doctrines of Intervening Causation

I. Hart's and Honoré's Attempt to Avoid both Policy Constructions and Traditional Metaphysics

Most of the older literature on causation was content with extracting consistent, usable legal rules of causation from the case decisions.[1] Very little attempt was made to justify such doctrines either by showing how as artificial constructions of the law they maximized desirable policies, or by showing how they captured the correct metaphysics of causation (and thereby maximized the policy of achieving retributive or corrective justice).

Hart's and Honoré's was the first sustained effort to justify the legal doctrines of intervening causation.[2] Hart and Honoré were refreshingly clear about eschewing any justification of such doctrines in terms of extrinsic policies (policies, that is, that were extrinsic to the tracking of moral blameworthiness via some notion of causation that was *not* of the law's creation). This was to be their most sustained attempt to roll back the Legal Realists' 'functionalist' approach to legal concepts, an approach that sought to construct a meaning for such concepts out of policies like deterrence, efficiency, or unfairness.[3]

---

[1] See the extensive case summaries in Joseph Beale, 'The proximate consequences of an act', Harvard Law Review 33 (1920), 633–58); Beale, 'Recovery for consequences of an act', Harvard Law Review 9 (1895), 80–9; Charles E Carpenter, 'Proximate cause', (Parts 1–3), Southern California Law Review 14 (1940), 1–34, 115–53, 416–51; (Parts 4–6), Southern California Law Review 16 (1941), 187–213, 304–21, 427–68; (Parts 7–8), Southern California Law Review 16 (1943), 1–23, 61–92, 275–313; Carpenter, 'Workable rules for determining proximate cause', California Law Review 20 (1932), 229–59, 396–419, 471–539; James McLaughlin, 'Proximate cause', Harvard Law Review 39 (1925), 149–99; Jeremiah Smith, 'Legal cause in actions of tort', Harvard Law Review 25 (1911–12), 103–28, 223–52, 303–27; Henry Terry, 'Proximate consequences in the law of torts', Harvard Law Review 28 (1914), 10–33.

[2] HLA Hart and AM Honoré, 'Causation in the law', Law Quarterly Review 72 (1956), 58–90, 260–81, 398–417; HLA Hart and AM Honoré, *Causation in the Law* (Oxford: Clarendon Press, 1959); HLA Hart and Tony Honoré *Causation in the Law* (2nd edn, Oxford: Oxford University Press, 1985).

[3] See eg, Edgerton, 'Legal cause', University of Pennsylvania Law Review 72 (1924), 211–44, 343–75. On the Legal Realists functionalist approach generally, see Felix S Cohen, 'Transcendental nonsense and the functional approach', Columbia Law Review 35 (1935), 809–49.

Less clear is the relationship of Hart's and Honoré's justificatory ambitions to the metaphysics of causation. It is unclear whether they were attempting to ground the legal doctrines of causation in (what they saw as) the correct metaphysics of causation; this is mostly because it is unclear what kind of an enterprise they took metaphysics, in general, to be.

In very general terms, their justification of the law's doctrines of intervening causation should be seen in terms of three premises. Premise one: such legal doctrines would be justified if they match the conditions of moral blameworthiness. Premise two: the conditions of moral blameworthiness include causation, in a sense of causation that is not a creation either of law or of morality. Premise three: this pre-legal, pre-moral notion of causation is the plain-man's concept to be found in unselfconscious usages of 'cause' and cognate terms in ordinary language.

Premise one strikes me as being entirely correct. It states no more than what I have said repeatedly throughout this book: *the* policy to maximize in criminal law is retributive justice, and *the* policy to maximize in tort law is corrective justice. These forms of justice require legal liability to track closely moral blameworthiness.[4]

Premise two is likewise true, as we explored Chapters 2 and 3. *Causing* the results one has culpably attempted to cause, foreseen to occur, or unreasonably risked, is more blameworthy than merely trying, foreseeing, or unreasonably risking when the events intended, foreseen or risked do not materialize. In short, causation matters to morality, and because it matters to morality, it matters to the law.

It is premise three that is the troublemaker. Suppose that Hart and Honoré were right about their claim of what the 'plain man' thinks; he thinks that causes are either voluntary human actions or abnormal natural events that are necessary elements completing a set of elements sufficient for the effect, so long as no other such event intervenes between the first and that effect. Why would this sociological truth justify legal doctrines in accord with such common sense views of 'cause'?

Reacting apparently to a sense that theirs was a very conventional approach to issues like causation, Hart and Honoré in the 1985 Preface to the second edition of their book urged that 'it is the ordinary man's conception of cause that is used by the law'; therefore, to understand 'the structure of ordinary causal statements was and is an indispensable first step towards understanding the use of causal notions in the law'.[5] Yet as thus far stated, this is just more sociology. The justificatory question, 'Why *should* the law look to the ordinary man's conception of cause?', is untouched by such sociology.

---

[4] On the retributive justice part of this claim, see Michael Moore, *Placing Blame: A general theory of the criminal law* (Oxford: Oxford University Press, 1997), Chapters 1–4.
[5] Hart and Honoré, *Causation* (2nd edn), xxxiv.

One might urge that what the ordinary person thinks about moral responsibility cannot be wrong, because morality is simply what most people in a given culture think it is. The plain man's view of the elements of moral responsibility like causation then becomes quite relevant because such elements, like responsibility itself, are constituted by the conventions of moral thought. It is pretty clear that neither Hart nor Honoré ever subscribed to this relativistic defense of their approach to causation.[6] Nor, incidentally, would it be a defensible approach, given the well-charted and crippling defects of any relativistic metaethics.[7]

Closer to home is the assumption that common-sense views of causation, as revealed by ordinary usage of words like 'cause', is all there is or can be to causation, the thing. The ordinary-language philosophy program (in which Hart and Honoré were steeped when writing of causation) often justified its attention to ordinary usage by making three claims, the first of which was that the meaning of words in natural language was to be found in their ordinary uses.[8] Second, the movement claimed that in finding the meaning in usage, one was looking for word/word relationships, not word/thing relationships. That is, one found the meaning of a word like 'cause' by seeing how it was related (by relations of sense and pragmatic appropriateness) to other words like 'consequence', 'explanation', and the like. Third, that once one discovered the meaning of words like 'cause' in this way, one also discovered all there was to be discovered about the thing, causation. To know what 'cause' means is to know what cause is.[9]

If one accepts this 1950s ordinary-language philosophy program, then Hart's and Honoré's sociology becomes highly relevant to the justification of legal doctrine. For if legal liability tracks moral responsibility, if moral responsibility tracks causal responsibility, and if causal responsibility is fully determined by ordinary thinking about it, then Hart and Honoré had all the justification they needed to rely on the plain man's view of causation.

Yet few today would subscribe to the idea that the thing, causation, has no nature save that reflected in ordinary usage of the word, 'causation'.[10] Imagine a similar claim made about other natural kinds or relations, like water, gold, proton-donor, heat, or dreams. Such a claim cuts off the possibility of further scientific insight about the nature of such things; for if all there is to such things is what is ordinarily known, as reflected in ordinary usage, then scientific

---

[6] An example is HLA Hart's review of moral skepticism in Hart, 'Morality and reality', *New York Review of Books* (9 March 1978), 35.

[7] See, eg, Heidi Margaret Hurd, 'Relativistic jurisprudence: Skepticism founded on confusion', Southern California Law Review 61 (1988), 1417–509.

[8] In a cryptic aphorism typical of Wittgenstein, 'Meaning is use': Ludwig Wittgenstein, *Philosophical Investigations*, trans GEM Anscombe (3rd edn, Oxford: Blackwells, 1958), 20.

[9] To dredge up another 1950s saying, 'the material mode and the semantic mode are really just two different ways of talking'. On the generally anti-metaphysical stance of ordinary-language philosophy, see Michael S Moore, 'The interpretive turn in modern theory: A turn for the worse?', Stanford Law Review 41 (1989), 927–34.   [10] Ibid.

hypotheses about kinetic energy, subatomic structure, rapid eye movements, molecular structure, and brain functioning are about something other than heat, protons, dreams, or water.

The alternative view in semantics is that we literally mean more than we know when we use words like 'cause.'[11] We intend to refer to a thing, whatever its nature might turn out to be. Such a semantics reverses the priority between word/word relations and word/thing relations posited by ordinary-language philosophy. Far from the relation of 'cause' to other words determining fully what causation is, on the newer semantics what causation is determines the meaning of 'cause'. The nature of causation—what causation is—is a matter of fact, inviting theoretical speculation. Such nature is not fixed by the conventions that have hitherto governed idiomatic English usage of the word, 'cause'.

Once we see the possibility that the nature of causation may differ significantly from the ordinary usage of 'cause' by the ordinary person, the need for justification for relying on the common-sense concept looms large. For on the moral views that justify the legal doctrines of causation, the law cares about causation only because morality cares about causation. Yet such morality does not assign responsibility according to the common-man's conception of cause; rather, it assigns responsibility to defendants who *actually cause* some harm. The nature of the causal responsibility that grounds both moral responsibility and legal liability could be considerably different than that revealed by ordinary usage of 'cause'.

This general objection to Hart's and Honoré's ordinary-language approach to justifying the legal doctrines of causation applies with full force to their more particular application of the method to explain and justify intervening causation in the law. The justification they offer for why the law should regard voluntary human actions and abnormal natural events as breaking off the causal responsibility of earlier actors lies in their use of the old 'paradigm case argument' of Oxford-style ordinary-language philosophy.[12] Like David Hume before them, Hart and Honoré believed that we (collectively and individually) learn of the existence of something called causation by our ability to manipulate objects in the world.[13] We move objects, hit people, twist, push, bend things. Our central paradigm case of *causing* is *doing* these simple actions with our bodies. We then analogize from simple doings to more complex manipulations; by doing one thing we can cause something more remote to occur.[14]

---

[11] See Hilary Putnam, *Mind, Language, and Reality* (Cambridge: Cambridge University Press, 1975), 215–71. See generally Michael S Moore, 'A natural law theory of interpretation' Southern California Law Review 58 (1985), 288–301, 322–38.

[12] For an introduction to paradigm case argument ('PCA') semantics, see Michael S Moore, 'The semantics of judging', Southern California Law Review 54 (1981), 281–91. Others besides Hart and Honoré adopted PCA semantics in their approach to causation. See John Borgo, 'Causal paradigms in tort law', Journal of Legal Studies 8 (1979), 419–55; Richard A Epstein, 'A theory of strict liability', Journal of Legal Studies 2 (1973), 151–204.

[13] Hart and Honoré, *Causation* (2nd edn), 28.   [14] Ibid, 28–9.

The embryonic notion of cause that we construct from these simple action paradigms and their first analogical extension is that causation 'is an interference in the natural course of events which *makes a difference* in the ways these develop . . . The notion, that a cause is essentially something which interferes with or intervenes in the course of events which would normally take place, is central to the common-sense concept of cause.'[15] With this embryonic concept of cause under our belts, we then analogize further: natural events, even when there is no human manipulation, may also be causes. In such cases 'the cause, though not a literal intervention, is a *difference* from the normal course which accounts for the difference in the outcome'.[16] And from here, we analogize even further, to include states as well as events, omissions as well as actions, in the kinds of things that can be causes.[17]

It is because voluntary human actions are our basic, central paradigms of causation that we trace causal chains to such actions.[18] Moreover, it is because of their paradigmatic status that we refuse *to* trace causal relations *through* such actions. Where another voluntary human action subsequently intervenes, we lose our ability to analogize the more complex causings to the paradigmatic and simpler doings.[19] We cannot so analogize our indirect manipulations to simpler cases of direct action because another, more paradigmatic cause has intervened. 'The intervenor did it' precludes us from analogically extending 'the original actor did it' to 'the original actor caused it'.

The same is true for abnormal natural events. These are already at a level of secondary analogy to the paradigm cases of causation, that of simple human actions. When some subsequent event intervenes, it is closer to the paradigm case of causation than is the original abnormal event. Therefore, it too breaks our ability to analogize the first abnormal event to the paradigm case of causation.[20]

One has to understand the general nature of the paradigm-case argument to appreciate the justificatory power Hart and Honoré were seeking with the foregoing tale of how we developed our common sense concept of causation. Believers in the paradigm-case argument in the 1950s believed that the meaning of words like 'cause' was to be found in the paradigmatic exemplars of such words shared by some linguistic community.[21] Sensible use of words such as 'vehicle', for example, depended on speaker and listeners both regarding blue 1958 Buicks as paradigmatic vehicles; skateboards, baby carriages, and bicycles might be vehicles too, but only by analogy to the paradigm case.[22]

To find the paradigmatic application of a word like 'cause' was to find a connection that could not be questioned. Such a connection was 'true-by-convention'.

---

[15] Ibid, 29.   [16] Hart and Honoré, *Causation* (2nd edn).   [17] Ibid, 31.
[18] Ibid, 41–4.   [19] Ibid, 73.   [20] Ibid, 77.
[21] See eg, JO Urmson, 'Some questions concerning validity', in Antony Flew (ed), *Essays in Conceptual Analysis* (New York: St Martin's Press, 1960).
[22] This example is Herbert Hart's in his justly celebrated debate with Lon Fuller. HLA Hart, 'Positivism and the separation of law and morals', Harvard Law Review 71 (1958), 607.

Anyone who questioned whether a blue Buick was a vehicle simply revealed that he did not know the meaning of 'vehicle'. Paradigms of words like 'vehicle' or 'cause' were necessarily instances of their respective labels, because they were what fixed the meaning of such words. And like the ordinary-language program in general, so here: things or relations like causation had no nature save that given by their paradigmatic exemplification and analogical extensions thereof; meaning (as paradigms plus analogies) totally fixed nature, rather than vice versa.

So if Hart and Honoré were right about the paradigms for causation, they would (according to the paradigm-case argument) have shown us all that need be shown to justify the legal doctrines of intervening causation. Where there are intervening voluntary human actions or abnormal events, the analogy to the paradigm case of causation (simple doings) is broken, and to break the analogy is to show that no causal relation exists.

The main problem both with the paradigm-case argument in general, and with Hart's and Honoré's use of it here, is the main problem with all of ordinary-language philosophy: it allows the nature of the thing, causation, to be fixed by the conventions of present usage (in this case, the paradigms and analogies). It thus purports to cut off scientific theorizing about such nature on the grounds that anything ordinary thought does not already recognize as causation cannot *be* causation.[23]

There are many other problems with the paradigm case argument, both in general and in Hart's and Honoré's hands. It is doubtful, for example, that people actually possess paradigms for very many of the words they use. Do you really have a standard instance of 'vehicle' that you use to judge all other items by analogy? If you do, is the paradigm of vehicle for you the same thing as is the paradigm for others, in the way that the standard instance of 'meter' is the iridium bar kept in the Bureau of Weights and Measures in Paris? Thirdly, it is bizarre to think that we possess any abilities to reason by primitive analogy to any paradigms that we do possess in common. Recall Potter Stewart being hooted out of accepting Nixon's offer of the chief justiceship[24] by his claim that he knew pornography when he saw it even though he could not define it.[25] We in fact have no magical abilities to sense 'innate similarity spacings', nor is there any clear meaning to be given to any primitive notion of similarity.

The upshot of these last objections is that we should put aside the paradigm case approach to describing our common sense conception of cause. The upshot more generally is that Hart and Honoré—or we—should be interested in the common-sense conception of cause itself only if we believe that conception to be accurate. Does the best theory of what the causal relation really is include the

[23] See generally Moore, 'The semantics of judging'; Moore, 'The interpretive turn'.

[24] See Bob Woodward and Carl Bernstein, *The Brethren* (New York: Simon and Schuster, 1979), 15–16.

[25] *Jacobellis v. Ohio*, 378 US 184, 197 (1961) (Stewart J, concurring).

features so prominent in ordinary thought: the power of voluntary human acts and abnormal natural events to break the chains of causation? That is the question requiring an answer, an answer that can be found only in the metaphysics of causation, not in ordinary usage of 'cause' and certainly not in supposed paradigms guiding such usage.

II. The Metaphysics of the Stone Age

Once we see the need for a metaphysics of causation to justify the legal doctrines of causation, and once we see that the common-sense conception of causation does not foreclose or answer the metaphysical inquiry into the nature of causation, then we can appreciate the danger of relying heavily on common sense and ordinary usage. As JL Austin recognized, ordinary usage may not prescind from metaphysics as much as it naively engages in it. In Austin's colorful phrase, the worry is that ordinary thought may merely enshrine a naive metaphysics, the 'metaphysics of the Stone Age'.[26]

The Stone Age metaphysics suggested by the legal doctrine of intervening causation, and by the common-sense conception of cause underlying such doctrine, seems to go like this. As a bumper sticker common in the 1990s had it: 'Shit Happens'. Sometimes, even at the macro level, events just go one way rather than another. Inexplicably, lightning strikes one person dead but leaves all others around him alive, or inexplicably, an evil impulse leads one person to kill another deliberately for no reason and with no cause. When such inexplicable coincidences or evil impulses intervene, they break the causal relations that would otherwise govern subsequent events.

The worry about intervening causation in the law is that such Stone Age (New Age?) metaphysics is about all there is to it. One might throw in a little theism—whatever science cannot explain, God does. This could help. If there is any uncaused cause in the universe, it would be God. If She deigns to jump into human affairs occasionally—say by tossing down a lightning bolt every once in a while, or allowing the Devil to do some ungodly brainwashing on human beings just to keep the contest interesting—that would explain fresh causal starts. Yet such theism is even more primitive than the brute inexplicability of certain events that it was designed to replace. It is not for nothing that such anthropomorphism is called 'primitive animisim', primitive because it so naively assumes that we can explain natural phenomena like gravitational attraction in terms appropriate to persons, such as love.

In fact, if we alternatively theorize such Stone Age approaches, we may find more serious candidates for a metaphysics that could rationalize the law of

---

[26] JL Austin, 'A plea for excuses', *Proceedings of the Aristotelian Society* 57 (1957), reprinted in Herbert Morris (ed), *Freedom and Responsibility* (Stanford: Stanford University Press, 1961), 10.

intervening causation. My own theoretical reconstruction follows, organized partly around the three sorts of intervening causes in the law (pre-emptive events, voluntary human actions, and abnormal natural events), and partly around different metaphysical accounts common to all.

III. An Opening Wedge: Pre-emptive Intervening Cause

The easiest sort of intervening cause for which to discover a plausible metaphysical basis is those subsequently arising, 'sufficient' events that pre-empt the ability of the defendant's action to have caused some harm. For what underlies the law and ordinary thought in such cases is pretty close to the surface.

We first need to rid ourselves of any illusion that talk of 'sufficient' conditions is all we need here. 'Sufficient' is one of those context-sensitive words that depends heavily on factors of particular application. In this it is similar to the notion of 'sameness'. When we say that one thing is 'the same' as another—and we mean qualitative, not numerical, identity—we never mean that the two things literally share all of the same properties. We always contextualize our judgments of sameness, so that we mean, implicitly, 'the same in *these* (relevant) respects'.

Similarly with 'sufficient', when we say 'X is sufficient for Y' we never mean 'X is sufficient all by itself', for we know that many other conditions must be present or must be absent in order for X to produce Y. A spark is not sufficient for an explosion, because oxygen and fuel are necessary as well. These three together are not sufficient for the explosion because the absence of large amounts of inert material is also required. And so on.

True, in the overdetermination cases of the pre-emptive kind, we can say that the fire that arrived first was sufficient, but it is also true that relative to a different set of things considered, it was not sufficient (and neither was some set of conditions of which the fire was a necessary element). What we are getting at when we call the first fire to arrive 'sufficient' is that the second fire to arrive was not *necessary*. And what we are really getting at in saying both of these things is that the second fire did not cause the damage—the first one did.

'Sufficiency' thus does not explain the causal conclusions in the pre-emptive overdetermination cases; it merely redescribes those conclusions. What is really going on in the pre-emptive overdetermination cases is that there are two causal processes at work whose nature we know well enough to know that one process was completed (the first fire) while the second was not (the second fire).[27] We

---

[27] Douglas Ehring too finds the preemptive overdetermination cases to be crucial to understanding causation; he also sees the metaphysics involved in such cases, namely, a mechanistic metaphysics capable of carrying causal influence across discrete sets of processes. See Douglas Ehring, *Causation and Persistence: A theory of causation* (Oxford: Oxford University Press, 1997), 50–70.

know enough about how poisons and burns work to cause death, and we know enough about how gunshots or blows to the head work to cause death, that, when we see cases like those described in the preceding chapter, we know that a particular victim was shot to death, not poisoned to death, or bludgeoned to death, not burned to death.

Indeed, once we limit our reliance on the unhelpful notion of sufficiency, we can also see that there is nothing unique, interesting, or especially problematic about pre-emptive *overdetermination* cases. Whenever we know enough of the underlying causal mechanism at work in a given case, we often see that one cause preempts some other factor from doing what it otherwise would have done. Consider the case where the victim dies from loss of blood; he is shot once by each of three defendants, and loses blood from all three wounds. Each defendant has caused the death, and this is true irrespective of whether: (1) each wound was sufficient to cause death by itself, so that no individual wound was necessary (but the three were jointly necessary);[28] (2) each wound was necessary by itself, so that no individual wound was sufficient (but the three were jointly sufficient);[29] or (3) no wound was either individually necessary or individually sufficient, but any two of the wounds was both jointly necessary and jointly sufficient,[30] or (4) one wound was sufficient, meaning the other wounds were not necessary (although these other wounds may or may not be collectively sufficient).[31] We know each defendant caused the death because we know the causal mechanism connecting each of the defendants' action to the death. In the colorful language of the California Supreme Court in a related sort of case, 'Drop by drop the life current went out from both wounds, and at the very instant of death the [earlier] gunshot wound was contributing to the event.'[32]

Contrast my three variations of concurrent-cause cases above with a parallel case of preemptive causation: As before, the victim dies of loss of blood; as before, each defendant shot the victim; but here, only one wound caused any bleeding, external or internal. If the victim dies of loss of blood, the cause of death is the wound whose effects can be traced to the death through the loss of blood; the other two actions lack this causal mechanism and are not causes of death. They are 'pre-empted' from doing their causal work, assuming they would eventually have killed the victim by some other mechanical process, such as organ failure or blood poisoning.

The pre-emption cases should be our model for a successful metaphysical underpinning for the law of intervening causation generally. In the pre-emption

---

[28] Standardly called an overdetermination concurrent-cause case.

[29] What I have called the 'garden-variety concurrent-cause case'.

[30] What I have called the intermediate or 'mixed' kind of concurrent-cause case, intermediate between the overdetermination and the garden varieties.

[31] What I dub the 'asymmetrical concurrent overdetermination' cases.

[32] *People v. Lewis*, 57 P 470 (Cal 1899). *Lewis* was the fourth variant, because the later knife wound caused a much greater blood loss than the earlier gunshot wound.

cases we bring to bear our detailed knowledge of the physical world in justifying the causal conclusion reached by the law. There is no very *general* metaphysical truth being relied upon in such cases—save perhaps the truths that nothing can cause an event or state to occur that has already occurred, and that merely hypothetical events that might have occurred but which did not occur cannot cause anything else to occur. Yet the metaphysical underpinning of the law is nonetheless quite secure in such cases. Our best scientific theories show us that there is no causal relation in such cases, and the moral and legal conclusions tag along behind such metaphysics unproblematically.

I turn now to the other two kinds of intervening causes—voluntary human actions and abnormal natural events—to see whether some equally respectable metaphysics can be found that could justify these legal doctrines as well.

IV. Causation and Explanation

There is a highly regarded tradition in the metaphysics of causation that follows the general lines propounded by David Hume.[33] The tradition recognizes that in ordinary speech we employ two quite different causal locutions. First, we cite a particular event as the cause of some other and later particular event, as in 'The spark caused the fire.' Second, we explain some type of event by the occurrence of some other type of event, as in, 'Sparks cause fires.' The former are called singular causal statements, the latter, statements of causal laws.

Hume proclaimed ordinary speech to be misleading in this regard. In particular, he urged that the existence of singular causal relations was an illusion. All that could be meant when we say, '*c* caused *e*', is: There was an event *c*, there was another event *e*, *e* did not precede *c* temporally, *c* is an instantiation of some type C and *e* is an instantiation of some type E, where C and E are connected by a C/E law, and the C/E law amounts to no more than the regular following of events of type C by events of type E. More recent variation of this tradition follows Hume in all of this, save the regularity view of causal laws. Certain 'Neo-Humeans' regard causal laws as primitive relations between universals,[34] and probability theorists regard causal laws as irreducibly probabilistic rather than exceptionless universal generalizations.[35]

Hume's regularity theory, the theory of the neo-Humeans, and the probability theory together make up the generalist approach to causation. For all three

---

[33] As I said earlier in Chapter 4, I am unconcerned with whether the theory sketched in the text was really believed by Hume. On this, see, for example, Galen Strawson, *The Secret Connexion: Causation, realism, and David Hume* (Oxford: Clarendon Press, 1989); Barry Stroud, *Hume* (London: Routledge and Kegan Paul, 1977), 42–95. The Humean theory is an interesting and influential one even if it turns out that Hume never held it.

[34] DM Armstrong, *What Is a Law of Nature?* (Cambridge: Cambridge University Press, 1983).

[35] Patrick Suppes, *A Probabilistic Theory of Causality* (Amsterdam: North Holland, 1970).

branches of the Humean tradition reduce singular causal statements to statements of causal laws. Thus, some particular event *c* cannot be a cause of *e*, unless *c* and *e* are instances of some C/E law, however construed. This reductionist metaphysical view of causation gives rise to two sorts of accounts of the law's notion of an intervening cause, both having some basis in Hart and Honoré's writings.

A. There are natural end points to explanations in term of causal laws

Hart's and Honoré's essential idea here is that causal explanations come to an end.[36] When we ask, 'What caused the fire?' we are satisfied with the answer, 'an arsonist'. We do not need or want further explanations, like a history of the arsonist's unhappy childhood, his need for money from fire insurance, and the causes of that, and so on. Where no further explanation is appropriate no statement of singular causal relations is appropriate either (for remember, on this view, singular causal statements are just disguised explanations in terms of causal laws). Thus any event that occurs before the event that is the subject of a satisfying causal explanation drops into the background as a mere condition, not in any sense a cause, of the event being explained.

To complete this line of thought, Hart and Honoré then urged that there were two sorts of satisfying causal explanations, those that stopped at voluntary human actions and those that stopped at unusual natural events.[37] When seeking an explanation for events like harms to victims, we search among the conditions necessary for such harms until we find one of these two types of items, and, when we find one, we search no further back in time for any other such items as may have preceded the item we already found.

There is no doubt that Hart and Honoré captured important features of our explanatory practices. In seeking an explanation, for example, of why the Spanish Armada was defeated, we are most interested in voluntary actions like Drake's decision to take advantage of the rather stupid Spanish decision to arrange their ships in the shape of a giant bird (pleasing to God in Heaven, no doubt, but exposed to concentrated fire at the tips of the wings). Add to this the great storm in the North Sea that dispatched a number of the ships that escaped Drake's fire, and we may well end up satisfied that we understand *why* the Spanish Armada was defeated . . . so satisfied, indeed, that we look no further for earlier 'underlying' or 'root' causes.

Yet even on the generalist accounts of causation of the Humean tradition, this surely will not do to account for the causal breaks posited by the legal doctrines of intervening causation. That is, even granting Hume's reductionist premise[38]—no explanation, no causal relation—there surely *is* an explanation behind the

---

[36] Hart and Honoré, *Causation* (2nd edn), 32–44.   [37] Ibid.
[38] I reject the reductionist version of this premise in Chapter 19, below.

decisions of Drake and of the Spanish, and behind the great storm. There just is no explanation *in which we are much interested*, given that our curiosity began with the defeat of the Armada. And surely *our* interest, or the lack of it, cannot determine whether the decisions of Drake and the Spanish, or the North Sea storm, were caused.[39] If we were to take any other view, no tree would fall in the proverbial forest so long as we had no interest in hearing about it.

B. There are literally inexplicable events

So Hart and Honoré needed a more radical use of Hume's reductionist metaphysics here. They needed to say (what they in fact came close to saying at times) that some events are truly inexplicable. What makes for an abnormal conjunction of natural events, for example, is just the lack of any causal law connecting the two types of events in question; what makes for an extraordinary natural event *tout court* is just the lack of any (ordinary) causal law explaining or predicting it. What makes for a fully voluntary human action is that there are no causal laws explaining or predicting such action. And now one could put Hume's reductionist metaphysics to good use: such inexplicable events are literally uncaused events (because they are inexplicable events), so that there are no causes of them that could be looked to to explain the harm they themselves cause.

Yet are 'acts of God,' coincidences, and 'free' human choices in fact inexplicable by causal laws? Consider first voluntary human actions. In the philosophy of social science generally,[40] and in the philosophy of history more particularly,[41] there is a respectable body of opinion holding that human behavior is not subject to 'covering laws.' It is notoriously difficult to frame universal causal laws about human behavior, because what people do and why they do such things seems too variable to be captured by such laws. People just are not as boringly repetitive as protons. For such reasons, Hart and Honoré distinguished the seeming causation of voluntary human action as in reality non-causal in any central sense:

---

[39] For another example of this line of criticism of Hart and Honoré, see JL Mackie, *The Cement of the Universe* (Oxford: Oxford University Press, 1974), 120 (explaining that while our interests determine what is satisfying by way of an explanation, such interests are irrelevant to a theoretical account of causation which does not distinguish cause from conditions). Hart and Honoré reject Mackie's interest-relative rejection of the cause/condition distinction as being only pragmatic and not truly causal. Hart and Honoré, *Causation* (2nd edn), xxxix. Yet it is very unclear how their own line of argument here is or can be anything other than 'merely pragmatic'.

[40] See Carl G Hempel, 'Aspects of scientific explanation', in his *Aspects of Scientific Explanation* (New York: Free Press, 1965); Leonard I Krimerman (edn), *The Nature and Scope of Social Science* (New York: Appleton-Century-Craft, 1969).

[41] Compare Carl G Hempel, 'The Function of General Laws in History', in his *Aspects of Scientific Explanation*, and Carl G Hempel, 'Reasons and covering laws in historical explanation', in Sidney Hook (ed), *Philosophy and History* (New York: NYU Press, 1963), with William Dray, 'The historical explanation of action reconsidered', *in Philosophy and History*.

Relationships between two persons' actions... do not depend upon 'regular connections' or sequence as the causal relations between physical events do. Hence the assertion that one person, for example, induced another to act is not 'covertly' general ... [G]eneralizations have a place here but a less central one.[42]

Yet surely one could grant all of this, and still protest. First, at the macro level, there are at least probabilistic laws. Hume himself gave a good example: leave a purse of gold at Charing Cross in London and come back an hour later; it probably will not be there because probably someone will pick it up.[43] Second, as we leave the macro level for the micro events making up human behavior and motivation, neo-Humeans like JL Mackie have urged that we will find universal 'laws of working' connecting stages in what at the macro level we call a single action.[44] That we do not know such micro laws of working reflect only our empirical ignorance; it does not reflect any brute inexplicability to human choice.

In dealing with the obvious fact that many human choices can indeed be explained, Hart and Honoré relied on a view quite prevalent in the ordinary-language philosophy of the 1950s.[45] This was the view that uncompelled human choices were explicable by *reasons*, not by *causes*; that only when choices were compelled was it appropriate to speak of them as caused;[46] that it was thus a category mistake to speak of caused but voluntary choices, the mistake of explaining something in one category (free choices) by something in a different category (causation).[47]

The main problem with this old view, like all variants of the category mistake argument, was that no amount of regimentation of ordinary speech into categories could seal off the insights of an advancing science. In particular, it has

---

[42] Hart and Honoré, *Causation* (2nd edn), 51–2; see also *Harton v. Forest City Tel Co,* 59 SE 1022, 1026 (NC 1907): 'The spontaneous action of an independent will is neither the subject of regular, natural sequence, nor of accurate precalculation by us.'; Sanford Kadish, 'Causation and complicity: A study in the interpretations of doctrine', California Law Review 73 (1985), reprinted in Sanford Kadish, *Blame and Punishment* (New York: Macmillan, 1987), 163: [E]very volitional actor is a wild card: he need never act in a certain way.... No laws of nature can settle the issue.'

[43] See David Hume, *Enquiry Concerning the Human Understanding* (Oxford: Clarendon Press, 1902), 93.

[44] Mackie, *Cement of the Universe*, 120–5, 210–12.

[45] See AR Louch, *Explanation and Human Action* (Berkeley: UC Press, 1966); AI Melden, *Free Action* (London: Routledge and Kegan Paul, 1961); Richard Peters, *The Concept of Motivation* (London: Routledge and Kegan Paul, 1958); Peter Winch, *The Idea of a Social Science* (London: Routledge and Kegan Paul, 1958). For Tony Honoré's sympathetic use of this old distinction, see Honoré, 'Necessary and sufficient conditions in tort law', in David G Owen (ed), *Philosophical Foundations of Tort Law* (Oxford: Oxford University Press, 1995), 382–4.

[46] See Hart and Honoré, 'Causation in the law', Law Quarterly Review 72 (1956), 80: 'When we do speak of a human action as caused, this is with the strong implication that the agent acted in one or more of those many different circumstances which are treated as inconsistent with his action being fully voluntary: we imply if we speak of an action as "caused" that the agent acted under coercion or domination or that he had lost self control or was submitted to some special stress or emergency... If it turns out that there were no such special circumstances the natural conclusion would be that nothing *caused* him to [so act]: he just deliberately did so.'

[47] See Gilbert Ryle, *The Concept of Mind* (London: Hutchins, 1949), 11–24.

become clear that 'reasons'—belief/desire sets of a certain content—are as much causal of behavior as is anything else in the natural world.[48] What sense are we to assign to the 'because' in sentences of the form 'He did it because he wanted the money' if it is not the usual causal sense? It is thus difficult today to take very seriously the claim that the only way to explain free human choices is by resort to the language of 'reasons' instead of 'causes'.

This more radical use of Hume fares no better if we move from voluntary human choices to abnormal natural events. After all, the 'shit happens' view of coincidences is pretty naive. As Hart and Honoré came to recognize,[49] even if there are no general causal laws connecting speeding in an automobile, for example, and a tree falling, surely there are Mackie's micro laws of working connecting successive stages of this larger conjunction and making the conjunction fully explicable. If we do not pursue such micro laws of working here any more than we do for human behavior, that is only because of our limited explanatory interests. It is not because there are no such explanations (and thus, on this view, no such chain of causes going back to defendant's action).

The probabilist branch of the Humean tradition about causation has tried to salvage things here.[50] Adherents of this view note, correctly, that in cases of coincidence, the conditional probability of the victim's harm, given the defendant's action, is very low. They also note that the intervening event dramatically increases that probability. If one identifies singular causal relations with probabilistic laws—which is one version of the probabilistic theory of causation—then the intervening event is a much bigger cause than even the defendant's original action. On a kind of *de minimis* principle one might thus relegate defendant's action to the status of a noncausal event, given that its contribution was below some threshold of significance.

One problem with this view is the implausibility of this version of the probabilistic theory of causation, an impalusibility we shall examine in Chapter 19. A second problem lies in the seeming over-inclusiveness of the suggested account of intervening causes. Surely it is not just extraordinary winds that dramatically increase the risk of a fire spreading; normal evening breezes that resuscitate a fire about to go out dramatically increase the conditional probability of fire damage as well. Similarly, it is not just intervening voluntary action that can dramatically increase the probability of some harm; a coerced gunshot can be just as deadly as a freely chosen gunshot. The probability account thus seems to make far too many events into intervening causes, and it seems blind to the criteria of intervening causation.

---

[48] See Donald Davidson, 'Actions, reasons, and causes', in his *Essays on Actions and Events* (Oxford: Oxford University Press, 1980).

[49] Hart and Honoré, *Causation* (2nd edn), xxxix.

[50] See Peter Lipton, 'Causation outside the law', in Hyman Gross and Ross Harrison (eds), *Jurisprudence: Cambridge Essays* (Cambridge: Cambridge University Press, 1992).

V. Libertarian Metaphysics for Human Choices and Acts of God

Surely at the root of many people's intuitions about uncoerced human actions breaking causal chains is a libertarian metaphysics. On this view, voluntary human choices are literally uncaused events. They are thus fresh causal starts, relegating all prior events to non-causal status vis-à-vis the chain of events such fresh starts cause.

James McLaughlin early on summarized this metaphysical basis for the law on intervening human actions:

Where human or animal action is purely involuntary so that an instantaneous response is made to the defendant's direct force without the exercise of choice, there is no reason for treating such response as constituting a new or intervening force. Where there is voluntary action or action involving choice on the part of any being other than the defendant, a basis for distinction is apparent . . . It may be a field for psychological speculation whether all such actions cannot be resolved completely in terms of physics and chemistry, but it is clear from all legal tradition and analogies that voluntary action must not be regarded as perfectly mechanical. The new element of conscious choice, which is elusive from a mechanical point of view, prevents causation from being direct.[51]

Hart and Honoré similarly attributed a libertarian metaphysics both to the law and to the common-sense notions they viewed as undergirding the law. In the article that preceded their book they held that 'whatever the metaphysics of the matter may be [a deliberate] human action is never regarded as itself *caused* or as *an effect*'.[52] In the two editions of their book they softened this line a bit; 'in some sense', they thought, a fully voluntary human action could be said to be caused, but not in the central sense of 'caused' used by the law to assign responsibility.[53] This is a kind of metaphysically dualist view about causation. The 'central' notion is of a relation that fully determines (is 'sufficient' for) that which is caused; the secondary notion is of a relation that only 'occasions', 'induces', 'enables', or 'inclines' that which it causes. The latter terms are used to connote a lack of determination and sufficiency in this kind of causation. Such lack is but another name for freedom, and so this softened line taken by Hart and Honoré remained libertarian in its metaphysics.[54]

Despite these antecedents, it is mostly Sandy Kadish who has explored the (metaphysically) libertarian roots of intervening-cause doctrine.[55] Like

---

[51] McLaughlin, 'Proximate causation', 168.
[52] Hart and Honoré, 'Causation in the law', 80.
[53] Hart and Honoré, *Causation* (2nd edn), 42–3, 51–9, 186–204, 363–88.
[54] I discuss Antony Flew's expression of this kind of dualistic determinism in Moore, *Placing Blame*, 513–14. For two other attempts to articulate a non-deterministic 'causation' of human actions, see Alan Donagan, *The Theory of Morality* (Oxford: Oxford University Press, 1977), 45; Antony Flew, 'Psychiatry, law and responsibility', Philosophical Quarterly 35 (1985), 425–32.
[55] Kadish, 'Causation and complicity'.

McLaughlin, Hart, and Honoré, Kadish does not tell us his own metaphysical views; rather, he too describes 'the beliefs that underlie the criminal law'.[56] Central to those beliefs is the idea that 'voluntary actions cannot be said to be caused', at least not in the sense that physical events are caused by relentless forces and necessary conditions.[57] Human actions may be 'influenced' by various events, 'but influences do not work like wind upon a straw'.[58] Rather, humans are total sovereigns over their own actions,[59] in the sense that, despite the influences of genes and environment, a person is free to choose to act contrary to such influences.[60]

This robustly libertarian metaphysics does allow that some human behavior is caused, and not merely influenced, by prior events. Such behavior is, however, the kind of non-voluntary behavior so fully explored by Hart and Honoré. Reflex reactions, involuntary motor movements, posthypnotic behavior, acts done under ignorance, duress, natural necessity, provocation, addiction, insanity, infancy, and the like, are all less than wholly voluntary because they are less than wholly free. Such less than wholly voluntary behavior is typically excused because in such cases 'my freedom to have acted otherwise was totally or partially impaired'.[61] More pertinently for our purposes, behavior that is the expression of such impaired freedom does not constitute an intervening cause; after all, being totally or partially caused itself, it could not represent a fresh causal start breaking causal chains. Such unfree, non-voluntary behavior is just another link in the causal chain, no different than other caused events.

Libertarian metaphysics is difficult to sustain, as we shall see. Perhaps for this reason, Kadish and his intellectual antecedents here all refuse to defend libertarian metaphysics as such. Rather, they defend the more modest, sociological claim that 'commonsense' (that is, other people) believe in such a metaphysics. Such sociology is fine if one wishes merely to *explain* why we have the legal doctrines of intervening causation that we do. If our ambitions are to *justify* such doctrines, however, we need to leave off doing the sociology of other people's metaphysics and start doing our own. Voluntary human actions have to *be* uncaused—not just *believed to be* uncaused—if they are justifiably to serve the sort of chain-breaking function they do serve in our law.

There is a hint in McLaughlin of a contrary view, for he seems to think that the law as an autonomous discipline can just *posit* human freedom even if psychology could show us otherwise.[62] The hint is developed into an explicit defense of 'autonomous legal metaphysics' by later criminal law theoreticians

---

[56] Ibid, 135.   [57] Ibid.   [58] Ibid, 141.
[59] Kadish, 'Causation and complicity'.
[60] Ibid.   [61] Ibid, 142.
[62] McLaughlin, 'Proximate causation', 168 (arguing that law must treat human choices as non-mechanical even if psychology shows that they are at bottom fully mechanical).

such as Jerome Hall[63] and Herbert Packer.[64] On this view, even if science tells us that voluntary human actions are fully caused, the law can presuppose just the opposite if it needs to do so for its own purposes. Such views of legal autonomy ignore the obvious here: if the legal doctrines (such as those of intervening causation) we seek to justify are based on the policy of fitting punishment to moral desert, and if moral desert itself depends on the facts of causation, then we cannot just *posit* any old 'facts' about causation that we need.[65] In particular, if the doctrines of intervening causation make sense only if voluntary human action is uncaused, then it will not do just to *posit* that, for legal purposes, we will assume such behavior is uncaused. For the legal doctrines in question to be justified, we need such behavior to *be* uncaused. A fictional freedom here is about as useful as is a fictional can opener to a starving man possessed of only tinned goods.[66]

There are three reasons to reject any libertarian defense of intervening-cause doctrines. One is that it does not account at all for acts of God. Even if human wills are free of being caused, that does not give any support to the doctrines of abnormal natural events and coincidences as intervening causes. Only a theistic view of such natural events can bring them under the umbrella of a free-will theory of intervening causation. (And even for theists, their God has to be only an occasional intervenor with a taste for the dramatic—He sends only freak winds, not normal evening breezes.)

The second reason to reject any libertarian basis for intervening-cause doctrines stems from the poorness of fit between the metaphysics and the legal doctrines. The legal doctrines, as we saw in detail in the last chapter, draw the line (of actions constituting intervening causes) at: (1) voluntary (willed) bodily movement; (2) itself motivated by an intention (or sometimes, accompanied at least by foresight) to do the harm done; (3) which intention or foresight is formed in the absence of coercive pressures making the choice difficult; (4) by one sufficiently possessed of his faculties as to be a generally responsible agent. As we have also seen, Hart and Honoré treat these conditions as the boundaries drawn by common sense around when an action is truly free in the sense of uncaused. They thus find a good fit between the plausible libertarian metaphysics of 'common sense' and the law's doctrines of intervening causation. I, on the contrary, think the fit to be quite poor.[67]

---

[63] Jerome Hall, *General Principles of Criminal Law* (2nd edn, Indianapolis: Bobbs-Merrill, 1960), 455.

[64] Herbert Packer, *The Limits of the Criminal Sanction* (Stanford: Stanford University Press, 1968), 74–5.

[65] I argue this at greater length in Moore, *Placing Blame*, 514–16.

[66] You know the old joke: the economist scornfully puts aside other suggestions about how to open the only can of food on a deserted island, saying that by his science it is easy: 'Assume a can opener.'

[67] The argument that follows is similar to my earlier argument, see Moore, *Placing Blame*, 491–502, 523–37, to the effect that a plausible boundary to when we are free and when we are caused poorly fits our legal doctrines of excuse. Herbert Hart himself came to question the fit between a libertarian metaphysics and the law's doctrines of intervening causation even before the publication of the second edition of *Causation in the Law.*

If I were a libertarian about free will (which I am not), I would draw the line of free versus caused action around items (1) and (4) above. That is, I would argue that what separates persons from all other creatures is their freedom of will; thus, (4) above. Further, I would argue that the immediate locus of the will is on those voluntary bodily movements that are the essence of human actions, and that what makes a mere behavioral routine into a human action is the will that causes such behavior, when such will is itself uncaused. Thus, (1) above.

So far so good for the libertarian defense of intervening-cause doctrine. Yet even as this hypothetical libertarian about the will, I can see no temptation to think that the willed bodily movements of a fully sane, adult human being become unfree if done in ignorance of certain properties of those movements. Consider the facts of *Watson*[68] again, the case discussed in the last chapter where a railroad negligently spilled gasoline that was then ignited by a third party's cigar. Whether Duerr, the intervenor, knew the gas was present when he threw his cigar, and whether he knew that the cigar would ignite the town, does not change the fact that he willed the movements that sent the cigar on its way. His act was intentional vis-à-vis the harm only if he had such knowledge, but surely his act was as *free* in the one case as in the other.

Moreover, on the most plausible mode of individuating actions and other events, Duerr did but one act when he threw the cigar.[69] There are many ways to refer to that one act, utilizing different types of actions: He moved his arm, he moved the cigar, he lit the gasoline, and he destroyed the town. If Duerr acted at all—if, that is, he willed the bodily movements that resulted in the cigar touching the gasoline—then necessarily he did certain types of actions intentionally.[70] If he did not intentionally destroy the town or ignite the gas, he did intentionally move his arm. Are we to imagine that his one act was free under the description, 'moved his arm', but caused under the description, 'destroyed the town?' That would lead the libertarian to a flat contradiction, namely, the very same act was both free and not-free.

Intention and foresight thus cannot be a line separating caused acts from free ones. Any plausible libertarianism must eschew condition (2) as marking such a boundary. Yet (2) is very much part of the boundary separating those acts that are not intervening causes from those that are. Thus, the charge of lack of fit between the legal doctrines and any plausible libertarian metaphysics.

Things are no better with regard to condition (3). It is true that when a choice becomes difficult because of some threat, natural necessity, overpowering craving, or unhinging emotion, we easily speak of the forces *causing* us to do what we did. Yet what of those cases where the capacities of the intervening actor remain

---

[68] *Watson v. Kentucky & Indiana Bridge & RR Co*, 126 SW 146 (Ky 1910).
[69] This 'coarse-grained' mode of event-individuation is defended in Michael Moore, *Act and Crime: The implications of the philosophy of action for the criminal law* (Oxford: Clarendon Press, 1993), 280–301.
[70] Ibid, 146.

undisturbed, intact, and fully functioning? Suppose such an actor finds himself at the top of a burning building, the fire having been set by an arsonist; having steeled himself to look death in the face without fear or even excitement, he coolly decides to jump rather than burn to death. In such cases, Herbert Hart would say, the actor's capacities to decide are intact but his *opportunity* to use his perfectly functioning *capacities* is diminished.[71] Such an actor has an excuse, when his own responsibility is at issue, and such an actor's constrained choice is said by the law to be less than fully voluntary and thus not an intervening cause when the arsonist's responsibility for the jumper's death is in question.

I should think that a sensible libertarian would find no temptation to regard such diminished-opportunity choices to be unfree. For in such cases the actor deliberates, decides, and executes his decision as rationally and as deliberately as in cases of greater opportunity. The phenomenology seems as free as any other case of deliberate choice, yet to fit the doctrines of intervening causation the libertarian would have to conclude that such choices were caused, not free.

Now let me stop pretending to be a libertarian about the will. In truth, I find libertarian metaphysics to border on the unintelligible. The closer one looks at this metaphysical position, the worse it looks. If 'common sense' indeed subscribes to such a metaphysics, so much the worse for 'common sense'. It can be no justification of legal doctrine to be based on error this fundamental, no matter how widely shared such error may be in our populace.

Take the best case for libertarians, situation (1) above, where the will admittedly plays a decisive role in the concept of human action. We *act* only if we *will*. The libertarian temptation is based on the idea that willing is necessarily incompatible with causation *of* the will (but not, of course, with causation of further events *by* the will).

The will as an uncaused causer is a very strange idea. How can there be an event that causes other events yet is itself not subject to causal influences by earlier events? Aquinas gave this role to God, but are we so divine in all of our actions? To sustain such an odd idea, libertarians usually invent another, even odder idea: The will (that is free) operates in a realm distinct from the realm of ordinary natural events. Ordinary events exist in both space and time, but mental events, like willings, exist in time only. This is what insulates willings from causal influences. Or so the dualist story goes. (Of course, there is the awkward question of how willings *cause* events in the natural world, given the insulation of willings within the distinct world of mind.)

Just how odd a story this is should become more apparent the more one thinks hard about what willings are. As we learn more and more about the brain, we are

---

[71] Hart's well-known account of when we are excused: when we lack capacity or when we are denied opportunity to use such capacity. See Hart 'Legal responsibility and excuses', in Sidney Hook (ed), *Determinism and Freedom in the Age of Modern Science* (New York: NYU Press, 1958). Hart put forward this account of excuses precisely to sidestep any issue of determinism; he saw that one could have capacity and opportunity even when one's choices were fully caused.

increasingly able to isolate certain brain structures as having some role in the mental act of willing. We know that the supplementary motor area of the cortex is involved in willing bodily movements.[72] We know that the brain functionally separates the initiation of motor movement from the regulation of movement once initiated and that this functional division is realized in different areas of the brain.[73] We know that in motor-movement initiation there are distinctive patterns of blood flow and electrical energy peculiar to willed (versus involuntary) motor movement.[74]

It is very unlikely that such physical events in the brain are uncaused. Therefore, if willings are uncaused ('free'), then they must be distinct from these brain events. Such brain events may be some other, distant event—one might call them 'schwillings'—but on this view they could not be *willings*.[75] But then, what are willings? Mental events, construed as existing in a special realm, that of the mind, existing in time but not in space, accessible through a special mode of observation known as consciousness.[76] By such route the libertarian in metaphysics is driven ineluctably towards dualism in metaphysics.

It is much more plausible to think that 'willing' refers to a functionally specified state of the brain, a state defined by its mediating and executing role between belief/desire/intention sets, on the one hand, and bodily movements, on the other.[77] Such a functionally specified state may have many different physical realizations, but in our brains the structural possibilities are far from infinite. Even though we only know part of the functional/structural story about willings, we literally mean more than we know when we speak of 'willing'. The same is true of other words, like 'water', 'gold', and 'tiger'. In all such cases we intend to refer to a kind whose nature is only partially glimpsed.[78] When scientists tell us more and more about that nature, they are not changing the subject—to 'schmater', 'schmold', 'schwilling'. Rather, they are telling us more about what water, gold, and willings are.

Taking this latter functionalist/physicalist view of mental states like willings, there is no reason whatever to think that willings are uncaused. Such functionally specified, physically realized events are both causes and effects of earlier causes, like all other events. They cannot, on such an account, be literal fresh causal starts breaking causal chains wherever they intervene.

[72] Gary Goldberg, 'Supplementary Motor Area Structure and Function: Review and Hypotheses', Behavioral & Brain Sciences 8 (1985), 567–88.

[73] Benjamin Libet, 'Unconscious Cerebral Initiative and the Role of Conscious Will in Voluntary Action', Behavioral & Brain Sciences 8 (1985), 529–39.

[74] Id.

[75] For such an ostrich-like reaction to the rapid-eye movement and EEG evidence produced in the 1950s about dreaming, see Norman Malcolm, *Dreaming* (London: Routledge, 1959). For the corrective, see Putnam, *Mind, Language, and Reality*.

[76] On the push of libertarianism to dualism, see Ryle, *The Concept of Mind*.

[77] Moore, *Act and Crime*, 113–65.

[78] Putam, *Mind, Language and Reality*; Moore, 'Natural law theory of interpretation'.

VI. Intervening Causes as Sufficiently Big Causes as to Relegate Earlier Events to De Minimus Causal Contributors

A common account of the metaphysics underlying the intervening causation doctrines of the law is in terms of 'forces'. The general idea is that causation is a matter of physical forces acting on one another, and that one force can cut off the operation of another force so as to preclude any causal relation between the latter and some harm. Most of the earlier writers on intervening causation expressed themselves in this way.[79] Hart and Honoré found such talk of 'forces' to be too metaphorical to be of any real use.[80] They rightly noted that writers such as Beale never attempted to translate such ideas of 'forces' into usable notions that could be applied to economic losses and other non-mechanical situations.

The continued use of such talk by contemporary legal theorists is not much more metaphysically self-conscious than was that of Beale or of his followers. Richard Epstein holds that 'force and dangerous conditions are still the only issues material to the causation question'[81] and fleshes out the notion of a dangerous condition in terms of stored and unstable energy.[82] An intervening cause for Epstein then becomes a subsequently arising 'big' force, while, by contrast, 'little forces never break the chain of causation'.[83] Yet none of this talk of forces and energy is fleshed out by Epstein because of his reliance on paradigms to give the meaning of 'cause'. As we recall, the paradigm case approach to meaning regards definitions of 'cause' to be otiose.

George Fletcher, to pick another contemporary example, willingly admits that his talk of 'causal energy' is metaphorical.[84] Yet such talk by Fletcher is worse than metaphorical or vague; it explicitly mixes in things that could not be aspects of force or energy in any sense. Fletcher supposes a case in which the victim ('Gabe') is negligently injured by defendant ('Jack'). While in the hospital, the intervenor ('Mike') executes Gabe. Fletcher's gives the following account of why Mike's act is an intervening cause:

When Mike enters Gabe's room and lays his hand on his intended victim, he invests more personality, more energy, into the unfolding of causes and events. This greater input of personal force brings his actions into the foreground...Jack's initial injury of Gabe is

---

[79] Beale, 'Recovery for consequences of an act'. Beale, 'Proximate consequences'; Francis Bohlen, 'The probable or the natural consequences as the test of liability in negligence', American Law Register 49 (1901), 79–88, 148–64;. Carpenter, 'Proximate cause'; Carpenter, 'Workable rules'; Albert Levitt, 'Cause, legal cause, and proximate cause', Michigan Law Review 21 (1922), 34–62, 160–73; McLaughlin, 'Proximate cause'.

[80] Hart and Honoré, *Causation* (2nd edn), 30, 96–7, 341.

[81] Epstein, 'A theory of strict liability', 180.   [82] Ibid, 177–8.

[83] Ibid, 183–4.

[84] George P Fletcher, *Basic Concepts of Criminal Law* (New York: Oxford University Press, 1998), 66.

merely negligent...Jack's contribution at the outset is less substantial and it is overwhelmed by Mike's committed and willful intervention.[85]

It should be apparent that Fletcher is exploiting the vagueness of 'energy' in these contexts to smuggle in notions of moral culpability. Because Mike is more culpable than Jack, his *causal* contribution is said to be greater. Yet as I argued in Chapter 6, causation is supposed to be one of the criteria by which we assess moral blameworthiness; if we allow moral culpability to guide our causal judgments, then causation cannot be such a criterion.

Fletcher is not alone in mixing moral blameworthiness with his idea of force and energy. Earlier writers too assumed without argument that intentional intervenors brought more 'force' to their interventions than did merely negligent intervenors, even when the physical behavior of each was identical. Without some metaphysical account of how this could be so, this looks for all the world like Fletcher's more explicit use of moral blameworthiness as a criterion of causation (rather than the other way around).

I shall defer until Chapter 20 discussion of what metaphysical sense we can make of the 'forces' translation of intervening causes. For now, let me use a singularist place-holder theory, one that accords primitive status to singular causal relations.[86] Perhaps we can use this place holder to at least strip some of the vagueness and metaphor from the forces approach, as well as rob it of its illicit moral subtext. The way to state a primitivist singularism about causation is in terms of three propositions. The first two are metaphysical, and the third is a distinctively moral doctrine. Proposition one: causation is a scalar relation.[87] Scalar relations are more-or-less affairs, not matters of black or white. Being 'redder than' is a scalar relation because one item can be more red than another. 'Dead', by contrast, is an all or nothing quality; one either is or is not dead, so that one person being 'more dead' than another makes little sense.

The idea here is that causation is a relation that can vary along a smooth continuum. One event can be more of a cause of some harm than another event, even if both events causally contribute to that harm. If two defendants each strike one victim, who dies of the loss of blood, it seems to make sense to say that the blow that caused a greater loss of blood was more of a cause of death than the

---

[85] Ibid.

[86] Causation is taken as a 'primitive' when it cannot be reduced to anything else. See Michael Tooley, *Causation: A realist approach* (Oxford: Oxford University Press, 1987).

[87] I discussed this aspect of causation in Chapter 5. Whether causation is scalar in nature is a disputed matter, particularly by those enamored of necessary or sufficient condition analyses of causation (which tend to be all or nothing analyses). *Compare* Richard A Epstein, 'Defenses and subsequent pleas in a system of strict liability', Journal of Legal Studies 3 (1974), 165–215, and Mario J Rizzo and Frank S Arnold, 'Causal apportionment in the law of torts: An economic approach', Columbia Law Review 80 (1980), 1399–429, and Smith, 'Legal cause' (all contemplating degrees of causal contribution), with Hart and Honoré, *Causation* (2nd edn), 223, and Mackie, *Cement of the Universe*, 128–9, and John Borgo, 'Causal paradigms', 448–52 (all questioning the sense of talk of degrees of causal contribution).

blow that resulted in a smaller loss of blood. Similarly with two fires that join: other things equal (there is no more precise information about the fuel and oxygen consumption patterns), the bigger fire is more of a cause of the harm than was the smaller fire. Similarly, when a town is flooded by waters, most of which would have flooded the town even if defendant had not negligently damaged the drainage wickets protecting the town, the flood is more of a cause of the damage than is the defendant's action.

Second proposition: the scalarity of causation is specifically such that the causal relation diminishes over time. This is the famous idea that causation peters out over time, much as the ripples from a stone dropped in a pond diminish as they travel outward. The basic idea here is of an inverted cone of causation pictured in Figure 12.1.

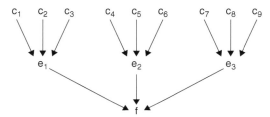

Figure 12.1 The inverted cone of causation

On this picture, every event has multiple causes so that the immediate effect of any given event is itself but one of numerous causes in the production of another event, and so on. At each successive period of time, the causal contribution of any given event diminishes in proportion to the number of other events contributing to the effect in question: c_1 may cause e_1, but its contribution to f (or to events f in turn causes) may be *de minimis*, on this picture of causal relationships. Third proposition: the amount of causal contribution needed for an actor to be morally responsible for some harm, is non-*de minimis* (or 'substantial').[88] When assessing an actor's blameworthiness, causation of a harm marks the difference between a serious degree of blameworthiness for the harm and a lesser degree of blameworthiness for only risking, foreseeing, or trying to cause, that harm. On the assumption that causation is a matter of degree, morality needs some line drawn on the continuum of possible causal contribution separating causers from mere riskers and attempters. The vague notion of 'substantial' is as good a line as we are likely to get. The vagueness of the idea of substantiality is not a defect but a virtue. As Aristotle remarked long ago, we should not demand greater precision than a subject matter can bear.[89] This is particularly true of attempting to

---

[88] The moral premise of Jeremiah Smith's 'substantial factor' test. Smith, 'Legal Cause'.
[89] See Aristotle, *Nicomachean Ethics*, Richard McKeon (ed) (Chicago: University of Chicago Press, 1973), Book I, Chapter 3, 347–8.

quantify exactly where a line is to be drawn on a smooth continuum. We can stipulate that the difference between a city and a town is at 50,000 inhabitants; but to do so usually hinders, not helps, our use of the terms defined, as in generalizing 'living in cities leads to higher levels of anxiety than living in towns'.[90] *Mutatis mutandis* for precise definitions of substantial degrees of causal contribution.

Assent to these three spare proposition allows one to see why the subsequent, preemptive cause cases are our clearest examples of intervening causation. In the hypothetical case where one defendant poisons the victim and an intervenor subsequently shoots the victim dead,[91] we know that the poison did not get the chance to do its work in causing death, so its degree of causal contribution was zero. This is the clearest case of de minimis or insubstantial causal contribution. Almost as easy are the cases where the intervening cause is a *vis major*, or 'act of God'. Gale-force winds, unprecedented floods, and the like are pretty straight-forwardly big forces that most of the time relegate earlier and smaller forces to *de minimis* or insubstantial status. Ordinary evening breezes, normal tidal movements, and other routine events do not overwhelm the causal contribution of wrongful action nearly so easily or so often.

More troublesome are the cases of coincidence and of fully voluntary human action. We understand that both such types of items draw our explanatory interest and that the second of these two draws in addition our moral attention. But such pragmatic accounts of our judgments are irrelevant to the metaphysics of causation. What is it about these types of interventions that overwhelms earlier causal contributions, relegating them to mere de minimis or insubstantial causes (Hart's and Honoré's 'mere conditions')?

My own provisional answers to these last queries go like this. About coincidences, I share Hart's and Honoré's (and the case law's) intuition of non-responsibility, but I do not think this conclusion can be defended on causal grounds. Rather, it is a culpability discrimination doing the work of *most of* these cases. Where harm consciously risked or intended occurs only because of extraordinary coincidence—such as a tree falling on a man only because of his earlier speeding—the harm as it happened is too far removed from the harm risked or intended for the actor to be held liable for it. There is a non-*de minimis* causal connection between the defendant's action and the harm that came about in most (but not all) cases of coincidence, but not enough of the causal route was within the contemplation of the actor to hold him responsible for the harm.[92]

---

[90] The example is William Alston's. See his discussion of the beneficial uses of vagueness, in William Alston, *Philosophy of Language* (Englewood Cliffs: Prentice-Hall, 1964).

[91] This is Richard Wright's example: see Wright, 'Causation in tort law', California Law Review 73 (1985), 1795.

[92] How much of the causal route must be within the contemplation of the actor when he acts is a vague matter in morality, but this matches the vagueness in the ideas of coincidence and abnormality. For the reasons given in Chapters 8 and 9, this culpability analysis is unavailable in torts/crimes of negligence; in such cases coincidences should not 'break causal chains' except in those cases where the causal contribution of the defendant's action has fallen below the *de minimis* line.

About voluntary human actions intervening between defendant's act and the harm: sometimes the same culpability criterion can explain the original actor's non-responsibility. Whether there is also a causal discrimination at work here is more troublesome. Prima facie, the choice to cause (or at least risk) the harm when made by the intervenor is a more substantial cause than the like choice made by the original actor. This is true because such choices, in the abstract, are on a par, but the intervenor's choice is in greater spatio-temporal proximity to the harm and is thus less diminished in its degree of causal contribution. Yet it is difficult to explain on causal grounds why choice itself is so significant. A negligent shot seemingly has as much causal power as an intentional shot, and even an involuntary movement can mimic exactly the physical characteristics of some voluntary movement. Absent some brute inexplicability or libertarian freedom for human choices, it is hard to see how metaphysics can explain these legal discriminations.

VII. Conclusion

As is probably evident even thus far in the book, my own bets on the metaphysics of causation are singularist and physicalist. Using such a metaphysics of force and energy, it is difficult to sustain some of the ordinary causal judgments we make not only in law but also in sociology, economics, and other of the human sciences. It is tempting at this point to issue a John Searle-like statement: 'This is as far as a philosopher need go; the rest is up to the physicists.'[93] After all, philosophy today is generally open to the insights of an advancing science in a way that would have shocked the Oxford ordinary-language philosophy that lay behind Hart's and Honoré's approach to causation. Yet from what has been done here, such an attitude is premature. Before he may pass off the project to the fact-grubbers, a philosopher at least has to see how the facts *could* go so as to sustain some moral or legal conclusion. That is a point we have not reached about intervening causation.

The most that can be said of this legal doctrine is that it serves a proxy function: what the law now calls 'intervening causes' are often such substantial causes that they relegate the earlier causal contribution of some defendant to a de minimis status. Yet such proxying function only yields a rule of thumb, not the bright line doctrines the intervening-cause notion purports to be. On a properly metaphysical notion of causation, these bright line doctrines should go. We substantially cause harms through the intervening, intentional actions of others

---

[93] Terry McDermott, 'No limits hinder UC thinker', Los Angeles Times (28 December 1999), A14: '[C]onsciousness is solved as a philosophical problem and has become a matter of science. "Let the brain stabbers figure out how it works..."'.

with enough frequency that the present doctrines of intervening causation are a poor proxy for what matters, substantiality of causal contribution.

The implications for tort law of eliminating the intervening-cause doctrines are pretty straightforward, and lie in the direction already being proposed by the new *Restatement (Third) of Torts*: tort liability should be apportioned amongst all substantially causing tortfeasors.[94] I would apportion such liability on purely causal grounds as well as on comparative fault grounds, but I suspect juries do this under comparative fault regimes anyway. The implications of eliminating intervening-cause doctrines for criminal law are less obvious, for criminal law has erected an entire theoretical edifice around the intervening-cause notions. What are we to make of the principal/accomplice liability distinction once intervening-cause doctrines are rejected? That is the topic of the next chapter.

---

[94] *Restatement (Third) of Torts: Liability for Physical Harm (Basic Principles)*, Chapter 6, Tentative Draft No 3 (Philadelphia: American Law Institute, April 7, 2003). See particularly the Comments to § 34, 99–104.

13

The Superfluity of Accomplice Liability

I. Introduction

We closed the last chapter with a query that will occupy us in the present chapter: what should criminal law do with accomplice liability once intervening-cause doctrines are repealed? Not surprisingly, my bottom-line answer in this chapter will match the bottom-line answer of the last chapter: we should get rid of accomplice liability as a special basis for liability in the criminal law, once we rid ourselves of the intervening-cause fiction.

That bottom line skips over a lot of nuances, however, that are worth exploring. Accomplice liability has long been found puzzling in criminal law, puzzling in ways going beyond any worries about intervening causation. Some of such puzzles are at the level of criminal-law doctrine, and some, at the level of criminal-law theory. I shall thus in this chapter step back a bit from the immediate aim of this book to explore the puzzles of accomplice liability on their own terms.

At the level of doctrine, there are two doctrinal puzzles about accomplice liability in Anglo-American criminal law. One is the puzzle about the mental states required for conviction as an accomplice. Hornbook law has it that accomplice liability is a 'specific intent' offense,[1] a requirement that the accomplice have 'purpose' and not merely 'knowledge', as those terms are used in the Model Penal Code.[2] Yet: are there two *mens rea* requirements here, a 'primary' *mens rea* having as its object the aiding of the conduct of another person, and a second requirement having as its object the elements of the underlying crime aided? If so, does the secondary requirement expand the liability otherwise permitted by the primary requirement, or limit that liability? What is the relationship between the *mens rea* required for conviction of guilty principals, and the secondary *mens rea* required for conviction as an accomplice? Does this vary,

---

[1] Eg, Wayne LaFave and Austin Scott, *Criminal Law* (St Paul: West Publishing, 1972), 506. Tony Duff rightly sees that one must probe these *mens rea* puzzles too to see whether there is anything truly distinctive about accomplice liability. RA Duff, 'Is accomplice liability superfluous?', University of Pennsylvania Law Review PENNumbra 156 (2008), 444–52.

[2] Model Penal Code, § 2.02, Proposed Official Draft (Philadelphia: American Law Institute, 1962).

depending on the kind of element (circumstance or result) of the underlying offense involved?

Interesting and important as these *mens rea* questions are, my doctrinal focus here is on a second puzzle about accomplice liability. This has to do with the *actus reus* of being an accomplice, not its *mens rea*. Put generally, what does one have to *do* in order to be guilty as an accomplice to someone else's crime? Again, the hornbook law answer (in the ancient language of the common law) is that one must 'aid and abet' another's commission of a crime in order to be guilty as an accomplice to that crime.[3] So one can put my question as a question about what it is to *aid* or *abet* another to do something.

Another way of approaching this puzzle can be seen by stepping away from criminal law *doctrines* and shift our focus to *theories* of liability in the criminal law. It is common to conceive of criminal law in terms of four 'theories of liability'. These legal theories are four alternative bases for holding someone responsible for a given legally prohibited harm or evil. One of these is the accomplice-liability theory. A good way of understanding this theory is by understanding the other three theories of liability. Most basic, it is thought, is liability as a principal for some completed crime. If I shoot and kill you I have committed the *actus reus* of homicide; if I drive away in your car without your permission, I have committed the *actus reus* of theft. In such cases, it is my agency that is involved, not someone else's; in addition, my agency has 'completed' the crime in the sense that it has produced each of the elements required for conviction of the offense.

As we saw in Chapter 1, the structure of non-omissive, principal liability for completed offenses is essentially causal. Sometimes this is obvious, as when a statute prohibits one from 'causing the death of a person' or 'causing the disfigurement of a person'. Yet this causal structure is only slightly less transparent when criminal statutes use causally complex verbs of action such as 'killing' or 'hitting' a person or 'abusing' a child. Such verbs transparently require that one cause death, contact, or abuse, respectively. This causal structure only becomes less obvious for what many criminal law theorists call 'conduct crimes'. It is commonly said that there are no 'result elements' (ie, no causal requirements) for crimes such as burglary, rape, theft, kidnapping, defacing public property, or drunk driving.[4] Yet there plainly are causal requirements to such offenses. Rape is done only when the perpetrator by his bodily movements causes penetration; burglary, when he causes a breaking and entering; theft, when he causes movement—'asportation'—of the thing stolen; kidnapping, when he causes confinement and movement of the person kidnapped; defacing, when he

---

[3] Eg, Rollin Perkins, 'Parties to crime', University of Pennsylvania Law Review 89 (1941), 584.

[4] Eg Glanville Williams, 'The problem of reckless attempts', Criminal Law Review (1983), 365–75. For other examples, see the discussion and citations in Moore, *Act and Crime: The implications of the philosophy of action for the criminal law* (Oxford: Clarendon Law Series, 1993), 208–9, 214–25.

causes marks constituting defacement to appear on public property; drunk driving, when he causes a car to be in the motion while he is drunk; etc.

There are two reasons why theorists have been mislead about the universal causal structure of non-omissive, principal liability for completed offenses. One is the immediacy of causal chains connecting acts of bodily movement and prohibited states of affairs in the kinds of crimes considered here, so called 'conduct crimes'. Because of the structure of such chains—between movements of the relevant sort, and penetration in rape, for example—there is little room for *complex* causal questions to arise. By contrast, causing death can be done in quite complicated ways. The upshot is that it is easy to miss the causal requirements in the former type cases; being un-problematically simple, these are too obvious for notice.

The second reason for not seeing the obvious here lies in the seeming triviality of saying things like 'to move some object is to cause the movement of that object'. That smells suspiciously like a famous definition of a rose. Yet the language misleads here. As we saw in Chapter 1, to use 'move' as a transitive verb, as in 'I moved the table', is different than using 'move' as an intransitive verb, as in 'the table moved'. To move a table does require that it move, but that does not prevent the bodily movements (that constitute my act of moving it) from causing the separate event that is the table's movement.

Obvious or not, non-omissive, principal liability for completed offenses is causal in structure. To be guilty as such a principal is to act in such a way as to cause some legally prohibited state of affairs. Contrast this form of liability with a second form, that of inchoate liability. Liability is 'inchoate' when the principal's act, while it may have to cause something, need not cause the state of affairs the law ultimately cares to prevent. Attempt crimes, crimes of reckless endangerment (when the danger is not known to the victim), solicitation, and conspiracy are the usual examples of inchoate liability. So are many specific intent crimes, such as traveling across state lines with the intent to bribe a state official.

Inchoate crimes lack the causal structure of completed crimes, in that the perpetrator need not cause the state of affairs the law seeks to prevent. Indeed, typically that undesired state of affairs has not occurred so one could not have caused it. But one does need to have that type of state of affairs in mind as one acts in order to be guilty of an inchoate crime. For example, one need not cause death to be guilty of attempted murder but one needs to have such a death as the object of one's purpose (or in some cases, belief), for such liability.

The third major theory of criminal liability is vicarious liability for the acts of others. In vicarious liability, one need not cause, nor even try to cause or risk causing, a legally prohibited state of affairs. If someone else has caused some such legal wrong, and if one stands in a certain relation to that perpetrator, then one is liable oneself for the offense committed. Vicarious liability is a form of agency well known to the civil law, in doctrines such as that of *respondeat superior* in torts. Criminal law is much more circumspect in imposing liability vicariously. Still, it is not unknown, the most notable example being liability of conspirators for the crimes of their co-conspirators even though there is no more than a general agreement between them.[5]

Accomplice liability is usually presented as a fourth and distinct theory of criminal liability, in addition to principal liability for completed offenses, inchoate liability for incomplete offenses, and vicarious liability for members of criminal combinations or groups. The puzzle is this: what relationship must exist between the act of the accomplice and the state of affairs the law seeks to prevent? We know, for example, that to be guilty of the completed offense of murder as a principal the accused must *cause* death; we also know that to be guilty of the inchoate crime of attempted murder the act of the accused must be in execution of an intention that has as its object such a death, and the act must go some distance towards causing such death even though no death is caused by such an act. And we know that to be guilty for the crimes of a co-conspirator, a conspirator must have established a relationship amounting to a conspiracy with that co-conspirator, who himself causes the legally prohibited state of affairs. What are we to say is the analogous relationship between the act of an accomplice and a result such as death that someone else has caused, if the accomplice is to be guilty of aiding and abetting murder?

A natural temptation is to assimilate accomplice liability, either to inchoate liability,[6] or to principal liability for completed crimes,[7] or to the vicarious liability of co-conspirators.[8] Consider first the last possibility: the assimilation to vicarious liability. The often-expressed idea is that complicity, like conspiracy, is an agency form of vicarious liability. For this form of liability, one need not have contributed in any way towards the occurrence of some legally prohibited result; one only need be a member of some group or combination, the other member(s) of which do cause some legally prohibited result to occur. On this view, an accomplice stands as the principal liable for the action of his 'agents', ie, the perpetrator.

There is some truth to this basis for complicity, at least as complicity is reflected in certain doctrines. Specifically, in some states merely agreeing with another that he will do some crime makes one liable as an accomplice to the crime that other commits.[9] Second, a number of states make one liable as an

---

[5] As in *Pinkerton v. United States*, 328 US 640 (1946).

[6] Richard Buxton, 'Complicity in the criminal code', Law Quarterly Review 85 (1969), 252–74; Buxton, 'Complicity and the Law Commission', Criminal Law Review (1973), 223–30; Daniel Yaeger, 'Helping, doing, and the grammar of complicity', Criminal Justice Ethics 15 (1996), 25–35; Spencer, 'Trying to help another person commit a crime', in P Smith (ed), *Criminal Law: Essays in honour of JC Smith* (1987). Recently Chris Kutz seems to have joined the view that accomplice liability is a form of inchoate liability. See his 'Causeless complicity', Criminal Law and Philosophy 1 (2007), 289–305.

[7] KJM Smith, *A Modern Treatise on the Law of Criminal Complicity* (Oxford: Clarendon Press, 1997); Francis B Sayre, 'Criminal responsibility for acts of another', Harvard Law Review 43 (1930), 689–723; Paul Robinson, 'Imputed criminal liability', Yale Law Journal 93 (1984), 609–76.

[8] Josh Dressler considers but rejects the vicarious basis for accomplice liability, in Dressler, 'Reassessing the theoretical underpinnings of accomplice liability', Hastings Law Journal 37 (1985), 109–11.

[9] The *Pinkerton* doctrine (see n 5 above) is a federal doctrine, but it is followed in a minority of American states.

accomplice, not only for crimes which one agrees should be committed, but for all crimes committed by any member of the group, so long as the commission of such crimes was foreseeable to the accomplice.[10] If one puts these doctrines together, a form of vicarious liability results: merely by joining a group, but doing nothing else oneself, one is liable as an accomplice for all crimes of that group's members that are foreseeably incident to those crimes that may have motivated the group's formation to begin with.

Yet this vicarious (or agency) interpretation of complicity does not begin to cover cases where accomplice liability has been imposed. There is no requirement that one be a conspirator to be an accomplice. If I aid you by finding a ladder, placing a gun where you can find it, make sure the victim is where you can find him, I am liable as an accomplice to whatever crimes I am trying to promote with such aid, even if there is no prior agreement between us. Moreover, in most states complicity requires more than mere agreement or group membership; one has to *aid* the commission of a crime to be an accomplice, and in such states the aiding required refuses to be reduced to mere group membership or general agreement.

Now consider the second assimilation, that to inchoate liability. The reasoning here is this. To be guilty as an accomplice requires the same *mens rea* towards the evil the law seeks to prevent (eg, death in homicide) as does inchoate liability—at least if one resolves in certain ways and not others the doctrinal ambiguities about the *mens rea* requirements for accomplice liability mentioned above. So, all that is different in the case of accomplice liability is that the evil the law seeks to prevent has occurred whereas typically for inchoate liability it has not. To be guilty as an accomplice to murder requires that a murder have taken place; ie, that there be a death. By contrast, for liability for attempted murder no death need have happened. So (on this view) accomplice liability is just inchoate liability in the special cases when the evil sought to be prevented by the law has occurred (even though the accomplice did not cause it to occur).

Such assimilation to inchoate liability plainly will not go through. Suppose I shoot at someone, intending to kill him. I miss, but at just the moment I would have killed him if I had hit him, another bullet fired by someone else arrives and kills him in just the way my bullet would have killed him. I have tried to kill the victim, and the result (broadly speaking) that I was trying to bring about has occurred, viz he was killed; yet it is plain that these two facts do not make me an accomplice to some form of homicide. I have only an inchoate liability, not accomplice liability, showing that accomplice liability requires something more than attempt plus occurrence of the result attempted. To be an accomplice, my act must have something to do with why, how, or with what ease the legally prohibited result was brought about by someone else.

Seeing this difference between accomplice liability and inchoate liability (even where the result attempted or risked does occur), tempts a third assimilation; my

[10] See, eg, *People v. Luparello*, 187 Cal App 3d 410, 231 Cal Rptr 832 (Cal Ct App 1987).

act of shooting above must in some sense *cause* the victim to be killed by the second bullet for me to be an accomplice in his murder.[11] Accomplice liability is thus likened to principal liability in that both require that an accused's acts *cause* some legally prohibited state of affairs. The *caveat* for accomplice liability would be that this (ie, the accomplice) way of causing death operates through the action of a third person, whereas principals may directly cause prohibited states of affairs like deaths.

By and large, this assimilation also will not go through. Yet why this is so is a complicated business. In the first two sub-parts of the next section I will explore two commonly voiced reasons for thinking that accomplice liability must be non-causal in its structure, concluding of them that they are bad. I will then explore reasons for thinking that causing-by-aiding another involves a different kind of causation than that needed for principal liability; concluding again there is no reason to think this. I will close the section by considering two commonly voiced reasons for thinking that even though accomplices cause death by aiding another to kill, they do not themselves *kill*, the prerequisite for liability for homicide as a principal. This line of thought too I by and large reject. In the section following I will begin again in the search for the bases for accomplice liability. The five bases I will explore involve the sometimes causal, sometimes non-causal relationship(s) that must exist between an accomplice's act and a legally prohibited state of affairs, for accomplice liability to attach. My conclusion is that *aiding* another to cause a harm is not a distinct basis for blame and punishment.

II. Some Bad Reasons for Thinking Accomplice Liability to be Non-causal or Otherwise Distinct in its Structure

Even paranoids have real enemies—or so the saying goes. True or partially true conclusions are indeed often supported by bad reasons. Such is the case here.

A. Liability as an accomplice does not depend on one being a necessary condition of the harm, but causation does

A very standard view of why accomplice liability is non-causal has two premises to it.[12] It firstly asserts that the criminal law's causal requirements include a 'necessary condition' (*sine qua non*, or counterfactual) element: for an act *a* to cause a harm *b*, *a* must be necessary for *b*, ie if *a* had not have happened, then *b* would not have occurred either. So if accomplice liability had a causal structure,

---

[11] The suggestion of Francis Sayre, 'Criminal responsibility'; Paul Robinson, 'Imputed criminal Liability'; and Keith Smith, *A Modern Treatise*.

[12] The view is held by Dressler, 'Reassessing the theoretical underpinnings', and by Chris Kutz, *Complicity* (Cambridge: Cambridge University Press, 2000).

then the act of an accomplice would have to be a necessary condition for the prohibited harm to occur. To be an accomplice to murder, for example, one would have to have done something necessary to the death occurring. The second premise is that there are many cases of accomplice liability when the act of the accomplice is not necessary to the occurrence of the harm. Ergo, the conclusion: accomplice liability is non-causal in its structure.

On the second premise, consider the well-known case of *State ex rel. Attorney General v. Tally.*[13] In *Tally,* the alleged accomplice, Judge Tally, learned of the plans of the four Skelton brothers to ride to the next town and to shoot and kill one Ross (who had seduced the Skeltons' sister). Judge Tally discovered that a warning telegram was to be sent to Ross; Tally ordered the telegraph operator not to deliver the warning telegram. Ross was not warned. He was found by the Skeltons, and killed.

On these facts it is possible that Judge Tally's action was necessary for Ross' death. Perhaps with a warning Ross could have fled, or defended himself successfully. But it is also possible that Tally's act was not necessary; whether warned or not, the Skeltons may well have caught up with Ross and killed him. (This may even be true if we focus in on the exact time, place, and manner of Ross' killing; even if the warning had been received Ross might well have been killed exactly when, where, and how he was actually killed.)

The important point is that under the law of accomplice liability it does not matter which of these scenarios is true. As the *Tally* court accurately stated the law on accomplice liability here: 'The assistance given . . . need not contribute to the criminal result in the sense that but for it the result would not have ensued . . .'.[14] If one assumes that the counterfactual ('but for') test must be satisfied for there to be causation in the criminal law, then one has the desired conclusion: 'the upshot of these cases is that causal responsibility is not necessary to complicituous criminal liability'.[15]

The problem with this argument lies in the first of its two premises. While theorists such as Kutz are not alone in thinking that the 'general causal requirements' of the criminal law are 'expressed in counterfactuals',[16] this in fact is not so. Saying why this is not so is a complicated business, but we shall go through the complications later in Chapter 17, so only a summary need be given here.

To begin with, it is very implausible to *identify* the causal relation as counterfactual dependence. When two names or descriptions that putatively are different nonetheless refer to one and the same thing, then what is true of that thing under one name or description must be true of it under any other name or description. Leibniz taught us as much about identity. To use Frege's

---

[13] *State ex rel Attorney General v. Tally*, 15 So 722 (Ala 1894).   [14] 15 So at 738.

[15] Kutz, *Complicity*, 217. Kutz has recently come to a somewhat more nuanced view of causation. See his 'Causeless complicity'.

[16] Kutz, *Complicity*, 215. See also Dressler, 'Reassessing the theoretical underpinnings'; Yaeger, 'Helping, doing'.

time-honored example: if 'the Evening Star' and 'the Morning Star' both refer to one and the same thing, viz the planet Venus, then if it is true that the Morning Star rises in the morning, so it must be true that the Evening Star does too, and so does Venus.

If causation *is* counterfactual dependence, then it can have no properties not possessed by counterfactual dependence, and vice versa. Yet causation is a transitive relation; with qualifications not here important,[17] if *c* causes *e*, and *e* causes *f*, then *c* causes *f*. It is well-known that counterfactual dependence is not transitive;[18] *f* may counterfactually depend *e*, and *e* may counterfactually depend on *c*, and yet *f* may not counterfactually depend on *c*. Moreover, causation (again with qualifications not here relevant) is an asymmetric relation; if *c* causes *e*, *e* does not cause *c*. Counterfactual dependence is not necessarily asymmetric; *e* can counterfactually depend on *c*, even while *c* counterfactually depends on *e*. Finally, causation relates temporally ordered states of affairs; if *c* causes *e*, then *e* must not precede *c* in time—causation does not work backwards though time. Whereas counterfactual dependence knows no such limitation; *e* can counterfactually depend on *c* without regard to whether *c* precedes or succeeds (or is simultaneous with) *e* in time.[19]

So there is little plausibility in identifying causation as counterfactual dependence. The more plausible claim is that counterfactual dependence is a good *test* of causation—which it certainly would be if '*c* causes *e*' is true when but only when '*e* counterfactually depends on *c*' is true. The weaker, more plausible claim here is of extensional equivalence between statements, not of identity between the things such statements are about.

Bi-conditionals such as, '*c* causes *e* if and only if *e* counterfactually depends on *c*', are the conjunction of two conditionals: (1) that the counterfactual dependence of *e* on *c* is *sufficient* for *c* to cause *e*; and (2) that the counterfactual dependence of *e* on *c* is *necessary* for *c* to cause *e*. Although the matter is hotly disputed in the philosophy of science, it is difficult to sustain either of these conditionals, as we shall see in Chapter 17.

The upshot is that some act may be causative of some harm even though it is not necessary to the occurrence of that harm. Legal theorists have simply been misled in their long-held view that the 'scientific' or 'factual' part of legal causation is counterfactual in nature. Now of course some legal theorists would claim a freedom for the law to define its notion of cause-in-fact as it pleases, to serve its own purposes. On this view, 'cause-in-fact' in the criminal law need not correspond to the actual nature of causation, but only need serve the artificial purposes of the law. Yet that old view, bequeathed to us by the Legal Realists and

---

[17] The qualifications are of the kind we explored in Chapter 5 having to do with the 'petering out' of causal contributions over extended chains.

[18] For reasons mentioned briefly in Chapter 16.

[19] At least this is true so long as one does not stipulate (as did David Lewis and his followers) that counterfactuals that 'backtrack' through time are 'deviant'. See the discussion in Chapter 17.

other skeptics discussed in Chapter 4, has no place here. Causation is one of those doctrines adopted by the criminal law because of its role in determining moral responsibility. If criminal liability is to track moral responsibility, the law cannot simply define items like causation as it pleases. It must discover, not stipulate, what causation is, so that the law can parcel-out legal liability on the same grounds as those that measure moral responsibility. The law thus has no Humpty-Dumpty-like freedom to mean what it pleases by 'cause-in-fact'. If counterfactual dependence does not constitute or even measure causation in reality, then it does not do so in the criminal law either.

The case law sustains this rejection of stipulative definitions of causation, whether by the highly influential American Law Institute, or by anyone else. Courts do what the more perspicuous first and second *Restatement of Torts* told them to do: when the 'but for' test leads to counterintuitive results in the various kinds of overdetermination cases we shall explore in Chapter 17, then they ignore the definition and go with some other, more intuitive notion of causation.

B. Accomplices cannot cause the results brought about by the actions of their principals because those latter actions are intervening causes

The second major explanation for why accomplice liability is non-causal stems from certain views about proximate causation (as opposed to views about cause in fact that motivated the explanation just examined). The pertinent views on proximate causation are those that we explored in the last two chapters, going under the label 'direct causation'. On the direct cause view, causal chains continue across considerable links but suddenly end whenever one of those special events constituting an intervening cause intervenes between the defendant's act and the harm. The direct cause notion is thus given whatever content it has by the notion of an intervening cause. As we saw in Chapter 11, an event is an intervening cause if and only if it is: (1) an event, not a state or an omission; (2) that occurs after the defendant's act but before the harm in question (ie, it 'intervenes'); (3) it is itself a cause of the harm; (4) it is causally independent of the defendant's act (ie, it is not an effect of that act); and (5) it is either such an extraordinary natural event as to amount to a 'coincidence', or it is the 'free, informed, voluntary act' of some third-party human agent.

It is this last bit that is of greatest relevance here. As we explored in Chapter 11 in greater detail, a human act is 'free, informed, and voluntary' only when: (a) it is the act of a responsible agent, meaning an adult, sane, rational, and autonomous person; (b) it is a chosen act in the sense that the bodily movements that constitute the act are willed by the agent (sleep-walking, reflex reactions, hypnotic behavior, etc, do not qualify); (c) it is not done in ignorance or under mistaken belief about the harm-producing aspects of the action; and (d) it is free in the sense that it is not coerced or otherwise compelled by external human threats or natural necessity, or by internal, ego-alien emotion.

Examples sometimes convey information better than generalities, so suppose I know that you are an extremely jealous, gullible and volatile person. I get you to assault your wife by: (a) getting you so drunk that you are barely rational; (b) hide your insulin while you are locked in a room with her so that you strike her when you go into a hypoglycemic episode; (c) deceive you about her presence behind a punching bag you are about to use; or (d) threaten you with the death of your children unless you strike her. In none of these cases is your hitting her an intervening cause; in all of them, therefore, I am 'guilty as a principal' because I have proximately caused her to be struck.

Contrast these with cases where I: (a) tell you where she is, knowing that you will hit her because you have just learned of her affair with another; (b) tell you about the affair, with the same expectation; (c) suggest to you that no red-blooded man should put up with such cheating behavior without some violence on his part; or (d) offer you money to go beat her up. In all of these last cases, your hitting of your wife will constitute an intervening cause, breaking any causal chain that might otherwise exist between my acts and her injury, and thus precluding any criminal liability on my part as a principal.

Enter, accomplice liability. As Sandy Kadish has shown in great and persuasive detail,[20] the doctrines of accomplice liability fit like soft clay around the shape of intervening causation. Wherever an intervening agent is himself guilty of crime and is an intervening cause vis-à-vis some earlier act by another, that other is eligible for accomplice liability; whereas if the intervening agent is not an intervening cause, then the earlier actor is eligible for liability as a principal. The picture is reminiscent of the hit tune by the former punk rocker, Blondie: we are going to get you, 'one way or the other'. Intervening-cause doctrines will determine which way it will be.

Notice that on the Kadish view accomplice liability is always and necessarily non-causal. Acts of accomplices cannot be causal because of the intervening causation of their principals. And if the acts of their principals are not intervening causes, then the would-be 'accomplices' cannot be accomplices—because they will be principals (ie, causers) themselves.

This is a quite accurate description of Anglo-American legal doctrine on accomplice liability. Yet making normative sense of this doctrine is much more challenging. Just because it is elegantly systematic does not mean it makes normative sense. It might mean instead the whole edifice falls to the ground once any of it is removed.

There are two routes one might take in seeking to make normative sense of the intervening-cause/accomplice-liability doctrines. One is to seek to ground the

---

[20] Sanford Kadish, 'Complicity, cause and blame: A study in the interpretation of doctrine', *California Law Review* 73 (1985), 323–410.

legal doctrines in the facts about causation. Because the dominant policy of the criminal law is to punish only those who are morally responsible and only in proportion to the degree of their responsibility, and because (as we argued in Chapters 2 and 3) the degree of moral responsibility is measured in part by the degree of causal responsibility, this first route can succeed in its normative task if it succeeds in grounding the legal doctrine in causal fact. That requires that the distinctions drawn by the legal doctrines of intervening causation turn out to be true, causal distinctions.

The second route to making normative sense of these legal doctrines, is quite different. This route admits that intervening actors do not break causal chains in fact; in fact, accomplices cause harms through the acts of their principals. But there are nonetheless reasons of policy justifying the law in treating intervening actors as breaking causal chains even when they do not do so in fact. This is the avowedly fictional approach that I eschewed about 'but for' causation above, but which has greater prima facie plausibility for intervening causation. (This is because all proximate cause doctrines have something of this fictional, constructed cast to them, in contrast to the prima facie literalist pretensions of cause-in-fact doctrines such as the 'but for' test.)

The first route was the subject of Chapter 12. As we saw there, literal chain-breakers are hard to find in science. 'Shit happens', as a popular 90s bumper sticker had it, but surely that does not mean that such bad things are inexplicable because uncaused. Aquinas' *prima causa* in theology gave us a picture of what such chain-breaking, un-caused causes would have to look like. Aquinas gave that power to God; libertarian metaphysics gives it each free human choice. We are all 'little gods', causing things while free of being caused to do so by anything else. Such libertarian metaphysics shows us what we need here if we are to make sense of the legal doctrines of intervening causation in causal terms,[21] as Kadish recognizes.

Yet to my mind this is like saying we need theism to be true for intervening causes to exist in fact. Indeed, is not such libertarianism a kind of theism—a pantheism? The libertarian is committed to there being lots of gods, namely, each person. These gods are like the ghost Casper in that they can cause things to move whilst themselves being immune to causal influences. This strikingly unscientific posture is a desperate and panicky metaphysics that should be put aside as not serious. Kadish himself does not subscribe to this desperate and panicky metaphysics. (He does not unsubscribe either—he simply does not tell us what he thinks to be true.) Rather, he *explains* why the law of accomplices/intervening causation has the shape that it does in terms of common belief: those who produced this legal doctrine believed in libertarian metaphysics.

---

[21] The fit of libertarian metaphysics to the legal doctrines of intervening causation is in fact a rough one, as I examined in Chapter 12.

This bit of sociological speculation by Kadish may well be true. Yet can we turn this plausible explanation for why we have such doctrines, into a plausible justification of why we should keep them? Suppose it is true, as Hart and Honoré also claimed, that 'the common man's view' of causation incorporates the libertarian metaphysics that alone could make sense of the legal doctrines of intervening causation[22]—would that justify those doctrines because supported by popular belief, no matter how false such belief might be? Moral responsibility does not depend on what most people believe about it. Nor are the natural properties on which such moral responsibility supervenes—such as intention, causation, rationality, voluntariness, etc—a function of popular belief. False beliefs if popular may win out in the democratic process that makes law. Such beliefs may thus explain why we have the legal doctrines we do. Such doctrines are still unjustified.

The second route to justifying judges in law cases *saying* that the intervening acts of principals break causal chains would admit that in fact this is not true.[23] But some reasons of legal policy justify legal doctrines that bid judges to treat it *as if* it were true. Some rivers are legally *navigable* (for various legal purposes such as federal admiralty jurisdiction) even though in fact one cannot float a canoe on them.

The problem with this fiction-based justification of treating accomplices as non-causal lies in finding the appropriate legal policies. Prima facie, proximate-cause doctrines (including those of intervening causation) serve a grading policy in the criminal law. We punish more severely those who (fully and unproblematically) cause the harm they intended to cause than we do those who try but fail to cause that same harm. Our proximate-cause doctrines exist to resolve the tough cases, where the harm intended or risked has come about but the causal route from defendant's act to the harm is freakish, attenuated, or in some other way abnormal. The doctrines serve to sort such cases, allocating some to be punished severely for causing harm, others less severely for only trying to cause (or risking the causation of) that harm.

This policy is one that seeks to get it right about the degree of moral blame attaching to the actions of defendants. Yet, since moral blame is here supervenient in part upon causation, this requires that we get it right about causation.

---

[22] HLA Hart and Tony Honoré, *Causation in the Law* (2nd edn, Oxford University Press, 1985).

[23] The 19th century's 'last wrongdoer rule' is an example of such an avowedly fictionalist approach to intervening causation: see Lawrence Eldredge, 'Culpable intervention as superseding cause', University of Pennsylvania Law Review 86 (1938), 121–35. On this rule, the law only need punish the (temporally) last wrongdoer in some complicated chain of causation leading to some legally prohibited result. Such 'last wrongdoer' thus cuts off all earlier wrongdoers from liability for that harm. The problems with the rule have been well known for the last one hundred years, starting with Holmes: (1) the cases do not actually fit the doctrine, especially in cases of merely negligent or reckless wrongdoers where the last wrongdoer often does not insulate others up the chain of causation from liability; (2) there is no policy that can justify the significance given such temporal ordering of wrongdoing. Ibid, 124–5.

There is no room for a fictional causation here. The one policy that is here operative demands that we *not* fictionalize causation, so that if the acts of principals do not really break the chain of causation between accomplices and some harm in fact, neither should they be said to break such chains in law.

One might grant all of this and yet think that morality itself can justify constructing a fictionalized intervening-cause doctrine. The idea would be that the structure of our moral obligations justifies such a fiction. That structure, the argument goes, gives each of us the permission to cause harm to others when done through the intentional agency of others. Tony Duff has argued recently that we are each morally privileged to do acts aiding others to cause harm, so long as we merely know (and not intend) that such harm will come about. 'The fact of intervening human agency'[24] then becomes important, not as a true causal doctrine, but because we have a moral right to be blind to the intentional wrongdoing of others:

[I]t is not my business that what I do makes it easier for P to commit the crime partly because it is P's business whether he commits the crime... it is up to P whether he commits the crime or not and—at least sometimes—I am not required to guide my actions by my knowledge of what P will do.[25]

As Heidi Hurd put this justification for the legal doctrines of intervening causation some years before, the doctrines 'appear to allow one to navigate through life without having to take causal responsibility for the harms that result when murderers, rapists, thieves, and arsonists seize on opportunities for wrongdoing that one's legitimate activities create'.[26] The moral principle is that 'the justifiable uses of one's time, labor, and property ought not to be thought relative to the unjustifiable uses to which those resources might foreseeably be put by slubberdegullions and shirkers'.[27]

One might think any such moral principle to be incapable of justifying intervening-cause doctrines when those doctrines are backed up by accomplice liability—for given the latter liability, it turns out one has no permission to ignore others wrongdoing in the framing of one's own obligations. Yet notice the claim of Hurd and Duff: one has no such permission if one *intends* the ultimate harm, for then (as Duff puts it) I have made it my business.[28] And in law, if one intends the harm one is criminally liable: as an accomplice, if I aid a third person, or as a principal, if I aid nature.[29] So the moral principle for which they contend does not prove too much for its own good.

---

[24] RA Duff, 'Is accomplice liability superfluous?', 451.   [25] Ibid.
[26] Heidi M Hurd, 'Is it wrong to do right when others do wrong?', Legal Theory 7 (2001), 314.
[27] Ibid, 308.   [28] Duff, 'Is accomplice liability superfluous?', 451.
[29] Recall the manipulation-of-nature exception to intervening-cause doctrines, discussed in Chapters 5 and 6, above.

Still, the principle is not plausibly broad enough to do the justifying work claimed for it. The principle is most plausible as applied to activities that will only harm oneself. Hurd's kinds of examples: women have a liberty interest in wearing low-cut red dresses even when would-be rapists lurk about; joggers have a liberty interest in jogging through Central Park even when they know they may well be assaulted; farmers may (on their own land) stack their flax close to railroad tracks even when they predict that the railroad will wrongfully operate with inadequate spark arrestors on its engines. In such cases one's own actions in enabling the harms in question do not constitute fault such as to relieve the later wrongdoer of the obligation to pay for the harm. Yet this is worlds removed from what is needed here, which is a principle entitling each of us to do actions enabling evils being done to others, not ourselves. There is no moral privilege: to dress an attractive woman in provocative garb when I know rapists will find her in isolated situations; no privilege to send a jogger across Central Park at night to buy me a pack of cigarettes; no privilege to stack *your* flax too close to the tracks of a railroad I know to have inadequate spark arrestors.[30] That not causing such rapes, assaults, and property destructions is indeed very much 'the business' of these intervening wrongdoers, goes no distance to saying that this is not also 'my business'. There is no liberty right to cause harm to others through the intervening agency of third parties, no more than there is to cause harm to others through the quirks of nature.

I conclude that there is no constructed notion of 'intervening causation' that can justify the law saying what is not literally true: that intentional human wrongdoing breaks causal chains.

C. Accomplices cause the harms they aid but only in a distinct, secondary, and anemic sense of 'cause'

A view that turns out to be related to the libertarian view just considered is what I shall call the causal-dualist view. On this view, the relation between an accomplice's act and some harm for which he is responsible is a causal one, but the kind of causation is said to be different when a second human agent is involved. Revert to the earlier examples where I got you to assault your wife by providing opportunity, information, encouragement, or financial reward. In such cases, Hart and Honoré tell us, you do not *cause* the apprehension of contact sufficient for an assault in the 'primary', 'strong', 'simple', or 'strict' sense of 'caused'. But there is a 'secondary', 'weak', 'complex', 'broad' sense of 'cause' by use of which you can be said to cause this apprehension. Such

---

[30] Indeed, American law generally denies the existence of any such broad privilege, as Hurd shows. See Hurd, 'Is it wrong to do right when others do wrong?'. If any such privilege existed, Hurd's title could better be phrased, 'It is right to do wrong when others do wrong too?'.

broad sense of cause is said to be captured by the expression 'he *occasioned* the harm'.[31]

It is important to see that this is not a merely quantitative distinction. The claim is not that there is but one type of causal relation, and that accomplices simply make a smaller causal contribution to some harm than do principals. Rather, the claimed difference is qualitative: there are 'two types of causal connections',[32] or 'two varieties':[33] a central type (or variety) that is broken by the intervening act of a guilty principal, and a secondary type (variety) that is not. The first is the causation between physical events, the second, causation between human agents. This then gives us an answer to our question about the relationship of accomplices to the harms they aid: 'The "causal connection" between a defendant's act and the harm may be succinctly described by saying that he has "occasioned it".'[34]

While admirably succinct, this answer is, less admirably, false. Indeed this answer is false for exactly the same reasons as is the answer just examined, that the intervening acts of principals break off the causal connection otherwise existing between accomplices and the harms they aid. For the only reasons given to support the existence of this weaker, lesser kind of causal connection ('occasioning') are the very same reasons as were given to support the idea of intervening causation: human beings are not billiard balls, but are free and not subject to the necessitation of causal laws. True enough, here the claim is not that the intervening human choices of a principal are *fully* free of the causal influence of the acts of an accomplice; rather the claim is only that the accomplice weakly causes ('occasions') the principal's acts. In Tony Flew's vocabulary, the accomplice *inclines* but does not *necessitate* that the principal so act.[35] Yet does this not make even less sense than a robust libertarianism? We might think libertarians can at least conceptualize an uncaused event; but what would it mean to speak of a *partly* caused event? It was 60 per cent caused, 40 per cent un-caused?[36] People have said such things, but that does not mean they make any sense.[37]

---

[31] Hart and Honoré, *Causation in the Law* (2nd edn), 6. Both Sandy Kadish ('Complicity, cause, and blame'), and John Gardner ('Complicity and causality'), Criminal Law and Philosophy 1 (2007), 134, have also explicitly endorsed this kind of causal dualism.

[32] Hart and Honoré, *Causation in the Law* (2nd edn), 186.

[33] Ibid, 388.   [34] Ibid, 195.

[35] Antony Flew, 'Psychiatry, law and responsibility', Philosophical Quarterly 35 (1985), 425–32.

[36] This is not to be confused with statements of comparative causation, as in: 'Factor X was 60% the cause, factor Y 40% the cause of harm Z.' Some of us (including as we saw in Chapter 5, above, standard tort law doctrine) think such scalar statements of degrees of causal contribution make perfectly good sense.

[37] For real world examples (Sheldon Glueck, Norvaal Morris), and an analysis of why this is truly metaphysical gibberish, see Moore, 'Causation and the excuses', California Law Review 73 (1985), 1091–149 reprinted in Moore, *Placing Blame: A general theory of the criminal law* (Oxford: Clarendon Press, 1997), 506–14.

D. The supposed inapplicability of the causative verbs of English to the causings of accomplices

The next argument I shall consider leaves the verbs referring to causation as such, for what linguists call 'causative' verbs—those verbs of action such as 'kill' that seemingly require the actor to have caused something (such as death). The idea is that although an accomplice may cause both their principal's actions and the harms those actions cause, nonetheless the accomplice does not herself *do* the action prohibited. On this view, thus: an accomplice who gives a principal a gun (which the latter uses to shoot some victim dead) may be said to be a cause of the victim's death, yet that accomplice did not *kill* the victim. Only the principal did that. And since standard criminal and tort law doctrine prohibits killings, hittings, maimings, etc—not causings of death, causings of contact, causings of disfigurement, etc—the idea concludes that accomplices cannot be guilty as principals even if they are causers of legally prohibited states of affairs.

The policies supporting this argument are two. First, there is the policy of legality. This policy regards the law we have as being a function of how ordinary people would understand it if they read it. If ordinary people distinguish killings from causing deaths, and if the law of homicide prohibits only killings, then accomplices cannot fairly be liable for the homicides they aid even if such aiding amounts to a causing of death.

The second policy is that of legislative supremacy. This policy regards the law we have as being a function of how legislators meant their words to be understood. Again, the claim is that legislators, like most native speakers of English, distinguish killings from causings of death; yet they explicitly only prohibited killings, so that accomplice-like causers of death were not meant to be included among those forbidden to *kill*.

Both policy arguments are premised on the truth of a linguistic claim, viz the claim that accomplices who cause death by aiding another to kill are not themselves *killers*. The claim is that 'killing' requires an act directly causative of death, a directness lacking when the principal's act intervenes. Yet we saw in Chapter 1 reasons to doubt the truth of any such linguistic claim. The equivalence thesis we there examined urges that 'X caused the death of Y' is true when and only when 'X killed Y' is also true.

In any case, the problem with this entire line of justification (for hiving off accomplices from principals in the context of criminal liability) is the arbitrary contingency on which this argument turns. If accomplices cause legally prohibited harms just as do principals, and if the causative verbs of English require more than mere causation, then it is a poorly drafted code that defines battery as hitting (rather than causing contact), or that defines homicide as killing (rather than causing death), or that defines mayhem as maiming (rather than causing disfigurement). The obvious remedy is not to use causatives in the drafting of penal codes, given their alleged divergence from what is important, causation.[38] Such more careful drafting of course alleviates any problem with legality or legislative supremacy that may exist under codes as currently drafted.

Such more careful drafting would of course be desirable only if it is indeed *causing* that is normatively important, not *killing* (hitting, maiming, raping, etc). One might think, for example, that the agent-relative obligations of morality (on which the *malum in se* crimes are based) are directed at killings, not at causing deaths; at hittings, not at causing contact; etc. If this were so, then the restriction of principal liability to killers, hitters, etc, (leaving accomplice liability for mere causers of death who are not killers) might well be justified. If, in other words, the linguistic difference between killers and causers of death is also a moral difference, then there may be good reason for there also to be a legal difference here.

Some of the British homicide cases that we looked at in Chapter 3 are seemingly illustrative of this line of thought. Unlike the Model Penal Code, British homicide law purports to mark the categorical nature of the obligation not to kill by refusing duress as a defense to murder, no matter how serious the harm threatened to the defendant. Yet at one point in time the House of Lords allowed an accomplice to murder to avail himself of the duress defense—the driver who aided the death of an innocent was not categorically obligated not to so cause death in the way the actual killers were so obligated.[39]

Yet it is not the killing/aiding another to kill distinction that is doing the moral work here. Rather, it is the degree of causal contribution. One who merely drives the IRA gunmen to where they can kill the British policeman is much less of a cause of the policeman's death than are the acts of shooting done by the gunmen themselves. One can see this by increasing the causal contribution of the aider— suppose he holds the victim in a position where the gunman can then shoot and kill. Now, the categorical obligation seems to be as much in force as it is against the literal killers.[40]

What makes this point harder to see is that killers (hitters, rapists, etc) are, as a class, more significant causal contributors than are those who enable others to do such acts. So killing, hitting, etc are proxies for the kind of significant causal contributions required for there to be a breach of our categorical obligations. But we must not confuse the proxy for the underlying desert-determiners; what matters morally is significant causal contribution, not the kinds of limitations perhaps marked by the causative verbs of English.

To see the same point from another vantage point, repair to another linguistic feature of causative verbs like 'kill'. Linguistically, we distinguish people who do acts enabling large forces of nature to kill, from people who *kill*, just as we distinguish

---

[38] Thus, for example, the Model Penal Code eschews the Biblical 'thou shall not kill' for one shall not 'cause the death of another human being'. Model Penal Code, §210.1 (1).

[39] *Director of Public Prosecutions for Northern Ireland v. Lynch* [1975] AC 653.

[40] As the House of Lords recognized by refusing the duress defense on these facts in *Abbott v. R* [1976] 3 All ER 140.

people who do acts enabling third parties to kill, from people who themselves *kill*. Suppose a freakish wind blows off the roof of a factory, blowing the roof weighing many tons a considerable distance; such freakish forces of nature are as regularly regarded as intervening causes as are the free, informed, voluntary acts of human agents.[41] Now suppose that the defendant foresees the wind and accurately predicts its effect on the roof; wanting some victim V dead, he drives V to just where the roof falls on him, crushing V to death. We might well be tempted to say that the defendant's driving V to a certain location *causally contributed* to V's death, but the defendant didn't *kill* V—the wind (or roof) did that.

Suppose one thought that such 'aiding of nature' in the case put was outside of morality's categorical obligation not to kill (ie, that such acts of driving a person to where he would be killed were eligible to be justified by good consequences). But would one nonetheless not distinguish the case of a more significant causal contributor? Suppose the defendant holds V in just the right position for the wind-driven roof to crush him.[42] Linguistically, it may still be the wind/roof that may properly be said to have *killed* V. But morality is not so formalistic and obtuse as to think that that matters. Those who manipulate nature in this way are as surely obligated categorically not to so cause death as are literal killers. Again, it is the degree of causal contribution doing the heavy lifting here, not the niceties in the semantics of the causative verbs of English.

E. Non-proxyable crimes and the need for accomplice liability

There is a related but distinct problem left unaddressed by this redrafting proposal. This is the problem Sandy Kadish refers to as 'non-proxyable crimes'.[43] Suppose (as many first-year Torts students tend to think) battery were defined, not just as causing contact with the body of another, but that it required that such contact be with the actor's own body. Then the crime would be non-proxyable, to use Kadish's term, because even if A caused P to hit V, he does not cause P to hit V *with A's own body*. Non-proxyable crimes, as Kadish defines them, are crimes that 'can be done only with his own body and never through the action of another'.[44]

Battery of course is not defined this way—causing contact of the victim's body with the floor, or a bat, some one else's body, or anything else, is enough. So consider some of Kadish's examples of non-proxyable crimes:

---

[41] See, eg, *Kimble v. Mackintosh Hemphill Co*, 59 A 2d 68 (Pa 1948).

[42] The hypothetical paralleling the facts of *Abbott*.

[43] Kadish, 'Complicity, cause, and blame', 373–85. In a recent paper John Gardner does not see this problem as distinct from the general semantics of causatives just discussed. 'Causation and complicity'.Gardner's mistake here is due to his bloated notion of 'proxyability'. Gardner mistakenly assumes all (or most) criminal prohibitions utilizing the causative verbs of English create 'nonproxyabile crimes'. As we will see shortly in the text, this is *not* Kadish's notion, which is much narrower and thus much more interesting.

[44] Kadish, 'Complicity, cause, and blame', 373.

A sober defendant may cause an insensate and disorderly drunk to appear in a public place by physically depositing him there. But we could hardly say that the sober person has through the instrumentality of the drunk, himself committed the criminal action of being drunk and disorderly in a public place. A defendant may cause a married person to marry another by falsely leading the married person to believe his prior marriage was legally terminated. But the defendant could hardly be held liable for the crime of bigamy, since one does not marry simply by causing another person to marry . . . a visitor to a prison who abducts a prisoner could not be said to have committed the crime of escaping from prison by forcing a prisoner to do so.[45]

Redrafting such statutes using 'cause' language (rather than causatives) will not make these crimes 'proxable', ie, do-able through the actions of another. Suppose we change the *actus reus* of bigamy, from 'marry while still married to another', to 'cause oneself to be married while oneself is still married to another'. This will not make Kadish's supposed deceiver guilty of bigamy, because *he* is not causing *himself* to get married (anymore than he is doing any marrying). This is because the event such non-proxable crimes seek to prohibit essentially involves reference to the actor being charged: it is not criminal to cause *another* to get married, only to cause *oneself* to get married.

This linguistic feature (of pronominal cross-reference) may also be arbitrary, depending on what one thinks about what is wrong about bigamy, public drunkenness, prison escapes, and the like. Is the evil sought to be prohibited by the escape statute, for example, the evil of prisoners being outside the prison walls, no matter how they got there? Or is it the evil of prisoners getting themselves out of prison? If the latter, then we would not rush to redraft because the class of persons we are aiming at—prisoners—are not involved in these visitors-caused-'escapes', except as victims. In such cases, we neither want to expand principal liability nor to use accomplice liability, because the evil we wished to prevent never happened.

As another example, consider rape. Is rape a non-proxable crime? Should rape be defined as causing penetration of another, or as causing penetration of another by one's own body?[46] That depends on what one takes the evil of rape to be. Suppose (as in one well-known case)[47] the defendant inserts the penis of another into the female victim. That should be rape, if the evil is violation of the female's body; not, if the evil is violation of the female's body *by the perpetrator's body*. In making the crime non-proxable, the Virginia Supreme Court implicitly took the latter view. On that view, there is no rape (and no aiding of rape) because the evil of rape did not occur.

Non-proxable crimes thus present no reason to require a separate form of liability called complicity. Doubtless most crimes should not be defined in such a

---

[45] Kadish, 'Complicity, cause, and blame', 373.
[46] The explicit definition in some states, such as North Carolina, where only penetration by the defendant's penis constitutes rape. See General Statutes of North Carolina 3, §§ 14.27.1–14.27.10.
[47] *Dusenbery v. Commonwealth*, 220 Va 770, 263 S E 2d 392 (1980).

way as to be non-proxyable—battery, homicide, and rape coming to mind. But for those crimes that are rightly so-defined, such as (perhaps) bigamy and escape, when the evil prohibited has not occurred—because the perpetrator has not caused himself to be in a certain state—then no form of liability should attach, accomplice or otherwise. For proxyable crimes, there is no need for accomplice liability, for principal liability will attach to accomplices who cause the prohibited harm by their aid; and for non-proxyable crimes, there is no need for liability of any kind for 'accomplices' who do not cause the prohibited harm (because that harm has not occurred at all). In short, the existence of non-proxyable crimes goes no distance in showing a need for accomplice liability.

III. Beginning Again: The Bases of Accomplice Liability

If we put aside these bad reasons for thinking accomplice liability to be non-causal (or not fully causal, or not describable with causative verbs), our puzzle recurs: is the relationship between the acts of accomplices and the legally prohibited state of affairs they aid, causal or not, and if not, what is the relationship?

We now need to employ the battery of distinctions argued for in this book. We need to distinguish: (1) true causation, from (2) counterfactual dependence (as we do in Chapter 17), and both of these from (3) probabilistic dependence (as we do in Chapter 19). We also need to distinguish: (4) what I shall dub 'Intentional dependence'—the kind of relation that exists between a harm and an act when that act is in execution of an intention having as its object a representation of that harm. The *actus reus* of accomplice liability is constructed out of one or more of these four relationships (between the accused's act and the prohibited result) being present in some combination—which is why that *actus reus* has so resisted easy characterization. Sometimes it is one thing, sometimes another, and sometimes it is a combination of two or more things. Let me begin with what I shall call the 'truly causal' accomplice.

A. Truly causal accomplices

As I shall argue in Chapter 17, it is not necessary that an accused's act be a necessary condition of some harm for that act (both in law and in actual fact) to be a cause of that harm. Nor is counterfactual dependence of the harm on the act a sufficient condition of causality. This means we need something other than the presence or absence of a 'but for' relationship to separate causal from non-causal accomplices. What might this be?

We do not yet need a fully worked out theory of causation at this point. Negatively, we do need causation *not* to be counterfactual dependence, probabilistic dependence, or Intentional dependence. We need this to have the distinctions organizing this discussion. But positively, we need only what the first and second iterations of the *Restatement of Torts* needed: treat causation as a primitive—a 'factor'—save for one characteristic, namely that there can be more or less of it. Causation needs to be a scalar quality, a matter of continuous variation, as opposed to a binary, black and white sort of relationship.[48]

Then—again with section 431 of the *Restatement of Torts First* and *Second*—we mark causal responsibility by using some quantitative measure; x causes y if and only if x is (say) a 'substantial' cause of y. *De minimis* amounts of causal contribution do not make for cause-based responsibility. This line (between substantial versus *de minimis* amounts of causal contribution) is not governed by counterfactual dependence; x can be a substantial cause of y without x being necessary for y—witness the fire that joins another fire of equal size, and the two together jointly burn down the victim's house. Moreover, x can be a de minimis causal contributor even though x was necessary for y—as where I remind you of how much you hate V, and (with that reminder) you go off and kill V, when otherwise you would not have.[49]

This spare notion of causation gives us all we need at this point to assess the causal contributions of accomplices. And, not surprisingly, if we apply this substantiality criterion, we find that some accomplices are causes of the harms they aid another to cause, whereas other accomplices either make no causal contribution to a harm by their aid, or they make quite small causal contributions to that harm.

Consider first the substantially causally contributing accomplices. It is perhaps helpful to follow the law here, dividing these cases along a temporal dimension—between those whose acts of aid are simultaneous with the acts of the principal causing the harm, and those whose acts of aid precede the relevant act(s) of the principal. The law makes this division because it treats simultaneous, substantial causal contributions as co-principals, not as aiders.[50] Thus, one who holds up the barrel of the gun so that a (weak) shooter can make the shot that kills, is treated as a concurrent causer of the death, not as an aider and abettor of another's causing of death. Likewise, the defendant who knifes the victim while another repeatedly strikes her with a saber, is held to concurrently cause her death, not be an accomplice.

---

[48] This 'causation-as-primitive-except for scalarity' approach was adopted by the American Law Institute from Jeremiah Smith, 'Legal cause in actions of torts', Harvard Law Review 25 (1911–12), 103–28, 223–52, 303–27. Cause-as-primitive is a respectable view within the contemporary philosophy of science. See, eg, Michael Tooley, *Causation: A realist approach* (Oxford: Oxford University Press, 1987); David Armstrong, *What Is a Law of Nature?* (Cambridge: Cambridge University Press, 1984).

[49] The currently proposed *Restatement (Third) of Torts* recognizes this in its commentary on the earlier *Restatements'* substantial factor test. See *Restatement of the Law of Torts: Liability for Physical Harm (Basic Principles)*, Chapter 6, Tentative Draft No 3 (Philadelphia: American Law Institute, April 7, 2003), § 36 Comment: 'The substantial factor test has revealed a tendency to be understood as permitting something less than a 'but for' cause or as demanding more than a 'but for' cause to constitute a factual cause.'

[50] See, eg, Perkins, 'Parties to crime', 594.

Some of the sequentially contributing cause cases also treat those who aid as co-causers and thus as principals, not accomplices. I refer to the innocent- (or partly innocent-) agent cases.[51] These are the cases where the putative accomplice: (a) gets the perpetrator so drunk that he barely knows what he is doing; (b) induces a hypoglycemic episode in another, who involuntarily does what is needed; (c) deceives the actor about the kind of act he is doing; or (d) coerces the actor with serious threats. In such cases there is no guilty principal, so there can be no accomplice liability. Yet the law here has no problem in seeing the first actor as a co-causer along with the second, thus treating that actor as a principal in his own right.

Whenever the present doctrines of intervening causation treat the second actor's choice as an intervening cause, then the sequential cases come out quite differently. In such cases, the law classifies earlier (but substantial) causal contributions as not amounting to causal liability; rather these actors are treated as accomplices. Yet once one sees that the doctrine of intervening causation does not mark a true causal distinction, there is no justification for treating the two classes of sequential causal contribution cases differently. Indeed, both sorts of sequentially co-causing cases are in reality no different than the simultaneous co-causer cases above. All of these three classes of cases represent the true causal liability of co-causers, despite the fictionally 'broken' causal chains supposedly existing in the last of these three sorts of cases.

Thus, one who picks the victim of the murder, orders a subordinate to do it, pays him well for it, locates the victim for the hit-man, brings the gun and ammunition, and drives the hit man to the location of the killing, substantially causes the death of the victim. We should thus say plainly that one way to be an accomplice is by *causing* the harm through the actions of another. Substantially aiding another to cause some harm *is* to substantially cause that harm oneself, whatever the pretensions of the intervening causation fiction.

Seeing the parallel between the various kinds of substantial causers—whether simultaneous or sequential—raises the question why the criminal law would distinguish between them. All substantially cause the harm, so why is one treated as an accomplice and the others treated as principals? One could say that, *on average*, accomplices are less substantial causers than are the principals they aid, and this is true enough. Yet this is only a rule of thumb of what is true in the general run of cases. It does not justify the bright-line rule marked by the distinction between principals and accomplices. Some very substantial causers will fall on the accomplice side of the line, as in the last example; conversely, some not-so substantial causers (such as one of 13 concurrent stabbers of a single victim)[52] will fall on the principal side of the line. Indeed, under current

---

[51] For a summary, see Kadish, 'Complicity, cause, and blame', 369–72.

[52] As in Agatha Christie's *The Murder on the Orient Express* (New York: Pocket Books, 1960). For a real-life, if scaled down version with only two wounders, see *People v. Lewis*, 124 Cal 551, 57 Pac 470 (1899).

doctrines the very same defendant will be treated as an accomplice or as a principal depending not on anything relevant to the degree of his causal contribution but only on the relative innocence of his co-causer.

Let us next examine the smaller causers of the harm aided. Take everyone's favorite here, the *Wilcox* case in England.[53] Wilcox was charged with aiding an alien saxophonist to perform for money whilst in England, in violation of the immigration laws then in effect. All Wilcox did is to buy a ticket and attend the concert where the saxophonist was playing, for the purposes of writing it up for his journal, 'Jazz Illustrated'. The court held that Wilcox's 'presence and his payment was an encouragement' sufficient for accomplice liability.

It is important first to see that Wilcox did causally contribute to the legally prohibited result here—the performance for pay of an alien musician. That is because Wilcox was a member of the paid audience, and presumably the presence of a paid audience entered into the motivations of the saxophonist who played. *Wilcox* is in this respect like others of what we earlier in Chapter 5 called mixed concurrent-cause cases, like pollution and elections. Suppose it requires five units of pollution to cause some harm, but each of several hundred polluters contributes one unit; or suppose it requires 51 votes to win an election, but 90 people vote for the winner. In such mixed, concurrent cause cases no individual polluter, voter, or audience member is necessary to the harm occurring, nor are they sufficient; still, they *are* causes of that harm.

Yet they are, considered individually, very small causal contributors to the result. At some point, surely, they become de minimis causes, to be treated for moral and legal purposes not as causers at all. Wherever that point is, it should be the same for cases where the result is the action of someone else (as in *Wilcox*) or where the result is an event that is not a human action (as in the pollution and election examples). Whatever is sufficient causal contribution for liability as a principal, in other words, should be sufficient for liability as an accomplice, and vice versa. Causal accomplices should again be treated like principals, because both groups equally cause the harm.

B. Necessary accomplices

Once one distinguishes causation from counterfactual dependence, then it becomes possible to see one non-causal basis for being an accomplice, namely, counterfactual dependence. Suppose in the *Tally* case earlier discussed the warning telegram would have saved the victim, Ross; this means that Tally's sending of the countermanding telegram was *necessary* to Ross's death—that is, but for Tally's act Ross would not have died. In such a case, Ross's death counterfactually depended on Tally's action even if that action in no sense caused

---

[53] *Wilcox v. Jeffrey* [1951] 1 All ER 464.

that death. Let us call such non-causal, counterfactually-related accomplices, 'necessary accomplices'.

What we wish here to examine is how the presence of counterfactual dependence can be a sufficient desert-basis for necessary accomplices, even in the absence of causation. For my somewhat hypothetical Tally case to be useful to us in this regard, two facts must be true of Tally. First, Ross's death in such a case does counterfactually depend on Tally's act, and second, that act did not cause that death.

The first point is obviously true, if for no other reason than that I stipulated it to be so—and it is my hypothetical! The second point is less obvious. The Tally we are now discussing is a double-preventionist, not a causer, of Ross's death. My hypothetical Tally prevented something (the warning telegram) from doing what it would have done (prevented Ross's death), and by preventing this prevention Tally allowed nature (here, the Skeltons) to take its course.

To see why such double-preventions are non-causal requires that we repair to the basic notion here, that of a simple prevention.[54] When I prevent someone's death by throwing them a rope, it is idiomatic to describe what I did as causing of something, namely, the would-be drowning victim's survival. Yet the victim's survival is not a positive event or state of affairs; surviving something is just the absence of dying because of that thing.[55] So, one might say we caused a negative event or state of affairs to exist, viz a not-dying of the victim.

Negative events, negative state of affairs, and negative properties are difficult items to admit into one's ontology. There are, of course, negative propositions (one of the meanings of the 'facts' explored in Chapter 14), such as the fact that V did not drown today. Yet such negative propositions do not demand negative entities or properties. Rather, what we rather transparently mean by 'V did not drown today' is 'It is not the case that there was some instance of the type of event, drowning of V, that occurred today.' We do not here refer to a negative event as a particular—a not drowning event—any more than we refer to a particular non-elephant in the sentence 'There were no elephants here today.' Rather, such statements are negative existentially quantified statements requiring reference only to types, either of events (like drownings) or objects (like elephants).

If there are literally no such things as negative events, etc, how can such 'items' enter into singular causal relations? More specifically, how could one cause

---

[54] The discussion that follows summarizes the discussion of this point in Chapter 3 and anticipates the somewhat longer discussion in Chapter 18.

[55] One need not agree with the example to agree with the point being illustrated. If to your sense of how things are, dyings are just not-survivings, then transpose the example. And if your view is that surviving and dying are both positive events or states of affairs, then (given the contradictory or at least contrary relation between them) your 'positive' events are at the same time 'negative' events—that is, you seem committed to there being negative events, negative states of affairs, negative properties.

something to exist (a not-dying) that we admit does not and never did exist? We cannot, so preventions of death cannot be causings of not-dyings.

What preventions are, is a somewhat tricky business to spell out. But part of their nature we already have before us: when I prevent the death of V, the fact that V did not die does counterfactually depend on the fact that I did what I did (such as throw a rope to V). Such counterfactual dependence does supervene (in part) on certain causal facts—such as that my throwing the rope caused it to be where V could reach it, and V's reaching of the rope and hanging on to it while it is raised out of the water is inconsistent with V's drowning then. But the details of this need not here detain us.[56]

Preventions themselves are not all that important to the issues that here concern us. But the (non-causal counterfactual) idea of a prevention is the basic building block for two items that do concern us. First, consider the notion of an omission. Although one can omit to do any type of action (such as killing, maiming, etc), the omissions of interest to us are failures to prevent something. Thus, in the much publicized New Bedford rape case of some decades past, several patrons of the bar where the rape took place stood by and did nothing. They did not cheer or in any other way positively aid the rapists; but they also did nothing to prevent the rape, such as intervening, calling the police, or whatever. They simply watched, and in so doing, omitted to prevent the rape. A much-discussed issue was whether such bar patrons' failure to prevent the rape should be sufficient for accomplice liability for the rape.

Suppose the chief stumbling block to accomplice liability in the actual case was here removed. Suppose, that is, that the bar patrons had a duty not to omit, as they would for example, if the rape victim were their child. How should we analyze their liability/blameworthiness for the rape? Not causally, from what we concluded about preventions. If preventing a rape is not to cause a non-rape, then not doing anything to prevent a rape is surely not to cause a rape. If there are no negative events that can be effects of some cause, surely there can be no negative events that can be causes of certain effects. 'Nothings' cannot cause somethings anymore than somethings can cause 'nothings'. Absent events cannot serve as relata (of either kind) of the singular causal relation.

Plainly what is sufficient for omission liability in such cases is counterfactual dependence. The fact that the victim was raped counterfactually depended on the fact that the bar patrons omitted to prevent it. Put more simply, they had the *ability* to prevent the rape and did not, and that is sufficient to ground their responsibility. Causation has no role to play in this kind of responsibility, ability (ie, counterfactual dependence) doing all of the work that needs doing.

Second, return to the notion of a double-prevention. If preventions and omissions are non-causal, then so too are double-preventions. Consider an old

---

[56] For more details, see Chapter 18, below.

example of mine.[57] D sees his old enemy, V, drowning in the ocean of natural causes. D rejoices. Then D sees L, the Mark Spitz of lifeguards, preparing to save V; to prevent this, D ties up L so he cannot swim out to save V, and V drowns. D's act of tying up L prevented L from preventing D's death. D is plainly responsible for V's death, but not because D caused that death. Rather, V's death counterfactually depended on D's act, and this is enough.

The conclusion that there is no causation here follows from what we said about prevention and omissions. D did not cause an absence of saving by L, and L's failure to save did not cause V's death. Double-preventions cannot be causal if preventions and failures to prevent are not causal.

D in my hypothetical is of course what I suggested in Chapter 5 might be called an 'aider of nature', not an accomplice to some human killer. Because of this, the law would thus classify D's liability as principal liability and not accomplice liability. Yet the difference is artificial and incidental. Tally's double-prevention would ground accomplice liability because he aided the Skeltons rather than a boulder or an ocean current; still, the basis of Tally's accomplice liability is no different than D's principal liability. Both are non-causal, double-preventionists whose liability is based on the fact that the deaths in question counterfactually depended on their actions.

An interesting question is whether such necessary but non-causal accomplices are less blameworthy as a class, when compared to causal accomplices. Does mere counterfactual dependence, unaccompanied by causation (because of the double-preventionist nature of such examples), make for a lesser blameworthiness? Perhaps it helps to creep up on this issue by considering a sub-class of such cases where there is plainly a large moral difference. I refer to what in Chapter 3 I called cases of *allowings*.

Consider the paradigm cases of non-omissive allowings, the passive euthanasia cases. When the doctor disconnects the respirator from a patient, he is said to let the patient die, not to kill the patient. More generally put, he *allows* the patient to die, he does not *do* the action of killing nor does he *cause* the patient's death. These are double-preventionist cases with counterfactual dependence. But such cases have a third property, one which makes a large difference morally. In Chapter 3 I called this third element the 'return to an appropriate moral base-line'. When the doctor unhooks the machine, she returns the patient to the state he would have been in had the machine never been hooked up to start with. What state was that? A dying state. What typically makes such state a morally appropriate baseline to which to return is that (with the advantage of the hindsight available at the time of disconnection) we can now see that the machine is incapable of doing any real good for this patient; so if we knew then what we know now, one would have been justified in not hooking the patient up to start with.

[57] Moore, *Act and Crime*, 278, n 42.

While the use of such baselines is close to the surface in many other standard instances of allowing, consider how it could be applied to variations in the facts of my hypothetical 'D' and of Tally. Suppose it was D himself who was about to swim out to save V; or suppose it was Tally himself who had sent the warning telegram. Suppose further there was no duty making it incumbent on either of them to do these things. Then when D ties himself up (so as not to yield to temptation to save V), and when Tally sends the countermanding telegram, I take it they only *allow* the death of V and of Ross. Because these acts do no more than return them to a morally appropriate baseline—one where they had no duty to intervene to start with—they have no liability; this, despite being double-preventionists whose later acts are necessary to the deaths of V and of Ross.

Indeed, in these revised scenarios their blameworthiness/liability seems no greater and not much different from simple omission cases, where they do not even begin to save their victims. To be sure, such allowers are not literally omitters: they do act. Yet their two actions together are almost self-cancelling. Hooking up a respirator which one then later unhooks allows the patient to die pretty much the death he was headed towards before there was any intervention. I say 'pretty much', because the patient's death is delayed somewhat by the combined actions of hooking/unhooking. Yet like the acceleration cases I discussed in Chapter 3, the allower leaves the world pretty much where it was headed without him. The accelerator makes such death slightly earlier—the allower makes it slightly later. Both are close to the pure omitter, who leaves things completely alone.

Now subtract the moral baseline element of allowings. On the actual facts of the *Tally* case, Tally was not the one who sent the warning telegram. So such a telegram unsent was not a morally appropriate baseline to which Tally could return. This crucial element of an allowing is missing. Tally is only what might be called a 'partial allower'—a double-preventionist whose acts are necessary to some harm but whose acts of prevention do *not* return the victim to some morally appropriate baseline (from which nature can take its course without blame). Still, are not partial allowers *somewhat* less blameworthy than causers?

Consider in this regard the much-discussed interrogation techniques used by American intelligence officers in the contemporary 'war on terror'. The core of these techniques were derived from those developed by the British in their own war on terror in Northern Ireland, labeled 'stress and duress' techniques. Some of these are cases of partial allowings, such as sleep deprivation and sensory deprivation. (Others are pure omission techniques, such as failing to feed, water, or medically treat.) Sleep deprivation techniques (such as bright lights, loud and irritating music) prevent sleep; and sleep 'knits up the raveled sleeve of care', ie it prevents a disoriented state. Sensory deprivation techniques prevent the perception of light, sound, touch, taste, etc; such perceptions again prevent disorientation of various kinds. So such techniques are double-preventions on which the disorientation, anxiety, etc, of the victim counterfactually depends.

And, there is no pretense that such states (of over- or under-stimulation, respectively) are morally appropriate baselines to which return may be made with impunity.

Even so, such techniques are distinguished from the kinds of causation of pain and distress involved in true torture (electric shocks, cuttings, beatings, and the like). The European Court of Human Rights termed these 'inhumane and degrading treatments', but not torture, in its review of British policies.[58] Even torture victims term these 'torture lite', as opposed to cause-based 'torture heavy'. Both, of course, merit heavy blame (in the absence of compelling justifications). Yet, is there not a difference in the degree of blame, just the same? Torture lite, like other partial allowings, involves the actor's agency less just because they are non-causal. Nature does the dirty work, so to speak, and the actor's agency merely removes the impediment that was holding nature back.

Notice that to so conclude is *not* to justify a differential punishment for accomplices vis-à-vis principals. That distinction I will get to at the end of this chapter. The pie-slicing here is different. The idea is that both necessary, non-causal accomplices and necessary, non-causal principals are somewhat less blameworthy than are both causal accomplices and causal principals. The difference here cuts across the accomplice/principal line, and cannot justify whatever moral difference that line is supposed to mark.

C. Chance-raising accomplices

We saw earlier that a common shibboleth in law about causation was that causation of *e* by *c* is identical with counterfactual dependence of *e* on *c*. An almost as common saying about causation within legal circles is this one: a cause is the raising of the probability of its effect.[59] More exactly:

'*c* causes *e*' means, $P(e/c) > P(e)$.[60]

The idea is that what causation amounts to is the chance-raising of an effect by its cause. We first need to show why this too is a myth in order to see the possibility of a third desert-basis for accomplices, that of a non-causal, chance-raising kind.

In considering the identity or extensional equivalence of causation with probability-raisings at this stage we need not take a position on the semantics of probability statements. I refer (as 'semantics') to the various interpretations of what probability itself is—whether it is subjective or objective, Baysian or

---

[58] *Case of Ireland v. The United Kingdom*, European Court of Human Rights, decision of 29 April 1976, Series A no 25.

[59] See, eg, *Restatement (Third) of Torts*, § 30, Tentative Draft No 3 (Philadelphia: American Law Institute, 2003), which requires that causes raise the chances of their effects.

[60] For those unfamiliar with the notation, '$P(e/c)$' means, 'the probability of *e* given *c*', whereas '$P(e)$' means 'the probability of *e*'.

non-Baysian, relative frequency or propensity, etc.[61] For now, we can do with a syntactic notion of probability: the probability function ('P' in the earlier statement) is one that obeys the axioms of the probability calculus. This puts aside the semantic question of what corresponds with that function in the world.

As with counterfactuals, it is implausible to *identify* causation with the raising of conditional probabilities. Again, if two descriptions refer to the same thing, then that thing will possess all the same properties no matter which description is used. And again, causation is a transitive, asymmetrical, and temporally ordered relation, whereas chance-raising (like counterfactual dependence) shares none of these properties. Suppose c causes e, and e causes f; then (with qualifications not relevant here) c causes f. Whereas if the probability of f given e is 50 per cent and the probability of e given c is 50 per cent, then (by the probability calculus) the probability of f given c is only 25 per cent, and transitivity is not fully preserved. Likewise, if c causes e, e does not cause c. Whereas if the probability of e given c is 50 per cent then the probability of c given e can also be 50 per cent. Symmetrical probabilistic relations are possible. Finally, if c causes e, e does not precede c in time. Whereas when c increases the conditional probability of e, c can succeed as well as precede e in time. Epiphenomenal forks provide frequent examples.

So *identification* of causation with an increase in conditional probability is implausible. But (again parallel to our discussion of counterfactuals), perhaps chance-raising is a good *test* of causation; perhaps there is an extensional equivalence of chance-raising with causation even if there is no identity. Again, we should examine the alleged equivalence in two steps: (1) is the chance-raising of e by c *sufficient* for the truth of 'c causes e' and (2) is the chance-raising of e by c *necessary* for the truth of 'c causes e'. This we will do in Chapter 19. To anticipate the conclusions of that chapter: singular causation is not to be identified with probabilistic dependence, nor is such dependence necessary or sufficient for causation. These metaphysical conclusions are enough to make possible the moral thesis I now want to advance: that chance-raising is an independent desert basis, along with causation and counterfactual dependence. And further, that some accomplices are only blameworthy on this basis, since they are neither causal nor necessary accomplices.

Liability for (non-causal) chance-raising is well known in both civil and criminal liability doctrines. Examples of the latter are the attempt and reckless endangerment liabilities in criminal law. An example of the former is the tort of 'lost chance', where a negligent doctor deprives terminal patients of what little chance of life they may have had.[62] Accomplice-liability doctrines are also often

---

[61] For an excellent summary, see Donald Gillies, *Philosophical Theories of Probability* (London: Routledge, 2000). In Chapters 19 and 20, below, we shall have to deal with the nature of probability in more detail.

[62] The leading case here is *Herskovitz v. Group Health*, 664 P 2d 474 (Wash 1983). Eric Johnson nicely shows how many putatively cause-based liability cases in criminal law, are in reality lost chance cases (because of laxity in the proof deemed sufficient for causation). Johnson, 'Criminal liability for loss of a chance', Iowa Law Review 91 (2005), 59–130.

stated in probabilistic terms: many cases conceptualize aid as acts that raise the chance of success of the principal's acts.[63]

Underlying all of these doctrines is the moral fact that risk imposition is a desert basis independent of causation and of counterfactual dependence. When I refer to risk impositions, I refer to some objective notion of risk. (A purely subjective version of inchoate liability I consider in a subsequent section.) Some contend that there is no objective notion of probability that can make sense of this objective idea of risk imposition. Such theorists urge that only subjective interpretations of probability make any sense. In this chapter I shall continue to suspend the debate about the correct interpretation(s) of probability, however. Even working with subjective probabilities alone, we can distinguish the wrong of risking from the culpability of the actor who subjectively thinks he is imposing risk.

To maintain neutrality about subjective versus objective interpretations of probability only requires that we idealize the subjective assessment of probabilities. Probability can then remain a purely epistemic notion, yet we can distinguish unreasonable risk impositions as judged from some idealized epistemic position, from unreasonable risks as judged from some particular actor's actual epistemic position. The former gives us all the objectivity to risk we need to distinguish this desert basis from the purely subjective desert basis next considered.

To assess how blameworthy one is, we need to add a culpability judgment to this judgment of objective risk. In cases of inadvertent risk creation (such as in the tort of negligent risk creation for terminal patients), we would ask, first, whether some act imposed an unreasonable risk from some idealized epistemic vantage point (which may well be the fact-finder's own, with the advantage of hindsight); and second, whether from the information base reasonably accessible to the actor, the act created an unreasonable risk. In cases of knowing-risk imposition (such as in the crime of reckless endangerment), we should ask the same 'objective' (ie, idealized) question about risk creation, and then ask the culpability question of whether the actor subjectively perceived such a risk. In cases of purpose (or 'specific intent'), such as in attempt liability, we again ask an 'objective' risk question: was the risk substantial enough to warrant liability. And separately we ask the culpability question of whether the actor either intended the harm risked, or (in rare cases) intended the risk itself.[64]

To say that riskings are wrongs in the sense just described is not to say that 'being hit with a risk' is a harm to the person risked. Nor is it to say that the victims of unrealized risk impositions have a right not to be risked. If the

---

[63] As Johnson documents: Johnson, 'Criminal liability for loss of a chance'. See, eg, the *Tally* case discussed above.

[64] An instance of the latter kind is *Hyam v. Director of Public Prosecutions* [1975] AC 55, [1974] 2 All ER 41. Mrs Hyam did not intend to kill Mr Booth, but she did intend to create a serious risk of death (in order to scare Mrs Booth).

probabilities involved in riskings are subjective only, then one's interests are neither harmed nor violated by risks that have not materialized. Risking a harm is not like causing a harm in these ways.[65]

Still, to unreasonably risk is to be blameworthy, the degree of blame here (like for causing) depending on the culpability with which the risking is done. On retributive principles the unreasonable risker deserves punishment as does the unreasonable causer. It may well be, as we argued in Chapters 2 and 3, such unreasonable riskers deserve substantially less punishment than causers of equal culpability. Even so, the risking is its own desert base.

Criminal law presupposes this as much in its accomplice liability doctrines as in its attempt/endangerment doctrines. In the actual *Tally* case, for example, the Alabama Supreme Court first noted that Tally need not have been either a causal or a necessary accomplice:

> The assistance given . . . need not contribute to the criminal result in the sense that but for it the result would not have ensued. It is quite sufficient if it facilitated a result that would have transpired without it. It is quite enough if the aid merely renders it easier for the principal actor to accomplish the end intended by him and the aider and abettor, though in all human probability the end would have been attained without it.[66]

The court then went on to define 'facilitating', 'aiding', and 'rendering easier' in probabilistic terms:

> If the aid in homicide can be shown to have put the deceased at a disadvantage, to have deprived him of a single chance of life, which but for which he would have had, he who furnishes such aid is guilty through it cannot be known or shown that the dead man, in the absence thereof, would have availed himself of that chance . . . where he who facilitates murder, even by so much as destroying a single chance of life the assailed might otherwise have had, he thereby supplements the efforts of the perpetrator, and he is guilty . . . notwithstanding it may be found that in all human probability the chance would not have been availed of, and death would have resulted anyway.[67]

On the facts of *Tally*, Judge Tally is guilty of aiding murder even though the warning telegram would not have saved Ross even if that telegram had been delivered to Ross; so long as Tally's prevention of the delivery of the warning telegram raised the chances of success of the Skeltons in their killing of Ross.

This is chance-raising (or risk-based) liability, pure and simple. See this clearly, and two fundamental features of the *actus reus* of accomplice liability at common law become very anomalous. The first of these is the firm common-law

---

[65] For the considerable debate here, see Heidi M Hurd, 'The deontology of negligence', Boston University Law Review 76 (1996), 262–5; Stephen R Perry, 'Risk, harm, and responsibility', in David Owen (ed), *Philosophical Foundations of Tort* (Oxford: Oxford University Press, 1995). For an exploration of the idea that exposing someone to a risk *is* itself to harm him, see Claire O Finkelstein, 'Is risk a harm?' University of Pennsylvania Law Review 151 (2003), 963–1001.

[66] 15 So at 738.   [67] 15 So at 739.

requirement that there be a guilty principal before there can be accomplice liability.[68] At common law, if the Skeltons had not killed Ross, then Tally could not be an accomplice to murder, no matter how much he raised the chances of Ross being killed. Nor, at common law, could Tally be guilty as an accomplice to attempted murder by such chance-raising, if the Skeltons themselves were not guilty of such a crime. The common-law mantra is that accomplice liability is essentially derivative, that is, dependant on there being someone else who is liable as a principal.

This is a very odd doctrine. To see the oddity, transpose such a requirement onto the liability of another class of culpable riskers, namely, attempters. We would then have the doctrine that to be guilty of attempted murder, the defendant must not only do an act substantially risking death while intending to cause that death by that act; but in addition, the victim risked must die. Not die by the act of the accused—for that would be cause-based murder liability. Rather, the victim must die gratuitously, that is, by means unconnected to the accused's attempt. This would be a ridiculous requirement for attempts, would it not? Attempters are blameworthy because they culpably risk. Whether the victim dies— by lightning, another assassin's bullet, old age, etc—is completely irrelevant to such risk-based blameworthiness.

The Model Penal Code sees this point with admirable clarity. Under § 5.01(3) that Code would make Judge Tally liable for his purposeful, chance-raising aid even if the Skeltons fail to kill Ross, fail to attempt to kill Ross, or fail to be guilty of any crime whatsoever. To put some words in the mouths of the drafters of that Code: culpable risking is blameworthy in its own right; such blame-worthiness does not depend on the fortuitous fact that the harm risked happens to occur or not. The liability is imposed for raising the chances of the harm, not for causing it, failing to prevent it, allowing it to occur, and especially not for the occurrence of such harm in a manner unconnected in any of these ways with the defendant's act.

The second common-law requirement pertinent here has to do with the details of *how* the accomplice's acts must do their chance-raising if they are to amount to aiding and abetting. Consider by way of example the common-law rule about what used to be called 'principals in the second degree', namely those present at the crime with the intent to assist the perpetrator if he needed it. The rule is that the would-be accomplice's intent to aid must be communicated to the perpetrator before presence without more can amount to aiding.[69]

The problem is that many cases of presence with uncommunicated intent to aid are cases of culpable chance-raisings. Suppose the would-be accomplice is present with intent to use his rifle to kill the victim if the principal perpetrator misses with his shot. Suppose the probability of each shooter hitting and killing the victim at their respective distances is 50 per cent. The existence of a back-up

---

[68] See, eg, Perkins, 'Parties to crime', 618.   [69] Ibid, 600.

mechanism—the would-be accomplice—increases the likelihood of the victim's death to 75 per cent, irrespective of any knowledge by the principal that there is such a back-up mechanism.

It is easy to see what tempts courts to the common-law rule here. If the accomplice does not communicate his intent to aid to the principal, then the principal's decision to shoot cannot have been influenced by the presence of the accomplice. Yet this is to require causal contribution of the accomplice to the result, even if indirectly (viz, the presence of the accomplices causally contributed to the principal's decision to shoot, which itself causally contributed to the death of the victim). Yet courts cannot consistently both say: causal contribution is necessary to be an accomplice, and that something else (such as culpable chance-raising) is sufficient by itself. Moreover, and passing by this inconsistency, culpable chance-raising *is* an independent desert basis, and criminal liability (either an accomplice or as a principal) should reflect this moral fact.

The Model Penal Code again sees all of this with admirable clarity. That Code's § 2.06(3)(a)(ii) makes attempting to aid a form of accomplice liability. As that Code's official commentary notes:

Where complicity is based upon agreement or solicitation, one does not ask for evidence that they were actually operative psychologically on the person who committed the crime; there ought to be no difference in the case of aid.[70]

Culpable chance-raising is sufficient aid without also (and inconsistently) requiring causal contribution.

This second common-law requirement for the *actus reus* of complicity is thus as anomalous as the first. The first requires the harm assisted to have actually occurred; the second requires that the assistance causally contribute to that harm. Neither requirement is consistent with the common law's own insight that culpable chance-raising deserves punishment on its own.

D. Necessary to chance accomplices?

If we attend carefully to the language earlier quoted from the Alabama Supreme Court's *Tally* opinion, we may think we see a somewhat distinct desert basis for accomplice liability. Note that the court does not talk in terms of Tally's act raising the chances of the Skeltons killing Ross. Rather, the court goes counterfactual on us: if but for Tally's act Ross would have had a 'single chance of life', then Tally has done the *actus reus* of aiding. Equivalently, if but for Tally's act Ross would have had a single chance *less* of death, then Tally has done the *actus reus* of aiding. We seem to be looking, not for chance-raisings in the actual world done by the presence of Tally's act, but for chance-lowerings in a possible world where Tally's act is absent.

---

[70] *Model Penal Code and Commentaries*, 314.

This might seem to be a fourth sort of desert base, one that in essence combines counterfactual with probabilistic notions. Thus, one might think some action *c* is necessary, not to the existence of some state of affairs *e*, but rather, to *e* having the probability that it possessed just after *c* occurred. But for *c*, in other words, there may well have been an *e* but the chances of *e* with no *c* would have been lower than in fact they were with *c* occurring. The absence of *c* is thus chance-lowering for *e* in some close possible world where *c* does not occur.

This could be an independent desert basis only if such counterfactual probabilities differ from causation, counterfactual dependence, and the kind of raising of the conditional probabilities I called chance-raising. Consider each of these in turn, beginning with causation. There is a well-known theory of causation that identifies causation with counterfactual probabilities.[71] According to the probabilistic counterfactual theory of causation:

'*c* causes *e*' means *c* is necessary to *e* having as high a chance of occurring as it does.

And, as before, a weaker form of the theory would make causation extensionally equivalent to probabilistic counterfactuals, even if the two relations are not identical:

c causes *e* if and only if but for *c*, the P(*e*) would be lower than it is.

As we shall see in Chapter 19, the probabilistic counterfactual theory of causation inherits the problems of both the counterfactual theory of causation, and the probabilistic theory of causation. I will not here anticipate those arguments but rather, assume causation is neither identical to, nor extensionally equivalent with, probabilistic counterfactuals.

The difference between probabilistic counterfactuals and the kind of counterfactual dependence earlier discussed should be apparent. Counterfactual dependence made *c* necessary for *e*; probabilistic counterfactuals only make *c* necessary for *e*'s chance of occurring, not *e*'s existence.

The difference with conditional probabilities is much more subtle. David Lewis (whose work on probabilistic counterfactuals is classic) put the difference this way: Lewis said that his 'analysis is in terms of counterfactual conditionals about probability; not in terms of conditional probabilities'.[72] What I gather Lewis means is that the conditional probability theorist looks for a conditional relation in this world, namely, the probability of *e* given *c*. The probabilistic counterfactualist looks for an unconditional probability of *e* in an only possible world, one very like this world save *c* is there absent.

---

[71] Namely, David Lewis. See his 'Postscripts to "Causation"', *Philosophical Papers* II (Oxford: Oxford University Press, 1986).
[72] Ibid, 178.

This difference does indeed make for some subtle differences between the two approaches to probability. One difference, for example, is the differential ability of the two theories to handle deterministic cases, where the probability of c occurring is one and so the probability of its not occurring is zero. Conditional probability theorists cannot define a raising of probability in deterministic cases (because the probability of *e* given no *c* is undefined and so cannot be less than the probability of *e* given *c*); but the probabilistic counterfactualist can define the chance of *e* occurring in a possible world where *c* is absent.[73]

Yet this is an in-house dispute about how best to conceptualize probability and risk. What is needed for there to be a distinct desert base here is something distinct from risk, not different analyses of what risk is. The only difference is for the counterfactualist probability theorist, the lowering of probability by the absence of *c* is tested in a possible world where all features that are the same as the actual world are held fixed, while for the conditional probability theorist only causally relevant factors are being held fixed.[74] That makes a difference in how we should conceptualize probability and risk; but it does not make for a new kind of desert basis.

It might seem that there is more of a difference here. It might look like there should be as much difference here as there is between sufficiency and necessity for a determinist. In the deterministic view of the world, if *c* is sufficient for *e*, that does *not* mean that *c* is also necessary for *e*. Analogously, it may seem, if *c* is sufficient to raise the chances of *e*, that does *not* mean that *c* is also necessary for *e* to have the chances of occurring that it has. Yet this analogy is an illusion. According to the conditional probability theorist, when *c* raises the chances of *e*, $P(e/c) > P(e/\text{not-}c)$. If we were to translate the probabilistic counterfactual theory into the language of conditional probabilities, the necessity of *c* to *e*'s chances would be given as $P(e/\text{not-}c) < P(e/c)$. Such chance lowerings (by *c*'s absence) is not different than what the conditional probability theorists asserts about chance-raisings. Chance lowerings of *e* in possible worlds where *c* is absent, are not different from chance-raisings of *e* in this world (where *e* is present).

E. Subjectively culpable accomplices

There is a class of persons traditionally held liable as accomplices that we have not yet accounted for. These are the individuals who do not causally contribute to some legally prohibited result, nor are their acts or omissions necessary to that result occurring. Further, their acts do not elevate the likelihood of the harm occurring. Still, they are held as accomplices, and rightly so.

---

[73] David Lewis, 'Postscripts to "Causation"', 178.
[74] See Christopher Hitchcock, 'Probabilistic causation', *Stanford Encyclopedia of Philosophy*, <http://www.plato.stanford.edu> (2002).

I refer to individuals, for example, who: seek to shout encouragement to some principal but the latter either does not hear them, mishears them so that he thinks he is being discouraged from his crime, or the principal discounts those who encourage him as untrustworthy fools to whom he pays absolutely no attention; replace a perfectly reliable get-away car with one that is, unbeknownst to them, about to break down; stand look-out for a bank robbery but get the time of the planned robbery wrong, so that they do their 'looking out' after the robbery has already occurred;[75] solicit a strangely silent hit man to do a murder for them by various inducements offered at a bar, when the hit man, unbeknownst to them, has already died of an overdose of heroin.

For some of these the common law would find there to be no aiding, and therefore no accomplice liability, whereas for others, rather inconsistently, there would be liability. The Model Penal Code would hold all of them for attempting to aid the commission of a crime.[76] When that crime was committed, the liability of the secondary party would be complicity; where there is no crime done by a principal, the liability would be for an attempt. Since the Code generally punishes attempts the same as completed crimes, the differing basis of liability would make no difference to punishment.

The Code here articulates a clear, consistent vision of what is truly a fourth ground of responsibility. Since on this desert basis there is no wrongdoing by the defendant, only culpability, I shall call this the 'subjective culpability basis' for holding accomplices and others blameworthy and liable.

One can see this desert basis most easily by leaving accomplice liability temporarily, and focusing on attempts. The common law of attempts does not belong here. Its vision is of a different sort, the kind of chance-raising, risk-imposition we saw before. This comes out clearly in the common law's 'dangerous proximity' requirement for the *actus reus* of attempts.[77] It also is evidenced by the common-law version of the defense of 'legal impossibility', according to which objectively non-risking behaviors are not regarded as attempts despite the actors' perceptions that they are likely to bring about some legally prohibited state of affairs.[78]

The Model Penal Code's version of attempt liability is strikingly different. It makes no bones about jettisoning any objective risk component; instead, the subjective perceptions of the actor are alone relevant. The desert-determiner for a Model Penal Code attempt is an executed intention. Attempted murder, for example, is simply the doing of some act motivated by an intent to kill. Thus, the Code's *actus reus* requirements are only that some step be taken strongly

---

[75] See the facts of *Larkin v. Police* [1987] 2 NZLR 282.

[76] Model Penal Code, § 2.06(3)(a)(ii).

[77] *People v. Rizzo*, 246 NY 334, 158 NE 888 (1927).

[78] Admittedly, it is difficult to discern any one policy intuition guiding the old common law defense of 'legal impossibility'. The requirement that there be a 'near miss'—a significant raising of objective chance—is the best sense I can make of the cases.

corroborative of the actor's intention; the step must be 'substantial', but this only means 'strongly corroborative'.[79] Such substantiality thus serves a purely evidentiary function, not a function of measuring degree of objective risk. Likewise, the Code explicitly jettisons the common law's version of legal impossibility. Sticking pins in a voodoo doll is attempted murder if the actor believes such action will kill the person the doll represents. Such extreme lack of any objective risk is to be taken into account, if at all, only as a matter of a court's sentencing discretion.[80]

The moral desert basis underlying this version of attempt law is even more severely subjective than the Code recognizes. What is deserving of punishment here is a *trying*. Notice there is no particular significance for this vision (as opposed to the objective risk vision) on how far the actor proceeds in his trying. That he tries—that he not only has an intention, but executes it—is all that matters. Such trying is a purely mental action.[81] When a defendant intends to kill V, and decides here and now to do it by pulling the trigger of the gun in his hand—which decision issues in a willing of the finger movement needed—he has *tried* to kill V. This is true even if: V receives immediate and exceptional medical treatment so that the normally mortal wound does not kill him; V receives a non-mortal wound; V is missed by the bullet; the gun misfires because the bullet is a dud; the trigger is stuck and cannot be pulled; someone holds defendant's finger so he cannot move it; a sudden paralyses besets the defendant so that no nerve signals go to his finger from his brain; etc. So long as defendant willed an act that he thought would cause death in the service of an intention to cause that death, he *tried* to kill.

This purely subjective desert basis is also broader than even the Model Penal Code recognizes in a second dimension, namely, in that it extends to the culpability of belief and negligence as well as to the culpability of intention. Take belief first. Suppose the would-be shooter hypothesized above does not intend to kill V. Rather, he intends to shoot out a light but he believes: (a) that he almost certainly will hit V (who is standing behind the light) if he hits the light; or (b) that there is a substantial risk that he will hit V if he shoots.[82] If the defendant then wills the movement of his finger on the trigger, he has again tried to do an act he believes would cause (or seriously risk) the death of V. Such mental acts of trying accompanied by one or other of these predictive beliefs, also make the actor culpable and deserving of blame on that basis alone.

Now negligence. Suppose the would-be shooter in the above hypothetical believes there is a person in close proximity to his target but he lacks any predictive belief about that person getting hit if he shoots at the target. He again wills the movement of his finger on the trigger, but now the willing is

---

[79] Model Penal Code, § 5.01(2).   [80] Ibid, § 5.05(2).

[81] The 'mental action' theorists saw this clearly. For a discussion see Moore, *Act and Crime,* 95–108.

[82] Roughly the facts of *Thacker v. Commonwealth*, 134 Va 767, 114 SE 504 (1922).

unaccompanied by either an intention to kill or any predictive belief that he will or might kill. Suppose further that, contrary to the shooter's belief, there is no one anywhere in the vicinity of his target. From the epistemic vantage point of the defendant (which includes his information base), what he tried to do was unreasonable (that is, negligent). He should have inferred there was a risk even though he in fact did not. This remains true even though from our epistemic vantage point, with our knowledge that no one could be hit, his trying to shoot at the target is perfectly reasonable. I take the would-be shooter even here to be culpable and therefore blameworthy on this exclusive culpability basis for blame.

It is interesting how this ground for blame presses our distinction between what Michael Zimmerman calls 'hypological' judgments—judgments of responsibility for harms real or imagined, and aretaic judgments—judgments of responsibility for character.[83] For those of us who distinguish these two kinds of judgments, and who refuse to relegate one to being a mere proxy for the other,[84] the puzzle arises because a usual ingredient of hypological judgments is here missing. Usually when we judge someone to be responsible for some harm, real or imagined, that hypological judgment is based in part on a deontic judgment. Deontic judgments are those judging actions as right or wrong. With this purely subjective desert basis, there is no wrongdoing. The actor neither causes the harm, nor does he allow it or fail to prevent it when he had the ability to do so; nor is there even wrongdoing in the anemic sense of objective risk imposition. The only wrongdoing is in the actor's mind—as *he* sees the world, he is doing something that morality regards as wrong and that the law forbids. Even so, this remains a hypological judgment of responsibility and therefore blameworthiness. Such judgments are not general as are aretaic judgments of character. Rather, such judgments are about what an actor did at one razor's edge of time: he tried to do something with the intent or beliefs that make him culpable.

This is enough for some lesser form of blameworthiness. Even for those of generally excellent character, such culpable tryings are an appropriate basis for blame. Our beliefs create a possible world, one that differs from the actual world by the degree to which our beliefs are false. In that possible world created by his own beliefs the would-be shooter is doing an act that he intends to cause (or believes will or might cause, or should believe it will or might cause in light of his other beliefs) a bad result. He is just as culpable[85] as one whose identical acts take place in a possible world much closer to the actual world, and merits blame on that basis.

---

[83] Michael Zimmerman, 'Taking moral luck seriously', Journal of Philosophy 99 (2002), 553–76. Chris Kutz plainly feels the tug toward aretaic theories in his inchoate interpretation of complicity. See Kutz, 'Causeless complicity'.

[84] Argued for in Moore, *Placing Blame*, 568–9.

[85] But not as blameworthy, because he has done nothing *wrong*. In my lexicon, culpability is but one of two ingredients in overall blameworthiness, the other being wrongdoing. See Moore, 'The independent moral significance of wrongdoing', reprinted in *Placing Blame*, 237–8.

We can now return to the accomplice-liability cases with which we began this section. On the common law's view of inchoate liability, limited as it is to objective risk imposition, there should be no accomplice liability in these cases. Yet on the subjective view of inchoate liability championed by the Model Penal Code, there would be liability in all such cases. On such a view, it is arbitrary whether one calls it accomplice liability or liability as a principal attempter; for this turns on the irrelevant fact of whether there is some second party who is a guilty principal.

F. Vicarious accomplices

Perhaps surprisingly, even with four distinct desert bases in play, we have not accounted for all of the cases in which courts have found accomplice liability. For there are those who have been held to be accomplices who have not causally contributed to some result, not allowed or failed to prevent a result that they had the ability to prevent, not risked the results, and not tried to do some action that in their own mind would have helped to cause some result. Yet they have been blamed and held liable because someone else did one of these four things.

This is vicarious liability. Liability is vicarious for some defendant D when: (1) someone else has caused, risked, tried, allowed, or failed to prevent some harm; and (2) D stands in some relation R to that person, so long as R does not make D himself stand in one of the four relations to that harm that would make him blameworthy. A threatening relation between D and the principal, for example, will not do, because then D causally contributed to the harm. But if R is mere group membership, then D's liability for what other members of the group do, is vicarious.

The well known *Pinkerton* case illustrates the extension of accomplice liability on a purely vicarious basis.[86] Walter and Daniel Pinkerton were brothers who lived on the same farm. They were whiskey runners, transporting and selling bootleg liquor. They each were convicted of their own separate acts of possession, transportation, and sales of the bootleg whiskey. In addition, they were convicted of conspiracy to do these things, that is, an agreement between them to cooperate in these ventures. Daniel was then sent to prison on unrelated charges, but Walter kept running whiskey. Daniel was convicted of Walter's transportation, possession, and sales of bootleg whiskey even though he (Daniel) was in prison.

The *Pinkerton* majority held that the agreement to cooperate created an agency relationship between the brothers, much like a legal partnership. And thus, 'so long as the partnership in crime continues, the partners act for each other in carrying it forward'.[87] As the dissent recognized, this basis for liability 'is a vicarious criminal responsibility as broad as, or broader than, the vicarious civil liability of a partner for acts done by a co-partner in the course of the firm's business...'.[88]

---

[86] *Pinkerton v. United States* (see n 5 above).   [87] 328 US at 646.
[88] Ibid, 651.

Vicarious liability is a derivative liability doctrine. It piggybacks on some true basis for responsibility such as the four we have examined. It is not, nor does it pretend to be, some distinct, fifth basis for blame. As such, it has no place in any punishment scheme linking legal liability to moral blameworthiness. This is as true of accomplice liability as of any other form of criminal liability.

Vicarious 'moral' blame is not unknown. It is said that Ghengis Khan issued standing orders to execute all ten members of any ten-membered cohort in his army, should any one member desert in time of battle. Some would hold present day Germans responsible for the evils of Hitler and other Nazis simply on the basis of membership in the class, Germans. Such vicarious blamings may make for efficient armies or compensation schemes; but surely on reflection there can be no doubt that blame is undeserved in such cases.

In a rightly conceived penal code there should be no vicarious accomplices. The Model Penal Code's rejection of the *Pinkerton* doctrine, now joined by a majority of American jurisdictions, is a step in that direction.

IV. Some Conclusions about the Four Kinds of Accomplices

So there are four kinds of accomplices in a rightly conceived penal code, corresponding to four kinds of general desert bases: causal contributors, necessary contributors (notably omitters and allowers, whether partial or full), objective riskers, and the culpable tryers. There are very large differences in degrees of blameworthiness within each of these classes, due in part to: the degree of causal contribution (of some bad result) the accomplice makes; the degree of necessity (to that result) possessed by an allower's act or an omitter's omission; the magnitude of the risk imposed by the accomplice; or the degree of culpability of the tryer. Even so, as a general matter, the degree of blameworthiness is descending as one goes down this scale. That is, on average, and holding the mental states of culpability constant, causing is worse than allowing, which is worse than omitting; causing is also worse than risking and worse than trying. It thus matters what kind of an accomplice one is—matters in the sense of, is relevant to the amount of punishment one deserves.

Given the four different desert bases grounding accomplice liability, it should be unsurprising that the *actus reus* of such liability—aiding—has proved so elusive. The accomplice liability cases and doctrines are not like the trunk, tusks, tail, feet, etc, of an unseen elephant. They are rather like the trunk, hooves, wings, stripes, spots, claws and talons of a rather difficult to picture animal. To search for some one thing that is aiding is to search for a will-o'-the wisp, because there are four distinct items sufficient for aiding under rightly conceived accomplice liability doctrines.

This might suggest a disjunctive definition of the *actus reus* of accomplice liability, a disjunction with four distinct desert bases for this liability.

Remembering the different degrees of blameworthiness attaching to these different desert bases, one would not want to define aiding as any one of the four, and leave it at that. Rather, one needs to separate degrees of complicity, reserving the highest degree of punishment for causal accomplices, less for double-preventionists, still less for omitters, etc.[89] The general statutory equation of accomplices with principals (in terms of deserved punishment) would also have to go, save perhaps for causal accomplices.

Yet any such reforms would be a mere tidying up of complicity, when what we have seen shows it to be in much too serious a trouble for such mere rearrangement of deck chairs. What we have seen should be sufficient to sink the good ship 'Complicity', not rearrange its furnishings. Notice that the four bases for accomplice liability are not unique to that form of liability. These four are the desert bases for moral blameworthiness generally. As the disjunctive proposal reveals, there is no unique desert basis for accomplice liability. Aiding another to cause some bad result is not an independent desert basis. It is a mere stand-in for one of the four general bases on which we are rightly blamed.

Another way of saying the same thing is to repeat what was said earlier: the existence of some second party who himself more directly causes some bad result is irrelevant when judging the blameworthiness of accomplices. Their blameworthiness is established by their own causal contribution to the result, their own allowing or failing to prevent that result, their own risking of that result, or their own culpable tryings. Their blameworthiness is just like any principal's in this regard. They are in no relevant respect different, and thus there is no need for a separate form or theory of liability for accomplices.

The most that might be said in favor of retaining an accomplice form of liability is this: those we now call accomplices, in general and on average, present lesser degrees of blameworthiness on each of the four bases for blame we have examined. That is: (1) causal accomplices on average are lesser causal contributors to some harm than those we now distinguish as principals; (2) necessary accomplices on average are less necessary to the harms they allow or fail to prevent than are those allowers or omitters we now call principals (where 'less necessary' means the relevant counterfacutal holds true only in possible worlds *closer* to the actual world);[90] (3) chance-raising accomplices on average raise the probability of some harm less than those riskers we now call principals; and (4) subjectively culpable accomplices are on average less culpable than those attempters we now call principals (because the former typically try to make lesser causal contributions than do the latter). But these are matters of degree and rules of thumb. One would need some good reason to magnify and rigidify these

---

[89] Josh Dressler, 'Reassessing the theoretical underpinnings', heads off in this direction, although with only two categories of accomplices, rather than four.

[90] On this notion of degrees of necessity, see Chapters 16 and 17, below.

differences into two distinct theories of liability, that of a principal versus that of an accomplice.

And if one believes that there are such good reasons and thus goes this route, then one still has more tidying up to do than I recommended a moment ago. Once one sees that the existence of a 'guilty principal' is merely a proxy for diminished causal contribution (diminished risk, etc) by the accomplice, then another equally good proxy presents itself in the form of 'guilty nature'. Recall that abnormal natural events metaphorically 'break' causal chains under standard intervening-cause doctrines just as do guilty human actors. This is because such large storms, extraordinary fires, etc are at least as good at showing some defendant's causal contribution (risk, etc) to be less than normal, as is the existence of some guilty principal. (Indeed, as we saw at the close of Chapter 12, they are often better.) So if accomplice liability is to be retained for cases involving guilty principals, such liability in all consistency should be created for aiding a 'guilty nature': that is, aiding nature should be a basis for complicity too, as I suggested in Chapter 5. If it were up to me, however, I would dump them both in favor of having no form of accomplice liability.

It might seem as if my skepticism about the principal/accomplice distinction should infect the completed/inchoate crime distinction as well. After all, inchoate liability is ultimately predicated on either objective chance-raisings *or* culpable tryings, and liability as a principal lumps harm-causing with harm-allowing and both together with failure to prevent harm. Yet notice that this is not the Chinese-cut chicken that is accomplice liability. Accomplice liability as it is presently constituted not only encompasses four (or five) distinct desert bases; it also *shares* these four distinct desert bases with principal liability. Like the Chinese way of hacking up a chicken, the law's blade here hits not a single joint in nature.

Whereas principal liability for completed crimes—once it includes accomplices—encompasses all three desert bases of causing, allowing, and failing to prevent. It may well be a good idea to tidy this up as well, separating causing from failing to prevent, and both from full and partial allowings. Yet whether we tidy up or not within principal liability for completed crimes, cases where an actor either causes a harm, or on whose acts the harm counterfactually depends, are neatly separated from cases where no such harm occurs (or, if it does occur, it is unconnected to the actor in either a causal or counterfactual way), ie cases of inchoate liability. Inchoate liability is thus worth distinguishing as a separate form of liability from that of a principal for a completed crime. The relationship(s) between an actor's act and the type of harm the law cares about is different for inchoate liability. It is non-causal, non-counterfactual; rather it is either that the type of harm was objectively risked or subjectively intended.

Within the category of inchoate liability, we also might tidy up, just as we could within the category of completed crimes. The complexity within the law we have on inchoate liability stems from our uncertainty as to which of two desert bases should govern. On the 'near-miss' view of it, inchoate liability only attaches when there is a substantial, objective risk of harm. On the culpability view of it, such liability attaches when there is a trying by the actor (modified only by the evidentiary demand of corroboration of that trying by real world events). This is a conflict in doctrine due to indecision about the most appropriate desert basis. A simple tidying up within inchoate liability would be either to resolve the indecision in favor of one desert basis or the other, or to embrace both disjunctively as sufficient for such liability.

In any case, tidied up or not, we have good reason to retain the completed crime/inchoate crime distinction. The bottom-line conclusion of this chapter is that we have no equally good reason to retain the accomplice/principal distinction. It only remains to say how eliminating the latter distinction would affect the shape of criminal liability.

Eliminating the distinction between principals and accomplices would not be 'academic' or 'theoretical' in the pejorative sense, making no doctrinal differences. Such elimination would not leave liability where it presently rests, only placing it under one label rather than another. Rather, such elimination would both decrease and increase liability from where it presently rests. The decrease in liability would come in cases like *Wilcox*, where the alleged accomplice is held for the crime of another despite de minimis aid being given. Defendants like Wilcox should be held to the completed crime only if the standard bases for such liability are present, viz they either substantially caused the criminal result or that result counterfactually depended upon their action. If defendants like Wilcox would not pass these tests for principal liability, they should not pass them as supposed 'accomplices'. That someone else completed the crime is irrelevant to the desert of such defendants who should be judged by what they and they alone contributed to the result. If their contribution is insufficient for liability for the completed crime, then they should be liable only for the lesser punishments of inchoate crimes, just like those now called 'principals'.

Greater liability would occur (once the principal/accomplice distinction is eliminated) in cases where a more culpable accomplice aids a less culpable principal. Under present law, accomplice liability is derivative of that of the principal, so that the accomplice can only be convicted of the crime of which the principal can be convicted. A much-discussed example is that of Isabel Richards, who hired two men to beat up her husband, with the intent they beat him severely; they in fact only hit him without causing any grievous bodily harm. Since they only intended to beat him in this moderate way, they were convicted only of misdemeanor assault. Isabel was convicted of assault with intent to cause grievous bodily harm, a crime for which a moderate beating was sufficient *actus reus* but which is a much more serious crime because of the more culpable *mens rea*. The conviction was reversed because of the derivative nature of Richard's accomplice liability.[91] Eliminating the accomplice/principal distinction would

---

[91] *R v. Richards* [1974] QB 776.

eliminate this limitation on Richard's liability; she would be judged by her own *mens rea*, which is as it should be.

Putting these last two points together allows us to see that eliminating the principal/accomplice distinction has very practical pay-offs, not just theoretical ones. Eliminating the distinction would allow each of us to be judged as we should be judged: by what we individually contributed to some legally prohibited result, and by the state of mind we had when we did what we did. Standing in the shoes of someone else and being blamed for what they did, and for the culpability with which they did it, violates proportionality between desert and punishment.

PART V
THE METAPHYSICS OF CAUSAL RELATA

14

A Prolegomenon to the Issue
of Causal Relata

I. Relationships and Things Related

It is time we transition from the law's suppositions about causation in its liability doctrines, to the true nature of the beast. It is time, in other words, that we leave off the third-person exercise of asking what the law must think causation is, for the first-person question of what it is. This first-person exercise is to ask after the true metaphysics of causation.

There are two metaphysical questions about causation. One is to ask after the nature of the causal relation itself: is it counterfactual dependence, nomic sufficiency, probabilistic dependence, regular concurrence, something else, or nothing at all? The other is to ask after the nature of the things related: are they events, aspects of events, facts, negative events, etc? This chapter and the next are on this second question, about the nature of causal relata; when we say 'x caused y', what are the values that the variables x and y can have?

These two metaphysical questions about causation form a pair of trousers, in the sense that they are so intimately related to one another that we cannot imagine answering the one without having answered the other. As I once complained about Judy Thomson's attempt to answer the relata question while not answering the relation question,[1] this is about as promising as would be a similar strategy about sentences of the form 'x loves y'. Arguments about what can be a loving or loved thing depend a lot on what love is, and arguments about what can be a cause or an effect depend a lot on what causation is—and vice versa.

Still—with the possible exception for those rare individuals possessed of gymnastic dressing abilities—we all have to put our trousers on one leg at a time. We thus may suspend the relationship question while we examine the things related question, even if in the course of our argument about relata we necessarily must issue many promissory notes about the relation that eventually will have to be paid. Such in any event is how I intend to proceed.

---

[1] Michael Moore, 'Thomson's preliminaries about causation and rights', Chicago-Kent Law Review 13 (1987), 512, reprinted in Moore, *Placing Blame: A general theory of the criminal law* (Oxford: Oxford University Press, 1997), 352.

There is one clarification of the causal relationship that we do need now, and that involves the distinction between two kinds of causal relationships. It is common to distinguish singular causal statements of the form '*x* caused *y*' from statements of causal generalizations of the form '*x*'s cause *y*'s'.[2] It should be intuitively obvious that, whatever are the values of *x* and *y* in the first statement, they will be different than the values of *x*'s and *y*'s in the second. More specifically, the second statement will require *types* of *x*'s and *y*'s as the values of its variables, whatever the instances (or 'tokens') *x* and *y* are ultimately taken to be. There is thus a seeming primacy to understanding the relata of singular causal relationships; we can derive the relata of causal generalizations simply by moving to *types* of singular relata. (This will be true even if the latter relata turn out to be universals themselves.) I shall therefore stipulate here an initial interest in singular causal statements only. Our question then is: what sorts of things are related by singular causal relationships?

II. The Law's Framing of the Issue

As we shall see shortly, the candidates for the sorts of things that can be causes (and usually also effects) are numerous and diverse: we commonly say that *persons* cause things, as in 'Jones caused Smith's death';[3] we also extend causal agency to other *objects*, as in 'the bullet caused Smith's death';[4] we often treat *events* as both causes and effects, as in 'the firing of the gun caused Smith's death',[5] we sometimes talk of aspects[6] or *features*[7] of events as causes, as when we say that it was the suddenness of the firing that so surprised Jones; we also commonly relate *states* by causal relations, as in 'the state of Jones' appearance (he was clean-shaven)

[2] The best-known proponent of there being a marked difference between statements of singular causal relations, and statements using causal generalizations in explanation, is Donald Davidson. See his *Essays on Actions and Events* (Oxford: Oxford University Press, 1980). For some of the reasons why Davidson's version of this view is controversial, see, eg, Peter Menzies, 'A unified account of causal relata', Australasian Journal of Philosophy 67 (1989), 64–7.

[3] Persons as causes is most prominently associated with the *sui generis* 'agent causation' postulated by Richard Taylor and others. See Richard Taylor, *Action and Purpose* (Englewood Cliffs: Prentice Hall, 1965).

[4] Judy Thomson flirted briefly with the idea of objects being causes (in a way not reducible to events-involving-such-objects being causes) in Thomson, 'Causation and rights: Some preliminaries', Chicago-Kent Law Review 63 (1987), 471–96.

[5] For three very different accounts of events as causal relata (because based on three very different theories of events), see Davidson, *Essays on Actions and Events*, Jaegwon Kim, 'Causation, nomic subsumption, and the concept of an event', Journal of Philosophy 70 (1973), 217–36; David Lewis, 'Events', in his *Philosophical Papers* II (Oxford: Oxford University Press, 1986).

[6] LA Paul, 'Aspect causation', Journal of Philosophy 97 (2000), 223–34. The aspect view is defended in law most prominently by Richard Wright, 'Causation in tort law', California Law Review 73 (1985), 735–1828.

[7] Fred Dretske, 'Referring to events', in P French, T Uehling, and H Wettstein (eds), *Midwest Studies in Philosophy* II (Minneapolis: University of Minnesota Press, 1977); David Sanford, 'Causal relata', in E LePore and B McLaughlin (eds), *Actions and Events* (Oxford: Basil Blackwell, 1985).

caused Smith not to recognize him';[8] we also speak of *states of affairs*[9] (or situations)[10] as causes, as in 'the situation Jones was in (he was subject to verbal abuse by his boss at any time) caused him many sleepless nights'; or we relate *facts* with causation, as in 'the fact that Jones was so excited caused Smith's death to be as brutal as it was';[11] we even sometimes say that an *abstract universal* caused something to occur, as in 'it was excitement that killed Smith'; more often we say that a concrete universal (aka abstract particular, or 'trope') is a cause, as in 'it was the excitement of the robbery that killed Smith'.[12] Even worse, each of these candidates for causal relata has competing theories as to its nature, events being a particularly notorious example of this.[13]

In legal settings this rather heterogeneous list is boiled down to two candidates: causal requirements for legal liability are framed either in terms of *events* (considered as whole particulars with many properties) or in terms of *facts*. To capture what will turn out to be a good deal of wisdom in the law's presupposed metaphysics, let us elaborate a bit on the legal distinction.

Consider first the cases in torts where the defendant's act violates a criminal statute (and is thus 'negligent per se').[14] The courts are split on how to frame the causal question. Some urge that we should ask whether the *fact* that the act had the properties making it violative of the statute caused the harm; others urge that we should ask only whether the *event* that was the act caused the harm, recognizing that that event possessed the properties making it a criminal act.

Illustrating the first approach is *Empire Jamaica*,[15] a case in which a ship collision occurred while a non-licensed officer was on watch. The *event* that was his driving of the ship unquestionably caused the collision; but because he was in fact as skilled in seamanship as if he had been duly licensed, the *fact* that he was unlicensed equally clearly did *not* cause the collision. The trial court justice in Admiralty saw this distinction with admirable clarity, resolving the ambiguity in favor of fact-causation:

this breach...had no causal connection with the collision. That it was a cause, in the sense of it being a *causa sine qua non*, there can be no doubt, because we know that Mr Sinon [the uncertificated officer] was in fact the officer of the watch at the time when the collision happened...But that, to my mind, does not conclude the matter...the mere fact of the officer of the watch not possessing a certificate does not by any means

[8] See Menzies, 'A unified account'. (Menzies misleadingly calls these 'states of affairs'.)

[9] David Armstrong, *A World of States of Affairs* (Cambridge: Cambridge University Press, 1997).

[10] Menzies, 'A unified account'.

[11] Jonathan Bennett, *Events and Their Names* (Indianapolis: Hackett Publishers, 1988). David Mellor, *The Facts of Causation* (London: Routledge, 1995); JL Mackie, *The Cement of the Universe* (Oxford: Clarendon Press, 1980).

[12] 'Tropists' include Keith Campbell, *Abstract Particulars* (Oxford: Basil Blackwell, 1990); Douglas Ehring, *Causation and Persistence* (Oxford: Oxford University Press, 1997).

[13] Compare, for example, Davidson, Kim, and Lewis on events (see n 5 above).

[14] The doctrine discussed in some detail in the last section of Chapter 9, above.

[15] *The Empire Jamaica* [1955] 1 All ER 452, affirmed [1955] 3 All ER 60.

necessarily involve that that was a cause of the collision ... it appears to me to be quite impossible to say that there was any causal connection between the fact of his not having a certificate and the fact of his negligent navigation [leading] to this collision.[16]

Likewise, the Court of Appeal framed the proper causal question to be the question of whether there was 'any causal connection ... between the fact of having no certificate and the fact of his negligent navigation.'[17] Framed as an issue of fact causation, the Court of Appeals too found the issue easy to resolve: 'clearly if the plaintiff's only fault was [the fact that their mate was uncertificated], that was not a fault which could have had any causal connection with the collision'.[18]

Illustrating the second approach are opinions like that of the dissent in *Brown v. Shyne*,[19] where an unlicensed medical practitioner paralyzed the plaintiff by a series of medical treatments. The treatments by the unlicensed defendant were clearly a violation of the law; equally clearly such acts of treatment caused the paralysis. Again, however, because the unlicensed practitioner did not lack the knowledge or skill of a licensed practitioner, the fact that he had no license seemed causally irrelevant to the analysis. Judge Crane in dissent took the proper causal question to be the question of whether 'his act, in violation of law, is the direct and proximate cause of the injury ... '.[20] Because the acts of treatment were the cause of the injury, and because those acts violated the law, Crane concluded that 'the violation of this statute has been the direct and proximate cause of the injury'.[21] The proper interpretation of the question of whether 'the violation was the direct and proximate cause of the injury',[22] according to Crane, was whether the act done both resulted in injury and was unlicensed.[23] The question for Crane was not whether the fact that the act was unlicensed caused the injury. The New York statute enacted after *Brown* appears to adopt Crane's view in dissent, requiring a court to ask whether the unlicensed *acts* were a cause of injury, not whether the fact that the acts were unlicensed was a cause of injury.[24]

This dichotomy of legal results is reproduced by the use of causation in torts generally, and not just when there is a statutory violation by a defendant. Here again the causal question asked is often whether a defendant's *acts* (which were negligent) caused the harm; perhaps as often, however, the causal question asked is whether the *fact* that the defendant's acts were negligent caused the harm.[25] Thus, suppose an unlabeled can of rat poison is placed next to food in the

[16] [1955] 1 All ER 452 at 454.　　[17] Ibid, 60.　　[18] Ibid, 68–9.
[19] *Brown v. Shyne*, 242 NY 176, 151 NE 197 (1926).　　[20] 242 NY at 187.
[21] Ibid, 188.　　[22] Ibid, 191.　　[23] Ibid.
[24] New York Civil Practice Law and Rules, § 4504(d) (1971).
[25] Cf *Victor Sparkler and Specialty Co v. Price*, 146 Miss 192, 111 So 437 (1927). (Although the manufacturing of phosphorus-containing fireworks caused the death of a child who ingested them, the fact that the fireworks were highly flammable—and dangerous for that reason—did not cause the child's death.)

kitchen of defendant's restaurant, and suppose further that it is largely the risk of accidental poisoning that makes such act negligent.[26] Although there is phosphorus in the rat poison, and although pure phosphorus is highly flammable, the phosphorus in the rat poison is so diluted that it is very difficult to ignite; so difficult that the risk of fire by itself did not make the placement of the rat poison next to a stove negligent. Despite the unlikelihood, the unlabeled rat poison on a shelf next to a hot stove is not ingested but does explode, as a result of which the plaintiff is injured.

Some legal theorists, such as Leon Green,[27] have urged that the correct causal question is whether the *act* of placing the rat poison on the shelf caused the injury. Others, such as Robert Keeton,[28] have urged that the correct causal question is whether the fact that the rat poison was unlabelled caused the injury. Since by hypothesis the negligence of the defendant consisted in placing unlabelled rat poison next to food (when it could mistakenly be ingested), Keeton phrases the latter, fact-oriented question as being the question of whether 'the negligence caused the harm'. In this terminology, the event-oriented question would be whether 'the act (that was negligent) caused the harm'.

It would be nice if the law crisply resolved this ambiguity, so one might use that intuitive result as the starting point for philosophical argument. However, there is no such dominant resolution of what should be causal relata in these contexts. It would, alternatively, be of some comfort if the law's irresolution in this regard was due to a policy difference unique to this legal context: viz that those courts favoring the fact interpretation do so because of their desire for contracted liability and that those courts favoring the event interpretation do so because of their desire for expanded liability. While there is some tendency in these directions, it is limited because anyone wishing for contracted liability can achieve that result by supplementing an event-cause view with a non-causal, 'harm-within-the-risk' requirement,[29] and anyone wishing for expanded liability can achieve that result by supplanting any fact-causation view (or any causal requirement, for that matter) with a non-causal, event-oriented counterfactual requirement for liability.[30]

So the law does not present us with a resolution of the fact/event ambiguity about causal relata, nor can one explain away the law's irresolution in ways making plausible that the law *has* uncovered such a resolution but simply covered

---

[26] A variation of the facts in *Larrimore v. American National Ins. Co*, 184 Okla 614, 89 P 2d 340 (1939).

[27] Leon Green, 'The causal relation issue in negligence law', Michigan Law Review 60 (1962), 543–76.

[28] Robert Keeton, *Legal Cause in the Law of Torts* (Columbus: Ohio State University Press 1963).

[29] As is done, for example, by Joseph Bingham, 'Some suggestions concerning "legal cause" at common law', Columbia Law Review 9 (1909), 16–37, 136–54, and by Warren Seavey, 'Mr Justice Cardozo and the Law of Torts', Harvard Law Review 52 (1939), 372–407.

[30] A suggestion I explore in Chapter 18, below.

it up for reasons of legal policy. Still, the law does unambiguously frame an issue that will turn out to be of philosophical significance: of all the sorts of things we *say* are causes or effects, there are only two real candidates for such status, events or facts. This leaves out many other candidates such as persons, properties, tropes, etc. In this, the law is roughly right, as we shall see.

III. The Cast of Characters Trying Out for the Role of Causal Relata

Like a good 19th-century Russian novel—typically filled with numerous characters with unfamiliar names—we need a list of characters up front. Before arguing which of this cast we should promote as the protagonist, we should first be clear about who has even tried out for the role. A preliminary word about the list that follows. It is common in the literature to argue for the existence of certain items, such as property-instances or 'tropes', on the ground that these are causal relata and causal relata certainly must exist if causation exists. Such arguments soundly beg the ultimate question I shall wish to examine (viz, what are causal relata?). So the list that follows is limited to those entities in whose existence we have reasons to believe, reasons that are independent of any role such entities may or may not have as causal relata. I do not pretend to answer the ultimate questions on ontology raised in forming such a list. To keep the argument about causal relata addressed to as wide an audience as possible (and also to disguise my current ignorance/agnosticism on some of these issues), I only require that there be some *plausible* metaphysical basis for the existence of the entities in question, a basis uncontaminated by any alleged causal role for such entities.

In ordinary speech, it is idiomatic to speak of a wide variety of things as causes and effects. I would group these possibilities into four major groupings, with various sub-groupings under each:

A. Objects as causes:
  1. Persons ('agent-causation')
  2. Other objects
B. Events (and states) as causes, conceived as:
  1. Quinean events
  2. Davidsonian events
  3. Thomson's componential events
  4. Kimian events or
  5. Dretskean events
C. Properties as causes, meaning either:
  1. Abstract universals or
  2. Concrete universals (tropes)
     but not as:

    3. Aspects or features of events because these are redundant to:
      a. Tropes (see C.2, above)
      b. Kimian events (see B.4, above) or
      c. Facts (see D, below)
D. Facts as causes, conceived as:
    1. True propositions or
    2. Mellor's 'facta', or Menzies' 'real situations', or Armstrong's states of affairs that make true propositions true.

The discussion proceeds by examining each of these items *seriatim*.

A. Whole objects as causes

It is a common observation that our acquaintance with causation began with the experience of our own agency.[31] We can cause the movement of our body by willing it to move; we also discover that our body is the only Archimedean lever we have with which to move the world, so that by moving our body we also cause other states of affairs to come about in the world. We can move our arm, etc, and so we can scare, kill, humor, signal, etc our fellows, and so we can cause avalanches, wars, train wrecks, etc. Some wish to turn this epistemic observation into a metaphysical one: we as persons can be causes. Generalizing, other objects possess such powers as well: trees can kill people (ie, cause their deaths) just like people can kill people.

    Richard Taylor is the best known expositor of such views within recent philosophy.[32] Yet Taylor's views have seemed to most philosophers (including myself)[33] to be far too mysterious to be taken seriously. Causal laws are not framed in terms of objects like fires and bullets, except elliptically, ie, insofar as such objects are involved in processes, events, and states. To say 'the bullet killed her', seems transparently elliptical for 'some event involving the bullet (such as a piercing of the victim's heart by the bullet) caused her death'. The same is true for supposed causation by persons: however much some philosophers are struck by the mystery of human agency,[34] surely to say 'Jones caused the death of Smith' is elliptical for 'some act of Jones (such as shooting) caused the death of Smith'. Human agency is no more irreducible to event (process state, fact, etc)

---

[31] As in, for example HLA Hart and Tony Honoré, *Causation in the Law* (2nd edn, Oxford: Oxford University Press, 1985), 28. The observation is of course originally David Hume's.

[32] Taylor, *Action and Purpose*.

[33] I should suppose confess I once had some sympathy for Taylor's views. See Michael Moore, *Law and Psychiatry: Rethinking the relationship* (Cambridge: Cambridge University Press, 1984), 56–7, 67–72. My rejection of 'agent-causation' is in Michael Moore, *Act and Crime: The implications of the philosophy of action for the criminal law* (Oxford: Clarendon Press, 1993).

[34] See, eg, Jennifer Hornsby, 'Agency and actions', in John Hyman and Helen Steward (ed), *Agency and Action* (Cambridge: Cambridge University Press, 2004).

causation than is the 'agency' of fires and bullets. I shall accordingly put aside the objects-as-causes view.

B. Whole events as causes and effects

What is perhaps still the standard view of causal relata in contemporary philosophy is the view that whole events are the only entities that can be causes or effects. I say _whole_ events to distinguish this view from other major views later discussed, such as, that it is aspects of events, or facts about events, that are causal relata.

One of the main factors making the whole event-view standard is the correspondence of the view with many ordinary intuitions about causation, intuitions connected to the apparent lawfulness of causal relations and to the change-in-the-world to which causation is apparently related. Another factor is the diversity of views allowed under the big tent of 'the' whole events view. That diversity stems from quite divergent views as to just what sorts of things events are.

One prominent axis along which to display these divergent views is that of individuation. Although individuation is something of the tail of the big dog of essence and identity, I shall honor philosophical convention to order theories of events by the coarseness of the grain of individuation of events that such theories entail. An overview is provided by the following chart of theories about events:

Extremely Coarse Grained	Coarse-grained	Moderately Fine-grained	Fine-grained	Extremely Fine-grained
D Williams,[35] Quine[40]	Anscombe,[36] Davidson[41]	Thomson,[37] Thalberg[42]	Kim,[38] Goldman[43]	Dretske,[39] Sanford[44]

Since I shall ultimately want to defend the Anscombe/Davidson view as to the nature of events, and since it is closest to common sense about events, let me start there. On this view, events are true particulars, like physical objects. They have

---

[35] Donald Williams, 'On the elements of being: I', Review of Metaphysics 7 (1953), 3–18; 'On the element of being: II', Review of Metaphysics 7 (1953), 71–92; 'Universals and existents', Australian Journal of Philosophy 64 (1986), 1–14.

[36] WV Quine, 'Events and reification', in E LePore and McLaughlin (eds), _Actions and Events: Perspectives on the philosophy of Donald Davidson_ (Oxford: Basil Blackwell, 1985).

[37] GEM Anscombe, _Intention_ (2nd edn, Ithaca: Cornell University Press, 1963).

[38] Davidson, _Actions and Events_.

[39] Judith Jarvis Thomson, _Acts and Other Events_ (Ithaca: Cornell University Press, 1977).

[40] Irving Thalberg Jr, _Perception, Emotion and Action_ (New Haven: Yale University Press, 1977).

[41] Kim, 'Causation, nomic subsumption'.

[42] Alvin Goldman, _A Theory of Human Action_ (Englewood Cliffs: Prentice-Hall, 1970).

[43] Fred Dretske, 'Referring to events'.

[44] David Sanford, 'Causal relata', in LePore and McLaughlin (eds), _Actions and Events_.

spatio-temporal location, like objects (even though their mode of occupying space is non-exclusive vis-à-vis other events, which is unlike objects, and even though the temporal duration of events is usually much shorter than for enduring objects). They also can have many properties, again like physical objects. However, many of such properties—the non-essential ones—are not parts of such events.

For example, suppose the snow in an avalanche begins moving down at t_1, it ceases moving at t_2, it dams a stream at t_3, it floods a village with the water backed up by the dam at t_4, and it is the most talked-about event in the region in which it occurred until the end of the year (t_5). On the Davidsonian view, the avalanche has spatio-temporal location. Temporally, it existed during the interval $t_1 - t_2$; spatially, it was located wherever the object avalanching (the snow) was located during $t_1 - t_2$. This spatio-temporally located particular also has numerous non-essential properties: it caused the damming of the stream, it caused the flooding of the village, and it caused people to talk about it a lot. We can successfully refer to it by using these properties, as in: 'the stream-damming avalanche', 'the cause of the flood of the village', or 'the most talked-about event of the year'. Yet neither the damming of the stream, the flooding of the town, nor the discussions about the avalanche, are proper parts of the event itself. The event that was the avalanche ended when the snow stopped moving, even though its effects continued on.

The role of properties in this account of events is crucial. On what I shall call the standard version, an event is a concrete particular consisting of an object undergoing change over an interval of time, such change in turn being analyzed as 'a having and then a lacking by an object of a static property at a time . . .'.[45] Notice there are three aspects of events, on this account: a (spatially located) object that exists in its own right; a change (the having then the absence) in some property or properties of that object; and a temporal interval during which the change takes place. It is the properties essential to an avalanche-type event that are crucial here, properties such as the movement of snow down a mountain. The snow was at rest at t_0, began moving at t_1, ceased moving at t_2, was continuously moving during the interval t_1–t_2, and was at rest at t_4. Movement is one of those 'static properties' the absence of which, the having of which, and the absence of which again, fixes the temporal location of the avalanche event.

It is the presence/absence of properties essential to events like avalanches that is the sense in the common view that events are *changes* in some object in the world. As Aristotle characterized this view:

There are three classes of things in connection with which we speak of change: the 'that which', the 'that in respect of which', and the 'that during which'. I mean that there must

[45] The Davidsonian view as characterized by Lawrence Brian Lombard, *Events: A Metaphysical Study* (London: Routledge, 1986). Lombard regards such change in static properties to itself be a 'dynamic' property so that one analyzes events in terms of the familiar triad of object, property, and time.

be something that changes, eg, a man or gold, and it must change in respect of something, eg, its place or some property, and during something, for all change takes place during a time.[46]

It is the standard view of events as changes in the properties of objects during an interval of time—a view as old as Aristotle and is modern as the contemporary metaphysics of events—that I favor.

The two main competitors for this standard, Davidsonian view of events can most easily be glimpsed via a problem for the standard view. The problem is this: since events on this standard view do not exclusively occupy the spatio-temporal region at which they occur, it is possible for two or more events to occur at the same place and during the same time. For example, the earth right now is both spinning on its axis, and cooling from core to crust. The object involved is but one thing, the earth. The time interval, let us assume, is the same; that is, the earth began spinning when it began cooling, and both will cease at the same time. Despite the identity of spatio-temporal location, it seems intuitively that there are two events here, involving the same object. If there are two events here, that can only be because of the distinct properties (of motion and of temperature, respectively) exemplified during the interval of time. It is because we think the properties of motion involved in spinning are distinct from the properties of temperature involved in cooling that we individuate the (spatio-temporally identical) events of the earth spinning and the earth cooling.

The problem for the standard view is partly the problem of property individuation. As mentioned earlier, it is notoriously difficult to individuate properties. Yet matters are even thornier for the standard view of events, because event individuation on the standard view often involves a clumping of properties into groups. Consider a parachutist coming down in such a way that his path is a spiral one. During the interval t_1 (when he jumps from the plane) to t_2 (when he lands) the parachutist is moving downward and he is moving in a spiral fashion. Is there one event here (a spiral descent) or two (a descent and a spiral motion)? If, as seems likely, the spiral motion is caused (in part) by the descent, we may be tempted to group the two properties and thus to find only one event to exist. The second aspect of the problem for the standard view of events stems from the fact that there are no obvious principles with which to group properties (even assuming that we can individuate the properties themselves). Jonathan Bennett concludes from examples such as these that on the standard view (as on Bennett's own view) 'our concept of particular event has a large dimension of vagueness . . .'.[47]

The second view of events, the fine-grained view of Jaegwon Kim,[48] finesses this grouping-of-properties problem by regarding almost every different property

---

[46] Aristotle, quoted in Moore, 'Causal Relata', Annual Review of Law and Ethics 13 (2005), 598.
[47] Bennett, *Events and Their Names*, 127.
[48] Kim, 'Causation, nomic subsumption'.

as making for a separate event-token—for then there can be no grouping-of-properties problem. On this view events just are exemplifyings of a property by an object over some duration of time. There are thus as many events going on in a space/time region as there are properties exemplified. Thus, when John kisses Mary, it is their first kiss, the kiss is a tender, short, but passionate one, Mary is both surprised and pleased by the kiss, and Mary catches cold from John via the kiss. There were eight events going on then and there: a kissing event, a first kiss kissing event, a tender kiss kissing event, a short kiss kissing event, a passionate kiss kissing event, a pleasing kiss kissing event, a surprising kiss kissing event, and cold-transmitting kiss kissing event. In the Kimian world, a lot goes on when John kisses Mary (!), which is why this is called a fine-grained view of events.

The third major view of events, by contrast is a very coarse-grained view. On the Quinean view of events,[49] event-tokens are simply the whole of what exclusively occupies a space/time region. Whatever properties may be instanced during an interval of time at some place together constitute but one thing, what Quine would call the material content of that space/time zone. Such a view not only finesses the grouping of properties problem, but it also eliminates the individuation of properties problem. For this view makes no use of properties in determining what exists. As Bennett recognizes, 'a Quinean event is . . . uniquely determined by the zone, with no need to mention properties at all'.[50]

Despite these benefits of Kimian and the Quinean views of events, we should hew to the standard, Davidsonian view of events. There are three reasons for this. One is my own metaphysical bet on where the truth of the matter lies about events. The standard view requires less revision of other things we rather deeply believe to be true than does its competitors. The Quinean view, for example, collapses events and objects together, regarding both as one thing, the material content of a space/time region. The Kimian view, on the other hand, collapses events in the other direction, making them simply properties as exemplified by a particular object at a particular time. Both the Quinean and the Kimian demote events to subsidiary roles in our overall ontology, and do so by placing events in the shadow of items that seem to ordinary thought to be very different from events (objects and properties, respectively). Moreover, each of these views leads to very counterintuitive modes of individuating events: on the Quinean view there is only one thing going on at any time and place, whereas for a Kimian an impossibly large number of things is going on. The world as we know it does not seem either this boring or this busy.

Thirdly, we can capture much of what may be intuitive about Kimian events by facts. Much of the attractiveness (as causal relata) of Kim's theory of events stems from the fine-grained nature of Kimian events, and this will be shared by

---

[49] Quine, 'Events and reification'.   [50] Bennett, *Events and Their Names,* 104.

the equally fine-grained facts. Being fine-grained, both facts and Kimian events allow familiar causal discriminations seemingly denied to Davidsonian events as causal relata. So we may suspend Kim's theory of events, returning to it if it is needed to rescue facts from various difficulties when considered to be causal relata.

C. Property instances, tropes, event-aspects and event-features as causes

A view that has gained considerable support in recent philosophy is what I shall generally call a trope metaphysics.[51] Tropes are often called 'abstract particulars', or also 'concrete universals'.[52] As these labels suggest, a trope is in some sense both abstract and concrete, both universal and particular. Consider the sentence, 'The dog is white.' Traditional metaphysics divides the truth-makers of such sentences into two kinds: particulars like the dog in question; and universals like the property, whiteness. Particulars have temporal/spatial location, whereas universals do not.

The tropist (if I may) adds a third sort of thing: the particular quality of whiteness that is this dog's. The whiteness-trope of this dog is a particular: it exists where and when the dog exists. Yet the whiteness trope is also universal: it is an instance, or token of the property-universal, whiteness. Actually, more ardent tropists do not think of tropes as a third kind of thing, on a par ontologically with substances and properties; on the contrary, typically it is tropes that are basic.[53] Objects are simply collections of tropes (all the property instances of caniness, whiteness, quickness, etc, making up this dog). And properties are simply resemblances between tropes (this whiteness trope will resemble all other whiteness tropes, which resemblance is what justifies us in constructing a complex whole, the property whiteness as an abstract universal).

Again, I shall prescind away from the detailed debates in metaphysics about whether tropes exist, and if so, whether their existence is basic while that of substances and properties is derived. Tropes are plainly plausibly enough existents to be granted a place at the table for the status of causal relata. The case that they are causal relata is also plausible enough. As a leading tropist puts it, when we are speaking of singular causal relations (and not causal generalizations), we seem to be using tropes as the relata: 'when you drop it, it is the weight of this

---

[51] 'Trope' appears to be Donald Williams' coinage. See Williams, 'On the elements of being: I–II'.

[52] As David Armstrong cheerfully notes, 'There is a truly horrifying number of terms for properties and relations conceived of as particulars. Each happy discoverer, it seems, names them anew.' Armstrong, *States of Affairs*, 21.

[53] 'Ardent tropists' include Williams, 'On the elements of being: I-II', and Campbell, *Abstract Particulars*. See generally Chris Daly, 'Tropes', in DH Mellor and Alex Oliver, *Properties* (Oxford: Oxford University Press, 1997), 141, for a discussion of ardent tropism.

particular brick, not bricks or weights in general, which breaks the bone in your particular left big toe'.[54]

The distinction between tropes and abstract universals seems clear enough: whiteness exists (for a realist about universals) without having spatio-temporal location, but this dog's whiteness lives and dies with this dog. More troublesome is the similarity of tropes to three other, equally plausible existents. First of all, tropes are easily confused with Kimian events. The latter as will be recalled, are exemplifyings of a property by an object at a time. Such exemplifyings are close to property-instances (or 'tropes'). Yet the difference between tropes and Kimian events is real enough. For Kim, events are ordered triples, where the ontological commitments are the traditional ones of particular objects and abstract universals, together with the relation of exemplifying. An ardent tropist, by contrast, rejects the traditional metaphysics divided between particular objects and abstract properties; both of these are mere constructions out of what is more basic, property-instances and the relation of primitive resemblance between them. These are quite distinct world pictures.

Causal relata thus differs for a Kimian and for a tropist. As discussed by another leading contemporary tropist, Douglas Ehring:

> Causal relata include, for example, the velocity of that ball and the whiteness of this page. And these expressions are understood not to refer to universals. Causal relata are individual properties of objects (and events), not the having of such particularized properties or the having of a universal by an object or an event. The cause of snow blindness is a particular whiteness, but not the exemplification of the universal 'whiteness' by the snow. Causes are individual properties, not exemplifications of properties.[55]

Tropes also have a troublesome similarity to the idea of *aspects* or *features* of events. On the Davidsonian view of events, it will be recalled that singular events have many properties. (This was opposed to Kim, for whom each property usually makes for a distinct event.) A familiar view of causal relata has it that causes and effects are not the (Davidsonian) events themselves; rather, it is said that it is some feature(s) or aspect(s) of an event that are both causes and effects. It is the heat of the fire, not the fire itself, that is said to cause destruction of a house (or more exactly, the quickness of that destruction).

In philosophy this view of causal relata is most famously associated with Fred Dretske,[56] and in law it is Richard Wright's extensive work on causation that most explicitly takes this view.[57] Although Dretske speaks of *features* of events while Wright talks of *aspects* of events, I take this difference in vocabulary to mark no difference between the views. Dretske does have a particularly fine-grained version of features—'*John* (of all people) kissing Mary' is different from

---

[54] Campbell, *Abstract Particulars*, 113.
[56] Dretske, 'Referring to events'.

[55] Ehring, *Causation and Persistence*, 83.
[57] Wright, 'Aspect causation', 244–5.

'John kissing *Mary* (of all people)' in that they pick out different aspects of the kissing event—yet such fineness of grain is incidental to the general nature of the features view.

There are two ambiguities to clear up about the aspect/feature view of causal relata and once we clear them up I think it will be shown that this view can be eliminated because it is fully redundant of other views. The first ambiguity is what the relation between an event and its aspects is supposed to be, on this view. There are two possibilities here. One, an aspect of an event could simply be identified as a trope. Alternatively, an aspect of an event could be the universal exemplified by the object involved in such an event. Consider Laurie Paul's recent restatement of the aspect-cause view, where she explicitly leaves open this ambiguity:

I shall use 'aspect' to refer to a property instance: an aspect is a particular's (a particular event's or individual's) having a property. Aspects are things that correspond one to one with thing-property pairs such that the property is had by the thing... Defined as such, aspects correspond to tropes (if there are any tropes), but the definition of 'property' is intended to be flexible: whether property instances involve exemplification of universals... or tropes I need not say or choose between.[58]

An aspect of an event, on the trope version, is the abstract particular constituting (along with other property-instances) the event. An aspect of an event, on the exemplification version, is the abstract universal exemplified by the object involved in the event.

On either reading of the aspect view, notice the view adds nothing to the trope or Kimian events accounts already considered. If this is all there is to the aspect/features view, it is fully redundant to the other two views and so merits no independent consideration as a view on causal relata.

There is, however, a third version of the aspect view. When Paul speaks of aspects as 'a particular's... having a property...' she is seemingly identifying aspects of events with neither Kimian events nor with tropes, but rather, with *facts*. Paul herself recognizes this, leaving open the possibility that an aspect of an event is just a fact about that event (what she calls a 'state of affairs').[59] Peter Menzies takes this view explicitly, urging that we can dispense with event aspects as causal relata because such aspects are best construed as states of affairs (what Menzies calls 'situations').[60] To assess this last suggestion requires us to have a good grasp of the fact-causation view, the fourth of the major candidates for causal relata. It is to that view that I shall now turn. Before doing so, however, we should note that even if aspects are likened to facts (rather than to either tropes or exemplifications of universals), still aspects are redundant when we are considering candidates for causal relata: facts will do so instead.

---

[58] Paul, 'Aspect causation', 244–5.   [59] Ibid, 244–5.
[60] Menzies, 'A Unified account', 74–8.

D. Facts, facta, states of affairs, and situations as causes

The traditional metaphysical view divides existents between particulars (such as objects or (Davidsonian) events) and abstract universals. Seemingly such a metaphysics requires that one also admit *states of affairs* into one's ontology. For as Ramsey pointed out, neither particulars nor abstract universals correspond to true sentences. Rather, it is the *having* (or the *being*, or the *instantiating*) of the universal by the particular that can correspond to a true sentence. 'The dog is wet' is not made true by there being the dog referred to and there being the abstract property, wetness; rather, the sentence is true only if in addition the dog has the property, wetness. Similarly, 'Fido is wetter than Bruno' is not made true by the existence of two particulars, Fido and Bruno and by the existence of the abstract relation, wetter than; rather, the sentence is true only if in addition Fido and Bruno have the relation, wetter-than, between them.

Thus begins the argument for the family of entities here considered. Again, it will be helpful to collapse differing terminology so as to keep the ontological clutter to a minimum. Let us start with Peter Menzies' term 'situation', a term used by him to denote the entities that are causal relata. Situations, according to Menzies, 'are the worldly correlates of *true* sentences or statements; situations are what true sentences or statements describe'.[61] So characterized, 'situation' is generically the same thing as what I have been calling a state of affairs. Since Menzies uses 'state of affairs' to refer to what I would call simply 'states', he has to use some new word ('situation') to refer to the having of a property by a particular. Not being similarly hamstrung in my vocabulary, I shall hew to the more philosophically standard, 'states of affairs', as the label for the complex, a-particular-having-a-universal, which complex makes a statement true when that complex exists.

'Facts' we can also deal with briefly: facts are simply actual states of affairs.[62] States of affairs are the having of a property by a particular; such complexes exist in the way all abstract things exist, namely, there is such a state of affairs even if there are no instances obtaining in the real world. States of affairs may be only possible, not real, in other words. Facts, on the other hand, are by definition actual; only if the particulars referred to has the property in question does such a fact exist.

The notion of 'facta'[63] (or what Menzies calls 'real situations')[64] requires some more extended discussion. One of the persistent objections to facts (or states of affairs, or situations) being causal relata is that they are insufficiently 'in the

---

[61] Menzies, ibid, 67.
[62] DH Mellor, *The Facts of Causation* (London: Routledge, 1995), 8.
[63] Mellor's coinage, DH Mellor, *The Facts of Causation*.
[64] Menzies, 'A unified account', 70.

world' to play that role.[65] The thought is that facts, etc are too propositional in nature to do any causal work. How, after all, can a sentence or a statement move a mountain?

Facts, etc are propositional because of their tight connection to truth. They are what correspond to true statements, which suggests that they are individuated precisely in the way such statements (or propositions) are individuated. This in turn suggests that facts are themselves propositional in nature: they are not *of* this world because they are *about* this world. As Jonathan Bennett, a leading proponent of facts as causal relata puts this objection:

> Some people have objected that facts are not the sort of items that can cause anything. A fact is a true proposition (they say)—it is not something *in* the world but is rather something *about* the world, which makes it categorically wrong for the role of a puller and shover and twister and bender.[66]

Bennett's own response to this objection is a curious one. It is to deny that causes do any pushing and shoving:

> I grant that facts cannot behave like elbows in the ribs, but we know what items do play that role—namely, elbows . . . . When an explosion causes a fire, what happens is that molecules bump into other molecules, increasing their velocity to the point where they react rapidly with the ambient gases, etc. The idea that the pushing is done not by the molecules but by the explosion is just the afterglow of ignorance about what an explosion is.[67]

I take it the suggestion is that facts relate objects to universals, and those objects are certainly in the world; so facts about those objects are sufficiently world-connected to serve as causal relata.

Yet facts etc are not objects; they are the having of a property by an object. That objects are admittedly in the world thus goes no distance towards putting facts about objects in the world. Moreover, objects are not causes in any basic sense. As we have seen, idiomatic statements of objects as causes are always elliptical for something else as the true causal relata.

A better response to the objection by a fact-causation theorist is to take the objection to heart, and even augment it. The augmentation is this one: without regard to the 'in-the-worldness' of causation, facts are too propositional to do other work demanded of them. More particularly, facts cannot be what makes true statements true. Facts cannot play this role precisely because of their propositional nature; facts *are* true propositions. They thus do not have a sufficiently independent existence to *make* such statements true. Facts 'make' true statements true only in the trivial sense that the truth of a true statement 'makes' that statement true.

---

[65] Jonathan Schaffer put this as the argument from immanence: causes must be 'immanent', whereas facts are 'transcendent'. Schaffer, 'The metaphysics of causation', *Stanford Encyclopedia of Philosophy*, <http://www.plato.stanford.edu> (2003), 3.
[66] Bennett, *Events and Their Names*, 22. [67] Ibid, 22–3.

Needed are entities with greater distance from true propositions, entities whose nature is not propositional. Such entities are sufficiently in the world that they can make true propositions true and can figure in causal relations. Such entities are what David Mellor calls 'facta' and that Peter Menzies terms, 'real (as opposed to "abstract") situations'. Mellor generally defines 'facta' as 'entities . . . whatever they may be, whose existence or non-existence makes true statements true'.[68] Similarly, Menzies notes that states of affairs (his 'situations') are often conceived of as 'quasi-linguistic entities that are posited merely to provide extra-linguistic correlates to true statements'.[69] Yet like Mellor, he sees that behind these there must be 'real entities existing in their own right independently of language'.[70] Such real situations will exist 'whether or not there are any linguistic expressions to denote them'.[71]

On my view the fact-causation theorist has to grant the force of the 'too linguistic' objection to viewing states of affairs as causal relata.[72] This robs her of Bennett's kind of shrug off of the objection, and demands a response more like that of Mellor and Menzies. The fact-causation view then becomes the view that causal relata are not proposition-like entities; rather, they are non-propositional entities like facta and real situations. The trick then becomes one of specifying just what these entities are like.

So far we know only two things about such entities: (1) they are language-independent in the sense Menzies describes; and (2) yet they are individuated in very much the same fine-grained manner as are their linguistic analogues (ie, facts in the 'true proposition' sense). This of course is not nearly enough, but before we ask for more we should see if we can get these two minimal requirements together. It should be obvious that there is some tension between these two requirements.

There is nothing metaphysically suspicious about fine-grained individuation as such. Both Kimians about events, and tropists about properties, can defend fine-grained individuation on metaphysically respectable bases. Properties are finely individuated—at least as compared to the Davidsonian events that have them—and these two property-based schemes reflect this fact.

Suspicion is aroused when the fine-grained individuation is made to match exactly the individuation of true propositions ('facts' in the linguistic sense). For then it looks like one is simply positing the existence of an extra level of entities, stipulating that these entities are *not* linguistic while nonetheless urging that their boundaries are exactly those of linguistic entities. Such a suspicion is well-founded, for it is unlikely in the extreme that the vocabulary of predicates in a natural language like English contains all and only the predicates that

---

[68] Mellor, *The Facts of Causation*, 162.   [69] Menzies, 'A unified account', 68.
[70] Ibid.   [71] Ibid, 68–9.
[72] As do, for example, both David Armstrong, *A World of States of Affairs*, 116, and Kit Fine, 'First order modal theories III—Facts', Synthese 53 (1982), 43–122.

correspond to the underlying properties that really exist. Much more likely is that if there is such a match (of predicate to property), it is a manufactured match: properties are posited to exist when but only when there is a predicate naming them in English. But this position—what Armstrong accurately calls 'predicate nominalism'[73]—collapses the having of properties by a particular into a purely linguistic phenomenon having no independent reality. One might as well have stayed with facts in the linguistic sense (as true propositions)[74] and not invented 'facta' ('real situations') which merely duplicate the ontological triviality of facts.

Most sophisticated fact-causation theorists (such as Mellor, Fine, Armstrong, and Menzies) rightly reject predicate nominalism. For them, facta (real situations) are language independent entities that will not fit perfectly the facts (true propositions) with which they sometimes correspond; and, when there is such fit, it will be contingently so, and not necessarily so.[75] Now the question is, what are these real situations, or facta? What else can we say about their nature other than that they are language-independent?

David Armstrong tells us that such facta are themselves particulars, not universals,[76] and this seems right. The truth-maker for the sentence, 'the dog is now wet', is that particular dog having the property wetness at the time of utterance. Such having is itself a particular, distinct from the particular (the dog) that does the having. Such having is also distinct from the universal (wetness) that is had. As Armstrong puts it, the having on a particular occasion is a non-repeatable particular, whereas what is had is a repeatable universal.[77]

Still, there is an intimate relation between this dog having now the property of wetness, and the universal wetness. Spelling out this relation will spell out further the nature of facta. There are two possibilities here. One is to identify the having of the property as an instance of the property, that is, a trope. On this view, the facta that the dog is wet is to be identified as the instance of wetness that that dog has. The plausibility of this identification lies in the fact that tropes (like facta) can be sentential truth-makers: while the existence of the abstract universal (wetness) does not make the sentence ('the dog is wet') true, arguably the existence of this dog's wetness does. Mellor and Oliver:

The trope that is Socrates' wisdom ... is not just a constituent of the fact that Socrates is wise, that may also occur in other atomic facts. Arguably it *is* an atomic fact, since Socrates' wisdom corresponds neither to 'Socrates' nor to 'is wise' but to the whole atomic sentence 'Socrates is wise' ... What this trope does is make that proposition true. In short,

---

[73] David Armstrong, *Universals and Scientific Realism* (Cambridge: Cambridge University Press, 1978), Chapter 2.

[74] As does Bennett, for example, who individuates facts as propositions simpliciter: Bennett, *Events and Their Names*.

[75] Eg, Armstrong, *States of Affairs*, 128–9.   [76] Ibid, 126.

[77] Ibid, 127.

tropes are facts not only in the weak sense of corresponding to (or being) true propositions but in the strong sense of *making* propositions true.[78]

Despite this, we should resist the identification of facta with tropes. For there are in fact two very different metaphysical views here. On one—the non-trope theory of facta—our fundamental ontology is the traditional one, consisting of particulars (objects and events) and abstract universals; in addition, it contains an especially important universal, the relation (having, being, etc) of a particular to an abstract universal.[79] The instances of this important universal are facta. By contrast, the trope theory rejects the traditional ontology. What is basic are property-instances (tropes), out of which objects, events, and abstract universals are constructed. On the trope view of it facta would be the simple, basic constituents of our ontology; whereas on the non-trope view, facta are complex constituents consisting of a relation between particulars and universals.

To be sure, one can force-fit tropes and facta together. As Chris Daly recognizes, there have been two interpretations of tropes, a strong interpretation holding tropes to be fundamental and a weak one simply adding tropes to the traditional view of fundamental ontology.[80] And as Daly also recognizes, on the weak 'interpretation it might be held that a trope is a substance having a universal'.[81] Yet, on the weak interpretation, we lose what is interesting (and interestingly different) about tropes. There is a distinct metaphysics of tropes, and even if we ultimately reject it (either in general, or at least as figuring in an account of causal relata), we should do so on the merits and not by a sleight-of-hand identification concealing its true nature.

Leaving tropes alone, the second and better identification of facta is with Kimian events. A Kimian event, it will be recalled is an exemplifying of a property by an object at a time. Peter Menzies, for example, explicitly adopts Kim's account in his explication of facta ('real situations').[82] With some minor modifications this seems to me to be the right construal of facta.

One modification is to cede events to the Davidsonians. Kim's account then becomes an account of facta but not of events. This move allows another: expand the analysis so that it is not just *objects* that can exemplify properties; let any particular, be it an object or a (Davidsonian) event, be eligible for this role. This allows *aspects* of events to be reduced to facta (or to tropes), as we did before. Thirdly, one wants to avoid the set-theoretic interpretation of Kim, according to which facts would be ordered triples (of objects, properties, and times); as Menzies observes, this set-theoretic entity is abstract and not a likely candidate to belong to the causal order.[83] What one wanted as facta 'are *real* parts of the

---

[78] DH Mellor and Alex Oliver, 'Introduction', in *Properties* (Oxford: Oxford University Press, 1997), 18.

[79] Puzzlingly Armstrong denies that he need posit such a universal: Armstrong, *States of Affairs*, 127.

[80] Daly, 'Tropes', 141.　　　[81] Ibid.　　　[82] Menzies, 'A unified account', 69.

[83] Ibid, 70.

world...[that] stand in causal relations to each other and are the objects of perception'.[84]

Finally, one does not want to put too much weight on the *exemplifying* nature of the relation that constitutes facta. As Menzies recognizes, what we need to say is that such facta 'consists in a certain primitive and unanalysable relation' holding between particulars and abstract universals at a time.[85] One might call this an exemplifying relation, as do Menzies and Kim. One might equally well call it an *instantiation* relation, as does David Armstrong.[86] Or one might label it with any of the diverse labels Armstrong charts through the history of philosophy (Plato's *participation* of a particular in a universal, Strawson's *non-relational tie* between them, John Anderson's *copula*, etc).[87]

* * * *

This completes our taxonomic prolegomenon of possible causal relata. Notice that we have returned pretty much to the legal wisdom with which we began. This was that there are only two real candidates for causal relata, events and facts. Hopefully we have improved on this legal wisdom in the following ways: first a clarification of events so that they are to be understood in the Davidsonian way, and not in any of the other ways events can be understood; second, a clarification of facts such that we distinguish facta (as actual states of the world making true propositions true) from facts (as those true propositions themselves) (This will prove to be a significant distinction for the fact-causation view.); third, a further clarification of facts so as to distinguish both facta and facts from tropes. Tropes should be added to the list of possible relata, a fine-grained entrant that is distinct from events but is also distinct from equally fine-grained facts and facta. Such a tropist possibility tracks closely the facta possibility (because of their shared fine-grained mode of individuation), yet it is a distinct metaphysical possibility meriting separate attention. We shall next enquire, in the chapter following, which of these four possible causal relata, are actually what stands in the causal relation.

---

[84] Ibid.   [85] Ibid, 69.
[86] Armstrong, *States of Affairs*, 115.   [87] Ibid.

15

The Facts, Events, States of Affairs, and Tropes Debate

I. The Transcendence Worry

With the reductions of the previous chapter, we arrive at a four-way competition between facta, facts, tropes, and events as the true causal relata. Facts (true propositions) face a hard, uphill battle to be considered as causal relata. True enough, as we shall see, facts would have some significant advantages over events, tropes, and even facta. Specifically, it is facts and facts alone that allow disjunctive relations to exist between them so that overdetermination cases become easy to solve; it is facts and facts alone that make causation by omissions unproblematic, given the sense to be made of negative facts (unlike negative events, etc).[1] Yet these advantages are possessed by facts only because of their propositional nature. Propositions can be disjoined, they can be negated, and propositions can be about absences as well as presences. Yet the nagging fact remains that propositions are not in the world and causation is; propositions are only about the world. For me this is disqualifying of facts as causal relata.

Even Jonathan Bennett, perhaps the leading proponent of (propositional) facts as causal relata, seemingly recognizes that purely linguistic entities do no causal work. He criticizes Davidson for sloppily talking of *descriptions* of events, rather than of properties of events, as instantiating causal laws. Bennett rightly sees that 'events could cause others even if there were no descriptions, no languages', so we should think of 'moving from language to what language is about'.[2] Exactly: we should move from facts about the world, to the facta that facts are about.

It is often difficult to argue for what one regards as obvious—for what can one appeal to that is even more obvious? One can, perhaps, broaden the appeal of a seemingly obvious conclusion by showing how it is part of some plausible, more general view. I take it my strong sense of a category mistake (occurring when one speaks of propositions causing anything) is part of a genuinely realist view about causation. The only way I can imagine making sense of propositions as causal relata

---

[1] These are two of the advantages that convince Jonathan Bennett to adopt facts as causal relata. See his summary in Bennett, *The Act Itself* (Oxford: Clarendon Press, 1995), 41–2.
[2] Bennett, *Events and Their Names* (Indianapolis: Hackett Publishers, 1988), 51.

is by thinking that the relation itself is merely a constructed thing. Then, on such a constructivist view, whether there is a causal relation between any pair of things depends on the propositions we believe to be true—so propositions as relata are not odd when compared to the propositional nature of the relationship itself.

Yet if causation is a merely constructed notion, what would not be? This kind of question I once directed at some graduate students who, eager to 'neuroscientize' causation, regarded it as a secondary property: my question was, what would then be left to be a primary property?[3] Causation seems to be too basic a constituent of the world to be regarded as an explicit construction out of more basic beliefs.

Perhaps thorough-going constructivists in the philosophy of science can make sense of propositions as causes. Not being one, I cannot. So unless the advantages possessed by facts as relata are so overwhelming that we should give up realism about causation, I would rule out true propositions ('facts') as causal relata.

II. Identity Conditions

Some seek to use identity conditions for the various candidates of causal relata the way I just used the requirement of immanence, namely, as a disqualifier of certain candidates. There is a tendency in the literature of casting general aspersions at the lack of identity conditions for each of the various candidates. It is common in such discussions to regard the other fellow's preferred entities as too mushy to be taken seriously. In Roderick Chisholm's discussion of Davidsonian events, for example, Chisholm pooh-pooh's there being any answer to the question of what properties are essential to an event being the event that it is. About a particular act of strolling, would it be the same event if it had been strolled later, elsewhere, or by someone else?[4] Or consider Peter Geach's utter dismissal of identity conditions for facts: 'Nobody really has the faintest idea of what he means when he says, the proposition that p is the same as the proposition that q.'[5] David Mellor finds this objection to be so common in debates about causal relata that he cannot ignore it.[6]

In truth, identity conditions for events, facts, facta, and tropes are vague; but none of them are vacuous. I shall in any event assume in what follows that vagueness in identity conditions, although of course a problem, is equally so far each of the candidates for causal relata. I thus put aside this problem, as I earlier did other issues of general ontology.

---

[3] 'Causation', University of California at San Diego Philosophy Department Colloquium, 2001. Menzies and Price explore this possibility as they consider 'manipulation' accounts of causation such as Nancy Cartright's. See Menzies and Price, 'Causation as a secondary quality', British Journal for the Philosophy of Science 44 (1993), 187–203.

[4] Roderick Chisholm, 'States of sffairs again', Nous 5 (1971), 182.

[5] Peter Geach, *Logic Matters* (Berkeley: University of California Press, 1980), 176.

[6] David Mellor, *The Facts of Causation* (London: Routledge, 1995), 111.

III. Fit with Ordinary Language

As we saw in the last chapter, there is a systematic, unresolved ambiguity in the law of torts and crimes as to what can be causal relata. Not surprisingly, ordinary usage of causal idioms reveals the same ambiguity (not surprisingly, because the law's causal notions are closely related to ordinary common-sense views, as Hart and Honoré were at such pains to point out).[7] It is equally idiomatic to make event or fact causation statements. To see this requires that we isolate what are event-referring, and what are fact-referring, expressions in English. Fortunately that task was nicely done years ago by Zeno Vendler's well-regarded work.[8] The seemingly easy cases are where the items come readily labeled, as in: 'the warehouse fire event of yesterday', or 'the fact that the warehouse burned down yesterday'. The reference of the former statement is indeed an event—a particular fire—and the reference of the latter statement is indeed a fact—the having of the property, burned down, by an object (the warehouse) at a time (yesterday). Yet much of the time idiomatic English does not use the explicit 'fact/event' labels, and even when it does, the labels can be misleading. Consider 'the event that was the warehouse burning yesterday',[9] and 'the fact of his negligent navigation'.[10] The first labels a fact, and the second an event, despite the opposite labels being attached to the expressions referring to them.

 Why this is so takes us deep into English grammar. Briefly, the nominalization of the verb 'to burn' can be used in one of two ways. We can form a perfect nominal with this gerund, as in 'the burning of the warehouse yesterday'; or we can form an imperfect nominal, as in 'the warehouse burning yesterday'. Imperfect nominals, Vendler persuasively shows, name facts, whereas perfect nominals name events. This does not change by mislabeling. 'The event that was the warehouse burning yesterday' refers to the fact that the warehouse burned yesterday notwithstanding the event label; 'the fact of his negligent navigation' refers to the navigation event, not to the fact that it was negligent nor to any other fact.

 Once we see how English can be used to refer to facts or events, it seems obvious that either facts or events are idiomatically used as causal relata. Both 'the fire caused the explosion', and 'the fact that the fire was so hot caused the explosion to be as violent as it was', are perfectly good English. Indeed, it is perfectly idiomatic to mix facts and events in the same relation, as in 'the fact that

---

[7] HLA Hart and Tony Honoré, *Causation in the Law* (2nd edn, Oxford: Oxford University Press, 1985).
 [8] Zeno Vendler, 'Facts and events', in his *Linguistics in Philosophy* (Ithaca: Cornell University Press, 1967), 122–46.
 [9] Bennett's kind of example, *Events and Their Names*, 6.
 [10] From the Court of Appeals'; opinion in *The Empire Jamaica* [1955] 1 All ER 452, affirmed [1955] 3 All ER 60.

the fire was so hot caused the explosion', and 'the fire caused the explosion to be as violent as it was'.[11]

Given the equally idiomatic use of facts and events as causal relata, it might be tempting to think that fact-causation and event-causation statements both relate the same information. Yet they plainly do not. 'The hot fire caused the violent explosion', and 'the fact that the fire was so hot caused the explosion to be as violent as it was', do not tell us the same thing. The hotness of the fire and the violence of the explosion are not causally related by the first statement; that event-statement could be true even if the extraordinary heat of the fire had nothing to do with the violence of the explosion (eg, a fire of lesser heat would have sufficed to set off the explosive material); whereas the fact-causation statement tells us precisely that the heat of the fire and the violence of the explosion are causally connected: it was because the fire was so hot that the explosion was so violent.

A second temptation is to think that one can show one of these locutions to be more basic than the other simply as a matter of degrees of familiarity in ordinary English usage. Fact-causation theorists, for example, often treat event-causation statements as elliptical expressions of fact-causation statements. Both Mackie[12] and Bennett[13] urge that sometimes a speaker's ignorance of what exactly it was about the fire that caused the explosion, leads the speaker to the event idiom. Analogously, sometimes the perception that the audience does not need to know precisely what it was about the fire that caused the explosion, motivates the event locution. In either case, event-causation statements are elliptical stand-ins for some more informative fact-causation statement that makes the event causation statement true.

I easily grasp how one could come to the Mackie/Bennett thesis here if one already possessed sufficient reasons to believe fact-causation statements to be basic. (Indeed, this is where I end up myself by the end of the chapter.) Given that belief, one would of course cast about for some explanation for the idiomatic appropriateness of event-causation talk. But what I do not see is anything *in language use* that could establish the primacy of fact-causation talk. Of course, if event-cause talk were otherwise senseless (because causation is not a relation between events), then such talk should be construed as elliptical for talk that does make sense, viz, fact-causation talk. But on Bennett's own showing there is nothing on the surface of event-causation talk that shows it to be senseless. (Indeed, Bennett rejects Vendler's attempt to show just this.[14]) Some substantive argument is needed (about causation's requirements on its relata) to establish the senselessness of event talk, for ordinary language, like the law, seems to make perfectly good sense of it.

---

[11] As Bennett explores in detail. *Events and Their Names*, 21.
[12] JL Mackie, *The Cement of the Universe* (Oxford: Clarendon Press, 1980).
[13] Bennett, *Events and Their Names*.   [14] Ibid, 28–31.

It is true that I have myself refused to take very seriously talk of persons or objects causing this or that. I argued that such talk is elliptical for, 'some event or fact involving the person or object causing . . .'.[15] Yet this was not a purely usage-based argument: I found the idea of irreducible agency metaphysically mysterious and ultimately unintelligible. In addition, 'the bullet caused his death' pretty much wears on its sleeve what is usually meant: 'The striking of his body by the bullet caused his death' (allowing that in some cases what might be meant is that the victim's swallowing of the bullet caused his death). Event-cause statements do not analogously wear on their sleeve the fact-cause statements for which they are supposedly elliptical.[16] 'The fire caused the explosion' seems complete in itself, in no need of paraphrase; and if one wants to parse further, it is unclear how to proceed; was it the extraordinary heat of the fire, its suddenness, its size, or something else about it, that caused the explosion?

Analogously, we should put aside event-causation theorists' attempt to explain away the apparently idiomatic fact-causation talk. Donald Davidson famously urged that all statements about singular causal relations apparently using facts as causal relata, could be paraphrased away to statements about causal explanations using facts.[17] So when we speak of the particular heat of the fire causing the particular violence of the explosion, we are really saying that the fact that the fire was so hot *explains* why the explosion was so violent. While there are many problems with this paraphrase, that is not my point here. Rather, the point is that language use does not motivate the attempt at paraphrase, here no more than in reverse. Only if one had independent grounds to think that fact-causation statements are senseless if taken literally, would one cast about for some other sense to be made of them. Our language goes no distance in forcing us to any such paraphrase. This leaves us still looking for substantive argumentation about what are proper causal relata.

IV. Causation by Omission

As Jonathan Schaffer recognizes,[18] the main argument for linguistic facts (ie, true propositions) being causal relata stems from the ease they have in accommodating absences as being involved in causal relations. Many think that the omission to feed a starving person can be a cause of his death, just as surely as hitting him

---

[15] Michael Moore, *Placing Blame: A general theory of the criminal law* (Oxford: Clarendon Press, 1997), 353–6.

[16] This is disputed in John Watling, 'Are causes events or facts?', Proceedings of the Aristotelian Society 80 (1980), 168–70.

[17] Donald Davidson, *Essays on Actions and Events* (Oxford: Oxford University Press, 1980). For a critical examination of Davidson's paraphrasing of fact locutions into explanatory ones, see Peter Menzies, 'A unified account of causal relata', Australasian Journal of Philosophy 67 (1989), 64–7.

[18] Jonathan Schaffer, 'The metaphysics of causation', *Stanford Encyclopedia of Philosophy*, <http//: www.plato.stanford.edu> (2003), 4.

over the head can. If one shares this thought (that omissions can be causes), then it is easy to think that (linguistic) facts can do the causal work here. 'The fact that Jones did not feed Smith caused Smith's death', seems unproblematic. It is more difficult to conceive of an event (that is the not-feeding of Smith) that could supply the needed cause here. Thus the argument for (linguistic) facts as causal relata.

There are two points we need to consider. The first is whether absences ever can be causes. If they cannot, then it is no advantage (and indeed, it would seem a disadvantage) for the facts-as-relata view that it readily admits absences as causes. The second point is this: if absences can be causes, does the facta/trope view have any easier time admitting them to be such than does the event view? On the face of it, negative facta, negative tropes, and negative events all seem equally lacking in sense, in which event none of *these* views have any leg-up in making sense of absences as causes, however much advantage linguistic facts may have in this regard.

In Chapters 3, 5, 6, 13, and elsewhere I have assumed that omissions and other absent events cannot be either causes or effects. We shall have occasion to re-examine this conclusion in Chapter 18. For now, let us make alternative assumptions. Suppose, first, that there is no such thing as 'negative causation', ie, causation of or by absences. Such a state of affairs would favor facta, events, and tropes, and disfavor facts. This is because facts can so easily be negative that it would be a puzzle why there is no negative causation: if facts are the causal relata, and facts can easily be negative or positive, why cannot the causal relation take either kind of fact as its relata? Since my ultimate view is that there is no 'negative causation', this permissiveness of facts counts against them as relata.

But now make the alternative supposition: suppose absences can be causes and effects. Would that advantage facta, tropes, or events? The answer, prima facie, appears to be no. Because facta, tropes, and events are real entities, there is no obvious sense to be assigned to the view that an absent thing—be it trope, factum, or event—can be a singular cause. The advantage here seems to be only with linguistic facts, that is, true propositions. For facts can be about absences as well as presences, and if facts are causal relata then facts about absences seem quite unproblematic.

When we say, 'that Jones didn't throw the rope caused Smith to drown', the causal fact seems unproblematic. After all, the proposition that is the fact—that Smith did not throw the rope—is true and unproblematically exists. It is only as a non-propositional thing, be it a trope, a factum, or an event, that we have problems. Tropists seemingly need to make sense of negative properties so that there can be an instance of them; facta theorists seemingly need negative properties to exist as well, so that an object like Smith can have one at a certain time; event theorists seemingly need negative events. Negative events and negative properties are not happy particulars or universals, so omissive causation seems equally problematic for all such theorists.

It is only facts as true propositions that can easily accommodate the idea of omissive causation. Yet as I mentioned at the beginning of this chapter, this advantage of facts is purchased by just what disqualifies facts as causal relata, viz their propositional nature. It is only because facts are not in the world in general that one can be nonchalant with respect to facts about absenses not being in the world either. Yet to repeat where I began this chapter: I can make no sense of propositions (which are not in but are about this world) causing things to happen in this world.

The task for theorists of tropes, facta, and events is tricky. Many such theorists wish to make sense of our talk about omissive causation, yet they must do so without committing themselves to unsavory entities like negative events or negative properties actually causing things to happen. If one of such theorists has an easier time of this than the other, that would be an advantage for the theory. Facta theorists, for example, might claim an advantage here. David Armstrong analyzes apparently omissive causation in terms of 'second-order' facta, what he terms 'totality' facta.[19] Such facta are conjunctions of first order facta with the stipulation that they are *all* the facts present on a given occasion. An omission by Smith to throw the rope at *t* would then just be the proverbial hole in the donut: the relevant totality factum is all the facta involving Smith at *t* (which totality will thus *not* include a factum of Smith throwing a rope). It is this totality factum that then stands in a causal relationship to Jones' death. Similarly, David Mellor engages in an extensive reconstruction of the relationship between negative facts and truly existing (ie, positive) facta to try and make sense of omissive causation.[20]

My own take on such efforts is that they are both unnecessary and give no leg-up to the theories being defended. Preferable is the conclusion that failures to prevent and double-preventions are simply non-causal relationships of a counterfactual or probabilistic nature. They are themselves independent desert-bases, and thus need not rely on some ghostly 'causation' by negative events, negative properties, or artificial constructions of true (positive) events or properties. There is thus no demand placed on a theory of *causal* relata to account for such relations—other than the demand to make sense of such alternative relationships and the entities they relate in order to explain away a lot of loose 'causal' talk about omissions, preventions, and double-preventions.

This strategy is equally available to theorists of events, theorists of facta, and tropists. Each can equally explain away talk of 'causation' by omissions (simple failures to prevent) and of 'causation through omissions' (double-preventions). Whatever causal relata are—tropes, facta, or events—where they are absent, any

---

[19] Armstrong, *A World of States of Affairs* (Cambridge: Cambridge University Press, 1997), 196–201. Armstrong's hole-in-the-donut approach seemingly fails because all the positive (ie, real facta) true of some omitter are usually not casually relevant to the harm that omitter fails to prevent, so it is hard to see how the totality of such irrelevant facta can become causally relevant.

[20] Mellor, *The Facts of Causation*, 131–9, 156–69.

difference between them disappears; the absence of any of them equally allows the substitution of counterfactual analysis for causal analysis.

V. Disjunctive/Conjunctive Propositions, Disjunctive/ Conjunctive Properties or Events, and Promised Help for the Overdetermination Cases

As we have seen, the overdetermination cases pose significant problems for most theories of causation. A concurrent, overdetermination case is one whereby two or more causal factors are independently sufficient to produce some effect *e*. Two fires, each capable of burning down plaintiff's house by itself, join together and the resultant fire burns down the house. Each fire is therefore independently sufficient and only jointly necessary for *e*. Contrast this to what I call a garden-variety concurrent-cause case: two small fires, neither of which is independently capable of burning down plaintiff's house, join to form a fire which does burn down the house; here, each fire was therefore necessary and only jointly sufficient for *e*.

As we shall explore in detail in Chapter 17, the overdetermination variety of concurrent-cause cases pose obvious problems for the counterfactual theory of causation. On the counterfactual theory, for *c* to be the cause of *e c* must be necessary for *e*; the problem in the concurrent overdetermination case is that neither fire is necessary for *e*. But for the first fire, the second would have burned down the house, and but for the second, the first fire also would have burned down the house. In a word, neither fire was necessary to the house's destruction (although both fires together were jointly necessary).

A popular solution here is to aggregate the putative cause events into one larger event, the mereological sum of the two fire events. This larger event—let us call it 'the fires of April'—now satisfies the demands of the counterfactual theory, for the fires of April were necessary to the house destruction. This popular solution then refuses to answer questions about the separate fires causing the destruction; they cause such destruction only insofar as they are parts of a larger whole that causes such destruction.[21]

There are severe problems with this popular solution. To begin with, notice that the solution fails to distinguish the garden variety from the overdetermination variety of concurrent-cause cases. In both there is a larger event that is the mereological sum of the two fires, and in both this larger event is necessary to the house destruction. Yet the cases are plainly different, for in the garden-variety case we can meaningfully and truthfully say that each fire was a cause of the destruction (because each was necessary to the destruction). We then just

---

[21] For an example of this popular solution, see Mackie, *Cement of the Universe*, 46–7, who talks of indissoluble 'event-clusters' as causes.

arbitrarily deny sense to that question for the overdetermination variety of concurrent cause cases.

The obvious thing to do to distinguish these cases is to distinguish larger events that are *conjunctions* of smaller events, from larger events that are *disjunctions* of smaller events. In the garden-variety concurrent-cause case it is a larger event (conjunctive) that is necessary to the house's destruction, in which event each conjunctive part of that larger event is also necessary. In the over-determination variety concurrent cause case it is a larger event (disjunctive) that is necessary to the house's destruction, in which event neither disjunctive part of that larger event is necessary for the destruction.

The problem for event-causation theorists is that there is no obvious sense to be assigned to a disjunctive event. Mereology makes tolerable sense of 'con-junctive events'—these are larger events that are wholes of which smaller events are parts. But there is no mereology of disjunctions. Moreover, even if one could make sense of there being disjunctive events, it appears to violate de Morgan's Laws in logic to say what wants saying here (viz, that the larger event caused *e* while neither of the disjuncts making up the larger event caused *e*). If one makes sense of negating and disjoining events, then from not (fire$_1$) and not (fire$_2$), one should be able to infer not (fire$_1$ or fire$_2$), and vice versa. This means $(F_1 \cdot \sim F_2) \equiv \sim(F_1 \vee F_2)$. If the negation of this larger event is equivalent to the conjunction of the negations of each smaller event, one might well conclude that whatever is not true of each fire considered separately is not true of the larger event that is the disjunction of these fires. (The uncertainty here because there is no clear sense to be assigned to logical relations of negation, disjunction, conjunction, and equivalence attaching to events rather than propositions.)

It is at this point that fact-causation theorists such as Jonathan Bennett promise some help. As he puts it, 'Move to fact causation and all is clear': the house was destroyed 'because *at least one*' of the fires occurred.[22] 'There is no unique event corresponding to the fact that at least one of the' fires occurred. On the other hand, there is such a unique fact: 'facts, being propositional, can be disjoined, conjoined, negated....This lets what we say in the language of facts, including fact causation, be more refined that the coarse "events" idiom can manage.'[23]

Bennett is right about facts. A disjunctive fact, made up of two lesser facts disjunctively related, makes perfectly good sense. Moreover, there is no violation of de Morgan's Laws in the following fact-statement: 'The fact that either fire$_1$ or fire$_2$ occurred was necessary for the house destruction, while neither the fact that fire$_1$ occurred, nor the fact that fire$_2$ occurred, was necessary to the house destruction.'

The problem for the fact-causation solution here is the general problem with fact-causation: it is purely propositional. As with negative facts, disjunctive facts

---

[22] Bennett, *The Act Itself*, 41.   [23] Ibid.

make the sense they do only because they are propositional in nature. But again, that means that such facts are not in the world and involve an unacceptably magical causation.

If one thinks (as I do) this is flat-out disqualifying, the question then is whether facta and trope theorists can reap the benefits of Bennett's fact solution here without paying the 'magic-causation' costs. As with negative facts, the answer is again no. Disjunctive properties make no more sense than disjunctive events;[24] this makes disjunctive property-instances (tropes) and disjunctive property exemplifyings (facta) equally problematic. Facta and tropes are in exactly the same boat with events: none of them are propositional in nature, so none of them can reap the benefits of Bennett's facts.

VI. Preserving the Limited Transitivity of Causation

Some philosophers regard transitivity to be a bedrock feature of causation and have skewed their theories of the nature of that relation accordingly. David Lewis was of this view, forcing him to some elaborate maneuvers in analyzing (transitive) causation by the non-transitive relation of counterfactual dependence.[25] Holding this 'bedrock view' of transitivity has similarly influenced theories of causal relata. Douglas Ehring: 'transitivity is a fundamental logical feature of the causal relation, along with irreflexivity and perhaps asymmetry'.[26] Since this leads Ehring to the view that 'causal transivity should be disavowed only as a last resort',[27] he uses transitivity as his Archimedean point from which he fashions a theory of causal relata.

The way that causal transitivity is thought to impact upon the debate about causal relata goes like this: suppose some event *c* causes another event *d*, and that *d* in turn causes a third event *e*. By transitivity, since *c* caused *d* and *d* caused *e*, *c* caused *e*. Yet what if *c* is the biting off of my right forefinger, *d* is my pressing the button on the detonator of a bomb with my left-forefinger, and *e* is the detonation of the bomb.[28] One might think that *d* was caused by *c* because, as a right-hander, I would have pressed the detonator with my right hand had the dog not bitten off that finger; one surely does think that pressing the detonator caused the bomb to go off; so (by transitivity) the dog biting off my left forefinger caused the explosion. Now the argument against Davidsonian events as causal relata, and in favor of tropes or facta: surely the causal conclusion above is absurd; in no sense was the dog bite a cause of the explosion. If transitivity is held constant, then the premise leading to such absurdity must be the assumption that the effect

[24] Armstrong so argues in his *Universals* (Boulder: Westview Press, 1989), 82–3.
[25] Maneuvers we shall examine in Chapter 17.
[26] Ehring, *Causation and Persistence*, 82.   [27] Ibid.
[28] The example is from Michael McDermott, 'Redundant causation', British Journal of the Philosophy of Science 46 (1995), 531.

of the dog bite is the very same thing as the cause of the bomb going off. If these are different things, then there need be no failure of transitivity in order to deny the absurd conclusion. Facta or trope theorists can hold these to be different things; on these theories, what the dog bite caused was not the whole event of the button-pushing (d) but only a having (or an instancing) of a property of that event, the property of being a left-handed button-pushing (d′); and the having (or instancing) of that property was not causally relevant to the explosion because the actor still would have pushed the button with his right hand had his left not been injured. The property relevant to causing the explosion was simply the property of being a button-pushing (d). Since d $\neq$ d′, there need be no violation of transitivity in denying that c caused e.[29]

Davidson's response to this argument was to bite the bullet: admit that c does (singularly) cause e in these kind of cases. But then, the oddity of saying so is attributed to the non-explanatory role of c's for e's: we do not explain explosions by dog bites. Causal explanations, according to Davidson, are much more selective in what can explain what, than are causal relations between particular events.[30]

Many philosophers, myself included, have found this response puzzling.[31] If the dog-bite did cause the explosion, then why is it not appropriate to explain the explosion, at least in part, by citing the occurrence of the dog bite? Must not causal *explanations* track closely causal *relations*? How can causal explanations be so intensional if causal relations are not? This puzzle is heightened by Davidson's insistence that causation is necessarily explanatory.[32]

I will assume the Davidsonian flight to explanations is unavailable. If this is right, then holding onto transitivity seems to mean rejecting whole events as causal relata. We should thus see whether we wish to hold on to the bedrock assumption that causation is a transitive relation.

One sense in which causation is not transitive has been explored by lawyers since Francis Bacon. The law for hundreds of years has required causes to be 'proximate' to be causes at all in legal contemplation. Factors that are spatially/temporally remote from some harm are not held to be causes of that harm, no matter how clearly necessary they might be to the harm occurring.

As we saw in Chapter 5, there is a plausible metaphysics underlying these legal doctrines of proximate causation. If one assumes that causation is scalar and that every event has multiple causes, then the more layers of events there are between an effect and its putative cause, the less the putative cause contributes to the effect

---

[29] For use of transitivity against Davidsonian events as causal relata, see Ehring, *Causation and Persistence*, 76–7; LA Paul, 'Aspect causation', Journal of Philosophy 97 (2000), 240–2; Daniel Hausman, 'Thresholds, transitivity, overdetermination, and events', Analysis 52 (1992), 156–63.

[30] Davidson, *Actions and Events*, 161.

[31] See, eg, Peter Menzies, 'A unified account of causal relata', Australasian Journal of Philosophy 67 (1989). 64–7.

[32] As Douglas Ehring explores in *Causation and Persistence*, 72–3.

vis-à-vis the contribution of other factors. At some point such a factor's contribution becomes de minimis so that we would not count it as a cause at all. If space/time remoteness is a pretty good proxy for layers of intervening events, then one can see the proximate cause doctrines as laying out a plausible metaphysics: causation peters out so that even though c causes d, d causes e, e causes . . . . n, yet for some n, c will not cause n.

Ned Hall sees clearly this sense in which causation may be non-transitive, yet finds such non-transitivity to be 'benign' because the alleged failures of transitivity in the examples devised by Paul, Ehring, McDermott, and Hausman seem to occur between closely linked series of events, not remote ones where gradual attenuation could explain the failure of transitivity.[33] Undiscussed by Hall is the following possibility: once we see that causation can peter out over time because of its scalarity, surely we should also see that some non-remote factors can also be so de minimis in the degree of their causal contribution (vis-à-vis their competitors at any one time) as to not be causes too. At some point in what I call the asymmetrical, concurrent, overdetermination cases, for example, a very small fire (wound, flood, noise, etc) that joins a much larger fire (wound, flood, noise, etc), the resulting fire causing an indivisible injury, is too *de minimis* in the degree of its causal contribution to be called a cause of the injury.

Seeing this then allows a Davidsonian about relata to deny causation across short chains in McDermott-like counter-examples. The dog bite was a cause of the explosion in the sense that it contributed to it; only, it was a de minimis contributor, below the threshold for any factor to be a cause. The dog bite was a de minimis contributor to the explosion because it was an *almost de minimis* contributor to the button-pushing—it just took one more set of other factors contributing to push it below the threshold for cause. It is transitivity thus that fails, not Davidson's whole events view of causal relata.

Notice one thing that is not being said here. When c is a big cause of d and d is a big cause of e, c cannot be only a *de minimis* contributor to e. If we could quantify degrees of causal contribution, suppose the dog bite was a 30 per cent contributor to the button pushing, and the button pushing, an 80 per cent contributor to the explosion; then seemingly the dog bite must be a 24 per cent contributor to the explosion, well over any plausible *de minimis* threshold.[34]

So the defense of Davidson turns on the initial link in the chain being a weak one, so weak that it is just above the *de minimis* threshold. One may well have just such a sense about the dog bite causing the button pushing. It is important to see why this is so: notice the dog bite prevents the use of my right hand and thus (given that I only have two hands) only in that sense 'causes' my left-handed button pushing. What we should say about such an example (once we adopt the view that preventings are not causings) is that transitivity is not in issue; c is only

[33] Ned Hall, 'Causation and the price of transitivity', Journal of Philosophy 97 (2000), 203.
[34] Ibid.

a preventer, not the cause, of *d*, so that even though *d* is the cause of *e* we have no reason to expect *c* to be the cause of *e*.

As Ned Hall shows in detail,[35] many of the supposed examples where fine-grained theorists hope to gain a leg-up on course-grained theorists (from apparent failures of transitivity from which only fineness of grain can rescue one) involve preventions and double-preventions in one of their links. Yet not all do. Consider this well-worn example of Jim Woodward: *c* = adding potassium salts to combustible materials, *d* = a fire of a certain purple hue, and *e* = the death of Elvis in the fire.[36] If we assume (probably contrary to the chemistry) that the potassium salts added no heat to the fire but only gave it its purple color, then the fine-grained theorist wants to say that *c* caused *d*, *d* caused *e*, yet *c* manifestly did not cause *e*.[37]

This time neither link of the causal chain is a case of prevention or double-prevention. The adding of the potassium salts contributed to the fire (by making it the fire it was, viz a purple fire) and the fire contributed to Elvis' death through known causal processes. Yet it is difficult to think that the adding of the salts caused Elvis's death. Ergo, if cause is transitive, then the fire as a whole event is not the correct relata; what the salts caused was a property of the fire, its purple color, but what caused Elvis' death was not that property of the fire but another property, viz the heat of the fire.

A Davidsonian may again feel some suspicions about the first link in this claim. Maybe it is already so close to being *de minimis* that but one more link sufficiently attenuates its contribution that it no longer is a cause. Yet is such suspicion not grist for the fine-grained theorist's mill? Is it not based on the thought 'the color of a fire is not one of its important properties so the event which gives the fire its color—the addition of potassium salts—is not very important either'. Yet surely 'importance' here is context-dependent: the color of the fire is not here important because the color of the fire was causally inert with respect to Elvis' death; whereas if Elvis died because, for example, he was so unfamiliar with purple fires that he failed to recognize the danger this one presented, then the color of the fire is one of its 'important' properties. What is doing all the work, of course, is just what the fine-grained theorist says should be doing the work: it is a *property* of the fire (not the fire itself) that is the effect of adding potassium salts, and it is a *property* of the fire (not the fire itself) that causes Elvis' death. When these are one and the same property (as in the last variation), transitivity is met, and when these are not the same properties (as in the original version), transitivity is not challenged. If what is *de minimis* by way of causal contribution is tied to the importance of properties in this way, then this *de minimis* defense collapses into the fine-grained view of causal relata.

[35] Ned Hall, 'Causation and the price of transitivity'.
[36] James Woodward, 'A theory of singular causal explanation', *Erkenntuis* 212 (1984), 231–62.
[37] Eg, Douglas Ehring, *Causation and Persistence*, 76.

Even the limited transitivity of the causal relationship thus proves to be a strong argument in favor of one of the fine-grained, property-oriented theories of causal relata. The course-grained theorists is committed either to asserting there to be implausible causal connections in order to preserve transitivity (Davidson's view) or to conceding that causation is not transitive even in the diminishing sense used here. The fine-grained theorists, by contrast, can explain why transitivity is not challenged in these cases.

It has been urged recently that the fine-grained theorist also cannot accommodate all of the apparent failures of transitivity (with her device of discovering different properties of an intermediate event). Consider, Ned Hall tells us, a variation of the dog-bite example: suppose the dog bite causes the would-be bomber to forego pressing the detonator button at all, with either hand; rather, what it causes is for him to order someone else to press the button; the order causes in turn the orderee to press the button which causes the bomb to detonate.[38] Hall's point: there is no property of the order in virtue of which it is the effect of the dog bite, different from a property of the order in virtue of which it is the cause of the explosion; so transitivity should lead us to conclude that the dog bite caused the explosion, which seems counterintuitive.

Consider a like example of Jonathan Schaffer's:

Suppose that the boulder begins to roll down the hill towards the hiker's head (c), which causes the hiker to duck (d), which in turn causes the hiker to survive (e). It seems that c causes d and that d causes e, yet it does not seem that c causes e or that slicing up d into different features or aspects or whatever will help.[39]

Such examples are intended to put the fine-grained theorist in the same pickle as is the course-grained theorist: either admit there is no transitivity to causation even in the diminishing sense,[40] or bite the bullet with Davidson and say there is causation through these chains.

My own view is that the fine-grained theorist does not lose the advantage here. Notice that both the revised dog-bite example, and the hiker example, do not challenge transitivity. The revised dog-bite example still involves a prevention, not a causing in its first link. The dog bite does not cause the order; it only prevents the button-pushing, which would have caused the explosion but it did not. Likewise, the ducking does not cause the hiker to survive; rather, the ducking prevents the hiker's death (and only in that sense does it 'cause' his survival). So for this reason no transitivity should be expected in these cases, and the fine-grained theorist has no burden to use her different-property device to account for this supposed lack of transitivity.

---

[38] Hall, 'Causation and the price of transitivity', 205.
[39] Schaffer, 'The metaphysics of causation', 7.
[40] The conclusion towards which such examples direct Chris Hitchcock. See his 'The intransitivity of causation revealed in equations and graphs', Journal of Philosophy 98 (2001), 273–99.

To be sure, if one holds a view about causation linking it to counterfactual dependence, so that cases of prevention and double-prevention are seen as causal, then the fine-grained view of relata does not rescue transitivity, and the Hall/Schaffer examples show this. This undoubtedly is a worry for fine-grained theorists who are also counterfactualists about the causal relation.[41] But if one rejects the counterfactual account of causation, as I urge in Chapter 17, then the limited transitivity of the causal relationship does argue strongly for some fine-grained view of causation's relata.

VII. The Implications of the Feature-driven Nature of Singular Causation

In addition to transitivity, the major feature of the causal relation arguing for fine-grained relata is its feature-driven nature. The basic idea is that properties have something to do with singular causation because causal laws are framed in terms of such properties; so a natural inference to draw is that causal relata are simply properties—not the universals themselves, but either the having of them (the states of affairs view) or the instances of them (the trope view).

This argument is usefully divided into four ideas: (1) every singular causal relationship is backed by a true causal law; (2) true causal laws connecting types of events will use some but not all the properties of those events; (3) singular causal relationships between whole events will therefore be 'feature-driven', that is, the causal relationships between two particular events will hold only in virtue of those events possessing the features required by the relevant causal law; and (4) if causation is feature-driven in this way, then the best explanation for why this is so is because the relata of the relationship are those features and not the events that possess them. I shall proceed by considering each idea in turn.

A. There is no singular causal relations without some general law

One can be a dedicated singularist about causation and not disagree with the first idea set forth immediately above. Singularism is not the view—at least it need not be the view—denying that for every singular causal relation there exists a true causal law. What singularism denies is a (broadly) Humean reductionism: that what is basic are causal laws connecting types of events, and that singular causal statements are misleading expressions of those laws (together with space/time locators of their instances). What singularism asserts is that there is (Hume to the contrary notwithstanding) a 'cement of the universe'—that is, causal relationships between particulars, that these relationships are basic, and that laws are derived inductively from these.

---

[41] As for example, Laurie Paul. See Paul, 'Aspect causation'.

So the idea that causal laws always accompany causal relations is available for the singularist no less than for the Humeans, neo-Humeans, probabalists, and counterfactualists about causation. The main reason for accepting the idea lies in our common experience. If this match lights (when struck, dry, etc), our experience gives us every reason to believe that other matches of exactly the same composition in exactly the same circumstances will do exactly the same thing, namely light. This experience inclines us to accept that, if 'striking this match in conditions c caused it to light' is true, then 'striking matches in conditions c causes them to light', is also true.

Despite this common experience, some philosophers are so rabidly singularist that they wish to deny the omnipresence of causal laws accompanying singular causal statements. In modern philosophy the best-known expositor of this denial is Elizabeth Anscombe.[42] As is true for me in moral philosophy, so here: considering an Anscombean argument against a view usually convinces me of that view. On the assumption that others share my negative reaction to Anscombean excesses, I shall consider her arguments by way of defending the view she is arguing against.

First, there is the question of who has the burden of proof. Anscombe attempts to shift it to philosophers (such as Donald Davidson) who believe causal relations presuppose causal laws:

It is over and over again assumed that any singular causal proposition implies a universal statement running, 'Always when this then that' . . . Even . . . Davidson will say, without offering any reason at all for saying it, that a singular causal statement implies *that there is* such a true universal proposition—though perhaps we can never have knowledge of it. Such a thesis needs some reason for believing it![43]

Anscombe dismisses in a sentence the common experience referred to above: ' "Regularities in nature": that is not a reason.'[44]

Why not, one wants to say. Perhaps because Anscombe believed that common experience also contains within it the experience of coming up short-handed when we try to produce good examples of laws behind singular causal statements we are confident are true: 'we often know a cause without knowing whether there is an exceptionless generalization . . .'[45] and, she elsewhere adds,[46] without knowing what the content of such a generalization might be. Consider in this regard causal accounts of why certain historical figures acted as they did—why did Henry VIII marry so frequently, for example. William Dray's familiar contention was that we often know things like why Henry did what he did

[42] GEM Anscombe, *Causality and Determination* (Cambridge: Cambridge University Press, 1971). I have in the text quoted from the excerpted portion of this lecture/booklet in Ernest Sosa and Michael Tooley (eds), *Causation* (Oxford: Oxford University Press, 1993), and the page references are to this excerpt.
[43] GEM Anscombe, *Causality and Determination*, 104.
[44] Ibid.　　　[45] Ibid.
[46] Ibid, 104.

without knowing, or having any confidence that there are, laws of psychology to which Henry's behavior conformed.[47] Yet to my mind Peter Hempel always had the better of it on these kinds of examples:[48] people are not as boring as protons, to be sure, but there are laws governing their behavior—not Toynbee's grandiloquent laws of history, but perhaps quite precise laws that neuroscience holds promise of discovering, and in any case a lot of probabilistic laws folk wisdom already has discovered.

So Anscombeans need some arguments, common experience *not* putting the burden of proof on the other side. Anscombe herself appears to have relied on three arguments. First, there is a quibble about *exceptionless* universal statements. Science continually refines its generalizations as it encounters exceptions in which the generalizations, if unqualified and exceptionless, are untrue. Science also presupposes that much else is held constant when it connects two or a few types of events in a single law. So, accurate statements of causal laws must include *ceteris paribus* clauses (the stipulation of 'in normal conditions'). Anscombe: 'That fact makes generalizations running "Always…" merely fraudulent…'.[49]

Surely the holistic and incomplete nature of scientific knowledge goes no distance towards establishing the non-existence of generalizations. Continuous refinements as we learn more should make one optimistic, not pessimistic, about there being such generalizations. The interdependence of scientific generalizations merely shows us that we put our epistemic trousers on one leg at a time, just like real trousers; it does not reveal us to be naked, ie to be without trousers altogether. Moreover, the most these observations could show us is something about the *form* that laws take—perhaps they are probabilistic, not universal; that is hardly to show that there are no laws at all.

Anscombe's second argument is subject to the same rejoinder. She relies on quantum physics to show that causes do not necessitate their effects and that therefore there can be no universal laws.[50] Okay—if that is how one reads contemporary physics, then there are probabilistic laws.

Anscombe lastly argues that we can directly observe singular causal relations and that therefore we have no need to rely on observations of constant conjunction in order to know what causes what.[51] Yet even if one swallows this hogchoker of a premise, that only would eliminate one reason for believing in the existence of causal laws behind singular causal relations. Such argument does not eliminate other reasons, still less does it constitute an argument the other way.

I conclude that Anscombe gives us no reason to doubt what I take to be a deliverance of common experience: behind every singular causal relation there

---

[47] William Dray, 'The historical explanation of actions reconsidered', in S Hook (ed), *Philosophy and History* (New York: New York University Press, 1963).
[48] Carl G Hempel, 'Reasons and covering laws in history', in S Hook (ed), *Philosophy and History*.
[49] Anscombe, *Causality and Determination*, 94.　　[50] Ibid, 101–3.
[51] Ibid, 92.

exists some true causal law. Given our experience, there being no reason to doubt it gives us some reason to believe it.

B. Not every property of causes or effects will figure in a law

If there are laws behind causal relationships, then the relata of those laws will be types of whatever those entities are that are the relata of singular causal relationships. Suppose the latter are whole events. Then causal laws will relate types of events. Yet events are instances of many types—indeed, as many types as there are properties of particular events. The striking of a match is not only a striking event; it is also an often-talked about event in the philosophy of science since Nelson Goodman, it is often a finger-moving, often a candle-lighting, etc. It is, as Douglas Ehring correctly observes, 'wildly implausible' to think that all of an event's properties are causally relevant and thus equally implausible to think that all types defined by such properties are covered by a causal law.[52] A match's price, for example, has nothing to do with its propensity to light when struck. We thus arrive easily at the second step of the argument: if causal relata are whole events, then it is some but not all of the properties of those events that figure in the causal laws necessarily accompanying each singular causal relation.

C. Singular causal relations are feature-driven

Third, if causal relata are whole events, then such events are causes in virtue of their possessing just those properties that figure in the necessarily accompanying causal laws. This is the idea that many philosophers call the 'feature-driven' nature of causal relata.[53] The idea is that it is not incidental that the things that are causal relata either are, or at least possess, features allowing causal laws to exist. Rather, what makes something be a cause is that it either is, or possesses features described by, a causal law.

Imagine the alternative with respect to events as causal relata. Suppose whole events could cause other whole events, yet there was no feature of the first by virtue of which such relationship held. This is more difficult to picture than the view just rejected, viz that *all* of an event's features are causally relevant and figure in some causal law. For here, the view would be that an event would have certain features which would figure in a causal law, yet the event's status as a cause of another event would in no way depend on those causally relevant features. This seems to suggest that the event could be a cause of some other event without such features, yet if the relevant causal law is true, how could that be?

---

[52] Ehring, *Causation and Persistence*, 77.		[53] Eg, ibid, 28.

D. That causal relata are features (and not the events that have them) best explains the feature-driven nature of the causal relation

So far we have not said anything with which a Davidsonian about relata need disagree, nor, for that matter, have we said anything with which Donald Davidson did disagree. What Davidsonians must resist is this fourth and final step: if causal relata must be feature-driven, then such relata are simply to be identified as those features. I find this quite intuitive: why is it not simplest to identify the relata as those features, and not as the whole events which have such features? Why is the driver (of a feature-*driven* relation like causation) not the better candidate for cause, rather than the passenger or vehicle driven? Less metaphorically: if what makes an event a cause of some other event is some feature that first event possesses, then why is the feature not really the cause? On the feature-driven view of causality, it is the feature that imparts to the event its causal character, so it is the feature that, at the most basic level, must be the cause.

The only reason that occurs to me not to draw this inference would be the thought 'but features are universals and universals cannot stand in singular causal relationships'. Yet we have seen two candidates for causal relata that are not universals and can fit the bill here: instances of properties (tropes), and the having of properties (states of affairs). Unless for reasons of general ontology one can deny that such things exist, they seem better candidates for causal relata than whole events.

Douglas Ehring advances a different argument against Davidson on this issue, an argument that is less intuitive and more systematic. Ehring urges that Davidson's acceptance of the feature-driven nature of causation and of whole events as causal relata, forces him to accept what Ehring calls the 'in virtue of' assumption: (whole event) c causes (whole event) e only if there is some property F of c in virtue of which c causes e.[54] And, Ehring concludes, the 'in virtue of' assumption ensures that Davidsonians must give up transitivity; in cases where c causes d in virtue of some property F, but d causes e in virtue of some property G, then there is no property in virtue of which c causes e—so it does not, and transitivity fails.

This argument, of course, is not independent of the argument of the preceding section. The force of each depends entirely on the need to hang onto the transitivity of causation. What Ehring's argument adds is a reason buttressing common intuition that c does not cause e in the class of cases considered: c cannot cause e, on the 'in virtue of' assumption.

VIII. Tropes or States of Affairs?

If we accept a fine-grained view of causal relata as against the whole events view, that leaves the question of which fine-grained view we should accept. Are causes

---

[54] Ehring, *Causation and Persistence*, 72 (this is not how Ehring formulates the assumption).

and effects property-instances, or are they the havings of such properties by an event? The issue is one on which a theorist on causation need have no strong views. To be sure, there are theorists in either camp who claim the contrary. David Mellor, for example, urges that only property exemplifications ('facta') yield the kinds required for there to be the chance-raisings by particulars that is the essence of the causal relation for Mellor.[55] Douglas Ehring, to take a contrasting example, urges that only tropes can fit the bill in his trope-persistence theory of the causal relation; this, because only tropes have sufficient particularity that their persistence through time is a significant fact (whereas exemplifyings are universals that of course persist through time).[56]

The difference between tropes and states of affairs are fine enough to doubt either of these claims. As to Mellor, the tropist metaphysical program in general claims to be able to aggregate classes of trope-particulars through some primitive resemblance relation, and then do anything with such classes that a realist about universals can do (such as frame probabilistic laws). As to Ehring, a states-of-affairs theorist surely can regard each exemplifying of a property by an object at a time as a particular, so that although the exemplifying relation itself is a universal, individual exemplifyings are sufficiently robust particulars that an 'exemplifying-persistence' theory of causation would not lack significance.

The choice between tropes and states of affairs as causal relata is thus not guided by the demands of the causal relation. Rather, the motives for adopting one or the other view lie in more general issues of ontology. Those who favor the traditional ontology of particulars and universals will favor states of affairs; those with more revolutionary ambitions will favor the nominalist ontology of ardent tropism. This is not an issue we need to resolve here, although my sympathies are with the traditionalists on this one.

IX. Epilogue

We now need to close the circle by returning to the point at which we began. If states of affairs—facts in the non-linguistic sense, or 'facta'—are the real relata of the singular causal relation, how are we to explain the completely idiomatic talk of event, as well as of fact, causation? When legal systems frame their liability requirements in terms of events, how are we to make sense of such laws (given that events are not causal relata)? We thus need to close with some account of how event-cause talk can be made sense of in terms of states-of-affairs-cause talk.

There would seem to be two possibilities here. One I shall call *holistic*. This asks of a given event, how many of its properties are causally relevant to the happening of some other event. If enough of them are—'enough' as measured by

---

[55] Mellor, *The Facts of Causation*, 180–2.
[56] Ehring, *Causation and Persistence*, 13, 100.

some quantitative threshold—then the (whole) event that has such properties may be called a cause of the subsequent event. The possibility is called holistic because it looks at all properties an event may possess to assess whether it is appropriate to use event-cause language.

The second possibility I shall call *contextual*. This asks of a given event, are any of its properties causally relevant to the happening of some other event? If there is at least one such property, then the (whole) event that has such property may be called a cause of the subsequent event. This possibility is called contextual because the fact that makes it appropriate to use event-cause talk is that it is inappropriate in certain contexts to say more than that some property of an event (without saying which one) is causally relevant.

Notice that a similar ambiguity pervades our notion of similarity. When we say that one object x is similar to another object y, we might mean: of all the properties possessed by the two objects, enough of them are shared—'enough' measured by some threshold—that we should adjudge them to be similar. Alternatively, we may mean: in the context in which this comparison is being made, some one property (or a small set) is the dimension along which similarity is to be assessed, and if x and y share this property then they are similar.

In the context of assessing David Lewis' use of a similarity metric for measuring the closeness of possible worlds to the actual world, I shall suggest in Chapter 16 that 'similar' in ordinary speech is almost always—and maybe always—used in the contextual manner, not the holistic manner. Similes, metaphors, analogies, colloquially qualitative identities, are all assessed relative to one property (or a small set of properties), the property often being implicit in the context of utterance.

The same is true of event-cause talk. When we say, 'the navigation caused the ships' collision',[57] we are not saying that there is some sufficient number of properties of the navigation-event that are causally relevant to the collision to justify us in ascribing the collision to the navigation. Rather, we are saying that there is at least one property of the navigation that caused the collision to have at least one of its properties.

In ordinary speech outside the law, we appropriately use event-cause talk in two situations. We may be ignorant of the causally relevant properties of an event, even though we are sure there are such. Or, our audience may not need the extra information of which property of some event is causally relevant, so it would be Griceanly inappropriate to tell them more than they needed to know or wanted to hear. Event-cause talk can be as usefully elliptical for states-of-affairs-cause talk as object-cause talk can be for event-cause talk.[58]

Legal-liability rules framed in terms of event-cause talk, if they are appropriate, are appropriate for the second sort of reason. As a matter of legal policy, one

---

[57] This is *The Empire Jamaica* example, with which we began Chapter 14, above.
[58] Watling, 'Are causes events or facts?'.

might favor a minimal causal requirement connecting a defendant's act to some harm: if any property of that act caused any aspect of that harm, then the defendant is prima facie liable for that harm. Rather than saying this explicitly, a liability rule might more economically (if elliptically) simply say: 'if the defendant's act caused the harm, then he is liable'.

Notice that nothing in the true metaphysics of causal relata makes illegitimate a legal rule framed in terms of event-causes. Such talk may be derivative of the metaphysically more basic states of affairs talk, but that hardly renders its use suspect in liability rules. Of course, the opposite is also true: nothing in the true metaphysics of causal relata precludes a more stringent causal requirement being framed by rules requiring that a particular property of a defendant's act be the causally relevant one to connect him to a certain harm. It is commonly urged, for example, that it must be that aspect of the defendant's action that made it negligent for him to perform it that must be causally connected to the harm.[59] If it is the lack of labeling of rat poison that makes it negligent to place the rat poison in the kitchen on the shelf next to a stove, then it must be that property of his act that causes the death of the victim; that *some* property of his act (such as it being a placement of phosphorus-containing rat poison next to heat) is causally relevant to the death is not enough.[60]

Which of these liability rules is to be preferred is not settled by the metaphysics of causal relata.[61] Because we can make sense of both event-cause talk and states-of-affairs-cause talk, either option is open, and other kinds of arguments are required to settle it. For the kinds of reasons advanced in Chapters 8 and 9, the law should favor an event-cause requirement over its more stringent alternative, at least in negligence cases.

---

[59] Eg, Richard Wright, 'Causation in tort law', California Law Review 73 (1985), 1735–828.

[60] The *Larrimore* example of the previous chapter. *Larrimore v. American National Ins Co*, 184 Okla 614, 89 P 2d 340 (1939).

[61] Of course, if the correct metaphysics of causal relata showed one of these forms of talk to lack sense, then that would be reason enough for law and morality to eschew such talk, no matter how idiomatic. My initial impetus for engaging in this inquiry was indeed the suspicion that fact or aspect cause talk made no metaphysical sense. Some of the colleagues thanked in the Preface have convinced me of the errors of my ways.

PART VI

THE METAPHYSICS OF THE CAUSAL RELATION

16
Counterfactual Conditionals

I. Introduction

In this and the succeeding chapters of Part VI we try on the other leg of the 'trousers' described in Chapter 14. We move from the nature of things related by causation to the nature of the relationship itself. In the first two chapters of Part VI, this and the following chapter, I focus on one theory of the causal relationship, the counterfactual theory. I start here for three reasons, one legal, one moral, and one metaphysical.

The law-related reason for this focus is the dominance of the counterfactual test in tort and criminal law, at least as that law views itself in its official theories. Whether the law calls it the 'but for' test, the '*sine qua non*' test, the 'necessary condition' test, or something else, it is plain as daylight that what is meant is the identification of the natural (ie, pre-legal) relation of causation with counterfactual dependence. Statements of the form '*c* caused *e*', are taken to mean '*e* counterfactually depended on *c*'. It is true, as we saw in Chapter 4, tort and criminal law heavily qualify their identification of cause-in-fact with counterfactual dependence, to the point that one can question whether the law is truly committed to the counterfactual theory of causation. Nonetheless, despite this quite real worry, what the law *says* its theory of causation is, is quite clear: causation is counterfactual dependence.

The second reason for the focus on the counterfactual theory lies in morality. It is often thought that the hard core of our moral obligations—the social minimum, so to speak—is that we do no harm. Regardless of what may be virtuous, supererogatory, or obligatory in making the world a better place, at a minimum we should not make it a worse one. Further, we make the world a worse place whenever we worsen it compared to the way the world would have been without our actions. On this view, our actions must make a difference for us to violate our basic obligations. What gets recorded in our moral ledgers are the bad states of affairs that would not have existed but for our actions. Our actions were, in a word, *necessary* to the bad states of affairs for which we are responsible. This view of our moral responsibility is naturally captured by a certain kind of counterfactual test, one that compares how the world is after our actions with how the world would have been if, contrary to fact, we had not done the actions in question.

The third reason lies in our intuitive metaphysics of causation. In daily life where responsibility is not in issue, we often enough test whether one thing (*c*) caused another (*e*) by asking 'if *c* had not have occurred, would *e* have occurred?' If we have any kind of 'verificationist' or 'operationalist' impulses, it may seem natural to identify the thing tested, causation, with the common test for it, counterfactual dependence.

Moreover, our intuitive causal metaphysics may incline us toward the counterfactual theory of causation in a second way. As we saw in Chapter 15, it is plausible to suppose that 'behind' every singular causal relation between token states of affairs there is a causal law linking types of states of affairs. One well respected account of how true causal laws are to be distinguished from accidental generalizations is by the ability of the former (but not the latter) to support counterfactual judgments. And if counterfactuals enter into causal laws, and causal laws are omnipresent whenever causation exists, then it may seem natural to regard counterfactuals as in some way intimately related to causation itself.

II. The Class of Counterfactual Statements

The division of labor between the present chapter and the next is as follows. Because the counterfactual theory of causation (in its most ambitious form, at least) seeks to *reduce* causation to counterfactual dependence, we do well to enquire into the nature of the reduction base; that is counterfactual dependence itself. The present chapter thus focuses on that relation by itself, without yet asking any questions about the relation of that relation to causation. It is Chapter 17 that takes up the relational question. It asks whether causation is in some way intimately related to the counterfactual dependence examined in this chapter.

It is said that undue syncretism is a symptom of various kinds of mental disease. Yet (to paraphrase the old saying about paranoids), even undue syncretists can encounter truly tangled webs where everything is related to everything else. Such is the case here. We need to understand counterfactual conditionals if we are to examine the purported reduction of causation to counterfactual dependency. Yet to understand counterfactual conditionals, we seemingly need to wend our way through the thorny philosophical thickets surrounding conditionals in general.[1] These preliminary thickets consist of the complexity of the issues, the amount of philosophical attention to such issues, and yet the lack of any consensus as to their resolution, on basic questions about conditionals. For example, do they have some unitary, general nature? Are there two basic kinds of

---

[1] See generally two recent monographs which build upon a quite extensive body of literature: Michael Woods, *Conditionals* (Oxford: Clarendon Press, 1997), and William G Lycan, *Real Conditionals* (Oxford: Clarendon Press, 2001).

conditionals, indicative and subjunctive? If so, how does one draw the line between them?

One hardly knows where to start. Perhaps we should first isolate the class of counterfactual statements. Usually the very name elicits the following sort of example:

(1) If the rocket were to have gone less than 18,000 miles per hour, it would not have escaped the earth's gravitational pull.

It is tempting to think that we can define the class of such statements by their grammar, namely, by the fact that they are framed in the subjunctive mood. Yet such a grammatical demarcation of the class of counterfactual statements is an unreliable guide.[2] Some subjunctive conditionals are not counterfactual conditionals, and some indicative conditionals are.

More promising is to frame the class of statements in which we are interested in terms of their conditional form conjoined with the falsity of both their antecedent and their consequent clauses.[3] With regard to (1), the rocket in question did not go less than 18,000 miles per hour, and it did escape the earth's gravitational pull. Therefore, when considered separately, both the antecedent and the consequent clauses of the conditional statement are false.[4] The statement is thus doubly contrary to fact, and is the classic sort of counterfactual conditional statement.

Suppose another massive body came close to the earth just where and when the rocket was speeding away from earth. Then this statement could be true:

(2) Even if, contrary to fact, the rocket did go less than 18,000 miles per hour, it would have escaped the earth's gravitational pull.

Unlike the classic example of counterfactuals, here the antecedent is false but the consequent is true. Nelson Goodman calls these statements 'semifactuals'.[5] Notice that the truth of (2) makes the truth of (1) impossible. As Goodman puts it, 'a semifactual conditional has the force of denying what is affirmed by the

---

[2] See Woods, *Conditionals*, 5: 'The subjunctive exists at best only vestigially in English...'.

[3] See, eg, JL Mackie, *Truth, Probability, and Paradox* (Oxford: Oxford University Press, 1973), 65. More exactly, as Mackie also notes (ibid, 71), counterfactual statements typically express the speaker's *belief* that the antecedent and consequent clauses of such statements are false.

[4] It takes some grammatical alteration to get determinate truth values to each clause of a counterfactual statement because usually such statements are put in the subjunctive mood and in the past tense. I follow convention here in translating the clauses into the indicative mood, and in rendering them tenselessly, thusly: 'the rocket goes less than 18,000 miles per hour' (the antecedent clause); and 'the rocket does not escape the earth's gravitational pull' (the consequent clause). The convention is controversial. See Woods, *Conditionals*, 9–10. But my use of it here is harmless because the very point of reformulating these clauses is to see if so construed the entire statement can be taken truth-functionally. The conclusion being that it cannot, the mood and tense shifts are merely by way of *arguendo* concession.

[5] Nelson Goodman, 'The problem of counterfactual conditionals', Journal of Philosophy 44 (1947), 114, reprinted in Nelson Goodman, *Fact, Fiction, and Forecast* (4th edn, Cambridge, Mass: Harvard University Press, 1983), 3–31.

opposite, fully counterfactual conditional'.[6] We thus cannot leave out semi-factuals from our analysis of counterfactuals for they seem to be one rendering of the contradictory, or at least the contrary, of counterfactuals.[7]

Neither can we leave out what Goodman calls factual conditionals,[8] which are conditional statements where both the antecedent and the consequent are true. For example:

(3) If the rocket escaped the earth's gravitational pull, then it did not go less than 18,000 miles per hour.

Note that (3) is just the contrapositive of (1) and it is true if (1) is true, and false if (1) is false. (It is a tricky question when contrapositives of true counterfacatuals are themselves true, but this one is.) Since counterfactuals like (1) can often be transformed into a factual like (3), such factual conditionals can no more be left out of an analysis of counterfactuals than can semifactuals.

The statements in which we are interested will thus not necessarily appear in explicitly counterfactual form. Still, it is the counterfactual form that highlights what seems most puzzling about this class of statements: what is it in the world that makes true a conditional statement, both clauses of which are false? What connects rockets that did not fall to earth with velocities that were never attained?

III. The Covering-law Account of Counterfactuals

Very generally speaking, there are two answers in the considerable literature of post-war, Anglo-American philosophy on counterfactuals.[9] One is given by the covering-law view. On this view, if statement (1) is true, it is made true at least in part by the truth of the general law that no object going less than 18,000 miles per hour escapes the earth's gravitational pull. The exact role of this general law in contributing to the truth of the singular counterfactual statement in (1) is a matter of some dispute. FH Bradley, at least as Roderick Chisholm once interpreted him, took the whole point of asserting a singular counterfactual like (1) to be to draw attention to, to emphasize, or to describe the underlying covering law.[10] Yet Chisholm himself declined this exclusive a role for covering laws in explicating singular counterfactual statements. Rather, Chisholm urged that the

---

[6] Goodman, *Fact, Fiction, and Forecast*, 5.   [7] Goodman's assumption. Ibid, 5–6.
[8] Ibid, 4.
[9] See generally David H Sanford, *If P, then Q: Conditions and the foundations of reasoning* (London: Routledge, 1989), 76–86, 101–18; Michael Tooley, *Causation: A realist approach* (Oxford: Clarendon Press, 1987), 64.
[10] Roderick M Chisholm, 'Law statements and counterfactual inference', Analysis 15 (1955), 102, reprinted in Ernest Sosa (ed), *Causation and Conditionals* (Oxford: Oxford University Press, 1975), 151–2. This is a revisiting of Chisholm's influential article, 'The contrary-to-fact conditional', Mind 55 (1946), 289–307.

assertion of a singular counterfactual statement presupposes the law statement without either describing it or having as the whole point of the assertion the drawing of attention to its existence.[11]

On the covering-law view, the truth of the law statement is one item which makes the singular counterfactual statement in (1) true. However, also necessary to the latter's truth are the truths of a variety of other singular statements, statements that rule out conditions wherein the law does not hold.[12] One such condition to be ruled out, for example, is that state of affairs making the semi-factual in (2) true, namely, that another body of large mass is near the rocket's path as it ascends from earth. On this enriched covering-law view the point in making singular counterfactual statements like (1) is to apply the covering law to the imagined situation described in the antecedent clause in (1): 'Supposing that this rocket is going less than 18,000 miles per hour, and supposing that certain other conditions C_1, C_2, C_n remain true, then we can infer that this rocket will not escape the earth's gravitation pull.' In other words, we use, but do not mention, the covering law which licenses the inference we wish to draw.

The covering law analysis of counterfactuals should not be taken to imply that we can translate counterfactual statements like (1) into the covering law(s) on whom the truth of (1) depends. The suggested translation would be arrived at by taking the covering law to be expressed in truth functional form as:

(4) (x) $(Fx \supset {\sim} Gx)$

Here, F is the predicate 'is traveling less than 18,000 miles per hour' and G is the predicate 'escapes from the earth's gravitational pull'. The singular counterfactual statement would then be translated as an open sentence instantiating the relevant law, namely:

(5) $Fx \supset {\sim} Gx$ (If the rocket is traveling less than 18,000 miles per hour, then the rocket does not escape from the earth's gravitational pull.)

The temptation to utilize such a translation is that it translates the troublesome counterfactual conditional into the familiar material conditional of modern logic.

Such a translation will not go through, however, because of the lack of connection between F and G in (4) and (5). The material conditional is a truth functional connective, meaning that the truth of '$Fx \supset {\sim} Gx$' turns exclusively on the truth of 'Fx' and of '${\sim} Gx$'. This gives rise to the well-known 'paradoxes of material conditionals', paradoxes making it difficult to translate any 'if...then...' conditional in English into the material conditional of logic.[13] It is sufficient for the truth of '$Fx \supset {\sim} Gx$' if either: (a) Fx is false or (b) Gx is false (meaning ${\sim} Gx$ is true). This leaves out what seems essential to counterfactual

---

[11] Roderick M Chisholm, 'Law statements and counterfactual inference', Analysis 15 (1955), 97–105, reprinted in *Causation and Conditionals*, 152.

[12] Goodman, *Fact, Fiction, and Forecast*, 8.

[13] See, eg, Wesley Salmon, *Logic* (2nd edn, Englewood Cliffs: Prentice-Hall, 1973), 38.

conditional statements, namely, that their truth depends on there being some connection between x being F and x being G. Only if such a connection exists is the counterfactual in (1) true, which is not at all captured by attempted translations like (5). Moreover, notice that since all counterfactual and semifactual statements like (1) and (2) have false antecedents, translating them into the material conditional would make all of them true. This is bad enough by itself, but it is particularly troublesome that (1) and (2) could both be true since they seem to be contradictories of one another.

The obvious suggestion to repair these difficulties is to turn to strict conditionals for the translation. This would be to translate (1) into:

(6) $\Box$ (Fx $\supset$ $\sim$ Gx) (Necessarily, if the rocket is traveling less than 18,000 miles per hour, the rocket does not escape the earth's gravitational pull.)

The strict conditional is almost as familiar to us as the material conditional,[14] so if counterfactual conditionals like (1) could be translated into strict conditionals like (6) that would lessen their uniqueness. Yet (6) suffers from the same defect as (5) in that it fails to capture the connectedness of F and G. The statement, '$\Box$ (Fx $\supset$ $\sim$ Gx)', will be true: (1) if x being F is impossible; or (2) if x being G is impossible (making '$\sim$ Gx' necessary). No connection between being F and being G is needed for the truth of the strict conditional in (6).

On the covering-law account, one can use the strict conditional to show that a statement of the antecedent (Fx), a statement of other conditions (S), and a statement of the relevant law $((x)((Fx \bullet S) \supset \sim Gx))$ entail the statement of the consequent, as in:

(7) $\Box$ $((x)$ $((Fx \bullet S) \supset \sim Gx) \bullet S \bullet Fx) \supset \sim Gx)$

Yet this is not to translate the counterfactual conditional in (1) into the strict conditional in (6). Statement (7) is no more than the logical truth known as *modus poneus*.

The covering-law account of counterfactuals thus cannot avail itself of the two familiar conditionals we know for any direct translations. Counterfactuals like (1) license us to infer $\sim$ Gx from Fx (together with other conditions and the covering law), yet the counterfactual conditionals themselves resist reduction to some statement of that law.

One of the pluses of the covering-law analysis of counterfactual statements is its ontological economy. Laws are ontologically no more mysterious than are universals generally—which is to say, a problem for nominalists perhaps but not the kind of problem besetting the alternative, possible-worlds account, to be discussed shortly. On the covering-law model there are no ghostly particulars existing in some other world related to particulars in this world in some

---

[14] See generally Sanford, *If P, Then Q*, 87–100.

recherché manner. Rather, there are only properties, kinds, and relations, and the laws that connect them.

Despite the plausibility of the covering law account, both generally and in terms of its ontology, there are a number of objections to the account. One is the objection that some counterfactuals seem to involve no covering laws in the background. Consider David Sanford's example:[15]

(8) If I had waited four more days to take out my loan, I could have borrowed at a lower interest rate.

As Sanford points out, there seems to be no law connecting the antecedent to the consequent. In other words, my taking the loan out early did not cause lower interest rates. It is true that a high volume of delayed loan applications should have the required effect by creating a lesser demand for loans, and thus a lower price in terms of a lower interest rate. Yet this law is not invoked by (4). Rather, there simply were lower interest rates four days later, due to some causes no doubt, but not necessarily to a drop in demand.

A defender of the covering-law account of counterfactuals might reply that there are laws in such examples, even though they are not laws connecting the state of affairs referred to in the antecedent to those referred to in the consequent. Rather, the laws are those connecting the rate I will get to the rates generally prevailing in the relevant loan market, and the conditions include that prevailing rate together with those things that have to be true in order for me to receive the prevailing market rate. Yet these laws do not license us to infer the consequent from the antecedent in (8). Rather, this only allows us to infer the consequent from some fact independent of the antecedent, namely, the fact about the pre-vailing interest rate. Thus, these laws do not help us to make out the covering law analysis for counterfactuals like (8).

What Sanford is plainly after is an example of a counterfactual that uses one 'just so' fact, such as the interest rate on a given date, as the basis for inferring the state of affairs described in the consequent clause, such as the interest rate on my loan. Yet to move from his example of a 'just so' fact to the desired conclusion in examples like (8), some laws seem to be necessary, although not laws connecting consequent to antecedent. A better counter-example would be:

(9) If I had waited four more days to take out my loan, the interest rate would still have been 100 basis points lower than it was when I, in fact, took out my loan.

Now the consequent refers to a 'just so' fact, the fact about the lower interest rate, so no laws are needed to infer a statement of the fact from statements of some other fact. Yet notice that (9) is a semifactual. That is, its antecedent is false

---

[15] Sanford, *If P, Then Q*, 86.

while its consequent is true. As we have seen, such semifactuals are the contradictories of counterfactuals like:

(10) If I had waited four more days to take out my loan, the interest rate would not have dropped 100 basis points but would have remained where it was four days earlier.

If (10) were true, it would only be true because of some law connecting my loan application to the interest rate. Similarly, if (9) is true and (10) is false, that will only be because of the laws determining interest rates, laws under which my single loan application makes no difference.

Consider another of example of Sanford's:

(11) If we had bought one more artichoke this morning, we would have had one for everyone at dinner tonight.[16]

Suppose we bought eight artichokes this morning, but nine people were at dinner tonight. Then what (11) is really saying is that:

(12) If we had bought 1 plus 8 artichokes this morning, we would have had 9 artichokes for dinner tonight.

Note that (12) is just the arithmetic analogue of non-causal counterfactuals, such as:

(13) If this rectangle were a triangle, then it would have one less side.

Or

(14) If this man were immortal, then he would live forever.

The laws behind such statements are not causal laws, to be sure. Yet, there are truths of a general sort at work in such statements.

There are a class of counterfactuals that Nicholas Rescher has dubbed 'purely hypothetical counterfactuals' that do not seem to involve any laws or other generalizations.[17] For example (from Quine):

(15) If Bizet and Verdi were compatriots, Bizet would be an Italian.

But the law-less character of such counterfactuals seems to be at one with the complete indeterminacy of such counterfactuals. One way Bizet and Verdi could have been compatriots would be for Bizet to have been an Italian. However, another would be for Verdi to have been a Frenchman. Yet another would have been for both to have been Argentineans, etc. If we eliminate the indeterminacy by supposing that only Italy allowed two such famous composers to be citizens of

---

[16] Sanford, *If P, Then Q*, 173.
[17] Nicholas Rescher, 'Belief-contravening suppositions', The Philosophical Review 70 (1961), 193–4, reprinted in *Causation and Conditionals*, 162.

the same country, then (15) is true, and the other suggestions are false. Yet the determinacy of such purely hypothetical counterfactuals is purchased by the law mentioned: only Italy allowed such famous compatriot composers.

I conclude that it is more difficult than is commonly supposed to find non-analytic, determinate counterfactuals that have no covering law as part of their truth conditions. This fact prepares the way for a second objection to the covering-law view, however. The objection is that the very idea of a law has the idea of counterfactuals built into it.[18] The worry is that the covering-law account of counterfactuals is circular, depending as it does on laws that themselves depend on counterfactuals.

The circularity worry begins by asking how do we distinguish an accidental generalization from a covering law? An accidental generalization shares with true laws a logically general form. For example:

(16) All pieces of pure gold are less than a cubic mile in size.[19]

This is universal in form predicating of anything, if it is a piece of gold, then it is less than one cubic mile in size. Yet such a generalization, while true, is true by the happenstance that no pieces of gold that large have ever formed. However, there is no reason that such huge pieces of gold could never have formed. Rather, it just so happens they did not. Contrast (16) to:

(17) All pieces of pure uranium-235 are less than a cubic mile in size.[20]

From what we know about the critical mass of uranium-235, there cannot be a cubic mile of the stuff. Note that (17) is a law of nature, whereas (16), while universal in form and true, is not.

The worry over circularity stems from the fact that the most obvious way to distinguish laws like (17) from accidentally true generalizations like (16), is via counterfactuals.[21] If, contrary to fact, geologic processes had occurred in certain ways, then there would be a cubic mile of gold. However, if analogous geologic processes had occurred with respect to uranium, there would not be a cubic mile of uranium. The causal law seems in some sense to be necessarily true whereas the accidental generalization is not. Furthermore, that necessity is tested by hypothetical cases that have not occurred.

To draw the sting from the circularity worry is to give an account of laws that does not depend on counterfactuals. If such an account is given, then we can use that notion of laws to explicate counterfactuals without circularity. Nelson

---

[18] Goodman called this 'the problem of law' for counterfactual conditionals. See Goodman, *Fact, Fiction, and Forecast*, 17–27.

[19] This example is taken from DM Armstrong, *What is a Law of Nature?* (Cambridge: Cambridge University Press, 1983), 17–18.

[20] Ibid.

[21] See William Kneale, 'Natural laws and contrary-to-fact conditionals', *Analysis* 10 (1950), 121–5, reprinted in TL Beauchamp (ed), *Philosophical Problems of Causation* (Encino: Dickenson, 1974).

Goodman's solution, to what may fairly be called his own problem, satisfies almost no one:

> What then does distinguish a law...from a true and general non-law...? Primarily, I would like to suggest, the fact that the first is accepted as true while many cases of it remain to be determined, the further, unexamined cases being predicted to conform with it. The second...is accepted as a description of...all cases, no prediction of any of its instances being based upon it.[22]

This social fact of acceptance, in the face of less than total data, is in turn based on the predicates contained within a generalization: if the predicate is 'projectable', the generalization is a law that can be used to predict unexamined cases. The projectability of a predicate, in turn, is a function of another social fact, namely, how 'entrenched' in past practice is the predicate?[23]

To be blunt, this amounts to saying that a law differs from an accidentally true generalization because we treat it as such. Anyone with a less conventionalist/relativist metaphysics will find this unhelpful. Realists about universals will have a quite different solution. Realists will suggest that laws describe relations between universals whereas accidental generalizations do not.[24] On this view, there is a relation between the size of a chunk of uranium and its existence, whereas there is no such relationship between the size of a chunk of gold and its existence. Of course, the realist has no more resources with which to verify the existence of a true law than does his relativist cousin. Nevertheless, at least he is not defining a law as simply the psycho-social fact that many have a willingness to project because they accept past projections.

Laws do sustain counterfactual judgments, whereas accidental generalizations do not. Yet if laws describe relations between properties, then what a law is is not given by counterfactuals describing projections onto unexamined cases. Then one can say, as the covering-law view of counterfactuals does, that a genuine law is part of the truth conditions for a counterfactual statement, without having the embarrassment that what makes the law in question a law is just its support of that counterfactual statement.

The third objection to the covering-law view of counterfactuals is perhaps the most discussed. I shall call this the problem of 'incomplete specification'. Nelson Goodman's famous example is of a match being struck.[25] There is some law to the effect that a match, if dry, made a certain way, oxygen is present, etc, will light if scratched on an abrasive surface. The law supports the counterfactual:

---

[22] Goodman, *Fact, Fiction and Forecast*, 20.   [23] Ibid.

[24] Eg, Armstrong, *What Is a Law of Nature?*, 16. When discussing singular causal relations, realists will also have a non-question-begging answer to Goodman's 'problem of law'. The distinction between a genuine law and an accidental generalization is already built into the distinction between a genuine singular causal relationship and a mere coincidence of spatio-temporal succession; induction over the former produces a general law whereas generalization over the latter produces an accidentally true generalization at best.

[25] Goodman, *Fact, Fiction and Forecast*, 8–17.

(18) If the match were struck, it would light.

Yet, as Goodman points out, the law equally as well supports the counter-factual:[26]

(19) If the match were struck, it would be damp.

To see this, reformulate the 'law of matches' as:

(20) $\sim$ (struck • well made • oxygen present • dry • unlit).

If a match were struck, then the law is equally satisfied by it being dry and lighting (18), and by it being wet and not lighting (19). What is it, Goodman asked, that justifies us in placing dryness in S (the set of conditions statements) and litness is the consequent, rather than unlitness in S and wetness in the consequent?

In retrospect it is puzzling that a generation or two of philosophers puzzled about this problem, conceiving the problem to be one of finding some formal characteristics of statements that made them assignable to the statement of conditions or to the consequent clause of the counterfactual.[27] It seems obvious that there can be no such formal characteristics and that the solution is wholly pragmatic.[28] Formally, the law in (20), together with an antecedent clause supposing a match to be struck, supports equally as well (18) and (19), together with other counterfactuals like:

(21) If the match were struck, then there was no oxygen present.

If (18) seems like the counterfactual, that is because most times the question we ask about a struck match is whether it lit or not. If matches were used as wetting agents, then struck but unlit matches would be our assumptions, and wetness, the state of affairs we cared about, would be in the consequent. We would then most typically derive some counterfactual other than (18) from the match law. Perhaps not (19), but:

(22) If the match were unlit (when struck, well made, with oxygen present), then it would be wet.

What Goodman's puzzle really reveals is the indeterminateness of our question when we ask after the truth of some counterfactual. Note that S, the crucial set of statements about background conditions being held constant, is not explicitly specified. What goes into S depends on the asserter of the counterfactual statement. Given the law of matches, if 'is dry' is put into S, then (18) is true.

---

[26] Ibid, 14.
[27] See, for example, Wilfrid Sellars, 'Counterfactuals, dispositionals, and the causal modalities', in Herbert Feigl et al (eds), *Minnesota Studies in the Philosophy of Science* 2 (Minneapolis: University of Minnesota Press, 1958), 225, 227–48 reprinted in *Causation and Conditionals*, 126.
[28] See Rescher, 'Belief contravening suppositions'.

However, if 'is wet' is put into S, then the following contrary semi-factual is true and (18) is false:

(23) If the match were struck, it would not have lit.

Only by making assumptions about what the speaker intends to place in S on the occasion of his utterance of (18) do we get determinate truth values to the statement uttered.

Even if only a problem in pragmatics, the problem thus revealed is a major one for counterfactuals. What goes into S to give determinateness to counterfactuals like:

(24) If Jefferson were alive today, he would disapprove of electronic eavesdropping.

Or:

(25) If Kaiser Wilhelm II were not so stupid, the First World War would never have happened.

The truth of these counterfactuals is so uncertain because what they assert is so indeterminate. How are we to unpack what is changed, and what is left the same, when we move Jefferson to today or when we up the Kaiser's IQ? For example, what are we picturing about Jefferson's education about the world of today? With no education, Jefferson's response to electronic eavesdropping is probably no more than a stupefied silence. However, with exactly our education, Jefferson's response is probably our own.

The problem of indeterminacy does not uniquely bedevil the covering law account of counterfactuals. The problem is endemic to counterfactuals and thus besets all accounts of them. Yet with what resources an account may attack the problem differs between accounts. On the covering law account, Goodman's point should be construed as this: laws, as such, do little to resolve such indeterminacies.

IV. The Possible Worlds Account of Counterfactuals

The second account of counterfactuals often begins with an analysis of conditional statements generally. According to this analysis, an assertion of a conditional is construed to be a conditional assertion.[29] The idea is to break apart all conditional statements, including counterfactual statements like (1), into a statement of the consequent by itself, with a condition attached to the assertion of the statement. As Von Wright described this approach, 'I shall never speak of the conditional as a proposition which is being asserted, but only of propositions

---

[29] See Woods, *Conditionals*, 14.

being asserted conditionally...'.[30] Likewise, as Quine has stated, '[a]n affirmation of the form "if *p* then *q*" is commonly felt less as an affirmation of a conditional than as a conditional affirmation of the consequent'.[31] In effect, 'if *p* then *q*' is taken to be '*q*', asserted whenever *p* is true.

One might well wonder how this general account of conditional statements could be applied to counterfactual conditional statements—that is, to statements where we know *p* is false. On its face, it would appear that such conditionals are all senseless because the speaker knows that the condition of asserting either the consequent or its negation—namely *p*—does not obtain. As Frank Ramsey put it:

If two people are arguing '*if p will q?*' and are both in doubt as to *p*, they are adding *p* hypothetically to their stock of knowledge and arguing on that basis about *q* ... in a sense, 'If *p*, *q*' and 'If *p*, ~ *q*' are contradictories... If *p* turns out false, these degrees of belief [in *q* given *p*] are rendered *void*. If either party believes ~ *p* for certain, the question ceases to mean anything to him except what follows from certain laws or hypotheses.[32]

For Ramsey, then, the conditional-assertion-of-the-consequent view of conditionals generally reverts to the covering-law view for counterfactual conditionals.[33]

In order to avoid this reverting back to the covering-law view, what is needed is something in the world to which the consequent clause *q* can refer. If so, then *q*'s truth value can be determined separately from its law-like connection to the antecedent clause *p*. Robert Stalnaker approached this problem by first asking after the justification for beliefs in counterfactuals.[34] Following this approach, one finds the justification conditions for belief in *q* by repairing to the total set of one's beliefs. As Stalnaker has stated, '[f]irst, add the antecedent (hypothetically) to your stock of beliefs; second, make whatever adjustments are required to maintain consistency (without modifying the hypothetical belief in the antecedent); finally, consider whether or not the consequent is then true'.[35] The totality of our beliefs, when revised in the way Stalnaker suggests, in effect creates a kind of world which Leibnitz called a 'possible world'. It is in that imagined world, created by our revised total beliefs, that we are to test the truth of the consequent of a counterfactual like (1).

If these are the conditions under which we are justified in believing in or asserting a counterfactual, then it is but a short step to the truth conditions for counterfactual statements. All we need is to move from the psychological notion

---

[30] Georg Henrik Von Wright, Logical Studies (London: Routledge and Kegan Paul, 1957), 131.

[31] Willard Van Orman Quine, *Methods of Logic* (4th edn, Cambridge, Mass: Harvard University Press, 1982), 21.

[32] Frank Ramsey, *The Foundations of Mathematics* (London: Routledge and Kegal Paul, 1931), 247.

[33] Ibid.

[34] Robert Stalnaker, 'A theory of conditionals', in N Rescher (ed), *Studies in Logical Theory* (Oxford: Blackwells, 1968), reprinted in *Causation and Conditionals*, 165.

[35] Ibid, 169.

of hypothetical beliefs to the ontological notion of the '*possible worlds*' such beliefs are about. As Stalnaker notes, '[t]he concept of a *possible world* is just what we need . . . since a possible world is the ontological analogue of a stock of hypothetical beliefs'.[36] The truth test is then analogous to the belief test quoted above. To paraphrase Stalnaker's earlier quoted statement, we must first add the state of affairs described in the antecedent of a counterfactual to the actually existing states of affairs of the world; second, we must make whatever adjustments are required to maintain consistency without denying the existence of the state of affairs added by the antecedent; finally, we must look to see whether the consequent is true in that possible world. As Stalnaker adds, when adjusting the actual world into a possible world in which the state of affairs described in the antecedent exists, we should look for a possible world 'which otherwise differs minimally from the actual world.'[37] It is in that minimally different, 'possible world' that we test the truth of 'if p, then q', by seeing if 'q' is true.

It is worth emphasizing how different this view is from the covering-law view. On the covering-law view, it is the lawful connection of p to q that governs the truth of, 'if p then q'. On the possible world view, it is the truth of q alone that governs the truth of this conditional, with the caveat that it is the truth of q not in this world, but in a merely possible world. Consider for example how the two accounts differ in their treatment of semifactuals, where q is true in the actual world. On the possible world account, adding p, which is false, to the actual world results in a possible world, but in that world q is true as it is in the actual world, so that 'if p, then q' is true. On the covering-law account, 'if p, then q' must depend on the connection between p and q. However, there is no connection. Those insisting on such a connection are forced to Goodman and Chisholm's assertion that the content of semifactuals is to *deny* a lawful connection between p and q.[38]

There are two very large problems with the 'possible world' conception of counterfactuals. One is the ontology demanded by the theory. The theory defines the truth of some counterfactual, 'if p, then q' in terms of the truth of q alone, in some possible world consistent with p. This seems to require that such possible worlds be quite real, real enough for us to ask whether q is true in them (even though false in the actual world). David Lewis has been quite upfront about the 'modal realism' required by the possible worlds interpretation of counterfactuals:

When I profess realism about possible worlds, I mean to be taken literally . . . Our actual world is only one world among others. We call it alone actual not because it differs in

---

[36] Robert Stalnaker, 'A theory of conditionals', 169.					[37] Ibid.

[38] Chisholm, 'The contrary to fact conditional', 298, revised and reprinted in H Fiegl and W Sellars (eds), *Readings in Philosophical Analysis* (New York: Appleton-Century-Crofts, 1949), 492; Goodman, *Fact, Fiction, and Forecast*, 6.

kind from all the rest but because it is the world we inhabit. The inhabitants of other worlds may truly call their own world actual, if they mean by 'actual' what we do . . . [39]

It is because such worlds are as real as the actual world which allows us to seek the truths of counterfactuals in those worlds.

As Lewis recognizes, many philosophers meet suggestions of such modal realism with 'incredulous stares'.[40] Such stares reflect a judgment that the doctrine is so counterintuitive that it ought to be rejected out of hand. Hilary Putnam, for example, dismisses such realism as no more than a 'dotty idea'.[41] Admittedly, the idea is a difficult one to accept, even for those of us with quite strong stomachs for supposedly queer ontologies.

A natural thought is that perhaps the possible world interpretation of counterfactuals could make do with a less extravagant ontology. David Armstrong, for example, being unable to 'believe in the literal reality of possible worlds' but knowing of no other way to deal with laws of nature except by considering possible worlds, 'cling[s] to the hope that an account of "possible worlds" can be given which does not assume the existence of *possibilia*'.[42] While Lewis has spent some time dashing various versions of such hope,[43] perhaps some such, less expensive, account of possible worlds will be found. I leave that question open, with some skepticism that a non-connectivist account of counterfactuals—one whereby we define the truth of the conditional solely in terms of the truth of its consequent clause in a possible world—can make do with anything less than Lewis' full-blown modal realism.

The second problem with the 'possible worlds' view of counterfactuals is the problem of incomplete specification that we encountered before in our discussion of the covering-law theory. To put this problem into the language of 'possible world' semantics, it is the problem of specifying the possible world in which we are to test the truth of the consequent of some counterfactual like (1). Stalnaker, as we saw, required that the 'possible world' selected 'differ minimally' from the actual world.[44] We know that the 'possible world' selected has to differ somewhat from the actual world, for in the actual world the antecedent is false, whereas we need a possible world in which it is true. Yet what changes in this selected world where we find, contrary to actual fact, that this rocket is going less than 18,000 miles per hour? Did it suddenly stop going 18,000 miles per hour? If so, was this

[39] David Lewis, *Counterfactuals* (Oxford: Blackwells, 1973), 85–6. Lewis' more sustained defense of modal realism will be found in David Lewis, *On the Plurality of Worlds* (Oxford: Basil Blackwell, 1986). Further defense is provided by John Divers, *Possible Worlds* (London: Routledge, 2002).

[40] Lewis, *Counterfactuals*, 86.

[41] Hilary Putnam, *Realism and Reason* (Cambridge: Cambridge University Press, 1983), 218.

[42] Armstrong, *What Is a Law of Nature?*, 163. For Armstrong's later thoughts about the need for modal realism, see Armstrong, 'The open door: Counterfactual versus singularist theories of causation', in H Stanken (ed), *Causation and Laws of Nature* (London: Kluwer Academic Pub, 1999), 175–6.

[43] David Lewis, *On the Plurality of Worlds*, 136–42.

[44] Stalnaker, 'A theory of conditionals', 169.

an ad hoc violation of the laws of inertia? If not, did it slow gradually for some reason? What reason? Moreover, there is even vagueness in specifying just what it is in the antecedent that changes. When we say 'contrary to fact, the rocket slowed to less than 18,000 miles per hour', how much did it slow? When we say 'if that hand-waving had not occurred, the auctioneer wouldn't have thought you were bidding',[45] how much of that hand-wave are we removing in the possible world we are to use? All of it? Half of it horizontally? Two-thirds of it vertically? That part of it necessary for the hand-wave to have been recognized by the auctioneer as a bid? Or, when we say 'but for the hammer blow, the chestnut would not have been flattened',[46] how much of the hammer blow is removed in the possible world we are to use? The whole blow? The actual contact only? The full force, or only the part of it necessary for the flattening of the chestnut?

With regard to the last mentioned vagueness problem (of specifying what in the antecedent we are supposing to change), JL Mackie urged that in ordinary speech:

we regard the hammer-blow as a unit, and simply do not consider parts or subdivisions of it or quantitative alterations to it. The alternatives considered are that I strike the chestnut in the way described and that I do not. In constructing possible worlds, in considering what might or could have happened, we either plug in the hammer-blow as a whole or leave it out as a whole.[47]

Similarly, David Lewis thought that in ordinary uses of '*c* caused *e*', when supposing counterfactually that *c* does not occur, 'we imagine that *c* is completely and clearly excised from history, leaving behind no fragment or approximation of itself'.[48]

---

[45] Jonathan Bennett, 'Event causation: The counterfactual analysis,' in JE Tomberlin (ed), *Philosophical Perspectives, I, Metaphysics* (Atascadero: Ridgeview Pub, 1987), reprinted in E Sosa and M Tooley (eds), *Causation* (Oxford: Oxford University Press, 1993), 219.

[46] JL Mackie, *The Cement of the Universe* (Oxford: Oxford University Press, 1974), 43–4.

[47] Ibid, 44. Mackie recognizes that a scientific reconstruction of ordinary speech might require some abandonment of this 'whole event' convention. Where strength of hammer-blows and flattening of chestnuts are matters of continuous variation that are functionally related (greater strength of blow, greater flattening), we could take '*c* causes *e*' to invoke this law of functional dependence; then there would be no worry about how precisely to specify how much of *c* to subtract in constructing a possible world in which to test the truth of the proposition, '*e* occurs'. For there would be a range of possible worlds equally relevant to the truth of the causal judgment, varying by how much of *c* is subtracted from the antecedent.

[48] Lewis, 'Causation as influence', Journal of Philosophy 97 (2000), 190. Lewis, like Mackie, *The Cement of the Universe*, 44, would ultimately regiment ordinary usage of counterfactuals so as to excise this 'whole event' convention. Also, like Mackie, Lewis came to urge that (at least for counterfactuals involved in causation) we should be taken to be specifying a range of variation in the antecedent: Lewis, 'Causation as influence', 189–90. When verifying such counterfactuals, we are then looking at a range of events in the consequent, hoping to discover a pattern of counterfactual dependence between the range of properties of consequent-events and the range of properties of antecedent events. Unlike Mackie, Lewis' 'pattern of counterfactual dependence' would be metaphysically prior to any causal law and not a product of it. This is because of the independence of Lewis' 'possible worlds' analysis of counterfactuals from Mackie's analysis of counterfactuals in terms of nomic sufficiency.

If we adopt this 'whole event' convention for what we are subtracting when we frame the antecedent of a counterfactual, that leaves the larger problem of specifying the possible world in which we are to test the consequent. Stalnaker tells us that we select a possible world where 'there are no differences between the actual world and the selected world except those that are required, implicitly or explicitly, by the antecedent'.[49] Alternatively, as Stalnaker puts it, 'among the alternative ways of making the required changes, one must choose one that does the least violence to the correct description and explanation of the actual world'.[50] Such lesser violence is done when a 'possible world' is selected that more closely resembles the actual world than does any other 'possible world' in which the antecedent is true.

Lewis relies on a similar criterion for selecting the 'possible world(s)' consistent with the antecedent of some counterfactual, in which we are to seek the truth value of the consequent of that counterfactual. We are to rely on an ordering of overall similarity between possible worlds consistent with the antecedent, and test the consequent in a 'possible world' that is high up in the ordering of possible worlds. In constructing this ordering of overall comparative similarity to the actual world, we trade off: (1) changes of particular fact against (2) ad hoc violations of laws (what Lewis refers to as 'small miracles'), and both against (3) wholesale changes in spatio-temporal regions of particular fact, and against (4) wholesale overturning of laws.[51]

It is an illusion to think that the 'possible world' that is overall closest to the actual world is one where only the state of affairs referred to in the antecedent changes. In the example of (1), this would be to think that the rocket just is going much slower in this possible world, but in all other respects that world is the same as the actual world. For this to be the case, at the very least, we need some laws not to hold in this possible world, namely, all the laws that connect the rocket going over 18,000 miles per hour in the actual world to earlier events that caused it to go that fast in the actual world. For, remember, if those earlier events all occurred in this 'closest' possible world too, then it must have been the laws that changed to produce the lesser speed of the rocket in this possible world. Once we grasp this fact, we will most likely withdraw the view that all other events being the same makes for a more similar world given that so many laws are miraculously suspended in that world.

Heavy lifting is done on this account of counterfactuals by the notion of overall similarity. It is a real question whether the notion is up to the work assigned to it. To begin with, similarity, like qualitative identity, is not a

---

[49] Stalnaker, 'A theory of conditionals', 171.
[50] Ibid.
[51] David Lewis, 'Causation', Journal of Philosophy 70 (1973), 556–67, reprinted in *Causation and Conditionals,* 184. Lewis more explicitly orders these four aspects of similarity in David Lewis, 'Counterfactual dependence and time's arrow', Noûs 13 (1979), 472, reprinted in Lewis, *Philosophical Papers II* (Oxford: Oxford University Press, 1986), 47–8.

primitive relation. It is not, that is, primitive like the relation 'redder than' which is parasitic on no property save redness itself. There is no simple property of similarity. Rather, one item is similar to another with respect to certain other properties. One diamond may be similar to another in that they both have the same cut, clarity, etc.

So, if the idea of overall similarity is to make sense, it must be done in terms of some combinatory function over the properties that two particulars share. There are two possibilities for such a function. One would be to utilize our ordinary notion of similarity, which is a highly contextualized notion. It takes a context of utterance to find the truth of statements of the form, 'x is similar to y', inasmuch as every particular is similar to any other particular in some respects and is dissimilar in others. It requires a context of utterance to isolate what the relevant respect(s) is for any given similarity statement.

Lewis recognizes the contextual nature of ordinary similarity judgments and at times urges that counterfactual utterances provide the needed clues about salient versus not-so-salient similarities between 'possible worlds'.[52] Yet the utterance of counterfactuals like (1) does not seem context-dependent as do ordinary similarity statements. Consider the statement 'this diamond is similar to that diamond', and imagine different contexts of utterance, for example by a husband replacing his wife's lost engagement stone, by an expert diamond cutter reporting on his copying of some cut on another diamond, or by an insurance executive assessing the value of a stolen diamond. The context may well reveal relevant respects by which similarity is to be judged such as overall appearance to the naked eye, cut, or value, respectively. By contrast, when one utters counterfactuals about rockets falling to earth when traveling at less than escape velocity, matches lighting when struck, chestnuts flattening when struck by a hammer, and the like, the relevant likenesses all seem to be drawn from the relevant scientific law. In which case, the possible-world approach just is the covering-law approach, albeit with a heavy-duty ontology as the preferred solution to the law problem.

The other possibility for making sense of similarity judgments about 'possible worlds' would be to take the 'overall comparative similarity' of such worlds literally. Literally, overall similarity is a function of all the properties there are and a summing of how many of them are shared by the two particulars being compared for similarity. 'More properties shared—more similar', would be the metric here. One has to be a realist about universals to make much sense of this proposed similarity metric, but, for some of us, that is not a problem.[53] Nevertheless, the calculability of such similarity is, to say the least, more than a

---

[52] Lewis, *Counterfactuals*, 91.

[53] David Armstrong, *A Theory of Universals: Universals and scientific realism* (Cambridge: Cambridge University Press, 1978). Realism about universals is presupposed because for nominalists, every particular shares exactly the same number of properties with every other particular. See Nelson Goodman, 'Seven strictures on similarity', in his *Problems and Projects* (Indianapolis: Bobbs-Merrill, 1976), 443.

bit mind-boggling. While recognizing this, Lewis nonetheless urges that 'somehow, we do have a familiar notion of comparative overall similarity…'[54] and that we form this notion 'by balancing off many respects of similarity and difference'.[55]

I think it is problematic whether we ever employ such an overall notion of similarity. But even if we do not, perhaps Lewis is entitled to construct such a notion. Arguably, that is exactly what he does when he prioritizes likeness of large spatio-temporal regions over likeness of laws over likeness of isolated, particular events.[56] However, this leads to two further questions. One is the question of motivation: what motivates the selection of a non-ordinary notion of similarity? Is it just an intuitive sense of how counterfactuals should come out in their truth values that drives a notion of similarity to achieve that result? In which case 'similarity' would be doing no epistemic work,[57] although it could denote the correct metaphysics of counterfactuals.

The second question is one of correctness. By Lewis' notion of similarity, what is the truth value of this counterfactual?

(26) If the Soviets had pushed the button to unleash a nuclear response to the blockade of Cuba in 1962, the world would have experienced nuclear winter.[58]

What is the set of closest 'possible worlds' in which we should see if the consequent is true? Is it one where the nuclear trigger was pulled but none of the systems worked because that is closer to the actual world than one where the systems worked and, as a result, the world as we know it is gone forever? Does Lewis' stipulated criteria of similarity not favor maintaining whole swatches of space/time regions over the 'small miracle' or two required for a nuclear trigger to fail?[59]

---

[54] Lewis, *Counterfactuals*, 92.   [55] Lewis, 'Causation', 184.   [56] Ibid.

[57] See Paul Horwich, *Asymmetries in Time: Problem in the philosophy of science* (Cambridge, Mass: MIT Press, 1987), 167, reprinted in Sosa and Tooley, *Causation*, 213.

[58] Paul Horwich, *Asymmetries in Time*. Like examples are provided by Kit Fine, 'Critical notice: *Counterfactuals*, by D Lewis', Mind 84 (1975), 452; and Jonathan Bennett, 'Counterfactuals and possible worlds', Canadian Journal of Philosophy 4 (1974), 395. The general form of such counterfactuals is where a small difference in what actually occurred would make a very big difference to the world.

[59] It may seem that we do not have to take the changes from the actual world described in the consequent into account when judging whether that consequent would be true in the sufficiently similar possible world. Rather, the thought might be, we are testing the consequent in a possible world constructed from changes worked by the antecedent clause alone. The problem with this thought is that the states of affairs described in the antecedent in (26) are connected by causal laws to the many other states of affairs (nuclear winter, etc) which make the world very different. Why would not a minimally different possible world be one where such laws are suspended but no nuclear winter takes place? David Lewis invites precisely this trade-off when he reformulates his test for counterfactuals this way: 'In other words, a counterfactual is non-vacuously true if it takes less of a departure from actuality to make the consequent true along with the antecedent than it does to make the antecedent true without the consequent.' Lewis, 'Causation', 184–5.

These are serious problems for the 'possible worlds' account of counterfactual conditionals. I raise them, however, not to reject the theory but to clarify it. In fact, in the chapter that follows I shall use the 'possible worlds' understanding of counterfactuals as we examine the counterfactual theory of causation. I do this partly because the counterfactual theory of causation is best worked out using the 'possible worlds' conception of counterfactuals.[60] In addition, in the covering-law conception counterfactuals are part and parcel of a larger theory about laws, raising issues extraneous to our present concerns.[61] In any case, much of what I shall say (in possible-worlds talk) about counterfactuals and their relation to causation and responsibility can be applied *mutatis mutandis* to the covering-law version of counterfactuals.

---

[60] Ibid.

[61] Counterfactuals, under the covering law view of them, are something of a mere tail on the dog insofar as causation is concerned. On the neo-Humean theory of causation (eg, Armstrong, *What Is a Law of Nature?*; Mackie, *Cement of the Universe*; and Richard Wright, 'Causation in tort law', California Law Review (1985), 1735–838), singular causal statements are reduced to a combination of causal generalizations (laws) together with space/time locaters. Such laws are then analyzed in terms of sufficient conditions for the happening of certain events ('effects'). Counterfactuals enter because they are an implication of the idea of laws and sufficient conditions. Some neo-Humeans, such as Wright and Mackie, find a slightly larger role for counterfactuals in this theory of causation, by adding that a cause must be a necessary element in the set of sufficient conditions that together form the antecedent of causal laws. Still, the main thrust of the neo-Humean theory of causation is nomic sufficiency, and the main problems for the theory stem from that dominant aspect of it, a point we shall examine in Chapter 19, below.

17

The Counterfactual Theory of Causation

I. The Nature of the Counterfactual Theory of Causation

The counterfactual theory of causation consists of two distinct parts. The first is showing that causation can be analyzed in terms of counterfactuals. The second is showing what makes counterfactuals themselves true. We have already addressed the second of these topics in the preceding chapter. In this chapter we shall address the first topic.

The counterfactual theory of causation is one of a family of theories of causation that may broadly be described as Humean. The label is appropriate because of the following characterization of causation by Hume: 'We may define a cause to be an object followed by another, and where all the objects, similar to the first, are followed by objects similar to the second. Or, in other words where, if the first object had not been, the second never had existed.'[1] In quoting this passage David Lewis urged that 'Hume defined causation twice over'.[2] Whether this is so, depends on which theory of counterfactuals one adopts.

On the covering-law view of counterfactuals, Hume defined 'causation' but once. A singular causal statement such as '*a* caused *b*', is analyzed in terms of the statements '*a* occurred', '*b* occurred', '*b* did not occur prior to *a*', and '*a* is an instance of some kind of event A, *b* is an instance of some kind of event B, where there is a covering law of the form $(x) (Ax \supset Bx)$'. Because under the covering-law view the truth of the A/B law requires the truth of the counterfactual, 'if *a* had not occurred, *b* would not have occurred', Hume's purportedly second definition of cause would, in reality, be no more than a restatement of his first.

Construing the counterfactual theory of causation in this way makes it less interesting because then the counterfactual implications of causal statements are but an aspect of the causal laws to which singular causal statements are to be reduced. These laws can be variously analyzed as mere regularities of nature (standard issue Hume), relations between universals (some neo-Humeans), or as relations of conditional probability (the probabilistic Hume). The problems that

---

[1] Hume, David, *Enquiry Concerning the Human Understanding* (Oxford: Clarendon Press, 1902) (Indianapolis: Bobbs-Merrill, 1955).
[2] David Lewis, 'Causation', Journal of Philosophy 70 (1973), 556, reprinted in Ernest Sosa and Michael Tooley (eds), *Causation* (Oxford: Oxford University Press, 1993), 193.

beset any of these reduction bases for singular causal statements then predominate in any discussion of the counterfactual theory of causation,[3] and problems unique to counterfactuals fade into the background. To avoid this, I shall focus on the possible-worlds construal of counterfactual conditionals and the reduction of causation to these.

On the 'possible worlds' construal of counterfactuals, Lewis is right to assert that Hume's second quoted statement gives a second and independent definition of causation. Again, 'if the first object had not been, the second never had existed'.[4] This second definition of Hume's is undoubtedly the historical antecedent to the law's dominant test for cause-in-fact in torts and criminal law, the 'but for' test of liability.

The counterfactual theory of causation is a reductionist theory: it seeks to reduce the causal relation to what seems to be something else, namely, a relation of counterfactual dependence. How strongly reductionist the theory is depends on what sort of reduction is being claimed. There are three possibilities.[5]

First, there is the analytic reductionist claim. This would be the semantic claim that 'c caused e' means 'e counterfactually depends on c'. Such a claim posits an analytic necessity of causation with counterfactual dependency. 'Causation' and 'counterfactual dependency' would then by synonyms of each other, much like 'bachelor' and 'unmarried male person' are thought to be synonymous.

Second, there is the metaphysically reductionist claim that the two putatively distinct relations are identical even if the words naming them are not synonymous. Water just *is* H_2O, on this view, even if 'water' and 'H_2O' do not have the same meanings. There is a necessity involved in such metaphysically reductionist claims, but it is not analytic necessity; Saul Kripke calls it 'metaphysical necessity'.[6]

Third, there is a nomologically reductionist version of the theory. This would be the claim that, necessarily, whenever c causes e, then e counterfactually depends on c, and vice versa. Causation and counterfactual dependence need not be identical for such law-like connection to exist between them,[7] nor need 'cause' and 'counterfactually depend' be synonyms. Rather, 'c caused e' and 'e counterfactually depended on e' would be extensionally equivalent expressions even though causation and counterfactual dependence are distinct relations.

---

[3] We examine these problems in Chapter 19, below.   [4] Hume, loc cit.

[5] These possibilities are explored by me in Moore, 'Legal reality: A naturalist approach to legal ontology', Law and Philosophy 21 (2002), 665–71, reprinted in Moore, *Objectivity in Ethics and Law* (Andershot, England: Ashgate, 2004).

[6] Sauk Kripke, *Naming and Necessity* (2nd edn, Cambridge, Mass: Harvard University Press, 1980).

[7] This is to deny one of Liebniz's principles of identity, what is usually called the 'identity of indiscernibles principle'. Such principle is much less accepted than Liebniz's other principle, the 'indiscernibility of identicals' principle.

If I were a counterfactualist about causation—ie, in some close possible world where my Moore counterpart believes the theory to be true—I would defend the second sort of reductionist view. Such an identity claim purports to tell us what causation is—it is counterfactual dependence. It does not leave us up in the air as to what causation is, as does the third view. (Of course, extensional equivalence would follow from the identity claim; as Leibniz taught us, identicals must share all of 'their' properties.) And the first view would embroil us in issues of semantics to the side of our present concerns; if causation is counterfactual dependence, then 'causation' and 'counterfactual dependence' have the same reference and extension, and on a plausible theory of meaning,[8] that is enough to say that the words mean the same thing.

So I shall examine the metaphysically reductionist claim in this chapter. I shall do this mostly by examining the work of David Lewis, who for the last 30 years of his life sought to work out the complexities of a counterfactual theory of causation. I do this because Lewis has been the most sophisticated, and the most influential, of the proponents of such a theory.

I do this despite the fact that Lewis did not straightforwardly adopt a metaphysically reductionist program identifying causation as counterfactual dependence. Lewis was too cautious to make this blunt an identification. Lewis proceeded by first introducing a notion of 'causal dependence' to serve as a kind of tertium quid between causation and counterfactual dependence.[9] Causal dependence is related to causation by an undefined notion of 'ancestry'. Causal dependence differs from its 'ancestral', causation, in two respects: (1) effects causally depend on their causes while the direction of causation is the reverse, from cause to effect; and (2) causation is taken to be a *chain* of causal dependencies. Lewis thought that there can be causation where there is no causal dependence, although it is rare.[10] Thus, for any given link in a causal chain, causal dependence is always sufficient for causation, and it is almost always present when causation exists.

Lewis could then identify causal dependence with counterfactual dependence. Being so identified, causal dependence necessarily shares with counterfactual dependence a lack of transitivity. If some state of affairs z counterfactually, depends on y, and y on x, it is not necessarily true that z counterfactually depends on x.[11] This is because the possible world in which one would test the counterfactual 'but for x, would z have occurred' is different from the possible world in which one would test the linking counterfactuals 'but for x, would y have occurred' and 'but for y would z have occurred'. Thus, under Lewis' view of possible worlds, it may be that in the closest possible world in which x does not

---

[8] Namely, K-P (Kripke-Putnam) semantics. See Kripke, *Naming and Necessity*; Hilary Putnam, 'The meaning of "meaning"', in his *Mind, Language and Reality II* (Cambridge: Cambridge University Press, 1985).

[9] Lewis, 'Causation', 187.   [10] Ibid.

[11] Michael Woods, *Conditionals* (Oxford: Clarendon Press, 1997), 44.

occur, z does occur. This could be the case because z could be caused other than by y. In this case, z does not counterfactually depend on x, and *mutatis mutandis* for the causal dependence of z on x.

Since Lewis staunchly held the view that the causal relation is transitive—if x causes y, and y causes z, then x causes z—there is a problem with causal dependence even being related by 'ancestry' to causation. So Lewis identifies causation, not with causal dependence simpliciter, but with a *chain* of causal dependencies. Thus, if z causally (and counterfactually) depends on y, and y so depends on x, then even if z does not causally (or counterfactually) depend on x, x does cause z. Causation between two states of affairs x and z is causal dependence *seriatim* down a chain of causal dependencies connecting x and z. Such chain-linked causal dependencies will exhibit the transitivity of the causal relation even though causal dependency itself is not a transitive notion.

II. Problems for the Counterfactual Theory of Causation

On the construal I favor, the counterfactual theory purports to tell us the nature of causation. It purports to tell us what causation is. Thus, it is best construed as an identity claim, namely, causation is counterfactual dependence, either direct or linked down a chain. As an identity claim, the theory is committed to an equivalence corollary, namely, anything predicable of causation is equivalently predicable of counterfactual dependence, and vice versa. Such equivalence makes (direct or linked) counterfactual dependence both sufficient and necessary for causation. The theory is thus subject to two sorts of objections. The first set of objections questions the sufficiency of counterfactual dependence for causation. The second questions the necessity of counterfactual dependence for causation. I shall consider each set of objections in turn.

A. The sufficiency of counterfactual dependence for causation

1. The existence of non-causal counterfactuals

The counterfactual theory is met initially by the observation that 'counterfactual dependency is too broad to pin down causal dependency'.[12] We saw examples of this in considering the covering-law account of counterfactuals in the last chapter. In statements (9)–(15) of that chapter we concluded that there is counterfactual dependence between consequent events and antecedent events, but there are no causal laws connecting such events. We should now add that there is also no causal relationship between such events. In a phrase, counterfactual dependence as such

---

[12] Jaegwon Kim, 'Causes and counterfactuals', Journal of Philosophy 70 (1973), 570–2, reprinted in Ernest Sosa and Michael Tooley, *Causation*, 206.

cannot be sufficient for causation. Something must be added for the account to rid it of this troublesome overbreadth.

Or so it seems. Just as the covering-law theorist may seek to discover hidden laws for all apparent counter-examples to his counterfactual theory, so the counterfactual theorist may seek to discover causal relations in such counter-examples. Consider this mereological counter-example of Jaegwon Kim:

If I had not written 'r' twice in succession, I would not have written 'Larry.'[13]

Kim fails to 'see a causal relation between these events'[14] but a defender of the counterfactual theory might purport to find a 'type of causation involved in mereological generation', what Ernst Sosa calls 'material causation'.[15] Indeed, one might seek to accommodate all purported counter-examples like (9)–(15) of the last chapter as instances of 'a form of necessary causation to be distinguished from its more familiar contingent counterpart'.[16]

Yet as we saw in Chapter 13 with regard to Hart's, and Honoré's causal dualism, it is unhelpful to invent special kinds of causation in order to deal with otherwise troublesome counter-examples. That is an old game smacking of the same irrationality that Bentham railed against in his attack on legal fictions.[17] It is all too easy to save a generalization from troublesome counter-examples by changing the meaning of the terms used in the generalization. The strategy is as unjustified here as it is in the hands of other causal dualists. Nothing can be gained by such ad hoc 'discovery' of special senses of terms that do not seem on the face of their usage to be ambiguous.

It is better to do one's repair work at the other end. Instead of playing with what causation is, limit the idea of counterfactual dependence. What is wanted is some exclusionary clause keeping out these unwanted counterfactuals that seem to be driven by some non-causal necessity. Perhaps the counterfactual theory can be supplemented by some requirement that the counterfactual dependence (with which causation is ultimately to be identified) must be between 'distinct events', as defenders of Lewis often say. Then the unwanted counter-examples, while being examples of counterfactual dependence *tout cour*, would not be examples of counterfactual dependence between *distinct events*. So, for example, writing 'r' twice in succession is part of the act of writing 'Larry', and thus, not distinct, and thus, not a counter-example.

Such a stipulated narrowing of the class of relevant counterfactuals needs not to be ad hoc. The limitation needs, in other words, not to be motivated merely by the desire to avoid counter-examples. Perhaps the counterfactualist could

---

[13] Jaegwon Kim, 'Causes and counterfactuals'.
[14] Ibid.
[15] Ernst Sosa, 'Varieties of causation', *Grazer Philosophische Studien* (1980) 99–100, reprinted in Sosa and Tooley, *Causation*, 240.
[16] Ibid.
[17] CK Ogden, *Bentham's Theory of Fictions* (Paterson: Littlefield, Adams and Co, 1959), 141–50.

motivate the limitation this way: since nothing is the cause of itself, causation only relates distinct events. It does not relate parts and wholes of the same thing. Therefore, in seeking a relation with which causation is identical, the counterfactualist is entitled to similarly restrict the counterfactual relation. It should be no surprise that c causing e, where c and e are distinct events, cannot be identified with y counterfactually depending on x, where x and y are not events (or distinct events) at all.

Yet does Kim's objection not retain force despite this rejoinder? The objection is that counterfactual dependence relates things that causation does not. Must not the relations then be non-identical, even if a sub-class of statements of counterfactual dependency is extensionally equivalent to statements of causation? Unless there is a distinct *kind* of counterfactual dependence with which we can identify causation—different than 'the causal kind of counterfactual dependence'—the counterfactual theory seems trivialized by the stipulated narrowing of the reduction base. I leave the issue open,[18] turning to more conclusive objections.

2. The continued overbreadth of counterfactual dependence

A long-recognized problem for the counterfactual theory of causation is the extremely non-discriminating notion of causation it generates. This is so even though we rule out mereological and other examples like those of Jaegnon Kim just considered. I have earlier called this the 'promiscuity' objection to the counterfactual theory.[19] There are two versions of this objection, one I shall call the '*the* cause' version and the other I shall call the '*a* cause' version. To illustrate the '*the* cause' version, reconsider Nelson Goodman's example in the last chapter of a match lighting because it was struck. As we there saw, the causal law involved in such examples includes more than striking the match in the conditions necessary for the match to light. In addition, the match needs to be dry, well-made, struck in the presence of oxygen, etc. On the counterfactual theory of causation, these equally necessary conditions have equal title with the striking of the match to be called the cause of the match lighting. Some find it absurd to think that *the* cause of the match lighting is as much due to the presence of oxygen, or the dryness of the match, as it is the striking of the match.

Lewis joins John Stuart Mill in not finding this absurd at all. On Mill's view the 'whole cause' includes all of these equally necessary conditions.[20] It is only pragmatic features of causal utterances that single out, say, the striking as 'the

---

[18] For further explanation of issues left open, see T Yagisawa, 'Counterfactual analysis of causation and Kim's examples', Analysis 39 (1979), 100–5.

[19] Michael Moore, *Act and Crime: The implications of the philosophy of action for the criminal law* (Oxford: Clarendon Press, 1993), 269.

[20] John Stuart Mill, *A System of Logic, Ratiocinative and Inductive* (London: Longman Group Ltd., 1970), Book 3, Chapter 5, Section 3, 214–18.

cause' of the lighting.[21] The striking is something we can perhaps control better, or it is the least expected and thus most surprising feature, or it is blameworthy because a human action, etc. Yet as I argued against certain Legal Realist, causal skeptics in Chapter 4, none of these pragmatic features of causal utterance go to the nature of the causal relationship itself. That, Mill said, is a relation holding equally between each of these conditions and their common effect. Indeed, as Lewis explicitly says, 'my analysis is meant to capture a broad and non-discriminatory concept of causation'.[22]

Despite the law's sometimes insistence to the contrary (explored in Chapter 5), Lewis and Mill are on solid ground in refusing to grant semantic status to the discriminatory principles by which we select amongst the various causes of the match lighting and thereby honoring one as '*the* cause'. These are merely pragmatic features of causal utterances which are dependant on the context of the utterance and the speaker's intent for their justifications. As we recognized in the last chapter with respect to the indeterminacy of the covering law account of counterfactuals, they are features which are irrelevant to causation itself.

More troublesome for the counterfactual theorist are the '*a* cause' versions of the objection. There are two such versions, what I shall call the 'at-a-time' version, and what I shall call the 'over-time' version. On the at-a-time version, very small causal contributors are rarely honored as 'a cause' of some event or state of affairs. One of thousands of polluters, one of thousands of paid attendees at an illegal concert, one of thousands who vote for a disastrously bad president, so minimally contribute to the indivisible injuries above described that they are not even a cause of those injuries. Yet notice that the counterfactual theory is committed to each of such *de minimis* contributors being a cause whenever their contribution was necessary to the injury occurring. In those rare cases where each vote, each unit of pollution, or each paid attendee is necessary to the harm, the counterfactual theory regards each as a cause, no matter the size of the contribution each makes.

As to the over-time version, we have seen that on Lewis' view causation is a fully transitive relation, so that if e counterfactually depends on d (so d causes e), and d counterfactually depends on c (so c caused d), then c causes e.[23] This means that the number of causes for any given event e is staggeringly large, in each case reaching back to the big bang that apparently began this whole show.

Both of these versions result in there being an absurd number of causes for any given effect. Our ordinary and legal conception of causation avoids this absurdity

---

[21] Joel Feinberg nicely taxonomizes some of these pragmatic features in Feinberg, *Doing and Deserving* (Princeton: Princeton University Press, 1970), 143–7.

[22] Lewis, 'Causation', 183.

[23] Remembering that this is not to say that e counterfactually depends on c. Counterfactual dependence is not transitive because the possible worlds in which one tests for e supposing the absence of c differ from the possible worlds in which one tests for e supposing the absence of d, and for d supposing the absence of c. Still, the *chains* of counterfactual dependence generate a fully transitive notion of causation, and that is the problem here.

through judgments of substantiality and of proximateness, as we saw in Chapter 4. Caesar's crossing of the Rubicon may well be a necessary condition for your loss of business on a given occasion, but that event will compete poorly with another, more proximate event, such as my breach of contract by revealing trade secrets, as the cause of that loss. The sheer size of Caesar's contributions disqualifies Caesar's act as a cause.

Lewis no doubt would wish to relegate the discriminatory principles by which we make such judgments to the pragmatics of causal utterances, just as he did for the principles involved in the '*the* cause' version of the objection.[24] Yet, that move is implausible here. What makes the move so plausible versus the '*the* cause' version of the objection is that we can imagine contexts of utterance where the dryness of the match, the presence of oxygen, etc, might well be appropriate answers to the question, 'what caused the match to light?' For example, when there was a fire in an Apollo test capsule years ago, the presence of oxygen was cited as the cause of the fire. This was appropriate because that presence was surprising, given the oxygen-free environment both usual and required in such settings. There seems no analogous context of utterance making Caesar's crossing the Rubicon an appropriate answer to the question of what caused your hypothesized loss of business.

The many lawyers who relegate problems of substantiality and proximateness to non-causal matters of 'policy', are making essentially the same kind of defensive move as the move to pragmatics by David Lewis. From the Legal Realists to the American Law Institute's *Restatement (Third) of Torts*,[25] the common lawyerly thought here is to concede that causation, on the counter-factual theory of it, is very promiscuous, but then to urge non-causal limitations on both moral responsibility and legal liability. These are the supposed 'policy'

---

[24] Lewis takes this tack in Lewis, 'Causation as influence', Journal of Philosophy 97 (2000), 196. To the suggestion that a cause of each of our deaths is our births, Lewis urges that even though this is indeed the case, 'it is understandable that we seldom say so. The counterfactual dependence of his death on his birth is just too obvious to be worth mentioning.' Ibid. Often, Lewis takes another tack, urging that there is nothing odd in attributing causation in cases like Caesar's mentioned in the text, in which event he has no need for discriminatory principles, be they semantic or pragmatic. See ibid, 195 (Lewis urges that historians trace causation 'over intervals of any length' and conclude 'without more ado' that the beginning of the chain *caused* the end). In an earlier article Lewis imagined such extended causal chains as, for example, those linking my writing a letter of recommendation to every death that occurs that would not have occurred without such letter, concluding that 'it would be strange to single out my acts as *the* cause of all those deaths. But it is *a* cause of them, under my analysis and also according to our common usage.' Lewis, 'Postscripts to "Causation"', in David Lewis, *Philosophical Papers II* (Oxford: Oxford University Press, 1986), 184. Lewis nonetheless adopts such discriminatory principles as part of the semantics of causative action verbs like, 'killing': Ibid. According to Lewis' analysis, I thus can cause death but not kill in these situations of extended causal chains: Ibid. My own view, expressed in Chapter 1, is that there is an equivalence between sentences using such causative action verbs and sentences using causation, and that therefore the discriminatory principles which form a part of the former are also a part of the latter.

[25] See the discussion in Chapter 4, above.

limitations on liability. Yet what are these policies? Suppose one has a corrective-justice theory of tort law under which one owes a legal and moral duty to correct the harm one has caused. If Caesar really did cause your loss of business, why is his estate not liable for that loss? What policy, in general, would justify leaving losses where they fall even when a culpable harm-causer causes harm to an innocent harm-sufferer? To my mind the policy arguments offered here, in terms of the inefficiency, unfairness or unforeseeably large liability, are so poor as to be but substitutes for what we actually believe on other grounds. No one really thinks that Caesar caused your losses, no matter how clearly his acts may have been necessary for them.

The upshot is that counterfactual dependence, by itself, cannot account for features causation seems to possess. Counterfactual dependence across chains of causes does not, as causation seems to, weaken or peter out. Also, counterfactual dependence does not take account, as causation seems to, of the substantiality of a factor's contribution. One might supplement the counterfactual account with some other feature of causation. However, for this to be anything other than ad hoc, such supplementary feature(s) had better flow from the supposed counterfactual nature of causation. No such showing comes to mind as at all plausible.

3. More overbreadth of the counterfactual theory: Omissions as causes

The counterfactual theory is blind to the difference between acts and omissions, and more generally, to the difference between actual and absent events. There can be counterfactual dependence between some particular harm and my omission to do some act preventing that harm, as easily as there can be counterfactual dependence of a harm on some positive action of mine. For example, 'had I not omitted to throw you the rope—that is, had I thrown you the rope—you would not have drowned' is a perfectly well-formed counterfactual. As good as the counterfactual 'had I not pushed you in, you would not have drowned'. More generally, there can be counterfactual dependence of some event on the absence, as well as on the presence, of certain other events. In this blindness, counterfactual dependence seems different than causation.

There are two routes to reconciling causation with counterfactual dependence on this issue. One is to deny that counterfactual dependence exists between harms and omissions. The other is to admit that omissions can be causes. Consider initially the first route.

If we think of omissions (as we should) as absent events, and if we refuse to countenance the existence of negative events (or negative states of affairs, negative properties) in fleshing out what we mean by 'absent event',[26] then the relevant counterfactual for an omission differs from that for an action. When we say 'my

---

[26] As Lewis rightly put it, 'absences are not events' and 'absences are bogus entities'. Lewis, 'Causation as influence', 195.

omission to throw her the rope caused her death', the phrase 'my omission to throw her the rope' does not refer to a particular, a ghostly non-rope-throwing. Rather, it is a negative existentially quantified statement about a type of action (rope-throwing), no instance of which I did on this occasion. More formally: 'It is not the case that there was something such that it was an instance of my throwing her the rope.'

As David Lewis noted, the counterfactual translation of such causation-by-omission statements cannot be quite the same as in his standard analysis:

> I cannot analyze this in my usual way, in terms of counterfactual dependence between distinct events. Instead, I have to switch to a different kind of counterfactual for the special case [of omissions]. The counterfactual is not: if event *c* (the omission) *had not* occurred ... it is rather: if some event of kind *k* (the omitted kind) *had* occurred ... '.[27]

Nonetheless the adjustment seems minor. On Lewis' own showing,[28] his standard analysis of counterfactual statements involving positive event-tokens construe such statements as being elliptical; although on their face they seemingly relate pairs of single events, in reality they relate *ranges* of such events in groups functionally related to each other. The same could be true for counterfactual statements about omissions: although they seem to relate a particular—'the omission'—they actually relate a *range* of particulars, namely, all instances of the kind of act omitted.

So amended, the counterfactual theory of causation unproblematically admits omissions as causes. This is where Lewis himself came to rest: 'it is not to be denied that there is causation by omission ... '[29] And again: 'absences can be causes'.[30] This is to embrace the second route to reconciling counterfactuals and causation distinguished earlier. Yet as I argued in Chapters 3 and 5, omissions are not happily regarded as causes. Since I will re-examine the issue in Chapter 18, I shall not do so here. Rather, I shall here assume omissions and other absences cannot be causes, so that it counts strongly against the counterfactual theory of causation that it is committed to such negative 'causation'.

4. Still more overbreadth: The counterfactual dependence between epiphenomenal events

The epiphenomenal objection is an old one, first developed against generalist theories of causation. Suppose some event *c* causes *e* at t_1, then *c* causes *f* at t_2, yet there is no causal relationship between *e* and *f*, which are merely 'epiphenomenal' of one another. For example, I run in the morning with my dog; this quickly lowers my anxiety; it eventually makes my dog tired; lowering my anxiety did not tire my dog.

---

[27] Lewis, 'Postscript to "Causation" ', 191–2.
[28] Ibid, 189–90.
[29] Ibid, 191.
[30] Lewis, 'Causation as influence', 195.

On the regularity theory of causation often attributed to Hume, events similar to e can regularly follow events similar to c, and events similar to f can regularly follow events similar to c. Unfortunately, events similar to f also can regularly follow events similar to e. Therefore, on the regularity theory e does cause f, contrary to our supposition. Similarly, on the counterfactual theory, c causing f means that c was necessary to f. Suppose that c causing e on a given occasion means not only that c was necessary to e but also that, given the laws and circumstances other than c, c could not have failed to cause e. That means that c, together with the other circumstances, was sufficient for e. This means that e was necessary for c. Yet, that means that e was also necessary for f—if e had not occurred, then c would not have occurred, and if c had not occurred, then f would not have occurred. Thus, on the counterfactual theory of causation, e did cause f, which is an embarrassing conclusion for that theory.

Lewis seeks to avoid this unwanted conclusion by getting rid of the sufficiency of c for e in the possible world(s) in which we are testing the counterfactual, 'If e had not occurred, f would not have occurred'. We rid ourselves of such sufficiency by giving up one or more of the other circumstances making c sufficient for e, or by giving up the law making c and these circumstances sufficient for e. Lewis argues that the possible world in which c occurs but e does not is closer to the actual world than is any possible world in which c occurs and e then occurs.[31] Lewis thus seeks to distinguish his account from generalist theories of causation, and from the covering law account of counterfactuals. The regularity account of causation, for example, is stuck with there being a causal law, that is, regularity, between c-type events and e-type events. Therefore, the troublesome sufficiency for e by c cannot be avoided, making e seemingly the cause of f. Lewis' possible-worlds account of counterfactuals frees him from holding the C/E law invariant in his closest possible world. As Lewis writes, 'the laws are not sacred'.[32] Better to posit a minor miracle after c has occurred so that e does not occur, than to allow f to depend counterfactually on e.

The usual rejoinder to Lewis here is that he has gerrymandered his idea of 'closest possible world' so as to get around the problem of epiphenomena. This may seem like a repeat of the ad hoc charge (in the preceding chapter) to Lewis's manipulation of 'similarity' so as to get intuitively acceptable truth values for counterfactuals. As we saw there, Lewis was entitled to respond that he is free to construct a notion of similarity that squares with our pre-theoretical intuitions about counterfactuals.

Here the charge is different, rendering that kind of answer much more problematic for Lewis. Notice that there is nothing counterintuitive about the counterfactuals, 'if e had not occurred, c would not have occurred', and 'if c had not occurred, f would not have occurred', both being true. All we need is that f not occur in a possible world very much like the actual world, save that neither e

[31] Lewis, 'Causation', 190.   [32] Ibid, 191.

nor *c* occurs. Lewis can stipulate that another possible world, one where *c* does not occur but *e* does, is closer to the actual world, because *e* occurs in both. However, what motivates the favoring of the retention of an event (*e*) over the retention of the C/E law? Why is Lewis' possible world closer to the actual world than my imagined possible world? Not because the earlier quoted counterfactuals are implausible by themselves, but only because they yield the wrong causal conclusion. Lewis may gerrymander his idea of closeness in order to get plausible counterfactuals, but surely he may not further gerrymander possible worlds in a way that eliminates independently plausible counterfactuals just to make the causal conclusion come out right. Such a secondary gerrymander of possible worlds would render the counterfactual analysis of causation vacuous. Indeed, one might as well define a cause as a cause, and be done with it.

Lewis would, no doubt, deny that he is doubly gerrymandering his notion of similarity. Yet that is far from obvious. Recall that, as a criterion of similarity, third in importance was a violation of causal laws and that fourth in importance, and being of 'little significance,' was preservation of isolated events. Prima facie, that would favor retaining the C/E law over retaining the *c* event as we select a possible world consistent with *e*'s absence. Lewis' apparent view is that some law(s) will have to be violated anyway, so why not violate the C/E law, thus allowing retention of *c*? Yet why is the amount of law violation a constant here? True enough, some law(s) will have to be violated when we select the possible world where *e* does not occur. Yet, why choose the C/E law, rather than the laws connecting *c* to some earlier events? Because, Lewis replies, later violations are to be preferred to earlier ones:

To get rid of an actual event *e* with the least over-all departure from actuality, it will normally be best not to diverge at all from the actual course of events until just before the time of *e*. The longer we wait, the more we prolong the spatio-temporal region of perfect match between our actual world and the selected alternative. Why diverge sooner rather than later?[33]

Yet perhaps the C/E law is a basic law, so that suspending it is a bigger deal than suspending the law(s) that connect *c* to earlier events. If so, then it is not at all apparent that we should wait until the last possible moment to have a law violation.

At this point, one is entitled to feeling a bit at a loss. The vagaries in the notion of similarity between possible worlds are such that it is difficult to tell whether Lewis is smuggling causal conclusions into his selection of possible worlds. Examples such as this one certainly give the appearance of such illicit smuggling. And we shall see further examples of this later on, as we examine Lewis' response to other objections.

---

[33] Lewis, 'Causation', 190.

Perhaps we can bring the ad hoc nature of Lewis' constructions here into focus by imagining two contrasting scenarios. The first is the one with which we have been working: I run in the morning (*c*), this causes my anxiety to drop (*e*), and it (*c*) also causes, later, my dog to become tired (*f*). In the second scenario, my dog stays home, I run in the morning (*c*), and this causes my anxiety to drop (*e*). In the first scenario, Lewis, as we have seen, tests the counterfactual, 'if not *e*, not *f*', by testing each link: 'if not *e*, not *c*', and 'if not *c*, not *f*'. The first of these links he holds to be false because it is a closer possible world where *c* occurs (I run) and *e* does not (my anxiety does not go down) than one in which neither *c* nor *e* occurs (I neither run nor have decreased anxiety). Would Lewis say the same in the second scenario where my dog stays home? That is, by hypothesis *c* causes *e*, and does so in a way that given *c*, together with other circumstances, *e* had to occur. Now when we test the counterfactuals 'if not *e*, not *c*', is the closest world one that suspends the C/E law (a world in which the counterfactual is false—*c* exists in such a possible world even without *e*)? Or is the closest possible world one in which the law holds and there is no *c* and no *e* (in which event the counterfactual is true)? If Lewis takes the latter option, then the fully ad hoc nature of these selections of possible worlds is naked for all to see.

Lewis has an alternative answer to the problem of epiphenomena, one that he in fact deploys, although not with any clear separation from the closeness machinations above described. This answer denies that the counterfactual, 'if not *e*, not *c*', follows from the sufficiency of *c*, and other circumstances, for *e*. This answer denies that counterfactual dependence can backtrack through time, so that an earlier event (c) can counterfactually depend on a later event (e). This Lewis has to deny anyway in order to defuse the next objection. Thus, I shall consider this response in conjunction with a like response to the next objection.

5. Overbreadth concluded: Back-tracking counterfactuals and the temporal asymmetry of causation

Two of our bedrock intuitions about causation are that it is asymmetrical (if *c* causes *e*, *e* does not cause *c*) and that it has a one-way direction in time (causes must not succeed their effects in time). An embarrassment for the counterfactual theory of causation is that, at least prima facie, counterfactual dependence does not seem to be bound by these limitations.[34] If some cause *c* is not only necessary but sufficient for some effect *e*, then *e* seems equally sufficient and necessary for *c*. To be at all plausible, the counterfactual theory has to deny this possibility. It must issue such denial, moreover, as something more than an ad hoc add-on to counterfactual dependence. That is, one cannot plausibly modify the counterfactual theory by saying that causation is counterfactual dependence plus the

[34] A long-noticed problem. See, eg, PB Downing, 'Subjunctive conditionals, time order, and causation', *Proceedings of the Aristotelian Society* 59 (1959), 125–40.

temporal condition that causes neither succeed their effects nor can they simultaneously be an effect of their effects. To be plausible, these additional restrictions have to be shown to follow from the counterfactual nature of causation, together with other plausible suppositions about the world.

David Lewis' initial answer to this problem was of a piece with his answer to the epiphenomenal problem. By managing the four criteria of closeness with care, he denied the truth of back-tracking counterfactuals.[35] Later, however, he supplemented this showing with an argument purporting to show why, in general, the closest possible worlds in which we should test back-tracking counterfactuals render them all false. I shall now explore this argument.

The conclusion of Lewis' argument here might be taken to be a kind of deliverance of common sense:

> The literal truth is just that the future depends counterfactually on the present. It depends, partly, on what we do now...The past would be the same, however we acted now. The past does not at all depend on what we do now. It is counterfactually independent of the present.[36]

This bit of common sense is not, and cannot, be the basis for Lewis' argument here. For the persuasive power of the truism that you cannot change the past is already loaded with the asymmetry of the causal relation precisely because causation does not work backwards through time. True enough, we cannot change the past. It is in that causal sense of 'depend' that the future *depends* on the past in a way that the past does not depend on the future. Lewis cannot just help himself to this cause-based deliverance of common sense. Rather, it is this causal conclusion that has to be matched by a like conclusion using 'depend' in Lewis' counterfactual sense. That is what needs showing: that the past cannot counterfactually depend on the future.

Lewis begins the argument with an empirical hypothesis: the causal structure of the world is such that there is an asymmetry of overdetermination. An overdetermination case is one where there are two or more sets of conditions sufficient for the happening of some event. If two independent fires are headed for the same property, and either is sufficient (when conjoined with other circumstances) for the destruction of the property, the destruction of the property is said to be overdetermined. While Lewis acknowledges the existence of such cases of causal overdetermination (where the past overdetermines the future), he thinks the converse is much more common. Namely, that the future typically overdetermines the past.[37]

The picture is that of a cone representing sufficient causes, each with many effects, but without overlap in the joint production of effects. Think of the

---

[35] Lewis, 'Causation', 190.

[36] Lewis, 'Counterfactual dependence and time's arrow', Noûs 13 (1979), 455–76, reprinted in D Lewis, *Philosophical Papers II* (Oxford: Oxford University Press, 1986), 32–52.

[37] Lewis, 'Counterfactual dependence and time's arrow', 49–51.

proverbial stone dropped into a quiet pond, sufficient for many ripples and other effects (see Fig 17.2 below). Those effects are not typically overdetermined. That is, absent this stone being dropped, there would have been no such ripples, for there were no ducks about to land in the pond, etc. Furthermore, given each ripple e_1, e_2, $e_3 \ldots e_{12}$ there had to have been a stone dropped, for the ripples would have come about in no other way. Each effect, in other words, is sufficient for the common event that was its cause.

It is important to see that Lewis need not deny the common picture of causation as an inverted cone, where it takes many causes to produce a single effect. The picture is:

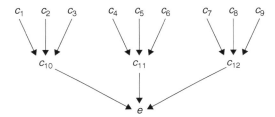

Figure 17.1 The inverted cone of causation

On the counterfactual conception of causation, there is no overdetermination by causes in this picture. There is one sufficient set for e (c_{10}, c_{11}, c_{12}), each member of which is necessary for e, and one sufficient set for each of the member of that set, and so on back through time. Nor is Lewis' overdetermination asymmetry thesis incompatible with the common view that every event has many effects, pictured as a cone of causation:

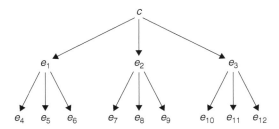

Figure 17.2 The cone of causation

This is just the stone (c) causing close-in ripples (e_1, e_2, e_3), which in turn causes further and wider ripples (e_4–e_{12}). Yet neither is Lewis' claim to be accepted just because one accepts this last view. Neither of these claims supports or refutes Lewis' claim here, which deals with an asymmetry of *sufficient* conditions.

Lewis's striking claim can be pictured by taking the arrows in figures 17.1 and 17.3 to represent sufficient conditions rather than necessary conditions. The claim is that the world looks more like figure 17.3 than like figure 17.1:

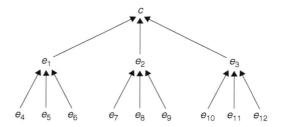

Figure 17.3 The cone of effects individually sufficient for their causes

Symmetry of overdetermination might sometimes be pictured as:

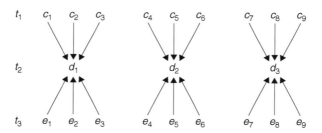

Figure 17.4 Symmetrically overdetermined effects and causes

Here causal overdetermination during the interval t_1–t_2 is matched by effect overdetermination during the interval t_2–t_3.

Lewis' empirical claim about the asymmetry of overdetermination is thus the claim that there are numerous effects for any given cause, each of which are sufficient for that cause, while for each such effect there is usually but one set of things sufficient as its cause.

If there is an asymmetry of overdetermination in the world, then the second step of Lewis's argument against back-tracking counterfactuals is to use that asymmetry to argue for the typical falsity of back-tracking counterfactuals. Such counterfactuals are usually false because in the possible world(s) in which they could be true, we have to allow for multiple violations of causal laws. This, because when we test the counterfactual: if the ripple had not occurred, the stone would not have been dropped in the pond, we must find a possible world in which the stone is not dropped. However, for such a world to exist, many links of nomic sufficiency will have to be broken, namely, the sufficiency of each effect for that common cause. There will be possible world(s) closer to the actual world where most of those links are preserved, so that the stone is still dropped; and in those possible worlds, back-tracking counterfactuals like that above come out false. Overdetermination thus feeds directly into Lewis's criteria of closeness of possible worlds. As Lewis puts it, 'The more overdetermination, the more links need breaking and the more widespread and diverse must be a miracle if it is to break them all.'[38]

Before questioning Lewis' account, we should pause to praise it. Not only is it ingenuous, but it is also the kind of account needed here. Notice there is no ad hoc stipulation just tacked onto counterfactual dependence so as to artificially inject temporal asymmetry into the account. Rather, it is the alleged nature of causation—counterfactual dependence—that is used to explain the asymmetry of causation through time, together with an empirical assumption.

Still, there is room to doubt either step of Lewis' argument here. With regard to the first step, the question is whether the empirical assumption is true. Recalling that there are two parts to this step, one might first question why we should think, in general, that effects are sufficient for their causes. Paul Horwich, for example, urges that 'Lewis does not…give grounds for a thesis of such generality, and I see no reason to accept it'.[39] Yet on standard logic, if c is necessary for e, then e is sufficient for c. If the counterfactual theory of causation is true, then every effect is sufficient for its cause. It may seem that Lewis cannot assume the truth of his theory in order to argue for that same theory. Yet, notice that the asymmetry argument is a kind of *reductio* argument against the counterfactual theory. It goes: assume the counterfactual theory is true; if so, then it has the absurd consequence that effects cause their causes. Lewis is thus here entitled to assume the truth of his theory in order to show that it does not generate this absurd consequence.

If on the counterfactual theory effects are generally sufficient for their causes, then one is still left with the other part of the first step of the argument, that is, with the counting question of whether causes have multiple effects (each of which is sufficient for its cause) more often than effects have multiple *sufficient* causes. Notice that this is not the question of whether there are more causes than there are effects. It is rather the question of whether there are more *sufficient* causes than there are (by Lewis' theory, necessarily sufficient) effects.

My own sense is with Lewis on this one. It is plausible that every cause has multiple effects, and equally plausible that every effect has multiple causes. Yet on the counterfactual theory of causation each of these multiple effects is sufficient for its cause, whereas, on the same theory, that is not necessarily true of each of

---

[38] Lewis, 'Counterfactual dependence and time's arrow', 50.
[39] Paul Horwich, *Asymmetries in Time: Problems in the philosophy of science* (Cambridge, Mass: MIT Press, 1987), reprinted in Sosa and Tooley (eds), *Causation*, 215.

these multiple causes. In fact, only rarely do we find redundancy mechanisms that ensure the existence of some effect even if what in fact causes it were to fail to cause it. On Lewis' theory of causation, which we are here assuming to be true arguendo, causal overdetermination cases are not the norm, but effect over-determination cases are.

More troublesome for Lewis is the second step of his argument, the step that moves from asymmetry of overdetermination to the falsity of back-tracking conditionals. Lewis' argument was that overdetermined events cannot easily be removed in selecting possible worlds because to do so involves numerous law violations.[40] Therefore back-tracking counterfactuals are almost always false, Lewis argues, because to be true the event referred to in their consequent must exist despite the non-existence of the event referred to in their antecedent. Yet, for a stone to still be dropped despite there being no ripples requires too many law violations for that to be the possible world closest to the actual world in which we are to test counterfactuals.

Yet if this is a good argument against back-tracking counterfactuals ever being true, is it not an equally good argument against forward directed counterfactuals ever being true in causal overdetermination cases? In the concurrent overdeter-mination case of the two fires that join forces to burn down plaintiff's house, consider the counterfactual: 'if defendant's fire had not been set, plaintiff's house would not have been burned to the ground.' Since this is an overdetermination case, we should find the possible world where plaintiff's house would have been burned to the ground closer to the actual world than the possible world in which the house would not have been burned. Therefore, this counterfactual is false, and defendant's fire did not cause the destruction of the house (and neither did the other fire). This would stick Lewis with the extremely unacceptable conclusion that in all causal overdetermination cases there is no causation of the destruction by any single fire—not 'too much causation' (that is, too many causes), but no causation at all. No theory of causation can accept this conclusion.

Worse, Lewis' theory also seems committed to backwards causation in the causally overdetermined cases. Imagine a possible world in which there is no burning of plaintiff's house to the ground. Keeping that world as close as can be to the actual world means not having multiple law violations. Therefore, in that world neither of the fires exist because, if they did, given the sufficiency of each, there would have been a destruction. So the back-tracking counterfactual, 'if plaintiff's house had not burned to the ground, there would not have existed

---

[40] 'Law violation' is the only sense I can make of Lewis' notion of the 'miracle' involved in breaking the 'link' between events, one of which is nomically sufficient for the other. Lewis, 'Counterfactual dependence and time's arrow', 50. I am thus at a loss to understand Lewis' later remark that in assessing the size of miracles (and thus the closeness of possible worlds), 'It's a blind alley to count violated laws.' Lewis, 'Postscripts to "Counterfactual dependence and time's arrow"', in Lewis, *Philosophical Papers II*, 55.

either fire', is true, and, on the counterfactual theory of causation, the house burning caused each fire.[41]

The upshot is that Lewis needs a notion of closeness of possible worlds that does not take the minimization of law-violations to make for a closer world per se. Perhaps there is a volume discount on multiple violations of the same law? If so, then perhaps Lewis can avoid these two absurd conclusions in the causal overdetermination cases. But by the same token, he will not have solved the original worry about the temporal asymmetry of causation in non-overdetermination cases.

What Lewis really needs is to argue that, appearances to the contrary notwithstanding, there are no true causal overdetermination cases. There is a very popular argument to this conclusion in both the legal and the philosophical literature.[42] It goes like this. If we look closely at supposed cases of causal overdetermination, we will see that there are never really duplicative sets of sufficient conditions for the same effect. There will always be differences in the effect if one or another of the sufficient conditions, or both together, cause 'it' so that, really, 'it' will not be numerically the same event at all.

In the two fires example, if fire one gets there first, that will be a different house destruction than if fire two gets there first, and both will be different destructions from the destruction that would occur from the fires joining and the resultant fire destroying the house. There will be qualitative differences in the destructions, for instance, different temporal locations or durations, different spatial occupations, different amounts of energy, etc. These qualitative differences will then make for numerical differences in destruction events across the three possible worlds imagined.

As I shall examine in the next section, there are good reasons to believe that this argument is false, root and branch. The only point needed here is a more modest one: Lewis could not avail himself of such an argument without destroying the asymmetry of overdetermination on which his theory rests. For if fine-grained individuation of effects works to dissolve problems of causal overdetermination, then fine-grained individuation of causes will also dissolve the apparent overdetermination of causes by their multiple effects. A fire that destroyed but one house would be a different fire from one that destroyed two houses, three, or a whole town. Lewis must thus reject this supposed dissolution of causal overdetermination, and, in fact, he does so.[43]

---

[41] A point nicely made by Horwich, *Asymmetries in Time*, 215.

[42] Richard Wright, 'Causation in tort law', California Law Review 73 (1985), 1777–80, describes some of the legal literature on this strategy. The drafters of the Model Penal Code, for example, thought they could utilize this strategy to defuse the counter-examples presented by overdetermination cases. See *Commentaries to the Model Penal Code*, § 2.03(1) (Philadelphia: American Law Institute, 1985). In philosophy this view is represented by JL Mackie, *The Cement of the Universe* (Oxford: Oxford University Press, 1974), 46–7, and Michael McDermott, 'Redundant causation', British Journal of the Philosophy of Science 46 (1995), 539–44.

[43] Sort of. Compare Lewis, 'Postscripts to "Causation" ', 197–9, with ibid at 205 n 26. See also the discussion to follow.

B. The necessity of counterfactual dependence for causation

We have been considering the question of whether counterfactual dependence is sufficient for the existence of causation. I turn now to the question of whether counterfactual dependence is even necessary to causation. Is it, in other words, even a part of the story about the nature of causation?

The principal reason for thinking that counterfactual dependence is not even necessary to causation stems from the causal overdetermination cases. The general form of the worry is easily grasped. A causal overdetermination case is one where two or more sets of conditions are independently sufficient for the production of some harm. For example, if each of two fires is sufficient for the destruction of a house, then it follows that neither fire is independently necessary for the house's destruction. On the usual counterfactual theory of causation, where it is at least necessary that a cause be a necessary condition of its effects, that means that neither fire caused the destruction of the house! This is an unacceptable conclusion, both metaphysically, because it goes against firm causal intuitions, and morally/legally, because it exonerates two culpable fire starters from liability for harm that they plainly caused.

It is also unacceptable because such a conclusion is hard to square with another implication of the counterfactual theory in these overdetermination cases, namely, the implication that because the two fires together are jointly necessary, they, considered together as a disjunctive unit, did cause the destruction.[44] If neither fire alone caused the destruction, how can the inclusive disjunction of them cause the destruction? As we saw in Chapter 15, above, our normal inference is that if $fire_1$ does not cause the destruction, and if $fire_2$ does not cause the destruction, then it is not the case that either $fire_1$ or $fire_2$ caused the destruction.

A common legal response to the overdetermination objection to the counterfactual theory of causation is, by and large, a puzzling response. Those many legal theorists who recognize that none of the defensive maneuvers (which we shall shortly examine) rescue the theory, nonetheless put aside the overdetermination

---

[44] Like many other philosophers—for example, David Armstrong, *Universals: An opinionated introduction* (Boulder: Westview Press, 1989), 82–3—Lewis finds disjunctive combinations of events with causal powers to be counterintuitive. Lewis, 'Postscripts to "Causation"', 212; Lewis, 'Events', in *Philosophical Papers II*, 266–9. Lewis thus proposes that we regard the two sufficient fires as parts of one larger event, 'the fires of April' say. Lewis, 'Postscripts to "Causation"', 212. Then one can say that this larger event was necessary for the destruction of the house. Still, even as a matter of mereology, there is a puzzle here. Some larger event c is a cause even though no part of c is a cause. More exactly: event c consists of two parts, c_1 and c_2. There is no other part to c; c_1 does not cause e; c_2 does not cause e; yet c does cause e? Suppose a hammer blow (of more force than needed) causes a chestnut to be cracked. Surely the hammer blow causes the chestnut to be cracked only if some part of that blow causes the chestnut to be cracked. It is only in the limiting case where c is a minimally sufficient condition that there would be no mereological puzzle here. Yet, there is nothing in the 'possible worlds' account of counterfactuals that requires c to be minimally sufficient as well as necessary to e.

cases as an unimportant and rare kind of aberrational side show. Yet the number of overdetermination cases that actually occur in real life is irrelevant to the problem they pose for the counterfactual theory. Unless appearances are deceiving, the overdetermination cases by themselves show that the counterfactual theory cannot be a theory of causation. At most, the theory could give a heuristic for the existence of causation. But what causation *is* would be untouched by the theory.

So I take such cases seriously as a challenge to the counterfactual theory. There are five kinds of cases that we should distinguish: ordinary garden-variety concurrent causation; symmetrically overdetermined concurrent; asymmetrically overdetermined concurrent; mixed concurrent overdetermination; and preemptive overdetermination.

The ordinary, garden-variety concurrent-cause cases are those numerous cases where several simultaneously present conditions are all individually necessary, and only jointly sufficient, for the production of some harm. Such cases are 'ordinary' or 'garden variety' in that they are not overdetermination cases, and thus do not pose any problems for the counterfactual theory of causation. I mention them because they form a helpful background against which to see clearly the four kinds of overdetermination cases. These are:

(1) Symmetrically overdetermined concurrent-cause cases are exemplified by the two fires, each sufficient by itself to burn the plaintiff's house, that join and together as one fire burn the house. Simultaneously noisy motorcycles, the noise of each of which would scare the plaintiff's horse, flood waters that join to flood a farm, mortal wounds simultaneously inflicted, etc, are further examples of such cases.[45] Such cases are overdetermination cases because each fire, flood, motorcycle, etc, is individually sufficient to produce the effect in question. They are concurrent because they cause such an effect only commingled into one fire, one sound, one flood, one wound, or one blood loss, and they are symmetrical in that each fire, etc, is equally potent—that is, sufficient.

(2) In an asymmetrically overdetermined concurrent-cause case, by contrast, one or more sufficient fires merges with one or more fires that are not individually sufficient. Or a small flood, insufficient to damage the plaintiff's land, is joined by a big flood that would have been sufficient by itself to damage the plaintiff's land. Or, one defendant inflicts a small wound, another defendant inflicts a major wound that causes such rapid loss of blood that the victim would have died from that alone but the victim in fact dies from loss of blood from both wounds.

(3) A mixed concurrent-cause case is one that stands half-way between the ordinary, garden-variety concurrent-cause case and the symmetrically

---

[45] Legal examples were given in Chapter 5, above.

overdetermined concurrent-cause case. For example, three equally sized fires join to burn the plaintiff's house, when any two of them would have been sufficient to do the job.

(4) Finally, a pre-emptive overdetermined-cause case is one where there are two conditions poised to do some damage, each being sufficient to do so, but one operates first, pre-empting the ability of the other to cause the harm. For instance, two independently set fires, each sufficient to burn the plaintiff's house, do not join. One fire reaches the house first and burns it to the ground, and then the second fire arrives but there is no house to burn.

Notice that all of these cases pose the same general problem for the counterfactual theory of causation: the presence of a sufficient condition renders the other condition not necessary, and thus, not a cause under the counterfactual theory. Still, the cases differ enough to have generated different attempts to wiggle around them, so I shall treat the four kinds of overdetermination cases separately below.

Before doing so, however, I shall first address the general defensive strategy commonly applied to them all. This is the fine-grained individuation of effects strategy mentioned before, a strategy that seeks to show that there really are no overdetermination cases of any kind. Earlier I addressed only the usability of such a strategy by someone such as David Lewis who relies on overdetermination of causes by their effects to answer the problem of asymmetry though time. Now, I shall address the correctness of the move, considered by itself.

There are three reasons to reject the move. The first is the extraordinary promiscuity introduced into the counterfactual theory by the fine-grained defense of it.[46] If any difference in properties of an event such as a house destruction makes for a different event across possible worlds, then the number of conditions necessary for that event with exactly these properties is staggering. To begin with, if one allows any difference in *relational* properties to make a difference in event-identity, then every event is a necessary condition for every other event. Consider the house destruction by fire. If this occurred three years after Princess Diana's death, then a relational property of the event is that it occurred

---

[46] David Lewis gave his own examples of promiscuity in (at one time) rejecting the move for this reason. Lewis, 'Postscript to "Causation"', 197–8. Yet Lewis ultimately came to think that there was no determinate answer to the question of event-individuation across possible worlds and that one could rescue the counterfactual theory from overdetermination counter-examples with the extremely fine-grained theory of 'event-alterations'. An 'event-alteration' is any change, no matter how minute, in the time, place and manner of event occurrence. Lewis then made causation depend on event alterations, and not on event identity. Lewis, 'Causation as Influence', 186–8. As Lewis recognized, his adoption of the fine-grained strategy leaves the counterfactual theory open to the objection that 'almost everything that precedes an event will be counted amongst its causes': ibid, 188. Lewis hoped one could deal with the flood of counter-examples by pragmatic considerations ruling out small differences in most contexts.

three years after Princess Diana died. Princess Diana's death was necessary for the event to have this property, so Princess Diana's death was one of the causes of the house destruction.

Even if one stipulates away changes in relational properties, the fine-grained move generates enormous promiscuity. Think of the conditions necessary for the house destruction that occurred to have had exactly the properties it did: the exact temporal duration of the burning of the house; the intensity of the heat generated; the sounds made by the destruction; etc. Facts such as how the house was built, what age wood was selected, the type of insulation material selected, etc, join a million other items to generate precisely the intensity of heat the house burning possessed. So a cause of the house-burning, along with defendant's negligent starting of a fire, was the degree of termite infestation? Surely not.

Even worse, as we saw in Chapter 4, many of the necessary conditions for the effect to have exactly the properties it in fact had are conditions that retarded and delayed the effect and thus seem in no sense to be the cause of that effect. For example, you throw gasoline on my house and light it up. I desperately try to put out the fire by throwing water on it. My water slows the fire somewhat but does not extinguish it and my house is destroyed. On the fine-grained view, my water-throwing is as much a necessary condition of my house's destruction as your gas-throwing and lighting; for, according to this view, that destruction would have been a different destruction had I not thrown the water.[47]

Second, the fine-grained move adopts a theory of numerical identity of event tokens across possible worlds that seems wrong on its face. In the actual world, it is true that at any one time, if two putatively distinct particulars do not share all of their properties, then they cannot be one and the same particular. This Leibnizian criterion of identity says that a difference in properties makes for a lack of identity between the particulars possessing such properties, and the

---

[47] I am assuming that the counterfactual theorist adopts Jonathan Bennett's proffered solution to the apparent asymmetry between hasteners (which intuitively seem to cause what they hasten) and delayers (which intuitively seem not to cause what they delay). Bennett's solution is to deny the asymmetry, so that events that either hasten or delay some event c are among its causes. Jonathan Bennett, *Events and Their Names* (Indianapolis: Hackett Publishing, 1988), 70. This, of course, exacerbates the promiscuity problem for the counterfactual theory by treating delayers as causers when common sense clearly rejects them as such. As to just why common sense is correct (and the counterfactual theory thus incorrect) here is a matter of some philosophical puzzlement. See Lawrence Lombard, 'Causes, enablers, and the counterfactual analysis', Philosophical Studies 59 (1990), 195–211; Penelope Mackie, 'Causing, delaying, and hastening: Do rains cause fires?', Mind 101 (1992), 483–500. It was Bennett who first raised the asymmetry problem against the counterfactual theory: Bennett, 'Event causation: The counterfactual analysis', in James E Tomberlin (ed), *Philosophical Perspectives I, Metaphysics* (Atascadero: Ridgeview Pub Co, 1987), reprinted in Sosa and Tooley, *Causation*. Despite this extensive literature, I do not raise the asymmetry between delayers and hasteners as a separate problem for the counterfactual theory. In truth, the problem is part-and-parcel of the problem posed for the counterfactual theory by omissions. That is, delayers (c) are mere preventions of events that, had they not been prevented by c, would themselves have caused some event e. Event c does not cause event e in such cases, not because c is an omission (which it is not), but rather because c would have to cause e *through* an omission (namely, the omission of some putative cause of e). See the discussion in Chapter 18.

principle is surely true at a given time in the actual world. However, it is just as surely false as a criterion of numerical identity over time. On the most plausible theories of personal identity, you are the same person now as you were two years ago even though the properties you possess differ somewhat. You are taller, shorter, heavier, smarter, nicer, etc, than you were then, but none of these are your essential properties. Over time it is only your essential properties that must remain unchanged for you to remain you.

The same is true for event-identity across possible worlds. Grant for the moment that there would be minute differences in duration, intensity, and sound, of the house destruction(s) in three different possible worlds: one where the defendant's fire burns the house by itself, another where the other fire does the job by itself, and a third possible world where both fires join to burn down the house. Unless these minute differences in house burnings affect the essential properties, there is but one house burning event here.[48]

The third reason takes away the arguendo concession just made: why must it be the case that there is any qualitative difference in the three house-burnings imagined? Surely it is possible that in every detail, save causal genesis, the 'three' house-burnings are qualitatively identical. In which case, even granting the erroneous extension of Leibniz to identity across possible worlds, there would be the unwanted conclusion of no causation in the overdetermination cases.

I conclude that the attempt to dissolve the problem here by showing that there are no overdetermination cases fails entirely. There are such cases and we should now see how the counterfactual theorist proposes to deal with them.

1. Symmetrically overdetermined concurrent-cause cases

There is an old saying in philosophy to the effect that one person's *reductio ad absurdum* is another person's valid inference. One response of the counterfactual theorist is to admit that there is no causation in the symmetrically overdetermined, concurrent cause cases. David Lewis came close to this when he professed to lack any firm pre-theoretical intuitions about such cases.[49] Even if this were true, still the counterfactual theorist has to account for the fact that his theory does not lack firm conclusions here. On the counterfactual theory, it is plain that in these cases neither sufficient condition is necessary to the occurrence of the

---

[48] Lewis, 'Causation as influence', 185–8. Lewis attempted to side-step this objection by granting its truth vis-á-vis actual event identity but substituting an extremely fine-grained notion of event-alteration. An event is altered by any change in its time, manner of occurrence, or spatial location, across possible worlds so that even though it is the *same* event it still would be an *altered* event if it would change to any degree in any of these dimensions. This is fine as far as it goes. The rub comes when Lewis then sought to alter the counterfactual analysis of causation so that event-alteration is important and event-identity is not. This altered counterfactual analysis I shall discuss shortly.

[49] Lewis, 'Causation', 191, n 12. Lewis later disavowed the lack of any common-sense judgments about such cases. Lewis, 'Postscripts to "Causation"', 208. The last word on this point by Lewis returned him to his earlier sense that we have no firm intuitions about these cases: Lewis, 'Causation as influence', 182.

harm. Thus, on the counterfactual theory, a firm conclusion of no causation fails to match Lewis' unfirm intuitions, which should not happen if Lewis' theory is to match our pre-theoretical intuitions about causation.[50] In any case, no one really believes such denials. Of course there is causation in such cases, and a theory that cannot account for that fact cannot be an acceptable theory of causation. The law of torts and of crimes joins common sense in finding causation in almost all such cases.

If we accept, as we must, two facts: (1) there is causation between c_1 and e, and between c_2 and e, in the symmetrically overdetermined concurrent cause cases; and (2) neither c_1 nor c_2 is a necessary condition of e (even though the inclusive disjunction of the occurrence of c_1 or c_2 is a necessary condition of e), then the counterfactual theorist needs some way of rescuing his theory. Very few strategies come to mind.

One possible strategy is to build on the intuition that surely independently sufficient conditions, when *considered together*, are the cause in the joint fire cases. Therefore, when considered separately, they must each be in some sense a cause as well. A number of lawyers and philosophers have thought that they can salvage the counterfactual theory by building on this intuition.[51] They insist that the counterfactual test works in these cases just so long as one restricts the causal question asked to the two fires, the two noises, etc, considered together. And of course, but for either fire occurring, there would have been no destruction of the house, so the counterfactual test yields the intuitively correct result. Yet how or why one imposes liability on the independent (not in concert) defendant without answering the question of individual causal contribution by that defendant, remains a mystery.

Another approach might be to adapt the strategy by which David Lewis seeks to rescue the theory in the pre-emptive-cause cases. This strategy utilizes his idea of a causal chain. Even if c is not a necessary condition of e, perhaps c is a necessary condition of d, and d is a necessary condition of e. Then there would be counterfactual dependence of e on d, and of d on c, and thus, links of causal dependence, and thus, causation between c and e. Consider the two fires again. Let c_1, c_2, be the independent setting of the two fires, d be the burning of the joint fire just before it reaches plaintiff's house, and e be the destruction of plaintiff's house. Then neither c_1 nor c_2 is necessary to e, yet they cause it because they are individually necessary to d, and d is necessary to e.[52]

The trick is to make sense of c_1 and c_2 being individually necessary to d, while c_1 and c_2 are not individually necessary to e. One would have to revert to the fine-grained individuation move put aside earlier. That is, here, one would be finely

---

[50] See Horwich, *Asymmetries in Time*, 210; McDermott, 'Redundant causation', 525–6.
[51] As we saw in Chapter 15, above.
[52] Event d might be called a 'Bunzl event', an event that is non-redundantly but jointly caused by c_1 and c_2, and which itself then causes e. See M Bunzl, 'Causal Overdetermination', Journal of Philosophy 76 (1979), 134–50.

individuating the intermediate event, *d*, rather than the ultimate effect, *e*, but the game is the same.[53] One has to say that the fire after joinder in the actual world is not the same fire as the fire that exists in the possible worlds when there is no c_1, or there is no c_2—the fire is bigger, stronger, etc. The three reasons given for rejecting this move earlier suffice to reject it here as well.[54] In particular, the third reason has bite: there is no reason to suppose that there will always be a qualitative difference between the *d* that actually occurred (the joint fire), and the *d* that would have occurred in the absence of c_1 or in the absence of c_2.

In addition, there is no reason to think that there always will be an intermediate event *d* in such cases on which one can work this 'Bunzling'. Take Lewis' own example of two neurons, C_1 and C_2, both firing and causing another neuron, E, to fire where the threshold for E to fire is below the energy level of the firing of either C_1 or C_2 considered individually.[55] Such cases of direct overdetermination seem not only conceivable but plentiful.[56] Thus, even if, contrary to fact, it worked when it was available, the Bunzl rescue of the counterfactual theory seems unavailable.

A third strategy is to retreat to John Mackie's 'INUS' analysis of causation[57] under which each fire is an insufficient but necessary part of set of conditions that is unnecessary but is sufficient for the effect. An event can be a cause of some event *e*, on this view, if it is not necessary to *e* so long as it is a necessary element of a sufficient set of conditions. Each fire, the argument goes, is a necessary member of a set of conditions sufficient for destruction of the house, and the fact that there is more than one sufficient set does not matter because there is no requirement that each *set* be necessary as well as sufficient for *e*.

Notice that this is not a counterfactual theory of causation, for the account gives up the crucial idea that a cause must be necessary to its effect. Rather, a cause is essentially a sufficient set of conditions with the afterthought that causes are members of minimally sufficient sets of conditions, that is, each member must be necessary for the sufficiency of the set. The idea that causation is a matter of lawful sufficiency is the hallmark of the Humean and neo-Humean theories of causation. Such theories have problems of their own (which I shall explore in Chapter 19), particularly with respect to the asymmetrically overdetermined

---

[53] Thus, Bunzl (in a case where *d* is an electric shock that caused *e*, the death of a person) resorts to very fine-grained individuation of the microphysics of the shock produced by c_1 (versus that produced by c_2) in order to conclude that the shock (or is it shocks?) counterfactually depended on c_1 individually (as well as on c_2 individually): ibid, 141.

[54] Lewis seems to favor a fine-grained solution to event-identity here. See 'Postscripts to "Causation"', 210–12.

[55] Ibid, 210. Lewis believed that we lack any clear intuitions in these cases. See Lewis' equivocation on this in n 49 above.

[56] McDermott, 'Redundant causation', 527–8. This point parallels the point to be made against Lewis' solution to cases of 'early pre-emption', as I discuss shortly.

[57] JL Mackie, 'Causes and conditions', American Philosophical Quarterly 2 (1965), 245–64. Richard Wright's NESS test is essentially the same as Mackie's INUS test. See Wright, 'Causation in tort law'.

concurrent-cause cases, the mixed concurrent-cause cases, and the pre-emptive-cause cases. Nevertheless, these are outside the domain of our present concern, which is the counterfactual theory of causation.

I conclude that the counterfactual theory of causation has no way of dealing adequately with the symmetrically overdetermined concurrent cause cases, as long as it remains a truly counterfactual theory of causation.

2. Asymmetrically overdetermined concurrent-cause cases

There are two varieties of asymmetrically overdetermined concurrent-cause cases. In one, the smaller causes that are not individually sufficient are nonetheless jointly sufficient. This variety is much like the symmetrically overdetermined concurrent-cause cases, the only difference being that one of the two or more individually sufficient conditions is an aggregate of smaller causes. For example, three smaller fires are set, each of which is necessary to form a fire sufficient to burn plaintiff's house. These fires then join another fire sufficient by itself to burn plaintiff's house, and the house is destroyed.

More interesting because more distinct are the second variety of asymmetrically overdetermined concurrent-cause cases. Here the smaller causes do not add up to a sufficient condition of the harm. For instance, a victim suffers two wounds from two blows by two defendants acting independently of one another. One wound is sufficient to kill the victim by loss of blood while the other wound is not. The victim dies from loss of blood, both wounds bleeding.

Here the initial response of David Lewis to the symmetrically overdetermined concurrent-cause cases may be more tempting. Lewis suggests that we deny that the smaller wound is a cause, so that the fact that it was not a necessary condition of the victim's death does not present a counter-example. Yet the California Supreme Court's causal intuitions in this actual case seem persuasive here: 'drop by drop' the blood flowed out of the victim 'from both wounds'.[58]

One way of buttressing this otherwise rather naked intuition is by likening these cases to the mixed concurrent-cause cases we shall consider shortly. One might think the two-wounds example to be like this five-wounds example: the victim dies from the loss of blood from five independently inflicted wounds, the loss of blood from each wound being exactly the same; the blood loss from any three of the wounds would have been sufficient for death, but no lesser number of wounds would have sufficed. When the victim dies from loss of blood, surely each wounding is a cause of that death. If that is so, then view the actual case as one in which the one big wound is equivalent in causal effect to three of the previous wounds and the smaller wound is equivalent in causal effect to two of the previous wounds. Surely, the smaller wound in the actual case, which is twice as big as each of the five wounds in the previous case, is also a cause. It should not

---

[58] *People v. Lewis*, 57 P 470, 473 (1899).

matter whether the other contributor to the death is one big wound or three smaller wounds, given that the blood-loss caused by each set is the same.

If the smaller factor is a cause in both varieties of the asymmetrically over-determined concurrent-cause cases, then these cases present the same problem for the counterfactual theory as does the symmetrical kind of case: these factors are not necessary conditions of some harm and thus should not be causes on the counterfactual theory. In fact, of course, they are causes. So much the worse for the counterfactual theory.[59]

3. Mixed concurrent-cause cases

The unique feature that makes mixed concurrent-cause cases of some interest is that none of the causes of some event *e* are either necessary or sufficient conditions for *e*. Consider for example, the five wounds case imagined earlier, where it requires a minimum of three wounds to cause death. Surely no one wishes to deny that each wound caused the death in such a case. Imagine a non-mixed, garden-variety concurrent-cause case, where each of five wounds is individually necessary, only jointly sufficient, for the bleeding to death of the victim. Holding everything else constant, these will be smaller wounds causing less loss of blood, than in the mixed case. If no one denies causation by each wound in the garden-variety case, it is hard to see how they could deny causation by each wound in the mixed case.

As an alternative example, consider the causal role of individual votes in generating the outcome of an election in which such votes are cast.[60] A garden-variety concurrent cause case is one in which the election's outcome was decided by just one vote which makes each vote for the winning side necessary for that outcome. Contrast this rare case with the mixed concurrent cause case in which there are multiple votes cast for the winning side in excess of what was needed for victory. In such a case no individual vote was necessary, or sufficient, to the election's outcome. Surely the causal role of each individual vote does not differ in these two kinds of cases. My vote is a cause of the outcome in both.[61] The problem for the counterfactual theory of causation is that it discriminates between these pairs of cases in a way that causation does not.[62]

---

[59] Notice that the second variety of these cases poses equal problems for the Humean and neo-Humean theories because the smaller causes are not necessary elements in a natural set of conditions sufficient for the harm.

[60] An example nicely explored in Alvin Goldman, 'Why citizens should vote: A causal responsibility approach', *Social Philosophy and Policy* 16 (1999), 201–17, reprinted in EF Paul et al (eds), *Responsibility* (Cambridge: Cambridge University Press, 1999).

[61] Assuming I cross the *de minimis* threshold of degree of causal contribution mentioned in Chapters 12 and 13, above.

[62] Incidentally, the Humean and neo-Humean theories fare no better with these cases because there is no non-arbitrary way to assign wounds or votes to sets of sufficient conditions such that any wound or vote is necessary to the sufficiency of that set.

4. Pre-emptive-cause cases

In pre-emptive-cause cases our causal intuitions are very clear: a pre-emptive cause causes all of the damage, and a pre-empted 'cause' is no cause at all. In the two fires cases, when both fires are independently sufficient to burn plaintiff's house, if the fires do not join, and one fire destroys the plaintiff's house before the other arrives, the first fire is the cause of the harm and the second is not. To my knowledge, no one denies these causal conclusions. The problem such conclusions present to the counterfactual theory is that prima facie neither fire is a cause under the theory. But for the first fire, the second would have burned down the plaintiff's house, and but for the second fire, the house still would have been burned to the ground by the first fire.

Pre-emptive-cause cases present a rather distinctive challenge to theories of causation. Unlike all three kinds of the concurrent-cause overdetermination cases we examined before, here there is an asymmetry between the putative causal factors—one is clearly the cause and one is equally clearly not. The problem for counterfactual and other theories of causation is that the facts on which they rely—facts of necessary or sufficient conditions—are symmetrical between the putative causal factors. On its face, this makes it tricky to line-up the causal facts with the underlying facts to which causation is to be reduced. Counterfactual theorists find it easy to characterize the second fire as not necessary to the harm, yet that also seems to make the first fire not necessary either. By contrast, those theorists who trade in nomic sufficiency find it easy to characterize the first fire as sufficient, but then the same characterization seems to apply to the second fire as well.

Lewis' initial response to pre-emptive-cause cases was to rely on the step-wise counterfactual dependence giving rise to a causal chain.[63] This allowed him to concede that the first fire was not necessary to the destruction of the house while concluding that the first fire nonetheless caused that destruction. To see this, let c_1 be the setting of the first fire, c_2, the setting of the second fire, and e, the destruction of plaintiff's house. In Lewis' theory, e depends counterfactually not on c_1, but on some intermediate events d_1, d_2, d_3; c_1 causes e if e counterfactually depends on d_3, d_3 on d_2, d_2 on d_1, and d_1 on c_1. The picture is then:

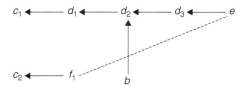

Figure 17.5 Stepwise counterfactual dependence in early pre-emptive cause cases

---

[63] Lewis, 'Causation', 191.

(The direction of the arrows is that of counterfactual dependence, so the direction of causation is opposite.) Notice that d_2 is a blocking event, because b is caused to occur by d_2, and b is the absence of what c_2 would need to cause e. For example, d_2 might be the burning of certain material located between c_1 and e, and it is this burning event (d_2) that both causes the material closest to the house to burn (d_3) and which causes the destruction of material (b) needed by the second fire (c_2) in order for it to reach the house. Now, Lewis can concede that c_1 is not necessary to e, for absent c_1, c_2 would have caused e. Yet c_1 still causes e because causation is step-wise counterfactual dependence, which exists between c_1 and e. There being no such dependence between c_2 and e, c_2 does not cause e.

The trick to understanding Lewis' first stab at a solution of the pre-emption problem is to see why d_3 is necessary for e. One might think that it is not because if there were no d_3, then e would still occur because caused by the chain initiated by c_2. Yet notice that by the time d_3 occurs, the c_2 chain is already blocked by d_2's causing of b. So without d_3, there will be no e, and the chain of counterfactual dependence from e to c_1 is unbroken. This rather neat solution is undone if there can be back-tracking counterfactual dependence. Look at what happens if d_3 turns out to be necessary for d_2, so that if there were no d_3, there would be no d_2. Since d_2 is necessary for b, the blocking event, without d_2 the causal efficacy of c_2 would not be blocked. This means that in the possible world where d_3 does not occur, neither does d_2 nor b, and in that world c_2 produces e after all. So e does not counterfactually depend on d_3, for e will come about even without d_3.[64] This yields the unwanted conclusion that c_1 does not cause e when we plainly know it does.

Lewis denies that d_3 is necessary to d_2. This is a back-tracking counterfactual which Lewis holds is always false. 'If d_3 had not occurred at t_5, d_2 would not have occurred at t_4' back-tracks through time and is the converse of the counterfactual dependence Lewis needs to assert (of d_3 on d_2). His denial is based on the judgment that the possible world in which the truth of such back-tracking counterfactuals is tested is one where the blocking-initiating event (d_2) occurs even if d_3 does not occur; then b occurs, c_2 does not cause e, and the counterfactual dependence of e on d_3 is preserved.

Notice that if Lewis allowed himself to test the counterfactual 'if d_1 had not occurred, d_2 would not have occurred' in the possible world in which he tests the back-tracking counterfactuals 'if d_3 had not occurred, d_2 would not have occurred', then c_1 would not be the cause of e (because d_2 would not counterfactually depend on d_1, and the step-wise dependence of e on c_1 would be broken). But Lewis does not test the former counterfactual in the same possible world in which he tests the back-tracking counterfactual. To see why not is to see, again, why Lewis thinks back-tracking counterfactuals are different.

[64] Lewis, 'Causation', 191.

Lewis thinks that it is of a piece with the asymmetry through time of counterfactual dependence. d_2 counterfactually depends on a prior event like d_1, but d_2 does not counterfactually depend on a later event like d_3. This is due to the greater commonality of the overdetermination of causes by their effects compared to the overdetermination of effects by their causes. This again turns on the impact of multiple law violations on the similarity of possible worlds. It would take more law violations to have d_2 absent in a possible world where d_3 was absent than it would to have d_2 absent in a possible world where d_1 was absent. Again, however, as we discussed before the worry is whether sheer numbers of law violations can so consistently determine the similarity of possible worlds, without regard to the relative importance or centrality of the laws being violated.

The killer problem for Lewis' step-wise solution to preemption stems from the fact that some pre-emptive overdetermination cases do not have the intermediary events, d_1, d_2, d_3 on which Lewis' step-wise dependence solution depends. In the two-fires scenario, suppose that the fires approach plaintiff's house from opposite directions so that there is no consumption by the first fire of the fuel necessary for the second fire to reach the house. There is, thus, no blocking events b or d_2. Rather, the first fire pre-empts the ability of the second fire to burn the house simply by virtue of the fact that there is no house left to be burnt by the time the second fire arrives at its location. The picture is then a simple one:

Figure 17.6 Counterfactual dependence in late pre-emptive cause cases

Now e does need to depend counterfactually on c_1, while e should not depend counterfactually on c_2. However, nothing we have said thus far goes any distance towards showing how this is possible.

Lewis' initial response to this problem was to deny the existence of such cases of 'late pre-emption'.[65] The argument was that the destruction of the house by fire two would have necessarily been a later destruction than the destruction that actually occurred because of fire one; and therefore a numerically distinct destruction; and therefore c_1 was necessary to e, the actual destruction that occurred. Yet as Lewis later recognized, this fine-grained theory of event-individuation across possible worlds is no better a solution in cases of late pre-emption than it is in cases of concurrent overdetermination.[66] In both cases such

[65] Lewis, 'Postscripts to "Causation"', 204.
[66] Ibid, 204.

fine-grained individuation multiplies the promiscuity problem to the point that 'they will give us lots of spurious causal dependence',[67] as we saw before.

Lewis then tried a different tack. On what he called his 'extended analysis',[68] we are to imagine two spatio-temporal regions in which what goes on (the events) is exactly alike and where the laws of nature that govern the two regions are exactly the same. In the example we have been working with, there is a fire just like 'fire one' in both regions, and there is a destruction of a house by burning in both regions. Lewis' take is that even though the regions differ in that in one of them there is a 'fire two' that would burn the house down if 'fire one' did not get there first, and in the other there is not, that difference should make no difference to our causal conclusions. If 'fire one' caused the house destruction in the region *without* 'fire two', then the analogous fire one caused the analogous house destruction in the region *with* a fire two.[69]

This response, to my mind, abandons the counterfactual analysis of causation. Lewis himself conceded that his 'extended analysis... is less purely a counter-factual analysis...'.[70] But it is a more radical a departure than that. Now causation is not to be identified as step-wise counterfactual dependence. Rather, a causal relationship between *c* and *e* is to be identified with such step-wise counterfactual dependence as would exist in a region with events and laws relevantly like the actual region in which *c* and *e* exists. Lewis found it 'intuitive' that the existence of a second, pre-empted causal factor is not a relevant difference between the actual world and this hypothetical world in which step-wise counterfactual dependence is to be sought. Yet if we look hard, surely the intuition about what makes the regions relevantly alike is wholly based on the laws in both regions, including the C/E law. It is these laws that make us so confident that if 'fire one' caused the house destruction when there was no 'fire two', then fire one caused the house destruction when there was a (pre-empted) 'fire two'.

This seems a wholesale abandonment of the possible world view of counter-factuals and a return to the covering law view. Moreover, by substituting the nomic sufficiency of the covering law model for the necessity of the counter-factual theory, Lewis' extended analysis suffers from the same problem as besets the neo-Humeans on pre-emption. Namely, if this analogy makes the pre-empting fire a cause, it equally makes the pre-empted fire a cause. After all, the pre-empted fire is just like a fire in another spatio-temporal region with the same relevant events and laws, save where there is no pre-empting fire, and in that region the pre-empted fire causes the destruction; therefore so does the pre-empted fire when there is a pre-empting fire? It can't be.

---

[67] Ibid.   [68] Ibid, 205–7.
[69] Lewis also thought that this extended analysis could also save him from concurrent overdetermination counter-examples: ibid, 211. It does not for the reasons I will address later.
[70] Ibid, 207.

Lewis himself came to accept a version of this last criticism of his solution to cases of late pre-emption,[71] although he thought the problem arose only in cases of 'trumping pre-emption'. Trumping pre-emptive-cause cases are those where the pre-empted causal factor runs its whole course—a course that normally produces some event *e*—yet it does not cause *e* because some pre-empting cause 'trumps' it. Lewis adopted an example from Jonathan Schaffer: a major and a sergeant both simultaneously order troops under their command to advance, which they do. Only the major's order causes the troops to advance since they always obey the higher-ranked officer; the sergeant's order would have caused them to advance if, contrary to fact, there had been no order from the major.[72]

Lewis accepted the idea that such trumping cases differ from cases of late pre-emption. If there is a difference here, it does not lie in the completeness of the causal chains (of the pre-empted factor) in the former cases and not the latter. In the two-fires case where there is no house to burn because the pre-empting fire burned it first, this is supposed to be only a case of late, not trumping, pre-emption. Whether trumping pre-emption truly differs from late pre-emption need not detain us, however, since it is Lewis' proposed solution to supposed 'trumping pre-emption' cases that should interest us. If the solution works for such cases, then the fact that there is no real difference between these and late pre-emption cases generally would be grist for the counterfactualist's mill.

Lewis' proposed solution begins with the fine-grained approach to event-alteration discussed before. Every slight difference in temporal duration, manner, or location of the troop's movement makes for an alteration in the event to be explained, namely the movement of the troops.[73] It is not that these changes would make it a different event. While sometimes that may be true, even when it is not, there is still an alteration in the very same event. Then notice, Lewis continues, that when, how, and where the troop movement occurs does depend counterfactually on the major giving his order—for if he had not, the troops still would have moved (in response to the sergeant's order) but that movement would have been an altered version of the movement that actually took place. Thus, the alteration of the troop movement counterfactually depends on the major's order even if the existence of the troop movement itself does not so depend.[74] The final step in Lewis' solution is to urge the sufficiency of the former counterfactual dependence for causation. Specifically, Lewis insists that it is sometimes enough for the truth of the causal judgment, 'the major's order caused

---

[71] Lewis, 'Causation as Influence,' 183–4.
[72] The example is from Jonathan Schaffer, 'Trumping preemption', Journal of Philosophy 97 (2000), 175.
[73] For another example see Lewis, 'Causation as influence', 185–6.
[74] Ibid, 186–7. Lewis is building on a similar analysis proposed by LA Paul, 'Keeping track of the time: Emending the counterfactual analysis of causation', Analysis 58 (1998), 191–8.

the troop movement', that how, when, or where the troop movement occurred counterfactually depends on the giving of the order by the major.[75]

It will be recalled that I advanced three arguments against the fine-grained dissolution of the overdetermination problem. Lewis' ideas about alterations of events, and about what he calls 'when, how, and where counterfactual dependence', speak only to the second of these problems, the problem of event-identity across possible worlds. As I noted earlier, Lewis' ideas here leave untouched the first problem, that of extreme promiscuity. Under such an analysis, as Lewis admits, 'almost everything that precedes an event will be counted among its causes'.[76] That strikes me as absurd, even if it does not so strike Lewis.

Also, untouched is the third problem: why should we suppose that there would be any alteration in *e* if it had been caused by the pre-empted factor rather than by the pre-empting factor?[77] Consider again the troop movement. The movement that would have been caused by the sergeant's order could have been qualitatively identical to the movement actually caused by the major's order. The troops need have no greater readiness to obey one versus the other, the decreased audibility of the sergeant's order, when not accompanied by the major's simultaneous order, need make no difference to the troops, since, for example, either order was quite audible, etc. On such suppositions, the counterfactual analysis still gives the wrong answer—neither order caused the troop movement—even when that analysis is amended in the way suggested.

The counterfactualist's only hope here is that there are no real-world pre-emptive-cause cases where there is no qualitative difference between the effect actually produced by the pre-empting cause and the effect that would have been produced by the pre-empted factor.[78] Yet, even if this were so, surely there are many possible worlds where there are such cases, possible worlds very similar to the actual world in which we live. If 'cause' names a real relation, say, of counterfactual dependency, then surely it does so in those possible worlds where the counterfactual theory comes out false.

---

[75] Lewis, 'Causation as Influence', 186–7.　　[76] Ibid, 188.

[77] As Ned Hall also concludes, 'it is child's play to come up with counter-examples' where the substitution of the pre-empted factor for the pre-empting cause makes absolutely no difference to the event caused: Hall, 'Causation and the price of transitivity', Journal of Philosophy 97 (2000), 221. Indeed, Hall presents quite a few in the course of his article.

[78] Lewis, at one time, thought that he could ignore such cases as being physically unrealistic because such cases invariably involved a temporal gap between the pre-empting causes and the effect. If Bob and Mary each throw a rock at a glass, Bob's rock arriving first to shatter the glass, Mary's rock thus harmlessly passing through the space formerly occupied by the glass, for the shattering that actually occurred (Bob's shattering) to have occurred at the same time as the shattering that would have occurred if Bob's rock had not been thrown (Mary's shattering) requires a delay in the actual shattering that is inexplicable; these have to be differently located (temporally) shatterings for Bob's rock to be a pre-emptive cause. See Lewis, 'Postscripts to "Causation"', 203. Against this, notice the trumping example given in the text is not inexplicable in this way: the major's order can cause exactly the same troop movement as that that would have been caused by the sergeant's order. For further examples, see McDermott, 'Redundant causation', 526, 530–1.

Quite apart from inheriting these problems of fine-grained individuation, Lewis' final solution to the overdetermination cases does not solve such cases on its own terms. Lewis supposes (contrary to fact, but assumed here arguendo) that there will always be some qualitative difference between the event caused by the pre-empting cause and the event that would have been caused by the pre-empted factor. Lewis then supposes that even in the actual case the pre-empted factor made some qualitative difference to the event caused.[79] In the example given, the troop movement that would have been caused by the major's order had there been no accompanying sergeant's order would have been different from the troop movement caused by the major's order where both orders were given. The difference between a pre-empting cause, and a pre-empted causal factor, then becomes one of degree.[80] The major's order is the cause, and the sergeant's is not, because the absence of the major's order would have made more of a qualitative difference to the troop movement that would the absence of the sergeants' order.[81]

This surely will not do. To begin with, there is nothing impossible about there being perfect symmetry here between the two orders—the absence of either one of them could make no qualitative difference whatsoever to the resultant troop movement. But assuming they both make some difference, then on Lewis' own showing both are concurrent, and not pre-emptive, causes of the troop movement. If one of them makes a bigger qualitative difference than the other, then we may have an asymmetrical concurrent cause case. Yet, there is no reason to think, as does Lewis,[82] that only when they make roughly the same difference that they should be considered concurrent causes.[83]

I conclude that the pre-emptive overdetermination cases join the three varieties of concurrent overdetermination cases in showing that counterfactual dependence is not necessary for there to be causation. Since such dependence is not sufficient for causation either, that reduces counterfactual dependence to something of a mere heuristic for causation. Often but not always, counterfactual dependence of some event *e* or some event *c* is good evidence that *c* caused *e*. But *c* can cause *e* without there being such dependence, either directly or in a step-wise fashion, and there can be such dependence without *c* causing *e*.

---

[79] Lewis, 'Causation as Influence', 189.   [80] Ibid, 189.
[81] Ibid.   [82] Ibid.
[83] I ignore Lewis' further complication in terms of varying the time, place, and manner of the causes as well as of the effects, (Lewis, 'Causation as Influence', 189–91), since it in no way diminishes the force of the objection.

18

The Role of Counterfactual Dependence as an Independent, Non-causal Desert-determiner

I. Introduction

The conclusion of the preceding chapter was that causation is distinct from counterfactual dependence. This is true as a matter of fact and as a matter of law (despite the legal pretensions to the contrary that were mentioned in Chapter 4). Yet that conclusion in no way precludes counterfactual dependence from being morally and legally relevant on its own hook, independently of causation.

To probe this independent role of counterfactual dependence as a desert-determiner it will be helpful to distinguish four sorts of cases in which some actor D does or fails to do some act A, and some victim V suffers some harm H:

1. A causes H but H does not counterfactually depend on A.
2. H counterfactually depends on A but A does not cause H.
3. H does not counterfactually depend on A, and A does not cause H.
4. H counterfactually depends on A, and A causes H.

I intend in this chapter to spend most of my time on cases of the second sort. These are the cases of omissions, preventions, allowings, and double-preventions that are not full allowings, that require more attention than we have yet given them, both as to the question of whether the relevant liabilities are non-causal and as to the question of whether it is counterfactual dependence that is the relevant desert-determiner for liability. I shall argue that those who mistakenly identify causation as counterfactual dependence can have most of the bottom-line conclusions about responsibility that they want, if they will but recognize counterfactual dependence to be a desert-determiner independent of causation.

Preliminarily, I shall spend some time on cases of the first sort, cases that raise some questions about whether causation can be a desert-determiner independent of counterfactual dependence. Unsurprisingly (in light of Chapters 2 and 3), my answer is in the affirmative, despite some occasional case-law intimations to the contrary.

Cases of the third sort require no attention at this point. As we saw in Chapter 13, these are cases of inchoate liability. If some defendant culpably tried or culpably risked some harm, and (independently of whether that harm does or does not eventuate) there is neither counterfactual dependence of the harm on the defendant's act nor is there causation of the harm by the defendant's act, then defendant's liability is inchoate. In such a case, the occurrence of the harm does not count in assessing the degree of his blameworthiness. We can thus ignore such cases for present purposes.

The same might seem to be true of cases of the fourth sort. Surely, one might think, these are as easy a case *for* liability for a harm as are cases of the third sort cases of *non*-liability for that harm. Cases where both desert-determiners are present should be as obvious as where neither are. Still, there is a surprising amount to be examined in such cases, so I shall close the chapter doing just that.

II. Causation without Counterfactual Dependence

The issue in the first sort of case distinguished above is whether counterfactual dependence is necessary to the sort of blameworthiness that takes into account the occurrence of some harm. Even if, in other words, some harm is caused by the defendant's act, if that same harm would have occurred anyway (even without defendant's action) the thought is that the defendant cannot be blamed for that harm's occurrence. (He may of course have a lesser inchoate liability, but that ignores the occurrence of the harm in question and is lesser for that reason.)

A. Three legal examples where causation seems in need of being supplemented by counterfactual dependence as a desert-determiner

Consider in this regard three sorts of cases. The first is a concurrent overdetermination case where the co-cause not attributable to the defendant is a natural event or some non-culpable human actor. As we have seen, an overdetermination case is one where two putative causal factors are in play and either is sufficient, by itself, to cause some single injury. A concurrent overdetermination case is one where such causal factors operate simultaneously. Our typical example has been that of two fires burning their way toward the plaintiff's house. Either fire, by itself, will be sufficient both to reach the plaintiff's house and burn it to the ground.[1] As it happens, the two fires join, and it is the larger, resultant fire that destroys the plaintiff's house. Suppose a defendant has negligently started one of the two fires, but the other fire is of natural origin caused, for example, by lightning, spontaneous combustion, or the like. Alternatively, suppose the second

---

[1] *Anderson v. Minneapolis, St Paul & S St Marie RR Co*, 179 NW 45 (Minn, 1920); *Kingston v. Chicago & NW Ry Co*, 211 NW 913 (Wis, 1927).

fire is the result of innocent human action. A minority of American courts deny liability of defendant to the plaintiff for his house in either of the sorts of cases just supposed.[2]

The stated rationale for this result is that the defendant's act of starting his fire did not *cause* the destruction of the plaintiff's house. As we saw in Chapters 5 and 6, however, this cannot be a causal distinction at work here. Whether the defendant's fire caused the harm cannot depend on the moral innocence of the origins of the second fire. Yet once we separate causation from counterfactual dependence, we can see the counterfactual rationale for this liability rule: if the defendant had not started his fire, the plaintiff's house would have been burnt to the ground regardless. The defendant's action, in other words, made no difference to what was going to happen anyway in the ordinary course of nature.

A second sort of case relevant here is the asymmetrical concurrent overdetermination case. As we saw in Chapters 5 and 17, an asymmetrical, concurrent, overdetermination case is one where there is one big cause ('big' meaning sufficient, by itself, to cause the harm), joined by one or more little causes ('little' here meaning, not big enough to cause the harm alone, either individually or jointly with the other little causes). Some examples: defendant's small fire joins a much bigger fire, and the resultant fire destroys the plaintiff's house; the defendant's acts stop-up the drainage wickets in a flood control levy, but such a big flood occurs that the harm to the plaintiff would have occurred even with the unstopped-up drainage wickets;[3] the defendant nicks a cable holding the plaintiff's cable car, a large force well in excess of the original carrying capacity of the cable without the nick causes the cable to break, but it nonetheless breaks at the nicked point, sending the plaintiff to his doom.[4]

There is some authority for the proposition that there is no liability in these cases.[5] The rationale is again counterfactual: these injuries would have happened anyway in the natural course of events. If contrary to fact, the defendant had not started his small fire, stopped up the drainage wickets, or nicked the cable, these injuries would still have occurred. Therefore, the defendant's act made no difference to the world and he cannot be made to pay for these harms.

The third sort of case is the pre-emptive overdetermination case. Recall that a pre-emptive overdetermination case is one where there are two events, each of which could be sufficient to cause some injury, yet unlike the concurrent cause cases, here one event pre-empts the other from becoming a cause of such injury.

---

[2] *Cook v. Minneapolis, St Paul & S St Marie Ry Co*, 74 NW 561 (Wis, 1898). This appears to be the majority rule in the English Commonwealth. See Peter Cane, *Responsibility in Law and Morality* (Oxford: Hart Publishing Co, 2002), 121–2. It is rejected by the weight of authority in America. See *Kyriss v. State*, 707 P 2d 5, 8 (Mont 1985); Charles Carpenter, 'Concurrent causation', University of Pennsylvania Law Review 83 (1935), 945–6.

[3] *City of Piqua v. Morris*, 120 NE 300 (Ohio, 1918).

[4] For a variation of the example see Richard Wright, 'Causation in tort law', California Law Review 74 (1985), 1794, 1800.

[5] Eg, *City of Piqua*, 120 NE at 303.

In the two-fires example, this is where the fires do not join, and the defendant's fire burns plaintiff's house to the ground before the other fire arrives. The first fire pre-empts the second, so the first fire is universally held to be the cause of the harm.

Despite such clear causation of the harm, often in tort law damages are limited to the value of just that temporal duration between the house's actual destruction and the destruction it would have had by the pre-empted fire if defendant's action had not existed. We measure, in other words, the amount of loss for which the defendant is liable by comparing what did happen to what would have happened had defendant not started his fire. In cases where that temporal interval is quite short, tort law eliminates damages entirely, on a kind of de minimis principle.[6]

In criminal law, of course, there are no damages recoverable by the victim to be limited in this way. It is no defense to homicide, for example, to show that if defendant had not caused the death of the victim something or someone else would have. Pre-emptive-cause killings are still fully homicides. Still, even in the criminal context, the lack of counterfactual dependency in the pre-emptive-cause cases makes for the difference we explored in Chapter 3 when we dealt with the 'acceleration cases': if the harm that defendant caused was about to be caused anyway by some natural occurrence, then defendant may have a consequentialist, balance of evils defense for his behavior that would otherwise be unavailable. In the lifeboat cases, for example, many find the result in *Dudley v. Stephens*[7] to be wrong. Many agree with Glanville Williams, and they do so for the reason that he pointed out: that the cabin boy, who was killed and eaten so the rest could survive until rescued, was about to die anyway of natural causes.[8] Really, the argument is, those who stabbed the cabin boy clearly caused his death but only by accelerating it. This idea of acceleration is fully a counterfactual notion: if the defendants had not stabbed the cabin boy, he would have died shortly anyway.

If these various legal doctrines reflect some underlying truth about moral blameworthiness, then causation would not be a desert-determiner independent of counterfactual dependence. Then, even if counterfactual dependency is a poor theory of the true metaphysics of causation, such dependency would nonetheless determine desert in just the way the counterfactual theory of causation says it does.

---

[6] *Dillon v. Twin State Gas & Electric Co*, 163 A 111, 115 (NH, 1932); *Jobling v. Association Dairies Ltd* [1982] AC 794 (HL 1991) (appeal taken from Eng).

[7] *R v. Dudley and Stephens*, 14 LR 273 (QBD 1884).

[8] Glanville Williams, *Criminal Law: The general part* (2nd edn, London: Stephens and Sons, 1961), 739–41. Williams' conclusion is an old one, reflecting the considered judgments of Cicero, Kant, Bacon, Holmes, and the drafters of the Model Penal Code. For discussion and citations see Michael S Moore, 'Torture and the balance of evils', Israel Law Review 23 (1989), 303, reprinted in Michael Moore, *Placing Blame: A general theory of the criminal law* (Oxford: Oxford University Press, 1997), 693.

None of these results, however, is morally compelling. Consider first the concurrent overdetermination cases where the other cause is a natural event or innocent human action. The intuitions that guide these cases are: (1) a sense that what was going to occur naturally is a morally significant baseline; and (2) that the counterfactual 'but for the defendant's action, the plaintiff would have lost his house to nature' is true. The baseline judgment in (1) is crucial here, because that is what distinguishes these cases from others where the second fire is of *culpable* human origin. In these latter cases (of culpable origin), plaintiff would have lost his house too, had defendant not set his fire, only not to natural circumstances but to another, perhaps equally culpable, human choice. If counterfactual dependence is necessary to the cases of a non-culpable origin for the second fire, why is it not equally necessary in cases of culpable origin? Prima facie counterfactual dependence cannot distinguish these cases any better than can causation. If causation is the sole desert-determiner, there is liability in both such kinds of case; if counterfactual dependence is necessary, then there is no liability in either sort of case.

Crucial is the baseline notion: we are invited to test the counterfactual in possible worlds where second fires of culpable origins are removed but where second fires of non-culpable origins are not removed. Nothing in Lewis' notion of similarity justifies this artificial construction of possible worlds. Nor is it morally very compelling. If it matters that the plaintiff was going to lose his house anyway, why should it matter whether that loss would have been due to nature, innocent human misadventure, or culpable human choice?

One might of course swallow hard here and deny liability in either kind of concurrent overdetermination case. But in torts that would leave plaintiff uncompensated despite the loss of his house because of two culpably set fires and two blameworthy defendants who could pay for the harm they caused; in criminal law that would result in a merely inchoate liability for the two culpable fire starters, despite the destruction of a house because of their actions. No jurisdiction has been able to stomach these results in torts or criminal law, and rightly so. Counterfactual dependence is not and should not be necessary in these cases. Causation of the harm is sufficient for liability for that harm.

The asymmetrical overdetermined concurrent-cause cases pit counterfactual rationales rather directly against cause-based rationales. When a court finds liability for a minor wound that together with a mortal wound produces death through loss of blood,[9] it is marching under the banner of causation. The minor wound was a cause of the death, even though that death would have happened anyway. When a court denies liability for negligently maintained drainage wickets on the ground that the flood was so large that it would have exceeded the capacity of the drainage wickets even if they had been properly maintained, it is

---

[9] *People v. Lewis*, 124 Cal 551, 57 P 470 (1899).

marching under the colors of counterfactual dependency.[10] The split in legal authority is wholly due to a divergence in rationale along these lines. Once one sees that causation and counterfactual dependency are not the same thing, one can at least see this split in its proper light.

My own view here too is that the culpable causation of harm should be sufficient for liability. The fact that the harm would have happened anyway, even without defendant's action should not change this result. True enough, this conclusion here is not buttressed by the *reductio* that supports a like conclusion in the symmetrical concurrent overdetermination cases. (That *reductio* was that if you cannot hold one culpable causer of the harm when there is an innocent co-causer of the harm, you cannot hold that culpable causer when there is another culpable co-causer, and if you cannot hold the second culpable co-causer you cannot hold the first because there is no difference between them—and that would be absurd.) We cannot use this exact *reductio* because in the asymmetrical cases there is a difference between the big and the little causes in that only the former was necessary; so that when that big cause is a culpable human agent we can hold him liable even though we do not hold the smaller, non-necessary, culpable causer liable.

Yet we can construct another, distinct but similar *reductio*: holding the size of defendant's causal contribution constant, imagine a case where the larger causal contribution comes from a combination of culpable human agents, each of whom was just like the defendant in terms of size of causal contribution. Now, if defendant cannot be held liable because his causal contribution was not necessary to the harm, neither can any other culpable harm-causer be held liable—for none of them, individually, were necessary to the harm either. And that too seems unacceptable. In torts, it would mean a plaintiff would suffer the loss uncompensated, despite the fact that he lost his house because of the culpable actions of several defendants. In criminal law, it would mean that each defendant can only be punished for the inchoate version of the crime of property destruction, despite the fact that each culpably caused the destruction of the property in question.

In the third sort of case, the pre-emptive overdetermination cases, courts that limit damages collectible from a pre-empting harm-causer often proceed under false colors. Often they talk as if this were a cause-based limitation: when the defendant's fire arrives first and burns the house to the ground, and thus pre-empts the ability of a second fire to have done so, the defendant is often said to have caused only the loss of the use of the house in the interim between the two fires. Once one divorces causation from counterfactual dependence, one can dispense with this fiction. The defendant clearly caused the destruction of the plaintiff's house, flat out. The only question is how we should value that house. There is no inconsistency in holding the defendant liable for causing a

---

[10] *City of Piqua v. Morris.*

destruction of the victim's house but then using the counterfactual judgment about what would have happened to plaintiff's house had the defendant's fire not destroyed it as a measure of the loss to the homeowner from that destruction.[11] Liability in such a case wholly turns on causation even when (if) the degree of harm suffered is measured by counterfactuals.

As we saw, criminal law doctrine differs from tort law doctrine here. In criminal law the pre-emptively causing defendant is liable for the completed crime because he caused the legally prohibited result; and this, despite the fact that his act was not necessary to that result occurring because another factor was about to cause it if he did not. In criminal law there is no second, independent judgment needed to value the victim's loss, as there is in tort law. There is thus no room in criminal law for counterfactual judgments to play a role in limiting damages.

Criminal law surely has it right here. Even as a tort-law damage-measurement rule, the role of counterfactuals in this way is highly problematic. If the tort-law damage rule is applied even to cases where the pre-empted factor is a culpable human action, the plaintiff cannot recover against anyone. Suppose two culpable defendants, D_1 and D_2, each try to kill some plaintiff, V; they do not act in concert; D_1 shoots a gun at V just as D_2 shoots an arrow at V. Both shots are true but D_1's bullet pierces V's heart before D_2's arrow does so, so that V is dead when D_2's arrow strikes V. V's estate has no basis for recovery against D_2—D_2's arrow did not cause death, nor was it counterfactually necessary. So if V cannot recover anything against D_1 (or recover only a de minimis amount equal to the value of a few seconds of life), V cannot recover at all. Yet V has suffered a loss he would not have suffered if D_1 had not done his culpable action. For D_1 both caused V's death, and prevented D_2 from having to compensate V (by preventing D_2 from causing V's death). So the loss D_1 has occasioned should be the sum of the harm he caused V, and the benefit (D_2's payment) he prevented V from receiving.

In any case, however one comes out on valuing the loss in these pre-emptive-cause cases in torts, counterfactual dependency is not required for liability, in torts no more than in criminal law. Even if counterfactual judgments, are necessary to measure damage in torts, they are not necessary to liability. Causation by itself is sufficient.

---

[11] On separately using counterfactuals to define the extent of damage (ie, the value of the harm rather than defendant's connection to it), see Stephen R Perry, 'Harm, history, and counterfactuals', University of San Diego Law Review 40 (2003), 1283–314. As Richard Fumerton accurately perceives, even if we do not use counterfactuals 'to determine at whose feet harm should be laid, we will almost certainly need to employ counterfactuals in deciding whether or not someone was harmed in the first place'. Even when causal connection determines who is responsible and liable for some harm, harm itself 'could plausibly be understood in terms of being placed in a state worse than that in which one would have been in the absence of that agent's action or inaction'. Fumerton, 'Moore, causation, counterfactuals, and responsibility', San Diego Law Review 40 (2003), 1273–4.

B. The general sufficiency of causation as a desert-determiner even when counterfactual dependence is absent

We now should step back from these three legal examples (the asymmetrical concurrent-cause cases, the symmetrical concurrent-cause cases where one sufficient cause is a natural event, and the damage-limitation rule in cases of preemptive causation). If we abstract a general principle from some courts' decisions of these cases, it would be that the absence of counterfactual dependence was sufficient for non responsibility—or, equivalently, that counterfactual dependence was necessary to responsibility, even in cases where there was causation.

It is the concurrent overdetermination cases which most clearly focus this general issue, for in these cases there is plainly causation of the harm and equally clearly that causing makes no difference to how bad the world ends up becoming. As we have seen, the law generally makes the causer liable in such cases, but that hardly settles the question of moral correctness. The moral question is, what matters here, causing a harm or making a difference?

My particular arguments so far have been in the form of *reductios* aimed at producing counterintuitive results as natural extensions of each of the three kinds of cases I discussed. What is now needed is something much more general. What are needed are arguments as general as the conclusion argued for, which is that culpable causation of a harm is by itself sufficient for being blamed for that harm; making a difference (ie, being necessary for the harm's occurrence) is not necessary.

In the better-known debate between causal theorists and subjectivists about responsibility that we addressed in Chapter 2, arguments for why causation matters are hard to come by. My earlier survey of my predecessors on this topic made me wonder whether there are any reasons capable of supporting the judgment that causation matters.[12] That it does may be more basic than anything we can adduce in support of it. So I am not sanguine about what can be said here. Still, the relation between the two debates can be seen as two nodes on a decision tree:

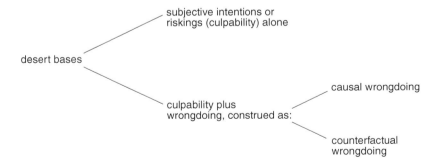

Figure 18.1 A decision tree about the competing grounds of responsibility

[12] Moore, *Placing Blame*, 196–211.

One gets to the second node—deciding between causation and counterfactual dependence as desert-determiners—only after one has rejected the purely subjectivist branch at the first node of the tree. So it is possible that whatever arguments there are that are capable of selecting objective wrongdoing as a desert-determiner (over subjectivism) are also capable of more particularly selecting the causal version of objective wrongdoing.

The main argument that I and others have used against subjectivists about responsibility has been a kind of *reductio ad absurdum* of an argument subjectivists deploy.[13] This subjectivist argument urges that we lack control over the results of our actions so that our blameworthiness cannot be increased by the happenstance of such results. Increased blameworthiness for factors over which we lack control would be a kind of 'moral luck', and morality, so the argument goes, cannot be so arbitrary as to admit the existence of such luck in determining the degree of our blameworthiness.

The *reductio* against this is based on the fact that we have no such control over what we intend, believe, or will either, so if this kind of control is necessary for blameworthiness there is no such thing as moral blameworthiness. This kind of response, while effective against subjectivists, cuts no ice against 'counterfactualists'. For proponents of counterfactual dependency as a desert-determiner do not rely on some supposed control actors have over what difference their actions make in the real world, a control over results such actors could then be said to lack. Counterfactual theorists are, in this respect, in the same boat with causal theorists, for it is implausible that there is any more control of 'what would have happened if...' than there is of what actually results from our actions.

The more positive argument that I have directed against the subjectivists is based on the epistemic power possessed by the twin emotions of guilt and moral hatred.[14] The general idea is that our emotional reactions, when they are virtuous, are good but not infallible guides to the truth of the moral judgments that such reactions cause.[15] Feeling guilty, for example, can be a good indicator that one is guilty. Against subjectivists, the argument is that there is a large difference in the emotional reactions to failed attempts and uninstantiated riskings, on the one hand, compared to successful attempts and realized riskings, on the other. It is the latter that gets the blood to the eyes, the former generating usually no more than relief at a 'near miss'.

This argument can be deployed against counterfactualists if we hone in more precisely on what it is that makes us feel so guilty for ourselves and so angry at others. Consider the pre-emptive overdetermination cases. If you have culpably caused a serious harm to an innocent, does it diminish your sense of guilt in the slightest that another person stood ready to cause that harm if you did not? True

[13] Moore, *Placing Blame*, 233–46.   [14] Ibid, 229–32.
[15] Ibid, 127–38.

enough, as a pre-emptive cause your action made no difference because right behind you someone or something else stood ready to cause the harm. Yet that fact seems to make no moral difference. Think how ill it lies in the mouth of a wrongdoer to try to lessen his responsibility by saying 'if I hadn't done it, someone else would have'. Similarly, if you were the pre-empted factor, should you feel the guilt of the actual doer of the deed? Or, is the reaction not still one of relief at a near miss: 'I almost did a great wrong, but as luck would have it, I didn't—someone (or something) else did.'

The principle to which these emotions and judgments point is a principle of 'ownership'—in some suitably extended sense, we *own* the results of our actions. Such results become a part of our history. They write an entry in our moral ledgers, for the good if they are good, otherwise if they are bad. Some such as Peter Cane[16] and Tony Honoré[17] wish to go further, arguing that our very identity depends on our being responsible for what we cause. Yet if we keep personal identity over time to truly essential properties, surely we could be the person we each are even if, contrary to fact, we had not caused some harm; what we cause is too contingent a feature of our lives to be plausibly listed as essential to personal identity.

It is true that often those who speak of 'personal identity' do not mean it literally. Rather, they mean what I have called elsewhere the *sense of* identity that we each possess.[18] We each do have a sense of the kind of person that we are and a sense of the kind of person we want to be, what psychoanalysts used to call our ego-ideal. These senses of self are impacted by what we culpably cause, for owning up to those items is what does and should shape our sense of who we are. I see this as another way of putting the 'ownership' metaphor mentioned above.

However this is put, it is not yet much of an argument. It will appeal only to those who have been horrified, ashamed, or numbingly distressed, by some awfulness of which they were the author. Such people know that causing things matters to responsibility in a way that requires no other argument. Those with either better characters or more fortunate opportunity sets will lack the relevant experience that makes this intuitively so plain to the rest of us.

III. Counterfactual Dependence without Causation I: Blameworthiness for Omissions

I turn now to the second sort of case distinguished in the introduction of this chapter. I refer to cases where there is no causation of a harm by a defendant yet

---

[16] Cane, *Responsibility in Law and Morality*, 57, 106, 117, 185.
[17] Tony Honoré, *Responsibility and Fault* (Oxford: Oxford University Press, 1999).
[18] Michael Moore, *Law and Psychiatry: Rethinking the relationship* (Cambridge: Cambridge University Press, 1984), 407–9.

the existence of that harm did depend counterfactually on the defendant. My first example, dealt with in this section, is omission.

In this section I need to defend three propositions:

(1) We do have positive moral duties. These are duties to do certain actions, as contrasted to negative duties *not* to do certain actions. Breach of such positive duties (by omitting to do the actions we have a duty to do) is blameworthy. In short, there is a moral responsibility for some omissions.

(2) A necessary condition for such blameworthiness for omissions is that the omitter could have prevented that which he omitted to prevent. He had to have, in other words, the *ability* to satisfy his positive duty. Such an ability is counterfactual: if, contrary to fact, he had not omitted to do some action A—if, that is, he had done A—then the state of affairs he was duty bound to prevent would not have existed. In a nutshell, counterfactual dependence (of the harm on omission) is necessary for responsibility for omissions.

(3) Causation (of the harm by the omission) is not necessary for responsibility for omissions. Indeed, causation could not be necessary for omissive responsibility, because omissions are not causes of the harms they fail to prevent.

These three propositions yield the conclusion I wish to defend in this section: counterfactual dependence, not causation, is the desert-determiner for omissive responsibility. I shall say little about the first two propositions here, because I think that they are uncontroversial. To deny the first would be to adopt a rabid libertarianism that is morally repellant. We have many positive duties, not just to the near and dear but also to strangers, even if Anglo-American tort and criminal law enforce only certain sorts of these. Yet (as the second proposition asserts) it would be patently unfair to demand the impossible of us: we can fairly be blamed only for not preventing what we had the ability to prevent. It is the third proposition that is the locus of serious disagreement. Whether omissions are or are not causes is hotly contested territory.

A. What is an omission?

It helps to remind ourselves what an omission is. Clarity here removes some needless controversy about the causal status of omissions. My stipulated sense of 'omission' in Chapter 3 was that an omission generically is an absent action.[19] An

---

[19] Argued for originally in Michael Moore, *Act and Crime: The implications of the philosophy of action for the criminal law* (Oxford: Oxford University Press, 1993), 22–31; Moore, *Placing Blame*, 262–6. I am continually surprised at how many of the critics of my generic concept of omissions do not see this, supposing instead that I defend some much more particular view such as that omissions are stillness's of bodily movement. See, eg, George Fletcher, 'On the moral irrelevance of bodily movements', University of Pennsylvania Law Review 142 (1994), 1443–53; Stephen Mathis, 'A plea for omissions', Criminal Justice Ethics (Summer/Fall, 2003), 15–31.

omission by me at *t* to save Jones from drowning is the absence of any act-token of mine at *t* that instantiates the type of action, saving Jones from drowning. Such an omission is not a particular event or a particular state of affairs, like a particular act of saving only existing as a particular *not*-saving. Omitting to save is no more a particular something than is an absent elephant a particular something, an odd and ghostly kind of elephant, a 'non-elephant'.

My stipulation is mostly for clarity and for the systematic argumentation it makes possible on the causal status of omissions. But I also take such a meaning to statements about omissions to be in conformity with ordinary usage and the semantic intentions of ordinary speakers when they speak of omissions.

This generic meaning to 'omission' will raise obvious problems for omissions being eligible to serve as causes. Seeing this, a number of theorists sympathetic to omissive causation seek to substitute a different generic meaning for 'omission', a meaning that takes omission to be some actually existent particulars (and not just absences of types, as I contend). I divide those who seek some such more positive meaning of 'omission' into three camps. First, there are those who wish to conceive of omissions as *mental* particulars that unproblematically exist. This is the view taking the phrase 'my omission at *t* to save Jones', to refer to my willing (deciding, intending, etc) not to save Jones. Second, others wish to construe omissions as referring elliptically to some one event that is going on in the spatio-temporal region in question. On this view, 'my omission at *t* to save Jones' refers to what I *was* doing at *t*. If I was sitting quietly, dancing a jig, conversing with a friend, or whatever, it is some such particular act to which reference is made. Third, one might take omission language to refer to everything else going on in the relevant spatio-temporal region. 'My omission at *t* to save Jones', on this view, refers to the totality of states of affairs in this region at *t*. Such a phrase refers to the omission in the same way that a donut isolates for us a donut hole—the omission (like the donut hole) is where nothing is going on (or where there is no donut).

There is nothing ontologically suspect about any of these three alternative conceptualizations of omissions. There are mental events, willings being one of them, and like all representational states there is nothing untoward or awkward about intending or willing *not* to do something. The content of such representational states is propositional, and as we saw in Chapters 14 and 15, negative propositions are unproblematic (as contrasted to negative properties or negative events). Similarly, conversing, dancing, etc, are unproblematically things we do, and such human actions are one species of events that unproblematically exist. Likewise, a totality of such events or states of affairs exists as robustly as does the events or states of affairs composing such a totality. Breaking a rack in billiards is a perfectly respectable event, as respectable as the events which compose it such as hitting the apex ball with the cue ball.[20]

---

[20] On fusing smaller events into fewer larger events, see Judith Jarvis Thomson, *Acts and Other Events* (Ithaca: Cornell University Press, 1977), 78.

Queer ontology is thus not the objection to any of these three proposals. Nonetheless we should reject each of them. There are two objections to the first construal, the mental state construal. One is Bentham's quite accurate observation that many of the omissions in which we have both explanatory interest and for which we blame people, are not willed omissions.[21] I can will myself to do nothing to save Jones; but I also can fail to advert (negligently or non-negligently) to Jones' peril, and *omit* to save him nonetheless. Secondly, even when some omission is willed, the semantic intentions of speakers who use the phrase 'my omission at *t* to save Jones' is *not* to refer to the willing. Their semantic intention is to refer to the fact that I did nothing to save Jones. We know this because of what they would say if I did will not to save Jones, but saved him nonetheless through misadventure: I did *not* omit to save Jones, even though the thing to which they were supposedly referring—my willing—was present.

The second and third construal of omissions are subject to this last objection too. My semantic intention in using the phrase 'my omission at *t* to save Jones' is not to refer to what I was doing at *t*. I know how to refer to what I was doing at *t*—I use words like 'sitting', 'reading', 'conversing', etc. True enough, Donald Davidson accurately pointed out that we often use descriptions of non-essential properties of an event to pick out that event.[22] We can refer to an avalanche event as 'the most talked about event of the year', without for a moment thinking that the talking was any part of the avalanching. What we do not typically do is use a property an event does *not* have to form a description with which to pick out that event. We do not pick out some avalanche at *t* by saying 'the non-red event at *t*'.[23] Imagine picking out *objects* by properties they do *not* have. Take the sentence, 'no dog was at dinner last night'. Is this elliptical for 'there *is* something such that (it is no dog and it was at dinner last night)'?[24] One can (just barely) imagine that this would be a way of picking out your attractive dinner companion of the previous evening—she certainly is no dog, you might think—but no one I know uses language this way. They mean, 'it is not the case that there was any token of the type, dog, at dinner last night'; which is how I construe talk about absent events too.

---

[21] Jeremy Bentham, *An Introduction to the Principles of Morals and Legislation* (Oxford: Oxford University Press, 1789), 72, n 1. See the discussion in Moore, *Placing Blame*, 262–6.

[22] Donald Davidson, *Essays on Actions and Events* (Oxford: Oxford University Press, 1980).

[23] There are of course circumstances where the absence of some property is so surprising or so uniquely true of some event that we pick it out by such absence. Eg: 'the least talked about event of the war' might refer to some surprisingly secret action.

[24] Jonathan Schaffer's construal. Schaffer urges that we 'regard the absence description as a way of referring to a present event, so that "the father's negligence" [in not watching his child] is just a way of referring to his actual nap, or whatever he actually did': Schaffer, 'Causes need not be physically connected to their effects: The case for negative causation', in Christopher Hitchcock (ed), *Contemporary Debates in Philosophy of Science* (Oxford: Blackwell, 2004), 212. At dinner at the 2006 Mt Hood Conference on Causation, Schaffer made explicit the paraphrase in the text, which moves the negation from outside the existential quantifier and places it inside that quantifier's scope.

There are two additional objections to the third alternative construal of omissions, objections not dependent on the semantic intentions with which we speak. One objection is that of indeterminacy: the hole in the metaphorical donut (of totality states of affairs) includes too much—indeed, it is as large as the universe surrounding the donut. Less metaphorically: what is *not* going on at *t* when everything that is going on at *t* *is* going on, is very very large. True enough, there is no saving of Jones by me going on at *t*; but the Martians are not invading, the moon is not disintegrating, the flies are not buzzing at *t* too. The totality of what is going on—even if we restrict the spatial region severely—does not uniquely isolate any non-saving of Jones by me. Second, much of what *is* going on (in the totality of states of affairs at *t*) is causally irrelevant to Jones' death. If the motive for reconstruing omission talk to be about something(s) is to have ontologically respectable relata for causal relations, this will not do it. On no plausible theory of the causal relation is my *conversing* a cause of Jones' death, even in the situation where that was what I was doing rather than saving Jones. On the counterfactual theory, for example, the closest possible world in which we should test the counterfactual, 'if I had not been conversing, Jones would not have died', is *not* the possible world in which we replace the conversing I did in the actual world with a rope-throwing.[25] If Jones is my old enemy, for example, and I noticed his plight but kept conversing, the closer possible world in which to test the counterfactual is one where we replace my conversing with my laughing, my dancing a celebratory jig, or my sitting quietly. And in those worlds, Jones dies all the same.

I conclude that my construal of omissions (as the absence of any instance of a type of action) is secure. This gives 'omission' what I call its *generic* meaning. Nothing in this construal precludes overlaying this generic meaning with many things lawyers in particular are often keen to add. The omissions (absent actions) we are interested in are often those generic omissions where in addition:

(1) there was an *ability* to make a difference
(2) there was a moral or legal *duty* not to omit
(3) there was some *expectation* of the action omitted so that the omission is surprising
(4) omitting was faulty (at least negligent) or
(5) omitting was intentional.

In various contexts we may well restrict the omissions that we wish to talk about to one or more of these subclasses of omissions. For my purposes, however, we need to work with the generic sense of an omission. For it is this sense that tests our question here, which is whether absent things—omissions—can ever be causes.

---

[25] Schaffer's strategy: 'Causes need not be physically connected to their effects'. I deal with this in Moore, *Act and Crime*, 29–31.

In addition to those who would substitute a different meaning for 'omission' for my stipulated, generic meaning, there are those who reject such a meaning because they doubt the coherence of *any* act/omission distinction. Omission talk is just a form of action talk, on this view, so that 'action by omission' versus 'action by commission' is no real distinction. The worry here is whether we can reliably distinguish actual events or states of affairs, from absent ones. There is a nest of worries here, so let me separate four of them. The first worry is the problem known as the problem of 'embedded omissions'.[26] The problem arises the moment one regards the individuation of act-tokens like an accordion, so that one can look narrowly or broadly in time for 'parts' of 'the same act'. Suppose a defendant starts driving his auto at t_1, accelerates to the legal speed limit at t_2, and is travelling in a straight line at that speed at t_3 when a child darts out in front of him. He fails to hit the brakes at t_3, the child is hit at t_4, and dies at t_5. The omission, it is said is 'embedded' within a larger 'course of conduct' for which the driver can be held responsible.[27] Now the skeptical worry: 'any omission can be characterized as part of a larger encompassing act'[28] if one is free to 'play the accordion' by expanding the time frame during which one looks for acts and not omissions.

The antidote to this form of the conceptual worry about omissions is not to be so sloppy in the formulation of the act requirement. Do not formulate that requirement in terms of some ill-defined 'course of conduct'; rather, ask at each relevant time whether there was some act or omission of the defendant with the relevant (causal or counterfactual) properties. In the driving example, there are acts at t_1 and t_2, but do they cause the death? There is an omission at t_3 (the duty with respect to which arose by defendant's acts at t_1 and t_2 placing the child in peril), but would the child not have died if defendant had not omitted to apply his brakes? These more precise questions do not allow one to conclude that 'any omission can be characterized as part of a larger encompassing act'.[29]

A second but distinct worry stems from what I have elsewhere called the 'true doctrine of "embedded omissions" '.[30] This is the doctrine holding that omissions to change some state of affairs can always be reconceptualized as the existence of the state of affairs not changed which is itself a circumstance present when the defendant performs some positive action. For example, the defendant who omits to obtain the woman's consent to sexual intercourse is not guilty of a crime of omission when he is convicted of rape; rather, his act of causing penetration took place in the circumstance that no consent had been given. That he could have

---

[26] Discussed by me in Moore, *Placing Blame*, 269; Moore, *Act and Crime*, 35–7.

[27] 'Course of conduct' is the term of art used by the American Law Institute's Model Penal Code, § 2.01. The English common law invites this same sloppy analysis. See, eg, *Fagen v. Metropolitan Police Commissioner* [1969] 1 QB 439, where the court debated whether not moving the car which earlier one had driven onto an officer's foot was an act or an omission (rather than seeing that there was an act at t_1 *and* an omission at t_2).

[28] David Fischer, 'Causation in fact in omission cases', Utah Law Review (1992), 1339.

[29] Ibid.   [30] Moore, *Placing Blame*, 269.

(perhaps) prevented this circumstance from existing but omitted to do so, is neither here nor there. His act took place in the circumstance of no consent, and it is for that act in that circumstance that he is rightly punished.

There is of course nothing whatsoever wrong with this conclusion or analysis for crimes like rape. Not fastening a seatbelt or not wearing a motorcycle helmet are not crimes of omission; driving or riding in a car or a motorcycle without these items are crimes and crimes requiring positive action. Likewise, operating a railroad engine without a spark arrestor is not a crime of omission; it requires the action of operating a locomotive in the circumstance that no spark arrestor is present.[31] Yet there is no general worry about the conceptual line between acts and omissions to be found here. From such examples one cannot generally conclude that any act can be characterized as an omission; nor can one conclude, as does Hyman Gross, that all 'crimes of omission are committed only when specified acts are done ... Even though liability is imposed *because* something was not done, liability nevertheless is *for doing* certain things without doing certain other things.'[32] The gross mistake here is overgeneralization: what is true of some crimes and of some moral failings is taken to be true of all. And it is not. Not rescuing a person in peril that one has a duty to rescue is *not* doing something else while not rescuing. Such omissions are as stubbornly omissive as the earlier examples were stubbornly active: it is the absence of doing any rescuing that is morally and legally prohibited.[33]

A third worry here is one that collapses my earlier distinctions between semantic intentions. Thus, Amit Pundik in a recent paper imagines a nurse who drinks tea rather than administering some medicine to a patient. Pundik supposes that the nurse's 'omission can be described as an action by emphasizing what the agent *actually did* (eg the nurse drank tea), or as an omission by emphasizing what the agent *failed to do* (eg the nurse did not administer the infusion)'.[34] The equal availability of these descriptions of course assumes that the descriptions describe the same thing. Rather patently, they do not. As I argued above, the referential intentions here are typically different. To use the first description is to intend to refer to an act-token, one of tea drinking; to use the second description is to intend to refer to an omission, the absence of any act-token instantiating the act-type of administering an infusion. There is no confusion of act/omission here,

---

[31] David Fischer's example, from which he concludes that 'this distinction between act and omission is meaningless because as a matter of semantics, any omission can be characterized as part of a larger encompassing act ... It is equally plausible to characterize the railroad's behavior as an act (carelessly operating a locomotive) or as an omission (failure to equip a locomotive with a spark arrestor).': 'Causation in fact in omission cases', 1339.

[32] D Hyman Gross, *A Theory of Criminal Justice* (New York: Oxford University Press, 1979), 65.

[33] Explored by me at greater length in Moore, *Act and Crime*, 31–4.

[34] Amit Pundik, 'Can one deny both causation by omission and causal pluralism? The case of legal causation', in Russo and Williamson (eds), *Causation and Probability in the Sciences* (London: College Publications, 2007), 25.

except in the mind of those who fail to distinguish these distinct semantic intentions and their correspondingly distinct speech acts.

The most troublesome of this nest of conceptual worries is a fourth one. It is that even when both forms of the embedding worries are put aside so that we are focusing on one discrete act or omission, and even when we do not elide two semantic intentions together by pretending they are the same when they are not, still (the objection is) it is arbitrary how we classify things into acts or omissions. Is death an event, but not-dying its absence? Or is surviving the event, and not-surviving (ie, dying) its absence? Is telling the secret an event, but not telling the secret its absence? Or is keeping the secret the event, and not-keeping it (ie, telling) the absence?

Examples like this might lead one to think that the positive/negative valencing of events is a purely arbitrary feature of language, not a feature of the world itself. Hart and Honoré seem to be hinting at this when they say that we are confused about negative statements: we easily think of omissions as 'negative events' and these in turn as 'simply nothing'. Hart and Honoré conclude 'that negative statements like "he did not pull the signal" are ways of describing the world, just as affirmative statements are, but they describe it by *contrast* not by *comparison* as affirmative statements do'.[35] One construal of this is that it is statements that are positive or negative, not the world; that both positive and negative statements describe something equally real, just by different techniques; and that for every seeming negative statement there is some positive translation, if one can but find the right word. 'Not telling a secret' sounds negative, but 'keeping a secret' sounds more positive; 'not throwing a rope' sounds negative, but 'ignoring the pleas of the drowning man' sounds more positive. 'Dying' sounds positive, while 'not surviving' sounds negative, just as 'surviving' sounds positive while 'not dying' sounds negative.

This suggestion is surely false. What is true is that the active/passive shifts of English are unreliable guides to presences versus absences. Keeping a secret is an absence, a not-telling, no matter how much idiomatic English may cover up this fact. Dying is also a presence, even if it can be described as a 'not-surviving', and surviving is an absence, even if it sounds like it is referring to some actual state of affairs.

Consider the following examples from a recent article. Amit Pundik, a skeptic about the conceptual coherence of the act/omission distinction, believes the problem to be exacerbated for what he calls 'quantitative omissions', which are not failures to act in a certain way in toto but are failures to *do enough* of the act in question. Contrast, Punkik tells us, 'the nurse administering *too little* infusion' with the nurse '*not* administrating *enough* infusion'; contrast 'driving too fast' with 'failing to drive slowly enough'; contrast 'providing too little information

[35] Hart and Honoré, *Causation in the Law* (2nd edn, Oxford: Oxford University Press, 1985), 38.

about an insurance policy', with 'failing to provide enough information'.[36] Believing these to be equally available descriptions that describe the same things, and believing each contrasting pair to contain an active and an omissive description, Pundik defies us to give a principled reason to prefer one description to another.

Yet surely these are no more difficult to classify than are the death/survival, keeping a secret/not-telling examples. If the referential intentions in each of these pairs of examples are the same,[37] then the single reference in each of these is clear. As to the nurse, these are two ways of referring to an omission; as to the driving, these are two ways of referring to an act; as to the insurance policy, these are two ways of referring to an omission. It is only the language that misleads; the reality is plain enough.

The only lack of clarity to be found in such examples lies in the semantic intentions of some speakers. In certain contexts of utterance one could refer to either an action or an omission with each of these pairs of descriptions. In response to a question of why the driver arrived too soon, for example, the utterer of the second pair of descriptions could be referring to an absence, a failure to drive at a certain speed. Yet this context-dependence of plausible referential intention proves nothing about the indeterminacy of the act/omission distinction. That on occasion we may be uncertain as to which a speaker may be referring does not at all confuse the two different things to which he could be referring.

JL Austin used to think that one could tell which of contrary pairs like 'dying/surviving' dominated ('wore the trousers', as he put it) by looking at the facts of ordinary usage.[38] What the foregoing examples do show is how unpromising is Austin's suggestion; to my ear at least, each of such pairs form equally idiomatic English. Rather, what is an actual event or state of affairs, and what is an absence, is a matter for science. It is up to our best science to tell us whether there are really dyings, or whether survivings is the actual event—just as it is up to our best science to tell us whether death is a natural kind of event, or only a nominal kind. It is up to science to tell us what there is and what there is not, here as elsewhere.

It is interesting why many people find this answer less plausible for events and states of affairs than they do for objects. If one thinks about whether there are elephants and whether there are Pegasus-like creatures, it does not seem that these are anything but questions that the best science, and the best science alone, should answer. The same is true about the question of whether a particular elephant was at a particular waterhole at a particular time (when, say, some grass

---

[36] Pundik, 'Causation by omission', 28.

[37] If they are not the same, then this is just another instance of the eliding of two distinct semantic intentions earlier discussed. In the context of blaming the nurse, the driver, and the insurance agent, I take the referential intention to be the same in each of these pairs of examples.

[38] JL Austin, 'A plea for excuses', *Proceedings of the Aristotelian Society* 57 (1956), 1–30.

was trampled). There is no room for any plausible skepticism about the distinction between actual elephants and absent ones, even if in particular cases there is of course room for considerable factual uncertainty.

This conceptual confidence is less for some people with respect to events and states of affairs that for objects. My own diagnosis of this is that such people are not realists about universals—properties, relations, types. They think that being a brother, and being a single child (that is, not having a sibling), are equally 'real' properties because their only criterion of what is a real universal is that some English predicate exists naming it.[39] On such a view, of course, the distinctions between not-being a brother and being a brother, not being a single child and being a single child, are illusory, depending as they do on the accidents of description-selection. Given the dependence of both events and states of affairs on properties, this view carries over naturally to a like skepticism about there being any real difference between absent or present events or states of affairs.

I shall *not* undertake a general defense of realism versus nominalism. (And while I *will* be doing something else, I am not referring to that with the omissive sentence just uttered!) Knowledge may be a seamless web, but we have to stop somewhere.[40] But since skeptics about universals are also necessarily skeptics about the act/omission distinction, their twin skepticisms must answer arguments suggesting that we need the latter distinction, both in our metaphysics and in our morals. It is to those arguments that I now turn.

B. Why omission liability cannot be cause-based liability: Omissions cannot be causes

Once we are secure that omissions are absences, we can address the main question of interest here: can absences be causes? There are four reasons for thinking that absences cannot be causes. The first lies in the fact adverted to before: we are not referring to a negative particular when we speak of omissions. Rather, we are referring to *types* of events only, saying that there was no instance of some type of action A at *t* when there is an omission to A at *t*.

One good reason for this semantic fact lies in the ontological fact that negative events, negative states of affairs, and negative properties do not exist. They are, as David Lewis rightly says, 'bogus entities'.[41] It would make for a very queer ontology to think that in addition to real tramplings of grass by real elephants, there were non-tramplings of grass by absent elephants. There are of course

[39] David Armstrong's name for this view is 'predicate-nominalism': Armstrong, *Universals and Scientific Realism I: Nominalism and realism* (Cambridge: Cambridge University Press, 1978), Chapter 2.

[40] David Armstrong argues generally *for* the reality of universals, and *against* there being negative universals, in Armstrong, *Universals and Scientic Realism II: A theory of universals* (Cambridge: Cambridge University Press, 1978), 23–9.

[41] David Lewis, 'Causation as influence', Journal of Philosophy 97 (2000), 195.

negative facts, in the sense of negated propositions that are true. It could be a fact that no elephants trampled the grass in the park today, for example. But it boggles the mind to think that the truth-maker for that negative proposition is some particular non-elephant and particular non-trampling 'done' by that non-elephant.

If negative events and negative states of affairs neither are referred to nor exist to be referred to by talk of omissions, it is baffling how there could be relata for singular causal relations involving omissions. In the (admittedly quite idiomatic) statement 'my failure to throw Jones the rope caused him to drown' we have a perfectly respectable drowning event to serve as the effect-relata. But what is the cause relata? Absences of certain things are not themselves some things (except in bad jokes and Heideggerean philosophy).

One possibility here is to take facts (in the true proposition sense) to be the relata of singular causal statements involving omissions. It was the fact that I did not throw the rope to Jones that caused him to drown. Yet this is too high a price to pay, as I argued in Chapter 15. Propositions do not cause changes in the world; the states of affairs such propositions are about cause changes in the world. It is a category mistake to regard propositions as causes, and if regarding omissions as causes drives us to this, it is an unacceptably high price.

It may seem that another possibility is to be found in the adoption of the reductionist view to be examined in Chapter 19: on this view, singular causal statements are but ellipses for statements of causal generalizations. Causal generalizations are only about types of events or of states of affairs, so no worries can arise about the lack of singular relata in singular causal relations. Yet this avenue affords no escape. Even such reductionist views require tokens for there to be types; causal generalizations about types of absent events require there to be token-absences.[42] Generalizations about how failure to water plants cause plants to die require commitment to there being individual absences of watering. And this is what is ontologically suspect.[43]

A second reason for thinking that absences cannot be causes lies in a widely shared metaphysical intuition Phil Dowe calls the 'intuition of difference':

There are cases where we have the intuition that . . . [the omission relation is] not strictly speaking a genuine case of causation. 'The father caused the accident by failing to guard the child'. It's natural enough to use the word 'cause' here, but when we consider the fact

---

[42] One might think one could make do with causal generalizations about absent types of events, not about types of absent events, and that absent types requires no absences as tokens. This I think reduces to the view that explanations using such causal generalizations relate facts in the propositional sense, where no commitments to negative events or states of affairs is needed, and thus is redundant to the first possibility considered in the text.

[43] I thus put aside as unpromising the Davidsonian temptation to find sense (for omission as cause talk) in explanatory uses of causal generalizations, a sense requiring no real commitment to negative relata for singular causal relations. Helen Beebee goes down this road in her 'Causing and nothingness', in J Collins, N Hall, and LA Paul (eds), *Causation and Counterfactuals* (Cambridge, Mass: MIT Press, 2004).

that the child's running into the road was clearly the cause of the accident, but that the father did nothing to the child, in particular that the father did not cause the child to run into the road, then one has the feeling that this is not a real, literal case of causation ... we do recognize, on reflection, that certain cases of ... omission are not genuine cases of causation. I call this the 'intuition of difference.[44]

Part of the popular appeal of the intuition of difference stems from the fact adverted to earlier: in omissions such as that of Dowe's hypothetical father, the father literally does nothing to guard his child. The intuition, put crudely, is that ' "nothing" cannot produce "something" '.[45] Or as Julie Andrews rephrased this in *The Sound of Music*: 'Nothing comes from nothing, and nothing ever could'.[46]

Put this way, the second objection to omissions as causes may seem wholly duplicative of the first objection (which was that there are no particular things to serve as the relata of singular causal relations in cases of omission). Yet there is more going on here. The 'intuition of difference' is based on an intuitive view of the causal *relation* and then, because of that view, only secondarily on an intuitive view of causal *relata*. The intuition is that the singular causal relation is most clearly revealed in cases of pre-emptive overdetermination, where we crisply and confidently conclude that the pre-empting cause (fire, noise, flood, shot, poison, whatever) completed its causal work while the pre-empted factor did not. However we characterize the relation that the pre-empted factor lacked that the pre-empting cause had, *nothing like that* is possessed by omissions. However we conceive of the father's *not* taking certain precautions, there is no relation between that not-doing and the child's death that is at all like the relation between shots causing death, noises scaring horses, floods inundating houses, etc—nor like (as in Dowe's example) a car hitting the child or the child running out in front of the car.

Humeans and neo-Humeans are wont to deride this intuition of difference as widely shared only because of a widely shared misconception about the causal relation. Logical positivists such as Moritz Schlick attributed such intuitions to the popular confusion of causation with a 'glue-like' relation whereby one event 'makes' (or forces, produces, or compels) another event to occur.[47] Whereas, Schlick thought, once we strip causation of these misconceptions and see with Hume that it is no more than regularity of succession, such intuitions will disappear. After all, a 'something' can regularly succeed a 'nothing', and if that is all we mean by causation then one *can* 'get something from nothing'.

---

[44] Phil Dowe, *Physical Causation* (Cambridge: Cambridge University Press, 2000), 217–18.
[45] Paul Ryu, 'Causation in criminal law', University of Pennsylvania Law Review 106 (1958), 779.
[46] 'Something Good', in Rogers and Hammerstein, *The Sound of Music*. Shakespeare got here first. In *King Lear*, Lear tries to prod his daughter Cordelia into speaking by admonishing her that 'nothing will come of nothing'.
[47] Moritz Schlick, 'Causality in everyday life and in recent science', University of California Publications in Philosophy 15 (1932), 99–125.

For reasons explored in Chapter 19, there are today few subscribers to the Humean regularity account of the causal relation. On most theories of the relation, causation does have some 'glue' to it, whether cashed out in terms of counterfactual necessity, nomic sufficiency, or something else. So the intuition of difference is not to be explained away on the ground that it was based on some naive confusion of causation with a compulsive making-happen. But the grain of truth in the Humean objection to the intuition of difference is this: the intuition is hostage to there being some theory of the nature of the causal relation that can explain why the intuition is well founded. The singularist theories explored in Chapter 20 attempt just that, whereas counterfactual and nomic sufficiency theories on their face seem incompatible with the intuition (both as it operates in the omission cases and as it shows itself in the pre-emptive overdetermination cases). To the extent that we have reason to favor singularist theories over their rivals,[48] we have reason to validate the intuition of difference by regarding omissions as non-causally related to the states of affairs that they fail to prevent.

With this caveat, is not the intuition of difference compelling? Omitted waterings kill plants no more than absent elephants grow grass. In each case, we may be confident: that some act of watering the plant would have kept the plant alive, and that some number of elephants walking to the waterhole would have killed the grass. Had those acts been done, the plant would have lived and the grass would have died; those acts would have thus *prevented* the death of the plant and would have *prevented* the continued growth of the grass. Such omitted waterings or tramplings are thus failures to prevent some event or state of affairs. But failing to prevent something does not seem anything like causing that thing to exist. Suppose you hold someone's head under water until they drown and I do not stop you. Have we each caused the victim's death? The metaphysical intuition I find compelling: you caused the death, whereas I only failed to prevent it.

This metaphysical intuition (of a difference between causings and failings to prevent) is matched by a moral intuition, which is my third reason for thinking omissions not to be causes. This is the intuition that there is a large moral difference between our positive duties of beneficence and our negative duties not to cause harm. I have a strong negative duty not to kill you even though you are a stranger to me; I either have no positive duty to prevent your death (for strong libertarians) or, more plausibly, a considerably less stringent duty to prevent your death when compared to my duty not to cause your death.

We explored several ways to test the relative stringency of duties in Chapter 3. One is the degree of seriousness with which we regard their breach. If I breach my negative duty not to kill strangers, I am rightly punished severely for some form of criminal homicide. By contrast, if I breach my positive duty to rescue strangers from deadly peril (when I can do so at no peril to myself), I am rightly

---

[48] This dependence of the intuition of difference on certain views of the causal relation and not others in stressed by Jonathan Schaffer in his 'The case for negative causation'.

punished much less severely—not perhaps as trivial as the $100 fine some states exact for such violations, but much less severely than for killing.

One can also test the relative stringency of paired negative and positive duties—such as the duty not to kill versus the duty to rescue from death—by asking the question we pursued at length in Chapter 3, namely: when do good consequences justify apparent violations of the duty? If one person is drowning in one location, three in another, and I can only throw a rope to the one or to the three, I may justify not throwing the rope to the one by the good consequences of saving the three. Whereas if in the same scenario the one has the rope in his hands and is saving himself with it, I may not justify holding his head under water long enough to drown him in order to get the rope so that I can again use it to save the three. My duty to prevent the death of the one is less stringent than my duty not to kill that one.

How are we to make sense of this moral distinction except with a metaphysical distinction between killing and not-saving, or more generally, between actions causing and omissions failing to prevent? If both are examples of causing death, how does one distinguish between them? Surely it is of no help to pretend that there are two kinds of killings, two kinds of causings; for that just returns us to the questions: what marks the difference and why does that difference make a moral difference? Categorical obligations not to cause death (kill) but only weaker, consequentialist obligations to prevent death (save), is a clear moral distinction based on a clear metaphysical distinction. Take away the metaphysics and it is hard to see how the morality here survives.

It may seem like I am letting the moral tail wag the metaphysical dog. And if I were arguing that because there was a metaphysical difference there must be a moral difference (between causing and failing to prevent) this would be true. But I am arguing the converse: because there is a moral difference there must be a metaphysical difference. The metaethics that makes sense of this last 'must' is a naturalist-realism that sees moral properties as supervening on natural properties (such as causation).[49] Supervenience is asymmetrical co-variance: the supervening property need not vary just because the base properties vary, because the supervening property can be alternatively realized by different base properties.[50] But every difference in the supervening property must be underlain by some difference in the base properties supervened upon. There cannot be a moral difference not reflective of some natural difference.

We must thus find some natural difference to account for the large moral difference between breach of our negative duties as against breach of our positive duties. The most intuitive natural difference is that between causation and non-causal failing to prevent. It is because causing death is so much worse than failing

[49] I defend such a naturalist realism in 20-odd years of essays collected in Moore, *Objectivity in law and ethics* (Aldershot: Ashgate, 2004).
[50] Ibid, 190–201, 376–9.

to prevent death that our negative duty here is so much more stringent than its positive counterpart.

Of course, one could locate the needed natural difference elsewhere. Jonathan Schaeffer, for example, would call both shooting someone and failing to prevent the shooting of someone, *causings* of death, but distinguish them on the basis of two kinds of causation: shooting is a kind of *physical* causation whereas failing to prevent a shooting is a kind of *non-physical* causation.[51] One could then explain the large moral difference by this difference, urging that physical causation gives rise to much more stringent moral duties than does non-physical causation.

Surely this is not very satisfying. It is a recurrent theme of this book that causal dualisms are always suspicious. We need some reason (other than saving a theory in trouble) for inventing second kinds of causal relations. They must share some essential features plausibly belonging to the genus, causation, yet that is rarely shown. Absent such feature common to both kinds of causation, the inclusion of non-physical with physical causation seems ad hoc and unjustified. Moreover, even if we were to concede the existence of two kinds of causation, physical and non-physical, in the context of moral blame it is *physical* causation that does the heavy moral lifting. The causal dualist would then have to admit that, 'while omissions may be causes of some kind, they cannot be *physical* causes, and that is what we care about in this context'. The significance of the distinction will not disappear just because we re-label it.

It is in fact preferable to keep the labels we have. If I *cause* death, I breach a stringent negative duty; whereas if I only fail to prevent death, I do not breach a stringent negative duty because I do not cause death. I may breach a less stringent positive duty—one built on counterfactual dependence, not on causation—but that is another matter.

My fourth argument for why omissions are not causes stems from the 'over-determination' omission cases mentioned in Chapters 5 and 6. Suppose a bus mechanic is under a duty to fix the brakes of a school bus in the morning but he fails to do so. The bus driver is of course obligated to use the brakes when coming to a stop sign, but he fails to do so on a given occasion (he either hits the clutch by mistake, or he fails to see the stop sign altogether).[52] Suppose further that if the bus driver had hit the brakes they would not have worked in their unfixed condition, and that if the mechanic had fixed the brakes the bus driver would not have used them anyway. The respective omissions of the mechanic and the bus driver were each sufficient for the accident that ensued when the bus ran the stop sign; meaning that neither omission was necessary.

We saw in Chapter 4 and again in the early part of this chapter that in the concurrent causal-overdetermination cases each causer is liable no matter how

[51] Schaffer, 'The case for negative causation', 211: 'Positive and Negative causation are different: the first involves physical connection and the second does not.'
[52] The example is from Fischer, 'Causation in fact in omission cases', 1349. It is adapted from the only slightly different facts of *Saunders System Birmingham Co v. Adams*, 117 So 72 (Ala 1928).

unnecessary may have been his contribution. If omissions were causes, that should be true in omission-overdetermination cases like the example above. Yet it is not.[53] From which I conclude there is no causation present in such cases. That makes the substitute for causation, counterfactual dependence, essential for omission liability. And since neither the bus driver nor the mechanic had the ability to prevent the accident, neither can be blamed for the accident. (They may of course both be blamed for their culpable omissions unconnected to the harm, but that would be an inchoate liability; the accident itself does not go in their moral ledger.)

I have noticed that there is some resistance to this conclusion among the theorists to whom I have presented it. Such resistance arises in cases of symmetrically culpable co-omitters, particularly if the culpability of each is that of intent (and not mere negligence). So: D_1 wants V to die, and so D_1 intentionally fails to fix V's brakes when he had a legal duty to do so; D_2, who also wishes V dead, intentionally fails to warn V of an unmarked danger on the road V will be driving when D_2 had a legal duty to warn V. Only if V had both known of the danger in advance, and had had the use of his brakes could he have saved himself. Each omission was thus sufficient to send him to his death. But neither D_1 nor D_2 did what they had a duty to do, so V died.

My resolution of such cases is to hold D_1 and D_2 only for some inchoate crime such as attempted murder. We should not hold them liable for V's death, not in criminal law and not even in torts, for that death was going to happen anyway, irrespective of the individual omissions of each defendant considered separately. There is thus no counterfactual dependence of V's death on each of D_1's and D_2's omissions, considered separately. There being no causation either, there is no desert basis for holding D_1 or D_2 responsible for V's death.

Those theorists inclined to decide cases the other way employ a kind of moral clumping principle.[54] One sees this clearly by asking for their resolution of contrasting overdetermination cases, those where one of the sufficient factors in

---

[53] The case law is actually ambiguous on this moral point. Many cases hold there to be no liability for either omitter, others impose liability, and still others treat the last omitter as pre-empting the liability of the first omitter. See ibid, 1349–60.

[54] Phil Dowe has tentatively suggested a metaphysical rather than a moral clumping principle. Perhaps we could say that when two omissions are individually sufficient and only jointly necessary, there is an 'indissoluble omission cluster' consisting of the two omissions. When the cluster is necessary for the harm (as it is in these cases), then any part of it is also necessary. This is essentially the suggestion by JL Mackie and others that I examined in Chapter 15, albeit under the guise of causation rather than counterfactual dependency as an independent desert-determiner. The suggestion is rife with the difficulties mentioned in Chapter 15, text at nn 21–2: (1) it is unclear how to represent Mackie's 'event-cluster', as a conjunction of O_1 and O_2 or as a disjunction; (2) as a conjunction, it is hard to see how (O_1 and O_2) could be necessary to some harm h when neither O_1 nor O_2 are necessary to h; (3) it is hard to give sense to a disjunction of negative events; (4) if sense can be made of it, the disjunctive version of the principle seems too broad: if O_1 or O_2 is individually necessary for h because the cluster (O_1 or O_2) is necessary for h, why is not *any* condition necessary for h? Eg, the disjunction of failing to apply the brakes or absence of fish in Lake Michigan is necessary for victim V's death, so the absence of fish is also necessary for V's death?

due to nature or non-culpable human misadventure. For example, V's brakes went out because of thrown gravel hitting the brakeline; or the sign warning of the hazard blew down in a windstorm. Now the conclusion is that neither D_2, who fails to warn (when there were no brakes anyway), nor D_1 who fails to fix the brakes (when there was no warning sign anyway), are responsible for V's death—because V was going to die irrespective of their omissions. It is only when there are symmetrically culpable human actors that this conclusion is reversed. They are then clumped together for purposes of asking after the moral responsibility of each of them.

Yet is this not just an unacceptable form of vicarious responsibility? We have doctrines of vicarious liability in both criminal law and torts: if D_1 and D_2 act in concert, then on agency grounds we attribute the acts and omissions of one to the other and vice-versa, with the result that the omissions of both of them (considered as a unit) were necessary for V's death. What the moral clumping principle above would do is extend vicarious liability to those who do not act in concert, do not rely on another's actions, and do not even know of the other's existence. D_1 and D_2 have no form of agency relationship and yet D_1 gets stuck with D_2's culpable omission and D_2 gets stuck with D_1's. We attribute one omission to the other, and then ask of the *two* omissions together: was that unit (of one or the other of them) necessary?

Rather than bloating our notions of vicarious responsibility in this way, surely it is better to explain away intuitions of responsibility for the harm in cases of symmetrically and seriously culpable omitters. Such intuitions are no more than the overweighting of culpability diagnosed before in Chapter 6: because we sense serious (if inchoate) culpability, we double-count it by using it as the basis of adding in responsibility for the harm. Such double-counting is illegitimate, here as elsewhere.[55]

C. The necessity of counterfactual dependence for responsibility for omissions

If omissions give rise to a moral responsibility for some harm that is not based on there being a causal relationship between the omission and the harm, it is pretty

---

[55] Another instance in which courts bloat our ideas of agency is in the Russian roulette and drag-racing cases. When the defendant puts the gun at his head and pulls the trigger to no effect and then the victim does the same, killing himself, some courts are dissatisfied with the result of applying the intervening-cause/accomplice-liability doctrines (which in their present form generate no liability as a principal because the victim's act is an intervening cause, and no liability as an accomplice, became the victim's suicide is not a form of criminal homicide). So such courts pretend that the victim and the defendant do but one act together, the act of 'playing the game', Then there is nothing that intervenes between that 'act' and the victim's death. See, eg, *Commonwealth v. Atencio*, 345 Mass 627, 189 NE, 2d 323 (1963). As Paul Robinson observes, such a 'combined effect' analysis (his phrase) paints with far too broad a brush beyond the confines of normal agency attributions: Robinson, *Fundamentals of Criminal Law* (2nd edn, Boston: Little, Brown, 1995), 235.

clear that counterfactual dependence is the relation between the omission and the harm that is doing the moral work here. If the defendant had no ability to prevent the harm in question—if in other words the harm's occurrence did not counterfactually depend on defendant omitting some act he had a duty to do—it is everywhere uncontroversial that he has no responsibility for that harm.[56] There may be an inchoate liability for such culpable but unsuccessful omissions. But there can be no responsibility for the harm without the counterfactual dependence in question.

IV. Counterfactual Dependence without Causation II: Preventions

One can omit to do any type of action, as we saw in Chapter 3. If one omits to *kill* Jones at time *t*, for example, then absent will be one or more features of any action at *t* that would have made that action an action of *killing*. One might have failed: to try to move one's body at *t*; to have had the willing of bodily movements actually cause those movements; to have had those movements actually cause the death of Jones at *t*. The causal nature of the act-type, killing, tells us what must not be present for there to be an omission to kill Jones at *t*.

The omissions we care about morally are typically not failures to *cause* something to occur. Rather, they are failures to *prevent* something from occurring. To understand these more typical omissions, we need to understand something other than causation, namely, the idea of a prevention.

We need to examine preventions anyway, for in their own right they present us with another example of where counterfactual dependence without causation can ground moral responsibility. One example of a prevention in Chapter 5 was of a property owner O building a tall building on his own land. Neighbor N heats the building on his adjacent property by both fireplaces with chimneys and solar panels. O's new building both shades N's solar panels and blocks the prevailing breezes so that N's fireplaces no longer draw properly. O has *prevented* the light from reaching N's solar panels, O has *prevented* the wind from drawing across the tops of N's fireplaces, and because of this, O has *prevented* the heating of N's premises.

As we saw in Chapter 5, tort and constitutional law reflect the kinds of distinctions I now want to urge morality recognizes as well. The primary mode of being responsible for some unhappy state of affairs is by causing it. Alternatively, however, a more occasional and lesser form of responsibility for some such state exists even without causation, and that is based on counterfactual dependence. If I prevent a benefit otherwise headed your way, I have not caused you a harm but I have deprived you of something of value that you would otherwise have had.

---

[56] As, for example, the Model Penal Code (§2.01) provides.

I may well be morally responsible for that unhappy state of affairs, although not as frequently or as seriously as I would be if I had made you that much worse off by causing you harm equal in value to your loss of benefit.

As with omissions, there are three points to consider here. The first is again uncontroversial: sometimes we are legally liable (as in nuisance) and morally responsible for benefits we prevent others from receiving. Also like omissions, the moral facts are nuanced: our responsibility for preventions is less frequent and (often) less serious than would be our responsibility for causing an equivalent harm, holding all else constant. This latter moral fact is less marked than in the cases of omissions, for duties to prevent (like duties not to cause) are negative duties, as a class more stringent than positive duties not to omit.

The second point should also be uncontroversial: responsibility for preventions requires counterfactual dependence. The benefit of which the victim is deprived must be one that he would have received if, contrary to fact, the defendant had not done his preventative act. In the ordinary run of cases this seems unproblematically true. As with omissions, the harder test cases are those analogous to causal overdetermination cases, cases where each of two or more acts of prevention are *sufficient* to deprive the victim of some benefit (thus making each act of prevention not *necessary*). We shall have occasion to consider one such case later in this section.

The third point in contention here is that preventions are not causes. One who prevents light and air from reaching land it otherwise would have benefited does not cause loss to the victim. It is because this conclusion is so controversial that I spend the balance of this discussion on the third point.

Preventions are not causes for much the same four reasons as were given for why omissions are not causes. First, there is no event or state of affairs to be caused in cases of prevention. *Not* receiving a letter is not an event or a state of affairs. Neither is *not* receiving light from the sun, nor is *not* receiving the wind one used to receive. If preventions were to be said to cause something, such 'somethings' would have to be absences like these. Absences can no more stand in the effect position of the causal relation than they can stand in the cause position (as would be required for omissions to be causes). To cause a nothing to exist makes no more sense that does nothing causing something to exist.

To be sure, some of the reference-shifting strategies we saw with omissions are also possibilities here. When speaking of preventing sunlight from coming onto solar panels, for example, one might urge either that: (1) the phrase 'sunlight not coming into solar panels', really refers to a state of affairs that does exist and that is caused by the defendant's acts, such as the construction of a high building on the defendant's land; or (2) the phrase isolates the absence of sunlight on the solar panel at *t* by referring to the totality of states of affairs in the vicinity of the solar panels at *t*, which totality (like the proverbial donut) does not include sunlight hitting the solar panels. Yet these reference-shifting strategies are as flawed here as they were for omissions, and for the same sort of reasons. First, the semantic intentions of all normal speakers when using phrases about sunlight and solar panels is *not* to refer to buildings and their construction. We have perfectly good words to refer to these items, and we use such words when we intend to so refer. Second, a totality of states of affairs at *t* fails to pick out just the absence of sunlight at *t*. Third, most of the items making up the totality of existing states of affairs at *t* are causally irrelevant: they are neither caused by defendant's action of building the building, nor do they in turn 'cause' the absence of sunlight (under any standard theory of the nature of the causal relation, such as the counterfactual theory).

The strategy of fleeing to facts (in the sense of true propositions) is of course also available here. As we saw before, negative facts (such as the fact that no sunlight hit the solar panels at *t*) are unproblematic, as unproblematic as any other negated proposition. Yet again, what makes negative facts unproblematic is just what makes them ineligible to serve as causal relata, viz their propositional nature.

The second argument against omissions being causes was Phil Dowe's 'intuition of difference', and that argument too applies to preventions. Admittedly, the intuition of difference is muted for preventions as contrasted with omissions. One does not write duets for musicals proclaiming that 'somethings cannot cause nothings, and somethings never can', for example.[57] Many people find it more acceptable to think that something real can produce an absence rather than vice versa. It does not have the flavor of something from nothing, as in the case of omissive causation.

Yet as we saw with respect to the Humean objection to the intuition of difference regarding omissions, this aspect of the intuition of difference was illegitimate anyway. That omissions cannot push, pull, or make things happen— while 'things' prevented can be pushed, pulled, or made not to happen—may seem intuitive, but only on an illegitimate picture of the causal relation. The intuition of difference remains after excising these extraneous features.

Even with this corrective in mind, the intuition of difference is lesser for prevention than for omissions, when each are contrasted with true causings. This sense of a lesser difference is easily explained. Recall that preventions *are* acts, unlike omissions. Moreover, they are acts that cause something (even if they do not cause the absences prevented). When I prevent you from receiving a letter of invitation you otherwise would have received, I act in such a way that I cause a state of affairs to exist that is incompatible with your receiving the letter: I cause a substitute letter (of rejection) to be in the envelope or I cause the letter to be misaddressed, or I cause the destruction of the letter. Such alternative ways of preventing your receipt of the invitation letter are acts causing states of affairs such as these.

Omissions depend wholly on counterfactual dependence to make a defendant responsible for a harm. To be sure, the content of the relevant counterfactual is

---

[57] In contrast with the earlier referenced (see n 46, above) Julie Andrews in the duet, 'Something Good', in *The Sound of Music*: 'Nothing comes from nothing and nothing ever could.'

about causation: when I am blamed for omitting to save you, the relevant counterfactual asserts that had I done a certain act (such as throw a rope) it would have *caused* a certain state of affairs (such as you being pulled ashore) that is incompatible with your drowning. Yet this is causation only in the possible world in which the counterfactual is tested.[58] Preventions, by contrast, require in addition that there be causation in this world, the actual world. It is because of the causal relationship between my act and the substitution/readdressing/destruction of the letter that the relevant counterfactual is true: if I had not so acted, you would have received the letter. Preventions, like omissions, are counterfactual and not causal in their nature; but unlike omissions, the relevant counterfactuals for preventions are true only because of an underlying causal relationship that exists in the actual world.

When the logical distance between the state of affairs caused and the type of state of affairs prevented is great, the intuition of difference is correspondingly great: my prevention of your having heat by my erecting a building tall enough to block the draft on your fireplaces, for example. But when the state of affairs caused is very close to the type of state of affairs prevented—as perhaps is my causing the destruction of your letter to your not receiving that letter—then the intuition of difference is much less. This scalar fact about preventions becomes crucial when we consider the moral difference between causing and preventing, as we shall now do.

The third consideration in favor of thinking there to be a metaphysical distinction between omittings and causings was a moral one: we typically are much less blamable for failing to prevent a certain state of affairs than we are for causing it. That consideration is present for preventions too. The metaphysical intuition of difference here too is matched by a moral intuition: the responsibility attached to a prevention is more occasional and less serious than for a corresponding causing. Legal reflections of this moral difference are to be found in the cause-based limitations of trespass and takings, as we saw before. As with the metaphysical intuition of difference above discussed, this moral difference is muted for preventions in contrast to omissions. It is both less blamable to block the draft of your chimneys (resulting in smoke from your own fires filling your house) than it is to blow (an equal amount of) smoke from my property into your home; it is also more easily justified. Still, the difference in this pair of cases is less than the corresponding difference in cases of omissions.

One might think that there is *no* moral difference between preventions and causings, and that the lesser blameworthiness in these pairs of cases is due to something else. The leading candidate for the 'something else' would be the differing entitlements involved in these pairs of cases. Causings giving rise to

[58] Phil Dowe calls such counterfactual dependencies who content includes causation, 'quasi-causation'. Dowe, *Physical Causation*; Dowe, 'Absences, possible causation, and the problem of non-locality', The Monist 91(4) (2008).

responsibility here involve the existence of *detriments* to the victim, whereas preventings involve the absence of *benefits*. The thought would be that we each have stronger entitlements to what we presently have than we do to what we presently do not have but which we would gain in the future (if there is no interference). On this view, it is the detriment/benefit asymmetry vis-á-vis a baseline of the status quo that is doing the moral work, not the presence/absence difference in causation/prevention.

Yet any serious consideration shows this thought to be untenable. Any right we might have to our present holdings just is a right not to have those holdings damaged; the correlative duty is not to cause such damage. Any right we might have to receive a benefit over and above our present holdings just is a right not to be deprived of that benefit; the correlative duty is not to prevent the receipt of such benefit. If one right is stronger than another, that is just another way of saying that one correlative duty is more stringent than the other, that breach of the one duty is morally worse than breach of the other. Our duties not to cause are stronger than our duties not to prevent.

Alternatively, one might urge that there is no moral difference between these pairs of cases, and thus, that one need not search for some explanation of that difference alternative to the causing/preventing distinction. Justice Antonin Scalia seems to take such a position in his takings opinions, urging that there is no conceptual distinction (and *a fortiori* no moral distinction) between harms caused and benefits prevented.[59]

One thing that motivates Scalia we should acknowledge just so we can put it aside. This is the well-charted human tendency to regard out of pocket costs as more serious than opportunity costs of equal value. Economists have long charted such 'framing effects' in popular psychology, but this is not what is involved in regarding preventings as less serious breaches than their corresponding causings. The preventing/causing distinction is not about the same state of affairs being differently valued, depending on whether one now has it or only expects it in the future. Indeed, in cases like that of smoke in one's room, the ultimate state of affairs is the same—smoke. The difference lies in how it got there—by being blown in, or by the non-drawing of the fireplace due to a blocked draught.

Even so, one pressing Scalia's objection would urge that route—via causing, or via preventing—is morally irrelevant. Yet as we saw in Chapter 3, except on a purely consequentialist morality, route often matters. I may have a strong, agent-relative permission to block your chimney's draughts whereas I have no such permission to blow smoke into your house; alternatively, I may have a weak

---

[59] In *Lucas v. South Carolina Coastal Council*, 505 US 1003 (1992), Scalia defies one to see a real difference between saying that the landowner's proposed use of his coastal property *caused harm* to South Carolina's ecological resources or saying that the use prevented the benefit of having an ecological preserve.

permission to block your draughts (and thus *allowing* smoke to envelope), if good consequences are in the offing, even though I have no such weak permission to *cause* smoke to enter your premises.

To my own mind, the cases differ considerably here. Indeed, the strength of the moral difference between causing and preventing seems to track closely the perceived strength of the metaphysical intuition of difference discussed earlier. In cases where the state of affairs caused by the preventative act is close to the type of state of affairs prevented, the moral difference (like the metaphysical difference) tends to evaporate. If I squeeze your neck blocking air from reaching your lungs, I have merely prevented air reaching your lungs. Yet what I had to cause to make the relevant counterfactual true is the state of closure of your wind pipe, a condition in which it is impossible for air to pass through. In such cases I cause a state of affairs to exist (wind pipe closure) that is very close to the type of state of affairs complained of, an absence of air passing to the lungs. Thus, I did not *cause* the absence; but what I did cause (to be a preventer of air) is so close to the absence of benefit that I may be as morally responsible as one who causes poisoned air to enter the lungs.

Contrast such cases with the preventings with which we began this section. If I do a series of acts that cause a tall building to abut your property, I have done a causing by virtue of which the counterfactual relevant to a preventing is made true: I have prevented your chimney from receiving the wind it would otherwise have received. Yet the state of affairs that I cause is not close to the type of state of affairs, about the absence of which you make complaint. Blocking draughts is a morally distinguishable prevention, in a way that blocking windpipes is not.

This raises large issues having implications well beyond the causing/preventing distinction. These issues have to do with the meaning of 'closeness' involved here, and the relationship between morality and metaphysics when the morality does not (quite) cut nature at its metaphysical joints. Since these same issues will be squarely before us with double-preventions, to be discussed shortly, I shall defer discussion of them briefly.

I come now to the fourth argument for not considering preventings to be causings of the absence prevented. This is the argument arising out of concurrent overdetermination cases; what we need to consider are cases of concurrent overdetermination *preventions*. Try a variation of the old McLaughlin hypothetical that I first introduced in Chapter 5.[60] The victim was sent a written offer of a valuable opportunity to join a scientific expedition that would have greatly furthered her career; she never learned of the offer and the opportunity it afforded her until after the expedition had completed its work. The reason for this loss lies with the actions of three rivals, D_1, D_2, and D_3, who did not know of each other's acts and thus did not act in concert. D_1 substituted a rejection letter for

---

[60] James McLaughlin, 'Proximate cause', Harvard Law Review 39 (1925), 155, n 25.

the acceptance letter that had been sent to her; D_2, thinking the acceptance letter was still in the envelope, readdressed the envelope and its return address so that the letter would end up lost in the Post Office's dead letter section; D_3, not knowing either of these facts, threw what he believed was a properly addressed acceptance letter into the fire. Each of these acts was sufficient for the victim to lose her opportunity to join the expedition; none was therefore necessary. Is the responsibility of D_1, D_2, and D_3 inchoate, or is their responsibility the more serious one of preventing her from receiving this benefit to which she was entitled?

If preventings were causings, there should be no doubt of a non-inchoate liability here. D_1, D_2, and D_3 were each a concurrent cause of her loss, and the fact that none of their acts (considered individually) were necessary for that loss to occur would be irrelevant. Yet this fact does not seem irrelevant. Counterfactual dependence seems necessary here. Each of course are blameworthy for *trying* to prevent her from receiving the benefit. And considered collectively, of course, they did *together* prevent her from going on the expedition. Yet judged as individuals they did not. D_1 did not in fact do what he was trying to do. D_1 did not succeed in preventing her from going, because she would not have gone even if D_1 had not done what he did. And *mutatis mutandis* for D_2 and D_3. Her loss counterfactually depended on none of their acts (considered individually), and that fact seems determinative of the degree of their responsibility in a way it would not be if preventings were causings.

As with omissions, there are those who do not find this resolution intuitive. Such critics want to hold D_1, D_2, and D_3 responsible for the loss of V's opportunity, both in torts and also in criminal law (if this were a crime of some sort). The considerations against this contrary resolution of such cases are the same as those against a like resolution of the overdetermination-omission cases: it is either a form of double-counting of culpability or it is an illegitimate extension of vicarious responsibility to not-in-concert actors. Being duplicative, I will not repeat the arguments.

There is, however, one new wrinkle in cases of overdetermining preventions. This stems from the fact mentioned before about preventions: although like omissions preventions create responsibility based on counterfactual dependence, unlike omissions, preventions require a counterfactual dependence that supervenes on a causal relationship in this, the actual world: for action A to have prevented benefit B, A must have caused some state S, where S is incompatible with the existence of B. As we have seen, as S gets very close to an absence of B, we are tempted to assimilate preventions to causings. Now suppose there are three actions A_1, A_2, and A_3 independently performed by three actors, each action being sufficient for S; in such circumstances, A_1, A_2 and A_3 are all causes of S; as causers of S, they also will be regarded as causers of the absence of B, where S is very close to such absence. So *in these cases* of overdetermined preventions, one might well hold each preventer jointly liable with the others for the loss of the benefit in question. (I do not think the altered/misaddressed/destroyed letter scenario is such a case, however, for each actor causes a different state S to exist incompatible with V's receipt of the offer letter.)

V. Counterfactual Dependence without Causation III: Blameworthiness for Double-Preventions

A third sort of situation making an actor morally responsible for some harm that he did not cause but which counterfactually depended on his act, is that of a double-prevention. As we saw in Chapter 3, these are cases where an actor does some act that prevents something else from happening which, if it had happened, would have prevented the occurrence of some harm. Thus the name, 'double-prevention'.

One of the examples in Chapter 3 was that of Judge Tally. Judge Tally acted in such a way as to prevent the delivery of a warning telegram to one Ross; had Ross received the warning telegram (on one version of the facts), he would have not been found and killed by the Skeltons. In such a way Tally prevented a preventer (the warning telegram) from preventing Ross' death.

As with omissions and (single) preventions, there are three points to establish: first, that we are morally responsible for the harms that at least some double-preventions make possible; second, that the connection between the defendant's act and the harm that grounds the actor's moral responsibility for that harm is the counterfactual dependency of the harm on the act; and third, that such acts do not cause the harms that they make possible in this way.

Judge Tally's case illustrates how obviously true is the first proposition: Tally and people like him are morally responsible for the harms their acts make possible. It is true that in Tally's case the legal form this responsibility takes in criminal law is that of accomplice liability; but as we saw in Chapter 13, that fact is due to the accidents of legal history. Tally is no more and no less responsible for Ross' death than was my hypothetical preventer (who prevented a lifeguard from saving a drowning victim in Chapters 3 and 13) responsible for the death of the drowning victim. Both defendants are seriously blamable for preventing something that would have prevented death. That the death of Ross was by human hands, whereas the death of the drowning victim was due to nature, is incidental.

As with omissions and preventions, however, the moral facts are nuanced for double-preventions. Two points arise. First, recall that there is a sub-class of double-preventions where both the degree of moral blameworthiness, and the availability of consequentialist justifications, parallel that of omissions. These are cases of *allowings*, where one is significantly less blameworthy and where the consequentialist justifications are much more available, than for the equivalent causings. In passive euthanasia cases, for example, when doctors who initiated the use of a respirator prevent that respirator from preventing a patient's death, their blameworthiness is less, and their justifications more available, than would be the case for an active killing.

Second, even for the double-prevention cases that are not (full) allowings—because the double-preventer does not return the victim to some morally appropriate baseline—the blameworthiness is less, and the justification more available, than in contrasting cases of causation. One of the examples of Chapter 3 were the stress and duress techniques—'torture lite'—employed in Northern Ireland, Israel, Afghanistan, and elsewhere.

The second proposition required to be established in this section was that counterfactual dependence is the relevant desert-determiner at work in these cases. This should be uncontroversial. Surely what makes Tally responsible for the death of Ross is that Tally's act (of preventing the delivery of the warning telegram) made it possible for the Skeltons to kill Ross. Tally did what was needed to get Ross killed, which was to remove an impediment to that killing. For that he is surely blameworthy.

One can see the necessity of counterfactual dependence to blameworthiness here most clearly in the allowing subspecies of cases. For what makes allowings so much different (morally speaking) from other double-preventions is the return-to-baseline aspect of them. As we saw in Chapter 3, if it was Tally who had sent the warning telegram, then it is much less blamable of him to countermand the delivery of that telegram and thus allow Ross to be killed. As we saw, such full-allowing cases largely remove the counterfactual dependency of the harm on that act of the defendant: Ross' two acts together—the sending of the warning telegram, and the sending of the countermanding telegram—pretty much cancel each other out, leaving Ross to die the death he was going to die anyway if Tally had done nothing. Such cases of full allowings thus show us the power of counterfactual dependency: when Tally's act makes a real difference (the bare double-prevention version of the facts), Tally is seriously blamable; but when Tally's act(s) make no real difference (the full allowing version of the facts), his blameworthiness is no greater than that of an omission.

The third proposition is again the controversial one; this was that double-preventionists like Tally do not cause the harms their acts make possible. In arguing for this third proposition, I shall rely again on four arguments, the same arguments deployed to show why preventions and failures to prevent (omissions) are non-causal.

First, there is the hard-to-dispute truth of general ontology: there are no negative properties, no negative events, and no negative states of affairs. Absences, thus, cannot stand in the singular causal relation—as either causes (omissions) or as effects (preventions)—for the simple reason that they are not particulars. This fact of general ontology may at first glance seem to be less damning of construing double-preventions as causal, than it is of a like construal of omissions or preventions. After all, in cases of double-prevention there is an act of the defendant that is real enough—an act such as Tally's sending the countermanding telegram. In such cases there is also an event that unproblematically exists such as the death of Ross. So one might think the ontological objection to be idle here. Yet it is not. In double-prevention cases the alleged causal intermediary is an absence, and that is problematic because such causal intermediacies need to be both effects of an earlier cause, and cause of yet later effects, and absences can be neither. If Tally caused something of relevance to Ross' death, it was the non-receipt by Ross of the warning telegram; it was this non-receipt that was necessary for Ross to be killed. Such non-receipt is an absence, and it can neither be the effect of Tally's act nor the cause of Ross's death, as it would have to be if double-preventions were causal in nature.

As with preventions and omissions, one can sidestep this worry by moving to facts (in the propositional sense) as causal relata. Yet as we saw in Chapters 14 and 15, that move comes at a high price. For those of us not willing to pay that price, double-preventions can be causal only if there are negative events, states of affairs, and properties—anethma to just about everyone.

Second, there is the argument stemming from the intuition of difference earlier discussed. This was the difference sensed to exist between the two relations, double-prevention and causation. 'Making possible' (by removing an impediment to nature or someone else causing) seems different than 'causing', is the intuition. As before, to the extent this intuition is not simply an expression of the sense (just mentioned) that negative relata do not exist, it is based on a sense about the causal relation. The intuition is singularist in its origins, premised on a view that sees the causal relation as not being counterfactual dependency, probabalistic dependency, or nomic sufficiency (since each of these seemingly can accommodate negative causation). To the extent that we have reasons to prefer some form of singularism to these theories—as I argue in Chapters 17, 19 and 20 we do—then Dowe's intuition of difference has adequate support.

Also, as in simple prevention cases, so in double-prevention cases, the intuition of difference seems scalar in its intensity. The intuition weakens in proportion to the closeness of the state caused (by the act of the double-preventer) to one of two things: either to the state causing the harm, or to the harm itself. Many of Jonathan Schaffer's telling counter-examples are on the 'close' end of this spectrum.[61] If some actor A causes a bullet to go through his victim's heart, the ultimate harm for which we hold the shooter responsible (the death of the victim) is immediately caused by cellular death in his brain and elsewhere. Such cellular death is close to the state the actor indisputably caused. A ruptured heart is not literally the same state of affairs as cellular death in the person whose heart it is; but it is pretty close. This is also true of Schaffer's other examples. Where A's willed bodily movements cause the trigger of a gun to move, which trigger movement moves a sear from the path of the spring behind the hammer of the pistol, what A has caused—the movement of the sear—is close to the state of affairs which caused the bullet to fire, viz the spring behind the hammer moving. Likewise in Schaffer's example of voluntary motor movement: A's willing to move his trigger finger unproblematically causes a calcium cascade through A's muscle fiber which in turn causes calcium-troponin binding; this is not literally the same state of affairs as actin-myosin binding (which is what immediately causes the finger muscle to contract) but it is pretty close.

Schaffer is right about all of these examples in two respects: (1) common intuition tells us that A *caused* the death of his victim, A's finger movement *caused* the bullet to fire, and A's willing of his finger to move *caused* his finger muscles to contract in such a way as to move his finger. The intuition of difference, in other words, evaporates for such examples. And: (2) at the micro level Schaffer specifies, these supposed 'causal chains' involve negative intermediaries: it is the *lack* of oxygen that makes possible cellular death, it is the *lack* of sear that enables the hammer spring to uncoil, it is the *lack* of tropomyosin on the actin binding sites that allows the myosin to bind there, etc.

In contrast to these cases of micro-double-preventions, the intuition of difference seems quite robust for the macro-level double-preventions that were our earlier examples: Judge Tally causing a countermanding telegram to be sent prevented the warning telegram from being delivered, only making possible (but not causing) the killing of Ross; the enemy of a drowning victim who ties up the lifeguard who otherwise would have saved that victim prevented rescue but did not himself cause the death of the victim. The intuition of difference is robust in such cases because what the defendant causes in each case—receipt of the countermanding telegram, an immobilized life guard—is at some remove both from the immediate cause of death—the shots of Ross' actual killers, or the ocean currents—and from death itself.

This problem should sound familiar. Recall that in Chapter 3 in discussing the doctrine of double-effect we encountered a similar problem about the other major desert-determiner there at issue, intention. Herod intends to please Salome, and as his means to this he intends John the Baptist to be decapitated and his head put on a platter. Yet one might think that Herod did not intend John's death; he foresaw that John would die from decapitation but would have been perfectly happy if John could have lived without his head.

As we saw in Chapter 3, anyone using intention as a marker of culpability or of permissability (of consequentialist justification) must resist this fine-grained characterization of what Herod intended. Decapitation, we said, was 'too close' to death to intend the one but not intend the other. This has long been noticed in the philosophy of intention. Philippa Foot: 'even if it be argued that there are here two different events—the crushing of the child's skull and its death—the two are obviously much too close for an application of the doctrine of double effect'.[62] Tony Duff: there is a 'logical connection' between decapitation and killing: ' "Brown is decapitated but survives" does not specify an intelligible possibility since it is part of the logic of our concept of "human beings" that decapitation kills them: if we could imagine a being who was not killed by decapitation, that would not be a human being.'[63]

In applying 'intention' we had quite self-consciously to 'get sloppy', as I put it in Chapter 3. The same is true of 'cause'. Decapitations and deaths are close enough that we should say that to intend the first is to intend the second. Analogously, we should say that to do an act causing the first is to do an act causing the second. In each case this is true irrespective of the actual metaphysics of event-individuation or the true identity of states of affairs and of mental representations. Even if Herod did not literally either cause or intend John's death, what he did cause and intend is close enough that his moral responsibility is that of an intender and a causer of death.

I am relatively confident of this as a truth of morality. Morality makes do with 'good enough for government work' intentionality and 'good enough for government work' causality rather than the finer-grained truths of microphysics. But it also seems that our folk psychological explanations, and our folk causal explanations, make do with this 'close enough' approximation. Moral blame aside, few people have any 'intuition of difference' between the Herod who intends John's death and the Herod who only intends John's decapitation, or between the Herod who causes John's death and the Herod who only causes John's decapitation.

This might lead one to proclaim a kind of causal dualism, according to which we have both a scientific concept of cause, and a popular concept. Some such as Phil Dowe indeed go this route.[64] Yet there are not two senses of 'cause' in play here, any more than there are two senses of 'intend' in play when we say that to intend *p* is to intend *q*. 'Intend' and 'cause' are univocal. What is being played with—and perhaps being played fast and loose with—is the identity of events, of states of affairs, and of representations. We know that literally being headless is not the same as being dead; yet for these purposes we will say that they are, so that to cause/intend one is to cause/intend the other.

This running roughshod over the true metaphysics of event-identity is not confined to applications of 'intend' and 'cause' in morality and in folk explanation. As we shall see in the Appendix, ordinary thought also utilizes a course-grained

---

[62] Philippa Foot, 'The problem of abortion and the doctrine of double effect', Oxford Review 5 (1967), 6–7.

[63] RA Duff, '*Mens rea* and the Law Commission report', Criminal Law Review (1980), 153.

[64] As noted before, Dowe allows that one might speak of a kind of 'quasi-causation' existing in cases where there is counterfactual dependency, no literal causation, but the counterfactual is about the causation that would exist in a close possible world. Dowe, *Physical Causation*. See also Ned Hall, 'Two concepts of causation', in J Collins, N Hall, and LA Paul (eds), *Causation and Counterfactuals* (Cambridge, Mass: MIT Press, 2004).

answer to event-identity in legal contexts such as double jeopardy and 'per occurrence' limitations in insurance contracts. Because of the mereological problem I address in the Appendix, the true metaphysics of events may be quite indeterminate in answer to the question 'How many events occurred with the collapse of the World Trade Center?' Yet the common sense relied on by the law in such contexts narrows the plausible answers to 'one' or 'two'. We confidently aggregate many fine-grained events/states of affairs, into the macro-sized events that we rightly think determine how much punishment or how much compensation the law should impose under 'single event' tests and the like.

I come now to the third argument for why double-preventions are not causal. This argument is based on the moral difference(s) between acts that prevent a prevention of a harm, and acts that cause that harm (or cause some state close enough to that harm). Double-preventions come in two varieties, as we saw in Chapter 3. Consider first what I called there full, non-omissive *allowings*. One example was where Tally himself had sent the telegram that would have warned Ross, but then, changing his mind, acted so as to prevent the delivery of that warning telegram. This hypothetical Tally's double-preventative act merely returned the world to a morally appropriate baseline, and we could properly characterize what Tally did as merely *allowing* (but not causing) Ross' death.

That Tally merely allowed Ross to die has the large moral consequences we adverted to in Chapter 3. If Tally was under no duty to warn Ross when he sent the warning telegram, then his later act (of sending the countermanding telegram) is not one that violates any duty and he is not blamable at all; if Tally had such a duty to warn, then Tally's sending of the countermanding telegram violates a duty no more stringent than his positive duty to warn (which is considerably less stringent than a duty not to kill Ross). In addition to these culpability differences, allowings make permissible consequentialist justifications that would be impermissible for the corresponding causings, as we saw in Chapter 3.

One might think that it is the return to a morally appropriate baseline that is doing all the work in making allowings so morally different than causings in these ways, in which case the causing/double-prevention distinction would be morally idle. There are two ways to test this. One is by making the double-preventing into a causing while retaining the moral baseline feature. For example, we transform passive euthanasia cases into active euthanasia cases, retaining the medical justification (say, a better use of the life-saving equipment for other patients with better prospects). Can we actively cause death (by knife in the heart, lethal injection, etc) in order to obtain the same good consequences? In the ducking cases of Chapter 3, if I may 'duck' by removing myself as your only defense against a pursuing grizzly, may I also shoot you dead so that the bear can feed on you (and thus save my life)? If some violinist is attached to me who will die if unattached within nine months, since I can allow him to die by removing myself as his defense against death, may I also shoot him dead (if that is the only way to get him unhooked)? I do not think the double-prevention/causing distinction is idle in these cases, however much work is being done by the return to a morally appropriate baseline feature.

The other way to test how much of the moral difference between causings and allowings is done by the causing/double-prevention distinction, is by eliminating the return to a morally appropriate baseline feature (but leaving the double-prevention feature) of a full allowing. Such 'partial allowings' (as I called them in Chapter 3) we should want to test anyway. These are the second subspecies of double-preventions where, if there is a moral difference with causings, it is considerably less than the difference between full allowings and causings.

Return to Judge Tally, the actual Judge Tally who was not the one who had earlier sent the telegram warning Ross that the Skeltons were on the way to kill him. In terms of degree of blameworthiness, Tally is indeed blameworthy for making it possible for Ross to be killed; but is he not *less* blameworthy than the Skeltons who actually caused Ross' death? It is true that formally in the criminal law Tally is an accomplice to the Skeltons' murder and is thus eligible for the same punishment as the Skeltons. The same is true in torts, where Tally would be an in-concert joint tortfeasor in any wrongful-death suit brought by Ross' estate. Yet as we saw in Chapter 13, the law-in-action is different than the law-in-the-books: Tally would almost certainly receive a lesser punishment than would Ross' actual killers.

In terms of the permissibility of consequentialist justification, suppose good consequences would follow from Ross' death; eg: Ross was the one person who knew of the British capture of the German Ultra coding machine in the Second World War and unless killed Ross was about to tell the Germans. Could not Judge Tally (or MI-6) make sure Tally is not warned and so that he goes to his grave with the secret? Is it not easier to justify letting others kill Ross than killing Ross yourself?

My example of this class of cases in Chapter 3 was so-called 'torture-lite', the stress and duress techniques that rely on nature to do most of the dirty work (sleep deprivation, sensory deprivation, and the like). The reason this is easier to justify than is true torture seems to lie in the double-preventionist nature of such interrogative techniques, a nature not shared by the cause-based techniques of 'torture-heavy'.

I conclude that even though there is less moral freight carried by the cause/double-prevention distinction than by the cause/failure to prevent (omission) distinction, still some is carried. It matters morally (and thus legally) whether people like Judge Tally are causers of death or are merely a preventer of something or someone who would otherwise have prevented that death.

It is admittedly disappointing that this moral difference does not track cleanly the metaphysical distinction between causings and double-preventings. As we have seen, to be morally plausible we need to expand the class of causings with the addition of those double-preventions that are 'near-causings'. We did this by getting deliberately sloppy and coarse in our mode of event/state/property individuation: when the counterfactual making the act A of defendant D a double-prevention is based on two causal truths—A having caused state S and state S' having caused harm H—and when S is 'close' either to S' or to H, then D's responsibility is that of a causer of H, not a double-preventionist. This was analogous to what we have to do with the other major desert-determiner in addition to causation, intention, as we saw in Chapter 3.

In both cases, the clean metaphysical distinctions of intention/belief and of cause/double-prevent only partly ground the moral distinctions. These two distinctions in natural properties need to be supplemented with the coarse-grained mode of event individuation at work in common thought, a mode that regards 'close' as good enough. This is not to abandon the supervenience of the moral on the natural; for closeness is still a natural property. The disappointment lies in its scalarity and thus the vagueness inherent in its application. It would be nice if the intention/foresight and cause/double-prevention applications were cleaner. But they are not.

The fourth and final argument for not thinking acts of double-prevention to be causes, again stems from the overdetermination cases. Consider in this regard James MacLaughlin's famous hypothetical.[65] The victim V is a prospector headed into dry desert country in which water will be necessary to his survival. V has two enemies (D_1, D_2) bent on his death, neither of whom know of the other's existence or activity. D_1 drains the water from V's kegs, replacing the water with rock salt for weight (so V will not notice). Later on, D_2, not knowing of the substitution of rock salt for water in the barrels, destroys the barrels. V dies in the desert of thirst. In Hart's and Honoré's[66] slight revision of this scenario (also discussed by JL Mackie[67] and Richard Wright[68]), D_1 does not drain the water, he poisons it; then D_2, not knowing the water to be poisoned, drains it out.

As we saw in Chapter 5, legal theorists are all over the map on this case. Some regard D_1 and D_2 as concurrent causers, in which event each are liable for V's death as intentional killers. Others regard D_1 as the causer of death, and D_2 only as an attempter (because death was inevitably headed Vs way after D_1's act (of either draining or poisoning the water). Still others regard D_2 as the pre-emptor, particularly in the second variation of the hypothetical where D_2 drains the poisoned water and V dies of thirst. Still others think D_1 and D_2 mutually preempt each other from being causes of V's death, but that each are responsible for that death anyway, on some unspecified ground.

As I argued in Chapter 6, these are all mistaken analyses because the use of such causal distinctions (concurrent/pre-emptive overdetermination) is misplaced.

[65] MacLaughlin, 'Proximate cause', 155, n 25.
[66] Hart and Honoré, *Causation in the Law*, 239–40.
[67] Mackie, *The Cement of the Universe*, 45–6.   [68] Wright, 'Causation in tort law', 1802.

These are also, as I now wish to argue, all mistaken bottom-line conclusions on responsibility for V's death. Neither D_1 nor D_2 are responsible for V's death. They are quite culpable, and each is liable for attempted murder. Yet their acts individually did not cause V's death, nor did such death counterfactually depend on either of their actions. They are no more responsible for V's death than they would be if some natural condition (such as naturally poisonous caulking in V's water barrels) had already poisoned V's water prior to anything D_1 or D_2 did to poison it, drain it, or destroy it. No one is tempted to think that D_1 or D_2 is responsible for V's death in such cases; the lack of counterfactual dependency is conclusive against such a conclusion. The same is true here, where there is no natural condition being sufficient for V's death. Only if one attributes the actions of one to the other, so that one asks the question of counterfactual dependency about *both* acts, can one sustain responsibility here. Yet this is to extend vicarious responsibility from in-concert actors to merely parallel actors.

If we are willing to make such vicarious attributions, why do not we also do so in true pre-emptive-cause cases? Suppose both D_1 and D_2 simultaneously fire at V, both hitting him in the heart with an instantaneously mortal wound. Because D_2 was at greater distance, his shot arrived too late, since V was already dead from D_1's earlier bullet. No one believes that D_2 is responsible for V's death on causal grounds. Yet why not clump D_2's behavior with that of D_1, say that the *combination* of D_1's and D_2's behaviors *was* necessary to V's death, and hold D_2 responsible for V's death, on a non-causal counterfactual basis? D_1's and D_2's behavior and culpability is exactly parallel; why not lump them together, ask the counterfactual question, and hold them both for murder? Anyone who believes in the kind of moral luck defended in Chapter 2 should find this conclusion absurd. They should accordingly reject the premise that generates it, viz that parallel actions done by separate actors not in concert can be attributed to each actor as we ask 'but for his action(s) would the victim have died'? And without this premise, there is no basis for holding D_1 or D_2 responsible for V's death in MacLaughlin's hypothetical. Neither caused V's death, and neither was necessary to V's death.

VI. The Interaction of Causation with Counterfactual Dependence when Both Are Present

We finally need to address the fourth of the possible combinations of causation and counterfactual dependence distinguished at the beginning of this chapter. This is where some action A causes some harm H *and* where H counterfactually depends on A. This is a very large number of cases. In the vast majority of instances in which A causes H, H will counterfactually depend on A; conversely, in a large percentage of cases where H counterfactually depends on A, A will have caused H.

As was said in the introduction to this chapter, this fourth combination of causation and counterfactual dependence may seem to be an easy class of cases to deal with, as easy as the class of cases where neither causation nor counterfactual dependence obtains. In the latter class of cases the actor is clearly *not* responsible for H (although she may have an inchoate form of responsibility). It may seem as unproblematically true here that the actor *is* morally responsible for H.

Sometimes, happily enough, the obvious is also the true; so here. The bottom-line conclusion is surely right: where both relations obtain, the actor is surely responsible for H, both in morality and in the law built on that morality. Yet this bottom-line conclusion glosses over some interesting and important nuances having to do with how these two relations interact with each other in determining the appropriate level of responsibility.

Blameworthiness and responsibility are matters of degree, and so are both causation and counterfactual dependence. This sets up the final question that interests me in this chapter: can the fact that some act A is strongly necessary for some harm H 'make up' for the fact that A is only a minor cause of H? Suppose, for example, that A is a minor wound in the victim compared to other wounds he has received but that he dies from loss of blood from all wounds.[69] As I argued in the first section of this chapter, A is responsible on a causal basis for the victim's death so long as the degree of his causal contribution crosses the *de minimis* threshold. Does it add to the actor's responsibility if his small wound was strongly necessary to the victim's death? (We might suppose, for example, medical help arrived too late to save the victim with all wounds, although the help would have been timely if the defendant had not added his small wound to the others.)

One thing should be plain about such cases, although it is worth making this explicit since doing so will forestall certain counter-examples being advanced against the conception of causation of this book. The fact that should be plain is that the presence of a minor causal contribution cannot detract from the responsibility that exists because of the counterfactual dependency of some harm such as death on the defendant's act of wounding. Polluters whose additional pollution just crosses the threshold for when harm occurs, voters whose votes are the deciding votes in some election, audience members whose attendance is just enough to ensure that some illegal performance takes place, all have a counterfactual-based responsibility undiminished by the fact that their causal contributions are quite small. After all, if a serious level of counterfactual-based responsibility exists when there is *no* causal contribution (as in cases of omission, prevention, and double-prevention), it surely exists when there is *some* causal contribution, as in these last sort of cases.

---

[69] The facts of *People v. Lewis*, 57 P 470 (Cal 1899).

I call these minor-cause sorts of cases the 'butterfly effect' kind of counter-example. The idea is to mention some quite trivial causal contributor to some large scale harm, much as the mythical flapping of a butterfly's wings in the Sahara is supposed to causally contribute to hurricanes in the Atlantic. Precarious boulders being given a slight nudge, powerful rockets being given slight course corrections, suggestions that place victims in the path of falling pianos, etc, are the common pattern of small (and sometimes *de minimis*) causal contribution. Then add counterfactual dependence: stipulate that none of these harms would have occurred without the butterfly doing its thing, etc. And finish with an evil manipulator: the defendant in each of these scenarios knows how necessary it is to get the proverbial butterfly to flap its wings, etc, and he causes just that to happen with the intent that such flapping produce the harm it does indeed produce. The sting of these examples is supposed to lie in the juxtaposition of *serious* blameworthiness with *tiny* causal contribution (if cause is taken in the singularist way this book defends).

The existence of a counterfactual-based responsibility removes the sting of such examples. There is serious blameworthiness in these cases; only it is not cause-based so it does not have implications for what causation must be like. There is no reason to think that counterfactual based responsibility is limited to cases where causation is absent—cases of omissions, preventions, and double-preventions. Counterfactual-based responsibility can exist for *acts* that cause harm as well, irrespective of whether such acts are large, small, or *de minimis* in the size of their causal contribution.

Seeing this possibility does raise the question of how causation and counter-factual dependence interact when both are present to determine responsibility for some harm. Granted, the small wound, minor pollution, single voter, and paid audience member of the earlier examples each have a serious counterfactual-based responsibility for the outcomes their actions make possible. Does it add to the degree of such actors' responsibility that they are also minor causers of the respective harms?

The problem in testing this is that we cannot get rid of the causal contribution and keep the examples parallel. (We can get rid of the counterfactual dependence easily enough, and that makes a large difference downward in the degree of one's responsibility.) Maybe this example will help.[70] The defendant wanted to kill his old enemy and so clubbed him on the head with a blow sufficient to kill most people. He then threw (what he took to be) the body over a high cliff in order to dispose of it. Seeing the body inert on the rocks below, he then left. In fact, the blow only rendered the victim unconscious. And the fall, which should have killed him, did not. The victim, weakened and injured because of the blow and the fall but nonetheless alive at the base of the cliff, could find no way up the cliff in his injured condition and so died of exposure.

---

[70] From the facts of *Thabo Mali v. R* [1954] 1 All ER 373 (Privy Council).

Suppose we get rid of the doctrines of intervening causation, as I urged in Chapter 12. Then the defendant's clubbing and his throwing causally contributed to the victim's death (it is my hypothetical so I can tell you definitively that it was his injuries and the exposure together that killed him). The defendant is seriously blameworthy for such causal contributions. Do we add responsibility for his having had the ability to prevent the victim's death (by rescuing him from the base of the cliff), an ability he (at least negligently) ignored?

The standard Anglo-American criminal-law answer is I believe the right moral answer here. On standard double-jeopardy grounds the defendant can be guilty of but one homicide here,[71] the degree depending on the most severe degree of any of the three possibilities. The causing of death done by the clubbing was done with an intention to kill, so that the negligent or reckless omission to save drops out as adding to the defendant's blameworthiness (as does the throwing). Such lesser counterfactual-based responsibility does not add to the greater cause-based responsibility.

If the converse is also true—that when the counterfactual-based responsibility is greater, a smaller cause-based responsibility does not increase blameworthiness—then we have the conclusion I think to be true. Causation and counterfactual dependence are not additive as desert-determiners. When both are present, the most seriously blamable relation governs, excluding the other from counting at all.

---

[71] See generally Moore, *Act and Crime*, Chapters 12–14.

19

Generalist Theories of Causation

I. Introduction: The Nature of Generalist Theories of Causation

As we saw in Chapter 14, we need to distinguish two kinds of causal statements: there are statements of singular causal relations, as in 'the spark caused the fire'; and there are statements of causal generalizations, as in, 'sparks cause fires'. The first statement is about the relation that holds between token events (or token states of affairs); whereas the second statement is about types of events or states of affairs. Even if one's aim is to reduce the first of these statements to the second—as is characteristic of the theories examined in this chapter—still one needs to appreciate the prima facie difference between them.

Generalist theories of causation (as I shall define them) are reductionist in their ambitions. What is metaphysically basic is a kind of universal, namely scientific laws. Statements of singular causal relations are to be translated into statements of these laws. This does not commit the generalist to regarding the statement, 'the spark caused the fire', as meaning simply, 'sparks cause fires'. After all, one cannot just ignore the reference to particulars in the first statement. So such generalists analyze the singular statement as meaning:

1. sparks cause fires, and
2. this spark occurred at t_1, and
3. this fire occurred at t_2, and
4. t_2 does not precede t_1.

Singular causal statements are thus unpacked as referring to *instantiations* of causal laws by spatio-temporally located particulars.

As we saw in Chapter 17's discussion of the counterfactual theory of causation, reductionist ambitions about anything come in various flavors. Most ambitious would be the analytical reductionist, seeking relations of synonymy between statements of singular relations and statements of instantiated causal laws. Less ambitious would be the metaphysically reductionist claim asserting an identity to exist between singular causal relations and instantiated causal laws. Less ambitious still is the nomological reductionist, who posits there to be an extensional equivalence between the two classes of statements even if there is neither identity nor synonymy.[1] For the reasons given in Chapter 17, I shall construe the reductionist claim here to be of the metaphysically reductionist kind.

So the generalist theories with which I shall here be concerned identify the singular causal relation with instantiated causal laws. In Chapter 20 I shall examine singularist theories of causation, theories that reject this identification. Clarifying what such singularist theories deny will further clarify what it is that generalist theories assert.

With respect to the law-reductionist claim of the generalist, there are two sorts of singularist theories. One is the extreme view that denies the necessity of there being some causal law behind every true singular causal statement. This is the rather wild-eyed singularism of Elizabeth Anscombe[2] that we examined and rejected in Chapter 15. Such an extreme singularism is counterintuitive because it allows that this spark can cause this fire without there being any general connection between sparks, fires, or anything else. It would not be in virtue of any property of sparks or of fires that this spark caused this fire; that it just did so, would be a brute fact.

A less extreme (and thus more plausible) singularism would allow that some law lies behind every singular causal relation. What is denied by this more moderate singularism is that the existence of such laws (together with space/time locators for instantiations of those laws) is sufficient for the truth of the corresponding singular statement. On this view, instantiated laws are necessary but not sufficient for there to be singular causal relations; there is no extensional equivalence, and hence, no identity.

Moderate singularism shall thus be my contrast case to the generalist theories here examined. Yet this opens up another ambiguity about the nature of generalist theories. One can get at this ambiguity by enquiring into the reduction base of generalist theories, viz what do they mean by 'laws?' When we examined the reductionist claims of the counterfactual theory of causation in Chapter 17, we preceded that discussion with Chapter 16's examination of the purported reduction base, viz the nature of counterfactual dependency itself. We should at least gesture at making some equivalent examination of laws here.

Suppose one meant by 'laws' to refer to all those true generalizations derived inductively from all true singular causal statements. Then it would be difficult to distinguish generalist from (moderately) singularist theories of causation. After all, if (as moderate singularism concedes) every singular causal relation is accompanied by some causal law, and if such causal laws exist only when there are instances of them that are genuine causal relations, then at least the

---

[1] These three ideas of reduction are explored by me in Moore, 'Legal reality: A naturalist approach to legal ontology', Law and Philosophy 21 (2002), 665–771, reprinted in Moore, *Objectivity in Law and Ethics* (Aldershot: Ashgate, 2004).
[2] GEM Anscombe, *Causality and Determination* (Cambridge: Cambridge University Press, 1971).

nomologically reductionist claim is made out: causal laws are not only necessary for causal relations, but they are also sufficient.

Yet this would be a trivial reductionism, for what makes a law causal is just what makes a singular relation causal. In which case, of course if there is a causal law, the relations which are its instances must also be causal in nature. What is wanted is a notion of causal laws that is not dependant on some prior notion of singular causal relations; then the reductionist claim distinctive of generalist theories of causation will not be trivial and will not fail to distinguish generalist from singularist theories.

Consider three sorts of items people have meant by 'law' in this context. One is owing to David Hume, who by 'law' meant only regularity of the concurrence of types of events. In Hume's famous language: 'We may define a cause to be an object followed by another, and where all objects similar to the first are followed by objects similar to the second'.[3] 'Sparks cause fires', on this account, is to be analyzed as the assertion of a uniformity of nature: when there are sparks, these are followed by fires.

A second view of laws is what I shall call the 'sufficiency' view of laws:[4] on this view, laws give sets of sufficient conditions for the happening of some sorts of events or for the existence of some sorts of states of affairs. The 'sparks/fire' law, for example, would be in terms of some set of conditions, such as: 'If there is a spark, in contact with combustible material, and there is oxygen, then *ceteris paribus* there will be a fire.' A further refinement of this view takes into account the worry that one could add any factor to a sufficient set and still have a sufficient set. So the refinement is to require *minimally* sufficient sets, that is, sets every member of which is necessary to the sufficiency of the set.[5] Richard Wright dubs these 'NESS' sets, 'NESS' abbreviating 'necessary elements of a sufficient set'.[6]

A third view of laws is the probabilistic view according to which laws are framed in terms of probabilistic dependence. Sparks are not sufficient for fires, nor are they universally followed by fires; but sparks do raise the conditional probability of fires, and the 'sparks/fire' law asserts just this.[7]

It is debatable which, if any, of these sorts of accounts is adequate as an account of the nature of scientific laws. There are serious objections to each of such types of accounts. Indeed, in the criticism of the three corresponding

[3] David Hume, *An Enquiry Concerning Human Understanding* (Indianapolis: Bobbs-Merrill, 1955), 87.

[4] One might also call this the 'deductive-nomological' view of laws, after the late Peter Hempel's famous articles with that title. See Carl G Hempel, *Aspects of Scientific Explanation* (Glencoel: Free Press, 1965).

[5] JL Mackie, *The Cement of the Universe* (Oxford: Clarendon Press, 1974), 62. See also Ned Hall, 'Two concepts of causation', in John Collins, Ned Hall, and LA Paul (eds), *Causation and Counterfactuals* (Cambridge, Mass: MIT Press, 2004), 260: 'S is *minimally sufficient* for *e* just in case S is sufficient for *e*, but no proper subset of S is.'

[6] Richard Wright, 'Causation in tort law', California Law Review 73 (1985), 1788–803.

[7] Hempel recognized the existence of what he termed 'statistical-inductive' laws, and distinguished them from 'deductive-nomological' laws, in his *Aspects of Scientific Explanation*.

theories of singularist causation—these derived from the Humean, the sufficiency, or the probabilistic theory of causal laws—it is common to attack such theories of causation in terms of criticism more properly directed at the specific account of laws being proposed. The Humean theory of causation is a case in point, because Hume's well-known difficulties in identifying laws as natural uniformities[8] are taken equally to refute his generalist approach to singular causal relations.

My hope is to prescind from these debates about the nature of scientific laws. So long as laws are not conceived so as to make the generalist theory of causation trivial (see above), I intend to leave open what might be the character of scientific laws. Such ecumenical approach is intended to focus on the range of arguments of interest here: whatever laws might be, can one identify singular causal relations as simply instantiations of such laws? I shall argue that the answer is no, hoping to deploy arguments good against the generalist reduction as such.

Still, it will be helpful to have some concept of laws before us as we proceed. I shall thus use the sufficiency conception of laws as my illustration. The points made against conceiving of singular causes as necessary elements of sufficient sets are intended to be equally applicable against the regularity or probabilistic view of laws. Where that is not the case, I shall note it.

II. The Nomic Sufficiency Theory of Causation

The crucial notion in the sufficiency theory of causation is that of sufficiency. Idiomatically, the idea is that a cause is something that guarantees that its effect will follow (and in that sense a cause 'makes' its effect happen). This stands in marked contrast to the counterfactual theory of causation, where the crucial notion is that of necessity (a cause is something necessary for the effect to occur, ie without which the effect would not have occurred).

One of the historically important reasons for adopting the sufficiency view is its apparent success in handling the concurrent overdetermination cases correctly.[9] As we saw in Chapter 17, these cases (of more than one sufficient condition for an effect) bedevil the counterfactual theory of causation, because if each of two or more conditions is sufficient for *e* then none of such conditions is (individually) necessary for *e*. Such cases present no equivalent problem for a sufficiency theorist; that each condition is sufficient is enough to count it as a cause, irrespective of the fact that such condition is not necessary.

[8] Nicely explored in David Armstrong, *What Is a Law of Nature?* (Cambridge: Cambridge University Press, 1984).

[9] See, eg, HLA Hart and Tony Honoré, *Causation in the Law* (2nd edn, Oxford: Clarendon Press, 1985), 124.

To emphasize this advantage, the late John Mackie formulated the sufficiency theory of causation in terms of an 'INUS' condition.[10] A cause is part of a set of sufficient conditions (thus the 'S'); but the set itself may be unnecessary to the happening of the effect (thus the 'U'); but the individual condition must be a non-redundant element of that set, ie, it must be necessary to the sufficiency of the set (thus the 'N'); yet that condition need not be by itself sufficient for the happening of the effect (thus the 'I' for 'insufficient'). In legal theory the negative elements are not emphasized; a cause is simply a necessary element of a sufficient set ('NESS').[11] But this is essentially Mackie's formulation, because it is still recognized by the NESS conception that a cause may be insufficient and unnecessary by itself and still be necessary to the sufficiency of a set of conditions.

Sufficiency theorists differ between themselves as to how much metaphysically heavy weather they wish to make of sufficiency. Mackie himself is usually classed as a neo-Humean, seeking to extract sufficiency from regularity.[12] At the other extreme, David Armstrong would back sufficiency with a primitive relation between universals.[13] For my purposes this will not matter. However sufficiency is cashed out metaphysically, the distinctive claim of the sufficiency theorist is that singular causes are simply necessary elements of sufficient sets.

What makes the sufficiency theorist a generalist about causation in his notion of sufficiency. 'Sufficiency' here means 'lawful sufficiency'.[14] A set of conditions on a particular occasion is sufficient in the required sense only if there is some law such that these *types* of conditions are sufficient to produce these *kinds* of effects. This spark is part of a set of conditions sufficient for this fire only if sparks are parts of sets of conditions sufficient for fires.

III. Problems for the Nomic Sufficiency Theory (and Generalistic Theories More Generally)

A common objection to nomic sufficiency theories is that no finite sets of conditions are ever truly sufficient for the happening of some putative effect, particularly if negative conditions are recognized.[15] One has to add *ceteris paribus* clauses to accommodate the open-endedness of scientific knowledge, yet these

[10] JL Mackie, 'Causes and conditions', American Philosophical Quarterly 2 (1965), 245–64, revised and reprinted as Chapter 3 of *The Cement of the Universe*.
[11] Eg, Hart and Honoré, *Causation in the Law*; Richard Wright, 'Causation in tort law'.
[12] Mackie, *The Cement of the Universe*.
[13] Armstrong, *What Is a Law of Nature?*
[14] That this is the best interpretation of the claims of the sufficiency theorist is argued in Richard Fumerton and Ken Kress, 'Causation and the law: Preemption, lawful sufficiency', and causal sufficiency', Law and Contemporary Problems 64 (2001), 89–95.
[15] Mortiz Schlick, a defender of a regularity version of the sufficiency theory, deals with this objection in his 'Causality in everyday life and in recent science', University of California Publications in Philosophy 15 (1932), 99–125.

clauses are themselves objected to as vacuous.[16] Relatedly, nomic sufficiency accounts are accused of parochialism in an indeterministic universe.[17]

These are the kinds of criticisms I intend to ignore, because they are directed specifically at the deductive-nomological view of laws. Wanted are problems for reducing singular causation to laws at all, however conceived. Fortunately we have a taxonomy of the right sort of problems ready-made for us. Such taxonomy is made up of the problems facing the counterfactual theory of causation, discussed in Chapter 17. A parallel set of problems exist for the sufficiency theory, problems which I shall examine *seriatim* in the same order as they were examined in Chapter 17.

A. The existence of non-causal laws

As we saw in Chapters 16 and 17, there are many kinds of counterfactual dependencies where intuitively it seems clear that there are no causal laws and no causal relationships. The analogous observation here is that there are many kinds of laws the instantiations of which are not causes and effects of one another. This is particularly easy to show for the Humean version of laws, where laws are simply observed uniformities of nature; for there are many such uniformities that are not causal (which is of course a damning criticism of the Humean account of laws). There are many accidentally true uniformities of nature, uniformities due to the accidents of sample selection or existence but having no necessity behind them: eg, there is no cubic mile of gold existing anywhere in the universe, no coin in my pocket is a nickel, and all lawyers in America are under seven feet in height.[18]

If laws are conceived in terms of probabilistic dependency (rather than in terms of Humean uniformities), laws are still too broad to pin down causal dependency. It could be that the comparative rarity of gold is such that if something is gold, it is less likely there is a cubic mile of the stuff than would otherwise be the case; and vice versa: if there is a cubic mile of the stuff, it is less likely that it is gold than would otherwise be the case. Neither of these probabilistic dependencies betoken there being any causal connection between being gold and there being a cubic mile of the stuff.

On the deductive-nomological view of laws, there is still overbreadth, although seeing that that is so can be trickier. Suppose the sun is presently casting a five foot long shadow on the ground while the angle from which the sunlight appears

---

[16] As in Anscombe, *Causality and Determination*.

[17] Ibid. See also Fumerton and Kress, 'Causation and the law'.

[18] The difficulty in hiving off accidentally true generalizations from true laws is of course one reason for rejecting a regularity view of laws, as both Hempel (in *Aspects of Scientific Explanation*) and Armstrong (in *What Is a Law of Nature?*) argue. The only point here is that if laws are conceiving as broadly as Humean uniformities, *laws* is far too broad a notion with which to explicate causality.

is at 45 degrees.[19] Given the laws of geometry, these facts are sufficient to guarantee that the flag pole is ten feet in length. Yet the nomic sufficiency (for the length of the flag pole) of the length of the shadow and the angle of the sun does not mean that the shadow's length and the angle of the sun caused the flag pole to be ten feet in length. It is not sufficient, in other words, for some set c to be the cause of some state of affairs e, that c is nomically sufficient for e.

What makes this point trickier to see under the nomic sufficiency view of laws is the hesitancy one might feel in granting the laws of geometry the status of scientific laws. One might relegate geometry to formal or mathematical laws, rather than laws of science. This is the same kind of temptation we saw before with respect to Jaegwon Kim's counter-examples of counterfactual dependencies that are not causal dependencies: the temptation is to regard counterfactuals like those of mereological or analytic necessity as not being of the right kind. Yet both temptations have to raise worries about whether one can specify the relevant kind of nomic sufficiency/counterfactual dependence, without soundly begging the question. It will not do to restrict the nomic sufficiency (or counterfactual dependency) sufficient for causation, to just those sufficiencies (counterfactual dependencies) that are the product of *causal* laws. For this would render the accounts viciously circular.

B. The continued overbreadth of nomic sufficiency

Even putting aside intuitively non-causal kinds of laws like those of mathematics, logic, or geometry, the generalist account of causality suffers from overbreadth. Indeed, it suffers from what I called 'the promiscuity problem' exactly as does the counterfactual theory of causation. In Chapter 17 I distinguished two major variants of this problem, the 'the cause' version and the 'a cause' version. I there put aside the 'the cause' version (on grounds that this version presents no real problem to any theory of causation), and I shall do so again here.

More troublesome was what I dubbed the 'a cause' version of which there are two variations. With the at-a-time variation, the problem lies in the sheer number of events and states of affairs that must be present for any truly sufficient law to be fully instantiated. My writing this paragraph is caused by my intention to convince you of its truth. But besides such intention other factors necessary to make the set sufficient to produce this paragraph are: oxygen for me to breathe, temperature in the room above what would otherwise freeze my fingers, a working supplementary motor area in my brain, ion pumps in the axon sheaths in the neurons that go through my pyramidal upper motor neuron system, etc, etc. Even the tiniest contributors, so long as they are necessary to the result, are all causes of my writing this paragraph; all factors that, if different, would have prevented me from writing, must also be included. The universe is not so

[19] The example of Fumerton and Kress, 'Causation and the law', 93, 101–2.

interrelated that the entire state of the universe at time *t* needs inclusion; but the list of the items needed to make a set truly sufficient is dauntingly large.

The list gets much longer on the over-time variation of the problem.[20] My parents having sex when they did, a variety of events in my educational history, probably Caesar crossing the Rubicon, and certainly the Big Bang, all are necessary elements of a set truly sufficient for me to write this paragraph. Such factors are necessary to complete the set of things sufficient for the writing of this paragraph: but in light of the millions of other factors necessary as well, the contribution of any of these remote factors is insubstantial and de minimis.

The nomic sufficiency theory of causation differs not a whit (in its riotously promiscuous willingness to consider factors as causes) from the counterfactual theory. Both count items as causes that neither law nor common intuition regard as causes. The probabilistic theories seem even in worse shape here, since there are even more probability raisers than there are necessary conditions or necessary elements of sufficient sets. While all three sorts of theorists can just bite the bullet here—as indeed, many of them do, as we saw in Chapter 17—it goes down hard. Any theory of causation having more discriminating power than these is to be preferred on this ground alone.

C. More overbreadth for the generalist theories: Omissions as causes

The promiscuity of sufficiency, like that of necessity, is vastly increased once one admits omissions and other absent events and states of affairs as possible causes. As we saw in the last chapter, omissions, properly conceived, are not causes, and any theory of causation committed to them being causes is in trouble.

Generalist theories are so committed.[21] A factor necessary to make some set sufficient can as easily be negative as positive. As Mill saw long ago, 'every fact or phenomenon which has a beginning invariably arises when some certain combination of positive facts exists, provided certain other positive facts do not exist ... The cause ... is the sum total of conditions positive and negative taken together ...'.[22] Bullets fired at hearts never kill by themselves; also necessary to complete a set of conditions sufficient for death of the victim is that: there was no bullet-proof armor on the victim; there were no large birds flying in just the wrong place at the wrong time; the victim did not get swallowed up by a large sink hole just before the bullet arrived; Martians did not land and stop the bullet;

[20] One might stipulate that every member of any minimally sufficient set S must occur simultaneously, as does Ned Hall, 'Two concepts of causation', 260: Given the transitivity of the causal relation, however, this does not reduce the promiscuity of the sufficiency theory (even if it does order it into a temporally sequenced series of sets).

[21] An exception is Ned Hall's recent interpretation of the sufficiency theory, where Hall explicitly aims to state a version of the theory that excludes absences as either causes or effects. Hall, 'Two concepts of causation', 260.

[22] John Stuart Mill, *A System of Logic* (8th edn, London: Longmans, 1872), Book III, Chapter V, sec 3.

etc, etc. As even Mill concedes about all this: regarding 'the negative conditions... a special enumeration would generally be very prolix...'.[23] Indeed! As prolix as all of the possible items that could have prevented the effect but did not do so on this occasion because they did not exist.

It might seem that the generalist could avail himself of the general truth of ontology so relied on in the last chapter, that truth being that there are no negative properties, no negative events, and no negative states of affairs. Can adhering to this general truth of ontology save the generalist from being committed to omissions as causes? Recall that generalists are so-called because they analyze singular causal relations in terms of general laws. At the level of laws, negative existential propositions are all that are needed, and these raise no ontological hackles. 'It is not the case that the victim was wearing body armor' can be a necessary element of a sufficient set because the only commitment is to the proposition stated (and negative propositions are not a problem). At the level of laws, there is no commitment to absent armor as a particular; only to there being a type of thing, body armor, that may or may not be present in particular situations.

Yet a generalist might counter that laws need to be instantiated at a time and place in order for there to be a *singular* causal relation, even on a generalist account of this relation. The thought would then be that negative conditions drop out of the sufficient sets because such negative conditions cannot be instantiated, the desired conclusion being that the theory is not committed to such negative conditions being considered as causes.

Whether this response is plausible depends on how literally one is to take the notion of 'instantiation' with which generalists state their theory. If 'instantiation' means that there must exist some token of the type instantiated, then the reply is a good one, and NESS and other generalists are not committed to omissions being singular causes. Yet this cannot be what generalists mean by 'instantiated'. When they are asking after the truth-makers for the negative conditions in laws, they are not looking for negative tokens of negative types. Rather, the truth-maker for negative conditions is the absence of any positive instances of some type. The law is 'instantiated' in this sense whenever its negative conditions are made true by the world. In that sense negative conditions can be 'instantiated', and so omissions will be causes.

Notice that this loosening of the sense of 'instantiated' is a move parallel to that made by the counterfactualist to accommodate 'negative causation'. As we saw in Chapter 17, the counterfactualist too does not want to be committed to there being negative events or negative states of affairs; he wants to avoid saying things like 'If Smith's omission to throw Jones a rope had not occurred, Jones would not have died.' Rather, David Lewis and his followers construed the counterfactuals relevant to negative causation to be: 'If some event of the kind throwing Jones a rope *had* occurred, then Jones would not have died.'

---

[23] Ibid.

Analogously, the sufficiency theorist wants to avoid saying: 'If someone is in the water and cannot swim . . . and if someone else's not throwing a rope occurs, then the first person drowns.' Rather, the generalization is: 'If someone is in the water and cannot swim . . . and if some event of the kind throwing a rope does *not* occur, then the first person drowns.' The sufficiency theorist thus commits only to *types* of acts the absence of which complete sufficient sets. His mode of conceiving of how such negative conditions can be 'instantiated' on particular occasions thus both allow omissions to be causes while keeping away from an ontology of negative events or negative states of affairs.

Most generalists think this threading of the needle to be a virtue of their theory. The late Herbert Hart, Tony Honoré, Richard Wright, and the late John Mackie all celebrated the allowance of omissions as causes by their sufficiency theory of causation. They recognized that their intellectual forebear here, John Stuart Mill, was more equivocal on this point. As Mackie notes, Mill was reluctant to call negative conditions a cause, conceiving negative conditions instead to be the 'absence of counteracting causes'.[24] (Mill's actual language is the 'absence of a preventing cause'.[25]) Yet Mackie quotes Mill on the cause being the sum total of conditions positive and negative, concluding to his own satisfaction that an individual instance (in the loosened sense above) of either sort of condition can be a cause.[26] Wright likewise bulls over Mill's reticence, urging that the 'complete', 'concrete', 'full' instantiation of a law will include those instances (in the loosened sense discussed above) of negative conditions no less than positive ones.[27]

Those generalists who are probabalists in their construal of scientific laws also both *can* be committed to omissions as causes, and they *are* in fact so committed. When formulated with the care exercised above so as to avoid commitments to negative events or negative states of affairs, probabilists can happily admit that absences can be probability raisers just like presences. A throwing of someone in the water increases the probability that they will drown; my not throwing them a rope does too.

I have said my piece in Chapter 18 why I do not think omissions or other absences can be causes. I there concluded that it is both morally and metaphysically absurd to think that my not saving Jones is a cause of Jones' death, just like your holding his head under water is such a cause (both being necessary elements of the set of conditions sufficient for his death). If that is right, then the commitment of generalist theories to counting omissions as causes counts heavily against them.

---

[24] Mackie, *The Cement of the Universe*, 63.
[25] Mill, *A System of Logic*, Book III, Chapter V, sec 3.
[26] Mackie, *The Cement of the Universe*, 64.
[27] Wright, 'Causation in Tort Law.' See also Wright, 'Once more into the bramble bush: Duty, causal contribution, and the extent of legal responsibility', Vanderbilt Law Review 54 (201), 1129–30.

D. Still more overbreadth: The lawful connection between epiphenomenal events

We should again start with the discussion of this problem in Chapter 17, which was: the epiphenomenal objection is an old one, first developed against generalist theories of causation. Suppose some event *c* causes *e* at t_1, then *c* causes *f* at t_2, yet there is no causal relationship between *e* and *f*, which are merely 'epiphenomenal' of one another. For example, I run in the morning; this quickly lowers my anxiety; it eventually makes my dog tired; lowering my anxiety did not tire my dog. On the regularity theory of causation often attributed to Hume, events similar to *e* can regularly follow events similar to *c*, and events similar to *f* can regular follow events similar to *c*. Unfortunately, events similar to *f* also can regularly follow events similar to *e*. Therefore, on the regularity theory *e* does cause *f*, contrary to our supposition.

As Mackie forthrightly recognized, the epiphenomenal problem equally besets the sufficiency and probabilist views of laws, along with the regularity view.[28] Mackie revised CD Broad's old example to illustrate this with respect to sufficiency views. Suppose the Manchester hooters sound as soon as Greenwich time records 5 pm. Suppose slightly thereafter (at 5:01 pm) London workers leave their work. Not only is the sounding of the Manchester hooters regularly followed by Londoners leaving their work; but such sounding is a necessary element of a set of conditions sufficient for Londoners leaving their work:

> the sounding of the Manchester factory hooters, plus the absence of whatever conditions would make them sound when it wasn't five o'clock, plus the presence of whatever conditions are along with its being five o'clock, jointly sufficient for the Londoners to stop work a moment later—including, say, automatic devices for setting off the London hooters at five o'clock, is a conjunction of features which is unconditionally followed by the Londoners stopping work. In this conjunction the sounding of the Manchester hooters is an essential element, for it alone, in this conjunction, ensures that it should *be* five o'clock.[29]

We should recall that the counterfactualist had two responses to the epiphenomenal problem. The first was to get rid of the sufficiency of the common cause *c* for its first effect *e*. As David Lewis wrote, when we construct those similar possible worlds in which to test the counterfactual (if not *e*, not *f*) the law

---

[28] Mackie, *The Cement of the Universe*, 81–7. Not all sufficiency theorists are so concessive. Where common cause *c* causes two effects *d* at *t* and *e* at (slightly later) *t'*, Ned Hall believes that it patently does not follow from the laws, together with the claim that *d* alone occurs at *t*, that *e* occurs at *t'*: Hall, 'Two concepts of causation', 261. Yet if the laws provide both that *c* could not occur if *d* did not occur and that if *c* occurred, *e* must occur, then the occurrence of *d* plus the laws is enough to guarantee the occurrence of *e*. To avoid this, Hall posits a causal intermediary, event *b*, that is caused by *c*, causes *e*, and is simultaneous with *d*. Now *d* is not necessary. But where there is no simultaneous causal intermediary such as *b*? Then *d* appears to be necessary to the sufficiency of its set.

[29] Mackie, *The Cement of the Universe*, 84.

connecting cs to es is not sacred.[30] Therefore the Greenwich time could mark 5 pm and yet the Manchester hooters not go off. A similar move here would make e (the Manchester hooters sounding) not a necessary element in a set sufficient for f (the Londoners getting off work).

Although in Chapter 17 I rejected this move by counterfactualists, notice that the same move is not even available to sufficiency theorists. For sufficiency theorists, the laws *are* sacred—these are the heart of their theory of causation. For c to cause e, c must be a part of a set sufficient for e, and if there is a law saying so, then in the actual world (where we seek causation on this theory) that is the end of the matter. Indeed, in the quotation just given Mackie concedes as much.

The second response of the counterfactualists to the problem of epiphenomena holds more promise for the sufficiency theorists. This response was to regard all 'back-tracking' counterfactuals as false. For if the counterfactualist can deny 'if not f, then not c', then he can avoid the seeming implication that e counter-factually depends on c and c on f; ie that on his theory one epiphenomenal fork, f, does cause another such fork, e.

Notice the sufficiency theorist wants here a like move. For what gives him trouble is that e—the sounding of the Manchester hooters—is seemingly an essential element in the conjunction of conditions sufficient for Londoners to leave work because (as Mackie says) 'it alone, in this conjunction, ensures that it should *be* five o'clock'. Event e thus alone guarantees that c exists, which guar-antees that f exists. So if Mackie denies either sense or truth to back-tracking sufficiencies, he too has what he needs to answer the epiphenomenal problem.

Mackie was refreshingly honest about this. Although he saw that one might stipulate a sense to 'sufficiency' such that back-tracking sufficiencies could be ruled out as deviant because not reflecting a 'causal priority' that could be read into 'sufficient', he also believed that this would be to run roughshod over what 'sufficient' usually means in this context:

there are senses of 'necessary' and 'sufficient' which do not include causal priority and which are exhausted by the appropriate conditional analyses, and I think it makes things clearer if we use 'necessary' and 'sufficient' in these simpler senses, and introduce causal priority as a further element.[31]

The result of such honesty is a confession by any honest generalist: in the normal meaning of the word, nomic *sufficiency* cannot be a sufficient account of caus-ation. What must be added to nomic sufficiency, Mackie concluded, is 'an additional distinguishing feature' of sufficiency sufficient for causation, a feature Mackie dubbed 'causal priority'.[32]

Thus Mackie's solution to the problem of epiphenomena is one with his solution to the problem of causation's asymmetry through time. (This was also

---

[30] David Lewis, 'Causation', Journal of Philosophy 70 (1973), reprinted in Ernest Susa and Michael Tooley (eds), *Causation* (Oxford: Oxford University Press, 1993), 190–1.
[31] Mackie, *The Cement of the Universe*, 53.   [32] Ibid, 86.

true of Lewis as we saw in Chapter 17.) I thus turn to that distinct problem for generalist theories of causation, considering it both as a problem in its own right and as a problem on which the solution of the epiphenomenal problem also turns.

E. Overbreadth continued: Backtracking sufficiency and the temporal asymmetry of causation

It is a bedrock feature of singular causation that it is an asymmetrical relation: if c causes e, then necessarily e does not cause c. Equally basic to the concept of causation is that the direction of causation is the same as the direction of time; ie, that causes cannot precede their effects. True enough, feedback loops can give an appearance to the contrary, as where overeating causes anxiety which causes overeating; yet in such cases, one event c_1 of event type C is causing another event e_1 of event type E, and e_1 is causing c_2, which is causing e_2, etc, but between individual event tokens each causal link is unidirectional (e_1 causes c_2, but not vice versa) and time-ordered.

A problem for the generalist about causation is that neither of these features is obviously true of laws. Regularities can be symmetrical—explosions can be preceded by sparks (etc) as regularly as sparks (etc) can be followed by explosions. Increases in probability can be symmetrical—a bullet entering a human body raises the conditional probability of that body dying, but a body dying raises the conditional probability that a bullet entered it.

Laws on the sufficiency view of them can also be symmetrical. Consider the laws governing the motion of a pendulum. Such laws, together with the location, length, mass, and velocity of the pendulum at t_1, can give sufficient conditions for the location of the pendulum at t_2; but equally such laws, together with the location, length, mass and velocity of the pendulum at t_2, can give sufficient conditions for location of the pendulum at t_1.

If laws give necessary as well as sufficient conditions for the happening of certain events, then of course the happening of those events will also be necessary and sufficient for the instantiation of the conditions mentioned in the laws. But even if laws only give INUS (or NESS) conditions, they can be (and often are) symmetrical even if logic does not require that they must be. As Mackie recognized, 'where A is an INUS condition of B, B is usually also an INUS condition of A ... so this relation will in general fail to introduce any asymmetry, and distinctive direction'.[33]

So generalists about causation face a real problem: the laws (to which they would reduce causation) do not share features that seem basic to causation. There are not a lot of options here for the generalist. Consider three possible responses.

---

[33] Mackie, *The Cement of the Universe*, 161.

One would be to play around with the notion of *laws* in a way that gets asymmetry and alignment with time's arrow into them. Mackie, as we have seen, was at one point tempted to build these features into the notion of sufficiency:

> The terms 'necessary' and 'sufficient' are often so used as to include a suggestion of causal priority: even when a cause is sufficient in the circumstances in the strong sense for its effect, we find it strange to say that the effect is necessary in the circumstances for the cause, just because the effect is not causally prior to the cause.[34]

In the sense of 'necessary' and 'sufficient' Mackie is here isolating, only temporally prior conditions can give INUS (or NESS) conditions, so the match between causation and sufficiency is restored. This seems to be a popular resolution in legal circles. Richard Wright, for example, has recently confessed that he has 'always viewed the NESS test as embodying not merely a requirement of logical or even empirical necessity or sufficiency, but also a notion of causal directionality...'.[35]

Mackie himself refused to go this route. The supposed notion of a 'directional sufficiency' is a thinly disguised version of what might more accurately be called, *causal* sufficiency.[36] What kind of sufficiency is that? Answer: the kind of sufficiency involved when there is a causal relation! The vicious circularity of this move should be apparent. The only criterion given for isolating the relevant sufficiency to which causation is to be reduced, is causation itself. This of course makes the supposed account of causation in terms of sufficiency completely trivial. Not false—a cause is a cause after all—but trivial.

The second move open to the generalist here is the stipulative move I mentioned in Chapter 17 as also being open to the counterfactualist. Admit that asymmetry and temporal directionality are not features of nomic sufficiency any more than they are features of counterfactual dependence. But causation is to be analyzed in terms of two distinct things. A cause is: (1) an INUS/NESS condition; and (2) where the effect caused by the INUS/NESS condition does not precede that condition. (I provisionally treated the generalist to some such stipulation at the beginning of this chapter, but now he needs to defend it.)

The second move at least has the grace of openness and honesty, in contrast to the sleight of hand practiced in the first move. Yet there are three worries about such a move. One is its lumpiness. It is often said that if you lump quite different things together the mixture is bound to be a bit lumpy. So here. On their own theory, generalists assert that causation is essentially lawfulness. Now we are told that causation is a *kind* of lawfulness, the running forward kind. This is like the counterfactualist telling us that causation is counterfactual dependence, then

---

[34] Mackie, *The Cement of the Universe*, 53.
[35] Wright, 'Once more into the bramble bush', 1103, n 113.
[36] Fumerton and Kress offer up the idea of causal sufficiency to generalists, recognizing that this is poisoned bait for such theorists because of the vicious circularity it introduces into their analysis: Fumerton and Kress, 'Causation and the law', 93–5.

qualifying that by throwing out back-tracking counterfactuals. Wanted in both cases is something in the nature of the thing (to which causation is to be reduced) that makes it plausible *why* the additional limitation is appropriate. Lewis, as we saw in Chapter 17, attempted just this with his empirical hypothesis of a temporal asymmetry of overdetermination. Needed is some equivalent hypothesis here, one showing temporally reversed INUS conditions to be either senseless or universally false.

Second, the stipulation proposed raises worries for those tempted by causal accounts of time. If the direction of time is to be analyzed in terms of the direction of causation, then clearly the latter cannot be analyzed, even in part, by the former.

Third, there is the worry (alternative to the second worry) nicely explored by Mackie: causal priority seems to be a notion distinct from temporal priority, and the proposed stipulation ignores this. Mackie's example is the debate about backwards causation.[37] Even for those of us who think that backwards causation does not exist, this seems a synthetic truth, not the analytic truth the stipulation proposed would make it.

The third option open to the generalist is to meet the challenge earlier addressed to him: show how the direction of causation flows naturally from nomic sufficiency plus some plausible empirical assumptions. Mackie helpfully surveyed many of the things that have been said in philosophy in an attempt to account for the direction of causation. These include: the manipulability of effects by their causes, but not vice versa; the explicability of effects by their causes, but not vice versa; the increase in disorder common from cause to effect, but not vice versa; etc.[38] Yet none of these flow from nomic sufficiency plus empirical hypotheses; they are stand-alone accounts of causation themselves. Indeed, this independence is particularly striking for the feature on which Mackie himself ultimately fastens, the fixity of the past in a way the future is not fixed.[39] As Mackie sees clearly, on the sufficiency account of causation, once (past) causes are fixed so are (future) effects. Only if some future events are *not* sufficiently determined—Mackie cites micro-physics and free will as the two places where this seems possible—can one explain causal priority in terms of comparative fixity.[40] Which is to say, only if causation is (sometimes) *not* nomic sufficiency that we can make sense of causation's asymmetry!

I conclude that there are no wiggles open to the generalist that allow him to escape the plain fact that lawful sufficiency does not exhibit the asymmetry and temporal direction so distinctive of causation.

[37] Mackie, *The Cement of the Universe*, 161–6.
[38] Ibid, 166–92.
[39] Ibid, 178. [40] Ibid, 182–3.

F. Overbreadth concluded: The pre-emptive and other overdetermination cases

As we saw in Chapter 17, there are five kinds of multiple cause cases. It will be helpful to reconsider them one at a time.

1. Garden-variety concurrent-cause cases

First consider the kind of case envisioned as typical by both the counterfactual and the sufficiency theories. These are cases where there are multiple causes of a single effect; each cause is necessary to the effect, and all the causes together are jointly sufficient. Three units of pollution are required for any harm to occur; the acts of each of these defendants simultaneously contribute one unit of pollution to a common stream, and harm results. Each act is a cause of the harm under the counterfactual theory, for each was necessary for the harm to occur; each act was also a necessary element in a set of conditions jointly sufficient for the harm to occur, and so is a cause under the sufficiency theory as well.

2. Overdetermination concurrent-cause cases

Historically *the* motive for preferring nomic sufficiency to counterfactual dependence as a theory of causation is the superior ability of the former over the latter to handle symmetrically concurrent overdetermination cases. As we saw earlier, these are cases of two fires (motorcycles, floods, etc), each of which would have been sufficient in the circumstances to have caused the destruction complained of, but which in fact join and together cause an indivisible injury. As we saw in Chapter 17, such cases present insurmountable problems for the counterfactual theory. Such cases are handled easily by the nomic sufficiency theory: each fire, flood, etc, can be an element necessary to the sufficiency of *a* set of conditions sufficient to destroy the house even though that fire is not necessary to the destruction. Recall that INUS and NESS do not require either that the individual condition, or the set of which it is an element, be necessary to the destruction; only that the set be sufficient and the individual condition necessary to that sufficiency. And each fire, flood, etc, in the class of cases here considered meets this requirement.

At least, such is the common thought of the proponents of nomic sufficiency. Whether this is in fact so depends on how each of the sufficient sets are constructed. What if, for example, the relevant set is determined to be one including both fires within it? Then neither fire would be a non-redundant part of that set, and thus not a cause, contrary to common causal judgment. Since the issue of set construction is the crucial issue to the resolution of the next two classes of cases, I shall defer discussion of it until after we have those cases before us.

3. Mixed (between garden-variety and overdetermination) concurrent-cause cases

What I termed in Chapter 17 the 'mixed' cases are cases in which no condition is either necessary or sufficient in the circumstances for some harm, but some set of such conditions (amounting to less than all of them) is sufficient for that harm. There are five polluters each of whose activities contribute to a single indivisible injury; it takes three units of such pollution to cross the threshold beyond which such injury occurs; no injury occurs below such thresholds and no additional injury occurs beyond such threshold. In which case each polluter's activity is neither individually necessary for the injury, nor is it individually sufficient.

On Richard Wright's application of the INUS/NESS theory, each of the five polluters' actions is a cause of the injury, for each is a necessary element of *a* sufficient set (consisting of two other polluting activities).[41] On these facts there are ten minimally sufficient sets, consisting of three polluting activities each; and each polluting activity is necessary to the sufficiency of six of such sets. So each is a cause of the harm, which Wright (correctly) surmises also agrees with common intuition about such cases.

Years ago Mark Kelman, raised what he termed the 'subset problem' for cases of this sort,[42] and to sort out what is and is not a problem here it is worth going through the Kelman/Wright exchange. One worry Kelman raised is that there is no uniquely right way to allocate polluters to subsets. With five polluters, and ignoring other conditions, there are very many possible sets (including sets of one). Most of these sets are not sufficient or if they are sufficient, they are not *minimally* sufficient because they include more than three polluters. So the nomic sufficiency theory is charged with indeterminacy; whether a given polluter's activity is or is not a cause of the harm depends on which division into subsets is selected.

This is a non-worry for the nomic sufficiency theorist. The theory is determinate in such cases, but not because it has some supplementary principle telling us how to divide the field up into discrete sets. Rather, the theory's determinacy is assured by regarding a condition as a cause of the harm if there is *any* sufficient set of which it is a necessary member.[43] All five polluters qualify as causes under this interpretation of the nomic sufficiency thesis.

The nomic sufficiency theorist has to be careful here, lest his loosened interpretation just given allows any condition to be a cause. Consider a sixth person in the above scenario, a person who does no polluting but who does do

[41] Wright, 'Causation in tort law', 1793.

[42] Mark Kelman, 'The necessary myth of objective causation judgments in liberal political theory', Chicago-Kent Law Review 63 (1987), 603–4.

[43] This is a fair interpretation of Mill, Mackie, and Wright. Ned Hall has very different ambitions for the sufficiency theory, and so posits a 'unique minimally sufficient set' for any given effect *e*, hoping that 'this *unique minimally sufficient set contains all and only the producers of e that occur at that time*': Hall, 'Two concepts of causation', 261 (emphasis in original).

some fishing in the stream at the relevant times. Let p_1, p_2, p_3, p_4, and p_5 be the propositions that polluting activities one to five occur; let q be the proposition that the injury (from the pollution) occurs; and let f be the proposition that the sixth person fished. Then f is a necessary element of *some* set sufficient for q. Consider the set described by $[(p_1$ and p_2 and $p_3)$ or not $-f]$. This disjunctive set is not sufficient for q, as it stands; but add the condition described in f to this set, it then becomes sufficient. So the fishing is also a cause of the polluting injury?[44]

A formal stipulation here is probably adequate to rule out this kind of *reductio* on the loosened interpretation of sufficiency given earlier. We cannot rule out absences as possible causal candidates, on the Millian interpretation of sufficiency we earlier adopted. Nor can we restrict negative conditions to absences of *preventers* without introducing a semi-causal notion (preventing) into our analysis of causation in terms of nomic sufficiency. What we can do is stipulate that the insufficient set (the addition to which makes some factor necessary to the enlarged set's sufficiency) may not contain as a disjunctive member a subset itself sufficient for the harm in question.[45] This rules out the artificially contrived necessity of the fishing to make some set sufficient for the harm.

Kelman appears to believe that, even without artificial construction of almost sufficient sets like that given above, the loosened interpretation of the INUS/NESS theory (according to which a condition necessary to the sufficiency of *any* set counts as a cause) results in any condition being a cause. Kelman appears to believe this because of the fact that we can indeed hypothesize some set that any condition, when added to that set, would make it sufficient for some harm. So in the pollution example, we can imagine that the fishing is a cause of the injury; suppose the world is such that polluters can only pollute after they fish the stream they are about to pollute, and that all who fish are irresistibly impelled to pollute after they fish. Suppose further that on a given day two (and only two) other fisherman/polluters are fishing. Now when the sixth person fishes, his fishing becomes a necessary element of a set sufficient for the pollution injury.

Yet this is of course entirely fanciful. That the world could have been arranged in a way that would make the fishing a necessary member of some set of conditions sufficient for polluting, is irrelevant to nomic sufficiency in the actual world. The nomic sufficiency theorist is entitled to limit causes to those actual conditions that, when joined with other actual conditions make for a set of conditions sufficient (under the laws of our world) for some other state of affairs. Kehman was mislead into thinking that the nomic sufficiency theory works with hypothetical sets, sets which could exist and for which the condition in question would be necessary.

There *is* a worry lurking here, but it is not any of those so far discussed. Indeed, it is no different than the worry I mentioned earlier in the chapter, the

---

[44] A version of a worry raised by Fumerton and Kress, 'Causation and the law', 95.
[45] Fumerton's and Kress' suggestion: ibid.

worry I called here (and in Chapter 17) the 'promiscuity' worry. Even without any of the machinations just gone through, there are an embarrassingly large number of INUS/NESS conditions for any event whatsoever, particularly if negative conditions are ruled eligible (as they are) by the theory. The quite remote and the quite insubstantial are as much causes as are the quite substantial and the quite proximate, and this is a problem for the nomic sufficiency view. However, it is not a new problem, so I shall leave it.

4. Asymmetrically overdetermined concurrent-cause cases

These are cases where one big factor sufficient by itself joins one smaller factor insufficient by itself, and the joint factor thereby produced itself causes some result. A large, mortal wound inflicted by defendant A joins a smaller, non-mortal wound inflicted by defendant B, and the victim dies from the loss of blood from both wounds, for example.[46]

The nomic sufficiency theorist has some choice as to how best to construe his theory vis-á-vis such examples. He could limit the conditions (to which some other condition is added to see if it is necessary to the sufficiency of the set so formed) to actually existing, whole conditions. This would be to say that the mortal wound was a cause of death, the non-mortal wound was not—for there were no other (actual, whole) conditions to which one could add the non-mortal stabbing to make a set sufficient for death. If one added the non-mortal stabbing to the (whole) mortal stabbing, then the non-mortal stabbing would not be necessary to the sufficiency of the resulting set; if one added the non-mortal stabbing to any thing else actually existing at the time, the resulting set would not be sufficient for death.

This is perhaps the most natural interpretation of the sufficiency theory, but so construed the theory implies an unacceptable result. As I argued in Chapter 17, asymmetrically overdetermined concurrent-cause cases are very much like the mixed concurrent-cause cases in that it is pure happenstance that the larger cause (sufficient by itself in the circumstances) is not itself the conjoined product of several smaller causes, each equal in size to the size of the non-mortal wound. If in the mixed variant of these cases each of these smaller contributors is a cause (as it is), then it would be desirable to reach the same result in the analogous asymmetrical case.

Richard Wright takes this tack, giving the sufficiency test a more liberal interpretation: some condition is a cause if it is a necessary element of a set of either actual, whole conditions or artificially separated parts of such conditions, that would together be sufficient for the harm.[47] This means that in the wounding example the minor wound is a cause, because that wound could make

---

[46] *People v. Lewis*, 57 P 470 (Cal, 1899).
[47] Wright, 'Causation in tort law', 1793–4.

sufficient a set consisting of itself and so much of the big wound as is needed to make sufficient for death the amount of blood lost.

This is a desirable interpretation of the sufficiency test if one can sustain it. The worry is that now 'being necessary for sufficiency' in getting so removed from reality that indeed anything will be regarded as a cause of anything else. Indeed, Mark Kelman focuses on this interpretation by Wright in urging just this *reductio*.[48] Yet Kelman's version of this worry is harmless. He assumes that one can just make up any old hypothetical set one wants in applying the theory, as we saw in the last subsection. To this Wright has an adequate answer: in applying the test one can ignore the actual individuation of units or degrees of a property that actual objects present in the particular situation happen to possess[49]— degrees of pollution, degrees of blood loss, degrees of weakening in the tensile strength of steel cable, and the like. But this does not mean that one ignores the kinds of properties themselves actually present in a given situation.[50] One does not get to hypothesize wholly new properties which, if present (which they are not) would make some condition necessary to the sufficiency of the set consisting of itself and such hypothetical properties.

A more refined version of Kelman's worry would be this one. The liberalization to which Wright's version of the sufficiency theory commits him, seems to commit him further to some mereological principle like: if any part of some condition c can be added to any part(s) of some other condition(s), so as to form a set minimally sufficient for e, then c is a cause of e.

Such a mereological principle is not a worry because of its ability to regard whole factors as causes when only a small part of them is necessary to the sufficiency of some set. As we saw in Chapter 16[51] with regard to counterfactuals, there are two answers to *that* worry: (1) in ordinary speech we employ what Mackie called a 'whole event' convention, regarding for example the whole event of a hammer blow as a cause of the flattening of a chestnut, even though we know only some part of the force of the blow was necessary. (2) Underlying ordinary speech, there is a more sophisticated counterfactual dependency (or nomic sufficiency) between a *range* of degrees of force, and a *range* of degrees of flattening. In which case there is nothing untoward about counting some condition as a cause even if only a small part of it was an INUS/NESS.

A more serious worry generated by the mereological principle is with regard to very small cases. If a pin prick can help itself to as much of a mortal stab wound's bleeding as it needs to form a sufficient set, then an infinitesimally small blood loss becomes a cause of death along with a sabre slashing across the chest. This is of course no more than the promiscuity worry, but exacerbated by the

---

[48] Kelman, 'The necessary myth', 603–4.

[49] Wright, 'Causation, responsibility, risk, probability, naked statistics, and proof: Pruning the bramble bush by clarifying the concepts', Iowa Law Review 73 (1988), 1036–7.

[50] Ibid.   [51] See nn 47 and 48 in Chapter 16, above.

(mereological) principle used to get the right answer in asymmetrically overde-termined concurrent cause cases.

5. Pre-emptive-cause cases

Pre-emptive-cause cases are those where one factor both causes some harm, and prevents some other factor (that without the pre-empting factor would have been sufficient for the harm) from causing that harm. Two fires, each large enough to destroy some victim's house, are coming right at the house from different dir-ections; the fires do not join; one fire burns the house before the other fire arrived. Only the first fire is regarded as a cause of the house's destruction.

Such cases give headaches to all theories of causation save the singularist theories examined in the next chapter. On the counterfactual theory, for example, such cases lead to the unwelcome conclusion that neither the pre-empted nor the pre-empting factors are causes, because neither was necessary to the harm. Probabalist versions of generalist theories have special problems with such cases, because the pre-empted factor could have been an instance of a much more highly probable type of event than the factor doing the pre-empting (making the pre-empting factor a chance-lowering, rather than chance-raising, event).

Generalist theories of all stripes are at their most vulnerable vis-á-vis such cases. Before getting embroiled in the details, it is important to see why this is so. In pre-emptive-cause cases, prima facie there are two or more sets of conditions each sufficient to bring about some event. This is indisputably true at the level of laws, for often it is the same law that covers both the pre-empting as well as the pre-empted factor; so if the factors mentioned in the law covering the pre-empting factor are sufficient (or probability-raising, or regular), then so are the factors mentioned in the law covering the pre-empted factor. Moreover, the relevant law(s) seems equally instantiated by the particular facts present in pre-emptive-cause cases. Yet this generates the unwelcome conclusion that the pre-empted factor was as much a cause of some harm as was the pre-empting factor. The second fire in the example above was as much a cause of the house destruction as was the first fire.

That being an unacceptable *reductio* to swallow, generalists must find some way to avoid it. Sufficiency theorists typically make two sorts of claims here: they say either that any set of which the pre-empted factor is seemingly a necessary member is *incomplete* (so that when the incompleteness is seen one can see that the set is in fact not sufficient); or they say that the set is not *actual, presently instantiated,* or *concrete,* by which they mean to deny that some condition gen-erally needed to make the set sufficient was present.[52]

---

[52] Both of such strategies are pursued, for example, by Richard Wright in all of the articles cited.

The organization of the discussion that follows is to follow the sufficiency theorist in his deployment of these two notions. It will be helpful to do so around each of the three sub-kinds of pre-emptive-cause cases that we distinguished in Chapter 17. These were: early pre-emption cases, late pre-emption cases, and trumping pre-emption cases. As we shall see, these two notions provide less and less plausible defenses for the sufficiency theorist as we move down this list. Preliminarily, however, there is one use of the completeness notion we need to address generally, for doing so will set the tone for the remainder of the discussion.

In Mill's discussion of the negative conditions that are always needed to make a complete (ie, sufficient) set, he innocently enough suggests that this 'very prolix' list of preventing or counteracting conditions 'may all be summed up under one head, namely, the absence of preventing or counteracting causes'.[53] If Mill means this summing up only to be abbreviatory of a 'special enumeration' of such conditions in *non-causal terms*, then it is harmless enough. But what if Mill meant that all purportedly sufficient sets were incomplete unless they included 'an omnibus negative condition, the absence of any preventing or counteracting cause',[54] where this omnibus negative condition is specified in irreducibly causal terms? Then the account of causation (in terms of nomic sufficiency) would be hopelessly circular and trivial.

At an incautious moment Richard Wright appears to take Mill in this latter direction.[55] Consider, Wright tells us, a case in which two defendants try to kill a single victim. At t_1 defendant one puts poison in the tea, and at t_2 (before the poison has finished its deadly work), defendant two shoots the victim dead instantly. One of the reasons Wright gives for concluding that the first defendant did not kill the victim is because 'the omnibus negative condition ... was not satisfied';[56] that is, the victims' death was caused by shooting and not by poisoning. But such an answer of course uses some causal notion that is prior to nomic sufficiency to construct a set complete enough to test whether poisoning was here a cause of death. This says obliquely what could be put more openly: 'no set is sufficient unless it includes an omnibus condition requiring the absence of causation by factors not in the set'. Here the circularity is open for all to see. Causation is analyzed by nomic sufficiency, but no set is sufficient unless it includes a condition ruling out *causation* by competing factors.

This is worth emphasizing, not because Millians like Wright place much reliance on this omnibus negative condition, but because it illustrates in striking fashion the ever present danger of circularity that I will now show bedevils all attempts by sufficiency theorists to get around the pre-emptive-cause cases.

[53] Mill, *A System of Logic*, Book III, Chapter V, sec 3.
[54] Wright, 'Once more into the bramble bush', 1130.
[55] Ibid, 1129–30.   [56] Ibid, 1130.

a. Cases of early pre-emption

As we saw in Chapter 17, cases of early pre-emption occur whenever the pre-emptive cause removes something needed by the pre-empted factor to do any causal work. In the two fires case, the first fire burns all the fuel around the house, so the second fire cannot get to the house to burn it. In the poison/shooting case, the shooter shoots the victim before he drinks any of the poisoned tea. As we saw, the counterfactualist had an easier time with such cases than he did with later and trumping pre-emption cases. The same is true for the sufficiency theorist.

One of the conditions needed to complete the set of which the second fire/poisoning was a part, was the fuel leading up to the house/the drinking of the tea by the victim. Therefore, there is no set (of which setting the fire/poisoning the tea are members) that is truly sufficient for death. Missing are some positive conditions, conditions not described in question-begging causal terms. Sufficiency theorists thus can get the right answer in cases of early pre-emption.

It is worth noticing that in some cases of early pre-emption such as that of the two fires, the condition needed to complete the pre-empted factor's set is present at some time t_1; it is only later, at t_2, that the fuel is destroyed by the pre-empting factor, which then allows it to destroy the house by itself at t_3. Judged at t_1, the pre-empted as well as the pre-empting fires are INUS/NESS conditions. This forces the sufficiency theorist to add another qualification to his theory: to be a cause, an INUS/NESS condition must be such *just before* the effect occurs of which it is the putative cause. The qualification can and should be made by the sufficiency theorist, but its necessity highlights something important. The general problem with generalist theories is that they are *general*, while what they purport to account for, singular causation, is not. To bridge this gap generalists must introduce the features of singularist causation, here the spatio-temporal contiguity characteristic of causal process and other singularist theories. This contiguity qualification is in this respect like the *ad hoc* stipulations of asymmetry and of temporal duration that we discussed before. One can make such qualifications and stipulations to bring generalist accounts in line with basic features of singularist accounts. Yet unless those stipulations and qualifications flow naturally from the supposed nature of causation—nomic sufficiency—it is hard to see the exercise as building a truly generalist theory of causation (as opposed to building a singularist theory in oddly ill-suited terminology which seems to be Ned Hall's ambition for the sufficiency theory).[57]

b. Cases of late pre-emption

In cases of late pre-emption there is no last event needed by the pre-empted factor and prevented by the pre-empting cause, save the ultimate effect itself. In

---

[57] Hall, 'Two concepts of causation'.

the two-fires case, the fires approach the house from opposite directions; the only reason the second fire did not destroy the house is because when that fire got to the site there was no house there to be burnt. In the poison/shooting case, the victim does drink the poison and it is well along in doing its deadly work in the victim's body when the shooter kills the victim. Indeed, the poison reaches toxic levels in the victim's body a split second after the victim dies from the bullet. The only reason the poison did not cause the death of the victim was because there was no live victim to be killed. (Despite the common homily that the coward dies a thousand deaths, in reality even cowards, like all of us, can die only once.)

The Millian move here is to add a condition alleged to be necessary for any set to be sufficient for destruction of a house or death of a person, *viz*, the house not already having been destroyed by something else, or the person not already having been killed by something else.[58] Yet is this not just to reintroduce the 'omnibus negative condition' already discredited? An INUS/NESS condition is a cause except when it is not because something else is!

Sometimes one can seemingly disguise the circularity by describing the added condition in seemingly non-causal terms: 'the house exists at the time the second fire arrived at the site', or 'the poison remaining in Mary's body a certain amount of time while she is still alive';[59] or 'P's being alive when the poison takes effect'.[60] Yet the house existing, or P or Mary still being alive, is just there not being a house destruction or a death—and this, in a deterministic universe, is to say that nothing else (other than the putative cause we are testing) caused such destruction or death. As Wright himself summarizes these supposed conditions: 'a necessary condition for the sufficiency of any set of actual antecedent conditions is that the injury not have occurred as a result of other actual conditions outside the set'.[61] This is just an analogue of the 'omnibus negative condition', turning the sufficiency analyses into a trivial (because circular) thesis.

c. Cases of trumping pre-emption
Things only get worse for the sufficiency theorist when we move to cases of trumping pre-emption. As we saw in Chapter 17, these are cases where the pre-empted factor runs its whole course—a course that normally produces some event *e*—yet that factor does not cause *e* on this occasion because some pre-empting cause 'trumps' it. Our earlier example was of a major and a sergeant simultaneously shouting orders to their troops to advance; ordinarily the troops would advance in response to the sergeant's order but on this occasion they advance solely because of the order of the higher-ranking major.[62]

---

[58] Wright, 'Once more into the bramble bush', 1104.
[59] Ibid, 1113.
[60] Wright, 'Causation in tort law', 1795.   [61] Ibid.
[62] The example is Jonathan Schaffer's in his 'Trumping pre-emption', Journal of Philosophy 97 (2000), 175.

A like example was discussed by Hart and Honoré (although I have altered the example slightly so as to excise its pre-emptive *prevention* aspect): suppose a riverboat is headed upstream, but the boat captain stops the engines at t_3. He does this because of what he sees: at t_2 he sees two bridges collapsed (both of which collapsed simultaneously at t_1 and both of which completely block the river). It is plausible to suppose he stops his engines solely because of the collapse of the first bridge, even though had the first bridge not have collapsed he would have stopped his engines just when he did because of the known collapse of the second bridge.[63]

Wright attempts to reach the correct causal conclusions here by denying that the second bridge's collapse is an INUS/NESS condition. Its set is supposedly not a sufficient set because missing is the condition 'the boat reaching the second bridge'.[64] Nothing further needed to happen to stop the boat (where and when it stopped), in conjunction with the second bridge's collapse; all that was needed was the non-intervention of the first bridge's collapse. The same is true of the troops' advance in the earlier hypothetical: nothing else needed to happen after the sergeant's order for that order to have caused the troops to advance; all that was needed was the non-intervention of the major's trumping order.

Sufficiency theorists could of course again add a condition supposedly necessary to complete the sets of which the sergeant's order and the second bridge's collapse are members. But think what this condition would have to require: nothing less than that the sergeant's order/the second bridge collapse *did not cause* the troops advance/engine stoppage. The circularity of any such response should be apparent.

Richard Wright's response to these sorts of problems is of a piece with his response to the inability of the sufficiency analysis to duplicate the asymmetrical and temporally ordered nature of the causal relation. He recasts sufficiency from *lawful* sufficiency to a special kind of sufficiency, *causal* sufficiency:

I have always viewed the NESS nest as embodying not merely a requirement of logical or empirical sufficiency, but also a notion of *causal directionality* according to which the conditions specified in the antecedent ('if' part) of the *causal* generalization are *causally* relevant conditions for the conditions specified in the consequent ('then' part), but not vice versa, and a notion of *causal* sufficiency which requires that all the conditions specified in the antecedent and consequent be concretely instantiated on the particular occasion.[65]

Well... this is not false, because a cause is, after all, a cause. But such response reduces the nomic sufficiency theory to exactly this level of triviality.

---

[63] Hart and Honoré, *Causation in the Law*, 250–1.
[64] Wright, 'Causation in tort law', 1797.
[65] Wright, 'Once more into the bramble bush', 1103, n 113 (emphasis added).

20

Singularist Theories of Causation

I. Introduction

The natural alternative to the generalist theories examined in Chapter 19 is some kind of singularist theory of the relation. In this chapter I seek to introduce singularist theories without purporting to offer knock-down arguments for the correctness of those theories. I address three preliminary concerns about singularist theories. First, I seek to clarify what is commonly meant by calling a theory of causation, a *singularist* theory. Second, a taxonomy of different types of singularist theories is laid out. Third, a very general overview is given of the kinds of arguments, pro and con, that have been addressed to singularist theories of causation.

II. What Is a Singularist Theory?

Before coming to the kinds or types of singularist theories on offer (the second topic of this introduction) and the arguments pro and con such theories (the third), we do well to revisit the singularist/generalist distinction. Doing so will clarify what we mean when we classify a theory of causation as *singularist*.

We should distinguish two brands of singularism, an extreme form and a moderate form. The axis of difference between these two forms is the degree of commitment to there being causal laws whenever there are singular causal relations. The extreme view, championed by Elizabeth Anscombe,[1] holds that singular causal relations could (and even do) exist even if there were no true causal laws that connected types of events of which these causes and effects were instances. A moderate singularism, by contrast, concedes that no singular causal

---

[1] GEM Anscombe, *Causality and Determination* (Cambridge: Cambridge University Press, 1971). Anscombe was arguing explicitly against Donald Davidson's view that singular causal relations resupposed causal laws, even if we did not know on a given occasion what the law might be. Bence Nanay, 'The properties of singular causation', The Monist 91(4) (2008), interprets Davidson not to hold the view that it is only in virtue of an event's properties that it can cause anything (even though the latter view is a common basis for Davidson's moderate singularism about laws).

relations can exist where there is not some true causal law connecting events of these types.

Both of these are recognizable forms of singularism about causation. Singularism can be, but does not have to be, the view that there are or can be lawless causal relations. What makes a theory singularist is not to be found along this axis of (either necessary or contingent) accompaniment. A theory can hold that every singular causal relation can (and even must) be accompanied by some casual law, and still be a singularist causal theory by my lights. This is because the more pertinent axis here is not accompaniment, but reduction.

In taxonomizing theories of causation, the introduction to a recent collection rightly observes that 'the most useful distinction to make at the outset is that between accounts that do and accounts that do not attempt to reduce causal facts to facts about what happens, together with facts about what the laws are that governs what happens'.[2] Put in my language, this is the distinction between accounts that do, and accounts that do not, reduce statements of singular causal relations to statements of instantiated laws (where the latter are taken to be statements of laws together with statements that particular events exist when those events are instances of the types of events connected by such laws). Singularism can be best seen as the account that does not reduce singular causal statements to statements of causal laws. Such a non-reductionist-defined singularism can then be agnostic about whether such laws are always present when there exist singular relations.

The generalist about causation who reduces singular causal relations to laws is not a two-way reductionist. Generalist theories regard the laws as basic, and singular relations as derived from these. A natural anti-reductionism is thus to reverse what is basic and what is derived. This view regards singular causal relations as basic, and laws simply as inductively derived generalizations from these. Chris Hitchcock calls this the 'generalization strategy' about laws,[3] which is a strategy pursued by one kind of singularist theory of causation.

Another kind of singularist theory, however, is to grant parity between singular causal relations and causal laws. According to this second kind of non-reductionist singularist theory, there are two different kinds of causal relationships, one between types (the relation of laws) and the other between tokens (singular relations).[4] To my mind, this position too is singularist: it admits that singular causal relations are not to be identified simply as instantiated causal laws (even if

---

[2] John Collins, Ned Hall, and LA Paul (eds), *Causation and Counterfactuals* (Cambridge, Mass: 2004), 12. This is also the dimension relied on in Michael Rota's 'An anti-reductionist account of singular causation', The Monist 91(4) (2008), in his discussion of the character of singularist theories.

[3] Christopher Hitchcock, 'The mishap at Reichenbach Fall: Singular vs. General causation', Philosophical Studies 78 (1995), 258.

[4] See ibid for citations to examples in the literature.

it also admits that causal laws are not to be identified simply as inductively derived generalizations of singular relations). Each, on this view, is equally basic.

The difference between these two kinds of singularist theories does not lie in their ontological commitment to the existence of singular causal relations. (It is this common commitment that makes them both singularist.) Rather, the only difference lies in how they regard causal laws (as either equally basic in their own right, or as derivative of the more basic singular relations).

A difficult test for this reductionist (to laws) criterion of singularism is provided by theories like that of David Armstrong. Early on Armstrong defended the view that causal laws are essentially primitive relations between universals.[5] Much later, however, Armstrong speculated about what an overt reductionism (of singular relations to laws) would look like when married to his views of laws as primitive relations between universals.[6] The upshot, he concluded, was a kind of singularism, even though there is a reduction to laws. As Armstrong cryptically put it, 'the law will be present *completely* in each instantiation', and hence 'singular causation will be a completely intrinsic relation'.[7]

A metaphorical way of putting Armstrong's thought would be to say that the 'glue' of causation, its necessitating power, resides as much in the singular relation as in the relation between types (the subject of a law).[8] Indeed, it is the same 'glue'. It is as completely present in singular causal relations as in causal laws. One is not more basic than the other, not because these are different but equally basic relations; rather, the mysterious ('primitive') element is the same thing in each relation. Even though reductionist, this by my lights counts as a singularist theory of causation. As we shall see, Armstrong's view here differs little from the primitivist singularism of Michael Tooley.[9] It too should count as a singularist theory of causation, just as Armstrong himself so classifies it.

III. Types of Singularist Theories

In clarifying singularist theories generically, we have along the way taxonomized singularist theories along two axes of differentiation. One was the axis of accompaniment, the extreme singularist denying that causal laws necessarily must be present if singular causal relations are present (and even denying that laws in

---

[5] David Armstrong, *What Is a Law of Nature?* (Cambridge: Cambridge University Press, 1984).
[6] David Armstrong, 'Going through the open door again: Counterfactual versus singularist theories of causation', in Collins, Hall, and Paul (eds), *Causation and Counterfactuals*, 456.
[7] Ibid.
[8] Put orally by me to Armstrong at the University of Illinois Conference on Causation and Responsibility, Mt Hood, Oregon, November, 2006.
[9] Michael Tooley, *Causation: A realist approach* (Oxford: Clarendon Press, 1987). See also Tooley, 'The nature of causation: A singularist account', in David Copp (ed), 'Causation Philosophers: Celebrating twenty years of the CJP', Canadian Journal of Philosophy Supp 16 (1990), 271–322.

fact are present for all existing singular relations), the moderate singularist admitting the omnipresence of laws with singular relations and perhaps even admitting the impossibility of there being singular relations with no accompanying laws.

The second axis of differentiation between singularist theories was in terms of reduction. Admitting (as does the moderate singularist) that causal laws always do or must accompany singular causal relations, it remains to ask which is more basic. To be a singularist at all, one must reject the generalist view which reduces the singular to the general. But two kinds of singularism can make this rejection, the generalizing singularist (who regards the singular relations as basic and the laws as derived) and the dualist singularist (who regards singular relations and laws as distinct, but equally basic, relations).

Now we need a third axis of differentiation, along another variable also (unfortunately) called 'reductionist/anti-reductionist'.[10] Here the singularist who is also an anti-reductionist in this second sense is a kind of primitivist. His slogan might be that 'each (at least metaphysically primitive) thing is what it is and no other thing'. The denial is not the denial of any reduction of singular relations to instantiated laws. Rather, the denial is much broader: singular causal relations cannot be reduced to anything else.

We shall come back shortly to primitivist kinds of singularism. But at this juncture it is more enlightening to examine the reductionist views the primitivist is denying. These are views that seek to reduce singular causal relations to singular relationships of other kinds. The most familiar of these reductionist theories are physicalist in the sense that the processes, qualities, or quantities to which causation is to be reduced, are all physical processes, qualities, or quantities. There is quite a variety here. One of the simplest is Humean in its inspiration: with Hume, identify causation as the succession of one event by another, but then, contra Hume, insist that simple spatio-temporally contiguous succession of event-*tokens* (rather than types) is all that causation amounts to.[11] Left out of this account, of course, is anything that looks like causal glue. The only connection between a cause and an effect, on this view, is that of immediate temporal succession and proximate spatial juxtaposition. This singularist version of Hume is subject to many of the objections that have been made to Hume's regularity account. Indeed, the 'accidentally true generalization' objection to Hume's theory is heightened against such a singularist Hume, for now *post hoc, ergo propter hoc* is true on this view for *single* successions in time, with no requirement of regularity of succession.

---

[10] Collins, Hall, and Paul lump this sort of reductionism together with a reduction to laws in their classificatory scheme. They nonetheless see that certain singularist theories may be non-reductionist about laws while reductionist about certain facts of nature, facts which 'appeal to fundamental laws only indirectly': *Causation and Counterfactuals*, 13.

[11] A reading of CJ Ducasse, 'On the nature and the observability of the causal relation', Journal of Philosophy 23 (1926), 57–68.

Physicalist singularisms that are more discriminating in their reduction bases prominently include transference theories, according to which causation is the transfer of some quantity from one object to another. The quantity transferred is a physical quantity—either energy and/or momentum,[12] or (more vaguely) different kinds of quantities of which momentum, velocity, kinetic energy, and heat are examples,[13] or the even vaguer notions of physical *force* and matter in motion.[14]

The idea of such transfers of physical quantities fits quite well with familiar paradigms of causation, such as one billiard ball hitting another, where one change immediately begets another change. Such transfers look more mysterious if they are across larger spatio-temporal regions. For such extended causal relations, causal chains need to be created, made up of a series of events or states of affairs, each pair of which is spatio-temporally contiguous. As Bertrand Russell put this assumption, 'when there is a causal connection between two events that are not contiguous, there must be intermediate links in the casual chain such that each is contiguous to the next, or (alternatively) such that there is a process which is continuous'.[15]

This Russellian denial of action at a distance poses a problem for any theory according to which causation consists only of these sorts of transfers, whether direct or indirect across a chain of direct transfers. The dangerous-condition cases, for example, long bedeviled force/energy theorists like Beale and Epstein in law, for no matter how dangerous a condition may be, and no matter how culpable may be a defendant for allowing it to continue, it is difficult to see how such persistence (sameness of state) can be a transfer of anything across long spatio-temporal intervals.[16] More broadly, all transfer theories are bedeviled by their difficulty in accommodating the 'quiet times' in causal chains, ie, the times during which objects simply persist. As Phil Dowe notes, 'there appears to be a type of causation . . . that is ruled out by the transference theory . . . [which is] persistence as causation'.[17]

Other physicalist theories respond directly to this worry. One is the causal process theory, a theory mostly associated with the work of Wesley Salmon.[18]

---

[12] David Fair, 'Causation and the flow of energy', Erkenntnis 14 (1979), 219–50.

[13] Jerrold Aronson, 'On the grammar of "cause" ', Synthese 22 (1971), 135–56.

[14] The early speculations in these directions by legal theorists, notably Joseph Beale and Richard Epstein. See Beale, 'Recovery for consequences of an act', Harvard Law Review 9 (1895), 80–9; Beale 'The proximate consequences of an act', Harvard Law Review 33 (1920), 633–58; Epstein, 'A theory of strict liability', Journal of Legal Studies 2 (1973), 151–204.

[15] Bertrand Russell, *Human Knowledge* (New York: Simon and Schuster, 1948), 491.

[16] Thus Beale made much of objects coming to rest, but such resting ends causal influence only when they come to rest 'in positions of complete safety'. Beale, 'The proximate consequences of an act'. Similarly, Epstein added to his notions of force and energy an idea of energy stored in unstable positions making it a continuant of causal influence via such 'dangerous conditions'. Epstein, 'A theory of strict liability'.

[17] Phil Dowe, *Physical Causation* (Cambridge: Cambridge University Press, 2000), 61.

[18] Wesley Salmon, *Scientific Explanation and the Causal Structure of the World* (Princeton: Princeton University Press, 1984); Salmon, *Causality and Explanation* (Oxford: Oxford University Press, 1998).

According to Salmon, causal influence is propagated by causal processes, and causal processes in turn are conceived of as spatio-temporally continuous sequences; the inertia of a bullet, for example, in such a process, as is the persistence of a physical object over time. For *processes*, according to Salmon, are anythings that display consistency of structure over time, and *causal* processes, are things displaying such consistency of structure when the structure in question is some local modification (what Salmon calls a 'mark').

Notice that the process theory is tailor-made to deal with the action at a distance worry because causal processes, so conceived, allow causal influence to be propagated with ease across the 'quiet times' (such as stable but dangerous conditions) of causal chains. Yet causal processes (as persisting structures), by themselves, do poorly in accounting for changes that introduce modifications in structures. The idea of a causal process thus has to be supplemented with some other idea to account for production and initiation of such changes, and this Salmon does with his idea of single case propensities (of which, more below).

A well-known variation in the process family of theories is the conserved-quantity theory of Phil Dowe.[19] On this theory, a causal process is the space/time points making up the history of a physical object through which some quantity is conserved according to the laws of science, and a causal initiation or production is where two objects exchange such a conserved quantity. Like Salmon's theory, the conserved-quantity theory sees the need to accommodate both change and persistence to maintain spatio-temporally continuous links in its causal chains.

A third sort of physically reductionist singularist theory also emphasizes persistence, but the persistence is not that of structure (Salmon) or of the conserved quantity of some object (Dowe). Rather, what persists are those concrete universals that are often called 'tropes', or as often called 'abstract particulars' or 'concrete universals'.[20] A trope is the instance of a property possessed by a particular object, such as the whiteness of some particular white car. The idea is that a trope literally persists across temporal intervals; a trope of a car's whiteness at t_2 is the very same thing as the car's whiteness at t_1. Causation, on this view, is a kind of property persistence (as it is for other reductionist singularisms), but for tropists this means trope persistence. Thus, the whiteness of some car at t_1 persists as the very same whiteness trope at t_2, and the propagation of causation

[19] Dowe, *Physical Causation*. See also Dowe, 'Absences, possible causation, and the problem of non-locality', The Monist 91(4) (2008). A critical review of Dowe's conserved quantity theory is Christopher Hitchcock, 'Problems for conserved quantity theory: Counterexamples, circularity, and redundancy', The Monist 91(4) (2008).
[20] See, eg, Keith Campbell, *Abstract Particulars* (Oxford: Basil Blackwell, 1990). As David Armstrong cheerily notes, 'each happy discoverer, it seems, names them anew': Armstrong, *A World of States of Affairs* (Cambridge: Cambridge University Press, 1997), 21.

consists just in this trope persistence. As Douglas Ehring notes of this form of causal process,

Unchange as well as change falls within the causal structure of the world. Unchanging persisting tropes are no less important as causal processes because of their simplicity. Indeed, this form of causal process is pervasive.[21]

If one steps back from the trees to the forest, it is plain that common to all such theories is the conception of causation as involving spatio-temporally continuous events or states of affairs. It is this idea that drives such theories both to think that 'causing is physical producing'[22] and to think that causing is also the persistence of something, be it a structure, a property, an object, or a trope.[23] It bears repeating that on these physically reductionist accounts both the producing and the persisting involve *physical* quantities, objects, properties, and tropes.

It is important to see that there are other reductionist singularisms that are not physicalist in the way these transference/process/conserved quantity/trope persistence theories are. Indeed, these other reductionist singularisms are close cousins of generalist versions of the counterfactual theory and of the probabalist theory. Despite their counterfactual/probabilist natures, they should be considered singularist.

Consider first the counterfactual theory of causation. On one well-known view of conditionals generally,[24] the sentence, 'if p, then q' does not typically assert a proposition that is conditional in form; rather, it makes a conditional assertion of an unconditional proposition, namely, q. As Stalmaker/Lewis applied this treatment of conditionals generally to counterfactual conditionals (where we know the supposition of the statement is false), this results in an assertion that q is true in some possible world that is close to the actual world (save that p is there true).[25] Conjoin this account of the truth conditions of counterfactuals with David Lewis' trenchant modal realism about possible worlds[26]—they are as actual to their inhabitants as our world is to us—and the counterfactual theory of causation can be seen as a reductionist, singularist theory.

What makes such a theory reductionist is that causal relations are reduced to counterfactual dependencies. What makes such a theory singularist is that causal

---

[21] Douglas Ehring, *Causation and Persistence* (Oxford: Oxford University Press, 1997), 122. See also Ehring, 'Abstracting away from pre-emption', The Monist 91(4) (2008).

[22] Jonathan Schaffer, 'The metaphysics of causation', *Stanford Encyclopedia of Philosophy*, <http://www.plato.stanford.edu> (13 August 2007), 15.

[23] Jonathan Schaffer, 'Causes need not be physically connected to their effects: The case for negative causation', in Christopher Hitchcock (ed), *Contemporary Debates in Philosophy of Science* (Oxford: Blackwell, 2003), 203–4.

[24] See Quine, *Methods of Logic* (4th edn, Cambridge, Mass: Harvard University Press, 1982), 21.

[25] Robert Stalnaker, 'A theory of conditionals', in N Rescher (ed), *Studies in Logical Theory* (Oxford: Blackwells, 1968); David Lewis, *Counterfactuals* (Oxford: Blackwells, 1973).

[26] Lewis, *On the Plurality of Worlds* (Oxford: Basil Blackwell, 1986).

laws play no essential role in the truth conditions of the relevant counter-factuals.[27] 'The short-circuit caused the fire' is made true by the non-existence of the fire in that close possible world where the short-circuit also is absent. Again, this is not a matter of extending the laws of our world to what would happen in this close possible world; rather, we use Lewis' similarity metric to isolate the relevant possible world and then we simply 'look' to see whether the fire is occurring in this close possible world.

What makes such a counterfactualist/singularist theory hard to see is the difficulty people have in accepting a full-blown modal realism, one that accepts the reality of possible worlds that exist in a sense more robust than as mere projections of the laws of our actual world. David Armstrong, for example, settled on an interpretation of Lewis according to which '*in his theory of causation* the possible worlds enter as mere calculational devices'.[28] The singularist/counter-factualist I am imagining is much bolder: for him, the truth-makers for counter-factual statements (and thus for causation on this theory) are *possibilia*, those real particulars that are actual in close possible worlds even though they are not actual in ours.

Another reductionist, singularist theory is a probabilistic one. Unlike generalist probabilistic theories, this theory does not reduce causation to probabilistic *laws*. Rather, causation is identified as single case chance-raising. The truth-maker for '*c* caused *e*' does thus not involve the probabilistic law, 'events of type C raise the chances of events of type E'. Rather, it is the chance of this particular event *e* occurring that was raised by *c*, another particular. The reduction base here is wholly singular.

Of course, like the singularist counterfactualist theory just imagined, such a singularist-probabilistic theory is ontologically very expensive. A holder of such a theory is committed to but one of the going interpretations of probability,[29] the propensity theory (for if he used the more standard relative frequency theory he would be using probabilistic laws ultimately for his reduction base). Moreover, propensities would be real properties of token events; a horse would have four hooves, a long nose, and a good chance of winning the Derby, all equally as its properties. As David Armstrong remarked about Hugh Mellor's version of such an ontology of chances, those who live in such ontological glass houses should throw few rocks at others'.[30]

---

[27] A query that Jaegwon Kim introduced to discussions of Lewis, in Kim's early reaction to Lewis' theory. See Kim, 'Causes and counterfactuals', Journal of Philosophy 70 (1973), 570–2. Recall that in Chapter 16, above, we separated the possible worlds account of counterfactuals from the older covering-law account.

[28] Armstrong, 'Going through the open door', 445.

[29] Donald Gilles helpful summarizes the going theories as to the semantics of the probability calculus in his *Philosophical Theories of Probability* (London: Routledge, 2000).

[30] David Armstrong, 'The open door: Counterfactual versus singularist theories of causation', in Harvey Sankey (ed), *Causation and Laws of Nature* (Dordrecht: Kluwer Academic Publishers, 1999).

We have thus far said little about anti-reductionist, singularist theories. These are theories of causation that take it to be in some sense 'primitive' or 'basic'. There are three sorts of 'primitiveness' we should distinguish:

(1) Some concept will be *analytically* primitive if it cannot be analyzed in terms of some other concepts. To say that causation is primitive in this sense is to say that the concept of causation cannot be defined or otherwise analyzed in terms of other concepts. This is because causation is so basic within our conceptual scheme. As John Carroll put this view, 'with regard to our total conceptual apparatus, causation is at the center of the center'.[31] Somewhat earlier Michael Scriven put it this way: 'The concept of cause is fundamental to our conception of the world in much the same way as the concept of number: we cannot define it in terms of other notions without... circularity.'[32]

(2) Some object, quality, or relation will be *epistemically* primitive if it is known non-inferentially; for empiricists this means known by direct observation, either by the ordinary senses or by our acquaintance with inner processes such as the pressure we feel on our skin when an object presses against us, or our willing of changes in the world which we then bring about. For Hume, of course, causation was not basic epistemically; for Hume famously held that all we ever observe is the occurrence of one event followed by another. Many contemporary philosophers have disputed this, holding either that in certain special cases such as willing we experience causation directly[33] or that in ordinary cases (such as watching a stone shatter a glass) we *see* the causing as much as the objects and their motions.[34]

(3) Some object, quality or relation will be *metaphysically* primitive if the type of which it is an instance is not identical to any (putatively different) type of thing. Causal relations will thus be metaphysically basic if there can be no reduction (or even any non-reductionist supervenience, if that is possible) to any non-causal properties or relations.

It is this third sense of 'basic-ness' that characterizes the primitivism about causation that opposes reductionism. Although arguments have been made from the supposed indefinability or non-observability of causation to the

[31] John Carroll, *Laws of Nature* (Cambridge: Cambridge University Press, 1994), 118.

[32] Michael Scriven, 'Defects of the necessary condition analysis of causation', in W Drey (ed), *Philosophical Analysis and History* (New York: Harper and Row, 1966), 358, reprinted in part in E Sosa and M Tooley (eds), *Causation* (Oxford: Oxford University Press, 1993), 56.

[33] Eg, Armstrong, 'Going through the open door', 454; Evan Fales, *Causation and Universals* (London: Routledge, 1990), Chapter 1.

[34] Eg, Anscombe, *Causality and Determination*. See also Ducasse, 'On the nature and the observability of the causal relation'.

metaphysical conclusion,[35] it is the latter conclusion that defines primitivism for our purposes.[36]

The advantages of a metaphysical primitivism about causation should be obvious. In a nutshell, primitivism frees us from having to deal with all the counter-examples adduced against generalist theories, counterfactual theories, and reductionist singularisms. Such counter-examples juxtapose our pre-theoretical causal intuitions against the seeming dictates of the preferred reduction bases for causation—counterfactual dependency, chance-raising, lawful sufficiency, regular concurrence, energy-transfer, trope-persistence, etc. By contrast, primitivism offers up no non-causal facts with which to compare our causal intuitions. Causation can be just what those intuitions say that it is, on the primitivist view.

Such flexibility comes with an equally obvious price, however, and that is the aura of mystery that surrounds all metaphysically basic things. It may be that 'a cause is a cause' is the most that can be said, but that does not make such a truth very informative. Consider in this regard the reception of such causal primitivism within legal circles. Early in the last century Jeremiah Smith despaired of finding any helpful legal test for causation.[37] He did this explicitly on grounds of analytic and epistemic primitivism, for he thought causation to be indefinable but that jurors would 'know it when they saw it'. (He may also have thought causation to be metaphysically primitive, but he did not make his metaphysics clear, probably even to himself.) He therefore proposed the intentionally circular 'substantial factor' test, according to which some act *c* is a cause of some harm *e* if and only if *c* is 'a substantial factor in the bringing about of *e*'.

This test, picked up by the first two iterations of the American Law Institute's *Restatement of Torts*, has long been criticized for its circularity and its vagueness.[38] Yet such criticism ignores the explicit primitivism that underlay the test. 'A cause is a cause' was all the jury could be told, and all they needed to be told, on such primitivist views. (The *only* thing the test adds is a measure of amount: only *substantial* causes make one liable.) The reaction to such primitivism in legal

---

[35] One might argue, for example, that because we can observe causation directly, therefore the concept of causation is indefinable, and from indefinability we move to lack of identity. Anscombe, for example, probably wished to make both of these moves.

[36] Metaphysical primitivists about causation include David Armstrong, 'Going through the open door'; Michael Tooley, *Causation: A realist approach*; John Carroll, *Laws of Nature*, and James Woodward, 'Supervenience and singular causal statements', in Dudley Knowles (ed), *Explanation and Its Limits* (Cambridge: Cambridge University Press, 1990), 211–46.

[37] Jeremiah Smith, 'Legal cause in actions in tort', Harvard Law Review 25 (1911–1912), 103–28, 223–52, 303–27.

[38] See, eg, Dan B Dobbs, *The Law of Torts* (St Paul: West Publishing, 2000), 416: 'The substantial factor test is not so much a test as an incantation. It points neither to any reasoning nor to any facts that will assist courts or lawyers in resolving the question of causation.' See also Richard Wright, 'Once more into the bramble bush: Duty, causal contribution, and the extent of legal responsibility', Vanderbilt Law Review 54 (2001), 1080: 'As a test for determining...causal contribution...the substantial factor formulation is completely useless.'

circles is symptomatic of the 'not informative' charge leveled at all primitivist theories.

IV. The Prospects for a Singularist Theory of Causation

Whether singularist theories of causation are viable depends initially on which brand of singularism one has in mind. I find either form of extreme singularism—according to which singular causal relations either do or at least can exist in the absence of any pertinent causal laws—implausible. Properties play too important a role in both events and states of affairs as causal relata to countenance extreme singularism.[39]

The choice between the generalizing and the dualist singularist is closer, depending only on how the singularist wishes to judge causal laws. My own sympathies are with the generalizing singularist, according to which causal laws are mere constructions inductively arrived at by generalizing over what is more basic, viz singular causal relations. The dualist, by contrast, faces an extra task at explicating the nature of laws even after he is done with explicating singular causal relations. Moreover, this extra task must overcome the puzzle of how the supposedly different causal law relation between types of states of affairs relates to the singular causal relation that exists between token states of affairs. Watching Davidson and Davidsonians undertake similar extra tasks (for *explanations* versus relations) does not give one confidence that it is do-able without residual mystery.[40]

The choice between the reductionist and the primitivist—our third taxonomical axis above discussed—is closer still. My suspicions are that even primitivists start with a presumption in favor of reductionism of some kind. We all prefer more informative analyses to less. But if no reductionist analysis ends up being plausible, yet singularism is to be preferred to alternative theories of causation, then primitivist singularism becomes one's theory by default. One might call this a reluctant primitivism. Yet one's backing into such a position can be comforted with the thought, common to primitivists, that if anything is primitive, causation is.

Wherever one comes out on these debates *inter se* between singularists about causation, there remains the generic question of whether singularism itself competes favorably with the generalist (nomic sufficiency, probabalist, Humean regularist) and counterfactualist theories of causation. Those latter theories have

---

[39] I argued this in Chapter 15, above.

[40] For doubts about the Davidsonian project of regarding generalizing explanations as very different than singular relations, see Peter Menzies, 'A unified account of causal relata', Australasian Journal of Philosophy 67 (1989), 64–7. Notice that the view of Armstrong and Tooley—that causal laws are the same primitive relation between universals as relates token states of affairs—does not involve one in this extra task.

had a familiar battery of arguments directed against them.[41] Vis-á-vis singularism, there are two ways of viewing the (roughly seven) arguments against these competing theories of causation. The first would be to say that these are merely negative arguments against these other theories, so that the fact that singularism survives such objections itself constitutes no positive reason to believe in singularist theories. On this view, surviving such arguments produces at most a kind of 'back-door singularism', a singularism that has only this to be said in its favor: since we have to adopt some theory of causation, and since the taxonomy of possible theories is exhausted by generalist, counterfactualist, and singularist theories, singularism wins by default.

Yet such a 'back door' construal of what can be said in favor of singularism has to make good on both of the conditions just expressed: is the taxonomy of theories complete?[42] And, perhaps various forms of skeptivism—such as having no *single* theory of causation,[43] or having no *theories* of causation at all (no matter how pluralistic),[44] or having no use for any concept of causation at all,[45] are to be preferred to singularism.

My own take on the standard arguments advanced against non-singularist theories is more positive for singularism. For those arguments have proceeded from firm intuitions about causation that generalist and counterfactual theories have difficulties in meeting. Just one example are the arguments developed from cases of pre-emptive causation. We all know (with a certainty that borders on the a priori) that in pre-emptive-cause cases (such as where two fires advance on the same house, each sufficient to destroy it, but one gets there first), the second fire did not cause the destruction of the house because the first fire did. Any theory that cannot accommodate this conclusion is a bad theory of causation. But more

---

[41] These are deployed against counterfactualist and generalist theories in Chapters 17 and 19, respectively.

[42] One might object, for example, to the exclusion of the powers/disposition theory of causation. See George Molnar, *Powers: A study in metaphysics* (Stephen Mumford (ed)) (Oxford: Oxford University Press, 2003); Stephen Mumford, *Laws in Nature* (London: Routledge, 2004). On the other hand, some powers theorists such as Stephen Mumford ('Passing powers around', The Monist 91(4) (2008)) regard such accounts as primitivist.

[43] See Chris Hitchcock, 'Of Humean bondage', British Journal for the Philosophy of Science 54 (2003), 1–25. Brian Skyrms also regards our concepts of causation to be an 'amiable jumble' of different ideas that resist unifying theory. 'EPR: Lessons for metaphysics', in P French, T Uehling Jr, and H Wettstein (eds), *Midwest Studies in Philosophy Vol IX* (Minneapolis: University of Minnesota Press, 1984).

[44] See, eg, Jane Stapleton, 'Perspectives on causation', in Jeremy Horder (ed), *Oxford Essays in Jurisprudence, Fourth Series* (Oxford: Oxford University Press, 2000), 72, n 24: 'the scientist ... does not need to use causal language. Indeed, [his] first order task neither requires nor is illuminated by "causal theories" ...'. Stapleton's own considerable body of work on causation in the law seeks to replace theory-laden talk of 'causation' with talk of 'historical involvement' and 'playing a role in the history of an outcome'. Stapleton, 'Legal cause: Cause-in-fact and the scope of liability for consequences', Vanderbilt Law Review 54 (2001), 941–1009.

[45] Bertrand Russell, 'On the notion of cause', in J Slater (ed), *The Collected Papers of Bertrand Russell: Vol 6, Logical and philosophical papers 1909–1913* (London: Routledge, 1992).

than that, any theory that generates such a conclusion is supported by that fact. It is, in the old language, *confirmed*.

The seven arguments that I deployed in earlier chapters are set out below.

1. General overbreadth in the proposed reduction base for causation

Uniformities in nature that are 'accidental generalizations', raises in conditional probability, nomically sufficient conditions, and counterfactual dependencies, all seemingly exist where there is no causation. This is not, on its face, a problem for singularist theories. Primitivists of course have the license to shape causation to their pre-theoretical intuitions, so their theory cannot suffer from overbreadth. Physicalist-reductionist singularisms, by contrast, are hostage to the nature of their various reduction bases; yet such singularist theories are quite narrow in the reduction bases to which they would reduce causation. On their face, they do not appear overbroad. Indeed, one of the worries about such theories is that they are too narrow, excluding the causal relations asserted to exist in history and the social sciences generally.

2. Promiscuity and de minumis causal contributions

The remote and the insignificant can all be causes on generalist and counter-factualist theories. Whereas a scalar primitivism or a quantitative reductionist singularism can handle this problem easily. Causation can 'peter out' over extended chains, and some co-present causes can be much smaller than others, on any scalar version of singularism.

3. Negative causation

Absences can be causes, they can be effects, and they can be causal intermediaries (where they are both an effect of an earlier cause and cause of a later effect), on generalist and counterfactual theories. Failing to prevent (omitting), preventing, and preventing preventions, are not causal, and the fact that generalist and counterfactual theories count them as causal counts against such theories.[46] One of the great strengths of most singularisms—namely, all forms of singularism that deny action at a distance—is that they get it right in how they classify omissions, preventions, and double-preventions as non-causal.

To be sure, some critics regard double-preventions as the Achilles heel of all forms of physically reductionist, and most forms of primitivist, singularism. Common intuition indeed treats double-preventions as causal, except in that subclass of double-preventions commonly called 'allowings' or 'letting die'. Yet a properly regimented common intuition—one recognizing that omissions and preventions cannot be non-causal unless double-preventions are also non-causal,

---

[46] Chapter 18, above.

and which recognizes that there is no causal distinction between double-preventions which are allowings and double-preventions which are not—must at the end of the day treat double-preventions as non-causal.[47]

4. Epiphenomena

No theory of causation can afford to collapse the distinction between epiphenomenal relations between events (which are co-effects of a common cause), and causal relations between events. Yet generalist and counterfactual theories have well-known difficulties in doing this. Singularists of all stripes have no such problem. There is no casual chain between co-effects of a common cause on any of these theories, making them invulnerable to objections along these lines.

5. The asymmetry and directionality of causation

Relations that permit symmetry, such as nomic sufficiency, chance-raising, regularity of concurrence, or counterfactual dependence, have a difficult time accounting for the necessary asymmetry of the causal relation. Relations that are not temporally ordered (the same group) also have difficulty in being the reduction-base for a relation that seems to follow the direction of time. On its face, the temporally ordered, asymmetrical relation of causation looks a poor fit with relations that are neither. Singularists do not face these problems. Primitivists, of course, can simply endow their primitive relation with temporal direction and asymmetry and be done with it. Physicalist reductionist singularists have to do a bit more work, here as elsewhere. The reduction-bases need to have these two features, but that seems unproblematic. Transfer, for example, occurs in one direction, and time-forward to boot; and persistence can be defined the same.

6. The transitivity of the causal relation

Moving to fine-grained states of affairs (rather than Davidsonian whole events) as causal relata alleviates much of the pressure transitivity puts on counterfactual and generalist theories. But not all. Generalists and counterfactualists have residual difficulties in accommodating the seeming transitivity of causation.[48] One can of course deny that causation is a transitive relation, and in a harmless sense this is true: causation can peter out over extended chains so that a cause of an early link is too de minimis a contributor to be a cause of a later link. But this scalarity-based limitation on transitivity is not what is needed by the generalist

---

[47] As I argued in Chapter 6, above, about the best reconstruction of the law's concept of causation.

[48] Explored in Ned Hall, 'Causation and the price of transitivity', *Journal of Philosophy* 97 (2000), 205; Jerome Schaffer, 'The metaphysics of causation', 9; and Christopher Hitchcock, 'The intransitivity of causation revealed in equations and graphs', *Journal of Philosophy* 98 (2001), 273–99.

and the counterfactualist,[49] so they still have problems in accounting for causation's transitivity, even so limited.

Singularist theories might also seem to have a problem here, given their common denial of action at a distance. One might construe such a denial to also be a denial of any causal relation between spatio-temporally remote events even when such events are connected by a causal chain. In some sense of 'cause', this will be true: when c causes d, and d causes e, then c cannot be a cause of e in the same sense that c is a cause of d, on these theories. Singularists need the distinction (ancient in the Anglo-American legal distinction between trespass and case) between direct causal relations, and indirect causal relations. Events like c and d are related directly, but c causes e only indirectly. Causation should thus be defined, Lewis style, disjunctively either as direct causation or as the end points of a causal chain, each link of which is a link of direct causation. This will suffice for preserving transitivity for singularists in the way that a like move by Lewis helps in the preservation of transitivity for counterfactualists.

7. Overdetermination problems

The overdetermination cases bedevil both generalist and counterfactual theories. In the symmetrically concurrent-cause cases, the counterfactualist theory gives the wrong answer (neither is a cause), and the probabilistic theory gives the wrong answer when the combined causes lower the probability of the effect (vis-á-vis that probability given only one of the causes). On the mixed concurrent-cause cases, where each cause is neither necessary nor sufficient, both the nomic sufficiency and the counterfactual theory give the wrong answer. And on the pre-emptive-cause cases, the counterfactual theory holds neither to be the cause, the nomic sufficiency theorist regards both as causes, and the probabilistic theory seems committed either to both being causes (if they are each chance-raising), or neither being causes (if they are chance-lowering). None of these theories give the right answer, which is that only the pre-emptive factor is a cause.

Singularist theories slice through these cases like the proverbial hot knife through butter. There are continuous causal chains for each factor in all of these cases, save for the pre-empted factor in pre-emptive-cause cases (which strong causal intuition does not regard as causal). Indeed, it would be fair to say that these cases motivate singularism as strongly as they demotivate generalist and counterfactualist theories. We know what the answers are here and it confirms a theory of causation if it yields these answers in these cases by implication.

The case for singularism is thus a strong one. What might be said against it? Several items are prominent in the literature. One stems from a different view on negative causation. If one thinks that omissions, preventions, and

---

[49] As Ned Hall points out, in his 'Causation and the price of transitivity'.

double-preventions are all causal in nature,[50] then one will reject all forms of singularism (which is most) requiring continuous causal chains, each link of which are pairs of spatio-temporally contiguous events. For such singularisms cannot 'skip over' absences and treat the more remote ends of the chain as standing in the cause/effect relation.

A second worry focuses on physically reductionist forms of singularism. The worry is that this seems to commit one to a rather grand vision of unified science. On their face, for example, the causal relations discussed in the social sciences do not seem to involve continuous physical processes; they relate things like the Great Depression to things like the First World War.[51] One has to think that economics, history, sociology, etc, all can be reduced to physics to hold the view that causation is nothing but continuous physical processes and yet that social science discovers genuinely causal truths. Such singularists, in other words, have to abandon the caution of those like Phil Dowe who offer up only a theory of *physical* causation; if theirs is to be a truly general theory of causation as such, they must embrace an old ideal: what used to be called the ideal of unified science.

A third worry is ontological. Some forms of singularism are committed to 'queer' entities, qualities, or relations. Singularist counterfactualists—those who embrace Lewis' full-blown modal realism so that 'possibilia' exist as robustly as 'actualia'—are one example. Another are those singularist probabilists who embrace ontologically primitive, single-case chance-raisings. To many, Armstrong's primitive relation between universals and Tooley's primitive singular relation look ontologically excessive as well. Physically reductionist singularisms, of course, are not queer in this way; their whole point is to reduce causation to some more familiar physical items. Yet such ontological respectability is bought at a price: often such reductionists give up the ambition to analyze causation (or even *physical* causation) as such. Rather, their stated ambition is to give an account of causation as it exists in our world, with our laws.[52] To critics of such singularisms, this is to give up the quest that a theory of causation should be undertaking.

Fourthly, there is Hume's old worry, a worry we might dub that of 'epistemological (as opposed to ontological) queerness'. The worry is how one could know of the existence of singular causal relations when our evidence is so limited. We can observe the existence of events, their spatio-temporal location, and thus, their order of succession in time; we cannot observe any glue-like relation between them. On the verificationist view that the meaning of our concepts can never exceed our evidence, Hume would thus conclude that causation is nothing other than the succession of events that we can observe.

---

[50] As does, for example, Jonathan Schaffer. See his 'The case for negative causation'.
[51] A worry fleetingly expressed in Collins, Hall, and Paul, *Causation and Counterfactuals*, 14.
[52] As in Phil Dowe, *Physical Causation*.

None of these worries comes without replies by singularists. Negative causation in all its forms is regarded as anathema by many. That most forms of singularism cannot accommodate it is thus no objection. Action at a distance is also anathema, so that my own bets are indeed with the reductionist vision of a unified science that that implies (as long as that vision makes due allowance for possibilities of emergence at the levels of laws for social sciences, and so long as one is not overly optimistic about the scientific status of some of the shibboleths of contemporary social science). Some ontologies are strange enough to wish to avoid them, although many doubt that primitive causal relations are among them; and if the form that is taken by a theorist's ontological modesty is that of metaphysically necessary truths, that is not too lacking in ambition to be called a theory of causation. Finally, epistemologically speaking, singular causal relations are not obviously queer. Not only does the theory-ladeness of perception (so studied these last 50 years) make what is observed versus what is inferred an unclear distinction, and not only are there good arguments for why we *do* observe causal relations, but the entire verificationist impulse behind Hume-style objections is now commonly rejected. There is a 'gap' between the evidence we possess, on the one hand, and the thing evidenced on the other, in all areas of knowledge—phenomenal properties and physical objects, behavioral dispositions and the psychological states of other people, the facts of the present and the facts of the past. The verificationist finds the gap intolerable and so identifies the thing evidenced with the evidence for its existence. Yet this impoverishes science, as is now widely recognized. If we can live with such 'gaps' about induction, other minds, the past, and external objects, seemingly we can do the same with causation.

Contract Law and Causation: An Illustration

I. Introduction

In relating the morality of responsibility for a harm to the metaphysics of causation and of counterfactual dependence, I have restricted the legal materials illustrative of both to the law of torts and crimes. I have not sought to illustrate either moral or metaphysical issues with examples or doctrines from the law of contract. The most obvious predecessor of the present book, Hart's and Honoré's *Causation in the Law*,[1] did not so limit itself, and so a note may be in order to say why I have.

Contract law does use some notions of causation and of counterfactual dependence in its liability rules, and some of those rules use tests strikingly similar to those used in torts and criminal law. In the famous *Hadley v. Baxendale* decision on consequential damages, for example, the court limited such damages to those 'arising naturally' from the breach of contract, or 'such as may reasonably be supposed to have been in the contemplation of the parties . . . as the probable result of the breach of it'.[2] This is close to the criminal law and tort rules of 'natural and probable consequence', 'foreseeability', and the like that we taxonomized in Chapter 4.

Yet contract law fundamentally differs from tort and criminal law in what it needs from the metaphysics of causation.[3] Contract liability is (by and large) self-imposed liability. The duties imposed by contract are typically duties one would not have except by having agreed to them. Because of this, it is reasonable to allow such self-imposed obligations to be limited in the remedies for their breach to just those remedies the contracting parties have agreed upon. Damage limitations, thus, will quite plausibly be a function of the understandings of the contracting parties; the correct moral/metaphysical rule will be the correct legal rule only if that was the understanding of the contracting parties (or would have been their understanding if they had thought about it).

The metaphysics of causation thus has a lesser role to play in contract law. One way in which it has some role to play is where the explicit terms of the contract refer to some causal ideas that are themselves best explicated by the metaphysics of causation and events. In such a case it is the parties' expressed intent that governs, but that intent is referential: it is to refer to the correct nature of causation. Alternatively, there will inevitably arise those instances of contract interpretation where some default rule must be

---

[1] HLA Hart and Tony Honoré, *Causation in the Law* (2nd edn, Oxford: Oxford University Press, 1985), Chapter XI.

[2] *Hadley v. Baxendale* (1854) 9 Exch 341, 354; 156 All ER 145, 151.

[3] As Hart and Honoré also note (for somewhat different reasons), 'some writers and judges have come to see an analogy between the rules limiting recovery for physical harm in tort and the rules in *Hadley v. Baxendale*. In truth the two are not comparable': *Causation in the Law*, 320.

supplied by a court. Here too of course the contracting parties' mutual intentions govern but in such cases the contents of those intentions are unclear or non-existent. In such cases courts have to supply hypothetical intentions: what would the parties have said about this if they had thought of it explicitly? It is in divining such hypothetical intentions that the metaphysics of causation may also enter. For sometimes the most reasonable default rule—the one most closely approximating what the parties would have said had they thought about it—will be a rule referring to the metaphysically correct interpretation. In which case, again, the policy of following the presumptive intentions of the parties may lead us back to the true nature of the causal relation and of its relata.

With this in mind I have included as an appendix the following in-depth study of a particular contract. This was the contract of insurance on the World Trade Center in New York City in 2001. This is a particularly apt illustration because the interpretive issue involved in the dispute was one of event-identity, and the test under New York insurance law was an explicitly 'causal test' of event-identity. As the essay that follows goes into in some detail, some of these insurance contracts are best construed as having terms explicitly referring to the causal test of event-identity of New York insurance law. Other contracts of insurance on the World Trade Center lacked the explicitly referring terms, but the default rule of New York insurance law supplies a causal test of event-identity to interpret the 'per occurrence' language of the contracts. In either case, causation and event-identity are at the center of the dispute about contract interpretation. The essay is intended to illustrate the subtle interplay between the correct metaphysics of events and of causation, on the one hand, with legal rules, social understanding, and presumptive intentions of the contracting parties, on the other.

II. The Facts of the Case

September 11, 2001 brought to legal awareness an issue that has long puzzled metaphysicians. The general issue is that of event-identity, drawing the boundaries of events so that we can tell when there is one event and when there are two. The September 11 version of that issue is: how many occurrences of insured events were there on September 11, 2001 in New York? Was the collapse of the two World Trade Center Towers one event, despite the two separate airliners crashing into each tower? Or were these two separate insured events?

Usually such puzzles are the stuff of academic debate amongst professional philosophers specializing in the metaphysics of event identity. Metaphysics is an arcane specialty carried on by 'those happy few who feel the intellectual fascination in . . . grubbing around in the roots of being'.[4] The metaphysics of events is a specialty within metaphysics, capturing the attention of many professional philosophers in the 1970s, but otherwise remaining esoteric even within the confines of professional philosophy. In 2001 such an issue emerged from the academic shadows into the bright light of a $3.5 billion legal controversy. For the owners of the World Trade Center lease, the Silverstein group, had obtained casualty ('first party') insurance for property damage with a limit of approximately $3.5 billion 'per occurrence'. The question in the recent lawsuits between those owners and the insurance companies, was whether there was one such occurrence or two

---

[4] David Armstrong, *Universals* (Boulder: Westview Press, 1989), 139.

when al Qaeda terrorists destroyed the World Trade Center. Such questions of individuation have often been scorned as pejoratively academic questions—like asking how
many angels can dance on the head of a pin, according to a long-standing parody[5]—but
now the financing of the rebuilding of a major American monument turns on the
question.

The basic facts of what transpired on September 11, 2001, are known to everyone.
Still, the details are important.[6] At 7:59 am on September 11 American Airlines Flight
number 11 departed Boston's Logan Airport. This Boeing 767 was hijacked shortly after
take-off by five members of al Qaeda, the terrorist organization headed by Osama Bin
Laden. At 8:46 am the plane crashed into the North Tower of the World Trade Center
and at 10:29 am that Tower collapsed because of the weakening of the steel columns, the
weakening itself due to the heat of the fire resulting from the crash. At 7:58 am that same
day United Flight number 175 departed Logan Airport. It too was hijacked shortly after
take-off by another five members of al Qaeda. In a co-ordinated attack, that plane, also a
Boeing 767, struck the South Tower of the World Trade Center at 9:06 am and at 10:00
am that Tower also collapsed from the weakened steel columns due to another fire
resulting from the second crash. The two Towers were completely destroyed, as were a
number of the other buildings comprising the World Trade Center that were also leased
to the Silverstein group. The reconstruction cost and lost rental income exceeds the
$7,073,600,000 dollars that were sought by the Silverstein group from their insurance
companies.[7]

Given the disparity between the foreseeably large loss if both Towers were completely
destroyed and the roughly $3.5 billion per occurrence limitation, the WTC leaseholders
were obviously taking a risk in underinsuring. Much was made of this fact in the controversy between the leaseholders and their insurance companies.[8] Yet that *a* risk was taken
by the Silverstein group does not answer the question of whether *this* risk was taken. The bet
being placed by insureds such as the Silverstein group who use 'per occurrence' limitations is
that no *one thing* is likely to destroy their property entirely; the most harm they can suffer
from any one thing, they might think, is the loss of half of their property (such as one
Tower). Whether the insureds win or lose in placing such bets is determined by the question
of whether indeed 'one thing' caused the whole loss—and that is determined by what the
parties meant by 'one thing', which is the subject of this appendix.

Because the WTC leaseholders had commenced ownership of the lease in July of 2001,
only months before September 11, the wording of their casualty insurance policy had not
been finalized. Instead, their insurance broker had obtained for them a 'binder' of
insurance, which is legally effective in initiating insurance coverage. The binder provided
for coverage against 'all risks of physical loss or damage' to a sum insured of

---

[5] Isaac D'Israeli, *Curiosities of Literature*, 1791.

[6] The details on the attack on the Twin Towers were reconstructed and presented in USA Today,
December 19, 2001, 1A, col 2–3, 3A–4A. The details on the exact nature of the collapse of the
Towers are given in the Affidavit of Matthys P Levy filed January 19, 2002, in support of
Defendant's Motion for Summary Judgment, in *SR International Business Insurance Co v. World
Trade Center Properties LLC, Silverstein Properties Inc et al* Civil No O1CV12738(JSM), United
States District Court for the Southern District of New York.

[7] Wall Street Journal, 2 November 2001, A-1, A-11.

[8] See, eg, the complaint of Swiss Re filed October 22, 2001, paragraphs 28, 46.

$3,536,800,000 *per occurrence*. The binder did not define the crucial 'per occurrence' language.

Earlier, however, on June 25, 2001, the WTC lease-holders' insurance broker had submitted a proposed policy form for the approval of the various insurance companies insuring or reinsuring the WTC lease. Those proposed terms of coverage did include the following definition of 'occurrence.'

'Occurrence' shall mean all losses or damages that are attributable directly or indirectly to one cause or to one series of similar causes. All such losses will be added together and the total amount of such losses will be treated as one occurrence irrespective of the period of time or area over which such losses occur.[9]

The lead reinsurance company, SR International Business Insurance Co ('Swiss Re'), did not sign off on this form. Instead, in its binder Swiss Re referenced two of its own forms (neither of which defines 'occurrence') and then added to its binder 'wording to be agreed by SRI'. Swiss Re executed its binder on July 9, 2001, adding that its agreement was 'subject to wording to be agreed'. No reference was made to the June 25 insurance form containing the definition of 'occurrence' quoted above.

Two other insurance companies, Ace Ltd and XL Capital, covering 365 million of the $3.5368 billion, did agree to the definition of 'occurrence' quoted earlier. Those two companies settled with the Silvestein group on a 'one occurrence' basis, namely, with a payout of only $365 million.[10] In addition, on September 25, 2002, three more insurance companies (totaling $112 million in coverage) obtained the same result by the granting of summary judgment in their favor; the liability of these three insurance companies was also held to turn on the definition of 'occurrence' quoted earlier. Such settlements and judgments reflect a consensus between the parties and the judge that the definition quoted above is 'definitive' of the issue. I question in section VI of this Appendix whether the definition makes the large difference the judge and the attorneys apparently thought that it did.

On October 22, 2001, Swiss Re filed for a declaratory judgment in federal district court in New York for a declaration of its liabilities under the binder of insurance.[11] This suit was joined with other lawsuits filed between the leaseholders and other insurance companies. In January 2002 the Silverstein group filed a motion for summary judgment, which was denied in June 2002. The matter was set for trial in November, 2002. The prediction at the time was that the amount of money involved, together with the murkiness of the issue, would require years' worth of appeals to resolve the issue.[12]

As of the date of this book that prediction has been borne out. In the two major trials (with different groups of insurance company defendants), the juries have gone each way, one deciding there was one occurrence, and the other, that there were two. Both such verdicts were taken on appeal.

---

[9] Quoted in Swiss Re complaint, paragraph 31.

[10] The Australian Financial Review, 18 February 2002, 44.

[11] The declaratory judgment action was set for expedited trial on 3 September 2002. Wall Street Journal, 14 December 2001, B-4; Wall Street Journal, 18 December 2001, B-6.

[12] Wall Street Journal, 2 November 2001, A16.

III. The General Insurance Law Understanding of 'Occurrence'

Not surprisingly, the 'per occurrence' language of the WTC binder is not unique to that contract. It is common in America to write both casualty and liability insurance policies with a 'per occurrence' or 'per accident' upper and lower limit in exposure.[13] What is surprising are the complexities in the treatment of this issue by American insurance law. As I shall explore shortly, there are some detailed causal doctrines and some sophisticated views of event-identity presupposed by American decisions in this context.

A. Simple, intuitive tests of 'one occurrence'

Before coming to the complexities, however, it may be well to put aside a tempting (because simpler) view. This is the view that takes at face value whatever bottom-line intuitions one might have about how many occurrences there were on the facts of particular cases. I have discovered, for example, that without knowing anything about insurance law many people have definite intuitions about how many occurrences took place when the Twin Towers were destroyed. The simple approach is to ask a judge or jury to resolve such cases by repairing to their own intuitions without further definition of, or instruction about, the meaning of 'occurrence.'

   The simple view in this insurance context is reminiscent of Justice Potter Stewart's famous 'test' for hard core pornography: 'I cannot define it', Steward opined, 'but I know it when I see it and this film is not that.'[14] The simple view is also reminiscent of Justice William Brennan's proposed test for when two criminal prosecutions are barred because they would prosecute 'the same offense': we should simply ask, Brennan urged, whether the 'same act, transaction, or episode' is being prosecuted in the two proceedings.[15] Arguably the New York Court of Appeals has also succumbed to the beguiling simplicity of intuitive tests in the present insurance context. For that court has said that all that needs asking in cases like that involving the World Trade Center is whether there is a 'single event' or not.[16]

   The problem with these simple intuitive tests is not that we are bereft of intuitions about such matters, for often we are not. Rather, the problem is that such unguided intuitions may be answering the wrong question. This was certainly true of Brennan's proposed 'single act, transaction or episode' test of double jeopardy: such a test elides two

---

[13] Although nuanced differences in meaning between 'occurrence' and 'accident', have been suggested, the tendency of the insurance cases is to equate the terms. See, eg, *Hartford Accident and Indemnity Co v. Wesolowski*, 33 NY 2d 169, 350 NY 2d 895, 305 NE 2d 907 (1973), where the New York Court of Appeals held there to be no distinction in meaning between 'per occurrence' and 'per accident' limitations in insurance policies—accord, *Truck Insurance Exchange v. Rohde*, 49 Wash 2d 465, 469; 303 P 2d 659, 661 (1957). For some suggestions regarding the differences between such terms when the issue is the kind of risks covered (not how many occurrences there were), see *Stauffer Chemical Co. v. Insurance Co of North America*, 372 F Supp 1303, 1307 (SDNY 1973) ('occurrence' a broader term than 'accident' in terms of the range of items covered).

[14] *Jacobellis v. Ohio*, 378 US 184, 197 (1961) (Stewart J, concurring).

[15] *Ashe v. Swenson*, 397 US 436 (1970) (concurring opinion).

[16] *Johnson v. Indemnity Insurance Company of North America*, 7 NY 2d 222, 196 NYS 2d 678, 164 N Ed 2d 704 (1959).

distinct questions that require separate answers in the double jeopardy context. A proper understanding of double jeopardy's concern with disproportionate punishment requires that we ask *both*: (a) whether the accused performed one or more than one particular act on the occasion in question; and, if the accused did perform but one particular act, (b) whether the particular act the accused performed instantiated one or more than one type of action prohibited by the criminal code.[17] Only individuals who suffer separate punishments for having done only one particular act instantiating only one prohibited act-type are multiply punished for 'the same offense', and Brennan's simple intuitive test ignored this.

The same is true of any simple, intuitive 'single event' test in the insurance law context. Such a test simply finesses the obvious question to ask about 'per occurrence' limitations in insurance policies. That question is, per occurrence *of what*? We can count instances of a kind only when we have some idea of the kind in question. Without specification of the kind, an untutored, intuitive approach may well count instances of very different (and very irrelevant) kinds.

B. The policies guiding a default rule about 'one occurrence'

As in the double-jeopardy context, the only way to get a handle on the relevant kind (whose instances we are to count) is by repairing to the policies that guide the law. Since in the insurance context we are dealing with a default rule of contract interpretation[18]—a rule that gives an interpretation of 'occurrence' in default of the parties' expressly supplying one—the dominant policy is that of freedom of contract.[19] Freedom of contract is the principle that recognizes the self-imposed nature of contractual obligations. Such principle dictates that parties be bound only to obligations that they have voluntarily undertaken (or at least that they could have been reasonably understood by their promisees to have undertaken).

Such a principle can be justified either on grounds of utility or on grounds of justice. That is, such a principle arguably furthers the maximization of utility by allowing those in the best position to judge the state of their own preferences to be legally obligated only by their own judgments. Alternatively, such principle is fair and just in that it limits their legal obligations to their moral obligations (and the latter are limited to those created by promise).

This principle has several implications for default rules of contract interpretation. One is that, insofar as the parties to a particular contract had the same actual expectations

---

[17] Argued at length in Michael Moore, *Act and Crime: The philosophy of action and its implications for criminal law* (Oxford: Clarendon Press, 1993), Chapters 12–14.

[18] The line between supplying an omitted term by a default rule, and finding the meaning of an express term by an interpretive process, is a vague one. For present purposes it does not matter how the issue is characterized, because the desiderata of a good supplied term match those of a good interpretation of an existing term. See generally E Allan Farnsworth, *Contracts* (3rd edn, New York: Aspen Law and Business, 1999), 461–6, 499–501.

[19] See Randy E Barnett, *The Structure of Liberty: Justice and the rule of law* (Oxford: Clarendon Press, 1998), 29–83 (explaining the need for freedom of contract and what its limits should be); Randy E Barnett, 'The sound of silence: Default rules and contractual consent', Virginia Law Review 78 (1992), 859–911 (explaining how default rules in contract law are consistent with contractual consent and should be chosen).

about how a term in the contract is to be understood, then that understanding should govern the contract's interpretation (so long as such understanding can be proven consistently with the parol evidence rule).[20] This follows from the self-imposed nature of contractual obligation. Second, if the parties to a contract have actual expectations about how a term of the contract is to be interpreted, but these expectations differ and one of them is reasonable and the other unreasonable, then the reasonably expected interpretation governs.[21] Third, if neither party has any actual expectations with respect to the matter in issue, but the parties do share the same hypothetical expectations—counterfactually, if they knew *ex ante* what they come to know *ex post*, what would they have thought about it?—then those hypothetical expectations should govern the contract's interpretation.[22] Fourth, if there are no actual or hypothetical expectations on the interpretation at issue, but there still is a contract,[23] then the best default rule is one that forms the best 'seed-crystal' around which the actual expectations of future parties to contracts of this kind can crystallize. In short, the best default rule of contract interpretation is one looking to the actual, reasonable, or hypothetical expectations of one or both contracting parties, or in the absence of these, looks to the expectations (for future contracting parties) foreseeably generated by the rule in this class of cases.

If we apply these general policies to interpret the undefined 'per occurrence' language specific to insurance policies, several desiderata of a good interpretation emerge. The first and by far the most important of these desiderata is to link the 'per occurrence' limitation to two items the parties to insurance contracts are certainly thinking about when they enter into such contracts. Insurance contracts are gambling contracts on future events about which the parties may have little or no control. The gamble in insurance contracts is two-fold: (1) what kind of loss or injury might the insured sustain during the policy period? And: (2) what kind of event that can cause the loss anticipated might occur during the policy period? In California, for example, homeowners typically purchase separate insurance policies insuring against: (1) property damage caused by (2) earthquake. Automobile liability policies, to take another example, insure against: (1) liability for personal injury damage and property damage to a non-insured, caused by (2) the tortious actions of the insured. Let us call the first of these the kind of *loss* insured against, and the second, the kind of *risk* insured against.

The parameters of loss and risk have to be the central focus of the actual expectations of parties to insurance contracts, for these two together define the gamble taken in such contracts. Hence, any reasonable party to an insurance contract containing a 'per occurrence' limitation in it has only one of two possible answers to the question, 'per occurrence of what?' It must be, per occurrence of the kind of loss insured against, or per occurrence of the kind of risk insured against. The 'per occurrence' limitation has to be read as part of these two larger limitations defining the gamble taken in insurance contracts.

---

[20] See Farnsworth, *Contracts*, 461, 499.

[21] Ibid, 462–3, 500–1.

[22] The hypothetical expectations of the parties tend to be the reasonable expectations parties generally to such transactions would have had. See ibid, 465–6, 500.

[23] As in the case of different and equally reasonable expectations, the absence of any expectations may preclude there being an enforceable contract. See, eg, *Ruckles v. Wicklehaus*, 2 H and C 906, 159 Eng Rep 375 (Exch 1864).

It is of course logically possible to divorce 'per occurrence' limitations from the kinds of losses or kinds of risks insured against. One might limit the insurance company's exposure by the occurrence of eclipses during the policy period, for example. But this would be deranged. Reasonable contractors have to mean what real contractors surely do mean: they mean per occurrence of those kinds of losses or risks that define the gamble they are taking.

Subsidiary desiderata of a good default rule of contract interpretation here are something akin to corollaries of the prime desideratum above. They are four in number. First, whatever test is used to determine whether a given *kind* of loss has occurred, or whether a given *kind* of risk has materialized, should be consistent with the test used to individuate occurrences under 'per occurrence' language. By way of illustration, suppose a single earthquake causes two separate fires (from ruptured gas lines) that destroy a house; under a property damage/earthquake policy, if one tests whether there is coverage for this kind of risk (earthquake risk) by looking to the original cause (the earthquake) rather than to the immediate cause (the fires), then one should test how many occurrences there are by counting earthquakes and not fires. Similarly, suppose two separate arsonists burn down two buildings of a company, the loss of both of which bankrupts the company; under a property damage/fire policy, if one tests whether there is coverage by looking to the initial damage suffered (building destruction) rather than the ultimate damage suffered (economic injury), then one should test how many occurrences there are by counting building losses and not bankruptcies.

Second, whatever test is used to determine whether a loss occurs, or a risk materializes, *during the policy period*, should be consistent with the test used to individuate occurrences under 'per occurrence' limitations. By way of illustration, suppose an earthquake occurs at t_1 this causes two aftershocks to occur at t_2, and all three cause a building to collapse at t_3. Under a property damage/earthquake policy whose period ends prior to t_2, if coverage is found to exist then one should be counting earthquakes at t_1, and not at t_2. (And of course one would not be counting building collapses at t_3.)

Third, 'per occurrence' limitations are commonly used to fix the upper limits of exposure and also to fix the threshold of exposure (the 'deductible') of a policy.[24] Whatever test is used to individuate occurrences for the upper limits of exposure should also be used to fix the thresholds of exposure.[25]

Fourth, 'per occurrence' limitations are used in both first and third party insurance policies (casualty and liability policies, respectively). Moreover, such limitations appear in both limited (or defined) risk, as well as in all-risk, casualty policies. Other things being equal, whatever test is used for individuating occurrences for one kind of policy should also

---

[24] See, eg, *Champion International Corporation v. Continental Casualty Co*, 546 F 2d 502 (2d Cir 1976), when the 'per occurrence' limitation was involved for both the deductible and the upper limit on liability.

[25] This is particularly true in cases like *Champion*, where both upper and lower limits are in issue. In such cases, if there are too many occurrences, then each separate loss falls below the deductible; if there is only one occurrence, there is only one recovery. The roofing company in *Champion* successfully avoided both the upper and lower limits by obtaining a finding of 27 occurrences for 27 batches of defective roofing materials—despite the materials going into hundreds of separate roofs, and despite the defect being one kind of defect of manufacture. One needs a common meaning to 'occurrence' in both the upper and lower limits of liability for this threading of the needle to be anything but arbitrary.

be used to individuate occurrences for the other kinds of policies.[26] This keeps the rule for interpreting insurance contracts simple enough that it can perform the 'seed-crystal' function mentioned earlier.

C. Per occurrence of what: Losses, risks, or both?

If we apply these desiderata to the present issue, it should be apparent that there are two main candidates for what kinds of occurrences we should be counting under 'per occurrence' limitations in insurance contracts. We could count occurrences of the kinds of losses insured against, or we could count occurrences of the kinds of risks insured against. These are said to be, respectively, the dominant approaches of English versus American insurance law.[27]

Under older English law, 'per occurrence' limits were interpreted to allow multiple recoveries by multiple parties who separately make claims for their injuries. By contrast, a 'per occurrence' limit in America is commonly held to focus on the event(s) that cause injuries, not on the number of injuries caused.[28] American insurance law thus focuses on the cause of injury, not on the effects of injurious behavior, in ascertaining when there is one or more occurrence. This is commonly termed the causal test (as opposed to the 'effects test') of whether two or more putatively distinct events are in reality one and the same occurrence.[29]

It is important to see what questions the causal test both does, and does not, purport to answer. The test resolves the basic question of interpreting the contracting parties' intentions: as we have seen, when contracting on a 'per occurrence' basis the 'per occurrence' language leaves open the question, 'per occurrence *of what?*' Per occurrence of the damage insured against, such as physical damage to a building? Or per occurrence of the kind of event that produces such damage and the risk of which was also insured against, such as earthquake, fire, or terrorist acts? By the majority position in American insurance law,[30] parties to an insurance contract are taken to refer to the number of covered kinds of damage-causing-events that occur, not the number of injuries or injured persons such events may cause and not the number of claims such injuries may spawn. What the test does not answer is how we are to individuate events. The test, in other

---

[26] As one court has observed, a liability policy is just a kind of casualty policy, one where the event insured against is liability to another for her losses as opposed to the losses the insured suffer directly by fires, earthquakes, and the like. See *Hyer v. Inter-Insurance Exchange of the Automobile Club of Southern California*, 77 Cal App 343, 349; 246 Pac 1055, 1057 (1926) ('Liability insurance is but a branch of accident and casualty insurance.').

[27] The English doctrine is set out in *Southern Staffordshire Tramways Co Ltd v. Sickness and Accident Assurance Association Ltd* (1891) 1 QB 402. It is discussed and rejected in one of the leading American cases, *Hyer*.

[28] One can, of course, write a 'per claim' version of 'per occurrence' limitations in American insurance contracts; but the default rule is that unless otherwise specified, 'per occurrence' limitations in American insurance contracts are per cause, not per claim. See, eg, *Champion International Corporation v. Continental Casualty Co*, 546 F 2d at 505–6; *Lamberton v. Travelers Indemnity Co*, 325 A 2d 104 (Del Sup Ct 1974), affirmed, 346 A 2d 167 (Del 1975).

[29] The 'effects test' is but another name for a 'per claim' or 'per injury' basis of coverage limitation. See, eg, *American Indemnity Co v. McQuaig*, 435 So 2d 414, 415 n 1 (Fla App 1983).

[30] There are occasional adoptions of the English per claim (or 'effects') view in America. See, eg, *Anchor Casualty v. McCaleb*, 178 F 2d 322 (5th Cir 1949).

words, tells us what sort of events must be individuated for insurance purposes, viz events that cause the relevant kinds of injuries. It does not even purport to tell us how to individuate such injury-causing events.

One might be tempted to regard the causal test of American insurance law as being more ambitious than this. In the philosophy of events there is a well-known view of event-identity which holds that any two putatively distinct events are in reality one and the same event if and only if such event(s) have the same causes and same effects.[31] On a modified version of this view one might think that the causal test of American insurance law *is* giving a test of event-identity for damage events, namely: two putatively distinct instances of physical loss or damage events are in reality one and the same physical loss or damage event whenever they have the same causes.[32] On such a view the answer to the interpretive question, 'per occurrence of what?', is the older, English answer: 'the kind of damages insured against' (and not the American answer, 'the kind of risks insured against'). The causal test would then be giving a theory of when two putatively distinct damage events are really one and the same event. Yet even if the causal test of American insurance law were this ambitious metaphysically, such test would still but regress the problem of event-identity: for to know when two damage events are the same, one would need to know whether they have the same cause-event, yet to know that, we must know when we have one cause-event versus two—and this the causal test cannot tell us, on pain of infinite regress.[33] In any case, the causal test of American law is not taken to be a metaphysical test of when two putatively distinct loss events are in reality one and the same event; rather, the causal test is regarded as the American answer to the basic question of contract interpretation in this class of cases, viz 'per occurrence *of what?*'

It is difficult to pinpoint any very plausible rationale for the American choice of the causal over the effects interpretation of 'per occurrence' language. One explanation (not justification) for the American doctrine lies in the accidents of case selection. In some of the early cases, the specific insurance policy language at issue suggested the causal test. For example, in a much-cited early California opinion the policy language was that the insurance company 'in no case shall . . . be liable with respect to claims . . . arising from one accident for more than one thousand dollars'.[34] As the California court pointed out,[35] such language plainly suggests that two or more injuries could nonetheless arise from but one accident. Moreover, the word 'accident' itself connotes something different than damage or loss; it

---

[31] Donald Davidson, *Essays on Actions and Events* (Oxford: Oxford University Press, 1980), 179. See also Laurence Lombard, *Events: A metaphysical study* (London: Routledge and Kegan Paul, 1986), 74–5.

[32] In construing state statutory bans against multiply punishing 'the same act', some courts have adopted a version of such a causal test of event-token individuation. See, eg, *People v. Neal*, 55 Cal 2d 11, 357 P 2d 839 (1960), where the California Supreme Court held two acts to be the same when they are the products of a single intention. See also *Spinnell v. State*, 83 Tex Crim App 418, 203 SW 357 (1918) ('A series of shots may constitute one act . . . where they are fired with one volition.') The same intent test of act-token individuation is discussed briefly in Moore, *Act and Crime*, 381–3.

[33] In addition the Davidsonian test itself seems false as a test of event identity. See Michael Moore, *Act and Crime*, 383; Myles Brand, *Intending and Acting* (Cambridge, Mass: MIT Press, 1984), 69; Judith Jarvis Thomson, *Acts and Other Events* (Ithaca: Cornell University Press, 1977), 70.

[34] *Hyer*, 77 Cal App at 345, 246 Pac at 1055.

[35] Ibid, 77 Cal App at 354, 246 Pac at 1059.

is not as easily taken to refer to an instance of kinds of loss insured against as is the more general word, 'occurrence'. Once 'per occurrence' limitations are equated to 'per accident' limitations,[36] these connotations of the latter were read into the former.

If we put aside these matters of historical accident and approach the matter afresh, it is difficult to see why one should think contracting parties would focus on the number of times the kinds of risks insured against materialize (to the exclusion of the number of instances of the kind of losses insured against) when they use undefined 'per occurrence' limitations. After all, both the kinds of risks insured against, and the kinds of losses insured against, form the core of the gamble taken by parties to insurance contracts. Presumably (prior to there being any legal rule on the matter, at least), the parties focus on both matters equally when they decide how much protection to buy or sell.

If this is so, then the preferable interpretation of 'per occurrence' insurance language is one asking *both*: How many *risked* events, and how many *loss* events, were there? Only if there were both two separate cause-events of the kind risked, and two separate loss-events of the kind covered by the policy, should there be two recoveries under a 'per occurrence' limited policy.[37]

Arguably this is in fact the correct reading of the causal test of American insurance law. The kind of case that tests this is a case in which there are two separate cause-events of the kind risked yet there is but one loss-event (of the kind covered) that is the common effect of the two cause-events. Imagine that it required the crashing of two airliners to bring down a single Tower. Suppose two airliners crashed into a single Tower, ignited the same portion of the Tower, causing its collapse by the fire-related weakening of the structural steel. We might display such a single, indivisible loss-event caused by two separate cause-events as in Figure A1:

Figure A1 One harmful effect of two causes

By the best reading of the causal test of 'occurrence,' there is but one occurrence here for purposes of insurance recovery. There is but one injury-event, the collapse of the Tower, even though there were two distinct causes of that collapse.

Part of my confidence that this is the right result stems from the commonness of (1). Events are rarely, if ever, caused by single, other events. Even where one airliner alone crashes into a tower which collapses, the crash of the Boeing 767 does not by itself cause the collapse of a skyscraper. Such collapse requires, in addition: the fueling of such aircraft with sufficient gasoline to fire the building sufficiently as to weaken its structural steel, the decision to use only such-and-such amount of steel columns in the center and at the

---

[36] See cases cited, n 13, above.
[37] I put aside (as too expansive of liability) the alternative, disjunctive combination of risk and loss.

perimeter of the skyscraper; the presence of sufficient ventilation to allow the flames to build to the required intensity; the use of combustible items in constructing and furnishing the part of the skyscraper hit by the airline; etc.

It is true that ordinary thought often distinguishes between various states and events equally necessary for the happening of the event to be explained, honoring only one as 'the cause' of the latter event.[38] Such thought thus rules out many conditions necessary to the happening of some event as eligible to be called its cause. The arson investigator who reports that the cause of some suspicious fire was 'oxygen in the air' will surely lose his job, just as the doctor who tells his patients that the cause of their tennis elbow condition is the playing of tennis, will lose his patients. Each of these items may be necessary to the events in question, yet no one singles them out as causes.

The factors that allow such discriminations, however, are no part of the notion of causation itself. Rather, these are pragmatic factors wholly dependent on context for their sensible use. Doctors, for example, list as causes those things they can treat, arson investigators list as causes of fires more unusual factors like sparks or human intervenors, historians tend to isolate extraordinary or surprising events, etc. These are matters having to do with the interest of the enquirer, not with the nature of the causal relation. There is nothing general to be found here, thus, that can be used to narrow the number of causes for any insured injury.

It is also not the case that the law narrows sufficiently the range of items eligible to be considered 'the cause' such that one and only one item is *the* proximate cause of an event such as a skyscraper's collapse. None of the dominant proximate cause tests that we explored in Chapter 4 even purport to limit the causes of any event to just one preceding event. Both simultaneous and temporally successive sets of events may contain numerous proximate causes for any given loss.[39]

Thus, in neither ordinary thought nor in the law is there any way to debar numerous events and states as the plural causes of any given injury event. It cannot be the case, then, that for an indivisible injury there can be more than one occurrence within the meaning of some insurance policy just because there are multiple causes of that injury—on pain of all accidents being such multiple occurrences.

Surprisingly, some American court opinions appear to assert the contrary. Consider, for example, this language of the Arizona Supreme Court:

The Fund also argues that there was only one 'occurrence' because there was only one injury. The cases, however, show that the number of causative acts, and not the number of injuries produced, determines the number of 'occurrences' . . . We conclude that the number of acts producing injury or damage, rather than the number of injuries caused, is the key on which the definition of 'occurrence' turns. *Multiple acts causing a single injury will constitute multiple occurrences*, while a single act will constitute a single occurrence even though it causes multiple injuries or multiple episodes of injury.[40]

---

[38] On the criteria used in ordinary thought for honoring one item as 'the cause' of some events see Joel Feinberg, *Doing and Deserving* (Princeton: Princeton University Press, 1970), 142–8.

[39] For examples of simultaneous proximate causes, see Chapter 5; for examples of successive proximate causes, see Chapter 11, above.

[40] *Arizona Property and Casualty Insurance Guaranty Fund v. Helme*, 153 Ariz 129, 735 P 2d 451, 457 (1987)

What the Arizona Supreme Court seems to be asserting is a broad principle of symmetry: just as one cause producing multiple injuries is but one occurrence, so multiple causes of but one injury constitutes multiple occurrences. Yet this language cannot be taken so broadly, however, on pain of the *reductio* about showing that all injuries are multiple occurrences because multiply caused.

At the very least, to avoid the *reductio* making all incidents into multiple occurrences, courts such as that in Arizona have to restrict their multiple cause/multiple occurrence idea to liability policies where the multiple causes are each acts of someone for whom the insurance company is liable. Thus, in *Arizona Property and Casualty Co v. Helme*,[41] quoted above, the multiple causes were acts of different doctors within the same professional corporation (the insured under the per occurrence liability policy); one doctor negligently diagnosed the victim and another doctor negligently operated on the victim, the victim dying as a joint result of an undiagnosed and untreated fracture dislocation of his cervical vertebra. Similarly, courts have held that other kinds of successive misdiagnoses by doctors insured under a liability policy,[42] as well as successive shots fired by a single insured under a liability policy,[43] constitute multiple occurrences despite their joint production of but a single injury.

Such a liability insurance doctrine avoids my *reductio* by limiting the multiple causes (that can lead to a 'multiple occurrence' characterization) to those negligent acts insured against by a liability policy. The apparent rationale of such a restriction is that the focus of liability policies is on the acts of the insured that generate liability; 'occurrences' can thus be taken to refer to such acts in measuring how many occurrences there were, not the loss(es) such acts cause. The idea is that the contracting parties to a liability insurance contract would contemplate a per-act-giving-rise-to liability basis in their per occurrence limitations.

If this is true, of course, such a rationale has no application to first party casualty insurance. In first party insurance there is no focus on acts of some insured or its employees; rather, under all risk policies, the focus is on the kind of loss suffered, such as physical property damage, not on the causes of such loss. Storms, rains, natural coincidences, as well as negligent acts of individuals, may cause a loss compensable under a casualty policy. Therefore, if a court were to count occurrences here by the number of causes alone, it would be fully subject to my earlier *reductio*: all cases would involve multiple occurrences.

In fact, my own view is that the liability-policy cases are mistaken even in the liability context. Negligent acts do not by themselves make for liability; only negligent acts that cause losses make for liability. The focus in the liability policy context should look to both separate losses and separate causes, on the more accurate assumption that contracting parties focus on both in setting limits of coverage. This is particularly clear in cases where the multiple causes of a single injury are overdetermining causes.[44] In the classic joint- fire cases,[45] for example, two fires of independent origin burn down some victim's house.

---

[41] *Arizona Property and Casualty Insurance Guaranty Fund v. Helme*, 153 Ariz 129, 735 P 2d 451, 457 (1987).

[42] *Insurance Corporation of America v. Rubin*, 107 Nev 610, 818 P 2d 389 (1991).

[43] *McQuaig*.

[44] The overdetermination cases are discussed in Chapters 5 and 17, above.

[45] *Anderson v. Minneapolis St Paul and S St Marie RR Co*, 146 Minn 430, 179 NW 45 (1920); *Kingston v. Chicago and NW Ry*, 191 Wis 610, 211 NW 913 (1927).

Each fire independently was sufficient for the job, but the joint fire they created was too. Suppose fire$_1$ was started by one of insured's employees and fire$_2$ was started by another employee of the insured. When the employer is held liable for the destruction of the house by fire, and seeks coverage of his liability from his liability carrier, surely this is only one occurrence for purposes of the per occurrence limitation in the employer's policy. The employer could not have expected to benefit by having more than one negligent employee causally contribute to some injury; for the employer has no more liability with the two negligent employees than he would have with only one.

What courts like those in Arizona may have mistakenly assumed is that where there is more than one negligent act causing injury for which an insured is liable, there must be more injury (even if not more separable injuries), thus, more liability, thus more need for a higher limit of insurance, thus, an intention by the purchaser of the policy for the higher coverage. Yet the overdetermination cases show that this is not true. Moreover, it is not even clearly true in the more ordinary kind of multiple cause cases, where each cause is necessary (and the causes together are jointly sufficient) for some indivisible injury. The only case where the assumption is clearly true are cases where each negligent act of employees cause separate injuries—but in such cases, there should be as many occurrences as there are such separately caused, separate injuries.

The correct interpretation of the American causal test is that fleetingly suggested by one federal district court: the question is whether multiple negligent acts or omissions of an insured doctor, or each act of treatment he prescribed, 'resulted in independent, compensable injuries.'[46] If they did, then each such act or omission should be a separate occurrence; but if, as in the actual case cited, each visit to the doctor and each treatment caused no separate damage but together jointly caused the blindness of the patient, then there is but one occurrence even for liability policy coverage purposes.[47]

In cases where there are two or more injuries *and* each injury has its own separate cause(s), then there should be two or more occurrences. Thus, if officers of a bank make a series of bad loans, each loan resulting in a loss equal to the amount of the loan, there are as many occurrences as there are acts of making a loan productive of loss of the money loaned.[48] Likewise, if a ship grounds its bow on a ledge, causing damage to its bow, and then it grounds its stern on the same ledge, causing damage to its stern, prima facie there are two acts causing two damages and thus there are two occurrences.[49]

This is not to say that the injury individuation question is always easy. If it could be proved that each administration of a chemical to the eyes of a patient caused some damage

---

[46] *Aetna Casualty and Surety Company of Illinois v. The Medical Protective Company of Fort Wayne, Indiana*, 575 F Supp 901 (ND Ill 1983). This federal district court better characterized the causal test as 'Whether the events in question are properly characterized as a single "occurrence" or multiple is a question of causation. A series of related injuries comprise a single "occurrence", for the purposes of an insurance contract, where they all flow from a single cause... *Where each injury results from an independent cause* [emphasis added], there are a series of occurrences': 575 F Supp at 903.

[47] The primary insurance carrier won in *Aetna Casualty*, because there were no separate injuries to the eyes of the patient with each application of the prescribed medicine to the patient's eyes. Ibid.

[48] *North River Insurance Co v. Huff*, 638 F Supp 1129 (D Kan 1985).

[49] *Newark Insurance Company v. Continental Casualty Company*, 46 App Div 2d 514, 363 NYS 2d 327 (1975). The 'prima facie' qualifier in the text, to leave open the possibilities discussed later in this section, that the second grounding was not causally independent of the first, and that there might be some common cause of both groundings in some general decision or policy of the captain or the ship owner.

to the eye and optic nerve, and all administrations together caused total blindness, is there one injury (blindness) or as many injuries as there were administrations causing some loss of sight?[50] Or if a bank employee writes forty bad checks, are there forty small losses or one big one?[51] Or if officers and directors make a series of bad decisions, each resulting in the loss of a certain amount of money to the company, and all such losses together bankrupt the company, are there numerous smaller losses or one big loss?[52] These questions are no easier to answer than are the similar individuation question about the events which cause such losses (both such questions will be considered in section V). The only point here is that both such questions of event-individuation need to be asked to properly apply the causal test for 'same occurrence'. I shall henceforth take the causal test of American insurance law to ask both of these questions of event-individuation.

D. The two kinds of metaphysical questions asked by the causal test

I shall call both these last questions the pure questions of event-identity: when is there one (versus two or more) events that cause injuries and when is there one (versus two or more) events of an injurious kind? Because the causal test makes the notion of 'same occurrence' as dependent on the causal relations between such events as on the question of whether these are separate events, the test requires that we answer an additional kind of metaphysical question.[53] This second question is what I shall call the causal relation question: even when there are distinct cause-events and distinct injury-events, are the causal relations between them such that they should be classified as one occurrence under the causal test?

Although these two kinds of questions each form a leg of a single pair of trousers, the causal question is logically prior to the pure event-identity questions. This is because it is the answer to the causal question that tells us how far back in time we are to look when we seek to individuate events. One possibility would be to look for occurrences of the kinds of events most proximate to the loss events insured against. In the destruction of the Twin Towers, for example, this would be to focus on fire kinds of events, since it was the fires that most immediately caused the collapse of the Towers. Another possibility would be to look to the causes of those fires, in terms of the airplanes crashing into the Towers. A third possibility is to look for more remote causes, such as the making of the decision within al Qaeda to destroy the Towers with passenger aircraft. It is only after we have used causal doctrines to settle on the temporal slice(s) on which to focus that we can then ask the pure event-identity question of how many collapse-events, crash-events, decision-events, etc,

---

[50] The facts of *Aetna Casualty and Surety Company of Illinois*, above.

[51] *Business Interiors v. Aetna Casualty and Surety Company*, 751 F 2d 361 (10th Cir 1984).

[52] *Okada et al v. MGIC Indemnity Corp*, 608 F Supp 383 (D Hawaii 1985), affirmed in part and reversed in part, 823 F 2d 276 (9th Cir 1986).

[53] Arguably, this point was obliquely recognized by the Appellate Division of New York when it stated that 'events of injury or loss are one "accident" within the meaning of the policy provided that they are (1) completely indistinguishable in time and space, or (2) that one event caused the other'. *Hartford Accident and Indemnity Company v. Wesolowski*, 39 App Div 2d 833, 333 NYS 2d 289, 292 (1972), reversed on other grounds, *Wesolowski*. Such a disjunctive test seemingly utilizes what I shall (in section V below) call a spatio-temporal test of event identity, uses the clumping of two events together as one if they are causally related (what I call in section IV, below, the causal chain doctrine), and sees that the test is disjunctive so that both questions must be answered to determine occurrence identity. Whether New York follows the causal test of occurrence identity is a matter requiring some discussion, pursued later in section IV, below.

there might have been at the relevant slice of time. For this reason I shall put on the causal leg of the trousers first.

IV. The Causal Relation Question

The causal test of American insurance law demands a great deal from our notion of causation, as we shall see. Let us start with four simple models where the implications of the causal test are thought to be plain. These are highly idealized models, freed of the complexities of most real world cases in order to keep the analysis simple. We can then seek to complicate the analysis in order to deal with the complexities of real world cases.

A. The four simple models

1. The common-cause model

The first of the models is what I shall call the 'common-cause', or 'epiphenomenal', cases. Suppose, for example, a single passenger airliner had crashed between the Towers, causing their collapse. Then a single cause-event caused two damage-events, which we might display as done below in Figure A2:

Figure A2 One cause of two harmful effects

If anything is clear from the causal test, it is that in epiphenomenal cases of this kind there is but one occurrence despite the existence of two damage events.[54] This is the pay-off of distinguishing the English from the American interpretation of 'per occurrence' insurance policies; under the latter scheme for interpretation, we focus on the number of causes of loss-events as much as on the number of such loss-events themselves.

2. The causal-chain model

The second simple causal pattern is that of a chain of dependent causes. Imagine that the al Qaeda plan had been (as it apparently was in 1993) to topple the second WTC Tower by crashing the first such Tower into it. Suppose both planes hit the same Tower with the

---

[54] The multiple car collision cases are illustrative: if one piece of bad driving causes three collisions with three motorcycles, injuring five separate motorcycle riders or passengers, there is but one accident for insurance limitation purposes under the causal test: *Truck Insurance Exchange v. Rohde*. The New York Court of Appeals in another multiple collision case, *Wesolowski*, reaches a like result with its so-called 'event test'.

result intended. Then we may schematize the relation between the two 767s crashing into the first tower (c_1 c_2), causing the toppling of that tower (e_1), which causes the collapse of the second tower (e_2), thus:

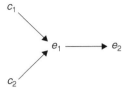

Figure A3 Two causes of a chain of two harmful effects

Notice that in such cases there are two cause-events of two injury-events, and yet the courts are uniform under the causal test in denying that there is more than one occurrence. The reason, it is said, is because e_1 and e_2 are not causally independent of one another; rather, e_1 causes e_2, and thus there is but one occurrence.

Illustrative of this causal independence aspect of the causal test are the multiple car collision cases.[55] When the insured's car hits multiple other cars, it matters whether he ricocheted off the first car into the second or whether, having regained control of his vehicle after the first collision, he then has a second collision. In the former case there is no causal independence between the successive collisions, so that there is a causal chain and thus but one occurrence; in the latter case the second collision is causally independent of the first and there are two occurrences.

The best way to think of this causal dependence notion is as a kind of clumping device: any cause-events that are causally linked are clumped together to count as one cause-event (even though as events they are in fact distinct), and any injury-events that are causally linked are clumped together to count as one injury-event (even though as events they are in fact distinct). The rationale for such clumping is of a piece with the rationale for the causal test of 'occurrence' in general: contracting parties using a 'per occurrence' (rather than a 'per claim') limitation of coverage are focusing on the events that cause injuries as much as they are focusing on the injuries themselves. In the former focus they are presumably using a causal notion of separateness of events, so that only events that are causally separate can count as separate occurrences; they are betting on how much damage they are likely to sustain with any one visitation of the whims of nature. In counting 'whims', any one event that causes numerous injuries via numerous intermediate events is but one visitation.

3. The common-injury model

As was discussed in section III, above, the best interpretation of American insurance law's causal test is that it counts instances of injury as well as instances of risked causes of injury. Under such an interpretation of American law, the third model precluding multiple

---

[55] See, eg, *Wesolowski*; *Rohde*; *Hyer*; *Olsen v. Moore*, 56 Wis 2d 340, 202 NW 2d 236 (1972).

recovery is one where were this is but one indivisible injury, the common effect of multiple causes. This was represented in Figure A1 above.

4. The separate causes of separate-injuries model

The common cause, common injury, and causal chain cases make up what I call the three idealized patterns to show but one occurrence under the causal test. These three contrast with the equally idealized pattern of two independent causes of two separate injuries, where there are two occurrences under the causal test:

Figure A4 Two causes of two unrelated harmful effects

B. Some real-world applications of the four models

To apply the four simple models to the complex facts of real world cases requires two kinds of knowledge: (1) knowledge of event-individuation, ie when there is one and when there are two or more distinct cause-events and injury-events; and (2) knowledge of the nature of the causal relation. The first kind of knowledge I deal with in section V; it is the second kind of knowledge on which I shall here focus.

The concept of causation that the courts adopt in 'per occurrence' insurance litigation is often said to be the same as is used throughout the law in assigning primary liability to actors. That is, 'cause' here is often taken to mean both of the notions explored in Chapter 4, cause-in fact and proximate cause. It is this latter notion, of proximate causation, that is of particular importance to the classification of real world cases into one of the four basic patterns:

Proximate cause is an integral part of any interpretation of the words 'accident' or 'occurrence' as used in a contract for liability insurance which indemnifies the insured for his tortious acts . . . [56]

Consider by way of illustration one of the cases of considerable interest to the Twin Towers litigation, *Arthur Johnson Corp. v. Indemnity Insurance Co.*[57] In that case the basements of two adjacent buildings (at 300 and 304 Fourth Avenue) were flooded by the waters from an extraordinary rainstorm. This was not a first party insurance case, but a liability policy case; the party whose actions were at issue was a contractor who had contracted with the City of New York to construct subway platform extensions for the various stations of the Lexington Avenue Subway. In constructing one such platform extension under Fourth Avenue, the contractor: (1) dug a continuous trench in the street before the two buildings, 300 and 304 Fourth Avenue; (2) removed the front vault walls

---

[56] *Rohde*, 49 Wash 2d at 471, 303 P 2d at 662.   [57] *Johnson*.

of each of the buildings, exposing their basements to the trench; and (3) constructed (in a manner stipulated not to be negligent)[58] a six-inch thick, cinder-block retaining wall sealing off the basement of each building from the trench in the street.

A rainstorm, characterized by the New York Court of Appeals as one of 'unprecedented intensity',[59] occurred, dropping 3.52 inches of rain in just two hours. The rain waters filled the trench, causing one retaining wall to collapse at 5:10 pm and causing the second to collapse at 6:00 pm. The collapse of the retaining walls resulted in the flooding of each of the two basements, causing water damage to each of the buildings.

The loss insured against by the contractor was liability for the property damage of others, so long as the property damage arose out of his work. As the policy recognized, the liability might be a tortious liability of the contractor to various building owners, or the liability might be a contractual liability of the contractor to the City of New York. The latter liability arose out of an indemnity agreement entered into between the contractor and the City of New York whereby the contractor agreed to indemnify the City against 'claims by persons, including abutting owners and their tenants for damage which . . . may be occasioned by the work of construction, even in cases where such owners have no legal claim against the City for such injuries or damage.'[60]

If the liability at issue in *Johnson* were a tort-based liability, then the kind of risk insured against would be easy to state: any acts or omissions of the contractor that under tort law would make him liable to the building owners are the kind of injury-producing events, the risk of which was insured against. In such a case, those acts or omissions of the contractor would have to be the in fact and proximate causes of the flood damage events suffered by the buildings, for only such acts or omissions could be the basis of the contractor's tort liability.

The kind of risk insured against is the same under a contract-based liability, which was the kind of liability actually at issue in *Johnson*. For that contract-based liability of the contractor was only for such liability the City might have to those building owners suffering property damage 'occasioned by the work of construction . . .'.[61] 'Occasioned' is one of those numerous synonyms in the English language for 'caused'.[62] Only property damage *caused* by the work of construction of the platform extension is insured against, so that the risk is again of injury-producing acts of the contractor.

The policy thus limited coverage to one kind of loss, property damage, and one kind of risk, viz work of the contractor causing such loss. The policy further limited the risk coverage to accidentally caused injury, and then limited such coverage to '$50,000 per accident'. The issue in the case was whether there was one or two accidents within the meaning of the policy.

One thing highlighted by a case like *Johnson* is the limited determinacy of the American causal test. The indeterminacy here does not stem from indeterminacies in the pure questions of event-individuation. There may be these latter indeterminacies as well— see section V below—but the causal test introduces its own indeterminacy. To isolate

---

[58] 7 NY 2d at 226, 196 NYS.2d at 681, 164 N Ed 2d at 705.
[59] 7 NY 2d at 225–6, 196 NYS 2d at 680, 164 N Ed 2d at 705.
[60] 7 NY 2d at 224, 196 NYS 2d at 679, 164 NE 2d at 704.   [61] Ibid.
[62] Action verbs of English are often 'causally complex' in this way, as we saw in Chapter 1, above. I disregard the analysis of 'occasioned' that treats it as naming a distinct, second kind of causal relation. See Chapters 12 and 13, above.

this latter source of indeterminacy, let us assume for now that we are clear on the relevant questions of event-identity: the digging of the one continuous platform trench was one event; that the destruction of the basement vaults at numbers 300 and 304 Fourth Avenue were two events; the construction of two cinderblock retaining walls in front of the two buildings constituted two events; the two-hour rainstorm was one event; that the filling of the trench was one event; the collapse of each retaining wall was each a separate event; and the flooding of each basement was a separate event. Then the causal relation of what happened in *Johnson* looks like Figure A5, with some simplifications such as making the paired events (vault wall destructions, retaining wall constructions, retaining wall collapses, floodings) simultaneous when in fact some were not:

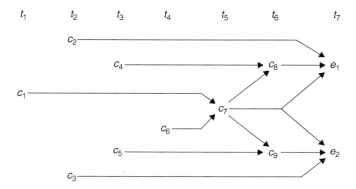

Figure A5 (Where c_1 = digging of trench in street; c_2, c_3 = removals of vault walls of the two buildings; c_4, c_5 = constructions of retaining walls before the two buildings; c_6 = rainstorm; c_7 = filling of trench with rainwater; c_8, c_9 = collapses of two retaining walls; e_1, e_2 = floodings of the two basements)

In English, what Figure A5 depicts is that each of the two flooding-of-basement events was caused[63] by: the removal of the basement vault walls (c_2,c_3), the collapse of the retaining walls (c_8, c_9), and the filling of the trench with water (c_7). The collapse of the retaining walls was caused in turn by the construction of them (c_4, c_5) with the strength they possessed, and the filling of the trench with water(c_7) to a depth where the pressure exceeded the strength of the walls. The filling of the trench with water was in turn caused by the digging of the trench (c_1) and the rainstorm (c_6).

The causal test tells us this much clearly: the fact that there were two injury-events (the two floodings) is not enough to make for two occurrences; for this could be a kind of common cause case where there is but one occurrence despite multiple separate injury-events. Still, while not sufficient, the separation of the two injury events is necessary for there to be two occurrences, as we have seen. There is no causal relationship between

---

[63] Both the removal of the vault walls and the collapse of the retaining walls 'caused' the flooding of the two basements only in the Pickwickian sense that these action and events removed preventers of the flooding. I would, however, construe the 'occasioned' language of the indemnity contract to include both literal causings and double preventions done by the 'work of the contractor'.

them; no water entered one basement through the flooding of the other.[64] Indeed, as the Court of Appeals noted,[65] probably the flooding of the first basement lessened the pressure on the retaining wall protecting the second basement, so that the first flooding retarded, not accelerated, the second flooding.

Yet the harder question about a case like *Johnson* is how many cause-events there might be. For there to be two occurrences we need there to be two separate cause events of two separate injury events. If we ask this question globally, over the entire time-span t_1–t_6 considered as a whole, there seems to be no answer. The two basement floodings were commonly caused by the one trench digging, the one rainstorm, and the one trench flooding; yet the two basement floodings were also separately caused by the removal of the separate vault walls, and the construction and collapse of the separate retaining walls. If we ask this question at any one time, we can get determinate answers (in terms of the two-wall collapses at t_6, for example), but how are we to pick the relevant slice of time on which to focus? Why not one rainstorm or one trench-digging as opposed to two wall collapses?

We might get some help here from the law's notion of proximate causation. If 'proximate cause' meant, 'cause nearest the injuries', then we would get a lot of help, for that would focus us on the question of how many wall collapses there were. Yet as we saw in Chapter 4, 'proximate cause' does not mean '*most* proximate cause'.[66] As one court noted in this context:

'Proximate cause' literally means the cause nearest to the effect produced; but in legal terminology it is not confined to its literal meaning. Though a negligent act or omission be removed from the injury by intermediate causes or effects, yet if, in a natural and continuous sequence, unbroken by any new efficient cause, it produces that injury...it is in law the proximate cause of such injury...[67]

Still, even with a plurality of proximate causes possible for any given harm, the help potentially given by the notion of proximate cause lies in the same court's idea of there being 'new efficient causes' that break causal chains. These are the familiar 'intervening', 'superseding', or 'extraneous' causes that we examined in Chapters 11 and 12, items which in law constitute fresh causal starts and thereby end any causal relation between earlier events and the harm. (That intervening causation is not part of the correct metaphysics of causation is here by-the-by; the parties are contracting with respect to the tort liability rules of New York, and those rules contain doctrines of intervening causation.)

The extraordinary rainstorm in *Johnson* is a good candidate for being an intervening cause. The rainstorm was conceded by the *Johnson* court to be one of 'unprecedented intensity'—3.52 inches in two hours.[68] The court further noted that the temporary retaining walls were not negligently constructed (or at least the parties so stipulated).[69] Although that leaves open the possibility that the walls were defective even if non-negligently made to be so, that seems unlikely given the failure of both walls and the great volume of water.

Such extraordinary natural events as an unprecedented rainstorm are good candidates for constituting an intervening or superseding cause under the legal doctrines examined in

---

[64] 7 NY 2d at 230, 196 NYS 2d at 684, 164 NE 2d at 708.   [65] Ibid.
[66] See generally, HLA Hart and Tony Honoré, *Causation in the Law*; Chapters 11 and 12, above.
[67] *Hyers*, 77 Cal App at 347, 246 Pac at 1056.   [68] See n 59, above.
[69] See n 58, above.

Chapter 11. So long as they are events that are: (i) subsequent to some earlier event, (ii) causally independent of that earlier event while (iii) themselves causally contributing to the harm, and so long as such event is (iv) 'extraordinary' or 'abnormal', while being (v) uncontrived by a defendant, then such states or events are intervening causes that break the causal chain between earlier events and the harm.[70] The rainstorm in *Johnson* is a good candidate for such an intervening cause, inasmuch as the only one of these five criteria for an intervening cause in doubt in *Johnson* is just how extraordinary a 3.52 inch downpour in two hours might be for New York City.

The Court of Appeals nonetheless found that 'The proximate cause cannot be said to be the heavy rainfall but separate negligent acts of preparing and constructing separate walls which, for all we know, may have been built at separate times by separate groups of workmen.'[71] Although the court does not tell us, perhaps the reason was that a rainstorm of that intensity was not so unusual for New York City (despite the court calling it 'unprecedented'). In any case, had the rainstorm been held to have been an intervening cause, that would focus our attention on times subsequent to the rainstorm. We would not have to worry about how many trench-diggings (t_1), vault wall destructions (t_2), or retaining wall constructions (t_3) there were because none of these would have legally caused the flood damage complained of. We would still have to choose whether we are counting rainstorms, (t_4), trench fillings (t_5), or retaining wall collapses (t_6), but at least our choice is lessened in these alternate possibilities. Whereas if the rainstorm is not an intervening cause, all of these slices of time are eligible for selection as the time to ask, 'How many cause-events were there *then*?'

What helps to reduce the indeterminacy here more than anything else is to remember what I called the prime desideratum of an interpretation of 'per occurrence' limitations in insurance policies: make sure you are counting events that instantiate the kind of risks covered under the policy; if it is an earthquake policy, do not count the fires caused by an earthquake even if they go on to cause the harms; rather, count earthquakes.

In *Johnson* recall that the type of damage insured against was liability for property damage and the risk taken was that such liability would arise from the work of the contractor. When counting occurrences, we must thus count how many acts or omissions of the contractor—his 'work'—were the causes of the two basement floodings. This focuses the enquiry at t_1–t_3, for it was the digging of the trench, the destruction of the vaults, and the construction of the retaining walls, that was the work of the contractor leading to the floodings.

Now consider again the rainstorm as an intervening cause under present law. If the rainstorm was an intervening cause, then the causal test is clear in its implication: there were *no* occurrences of work by the contractor causing the floodings. If the rainstorm was an intervening cause, then it and the events that followed it alone caused the floodings; and yet neither the rainstorm nor what followed it were the work of the contractor for which he could be liable in either torts or under his contract of indemnity. On the other hand, if the rainstorm is not an intervening cause, then the implications of the causal test are not so clear. To be sure, now we restrict our focus to t_1–t_3, but even so restricted the *Johnson* case could be construed as a common-cause case (one trench digging) or as a

---

[70] HLA Hart and Tony Honoré, *Causation in the Law*, 79–80. See generally Chapter 11, above.
[71] 7 NY 2d at 230, 196 NYS 2d at 684, 164 NE 2d at 708.

separate causes of separate injuries case (two vault wall destructions and two retaining wall constructions).

The application of standard proximate-cause notions, conjoined with the reminder that we only count cause-events of the kind risked in a policy, thus reduces but does not eliminate the indeterminacy of the causal test for liability policies like that in *Johnson*. A proper understanding of this highlights an important difference between liability and all-risk casualty policies. For notice in *Johnson* what makes possible a non-arbitrary selection of a time at which to ask 'How many cause-events were there?' was the basis of the liability insured against: for an ordinary tort-liability policy, that would mean negligent acts by the insured; for a contract-based strict liability, as in *Johnson*, that would mean any act of the insured—so long as such acts were among the proximate causes of the injuries.

For all risk policies such as that issued to the World Trade Center leaseholders, there was nothing analogous pinpointing *when* one should ask 'How many causes were there?' For any kind of injury-causing event is the risk covered under an all-risk policy. Suppose in *Johnson* the two adjacent buildings were owned by one owner, who purchased a casualty policy, insuring against property damage from all risks, at $50,000 per occurrence. Suppose further we grant the New York Court of Appeals its conclusion that the rainstorm was not so extraordinary as to be an intervening cause under present tort law. Whether there was one or two occurrences depends on whether we look at how many collapses there were (t_6), how many trench fillings there were (t_5), how many rainstorms there were (t_4), how many buildings of retaining walls there were (t_3), etc. Since all of these equally proximate causes of the physical damages suffered are covered risks, each seems equally eligible to be considered; and this has the embarrassing consequence that the causal test is much more indeterminate as a test of how many occurrences there might be for all-risk casualty policies than for liability policies.

C. Three approaches to reduce the indeterminacy of the causal test

Given the indeteminacy of the causal test that remains even after one has both focused exclusively on events that instantiate covered risks and applied standard intervening cause doctrines, it is tempting to supplement the causal test with some more determinate subtest. Two obvious possibilities are temporal: pick the earliest of a series of covered, proximate causes, or pick the latest. The third possibility is more substantial: pick the 'most important' of a series of covered, proximate causes. I shall consider each such suggestion *seriatim*.

1. The earliest proximate cause approach

There is considerable case law support for the view that in cases where there are multiple proximate causes (of the kind that instantiates a covered risk) of damages (of the kind also covered by a policy) one should count occurrences by the *earliest* of the sequence of covered, proximate causes. Suppose an insured purchases an earthquake policy protecting against property damage. Suppose that insured's house is damaged by two aftershocks (c_2, c_3) of an earlier earthquake (c_1), each aftershock inflicting separate damage to a separate part of the house (e_1, e_2) but the initial earthquake causing no damage to these parts of the house. The picture is thus that of Figure A6:

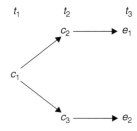

Figure A6 One remote cause of two harmful effects where there are two causal intermediaries

In such circumstances there is considerable authority for the view that there is one occurrence, not two: c_2 and c_3 are causally dependant on c_1, and therefore can be regarded as a mere means by which one earthquake caused multiple harms. Figure A6 thus reduces to Figure A2, the common-cause model for but one occurrence under the causal test.

The best case-law support for the view that we are to look to the earliest proximate causes of harm when we are counting occurrences is to be found in the context of liability policies for automobile collisions.[72] The typical fact scenario involves the insured driving in a negligent manner at t_1 (typically a crossing of the center line); this results in a collision with victim number 1 at t_2; this collision ricochets the insured's vehicle into colliding with one or more other vehicles at t_3. The pattern is thus that of a causal chain (Figure A3 above), and the courts uniformly hold there to be but one occurrence under the causal test.

The rationale for this *first* proximate-cause interpretation of the causal test is the same as the rationale for the 'one occurrence' construal of causal chains generally: so long as the subsequent causes of injury are dependant upon the earlier cause, that event is the one to count in deciding how many times the insured suffered one of the risks he insured against. All events produced by that earliest proximate cause are the mere means or mechanism by which that earlier event causes the multiple injuries that are its (covered by insurance) effects.

The limits of this rationale, and the limits of this first proximate-cause doctrine, are shown in cases where the later causes of injury are not causally dependant on the earliest proximate cause. We should thus contrast the causal-chain multiple-collision cases discussed above with a case where a negligent insured driver does not ricochet off the first car he hits nor does he make one mistake only. In *Liberty Mutual Insurance Co. v. Rawls*,[73] the insured was recklessly speeding because he was attempting to outrun two pursuing deputy sheriffs. He hit the left rear of one automobile in his own lane of travel, apparently in an attempt to pass it. Without losing control of his vehicle, he continued for several

---

[72] See the cases cited nn 54 and 55, above.   [73] 404 F 2d 880 (5th Cir 1968).

seconds across the center line, hitting a second vehicle head-on. Prima facie there were two acts of speeding, causing two separate injuries, as depicted in Figure A7:

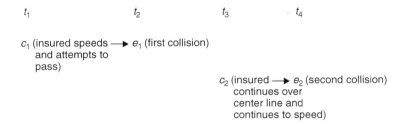

Figure A7 Two independent causes of two harmful effects

As the Fifth Circuit emphasized in reaching its conclusion that there were two accidents, the insured 'had control of his vehicle after the initial collision'.[74] As subsequent courts have emphasized,[75] such control and continued reckless driving makes the second collision causally independent of the first. Therefore the model is that of Figure A4, where there are two causes of two separate injuries, and thus, two occurrences under the causal test.

One way of construing cases like *Rawls* so as to make it fully consistent with always picking the earliest proximate cause when counting occurrences, is to regard the second act of speeding by the insured as an intervening cause. Then the act of speeding and veering over the center line at t_3 is the earliest proximate cause (of the kind instantiating the covered risk) of the second injury at t_4, just as the first act of speeding at t_1 is the earliest proximate cause of the first injury at t_2. Yet suppose we were to think that the second act of speeding at t_3 was not an intervening cause. The control exercised by the injured in continuing to attempt to outrun the deputies at t_3 makes the second act of speeding causally independent of the first collision—this is not a ricochet case, in other words where the first collision causes the second via an out-of-control automobile. But a later event that causally contributes to some harm can be causally independent of an earlier event without breaking the causal relationship between the earlier event and that harm. This is possible because causal independence is only a necessary condition for an event to be an intervening cause; it is not a sufficient condition.[76] Also necessary for a subsequent human action to be an intervening cause is that a human act intentionally takes advantage of the opportunity afforded by the earlier act so as to bring about the harm that resulted.[77]

Suppose that we were to think that the insured's decision to continue to evade the deputies in *Rawls* was not sufficiently intentional vis-á-vis the second collision as to be an intervening cause. The picture of the facts of *Rawls* then would be that of Figure A8:

---

[74] Ibid, 880.
[75] Eg, the Supreme Court of Wisconsin in *Olson v. Moore*, 56 Wis 2d at 349, 202 NW 2d at 240.
[76] See Chapter 11, above.   [77] Hart and Honoré, *Causation in the Law*, 74–7.

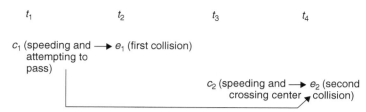

Figure A8 Two independent causes of two harmful effects where the first cause is a common cause of both effects

Because c_2 is not an intervening cause, the second collision can be a product of both the initial speeding at t_1 and the later swerving across the center line at t_3.

If one applied the 'pick the earliest proximate cause' idea to such a case, then this is but one occurrence—for there is one cause (c_2) of both collisions, and we have an instance of Figure A2, the common-cause model. Yet it seems quite doubtful that 'one' is the correct answer to such a case. Given the causal independence of c_2 from c_1, this is not a chain kind of case where one can say 'The earliest proximate cause counts as one because it caused everything else.' Given the causal independence of c_2, there was not just one instance of the risk insured against materializing—there were two. And so long as each occurrence of the risk materializing caused its own separate injury (to put aside the common injury cases), there should be two occurrences here. Such a result is closer to the gamble the parties presumably took in affixing per occurrence limits to the kinds of events risked.

We can see the plausibility of the same point with the facts of *Johnson*. In *Johnson*, we should focus only on those events that constitute the work of the contractor that caused the flooding of the two basements. On the assumption that the rainstorm was not an intervening cause, there were three sorts of such causally relevant work: the digging of the one trench, the destruction of the two basement vault walls, and the construction of the two retaining walls. The earliest of these events was the digging of the trench, and on the 'earliest proximate cause counts' view, we should count events at t_1, in which case there was but one occurrence. Yet this to my mind is counterintuitive. Given the causal independence of the vault destruction and the retaining-wall construction from the trench digging, one cannot say that everything leading to the flooding was caused by the trench digging. That event was first in time but equally important to the subsequent flooding was the replacement of strong vault walls with weaker cinder-block retaining walls.

The upshot is that one cannot extend the first proximate-cause doctrine to cases where the other proximate causes are causally independent of the first proximate cause of some injuries. The causal test under this interpretation should be regarded as still indeterminate with regard to this class of cases.

2. The last proximate-cause approach

The other interpretation of the causal test having some explicit support in the case law is to pick the proximate cause(s) nearest in time to the harms and count how many of those there might be. This is the interpretation of the causal test accepted by the New York Court of Appeals as the main rationale for its decision in *Johnson*.[78]

There are two ways of taking this suggestion. One is to focus exclusively on the proximate cause(s) nearest the harm *no matter whether such events instantiate the risk insured against*. This was apparently the view of the majority opinion in *Johnson*, for that opinion held there to be two occurrences because there were two wall collapse events. It was the collapse of the retaining walls that were the proximate causes most immediately preceding the flooding of the two basements, and because there were two such collapses, each causing a separate flooding-injury event, the court held there to be two occurrences under the policy. The court simply ignored how many trench-floodings, how many rainstorms, how many retaining-wall constructions, how many vault-wall destructions, and how many trench diggings there were, because these (admittedly proximate causes) were not the '*most* proximate', or immediate, causes of the flooding.

This 'last cause' interpretation is surely a very bad reading of per-occurrence limitations in insurance contracts. As I argued earlier in section III, both liability and casualty policies are issued against the risk of there being certain kinds of causes of certain kinds of injuries. 'Per occurrence' limitations on coverage have to be read in light of this fact. The two kinds of occurrences of interest to parties to insurance contracts are occurrences of injuries and occurrences of causes of injuries, for these are the things (kinds of losses and kinds of risks) generally defining coverage.

There is thus only one sensible answer to the question, 'per occurrence of what?' That is the answer of the causal test (properly construed as above): 'per occurrence of injurious events of the kind covered in the policy, so long as each such injury is caused by a separate occurrence of the kind of event the risk of which was also covered in the policy'. One might argue for either a pure effects test, or a pure causal test, focusing respectively on covered kinds of damage or on covered kinds of risks. Although I argued earlier this would be erroneous, either of these arguments is at least intelligible. But focusing on events that are neither losses nor risks makes no sense. In particular, there is no sensible test focusing on events located temporally between the covered cause events and the covered damage events, such as the collapse of retaining walls in *Johnson*; for no contracting party is limiting coverage based on those events. Such events are neither covered types of injuries nor covered types of risks. One might as well construe 'per occurrence' limits in insurance contracts based on the number of eclipses that occur during the policy period; such eclipses have as much to do with damages and risks insured against as do other non-covered events like retaining wall collapses.

Imagine buying a property-damage policy covering the risk of earthquakes. Suppose an earthquake occurs, this causes two fires to break out in two separate parts of the building insured, and this results in separate injuries to the different parts of the building. Suppose further a court would construe the policy to cover this property damage, on the ground that it is still earthquake-caused damage even though the means by which the earthquake caused the damage was by two fires. If one were to apply the last-proximate-cause test in the manner of the court in *Johnson*, then one would conclude that there were two occurrences because there were two fires; this, despite the fact that fires are not risks covered by an earthquake policy. Such an approach divorces what one is counting under

---

[78] *Johnson*.

'per occurrence' limitations from what is covered by the policy, and that surely no party to an insurance contract either intends or expects.

The cases cited by the New York Court of Appeals do little to support its view in *Johnson* that there is some test of 'same occurrence' focusing exclusively on the last proximate cause of the injuries. The case that court considered 'most similar'[79] to *Johnson* was *Kuhn's of Brownsville*,[80] a case in which four buildings collapsed because of the excavation work done by the insured. Yet in the latter case the Supreme Court of Tennessee did not see itself as applying some last proximate-cause kind of test. Rather, the court engaged in standard proximate-cause analysis (called for by the causal test) to find that the insured's excavation(s) had caused the collapse of the four buildings. That court then mistakenly found there to be two excavation events to cause the two injury events,[81] but this mistake had nothing to do with any supposed invention of a last-proximate-cause test for 'per occurrence' limitations.

The subsequent application of the New York last-proximate-cause test also does little to support the idea that this is truly the test for 'same occurrence' being followed in New York. In the *Wesolowski* decision[82] issued 14 years after *Johnson*, the New York Court of Appeals purported to be applying the *Johnson* last event test. Yet in this ricochet-type multiple-car-collision case, the court in fact engaged in the standard proximate-cause analysis. Because 'the continuum between the two impacts was unbroken, with no intervening agent or operative factor',[83] the court held there to be but one occurrence despite the multiple car collisions. This is precisely the result and the reasoning dictated by the standard version of the causal test.

I conclude that in reality New York cannot be following any last-proximate-cause test of 'same occurrence'. There is no such test that makes any sense in light of contracting parties presumed intentions, there is no such test to be found in the non-New York case law relied on by the New York courts, and the New York courts themselves have had the good sense to apply no such test in their multiple-collision cases, despite what they may say. There is also a fourth reason to think that New York cannot be following any such last-proximate test. This reason is supplied by a *reductio* suggested by the dissent in *Johnson*. Justice Van Voorhis noted in that dissent that 'something analogous to the collapse of these two walls can always be found, and would necessarily occur whenever damage is effected to more than one person'.[84] This would collapse the causal test supposedly distinctive of American insurance law, into the English effects test.

Justice Van Voorhis' point can be illustrated by one of the multiple-collision cases, *Truck Insurance Exchange v. Rohde*.[85] In that case a truck negligently driven by the insured ran into three motorcycles successively. On two of the motorcycles there was a passenger in addition to a driver. All five persons on the motorcycle suffered serious injuries. Given the lack of causal connection between the collisions, this was not a ricochet case but rather, a common cause sort of case as depicted in Figure A9:

---

[79] 7 NY 2d at 229, 190 NYS 2d at 683, 164 NE 2d at 707.

[80] *Kuhn's of Brownsville v. Bituminous Casualty Co*, 197 Tenn 60, 270 SW 2d 358 (1954).

[81] See the discussion, text at nn 123–7, below.   [82] *Wesolowski*.

[83] 33 NY 2d at 174, 350 NY S 2d at 900, 305 NE 2d at 910.

[84] 7 NY 2d at 232, 196 NYS 2d at 686, 164 NE 2d at 709.   [85] *Rohde*.

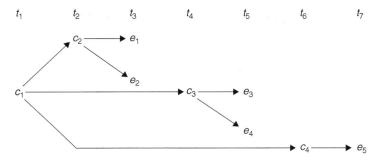

Figure A9 (Where c_1 = negligent crossing of center line; c_2 = collision with first motorcycle; c_3 = collision with second motorcycle; c_4 = collision with third motorcycle; e_1 = injury of driver$_2$; e_2 = injury of passenger$_1$; e_3 = injury of driver$_2$; e_4 = injury of passenger$_2$; e_5 = injury of driver$_3$)

If we look to the last proximate cause of the injuries (despite the fact that it is not a kind of risk covered in the policy), this was arguably the impact of the truck on each motorcycle—and there were three of those. Yet there should be but one occurrence here, as the Washington Supreme Court properly held.

But van Voorhis's *reductio* does not stop here. Once we free ourselves from looking only for proximate causes of injury that instantiate a covered risk, why not see *Rohde* this way:

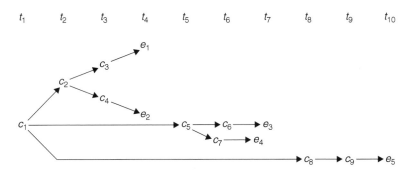

Figure A10 (Where c_1 = negligent driving; c_2, c_5, c_8, = the three collisions; e_1, e_2, e_3, e_4, e_5 = the five injuries, as before; c_3, c_4, c_6, c_7, c_9 = the impact of a passenger or a driver onto the pavement)

Now there are five last proximate causes—the impact of each of the five motorcycle riders on the pavement—to match the number of persons injured. So long as the major injuries resulted from such impacts with the pavement, there will be as many of those as there are persons injured, and the causal test merges fully into the effects test avowedly rejected by American insurance law.

A second and much more sensible way of taking the suggestion about last proximate causes, would be to restrict the causes eligible to those that instantiate a covered risk. Then at least we would not be counting fires under earthquake policies, nor would we be counting non-acts like wall collapses or rainstorms under liability policies covering only actions of the insured.

Even this much more sensible version of the last proximate cause doctrine faces two problems. One is the problem that in cases where the last proximate cause is itself causally dependent on earlier proximate causes, the rationale for the *first-proximate-cause test* seems correct: all that is produced by this first proximate cause is the mere means by which it causes damages even though those means may be causes too of those damages. Suppose again a property damage/earthquake policy, and suppose one earthquake produces two aftershocks, each of which causes separate injury to the insured's building. The schema in such a case is:

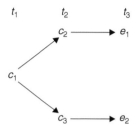

Figure A11 (Where c_1 = the initiating earthquakes; c_2 and c_3 = the two aftershocks; e_1 and e_2 = the two injury events)

Intuitively the first proximate cause doctrine seems correct for this class of cases: there was one occurrence of an earthquake even though it caused two separate injuries via two separate aftershocks.

If this is right, it suggests restricting the last-proximate-cause test even further, namely, to those cases where there are two or more proximate causes (each of which instantiate a covered risk) *and* those causes are causally independent of one another. In a case like *Johnson*, for example, that would suggest a focus on the retaining wall constructions—and not the trench digging or the vault wall destructions—when counting occurrences. This was in fact the alternative focus of the New York Court of Appeals in *Johnson*, who in the alternative held there to be two acts of retaining-wall construction causing two separate instances of flood damage.

The problem with even this restricted an application of the *last* proximate cause doctrine is the same problem as beset the application of the *first*-proximate-cause doctrine to this class of case: it seems an arbitrary stipulation having no salience in the likely expectations of the contracting parties. It seems as arbitrary to focus on the retaining-wall constructions alone as it is to focus on the trench digging alone when asking 'How many instances of the work of the contractor were there that resulted in the two instances of flood damage?' Seemingly needed is some more holistic approach for this class of cases.

3. The most substantial proximate-cause approach

It may seem that with the restrictions hitherto imposed we are dealing with a small and not very significant class of cases. To review, these are cases where: (1) standard inter-vening-cause doctrines leave open the possibility that there is more than one proximate cause for a set of injuries; (2) when such proximate causes each instantiate the kind of risk insured against; and (3) when such proximate causes are each causally independent of one another. Yet these three restrictions in fact leave open a large number of cases, including both the *Johnson* case in New York and the World Trade Center litigation.

Take the facts of *Johnson* again, and suppose we are dealing with an all-risk casualty policy purchased by the common owner of both of the buildings flooded. Such an all-risk policy means that limit (2) above does very little work, for all risks are insured against, rainstorms as much as negligent contractors. Still, items (1) and (3) above do some work. Events prior to the digging of the trench on Fourth Avenue may be cut off by standard intervening-cause (or other proximate-cause) doctrines, and we should lump vault-wall destructions with retaining-wall constructions with retaining-wall collapses under the causal dependence idea. Nonetheless, that leaves the digging of the trench, the wall replacements, and the rainstorm as equally proximate causes of the two floodings. That results in one or two occurrences, depending on which of these one counts as occurrences.

The way out of this indeterminacy is to leave temporal tests (of first or last proximate causes) for a more substantive test. Roughly: focus on the most important cause(s) of the floodings and count how many of those kinds of events there were. By the facts given in the *Johnson* opinion, that seems to be the 'unprecedented' rainstorm; there was one of those and so one occurrence under a single casualty policy purchased by the owner of the two buildings. True enough, there would have been no flooding if there were no trench dug or no vault walls replaced with weaker retaining walls, no less than if there had been no rainstorm. Each of these three factors, in other words, was equally necessary to the damage events, the floodings. Yet so long as the retaining walls were not defective in any way, the rainstorm was more of a cause of the floodings than was either the trench digging or the retaining wall substitution.

The argument for this approach is simple. If causation is as this book describes it, it is a scalar relation that admits of degrees and it is so understood in popular understanding. In cases where there is one salient sort of event in the role of cause, we should expect contracting parties to be counting occurrences of these. Since size of causal contribution is the best proxy for salience in the parties' understanding, this sort of event should be focused on by the courts when they are counting occurrences in all-risk, first-party policies.

There is an objection to this idea that should be dealt with here. This is the objection that has been voiced in legal circles ever since a scalar notion of causation was defended by Jeremiah Smith in his introduction of a 'substantial factor' test for causation in tort law in 1911.[86] The objection is that there is a large area of indeterminacy introduced into causal questions if the causal relation can be one of degree. How much of the stuff must there be to be substantial? How do we individuate the units of the stuff so that we can compare degrees of causal contribution and pronounce one (of a set of causes) to be 'most substantial?'

---

[86] Jeremiah Smith, 'Legal cause in actions of tort', *Harvard Law Review* 25 (1911), 103–28, 223–52, 303–27.

The vagueness objection is a rather toothless objection here. As Aristotle once admonished us, it is folly to demand more precision than the subject matter at hand affords.[87] If causation is scalar then it is a matter of degree, and the matching of the continuous variation of the relation with the vagueness of the concept is a virtue for an analysis, not a vice. This is particularly true for the concept of causation used in the interpretation of contracts. Insofar as the parties limit their coverage by occurrences of certain sorts of risks that, when they materialize, cause injuries of certain sorts, the notion of cause employed should be no more precise than that understood by the parties. Big rainstorms, like terrorist acts, are big causes in ordinary understanding, in a way that non-defective retaining wall construction (and non-defective skyscraper design) are not.

D. Applying the causal test to the destruction of the Twin Towers

It is now time to apply this analysis to the Twin Towers litigation. To begin with, that litigation involved an all-risk policy on the Towers. All proximate causes of the Towers' destruction are thus eligible to be considered under the 'covered risk' criterion. That leaves the proximate cause, the causal dependence, and the most substantial cause criteria, to do all of the work in determining what kind of events we should be counting in this case.

Consider first the causal-independence criterion. Many of the events included in the Twin Towers litigation are clear instances of causal dependence. The Twin Towers causal picture may be schematized as:

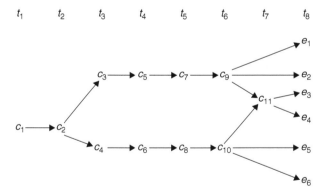

Figure A12 (Where c_1 = the decision at the top of al Qaeda to destroy both of the TwinTowers, c_2 = the agreement of the two pilots to destroy the Twin Towers, c_3, c_4 = the decision of the two pilots after hijacking to crash the two 767s into the two Towers, c_5, c_6 = the crashing of the two 767s into the two Towers, c_7, c_8 = the intense fires that raged in each tower, c_9, c_{10} = the collapse of each tower, c_{11} = the collapse of other WTC buildings also leased by Silverstein, and e_1 - e_6 = the reconstruction costs and non-payment of rent otherwise due on each Tower and on the other collapsed WTC buildings)

---

[87] Aristotle, *Nicomachean Ethics*, Book 1, Chapter 3, in Richard McKeon (ed), *Introduction to Aristotle* (2nd edn, Chicago: University of Chicago Press, 1973), 347–8.

Despite the two different kinds of damage—property damage and lost income—these are the effects of a common cause (the collapse of each Tower) and there are thus at most two occurrences of injury-events. Furthermore, despite the separate injuries flowing from the collapse of other WTC buildings also leased by the Silverstein group, the collapse of those buildings was caused by the collapse of the Towers and (under the causal chain model) cannot constitute a separate occurrence. The fires at t_5 are causally dependant on the crashes at t_4 which are themselves the result of the decisions of the pilots on board each aircraft at t_3; there are thus at most but two occurrences of risked events to be found here as well. Further, if the decisions of the two teams was causally dependant on one earlier decision by the pilots themselves (t_2) or by the al Qaeda leadership (t_1), then all other causes in the chains (c_3–c_{11}) are the mere means or mechanisms by which one terrorist decision caused two injuries; this reduces to the common cause model for one occurrence. The trick, however, is to decide whether the decisions of the two pilots at t_3 causally depended on the general decision to destroy the Towers made by themselves or by the al Qaeda leadership.

When we are dealing with human actions and decisions to act, causal independence under standard intervening cause doctrine means motivational independence, as we saw in Chapter 11. Put simply, if one person supplies the motivation for another to do a certain act, the latter act is causally dependant on the act of the first person supplying the motive; whereas if the second actor has his own reasons for wanting to do the act in question, then the later action is (regarded by the law as being) causally independent of the earlier suggestions. This is true even if the first actor's actions suggest or request the later action of another, and are in that sense a 'but for cause' of that later act. A clear case of supplying motivation to another is coercion by threats. Another is brainwashing. A clear case of the later actor bringing his own motivation to his action is where a suggestion or request is made to the second actor who decides for his own reasons to do the action suggested or requested.

From what we know thus far about the structure of al Qaeda it would appear most likely that the decisions of the two terrorist teams was causally independent of the decision of the leadership to destroy both Towers. There are three reasons for this. First, the pilots involved in crashing the planes were not the indoctrinated 18-year-olds typical of Palestinian suicide bombers. They were fathers, aged 23 and 33; they presumably had the maturity to reflect on what they were doing. They were thus far removed from the brain-washed automatons perhaps typical of some of the terrorist acts currently taking place in the Middle East. Second, al Qaeda is said to be an example of the new form of terrorist organization. It is said to consist of semi-autonomous cells, different from the more hierarchical structure of older terrorist organizations. If this is true then even the mild form of coercion supplied by military orders (not backed by threats) was not present in the suggestion by the leadership about destroying the Twin Towers. The pilots supplied their own motivations for their crashing of the planes (motivations consisting of their subscribing to a certain religious ideology); they were not moved to act by the coercive effect of threats, orders, or 'offers they could not refuse'. Third, the details of just how to bring down the Twin Towers seem to have been left to the 33-year-old leader of the terrorist teams. The speed of the aircraft differed (the second was at full throttle, while the first was operated at a more normal speed for that low altitude), as did the timing and the precise targeting of impact. The teams may also have picked which flights to hijack (so long as they were 767s loaded with fuel for a cross-country flight). Such independent fixing of the content of the decisions by each team to hijack and crash the aircraft lessens (under the law) any causal dependence of those decisions on some general decision to destroy the Twin Towers with aircraft. Not only were the pilots bringing their own motivation to bear on their decisions to crash, but they also were exercising their independent cognitive abilities in deciding precisely how and when to crash.

The causal independence of the pilot's decisions to crash from the more general decision of the leadership to destroy the Twin Towers with aircraft, means that one cannot disregard the former decisions in counting occurrences. Such causal independence does not tell us to look to those decisions alone in counting occurrences, for perhaps both these decisions and the more general decisions are causes of the damage events. Whether this is so depends on whether we apply our intervening cause analysis here and whether, under that analysis, the pilots' decisions meet the other conditions (in addition to causal independence) for being intervening causes.

In addition to c_2, c_3 being causally independent of c_1, for c_2 and c_3 to be intervening causes they must be intentional with respect to the harms suffered. This too seems to be satisfied here, from what we know or can surmise about al Qaeda's planning of these attacks. It is true that Osama bin Laden in one of the videos released during the recent war in Afghanistan laughed about the degree of ignorance of some of the hijackers of just what they were about to do. Insofar as those hijackers were ignorant dupes of al Qaeda's central leadership, their actions and choices would not be intentional with respect to the crash into, and damage to, the Twin Towers under standard doctrines.[88] Yet the pilots surely knew what they were about and decided to go forward anyway. The pilots' decisions and actions, at least, were sufficiently intentional so as to constitute intervening causes.

A way to test this claim is to imagine that the pilots and bin Laden survived and were indicted for murder. Would the central leadership—bin Laden—be charged as a principal or as an accomplice? (If we retain intervening cause doctrine, then we retain this distinction, despite the conclusions of Chapter 13.) If the pilots' decisions were intervening causes, bin Laden could only be charged as an accomplice—one who intentionally *aids* another to cause some legally prohibited state of affairs but who does not himself *cause* such state of affairs. If the pilots were duped by bin Laden about what they were doing, then they would be like the innocent or partly innocent agents whose actions do not break causal chains; then bin Laden could be indicted as a principal.[89] From what we know thus far, it seems quite unlikely that the al Qaeda leadership would be charged as principals— this, because they procured others to act but did not themselves legally cause the harms the criminal law prohibits.

It should thus be relatively easy to reach the conclusion that the decision by the pilots to crash the planes constituted intervening causes robbing the earlier decision of the al Qaeda leadership (to destroy the World Trade Center) of the potential of being the common cause of both injuries. Yet this does not end the enquiry because of a second candidate for a common cause emerging from the facts behind September 11. One of the pilots, Mohamed Atta, was himself (apparently) the principal architect of the details of the plan as it evolved in the United States. If it was not his idea originally (which it appears it

[88] On the use of innocent agents and their status as non-intervening causes, see Sanford Kadish, 'Causation and complicity: A study in the interpretation of doctrine,' California Law Review 73 (1985), 323–410.
[89] Ibid.

was not), it was his to plan in detail. Atta co-ordinated all of the other teams of terrorists in America, traveling constantly between the various groups.[90] Perhaps Atta's earlier, detailed intention constitutes the common cause of all injuries.

This event too, seems remote (in the law's sense) from the collapse of the Towers. Again, the decisions of the pilots (including Atta's) prima facie meets the standard criteria for an intervening cause: they were subsequent to Atta's planning activities, causally (motivationally) independent of those activities, causally significant themselves, intentional with respect to the damage, and voluntary in the sense of uncoerced by Atta as well as done by those in full possession of their faculties.[91] Hence, if we read the law's standard doctrines of intervening causation into this insurance contract's causal test for 'occurrence', Atta's pre-flight intention was no more a common cause of the collapse than was bin Laden's much earlier intention.

In liability policies there is good reason to read tort law's detailed doctrines of intervening cause into the causal test of insurance law.[92] For liability policies, the liability of the insurance companies is for the liability of the insured to some third party, and the latter liability itself is based on the tort law's doctrines of proximate causation. When the loss insured against—liability in tort—itself is based on certain ideas of causation, it makes sense to read those ideas into the test for liability of the insurance company for that loss. The reasonable expectations of both parties to insurance contracts should be focused on these doctrines (even if the doctrines get the metaphysics of causation wrong).

With casualty policies the issue is different. In a first-party casualty policy insuring against property damage caused by earthquakes, for example, the risk insured against is earthquakes. Unlike tort liability, earthquakes do not have the legal notion of intervening causation built into them. Of course, even in casualty policies earthquakes must *cause* damage of the requisite sort and it is *open* to us to read the law's notions of intervening causation into that requirement.

Whether such reading is a good idea depends in part on what one thinks is the status of the legal idea of intervening causation. If that legal idea is no more than a reflection of the ordinary person's conception of causation used throughout daily life, or if that legal idea captures the metaphysics of the causal relation, then there is some reason to read such ideas into the causal test for casualty policies as well as for liability policies. Yet despite the distinguished defense of one or both of these bases for the legal idea of intervening causation by Herbert Hart and Tony Honoré,[93] I have sought to give reasons to doubt these claims in Chapter 12. There is simply no plausible metaphysics that can make sense of the law's idea that intervening (free, voluntary, informed) human choices always break causal chains, relegating what went before to mere background conditions (rather than causes) of the harm.

It is true that there are many applications of the law's notion of intervening cause that common folk find intuitively compelling even outside legal contexts. Yet these are accounted for by a metaphysically more plausible concept of causation, the 'substantial

---

[90] The evidence is summarized in the New York Times' anniversary retrospective, 11 September 2002.

[91] See generally Hart and Honoré, *Causation in the Law*, 74–7, 136–62, 326–40; Chapter 11, above.

[92] As many courts do. See text at nn 56 and 57, above.

[93] Hart and Honoré, *Causation in the Law*, *passim*, but particularly the 'Preface to the Second Edition'.

cause' idea adverted to throughout this book. What makes both 'acts of God' and free human choices act like intervening causes in popular understanding is that such factors often (but not always) swamp earlier causal factors in importance. Put crudely, such later factors are so much *more* of a cause than the earlier items that they dominate any causal account of the harms in question.

If such 'substantial causation' idea better captures both the true metaphysics and the popular understanding of the causal relation, then we might read this idea into the causal test for casualty policies, in preference to using the legal doctrines of intervening causation. If we frame the issue this way, then the question in the Twin Towers litigation is this one: when was (were) the decision(s) that had the largest role in causing the destruction of the Twin Towers, actually made? Was bin Laden's decision the major factor, or was it Atta's planning in America, or was it the decisions of each pilot, that played the dominant role? This approach involves the following sub-questions. First, of content: how much of *what* was decided (the content) at the later time was identical to what was already decided at the earlier time? Were the details all worked out earlier, or was much planning done later? Second, there is the sub-question of resolve: how firm was the earlier intention? Except for some forms of mental disease, intentions are never fixed come hell or high water. Their firmness is rather a matter of degree, measured by their resistance to change even if it should turn out the action intended will conflict with other desires and intentions of the agent. Third, there is the sub-question of what could be called the counter-instinctual nature of the action intended. Some choices necessarily run counter to nearly universal human needs that are almost always deeply felt, and are in that loose sense 'instinctual'. Soldiers often say, for example, that one never knows how one will perform in battle until one is there. In such cases even firm general intentions may call for fresh judgment when it comes time to execute them, for only then does the actor really face (emotionally) the costs of his action.

All three of these matters—of content, resolve and instinct—are matters of degree, but that hardly cuts against this approach, for the nature of the issue itself necessarily involves drawing lines on a matter of continuous variation. Without saying so, this is implicitly the approach adopted in some of the insurance cases dealing with the issue of later, multiple decisions of an agent supplanting earlier, single decisions by that same agent. Consider again in this regard the *Rawls* case, where the insured attempted to outrun two sheriff's deputies and successively collided with two cars. One might schematize the case as a kind of common cause case:

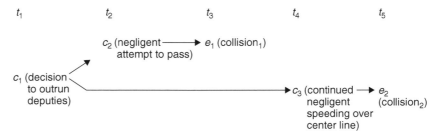

Figure A13 One remote cause of two harmful effects where there are two causal intermediaries

To decide the case as it did, the Fifth Circuit implicitly had to reject the earlier decision of the insured (to outrun the deputies) as the common cause of the two collisions; yet it could not do this on standard intervening cause notions. The insured's later decisions (to pass the first car, to continue to speed and to cross the center line) were not intentional or knowing with respect to the collisions that resulted; they were at most reckless and more likely only negligent. Usually negligent subsequent decisions do not constitute intervening causes, as we saw in Chapter 11. To prevent the earlier, more general decision being considered the common cause of all injuries required the court to use some other approach.

Enter the most-substantial-cause approach. *When* was the decision(s) really made that resulted in the collisions? In *Rawls*, the resolve of the earlier decision may have been quite firm, but the content was hardly identical to the content of the later decisions; they were responsive to situations unforeseen at the earlier time and about which no decision had therefore been taken. The later decisions were *more of a cause* of their respective collisions than was the earlier, more general decision to outrun the deputies.

Consider these variations. A mentally disturbed indivdual fires his shotgun three times at arresting officers, the shots separated by about a minute apiece—is there a common cause in the initial decision to resist arrest, or several causes with each pull of the trigger?[94] Directors and officers of a savings-and-loan association (insured under a directors and officers liability policy) instituted a loan-swap program under which four bad loans were made—is there a common cause in the initiation of the general loan-swap policy, or several causes in the decision to make each individual loan?[95] Under another directors and officers ('D and O') liability policy, when officers of the insured separately authorize spot loans to unqualified home buyers, authorize five separate large condominium project loans that go bad, and authorize the move and renovation of corporate headquarters without having sufficient funds to pay for it, was there one common cause of all losses in the general ineptitude of the directors; three causes of three unrelated series of losses; or as many incidents of loss as there were bad spot loans, bad condominium loans, and unfundable moves and unfundable renovations?[96] Under an insurance policy against losses caused by dishonest employees, when the insured's employee embezzled a large sum of money by writing forty separate checks, was there one common cause in the employee's general decision to embezzle money via bogus checks, or forty causes of forty losses in the decision to write each bogus check?[97] Under a general liability policy for a business, when the insured company is held liable in a class action suit for sex discrimination in the hiring, promoting, and compensation of numerous of its female employees, was there one common cause in the initiation of a general company policy of discrimination or as many causes of separate injuries as there were acts of discrimination on particular occasions?[98]

In the first three of these five cases the courts held for multiple causes, in the last two, for a single common cause. The difference lies in the degree of firmness of the earlier decision and in the degree of content-independence to be found in the individual decisions, an independence increased by the lack of identity of content between the later decisions and some more general background policy or decision. As the Tenth Circuit

[94] *McQuaig.*   [95] *Huff.*   [96] *Okada.*   [97] *Business Interiors.*
[98] *Appalachian Insurance Co v. Liberty Mutual Insurance Co*, 676 F 2d 56 (2rd Cir 1982).

noted in *Business Interiors* (the 40 bogus checks case),[99] the question is whether the initial decision (eg, to embezzle money) effectively decided that issue on each of 40 occasions where the opportunity arose to embezzle money, or whether each transaction required some kind of fresh decision. If the individual decisions (to make loans, write checks, offer less money to female employees) are each sufficiently unique as to call for fresh judgment, or if the original decisions were sufficiently shaky in their resolve as to call for fresh judgment, then the most substantial causes are the later decisions; whereas if such individual judgments are the routine application of one's own established policy, less judgment is called for and the less such individual decisions look like the most substantial causes of the injuries they admittedly do cause.

Suppose (as seems possible from the facts thus far revealed) that one decision was made by Mohamed Atta to destroy the World Trade Center by using two passenger aircraft, and that that decision was firmly fixed in his mind when he directed his own and the other teams. Whether that decision is a common cause of the two collapses of the Twin Towers then depends in part on whether the subsequent decisions of Atta and the other pilot while on their airplanes made significant additions or changes to what was originally decided. How much choice was left (by the general decision to destroy the World Trade Center) to the individual terrorist teams as to *how* such destruction was to be accomplished—was every detail decided in advance by the al Qaeda terrorist network or was much independent judgment required by the separate terrorist teams? Were the targets pre-assigned to each of the planes, or was choice required between alternative targets? Second, there is the question of a fresh judgment being made by each of the pilots because of the nature of the actions contemplated. It is one thing to form a firm intention to crash a plane into a building for the greater glory of God when that event is yet in the future; it must be something else to actually pilot a plane right at the face of that building. While in a general sense the pilots chose to do exactly what they earlier intended to do, it may well have required the kind of fresh decision just because of the counter-instinctual nature of the act chosen.

Some of these facts we will undoubtedly never know.[100] Such as we can know them, however it is these kinds of facts that should determine how substantial a cause was the earlier (versus the later) decisions of the two pilots. This approach is thus somewhat less determinant than is the intervening cause approach, where the result seems pretty plain: the pilots' on-board decisions were intervening causes cutting off any earlier, common cause, and there were two of such decisions.

V. The Pure Questions of Event-identity

In discussing and applying the causal test we assumed we knew how many events were involved in any given situation—one trench digging, two wall destructions, two wall constructions, one rainstorm, one trench filling, two wall collapses, two basement

---

[99] *Business Interiors*, 751 F 2d at 363.
[100] Suggestive, however, are facts such as the two pilots routinizing their crashing of an airliner into a building by using the publicly available software simulating flying an airplane between and into the Twin Towers. See Time, special issue of 11 September 2001, 28.

floodings, for example in *Johnson*.[101] We made such assumptions in order to focus on the causal relations between such events. Now we need to examine what I earlier called the pure questions of event identity: when do we have one event, such as the flooding of the basements of New York City,[102] and when do we have two floodings, or many?

I shall proceed in the following way. Since it is easy to confuse qualitative identity with numerical identity in ordinary speech and in the law, I shall first examine these two notions, the relations that hold between them, and argue that only numerical identity is meant by the same occurrence limitation in insurance policies. Second, since the (numerical) identity conditions for a class of things like events depends on the essential nature of such things, I shall explore several different theories as to the nature of events, as well as their corresponding notions about the identity conditions of events. Third, I will then address what I shall call the sizing question: under the theory of the essential nature of events that I believe to be correct, there are three dimensions of indeterminacy in how big or small natural events might be. An answer to the sizing question should defend some point in each of these three areas of indeterminacy.

A. Numerical and qualitative identity

When we talk of identity, we are often ambiguous between two different ideas of identity. Consider statements about the identity of persons. We often say of a reformed criminal, for example, 'Smith is no longer the same person.' We sometimes say the same of a multiple-personalitied person when he shifts to his alter ego. In such statements we could mean that Smith is no longer numerically the same person, so that, for example, the person he now is: cannot be punished for the crimes of someone else, cannot benefit from contracts made by someone else, or wills leaving property to someone else, is not married to the Mrs Smith the other guy was married to, cannot trespass on the other's person's real property, etc.[103] More likely such statements should be taken to refer to qualitative, not numerical, identity. We likely mean that 'Smith is not quite himself' in the sense that his personality traits are markedly different from those that are usually in character for him. We mean, that is, that Smith is not the same *kind* of person today, not that he is not literally the same person as he was yesterday.[104]

True qualitative identity—where two numerically distinct particulars share all the same properties—is rare to the point of non-existence. The 17th-century German logician, Leibniz, noticed this with his famous two principles of identity.[105] The first is called the Indiscernability of Identicals, or sometimes called Leibniz's Law. This principle asserts that if two putatively distinct particulars are in reality one and the same thing, then necessarily they (it) share all the same properties at any given point of time. (Over an

---

[101] *Arthur Johnson Corp. v. Indemnity Insurance Co.*

[102] Cf Lombard, *Events*, 123–4, where Lombard considers the singleness of very large, composite events like the melting of the Antarctic ice cap, or even the melting of all the world's snows.

[103] Rebecca Dresser examines the sense of taking statements of personal identity over time in this numerical sense of identity. See Dresser, 'Personal identity and punishment', Boston University Law Review 70 (1990), 395–446.

[104] I so construe most of such statements in Michael Moore, *Law and Psychiatry : Rethinking the relationship* (Cambridge: Cambridge University Press, 1984), 398–407.

[105] A brief introduction to these principles of identity may be found in Baruch Brody, *Identity and Essence* (Princeton: Princeton University Press, 1980), 6–10.

interval of time, they (it) necessarily share only their (its) essential properties.) In a phrase, at any one time numerical identity implies true qualitative identity.

Leibniz also thought the converse was true, namely, that if two putatively distinct particulars shared all of their properties, then such particulars were in reality one and the same thing. Leibniz thought, in other words, that no two truly distinct items could share all of their properties. This is usually called the Identity of Indiscernibles principle.

The former of these principles, Leibniz's Law, is usually thought to be partly constitutive of the idea of identity. If two descriptions literally describe the same thing, it is difficult to conceive how that thing could possess different properties depending on how it is described. As philosophers often put it, 'if identity does not mean universal interchangeability, then I do not really understand identity'.[106] Or again, 'tampering with the substitutivity of identity may easily make the notion of identity unintelligible'.[107] By contrast, the second principle, the Identity of Indiscernibles, seems less likely true and, even if true, less closely connected to the very meaning of identity.

As we saw in Chapter 16's discussion of similarity, when we speak in most contexts of two numerically distinct particulars being the same kind of things, we almost never mean 'the same in all respects'. Rather, we mean 'the same in certain respects relevant to this context'. One diamond may be 'the same' as another in terms of its monetary value; its color and cut; its clarity and degree of imperfections; its source of origin; etc. In assessing qualitative sameness, usually the context picks out the relevant qualities. A husband replacing his wife's lost engagement ring may focus on the value, the wife on the appearance, the jeweler on the rated quality, and the customs inspector on the country of origin.

Judgments of qualitative identity thus focus on one or a few properties and ask whether two particulars do or do not share those properties. Of course, particulars 'share' a property only if the property each particular possesses is 'the same'. Qualitative identity judgments thus require judgments about the numerical identity of properties (or types). The elusiveness of the identity conditions for universals (properties and types) makes this question often a perplexing one.[108]

Nonetheless, this question of the numerical identity of properties lies at the root of judgments of the qualitative identity of particulars, which in turn impacts upon judgments about the numerical identity of particulars. To distinguish between the two uses of numerical identity, we should introduce a standard convention. When speaking of the numerical identity of particular events, we shall call them 'event-tokens'; when speaking of the identity of the properties that events may possess, we shall call them 'event-types'.[109]

Having distinguished numerical from qualitative identity, it remains to enquire which notion of identity is involved in insurance law's question of 'same occurrence'. It is of course possible that insurance law elliptically asks both sorts of identity questions when it asks after 'same occurrences'. In double-jeopardy contexts, for example, the law rather plainly asks both sorts of questions when it asks whether an accused has been prosecuted or punished twice for 'the same offense'. In the latter context the law asks first, whether

---

[106] Neil Wilson, *The Concept of Language* (Toronto: University of Toronto Press, 1959), 39.

[107] D Follesdal, 'Quantification into causal contexts', in L Linsky (ed), *Reference and Modality* (Oxford: Oxford University Press, 1971), 56.

[108] See Armstrong, *Universals*.   [109] See Moore, *Act and Crime*, 80.

the same type of act is being twice prosecuted or punished,[110] and second, whether the same instance of each type (ie, the same act-token) is being twice prosecuted or punished.[111] Double jeopardy attaches only if the same act-token is being multiply prosecuted or punished for instantiating the same act-type.

In insurance law, by contrast, 'same occurrence' is univocal: it asks only after the numerical identity of event-tokens. There is a concern with types of events in insurance law: the injury event-token must be an instance of the type of injury ('physical damage to property', for example) covered by a policy; in addition, the cause event-token must be an instance of the type of causes (earthquake, fire, liability for negligence, etc) covered by a policy. Yet there is no concern with the identity of types in insurance law analogous to the concern with types of acts in double jeopardy law. The usual concerns in insurance law are the concerns about the numerical identity of both injury event-tokens and cause event-tokens. So long as each such event-token is an instance of the types (of damage and risks, respectively) covered by the policy, the enquiry into types of events is usually satisfied.[112]

B. The essential nature of events

We shall here examine several different views of when two putatively distinct event-tokens are in reality one and the same. Such theories each purport to give the identity conditions of event-tokens. The first such theory utilizes the Leibnizian principles above discussed. More specifically, Baruch Brody has urged that the identity conditions of event-tokens are no different than the identity conditions for all particulars, namely: two putatively distinct event tokens x and y are in reality one and the same event token if and only if x and y share all of their (its) properties.[113]

If both of the Leibnizian principles are true of identity generally, then of course they are true of the identity of event-tokens. I nonetheless shall put aside the Leibnizian criteria, not on the grounds of falsity, but rather on the grounds of generality.[114] More powerful identity conditions for event-tokens are wanted, conditions that are distinctive of events as a class of things. Such more specific and more powerful identity conditions for events will focus on some properties that, if shared, make for identity of event-tokens. Such more powerful identity conditions do not require us to examine all properties in order to reach conclusions of sameness when faced with questions of identity and individuation of act-tokens.

The properties on which to focus in building more powerful identity conditions for events are the essential properties of something being an event. If two putatively distinct items x and y are events, and if they share the properties essential to events, then they are one and the same event. This means they of course do share *all* of their properties (by

---

[110] Ibid, Chapter 13.

[111] Ibid, Chapter 14. In double-jeopardy adjudication, this is called the 'unit of offense' question.

[112] As we shall see, however, questions about the identity of particulars quickly involve one in questions about the identity of properties.

[113] Baruch Brody, *Identity and Essence.*

[114] For variations of this critique, see Moore, *Act and Crime*, 366–7; Lombard, *Events*, 23–30; Brand, *Intending*, 59–65.

Leibniz's Law), but one advantage of these more powerful identity conditions is that we do not have to look at all properties to reach conclusions on identity.

Another advantage of seeking more powerful identity conditions for events based on their essential properties lies in the capacity of such conditions to make identifications over time. For events exist over intervals of time[115] and it is possible for a single event to have some property P at the beginning of the interval but to lack it at the end. The Leibnizian criteria of identity hold only for identity at a time; for identity over time, we need the more powerful identity conditions of events that focuses exclusively on their essential properties—for these cannot change over time for the same thing.[116]

If we put aside the general Leibnizian criteria of identity as too broad for a useful theory of event-identity, then we need a theory about the essential nature of events in order to know how many of them may exist at any given time. If we generalize the discussion of Chapter 14 considerably, we can say that ordinary thought and most metaphysicians conceive of events as spatio-temporally located particulars. As we saw, there are three main variants of this view, the middle-sized view of events of Donald Davidson,[117] the fine-grained view of Jaegwon Kim,[118] and the coarse-grained view of Willard Quine.[119] In Chapter 14 I urged that we adopt the Davidsonian view of events. On this view events have many properties, unlike the Kimian view according to which each exemplification of a distinct property is a distinct event and unlike the Quinean view according to which properties are irrelevant to the nature of events. I gave three reasons for adhering to the Davidsonian line on events. In the context of this essay, let me now add a fourth reason.

This reason lies in the case-law on event individuation. Courts too are not immune to the pull of common-sense views of deep metaphysical puzzles like the nature of events. Insofar as there is any insurance law on what I have been calling the pure questions of event-individuation, that law tends toward the Davidsonian view of events. Thus, for example, the New York Court of Appeals in *Johnson*[120] rather easily found there to be two retaining wall collapse events because: (1) there were two objects (the two separate buildings with the two separate walls in front of them); and (2) there were two separate time intervals involved; even though (3) there was (arguably) the same group of properties involved in the collapses. A Quinean about events would not rely on the separateness of objects in deciding how many events took place in *Johnson*, but would individuate the space/time zone differently (leading perhaps to a big enough zone in which there was but one event). A Kimian

---

[115] Moore, *Act and Crime*, 72.

[116] For Brody's attempt to deal with this, see Brody, *Identity and Essence*, 20–3.

[117] Davidson, *Actions and Events*.

[118] Jaegwon Kim, 'On the psycho-physical identity theory', American Philosophical Quarterly 3 (1966), 227–235; Kim, 'Causation, nomic subsumption, and the concept of event', Journal of Philosophy 70 (1973), 217–36; Kim, 'Events as property-exemplifications', in M Brand and D Walton (eds), *Action Theory* (Dordrecht: Reidel, 1976). Alvin Goldman also adopts this view in his *A Theory of Human Action* (Englewood Cliffs: Prentice-Hall, 1970).

[119] Willard Quine, 'Events and Reification,' in E Le Pore and B McLaughlin (eds), *Actions and Events: Perspectives on the Philosophy of Donald Davidson* (Oxford: Oxford University Press, 1983); Quine, *Word and Object* (Cambridge, Mass: MIT Press, 1960), 171; Quine, *Theories and Things* (New York: Columbia University Press, 1981), 11–12. Davidson came to have some sympathy for Quine's view of events. See Davidson, 'Reply to Quine on events', in Le Pore and McLaughlin (eds), *Actions and Events*.

[120] *Johnson*.

about events would presumably find there to be many events (not just two) in *Johnson*—as many as there were properties instantiated when the walls collapsed.

Consider also the court's conclusion in the *Okada* case mentioned earlier,[121] where the officers and directors under a D and O liability policy voted to authorize several bad spot loans to home buyers, five large condominium project loans, and the move and renovation of corporate headquarters. In holding these to be 'distinct acts',[122] the court focused on the properties of the authorizing decision, not the place or time at which they were made. The decision on one of the condominium project loans, for example, was a decision to waive a participation requirement on the loan, immediately obliging the savings and loan association to fund the entire loan commitment.[123] This was a property not shared by other acts of the officers and directors, even if (the facts are not given) those other acts of authorization took place where and when this one did, *viz.* in one Board resolution. A Quinean about events could not so finely individuate these authorization events, and a Kimian would even more finely individuate them.

Occasionally courts stray from the Davidsonian view of events. Consider, for example, the facts of *Kuhn's of Brownsville v. Bituminous Casualty Co.* Kuhn's excavated beneath two adjoining buildings in an effort to remodel them. As part of the excavation Kuhn's removed the wall between the two buildings. The excavation and/or the removal caused the two buildings to collapse, which also caused the immediate collapse of the building to the east of the two buildings worked on by Kuhn's. Two days later a fourth building collapsed, the one to the west of the first two buildings. The court assumed there was liability of Kuhn's to property owners in all four buildings, because 'the excavation work . . . was the proximate cause of the collapse of the [three] buildings on May 27th and the collapse of the [fourth] building on the west side on May 29th'.[124] The court held there to be two accidents within the meaning of Kuhn's policy with Bituminous Casualty Co. The reason given by the court was pure Kimian event theory. The court recognized the policy covered only liability of the insured for property damage caused by 'the collapse of or structural damage to any building or structure due to excavation . . . or removal . . . of any structural support . . . while such operations are being performed by the named insured'.[125] Such coverage required the court to focus on the excavation/removal work of Kuhn's as it asked, how many covered accidents there were. The court apparently thought that there were two such excavation events:

If the excavation was a single act, and constitutes a single accident, then the question comes as to when the accident occurred. The owners on the west suffered no loss and experienced no unforeseen event until the 29th.[126]

Only a Kimian about events could think that the losses of the west side property owners was part of a separate excavation event.[127] For it is only Kimians who think that because an excavation event seemingly has two properties—a causing of the collapse of the east

---

[121] *Okada*. [122] Ibid, 388. [123] Ibid, 388.
[124] 197 Tenn at 61, 270 SW 2d at 359.
[125] 197 Tenn at 64, 270 SW 2d at 360.
[126] 197 Tenn at 65–6, 270 SW 2d at 360.
[127] The statement in the text is not quite true. One might construe the 'componential' theory of events of Judy Thomson and the late Irving Thalberg to hold there to be two distinct events here. See Thomson, *Acts and Other Events*; Thalberg, *Perception, Emotion, and Action* (New Haven: Yale University Press, 1977).

side building, and a causing of the collapse of the west side building—that there must in reality be two excavation events. This is a piece with the Kimian conclusion that when a defendant moves his finger on the trigger of a gun, and such finger movement causes the death of two people with a single bullet, there are at least three act-tokens by the defendant here—the act of finger movement, the act of killing the first victim, and the act of killing the second victim.[128]

Surely the reasoning in *Kuhn's* is as counterintuitive as is the Kimian theory of events generally. There was only one excavation in *Kuhn's* even though that event had numerous properties. What happened after Kuhn's ceased digging is no part of Kuhn's excavation event, even though we might use that later happening as a means of referring to Kuhn's excavation (as in, 'the four-building-destroying excavation').

Kuhn's is as aberrational as it is counterintuitive. Most of the time courts adopt the standard view of events that has captured common sense since Aristotle: an event is the change in some property (or group of properties) of some object during some interval of time. To individuate events on this dominant view is to individuate: (1) both properties and groups of properties; (2) objects; and (3) temporal intervals.

C. The sizing of events

If one adopts the standard view on the nature of events, then the individuation question at issue in the Twin Towers litigation has three parts to it, corresponding to the three attributes of events: (1) When is there one, or more than one, physical object? (2) When is there one property or one group of properties, and when are there two or more? (3) When is there one interval of time, and when are there two or more?

Here the happy coincidence of ordinary, legal, and true metaphysics comes apart. For the true metaphysics on the size of events is unhelpful in this context. There are two plausible views of such true metaphysics of event sizes (assuming we restrict ourselves to the possibilities under a Davidsonian theory of the nature of events). One I shall call the *atomic* view.[129] On this view there are 'atomic events', defined as events out of which other larger events may be constructed but which themselves have no parts because they are the smallest events that exist. Such atomic events are thus basic, whereas all larger events are secondary constructions of the more basic events.

For atomic events to exist, three things must be true (corresponding to the three attributes of events). First, there must be atomic objects, that is, physical objects ('atoms' in the ancient Greek sense) that are composed of no parts. Second, there must be simple properties; that is, properties not themselves composed of combinations of other properties. Third, there must be atomic event-intervals, being the minimum amount of time it

---

[128] The explicit conclusion in double-jeopardy contexts by a leading Kimian about events, Alvin Goldman. See his critique of my Davidsonian views on event-identity, in Goldman, 'Action and crime: A fine-grained approach', University of Pennsylvania Law Review 142 (1994), 1563–86, and my response, 'More on act and crime', University of Pennsylvania Law Review 142 (1994), 1749–840, revised and reprinted as Chapter 6 of Michael Moore, *Placing Blame: A general theory of the criminal law* (Oxford: Oxford University Press, 1997), 318–29.

[129] Lawrence Lombard adopts this view in his *Events*, 168. Lombard's attempt to find metaphysically correct sizes for events is taken to task in Jonathan Bennett's *Events and Their Names*, 149–51, 155–6.

takes to cross an 'atomic quality space' (ie, to constitute a *change* in some single properties).

The second plausible metaphysical view denies that there are any atomic events and also denies that there is any limit to the size of an event. The universe is one object, all of its parts are objects, and every change to every object (no matter what its size) is equally an event. We can fuse smaller events into bigger ones, and divide bigger ones into smaller ones, without limit, on this view.[130]

Neither of these possibilities as to the true metaphysics of event size can be of much use to the law of insurance. The second view yields no answer to the question of how many events took place in the collapse of the Twin Towers, for example, because the 'how many' question fully depends on the size of objects, properties, and time intervals selected for individuating *an* event. The first view, by contrast, yields *an* answer (in terms of atomic event sizes) to the 'how many' question, but it is surely the wrong answer. Surely no party to a 'per occurrence' insurance contract means to be counting atomic-sized events when pay-offs per occurrence are being calculated. Presumably there were millions of such atomic events involved in the collapse of just one Tower, but that answer would make a 'per occurrence' limit on liability no limit at all.

The answer needed is one plausibly attributable to the actual or hypothetical expectations of the parties to insurance contracts. Such expectations are framed with neither very small nor very large sized events in mind; rather, they are framed with the middle-sized events of daily life in mind—events like a conversation, a speech, a wedding, a death, etc. There being no true metaphysics of events that can yield a determinate, intuitive mode of individuating such middle-sized events,[131] we do better to repair to the common-sense metaphysics of event-individuation, if there is one.

Consider each of the attributes of an event (on the Davidsonian metaphysics of events) with an eye to sizing that event along the lines accepted by common sense (or, as the English courts are wont to say, 'the plain man's view'). Take the object question first. The ordinary notion of physical objects gives some hope of offering up some determinate, non-arbitrary answers. The hope remains despite the fact that the identity conditions for physical objects are standardly given in terms of such objects exclusively occupying spatio-temporal zones.[132] The hope is that physical objects like ships, tables, buildings, human bodies, etc, have natural sizings in a way that spatial zones do not.

Such hope is not dashed by recognition of the vagueness of the concept by which we clarify objects. Quine used the example of mountains: when two higher pieces of rock are joined by a high saddle, do we have one mountain or two?[133] Such vagueness diminishes

---

[130] Arguably the view of Judy Thomson in her *Acts and Other Events*. See particularly ibid, 78, where she accepts a 'fusion principle' according to which there always exist larger events that are the fusion of smaller events sharing any given property.

[131] Lombard appears to believe the contrary, urging that there is a metaphysics of events such that we can resist fusions such as the fusion of Jones saying 'hello' and Smith saying 'hello' into one larger event, Smith's and Jones' greeting each other. For Lombard, Smith and Jones are separate objects, and the pair of them is in no sense an object, so there is no such event as a greeting between them. Similarly, although there can be a horse in the field, 'the horse in the field' does not name an object that can undergo change over an interval of time (and thus be a larger event). *Events*, 238–9. I shortly defend similar conclusions, but not based on any supposed true metaphysics of events and their objects.

[132] See Moore, *Act and Crime*, 368.

[133] Willard Quine, *Word and Object* (Cambridge, Mass: MIT Press, 1960), 126.

but does not eliminate the determinateness in the boundaries of physical objects. If there are cases like Marian Peak and Jean's Peak in the San Jacinto Mountains of California— two barely discernible high spots on a 10,000 foot ridge[134]—where we are unclear, there are also easy cases like Chomolunga and Sagamantha (the Tibetan and Nepalese names for Mt Everest, one peak), and like Annapurna and Daligari (two 8,000 meter peaks separated by the deepest valley on earth).

More pernicious than vagueness for the hoped-for determinacy in the boundaries of common-sense objects is the mereological problem I adverted to before in discussing true metaphysics: in ordinary thought, are not parts of objects, and aggregations of objects, often objects in their own right? A glacier is a physical object. But are not parts of glaciers, such as the Bergshrund at the top, the ice-fall in its middle, and the calving tip of it at its base in the ocean, also physical objects? Indeed, are not all the worlds glaciers in some sense one object, viz the earth's glacial ice?[135] If so, then there is no more determinacy in the ordinary usage of an event than there is on the true metaphysics of the matter.

Yet in ordinary thought—the touchstone in contract interpretation—there is a primacy to ordinary-sized objects. In most contexts a table is an object in a way that the table's legs, or the furniture in the dining room that includes the table but more besides, are not. Hilary Putnam imagines taking 'someone into a room with a chair, a table on which are a lamp and a notebook and a ballpoint pen, and nothing else, and I ask, "How many objects are there in this room?" My companion answers, let us suppose, "Five." '[136] Although Putnam himself views 'Five' as just one answer metaphysically no better than others (such as 'one', for the mereological sum of these five objects, or 'twenty', viewing each of the five objects as itself being the mereological sums of four other objects),[137] surely Putnam's companion is closer to ordinary thought than Putnam himself. If someone had contracted to pay one dollar for every object found in the room, the best interpretation of that contract would be that there is an obligation to pay five dollars.[138]

In a case such as the *Johnson* case mentioned earlier, the New York Court of Appeal's characterization of a building as one object, and a retaining wall as one object, seems in accordance with the primacy given ordinary size objects in ordinary thought. The basement of a building, the front of a building, the front half of the basement of a building, are in some sense objects in their own right; two adjoining buildings, or a cluster of buildings such as the Rockefeller Center, are also objects in some sense; yet separate buildings seem primary in most contexts of ordinary thought, in a way that the parts of such buildings, or the aggregation of such buildings, do not.

[134] Named separately, incidentally, because the surveyor of the area in the 1890s had two lady friends at the time of his survey and did not wish to insult either one by naming *the* peak with just one of their names.

[135] Lombard's kind of puzzle. Lombard, *Events*, 123–4.

[136] Hilary Putnam, *Representation and Reality* (Cambridge, Mass: MIT Press, 1989), 100.

[137] Ibid, 100. See also Putnam, *The Many Faces of Realism* (La Salle: Open Court, 1987), 18–19; Putnam, *Renewing Philosophy* (Cambridge, Mass: Harvard University Press, 1992), 120.

[138] Perhaps Putnam does not disagree with this, as a matter of common sense (not true metaphysics): 'Certain things are paradigmatically objects, for example tables and chairs but . . . there is no fact of the matter as to whether . . . mereological sums are objects or not.' Putnam, *Renewing Philosophy*, 120.

More troublesome was how one should consider the subway station platform extension trench dug by the contractor-insured in the *Johnson* case. Was there one trench running the entire length of the block? Or as many trenches as there were buildings fronting the street in which the trench was dug? Common sense would probably consider the trench one object, at least until it intersected another trench. This is particularly true given the free flow of rainwater up and down the full length of the trench. If the relevant work of the contractor covered by the insurance were solely the digging of the trench, prima facie there was only one such event of trench digging because only one trench was dug. Such individuation of work-events is prima facie only, however, because perhaps one could show either temporally discontinuous bits of trench digging, and/or different properties of the trench-diggings when done in front of the two different buildings. As the Court of Appeals mentioned with respect to the cinder-block retaining walls, even if they were spatially continuous (which they were not), perhaps they had been 'built at separate times by separate groups of workmen'.[139] As the court here implicitly reminds us, the singleness of an object is only one of the three things we need to look at in individuating events (on the standard account of the nature of events); in addition, we must look at both properties and temporal locations.

About the temporal location of events, we seem to have a greater sizing problem than we did for spatial location. For the latter sizing problem, we can rely on the primacy given by ordinary thought to the familiar objects of everyday life. For temporal sizings, we have no such natural sizings.

If the temporal locations of events were points in time, there would be no temporal sizing problem for events. Then *any* difference in temporal location would make for a difference in events. Yet the temporal locations of events are not points in time; they are intervals of time, intervals having a duration.[140] The 'how much' question is inevitable once one sees this fact about the temporal location of events. Squeezing five quick shots off only seconds apart has been held to be but one event in certain contexts,[141] but firing a shotgun three times, a minute between each blast, counts as three events in other contexts.[142] What is the natural sizing of temporal duration that makes these results justifiable?

Fortunately we get considerable help in the temporal sizing of events by repairing to the third aspect of events, the property or properties making each event-token the kind of event it is. Consider again the excavation events at issue in *Kuhn's of Brownsville*. What makes an excavation event the kind of event it is—an excavation kind of event—is a change in the earth beneath a building: at t_1, it was there, at t_2 the first earth was removed, at t_3 it all was removed, and at t_4 buildings collapsed. On the standard account of events, we focus on the essential properties of the excavation event, here earth-removal. (Causing the collapse of buildings is a property of the excavation, but it is not an essential property of it.) The essential property, earth removal, began at t_2, and ceased at t_3. Therefore, the relevant temporal interval is t_2–t_3.

Such examples might suggest that the temporal dimension of events is simply the tail wagged by the dog of the property dimension of events. In cases where there is no

---

[139] 7 NY 2d at 230, 196 NYS 2d at 684, 164 NE 2d at 708.
[140] Moore, *Act and Crime*, 72.
[141] *Davis v. Herring*, 800 F 2d 513 (5th Cir 1986).
[142] *American Indemnity Co v. McQuaig*.

difference in essential properties between two putatively distinct events, however, the temporal dimension can do all of the individuating work. Consider the facts of *Newark Insurance Co* again, the case in which a tanker grounded itself twice on the same underwater ledge. In that case it is plausible to suppose that there were the same objects (ship, ledge) and the same essential properties involved (contact between ship and ledge). Nonetheless, the court was on solid ground (so to speak) in holding there to be two grounding events 'differentiated by the passage of time'.[143] Even if there had been no difference in properties between the two groundings,[144] the temporal separation made these two grounding events, not one.

Where the temporal dimension of events does depend on the duration of the change in essential properties making an event the kind of event that it is, the temporal dimension will be as vague as is the property dimension. As noted before, such vagueness in property individuation and property aggregation prevents determinate answers being given in all cases to the how many events question. As with the spatial sizing problem, however, there will also be clear cases, even though there are also unclear cases, of property (and thus temporal) individuation.

It might be thought that these three indeterminacies in event-individuation can be reduced considerably in the context of insurance law. Sometimes such contextualization of the event-individuations question surely does reduce these indeterminacies. When individuating events for purposes of answering the 'unit of offense' question in double jeopardy, for example, we use the type of act that is the offense in question and ask 'how many instances of that type of act were there?'[145] This is a lot easier than asking how many events took place there and then, without regard to type. The difference is illustrated by comparing the question, how many kissings of Mary by John there were in a given space/time region, with the question asking how many events took place in that region.[146] The event-type, kissing, has its own essential nature to help in guiding the individuation of kisses, in addition to the identity conditions for events generally. As Helen Steward also notes, 'it seems clear that each event sortal [like 'kiss'] brings with it its own bundle of relevance considerations'.[147]

Sometimes this aid is available in the insurance context, particularly when first-party defined-risk policies are in issue. In a war-risk policy limiting coverage by occurrences of acts of wars, for example, many events that played a causal role in the production of the damage insured against would be irrelevant in counting acts of war. As Steward notes, 'The concept "war" . . . suggests that we need to exclude most civilian activity events in the plant and animal kingdoms, and geological and meteorological events, and demands that we include all offensive and defensive operations.'[148] Similarly, for defined-risk policies about earthquakes, floods, fires, and the like, we need count only causally relevant earthquakes, floods, fires, etc; we need not count causally relevant events in general.

Similarly, for some liability policies like that in *Kuhn's*, the liability insured against is limited to liability for harms caused by specific types of acts of the insured only, such as 'excavation or removal work'. As I noted earlier, we can count excavations more easily

---

[143] 46 App Div 2d at 517, 303 NYS 2d at 330.
[144] In fact, one was a bow grounding and the other was a stern grounding.
[145] Moore, *Act and Crime*, 371.   [146] Ibid.
[147] Helen Seward, *The Ontology of Mind* (Oxford: Oxford University Press, 1997), 68.
[148] Ibid.

than events in general. For other liability policies like that in issue in *Johnson*, however, notice that such help is only minimally available; for the defined risk of a liability policy is any act by the insured that causes damage of the kind insured against. This restricts the kinds of events we must count to actions by one human agent (and its agents)—but this is not much of a restriction. It is not like counting occurrences of excavations, kisses, burglaries, or weddings, for example.

The situation is even worse with all-risk casualty policies, for such policies make all types of events part of the risk insured against (so long of course as such events cause damage of the kind insured against). 'All risk' robs us of the greater determinacy promised by types like, 'earthquake', 'fire', etc. All-risk policies throw us back to individuating events simpliciter, without regard to any particular types of events that must be instantiated. In the Twin Towers litigation, for example, we do not get to ask 'how many acts of war caused the destruction of the World Trade Center?' (as would be asked under a war-risk policy). Rather, we must ask 'how many events caused the destruction of the World Trade Center?, a much more open-ended question.

D. Applying the criteria of event-identity to the destruction(s) of the twin Towers

If we apply these general observations to the facts of the Twin Towers litigation, we must do so separately with respect to the several different possibilities as to where in the causal sequence we are seeking to individuate events. If we focus on the last cause events and ask, how many building collapses were there, the answer rather patently seems to be, two. As to the object dimension of this conclusion, two 110-story towers, connected only by a subterranean shopping mall, undoubtedly constitute two buildings, on any ordinary concept of a building. Their common plan of construction, their common ownership, their common designation ('The World Trade Center'), and the single insurance policy issued on them, is not enough to overcome this conclusion. Even their popular name, 'The Twin Towers', betokens the only qualitative but not numerical identity of the two buildings. Thus, even if these collapses were both qualitatively identical (which in fact they nearly were) and temporally coincident (which they were not), there would have been two collapse events.

As it happened the collapses were separated by 29½ minutes. Even if the two towers were each considered part of the same building, this temporal separation would make for two collapses. If part of a building collapses from one cause, and 29½ minutes later another part of a building collapses from a distinct cause, with no causal connection between the collapses, there would be two collapses.

Moving back in time, if we focus on the dominant immediate causes of the two collapses, we get the same result. The immediate cause of each collapse was an intense fire that degraded the structural integrity of the columns of steel holding up the towers. Assuming there were two buildings (see above), there were then two fire events. This conclusion is reinforced by the slight lack of qualitative identity between the fires: the fire in the South Tower did not completely cover the floors involved in the impact, whereas the fire in the North Tower did completely seal off its impact floors.[149] The two

---

[149] See USA Today, 19 December 2001, 4A.

fire-events conclusion is more strongly reinforced by the temporal distinctness of the fires: the South Tower fire existed for approximately 56 minutes, from 9:03 am to 9:59 am, whereas the North Tower fire existed for approximately 1 hour 42 minutes from 8:46 am to 10:28 am.

Moving further back in time, to the dominant, immediate causes of the two fires, we also get the same result. There were two crash-events, first, because there were two sets of objects involved (two planes, two buildings), second, because there were some qualitative differences between the crashes (eg, the floors hit, the speed of the airplanes and the resulting force of the impacts, the squareness of the hits[150]), and third, because the temporal locations of the crashes was distinct (8:46:26 am on the North Tower, 9:02:54 am on the South Tower).

My analysis in section IV earlier would lead one to focus on none of these kinds of events when individuating occurrences under the WTC insurance policy. For each of these events causally depends on earlier events, and the real question is whether those earlier events were singular (and thus a common cause) or plural. The events on which we should focus are probably (see section IV) the decision(s) to crash made by the terrorist pilots aboard each aircraft. There is an easy sense, of course, in which those decisions were 'the same'. This is the sense we use in contract law, for example, when we ask whether there was a 'meeting of the minds', meaning by that phase that the intentions of the contracting parties were 'the same'.[151] What contract law means by 'the same', however, is qualitative, not numerical, identity. Two numerically distinct people do not have numerically the same intention; they can only have qualitatively identical intentions.[152] Thus, the decisions of the two terrorist pilots when aboard their separate aircraft are two, no matter how similar such decisions might have been in terms of their properties and no matter how identical such decisions might have been in terms of their temporal location (eg, 7:58–7:59 am at Boston's Logan Airport, the place and times of departure of both flights).

The only seriously contestable event-individuation issues are to be found if one moves even further back in time, as one might do if that is where the most substantial cause(s) of the crashes is to be found (see section IV). Suppose our causal analysis in section IV leads us to focus on either the pre-hijacking decision of Mohamed Atta or on the even earlier decision(s) of the al Qaeda leadership in Afghanistan, presumably Osama bin Laden or Ayman al-Zawahiri.[153] Considered as individual decisions (or intentions) in either case there was but one intention-token as there was but one person making the decisions. Yet as the law of conspiracy shows us, we might not conceptualize this as a matter of individual decision; rather, we might conceptualize this as a matter of *agreements*, between

---

[150] USA Today, 19 December 2001, 4A.

[151] As in the classic contract formation case involving the good ships, *Peerless*, *Raffles v. Wichelhaus*, 2 H and C 906, 159 Eng Rep 375 (Exch 1864).

[152] Some aspects of the individuation of intentions can be quite tricky, namely, those aspects having to do with the content of such intentions. But on the objects involved with intentions—persons—the issues are easy: absent a group mind, different person makes for different intention. See Michael Moore, 'Intentions and *mens rea*', in R Gavison (ed), *Issues in Contemporary Legal Philosophy* (Oxford: Oxford University Press, 1987), reprinted as Chapter 11 of Moore, *Placing Blame*.

[153] On al-Zawahiri's leadership role within al-Qaeda, see 'The man behind Bin Laden', The New Yorker, 16 September 2002, 56–85.

bin Laden, al-Zawahiri, and their associates, or between Atta and his associates, or between all of them. We might well do that here (in the context of insurance law) for the same reason criminal law conceives of conspiracies as a crime separate from those crimes that are the objects of conspiratorial agreements: there is a special danger presented by group criminality. That special danger is often cashed out in causal terms: each individual's intention to do some criminal act in furtherance of a conspiracy is reinforced by the group-reinforcements created by a common design involving others. Even if a sole pilot might have turned back if on his own, the reliance by others involved in a group action may have made the difference.

In any case, if we are counting agreements, seemingly there is only one. In double-jeopardy contexts, as in ordinary thought, agreement events are individuated by the three attributes of events in metaphysics: the objects involved, viz the parties to the agreements; the time(s) of the agreeing acts; and the properties of the agreeing acts—and particularly those properties having to do with the content of the agreement(s), viz *what* was agreed upon. By these criteria there would appear to be but one agreement between the relevant parties.

This conclusion about individuation makes even more crucial the resolution of the causal issues at the end of section IV. If the tentative conclusion favored there is followed—that we should look at the in-flight decisions of the pilots but no earlier—then there were two occurrences, not one. If, however, we look past the decisions of the pilots, there was but one decision or but one agreement operating as the common cause of all else that followed on September 11; this then would be but one occurrence.

VI. Does a Definition of 'Occurrence' as 'One Series of Similar Causes' Alter the Causal Test?

One of the issues addressed in the World Trade Center litigation was whether the definition of 'occurrence' (quoted in section II above) was or was not part of the contract of insurance between the parties. Although there is a strong argument vis-á-vis most of the insurers that the definition is not part of the contract of insurance, I shall here assume the contrary. This allows us to reach the question of whether or not such a definition alters the meaning of 'occurrence' from the kind of meaning analyzed in sections IV and V of this essay. For two reasons I conclude that such a definition, even if it were part of the contract of insurance, likely works no change in the meaning of 'per occurrence' limitations in insurance contracts.

A. The language of the definition is consistent with the causal test

The first reason lies in the language of the definition itself. Part of that definition provides that '"occurrence" shall mean all losses or damages that are attributable ... to one cause ... All such losses will be added together and the total amount of such losses will be treated as one occurrence irrespective of the period of time or area over which such losses occur.' This part of the definition does no more than state the causal test for 'occurrence'. That is, such language affirms that the occurrences limiting coverage are cause-events, not injury-events. Moreover, the language simply states the common-cause doctrine, the essence of the causal test of 'occurrence': if there is one cause of numerous injuries, there is but one occurrence, no matter how distinct the injuries may be *inter se*.

The language of 'damages . . . attributable *directly or indirectly* to one cause . . .' does not take the definition any distance from the causal test's standard formulation. Damages that are attributable indirectly to one cause are damages caused by some one cause-event through some intermediate cause-events. This is just the causal chain doctrine we examined earlier in section IV.

The only language in the definition raising a serious issue of divergence from the causal test is the language 'damages . . . attributable . . . *to one series of similar causes*'. A possible reading of this language is that multiple causes of multiple injuries could count as one occurrence even if there are no causal relationships between such cause-events and even if they share no common cause. This is an interpretation diverging from the standard formulation of the causal test.

Any such interpretation of this language, interpreting it to diverge from the causal test, should have been rejected. To begin with, the definition states that the causes must be similar. That leaves open the question we looked at in Chapter 16, namely in what respect must two distinct cause-events be like one another to be relevantly 'similar'? Everything is similar in some respect to everything else, and everything is dissimilar to everything else in some respect.[154] So an interpreter must choose the respect or respects in which one thing must be like another to be adjudged 'similar'.

The best reading of the definition is that two distinct cause events are 'similar' if they possess similar causal properties. For example, if the employee of the insured writes 40 bogus checks in his general scheme to embezzle money from his employer, the 40 cause-events (the writing of each check) are similar in that they are the effects of a common cause, which was the general decision of the employee to embezzle the money.[155] As another example, in the ricocheting-car-collision cases,[156] two collisions are similar if one causes the other; they are then alike in sharing a causal relationship, one being the cause and the other being the effect of the same causal relationship.

This causal reading of 'similar', of course, diverges not at all from the result reached under the causal test for 'occurrence' of standard American insurance law. The above examples of similarity are no more than applications of the common-cause and causal-chain doctrines discussed in section IV. Such a reading of 'similar' in the definition thus would change the causal test not at all.

This causal reading of the definition was adopted by the Arizona Supreme Court in *Arizona Property and Casualty Insurance Guaranty Fund v. Helme*, discussed earlier. In that case the definition of 'occurrence' was 'any incident, act or omission, or series of related incidents, acts or omissions resulting in injury . . .'.[157] As the court recognized, 'neither the Imperial policy, the parties, nor the Court of Appeals have defined the word "related" and our research does not reveal any generally accepted legal meaning . . .'.[158] The court proceeded to give the word 'related' a causal reading:

> We think it clear that Imperial limited 'occurrence' by using the term, 'series of related incidents . . .' to protect itself from the contention that multiple, causally-connected negligent acts constituted more than one occurrence.[159]

---

[154] Nelson Goodman, 'Seven strictures on similarity', in his *Problems and Projects* (Indianapolis: Bobbs-Merrill, 1976).

[155] The facts of *Business Interiors*.   [156] See nn 54 and 55, above.

[157] 153 Ariz at 134, 735 P 2d at 456.   [158] 153 Ariz at 134, 735 P 2d at 456.

[159] 153 Ariz at 135, 735 P 2d at 457.

The court thus held that two doctor's qualitatively similar negligent acts constituted two occurrences because those acts were causally independent of one another.

This causal reading of the definitions in both the World Trade Center litigation and the *Helme* case, is reinforced by the use of the word 'series'. Cause-events linked as a sequence in a causal chain is a natural reading of 'series'; cause-events related as epiphenomena of a common cause is another natural reading of 'series'. Both of such readings are again no more than standard applications of the causal test of general insurance law.

A second interpretation of the definition's language, 'one series of similar causes', is alternative to the causal reading. This is an interpretation addressed to the indeterminacy in event-individuation we explored in section V. More specifically, as I there mentioned, activities of a more or less continuous nature carried on over a long period of time are notoriously difficult to individuate. For double-jeopardy purposes, for example, how many units of the offense of joy-riding take place when the defendant drives another's car without permission continuously over a 24-hour period?[160] For insurance purposes, how many insured events take place when a continuous trench the length of a street is dug by the same crew of workmen over the course of several weeks,[161] or when a continuously dug hole is excavated under two buildings over several days.[162] Definitions like that used in the World Trade Center situation can reduce the vagueness of event individuation in dealing with such continuing events.[163] What such definitions then do is not supplant the causal test but supplement it. They reduce the indeterminacy otherwise latent in the causal test with respect to continuous events of long duration.

The Texas Supreme Court has given such reading to a definition of 'occurrence' similar to that involved in the World Trade Center litigation. In *American Physicians Insurance Exchange et al v. Garcia*,[164] a medical malpractice policy defined 'occurrence' as including 'a series of acts or occurrences arising out of one event'.[165] The court's construal of this definition was:

[a] series of acts or occurrences', is apparently intended to have a coverage effect similar to the 'continuous or repeated exposure' unifying directive in commercial liability policies—but in a manner that is meaningful in the medical context. For example, medical malpractice frequently involves an operation or an extended course of treatment. A malpractice event may involve numerous independent grounds of negligence that cannot be unified as 'repeated exposure to substantially the same conditions', but that nevertheless constitute 'a series of acts or occurrences' that are related and form a single malpractice claim.[166]

Both of the above two readings of a definition of 'occurrence' (as a series of similar causes) are acceptable readings; indeed, one could give the definition both readings. Unacceptable would be a third reading, the one that would change the causal test in significant ways.

---

[160] One of the issues in *Brown v. Ohio*, 432 US 161 (1977), discussed in Moore, *Act and Crime*, 320–3.

[161] One of the relevant events in *Johnson*.

[162] The relevant event in *Kuhn's of Brownsville*.

[163] On the ability of definitions to reduce or at least reallocate vagueness, see Michael Moore, 'The semantics of judging', Southern California Law Review 54 (1981), 196–7.

[164] 37 Tex Sup J 561, 876 SW 2d 842 (1994).

[165] 37 Tex Sup J at 573, 876 SW 2d at 854.   [166] Ibid.

On this reading one interprets 'similar' to mean any qualitative similarity between numerically distinct cause-events, and one would read 'one series' to mean any temporally ordered sequence of qualitatively similar events. What makes such a reading unacceptable are three factors.

One is the great indeterminacy opened up by such a reading. If any qualitative similarity counts—not just causal similarities or the similarity of being spatio-temporally contiguous and involved in continuous events—then no principled line-drawing is possible. For every event is similar to every other event in some respects. Moreover, a similar indeterminacy would affect the 'one series' language. How large a temporal slice should one use to find one series? The question has no obvious answer, once one abandons proximate-cause doctrines or the limits of those spatio-temporally contiguous events making up one continuous event.

The second reason to reject this third reading of the definition lies in the reasonable expectations of insureds under a 'per occurrence' limitation in a policy. Suppose a building were hit on the same day by two aircraft. The crashes are qualitatively as similar as you please, involving the same kind of aircraft, the same kind of negligent inadvertence by the pilots, the same kind of damage and injury, etc. Yet if each crash is causally independent of the other—it is a freak accident that they happened the same day to the same building—and if each crash causes its own separate damage, could anyone doubt that there would be two occurrences under the building owner's casualty policy? Yet the third reading of the definition at issue here—focusing as it does only on qualitative similarity and temporal sequencing—would hold this to be but one occurrence. That is so contrary to the reasonable expectations of the parties to insurance contracts that it is a sufficient reason to reject that reading.

The third reason to reject this reading lies in the language of the insurance form which contains the definition, for this language gives a partial definition of the phrase, 'one series of similar cases', that is itself used to define 'occurrence'. With regard to perils of nature including floods or earthquakes, the insurance form in question defines 'one cause or a series of similar causes' explicitly to mean 'one single atmospheric disturbance as designated by the National Weather Service . . . '.[167] Notice that a close temporal sequence of qualitatively identical storms would not qualify as a 'series of similar causes' under this definition, thus rejecting the third, most expansive reading of 'series of similar causes' for storms and other natural perils.

The stipulations for floods caused by tidal movements also rejects the expansive reading. If property is inundated with ocean water by a series of waves, tides, or tidal waves, there 'shall be deemed to be a single occurrence', but only so long as each wave or tidal movement was 'caused by any one disturbance'.[168] Again, if one tidal wave hits, and then sixteen minutes later another tidal wave hits, and the waves are qualitatively as similar as you please, there are two occurrences because there is neither a causal connection between the waves nor a causal relationship between each wave and some one storm as a common cause.

Inland or stream flooding is handled differently. Here the problem is that adverted to before: how does one draw boundaries on matters of continuous variation (such as the

---

[167] Willis North America, WILPROP 2000 sm, 3.
[168] Ibid, 4.

gradual rise and fall of flood waters over an extended period of time)? As one philosopher of events noted recently, 'continuous, gradual change gives anyone trying to count [events] a headache . . . '.[169] It is precisely to alleviate such headaches that stipulations such as 'series of similar causes' are introduced. For stream floods, the insurance form stipulates that any flood(s) occurring 'within a period of the continued rising or overflow of any natural or man-made bodies of water and the subsidence of same within their banks' shall be deemed to be a single occurrence.[170] Note this is the second use of the definition (the one adopted by the Texas Supreme Court), not the third.

Earthquakes are treated differently: 'if more than one earthquake occurs within any period of 168 hours during the term of this policy, such earthquakes shall be deemed to be a single occurrence . . . '.[171] This might seem to lump qualitatively similar but causally unconnected events together as a 'series of similar causes' and thus to support the third reading of that last phrase. This would be a mistake, however. What the 168-hour stipulation is doing is drawing a circle within with the following evidentiary presumption applies: any earthquakes in the same area following within one week (168 hours) of another earthquake are presumed to be aftershocks of the first quake. Seismology being the inexact science that it is, it is hard to prove that a later quake is an aftershock of an earlier one, but if they are in the same area, and occur within days of each other, almost always (and perhaps always) the later quakes are mere aftershocks of the earlier one. The causal test is thus once again intended by the 'series of similar causes' language, only aided by a conclusive presumption about relations of causal dependence between spatio-temporally close earthquakes.

To summarize, none of the language contained elsewhere in the insurance form at issue in the World Trade Center litigation goes any distance to support the third, expansive reading of the 'series of similar cause' definition of 'occurrence'. On the contrary, most of that language supports the first reading where 'similar' means, causally related. (What does not support the first reading does support the second reading, where the 'series of similar causes' language is taken to draw lines on matters of continuous variation.) Since the third reading also seems contrary to any reasonable expectations parties to such contracts could have, and because that reading results in greater vagueness than that it was designed to reduce, the third reading of the definition of 'occurrence' should be rejected.

B. The intention could be to refer to the causal test even if the language of the definition were inconsistent with the causal test

Suppose (contrary to the argument of the immediately preceding subsection) that the most natural reading of the language, 'one series of similar causes', is the third, most expansive reading. Even so the language should not be given that reading.

There are two ways that we use descriptive words and phrases, both in ordinary speech and in the law. One use is to fix the class of things being referred to by the description. In this use, a description gives a set of properties and those properties fix the reference entirely in the sense that anything possessing the properties mentioned in the description is meant as the subject being discussed. An example of such usage is to be found in the

---

[169] Keith Campbell, *Abstract Particulars* (Oxford: Basil Blackwell, 1990), 140.
[170] WILPROP 2000 sm, 4. [171] Ibid, 3.

'unborn widow' cases under the rule against perpetuities.[172] In such cases gifts over are made to a named person's 'widow'. The issue is whether the description, 'so-and-so's widow', should be taken to refer to the present wife of that person (who is a life in being), or whether the property of widowhood fixes the reference so that whoever is married to the husband when the latter dies is the one meant to take (who may not be a life in being). The right answer depends on the intention of the user of the word 'widow', in this case, the testator: did he intend to make a gift to the present wife, using the phrase, 'John's widow', to refer to her, or did he intend anyone to take the property so long as she turned out to be the widow of John? Courts reasonably enough interpret the description so that the property of widowhood fixes the reference, meaning whoever meets that description takes the property.

The second way to use a description is as a heuristic, a learning device that helps audiences pick out the thing(s) being described. In such use, the description does not fix the reference, however; what is referred to is fixed by the intention of the speaker, and the description is given to help the audience grasp the speaker's referential intention.[173] An example of this latter usage is given by Leo Katz:[174] your spouse directs you to go meet that man over there, described as, 'the one in the Brooks Brothers suit, Yves St. Laurent tie, and Gucci shoes'.[175] As Katz points out, typically this list of properties is not to be taken to fix the reference of the phrase 'that man over there'. That is, your spouse probably intends you to meet a certain person irrespective of whether that person is wearing what your spouse thinks he is wearing. In such cases the description is not to be taken as fixing the reference of who it is you are to meet, but is used as a heuristic to get you to see to whom your spouse intends to refer.[176]

Definitions do not differ from descriptive phrases in having these two distinct usages,[177] which is not surprising since definitions are simply descriptions framed in terms of properties the thing defined is supposed to possess. Consider the explicit definition of 'death' prevalent in American law pre-1970, which law defined death in terms of loss of consciousness and cessation of spontaneous heart and lung functioning.[178] Such definition could be taken to fix the reference of 'death' in the sense that any event that has the properties described necessarily is a death and anything lacking them is not. Alternatively, such definition could be taken as a heuristic to picking out the cases when someone is

---

[172] Eg, *Dickerson v. Union National Bank of Little Rock*, 595 SW 2d 677 (Ark 1980).

[173] Of the considerable literature on this topic, the classic article is Keith Donnellan, 'Reference and definite descriptions', The Philosophical Review (1966), 281–304. One of Donnellan's examples: 'Smith's murderer is insane.' Are we using the phrase, 'Smith's murderer', to pick out some one person, Jones say, who may or may not actually be Smith's murderer? Or are we using the phrase to pick out whoever turns out to be the murderer of Smith?

[174] Leo Katz, *Bad Acts and Guilty Minds* (Chicago: University of Chicago Press, 1987), 85–7.

[175] Ibid, 85.

[176] Alternatively, a spouse who is concerned to point out an example of a well-dressed man may well take the properties to fix the reference; she wants her husband to see someone dressed in just the outfit described.

[177] On these two usages of definition, and on the law's frequent use of the second sort, see Michael Moore, 'Justifying the natural law theory of constitutional interpretation', Fordham Law Review 69 (2001), 2090–8; Moore, 'Do we have an unwritten constitution?', Southern California Law Review 63 (1989), 134–5; Moore, 'A natural law theory of interpretation,' Southern California Law Review 58 (1985), 291–301, 322–38, 340–1.

[178] See Moore, 'A natural law theory of interpretation', 293–300, 322–8, for an extended discussion of the definition of 'death'.

actually dead, but whether someone is or is not dead is not determined by the possession of these properties.

It is remarkable that despite the long-known marking of this distinction in linguistics, judges and lawyers regularly assume that definitions are used in legal documents only in the first way. Yet the reverse is actually true: usually definitions are used as heuristics, not determiners of reference. Take 'death' again. If we were to take the pre-1970 definition of 'death' to fix the reference of the word, a judge should find that a person submerged in very cold water for 40 minutes, who had lost consciousness and whose heart and lungs had ceased functioning, was legally dead—after all, the state of such a 'corpse' meets the legal definition of 'death'. Therefore a judge (in an organ transplant case, for example) should exclude medical testimony purporting to show that such a person is not really dead (as we know some such persons are not)—for if the proposed organ donor meets the legal definition of 'death', he must be dead. Yet so to rule would be absurd.[179] The absurdity of the conclusion stems from the absurdity of thinking that the legal definition of 'death' fixes the class of things referred to by the word 'death'. The absurdity lies in the fact that the legal definition of 'death' was intended to help judges pick out the natural class of events that really are deaths, irrespective of whether or not all of the members of that class possess the properties contained in the legal definition.

It was this insight into the judicial tendency to take definitions the wrong way that lead the Presidential Commission on the Definition of Death in the 1980s to recommend that *no* statutory definition of death be given; for the Commission foresaw that judges might mistakenly think that a new definition of death (in terms of brain function) fully determined what legal death was, rather than being simply another heuristic for judges (to be added to the heart/lung heuristic) that might be helpful to finding out when someone was really dead.[180]

Two law students at the Toronto Law School nicely captured the absurdity of taking definitions the wrong way, as judges often do, in creating the imaginary case of an Ojibway Indian who shot his pony because it was lame.[181] The defendant was prosecuted under the Ontario Small Birds Act, section 2 of which prohibited the killing of small birds. To the accused's objection that he had killed a horse and not a bird, the judge's reasoning was impeccable: section 1 of the Act defined a bird as a 'two-legged animal covered with feathers'; the pony met the definition, for it was: (a) an animal; (b) two-legged (indeed any four-legged creature necessarily has two legs); and (c) was covered with feathers (because the accused had placed a feather pillow on the pony's back in lieu of a saddle and anything artificially covered with feathers is *a fortiori* covered with feathers).

The absurdity of the judge's conclusion is fully generated by taking the legal definition to fix the class of things referred to by the word 'bird'. Had he taken the definition to be used only as a heuristic, then he could have recognized that some things that met the definition (eg, ponies with pillows) were not birds and that some things that failed to meet the definition (eg, featherless birds) were still birds. In short, the use of the definition to fix the class referred to by the legislature ignores the legislature's own intention, which is

---

[179] Moore, 'A natural law theory of interpretation', 293–300, 322–8.
[180] Report of the President's Commission, 'Defining Death: The Medical, Legal, and Ethical Issues in the Determination of Death', excerpted in T Beauchamp and L Walters (eds), *Contemporary Issues in Bioethics* (2nd edn, St Paul: West Pub Co, 1982), 301–5.
[181] 'Judicial humour: Construction of a statute', Criminal Law Quarterly 8 (1966), 137–9.

to pick out *birds*—even if that very same legislature partly misdescribes that class with its definition.

The trial judge in the Twin Towers litigation, Judge John Martin, unfortunately joined the long list of judges who assume that legal definitions must be taken to fix the class of things referred to. In granting summary judgment in favor of three insurance companies whose contract of insurance was held to contain the definition of 'occurrence' earlier quoted, Judge Martin assumed there could be no triable issue of fact about how the definition of 'occurrence' was used.[182] But of course there was such an issue of fact: were those who used the definition—the contracting parties—using it to fix the class of things referred to by 'occurrence'? Or were they using the definition only as a heuristic, a way of directing attention to the fact that the intention was to refer to the causal test—a test whose nature is (perhaps) partly misdescribed by the very definition referring to it?

Not only was this factual issue open, but linguistics teaches us that the answer is probably the opposite of the one assumed by the federal district judge who tried the case. That is, usually definitions are used as mere heuristics, aids to referring to something whose nature only approximates the properties described in the definition.[183] This usage fact is true even of phrases used to refer to legal tests, such as the causal test in insurance law. Consider in this regard the initiative in California that sought to return the state to the McNaughten test for legal insanity, yet defined that test badly: in lieu of McNaughten's 'or' the initiative used 'and'.[184] Nonetheless, the California Supreme Court properly held the definition to be a heuristic, aiding judges to pick out the thing referred to—the McNaughten test—even though that thing was very badly described by the definition.[185]

Another example is afforded by the British prohibition of *witchcraft* in their African colonies in the 19th century.[186] With their customary penchant for precision, the British not only prohibited witchcraft, they also defined it. Among other things, witchcraft was defined as the throwing of bones. Yet the social practice of witchcraft did not actually include the throwing of bones—such actions were part of the supposed antidote to witchcraft, not the practice of it. If the British courts had taken the definition to fix the class of things referred to by 'witchcraft', then they should have acquitted witchcraft's practitioners and convicted its victims. They of course had the good sense to do no such thing, taking the definition to be a heuristic (a poor one, to be sure) to aid them in picking out 'true' witches (ie those regarded as witches by the test embedded in the social practices of the tribes in question).

The important lesson to be drawn in the present context from these two uses of definitions is this: a definition used in the first way cannot misdescribe the phenomenon to which it refers—because the phenomenon to which it refers is wholly fixed by the descriptions making up the definition. That is how Judge Martin used the definition of 'occurrence' in the World Trade Center litigation. Whereas a definition used in the

---

[182] Reported in The Wall Street Journal, 26 September 2002, B4, col 3–4; The New York Times, 26 September 2002.

[183] Hilary Putnam argues that most words are used referentially ('indexically') so that definitions of them give only stereotypes, but not the meanings of such words. 'The meaning of "meaning"', in Putnam, *Mind, Language, and Reality* (Cambridge: Cambridge University Press, 1975), 215–71.

[184] The initiative is quoted in *People v. Skinner*, 704 P 2d 752 (Cal, 1985).

[185] Ibid.

[186] The tale of witchcraft is nicely told by Leo Katz in his *Bad Acts and Guilty Minds*, 82–96.

second way can misdescribe the item meant by the word being defined, and yet the reference remains the same despite the misdescription in the definition—because again, the definition used in this second way does not fix the reference of the term being defined.

It thus should have remained an open issue in the World Trade Center litigation whether the contracting parties or their agents intended to refer to the causal test in their definition of 'occurrence', even supposing that the definition partly misdescribes that test. If they did, then their intentions are honored by using the thing referred to—the causal test—and not some misdescription of that test.

VII. Conclusion

So, was there one occurrence, or were there two occurrences within the meaning of the insurance policy covering the destruction of the World Trade Center on September 11, 2001? On the facts presently available to us, my own conclusion is that there were two occurrences. This is a relatively clear conclusion if one applies New York's supposed last-proximate-cause version of the causal test, almost as clear if one applies an 'intervening-cause version of the test, but also true (although less clearly so) under the version of the causal test this book's analysis of causation would favor, the most-substantial-cause version.

This conclusion is less important, at least in academic settings, than is the route used to reach it. My hope for this essay, as for some of my earlier efforts, is to illustrate the potential help that philosophy can give to law. Everyone understands that at high levels of abstract legal theory—such as the general theory of punishment, the nature of corrective or distributive justice as the point of tort law, the nature of liberty as a restraint on legislation, the nature of law itself, and the like—philosophical analysis is an integral part of any legal analysis. Less generally accepted is the view sought here to be illustrated: even at the level of particular cases there is no escaping from doing some philosophy. To resolve this case, strictly legal analyses (of the causal test, the policies behind it, the intervening cause doctrine) must be blended with a philosophy of causation that is itself a blend of a metaphysical theory about the nature of the causal relation and a sociology of the popular conception of that relation; a philosophy of events that is similarly a blend of a metaphysical theory about the nature of events and a sociology of the popular conception of those entities; and a philosophy of language that distinguishes between referential and attributive uses of definitions. Legal decision-makers cannot afford the luxury of ignoring these kinds of philosophical analyses. Their only choices are whether to engage in such analyses consciously or unconsciously, with the help of another discipline (such as philosophy or linguistics), or without such help—ultimately, whether to do such analyses well, or to do them badly.

Bibliography

Abraham, Kenneth, *The Forms and Functions of Tort Law* (New York: Foundation Press, 1997).
—— *The Forms and Functions of Tort Law* (2nd edn, New York: Foundation Press, 2002).
Alexander, Larry, 'Crime and culpability', Journal of Contemporary Legal Issues 5 (1994), 1–30.
—— 'Deontology at the threshold' San Diego Law Review 37 (2000), 893–912.
Alexander, Larry, and Kimberly Kessler Ferzan, with the assistance of Stephen J Morse, *Crime and Culpability: A theory of the criminal law* (Cambridge: Cambridge University Press, 2008).
Alston, William, *Philosophy of Language* (Englewood Cliffs: Prentice-Hall, 1964).
American Law Institute, *Model Penal Code* (Philadelphia: American Law Institute, 1962).
—— *Commentaries to the Model Penal Code* (Philadelphia: American Law Institute, 1985).
—— *Restatement (Second) of Torts* (St Paul: American Law Institute, 1965).
—— *Restatement of Torts* (St Paul: American Law Institute, 1934).
—— *Restatement of the Law of Torts (Third)*, tentative draft No 3 (St Paul: American Law Institute, 2003).
Anscombe, GEM, 'War and murder', in Walter Stein (ed), *Nuclear Weapons: A catholic response* (New York: Sheed and Ward, 1962).
—— *Intention* (2nd edn, Ithaca: Cornell University Press, 1963).
—— *Causality and Determination* (Cambridge: Cambridge University Press, 1971).
Aquinas, Thomas, *Summa Theologica* (Benziger Bros, 1947).
Aristotle, 'On interpretation', in John Lloyd Ackrill (trans), *Aristotle's Categories and De Interpretatione: translated with notes* (Oxford: Clarendon Press, 1962).
—— *Nicomachean Ethics*, Richard McKeon (ed) (Chicago: University of Chicago Press, 1973).
Armstrong, DM, *Universals and Scientific Realism I: Nominalism and realism* (Cambridge: Cambridge University Press, 1978).
—— *Universals and Scientific Realism II: A theory of universals* (Cambridge: Cambridge University Press, 1978).
—— *Universals: An opinionated introduction* (Boulder: Westview Press, 1989).
—— *What Is a Law of Nature?* (Cambridge: Cambridge University Press, 1983).
—— *A World of States of Affairs* (New York: Cambridge University Press, 1997).
—— 'Going through the open door again: Counterfactual versus singularist theories of causation', in John Collins, Ned Hall, and LA Paul (eds), *Causation and Counterfactuals* (Cambridge, Mass: MIT Press, 2004).
—— 'The open door: Counterfactual versus singularist theories of causation', in H Stanken (ed), *Causation and Laws of Nature* (London: Kluwer Academic Pub, 1999).
Aronson, Jerrold, 'On the grammar of "cause"', Synthese 22 (1971), 414–30.

Austin, J L, 'A plea for excuses', Proceedings of the Aristotelian Society 57 (1957), reprinted in Herbert Morris (ed), *Freedom and Responsibility: Readings in philosophy and law* (Stanford: Stanford University Press, 1961).

Bacon, Sir Francis, 'Maxims of the law', in F Bacon, *The Elements of the Common Law of England* (London: Assigns of I Moore, 1630).

Barnett, Randy E, 'The sound of silence: Default rules and contractual consent', Virginia Law Review 78 (1992), 859–911.

—— *The Structure of Liberty: Justice and the rule of law* (Oxford: Clarendon Press, 1998).

Beale, JH, Jr, 'Recovery for consequences of an act', Harvard Law Review 9 (1895), 80–9.

—— 'The proximate consequences of an act', Harvard Law Review 33 (1920), 633–58.

Beauchamp, Tom (ed), *Intending Death: The ethics of assisted suicide and euthanasia* (Upper Saddle River: Prentice Hall, 1996).

Beebee, Helen, 'Causing and nothingness', in John Collins, Ned Hall, and LA Paul (eds), *Causation and Counterfacuals* (Cambridge, Mass: MIT Press, 2004).

Bennett, Jonathan, 'Event causation: The counterfactual analysis', in JE Tomberlin (ed), *Philosophical Perspectives I: Metaphysics* (Atascadero: Ridgeview Pub, 1987), reprinted in E Sosa and M Tooley (eds), *Causation* (Oxford: Oxford University Press, 1993).

—— *Events and Their Names* (Indianapolis: Hackett Publishing, 1988).

—— 'Counterfactuals and possible worlds', Canadian Journal of Philosophy 4 (1974), 381–402.

—— 'Morality and consequences', *The Tanner Lectures on Human Values* II (Salt Lake City: University of Utah Press, 1981).

—— *The Act Itself* (Oxford: Clarendon Press, 1995).

Bentham, Jeremy, *An Introduction to the Principles of Morals and Legislation* (Oxford: Oxford University Press, 1789).

Bernstein, Richard, 'Kidnapping has Germans debating police torture', New York Times, International, Thursday, 10 April 2003, A-3.

Bingham, Joseph, 'Some suggestions concerning "legal cause" at common law', Columbia Law Review 9 (1909), 16–37, 136–59.

Bishin, Bill and Stone, Chris, *Law, Language and Ethics* (Mineola: Foundation Press, 1972).

Bishop, John, *Natural Agency* (Cambridge: Cambridge University Press, 1989).

Bohlen, Francis H, 'The probable or the natural consequence as the test of liability in negligence', American Law Register 49 (1901), 79–88, 148–64.

Boorse, Christopher and Sorensen, Roy, 'Ducking harm', Journal of Philosophy 85 (1988), 115–34.

Borgo, John, 'Causal paradigms in tort law', Journal of Legal Studies 8 (1979), 419–55.

Bradley, FH, *Appearance and Reality: A metaphysical essay* (2nd edn, Oxford: Oxford University Press, 1897).

Brand, Myles, *Intending and Acting* (Cambridge, Mass: MIT Press, 1984).

Brody, Baruch, 'Withdrawal of treatment versus killing of patients', in Tom Beauchamp (ed), *Intending Death: The ethics of assisted suicide* (Upper Saddle River: Prentice Hall, 1996), 99.

Bunzl, M, 'Causal overdetermination', Journal of Philosophy 76 (1979), 134–50.

Burke, Norris J, 'Rules of legal cause in negligence cases', California Law Review 15 (1926), 1–18.

Buxton, Richard, 'Complicity and the law commission', Criminal Law Review (1973), 223–30.

—— 'Circumstances, consequences, and attempted rape', Criminal Law Review (1984), 25–34.

—— 'Complicity in the criminal code', Law Quarterly Review 85 (1969), 252–74.

Calabresi, Guido, 'Concerning cause and the law of torts: An essay for Harry Kalven Jr', University of Chicago Law Review 43 (1975), 69–108.

—— 'Some thoughts on risk distribution and the law of torts', Yale Law Journal 70 (1961), 499–553.

Campbell, Keith, *Abstract Particulars* (Cambridge, Mass: Blackwell, 1990).

Cane, Peter, 'The general/special distinction in criminal law, tort law and legal theory', Law and Philosophy 26 (2007), 465–500.

—— *Responsibility in Law and Morality* (Oxford: Hart Publishing Co, 2002).

Cardozo, Benjamin N, *Law and Literature: And other essays and addresses* (New York: Harcourt, Brace and Company, 1931).

Carpenter, Charles, E, 'Workable rules for determining proximate cause', California Law Review 20 (1932), 229–59, 396–419, 471–539.

—— 'Concurrent causation', University of Pennsylvania Law Review 83 (1935), 941–52.

—— 'Proximate cause', (Parts 1–3), Southern California Law Review 14 (1940), 1–34, 115–53, 416–51; (Parts 4–6), Southern California Law Review 15 (1941), 187–213, 304–21, 427–68; (Parts 7–9), Southern California Law Review 16 (1943), 1–23, 61–92, 275–313.

Carroll, John, *Laws of Nature* (Cambridge: Cambridge University Press, 1994).

Chisholm, Roderick, 'The contrary to fact conditional', Mind 55 (1946), 289–307, revised and reprinted in H Fiegl and W Sellars (ed), *Readings in Philosophical Analysis* (New York: Appleton-Century-Crofts, 1949).

—— 'Law statements and counterfactual inference', Analysis 15 (1955), 97–105, reprinted in Ernst Sosa (ed), *Causation and Conditionals* (Oxford: Oxford University Press, 1975).

—— 'States of affairs again', Noûs 5 (1971), 179–89.

Chomsky, Noam, *Studies on Semantics in Generative Grammar* (The Hague: Mouton, 1972).

Christie, Agatha, *Murder on the Orient Express* (New York: Pocket Books, 1960).

Coase, RH, 'The problem of social cost', Journal of Law and Economics 3 (1960), 1–69.

Cohen, Felix S, 'Transcendental nonsense and the functional approach', Columbia Law Review 35 (1935), 809–49.

—— 'The problems of a functional jurisprudence', Modern Law Review 1 (1937), 5–26.

Cole, Robert, 'Windfall and probability: A study of "cause" in negligence law', California Law Review 52 (1964), 459–512, 764–821.

Collins, John, 'Preemptive prevention', Journal of Philosophy 97 (2000), 223–34.

——, Hall, Ned, and Paul, LA (eds), *Causation and Counterfactuals* (Cambridge, Mass: MIT Press, 2004).

Cooperrider, Luke, 'Causation in the Law,' Michigan Law Review 59 (1960), 501–14.

Costa, Michael, 'The trolley problem revisited', in John Martin Fischer and Mark Ravizza (eds), *Ethics: Problems and principles* (New York: Harcourt, Brace, 1992).

Costa, Michael, 'Another trip on the trolley', in John Martin Fischer and Mark Ravizza (eds), *Ethics: Problems and principles* (New York: Harcourt, Brace, 1992).

Daly, Chris, 'Tropes', Proceedings of the Aristotelian Society 94 (1994), 253–61.

—— 'Tropes', in DH Mellor and Alex Oliver, *Properties* (Oxford: Oxford University Press, 1997).

Dan-Cohen, Meir, 'Causation', in Sanford Kadish (ed), *Encyclopedia of Crime and Justice* 1 (New York: Macmillan, 1983).

Davidson, Donald, 'Actions, reasons, and causes', in his *Essays on Actions and Events* (Oxford: Oxford University Press, 1980).

—— *Essays on Actions and Events* (Oxford: Oxford University Press, 1980).

—— 'Reply to Quine on events', in E Le Pore and B McLaughlin (eds), *Actions and Events: Perspectives on the philosophy of Donald Davidson* (Oxford: Oxford University Press, 1983).

Dennett, DC, *Elbow Room: The varieties of free will worth wanting* (Cambridge, Mass: MIT Press, 1984).

D'Israeli, Isaac, *Curiosities of Literature* (London: J Murray, 1791).

Divers, John, *Possible Worlds* (London: Routledge, 2002).

Dobbs, Dan B, *The Law of Torts* (St Paul: West Publishing, 2000).

Domsky, Darren, 'There is no door: Finally solving the problem of moral luck', Journal of Philosophy 101 (2004), 445–64.

Donagan, Alan, *The Theory of Morality* (Oxford: Oxford University Press, 1977).

Donnellan, Keith, 'Reference and definite descriptions', The Philosophical Review (1966), 281–304.

Dowe, Phil, *Physical Causation* (Cambridge: Cambridge University Press, 2000).

—— 'Absences, possible causation, and the problem of non-locality', The Monist 91(4) (2008).

Downing, PB, 'Subjunctive conditionals, time order, and causation', Proceedings of the Aristotelian Society 59 (1959), 125–40.

Dray, William, 'The historical explanation of actions reconsidered', in S Hook (ed), *Philosophy and History* (New York: New York University Press, 1963).

Dresser, Rebecca, 'Personal identity and punishment', Boston University Law Review 70 (1990), 395–446.

Dressler, Joshua, 'Reassessing the theoretical underpinnings of accomplice liability', Hastings Law Journal 37 (1985), 91–140.

—— *Understanding Criminal Law* (New York: Mathew Bender, 1987).

—— *Understanding Criminal Law* (2nd edn, New York: Mathew Bender, 1995).

Dretske, Fred, 'Referring to events,' in P French, T Uehling, and H Wettstein (eds), *Midwest Studies in Philosophy* II (Minneapolis: University of Minnesota Press, 1977).

Ducasse, CJ, 'On the nature and the observability of the causal relation', Journal of Philosophy 23 (1926), 57–68.

Duff, RA, 'Intention, mens rea and the law commission report', Criminal Law Review (1980), 147–60.

—— 'Is accomplice liability superfluous?', University of Pennsylvania Law Review PENNumbra 156 (2007), 444–52.

Dworkin, Ronald, *Taking Rights Seriously* (Cambridge, Mass: Harvard University Press, 1978).

Edgerton, Harry, 'Legal cause', University of Pennsylvania Law Review 72 (1924), 211–44, 343–75.

Ehring, Douglas, *Causation and Persistence* (Oxford: Oxford University Press, 1997).

Ehring, Douglas, 'Abstracting away from preemption', The Monist 91(4) (2008).

Eldredge, Laurence, 'Culpable intervention as superseding cause', University of Pennsylvania Law Review 86 (1938), 121–35.

Enoch, David and Marmor, Andrei, 'The case against moral luck', Law and Philosophy 26 (2007), 405–36.

Epstein, Richard A, 'A theory of strict liability', Journal of Legal Studies 2 (1973), 151–204.

—— 'Defenses and subsequent pleas in a system of strict liability', Journal of Legal Studies 3 (1974), 165–215.

—— *Cases and Materials on Torts* (6th edn, New York: Aspen Law & Business, 1995).

Fair, David, 'Causation and the flow of energy', Erkenntnis 14 (1979), 219–50.

Fales, Evan, *Causation and Universals* (London: Routledge, 1990).

Farnsworth, E. Allan, *Contracts* (3rd edn, New York: Aspen Law & Business, 1999).

Feinberg, Joel, 'Action and Responsibility', in his *Doing and Deserving* (Princeton: Princeton University Press, 1970).

—— 'Equal punishment for failed attempts: Some bad but instructive arguments against it', Arizona Law Review 37 (1995), reprinted in his *Problems at the Roots of Law* (Oxford: Oxford University Press, 2003).

—— *Doing and Deserving: Essays in the theory of responsibility* (Princeton: Princeton University Press, 1970).

Ferzan, Kimberly Kessler, and Larry Alexander, with the assistance of Stephen J Morse, *Crime and Culpability: A theory of the criminal law* (Cambridge: Cambridge University Press, 2008).

Fine, Kit, 'First order modal theories III: Facts', Synthese 53 (1982), 43–122.

—— 'Critical notice: *Counterfactuals*, by D Lewis', Mind 84 (1975), 451–8.

Finkelstein, Claire O, 'Is risk a harm?', University of Pennsylvania Law Review 151 (2003), 963–1001.

Fischer, David, 'Causation in fact in omission cases', Utah Law Review (1992), 1335–84.

Fischer, John Martin and Ravizza, Mark, *Responsibility and Control: A theory of moral responsibility* (Cambridge: Cambridge University Press, 1998).

—— *Ethics: Problems and principles* (New York: Harcourt, Brace, 1992).

Fischer, John, Ravizza, Mark, and Copp, 'Quinn on double effect: The problem of "closeness" ', Ethics 103 (1993), 707–25.

Fleming, James and Perry, Robert, 'Legal cause', Yale Law Journal 60 (1951), 761–811.

Fletcher, George P, 'Fairness and utility in tort theory', Harvard Law Review 85 (1972), 537–73.

—— 'Proportionality and the psychotic aggressor: A vignette in comparative criminal theory', Israel Law Review 8 (1973), 367–90.

—— *Rethinking Criminal Law* (Boston: Little, Brown, 1978).

—— 'On the moral irrelevance of bodily movements', University of Pennsylvania Law Review 142 (1994), 1443–53.

—— *Basic Concepts of Criminal Law* (New York: Oxford University Press, 1998).

Flew, Antony, 'Psychiatry, law and responsibility', Philosophical Quarterly 35 (1985), 425–32.

Fodor, Jerry, *The Language of Thought* (Cambridge, Mass: MIT Press, 1975).

—— *Psychosemantics* (Cambridge, Mass: MIT Press, 1987).

Follesdal, D, 'Quantification into causal contexts', in L Linsky (ed), *Reference and Modality* (Oxford: Oxford University Press, 1971).

Foot, Philippa, 'The problem of abortion and the doctrine of double effect', originally published in *The Oxford Review* (1967), reprinted in PA Woodward, *The Doctrine of Double Effect: Philosophers debate a controversial moral principle* (Notre Dame: University of Notre Dame Press, 2001).

—— 'Morality, action, and Outcome', in T Henderich (ed), *Morality and Objectivity* (London: Routledge, 1985), reprinted in PA Woodward, *The Doctrine of Double Effect: Philosophers debate a controversial moral principle* (Notre Dame: University of Notre Dame Press, 2001).

Foster, Henry, Grant, William H, and Green, Robert W, 'The risk theory and proximate cause: A comparative study', Nebraska Law Review 32 (1952), 72–102.

Fried, Charles, *An Anatomy of Value* (Cambridge, Mass: Harvard University Press, 1970).

—— 'Right and wrong: Preliminary considerations', Journal of Legal Studies 5 (1976), 165–200.

—— *Right and Wrong* (Cambridge, Mass: Harvard University Press, 1978).

Fumerton, Richard, 'Moore, causation, counterfactuals and responsibility', San Diego Law Review 40 (2003), 1273–81.

Fumerton, Richard and Kress, Ken, 'Causation and the law: Preemption, lawful sufficiency, and causal sufficiency', Law and Contemporary Problems 64 (2001), 83–104.

Gardner, John, 'Complicity and causality', Criminal Law and Philosophy 1 (2007), 127–41.

—— 'Moore on complicity and causality', University of Pennsylvania Law Review PENNumbra 156 (2007), 432–43.

Geach, PT, 'Ascriptivism', Philosophical Review 69 (1960), 221–5.

—— *Logic Matters* (Berkeley: University of California Press, 1980).

Gillies, Donald, *Philosophical Theories of Probability* (London: Routledge, 2000).

Ginet, Carl, *On Action* (Cambridge: Cambridge University Press, 1990).

Goldberg, Gary, 'Supplementary motor area structure and function: Review and hypotheses', Behavioral & Brain Sciences 8 (1985), 567–615.

Goldberg, John, and Zipursky, Benjamin, 'The Restatement (Third) and the place of duty in negligence law', Vanderbilt Law Review 54 (2001), 657–750.

Goldman, Alvin, *A Theory of Human Action* (Englewood Cliffs: Prentice-Hall, 1970).

—— 'Action and crime: A fine-grained approach', University of Pennsylvania Law Review 142 (1994), 1563–86.

—— 'Why citizens should vote: A causal responsibility approach', Social Philosophy and Policy 16 (1999), 201–17, reprinted in EF Paul et al (eds), *Responsibility* (Cambridge: Cambridge University Press, 1999).

Goldstein, Abraham, *The Insanity Defense* (New Haven: Yale University Press, 1967).

Goodman, Nelson, 'Seven strictures on similarity', in his *Problems and Projects* (Indianapolis: Bobbs-Merrill, 1976).

—— 'The problem of counterfactual conditionals', Journal of Philosophy 44 (1947), reprinted in Nelson Goodman, *Fact, Fiction, and Forecast* (4th edn, Cambridge, Mass: Harvard University Press, 1983).

Grady, Mark, 'Untaken precautions', Journal of Legal Studies 18 (1989), 139–56.

Gray, John Chipman, *The Nature and Sources of Law* (New York: Columbia University Press, 1909).

Green, Leon, 'Are negligence and "proximate cause" determinable by the same test?', Texas Law Review 1 (1923), 243–60, 423–45.

—— 'Are There Dependable Rules of Causation?', University of Pennsylvania Law Review 77 (1929), 601–28.

—— 'The causal relation issue in negligence law', Michigan Law Review 60 (1962), 543–76.

—— 'The Wagon Mound No 2: Foreseeability revised', Utah Law Review (1967), 197–206.

Gross, Hyman, *A Theory of Criminal Justice* (New York: Oxford University Press, 1979).

Hall, Jerome, *General Principles for Criminal Law* (1st edn, Indianapolis: Bobbs-Merrill, 1947).

—— *General Principles of Criminal Law* (2nd edn, Indianapolis: Bobbs-Merrill, 1960).

Hall, Ned, 'Causation and the Price of Transitivity,' Journal of Philosophy 97 (2000), 198–222.

—— 'Two concepts of causation', in John Collins, Ned Hall, and LA Paul (eds), *Causation and Counterfactuals* (Cambridge, Mass: MIT Press, 2004).

Hart, HLA, 'The ascription of responsibility and rights', Proceedings of the Aristotelian Society 49 (1948), 171–94.

—— 'Positivism and the separation of law and morals', Harvard Law Review 71 (1958), 593–629.

—— 'Legal responsibility and excuses', in Sidney Hook (ed), *Determinism and Freedom in the Age of Modern Science* (New York: NYU Press 81, 1958), reprinted in HLA Hart, *Punishment and Responsibility* (Oxford: Oxford University Press, 1968).

—— 'Intention and punishment', The Oxford Review 14 (1967), reprinted in his *Punishment and Responsibility* (Oxford: Oxford University Press, 1968).

—— *Punishment and Responsibility* (Oxford: Oxford University Press, 1968).

—— 'Morality and reality', New York Review of Books 9 March 1978.

Hart, HLA, and Honoré, Tony, 'Causation in the law', Law Quarterly Review 72 (1956), 58–90, 260–81, 398–417.

—— *Causation in the Law* (Oxford: Clarendon Press, 1959).

—— *Causation in the Law* (2nd edn, Oxford: Oxford University Press, 1985).

Hartmann, Ernest L, *The Function of Sleep* (New Haven: Yale University Press, 1973).

Hausman, Daniel, 'Thresholds, transitivity, overdetermination, and events', Analysis 52 (1992), 159–63.

Hempel, Carl G, 'Reasons and covering laws in historical explanation', in Sidney Hook (ed), *Philosophy and History* (New York: NYU Press, 1963).

—— 'The function of general laws in history', in Carl G Hempel (ed), *Aspects of Scientific Explanation* (New York: Free Press, 1965).

—— 'Aspects of Scientific Explanation,' in his *Aspects of Scientific Explanation* (New York: Free Press, 1965).

—— *Aspects of Scientific Explanation* (New York: Free Press, 1965).

Herman, Barbara, 'Feinberg on luck and failed attempts', Arizona Law Review 37 (1995), 143–9.

Hitchcock, Christopher, 'The mishap at reichenbach fall: Singular vs. general causation', Philosophical Studies 78 (1995), 257–91.

Hitchcock, Christopher, 'The intransitivity of causation revealed in equations and graphs', Journal of Philosophy, 98 (2001), 273–99.

—— 'Probabilistic causation', *Stanford Encyclopedia of Philosophy* (2002), available at <http://www.plato.stanford.edu>.

—— 'Of Humean bondage', British Journal for the Philosophy of Science 54 (2003), 1–25.

—— 'Problems for conserved quantity theory: Counterexamples, circularity, and redundancy', The Monist 91(4) (2008).

—— 'The conserved quantity theory: Between circularity and redundancy', The Monist 91(4) (2008).

Hohfeld, Wesley, 'Some fundamental legal conceptions as applied in judicial reasoning', Yale Law Journal 23 (1913), 16–59.

—— 'Fundamental legal conceptions as applied in judicial reasoning', Yale Law Journal 26 (1917), 710–70.

—— *Fundamental Legal Conceptions* (New Haven: Yale University Press, 1919).

Holmes, OW, Jr, *The Common Law* (Boston: Little, Brown, 1881).

—— 'The path of the law', Harvard Law Review 10 (1897), 457–78.

Honoré, Tony, 'Necessary and sufficient conditions in tort law', in David G Owen (ed), *Philosophical Foundations of Tort Law* (Oxford: Oxford University Press, 1995).

—— *Responsibility and Fault* (Oxford: Oxford University Press, 1999).

Honoré, Tony, and HLA Hart, 'Causation in the law', Law Quarterly Review 72 (1956), 58–90, 260–81, 398–417.

—— *Causation in the Law* (Oxford: Clarendon Press, 1959).

—— *Causation in the Law* (2nd edn, Oxford: Oxford University Press, 1985).

Hornsby, Jennifer, *Actions* (London: Routledge, 1980).

—— 'Agency and actions', in John Hyman and Helen Steward (ed), *Agency and Action* (Cambridge: Cambridge University Press, 2004).

Horwich, Paul, *Asymmetries in Time: Problem in the philosophy of science* (Cambridge, Mass: MIT Press, 1987), excerpts reprinted in Ernest Sosa and Michael Tooley (eds), *Causation* (New York: Oxford University Press, 1993).

Hume, David, *An Enquiry Concerning Human Understanding* (Oxford: Clarendon edn, 1902) (Indianapolis: Bobbs-Merrill, 1955).

Hurd, Heidi M, 'Relativistic jurisprudence: Skepticism founded on confusion', Southern California Law Review 61 (1988), 1417–510.

—— 'Correcting injustice to corrective justice', Notre Dame Law Review 67 (1991), 51–96.

—— 'Justifiably punishing the justified', Michigan Law Review 90 (1992), 2203–324.

—— 'What in the world is wrong?', Journal of Contemporary Legal Issues 5 (1994), 157–216.

—— 'The deontology of negligence', Boston University Law Review 76 (1996), 249–72.

—— 'Is it wrong to do right when others do wrong?', Legal Theory 7 (2001), 307–40.

Johnson, Eric, 'Criminal liability for loss of a chance', Iowa Law Review 91 (2005), 59–130.

Kadish, Sanford, 'Causation and complicity: A study in the interpretation of doctrine', California Law Review 73 (1985), 323–410.

—— *Blame and Punishment* (New York: Macmillan, 1987).

Kadish, Sanford, 'A theory of complicity', in R Gavison (ed), *Issues in Contemporary Legal Philosophy: The influence of HLA Hart* (Oxford: Oxford University Press, 1987).

—— 'Foreword: The criminal law and the luck of the draw,' Journal of Criminal Law and Criminology 84 (1994), 679–702.

Kadish, Sanford H, and Schulhofer, Stephen J (eds), *Criminal Law and Its Processes* (6th edn, Boston: Little, Brown, 1995).

—— (eds), *Criminal Law and Its Processes* (7th edn, Boston: Aspen Publishers, 2001).

Kafka, Greg, 'The toxin puzzle', Analysis 43 (1983), 33–6.

Kamm, Frances, 'Action, omission, and the stringency of duties', University of Pennsylvania Law Review 142 (1994), 1492–512.

—— *Morality, Mortality Volume II* (New York: Oxford University Press, 1996),

Kant, Immanuel, *The Metaphysical Elements of Justice*, tr J Ladd (Indianapolis: Bobbs-Merrill, 1965).

Katz, Leo, *Bad Acts and Guilty Minds* (Chicago: University of Chicago Press, 1987).

—— *Ill-Gotten Gains: Evasion, blackmail, fraud, and kindred puzzles of the law* (Chicago: University of Chicago Press, 1996).

Keeton, Robert E, *Legal Cause in the Law of Torts* (Columbus: Ohio State University Press, 1963).

—— 'A Palsgraf anecdote', Texas Law Review 56 (1978) 513–18.

Keeton, W Page, et al, *Prosser and Keeton on the Law of Torts* (5th edn, St Paul: West Pub Co, 1984).

Kelley, Patrick, 'Proximate cause in negligence law: History, theory and the present darkness', Washington University Law Quarterly 69 (1991), 49–105.

—— 'Who decides? Community safety conventions at the heart of tort liability', Cleveland State Law Review 38 (1991), 358–9.

—— 'Restating duty, breach and proximate cause in negligence law', Vanderbilt Law Review 54 (2001), 1061–2.

Kelman, Mark, 'The necessary myth of objective causation judgments in liberal political theory', Chicago-Kent Law Review 63 (1987), 603–4.

—— *A Guide to Critical Legal Studies* (Cambridge, Mass: Harvard University Press, 1987).

Kenny, Anthony, *Action, Emotion, and Will* (London: Routledge, 1963).

Kessler, Kimberly, 'The role of luck in the criminal law', University of Pennsylvania Law Review 142 (1994), 2183–237.

Kim, Jaegwon, 'On the psycho-physical identity theory', American Philosophical Quarterly 3 (1966), 227–35.

—— 'Causes and events: Mackie on causation', Journal of Philosophy 68 (1971), 426–41.

—— 'Causation, nomic subsumption, and the concept of an event', Journal of Philosophy 70 (1973), 217–36.

—— 'Events as property-exemplifications', in M Brand and D Walton (eds), *Action Theory* (Dordrecht: Reidel, 1976).

—— 'Causes and counterfactuals', Journal of Philosophy 70 (1973), reprinted in Ernest Sosa and Michael Tooley (eds), *Causation* (New York: Oxford University Press, 1993).

—— 'Epiphenomenal and supervenient causation', in Peter French, Theodore Vehling, and Howard Wettstein (eds), *Midwest Studies in Philosophy IX: Causation and causal theories* (Minneapolis: University of Minnesota Press, 1984).

Kneale, William, 'Natural laws and contrary-to-fact conditionals', Analysis 10 (1950), 121–5 reprinted in T. Beauchamp (ed), *Philosophical Problems of Causation* (Encino: Dickenson, 1974).

Knowles, Dudley (ed), *Explanation and Its Limits* (Cambridge: Cambridge University Press, 1990).

Korsgaard, Christine, 'Acting for a reason', Illinois Philosophy Dept paper (2005).

Krimerman, Leonard I (ed), *The Nature and Scope of Social Science: A critical anthology* (New York: Appleton-Century-Crofts, 1969).

Kripke, Saul, *Naming and Necessity* (2nd edn, Cambridge, Mass: Harvard University Press, 1980).

—— *Wittgenstein on Rules and Private Language: An elementary exposition* (Cambridge, Mass: Harvard University Press, 1982).

Kutz, Chris, *Complicity* (Cambridge: Cambridge University Press, 2000).

—— 'Causeless complicity', Criminal Law and Philosophy, 1 (2007), 289–305.

LaFave, Wayne and Scott, Austin, *Criminal Law* (St Paul: West Publishing, 1972).

Lakoff, G, 'On generative semantics', in D Steinberg and L Jakobovits (eds), *Semantics: An interdisciplinary reader in philosophy, linguistics and psychology* (Cambridge: Cambridge University Press, 1971).

Landes, John and Posner, Richard, 'Causation in tort law: An economic approach', Journal of Legal Studies 12 (1983), 109–34.

Lehman, Warren, 'How to interpret a difficult statute', Wisconsin Law Review (1979), 489–507.

Levitt, Albert, 'Cause, legal cause and proximate cause', Michigan Law Review 21 (1922), 34–62, 160–73.

Lewis, David, 'Causation', Journal of Philosophy 70 (1973), 556–67, reprinted in Ernest Sosa and Michael Tooley (eds), *Causation* (Oxford: Oxford University Press, 1993).

—— *Counterfactuals* (Oxford: Blackwell, 1973).

—— 'Counterfactual dependence and time's arrow', Noûs 13 (1979), 455–76, reprinted in David Lewis (ed), *Philosophical Papers II* (Oxford: Oxford University Press, 1986).

—— *On the Plurality of Worlds* (Oxford: Basil Blackwell, 1986).

—— 'Postscripts to "causation"', in *Philosophical Papers* II (Oxford: Oxford University Press, 1986).

—— *Philosophical Papers* (Oxford: Oxford University Press, 1986).

—— 'Events', in his *Philosophical Papers* II (Oxford: Oxford University Press, 1986).

—— 'The punishment that leaves something to chance', Philosophy and Public Affairs 18 (1989), 53–67.

—— 'Causation as influence', Journal of Philosophy 97 (2000), 182–97.

Libet, Benjamin, 'Unconscious cerebral initiative and the role of conscious will in voluntary action', Behavioral & Brain Sciences 8 (1985), 529–39.

Lipton, Peter, 'Causation outside the law', in Hyman Gross and Ross Harrison (eds), *Jurisprudence: Cambridge essays* (Cambridge: Cambridge University Press, 1992).

Lombard, Lawrence Brian, *Events: A metaphysical study* (London: Routledge, 1986).

—— 'Causes, enablers, and the counterfactual analysis', Philosophical Studies 59 (1990), 195–211.

Louch, AR, *Explanation and Human Action* (Berkeley: University of California Press, 1966).

Lycan, William G, *Real Conditionals* (Oxford: Clarendon Press, 2001).

Macaulay, Lord, *Notes on the Indian Penal Code* (1837), reproduced in *The Works of Lord Macaulay*, Vol 7 (New York, 1897).

Mack, Eric, 'Bad Samaritanism and the causation of harm', Philosophy and Public Affairs 9 (1980), 230–59.

Mackie, John L, 'Causes and conditions', American Philosophical Quarterly 2 (1965), 245–64.

—— *Truth, Probability, and Paradox* (Oxford: Oxford University Press, 1973).

—— *The Cement of the Universe: A study of causation* (Oxford: Clarendon Press, 1974).

—— *Ethics: Inventing right and wrong* (London: Penguin, 1977).

Mackie, Penelope, 'Causing, delaying, and hastening: Do rains cause fires?', Mind 101 (1992), 483–500.

Malone, Wex Malone, 'Ruminations on cause-in-fact', Stanford Law Review 9 (1956), 60–99.

Mathis, Stephen, 'A plea for omissions', Criminal Justice Ethics (Summer/Fall, 2003), 15–31.

Mayer, Jane, 'Outsourcing torture', The New Yorker, 14 February 2005.

McCawley, JD, 'Prelexical syntax', in Pieter AM Seuren (ed), *Semantic Syntax* (Oxford: Oxford University Press, 1974).

McDermott, Michael, 'Redundant causation', British Journal for the Philosophy of Science 46 (1995), 523–44.

McDermott, Terry, 'No limits hinder uc thinker', Los Angeles Times, 28 December 1999, A14.

McIntosh, Andrew C, 'Intervening criminal act as breaking causal chain', Law Notes (1931), 109.

McIntyre, Alison., 'Doing away with double effect', Ethics 111 (2001), 219–55.

McLaughlin, James Angell, 'Proximate cause', Harvard Law Review 39 (1925), 149–99.

Melden, AI, *Free Action* (London: Routledge and Kegan Paul, 1961).

Mellor, DH, *The Facts of Causation* (London: Routledge, 1995).

Mellor, DH and Oliver, Alex, 'Introduction', in their *Properties* (Oxford: Oxford University Press, 1997).

—— (eds), *Properties* (Oxford: Oxford University Press, 1997).

Menzies, Peter, 'A unified account of causal relata', Australasian Journal of Philosophy 67 (1989), 64–7.

Menzies, Peter and Price, Huw, 'Causation as a secondary quality', British Journal for the Philosophy of Science 44 (1993), 187–203.

Michelman, Frank, 'Property, utility, and fairness: Comments on the ethical foundations of "just compensation" law', Harvard Law Review 80 (1967), 1165–258.

Mill, John Stuart, *A System of Logic* (8th edn, London: Longmans, 1872).

Minahan, Victor I, 'The doctrine of intervening cause in the law of negligence', Marquette Law Review 4 (1919–1920), 75–80.

Molnar, George (as edited by Stephen Mumford), *Powers: A study in metaphysics* (Oxford: Oxford University Press, 2003).

Montague, Phil, 'Self-defense and choosing between lives', Philosophical Studies 40 (1981), 207–17.

Montmarquet, James, 'Doing good: The right way and the wrong way', Journal of Philosophy 79 (1982), 439–55.

Moore, Michael S, 'The semantics of judging,' Southern California Law Review 54 (1981), 246–70.

—— 'Moral reality', Wisconsin Law Review (1982), 1061–156.

—— *Law and Psychiatry: Rethinking the relationship* (New York: Cambridge University Press, 1984).

—— 'A natural law theory of interpretation', Southern California Law Review 58 (1985), 338–58.

—— 'Intention and mens rea', in Ruth Gavison (ed), *Issues in Contemporary Legal Philosophy* (Oxford: Oxford University Press, 1987), reprinted in Michael S Moore, *Placing Blame: A general theory of the criminal law* (Oxford: Clarendon Press, 1997).

—— 'Causation and the excuses', California Law Review 73 (1985), 1091–149, reprinted in A Eser and G Fletcher (eds), *Justification and Excuse: Comparative perspectives*, Vol II (Freiburg: Max Planck Institute, 1987).

—— 'Thompson's preliminaries about causation and rights', Chicago-Kent Law Review 63 (1987), 497–521.

—— 'The interpretive turn in modern theory: A turn for the worse?', Stanford Law Review 41 (1989), 927–34, reprinted as Chapter 10 in Michael Moore, *Educating Oneself in Public: Critical essays in jurisprudence* (Oxford: Oxford University Press, 2000).

—— 'Do we have an unwritten constitution?', Southern California Law Review 63 (1989), 127–30, 134–5.

—— 'Choice character, and excuse', Social Philosophy and Policy 7 (1990), 219–48, reprinted in E Frankel-Paul (ed), *Crime, Culpability, and Remedy* (Oxford: Basil Blackwell, Ltd, 1990).

—— A Theory of Criminal Law Theories', Tel Aviv University Studies in Law 10 (1990), 115–85.

—— 'Moral reality revisited', Michigan Law Review 90 (1992), 2424–533.

—— *Act and Crime: The implications of the philosophy of action for the criminal law* (Oxford: Clarendon Press, 1993).

—— 'More on act and crime', University of Pennsylvania Law Review 142 (1994), 1749–840.

—— 'Prima facie moral culpability', Boston University Law Review 75 (1995), 319–33.

—— 'Torture and the balance of evils', Israel Law Review 23 (1989), 280–344, reprinted in Michael Moore, *Placing Blame: A General Theory of the Criminal Law* (Oxford: Oxford University Press, 1997).

—— 'Foreseeing harm opaquely', in John Gardner, Jeremy Harder, and Stephen Shute (eds), *Action and Value in Criminal Law* (Oxford: Oxford University Press, 1993), reprinted in Michael Moore, *Placing Blame: A general theory of the criminal law* (Oxford: Oxford University Press, 1997).

—— 'The independent moral significance of wrongdoing', Journal of Contemporary Legal Issues 5 (1994), 1–45, reprinted as Chapter 5 in Michael Moore, *Placing Blame: A general theory of the criminal law* (Oxford: Oxford University Press, 1997).

—— *Placing Blame: A general theory of the criminal law* (Oxford: Clarendon Press, 1997).

—— 'Justifying the natural law theory of constitutional interpretation', Fordham Law Review 69 (2001), 2090–8.

Moore, Michael S, 'Legal reality: A naturalist approach to legal ontology', Law and Philosophy 21 (2002), 665–77, reprinted in Michael Moore, *Objectivity in Law and Ethics* (Aldershot: Ashgate, 2004).

—— *Objectivity in Law and Ethics* (Aldershot: Ashgate, 2004).

—— 'The mysterious agency of the mysterians', forthcoming in JH Aguiler and AA Buckareff (eds), *Causing Human Action: New perspectives on the causal theory of action* (Cambridge, Mass: MIT Press, a Bradford Book, 2009).

Morgan, JL, 'On arguing about semantics', Papers in Linguistics 1 (1973), 49–70.

Morris, Clarence, 'Custom and negligence', Columbia Law Review 42 (1942), 1147–68.

Morris, Herbert, *On Guilt and Innocence* (Berkeley: University of California Press, 1976).

—— (ed), *Freedom and Responsibility* (Stanford: Stanford University Press, 1961).

Morse, Stephen, 'Culpability and control', University of Pennsylvania Law Review 142 (1994), 1587–660.

—— 'Reason, results, and criminal responsibility', Illinois Law Review (2004), 363–444.

Mumford, Stephen, *Laws in Nature* (London: Routledge, 2004).

—— 'Passing powers around', The Monist 91(4) (2008).

Nagel, Thomas, 'Moral luck', Proceedings of the Aristotelean Society, Supp 50 (1976), 137–52, reprinted in his *Mortal Questions* (Cambridge: Cambridge University Press, 1979).

—— *The View from Nowhere* (New York: Oxford University Press, 1986).

—— 'War and massacre', in S Scheffler (ed), *Consequentialism and Its Critics* (New York: Oxford University Press, 1988).

Nanay, Bruce 'The properties of singular causation', *The Monist* 91(4) 2008.

Nelkin, Dana, 'Moral luck', *Stanford Encyclopedia of Philosophy* (2004) available at <http://www.plato.stanford.edu>.

Nozick, Robert, *Anarchy, State and Utopia* (New York: Basic Books, 1974).

Ogden, CK, *Bentham's Theory of Fictions* (Paterson: Littlefield, Adams and Co, 1959).

Owen, David, 'Duty rules', Vanderbilt Law Review 54 (2001), 767–86.

Packer, Herbert, *The Limits of the Criminal Sanction* (Stanford: Stanford University Press, 1968).

Paul, LA, 'Keeping track of the time: Emending the counterfactual analysis of causation', Analysis 58 (1998), 191–8.

—— 'Aspect causation', Journal of Philosophy 97 (2000), 223–34.

Perkins, Rollin, 'Parties to crime', University of Pennsylvania Law Review 89 (1941), 581–623.

Perkins, Roland and Boyce, R, *Criminal Law* (3rd edn, Mineola: Foundation Press, 1982).

Perry, Stephen R, 'Risk, harm, and responsibility', in David Owen (ed), *Philosophical Foundations of Tort* (Oxford: Oxford University Press, 1995).

—— 'Harm, history, and counterfacutals', San Diego Law Review 40 (2003), 1283–314.

Peters, Richard, *The Concept of Motivation* (London: Routledge and Kegan Paul, 1958).

Plato, *The Laws* IX, s 876, in *The Dialogues of Plato*, tr B Jowett, Vol 4, 445 (1953).

Pollock, Frederick, *A Treatise on the Law of Torts in Obligations Arising From Civil Wrongs in the Common Law* (St Louis: FH Thomas Law Book Co, 1894).

—— *Handbook of the Law of Torts* (11th edn, London: Stevens, 1920).

—— 'Liability for consequences', Law Quarterly Review 38 (1922), 165–7.

—— *Torts* (6th edn, New York: Banks Law Publishing Co, 1901).

Pomerantz, H, and Breslin, S, 'Judicial humour: Construction of a statute', Criminal Law Quarterly 8 (1966), 137–9.

Posner, Richard A, 'Statutory interpretation: In the classroom and in the courtroom', University of Chicago Law Review 50 (1983), 800–22.

Prosser, William, 'Palsgraf revisited', Michigan Law Review 52 (1953), 1–32.

—— *Handbook of the Law of Torts* (3rd edn, St Paul: West Pub Co, 1964).

—— 'Transferred intent', Texas Law Review 45 (1967), 650–62.

—— *Handbook of the Law of Torts* (4th edn, St Paul: West Pub Co, 1971).

Pundik, Amit, 'Can one deny both causation by omission and causal pluralism? The case of legal causation', in Russo and Williamson (eds), *Causation and Probability in the Sciences* (London: College Publications, 2007).

Putnam, Hilary, *Mind, Language, and Reality* (Cambridge: Cambridge University Press, 1975).

—— *Realism and Reason* (Cambridge: Cambridge University Press, 1983).

—— 'The meaning of "meaning"', in his *Mind, Language and Reality II* (Cambridge: Cambridge University Press, 1985).

—— *The Many Faces of Realism* (La Salle: Open Court, 1987).

—— *Renewing Philosophy* (Cambridge, Mass: Harvard University Press, 1992).

—— *Representation and Reality* (Cambridge, Mass: MIT Press, 1989).

Quine, WV, *Word and Object* (Cambridge, Mass: MIT Press, 1960).

—— *Theories and Things* (New York: Columbia University Press, 1981).

—— 'Events and reification', in E LePore and McLaughlin (eds), *Actions and Events: Perspectives on the philosophy of Donald Davidson* (Oxford: Basil Blackwell, 1985).

—— *Methods of Logic* (4th edn, Cambridge, Mass: Harvard University Press, 1982).

Quinn, Warren, 'Action, intentions, and consequences: The doctrine of double effect', Philosophy and Public Affairs 18 (1989), 334–51.

Rabin, Robert L, 'The historical development of the fault principle: A reinterpretation', Georgia Law Review 15 (1981), 925–62.

—— 'The duty concept in negligence law: A comment', Vanderbilt Law Review 54 (2001), 787–802.

Rachels, James, 'Active and passive euthanasia', New England Journal of Medicine 292 (1975), 78–80.

—— 'Killing and starving to death', Philosophy 54 (1979), 159–71.

Ramsey, Frank, *The Foundations of Mathematics* (London: Routledge and Kegan Paul, 1931).

Rawls, John, *A Theory of Justice* (Cambridge, Mass: Harvard University Press, 1971).

Report of the President's Commission, 'Defining Death: The Medical, Legal, and Ethical Issues in the Determination of Death', excerpted in T Beauchamp and L Walters (eds), *Contemporary Issues in Bioethics* (2nd edn, St Paul: West Pub Co, 1982), 301–5.

Rescher, Nicholas, 'Belief-contravening suppositions', The Philosophical Review 70 (1961), 193–4.

Rizzo, Mario J and Arnold, Frank S, 'Causal apportionment in the law of torts: An economic approach', Columbia Law Review 80 (1980), 1399–429.

—— 'Casual apportionment: Reply to the critics', Journal of Legal Studies 20 (1986), 219–26.

Robinson, Paul, 'Imputed criminal liability', Yale Law Journal 93 (1984), 609–76.

Rota, Michael, 'An anti-reductionist account of singular causation', The Monist 91(4) (2008).

Royal Commission on Capital Punishment, *Royal Commission on Capital Punishment 1949–1953 Report* (London: Her Majesty's Stationary Office, 1953).

Russell, Bertrand, *Human Knowledge* (New York: Simon and Schuster, 1948).

—— 'On the notion of cause', in J Slater (ed), *The Collected Papers of Bertrand Russell: Vol 6, Logical and philosophical papers 1909–1913* (London: Routledge, 1992).

Ryle, Gilbert, *The Concept of Mind* (London: Hutchins, 1949).

Ryu, Paul K, 'Causation in criminal law', University of Pennsylvania Law Review 106 (1958), 773–805.

Salmon, Wesley, *Logic* (2nd edn, Englewood Cliffs: Prentice-Hall, 1973).

—— 'Probabilistic causality', Pacific Philosophical Quarterly 61 (1980), 50–74.

—— *Scientific Explanation and the Causal Structure of the World* (Princeton: Princeton University Press, 1984).

—— *Causality and Explanation* (Oxford: Oxford University Press, 1998).

Sanford, David, 'Causal relata', in E LePore and B McLaughlin (ed), *Actions and Events* (Oxford: Basil Blackwell, 1985).

—— *If P, then Q: Conditions and the foundations of reasoning* (London: Routledge, 1989).

Sayre, Francis B, 'Criminal responsibility for acts of another', Harvard Law Review 43 (1930), 689–723.

Schaffer, Jonathan, 'Trumping preemption', Journal of Philosophy 97 (2000), 165–81.

—— 'The Metaphysics of causation', *Stanford Encyclopedia of Philosophy* (2004) available at <http://www.plato. Stanford.edu>.

—— 'The metaphysics of causation', *Stanford Encyclopedia of Philosophy* (2007) available at <http://www.plato.stanford.edu>.

—— 'Causes need not be physically connected to their effects: The case for negative causation', in Christopher Hitchcock (ed), *Contemporary Debates in Philosophy of Science* (Oxford: Blackwell, 2004).

Scheffler, Sam, *The Rejection of Consequentialism: A philosophical investigation of the considerations underlying rival moral conceptions* (Oxford: Oxford University Press, 1982).

—— (ed), *Consequentialism and Its Critics* (Oxford: Oxford University Press, 1988).

Schlick, Moritz, 'Causality in everyday life and in recent science', University of California Publications in Philosophy 15 (1932), 99–125.

Schulhofer, Stephen, 'Harm and punishment: A critique of the emphasis on results of conduct in the criminal law', University of Pennsylvania Law Review 122 (1974), 1497–607.

Scriven, Michael, 'Defects of the necessary condition analysis of causation', in W Dray (ed), *Philosophical Analysis and History* (New York: Harper and Row, 1966), reprinted in part in Ernest Sosa and Michael Tooley (eds), *Causation* (Oxford: Oxford University Press, 1993).

Seavey, Warren, 'Mr Justice Cardozo and the law of torts', Harvard Law Review 52 (1939), 372–407.

—— 'Principles of tort', Harvard Law Review 56 (1943), 72–98.

—— 'Negligence, subjective or objective', Harvard Law Review 41 (1927), 1–28.

Sellars, Wilfrid, 'Counterfactuals, dispositionals, and the causal modalities', in Herbert Feigl et al, eds) *Minnesota Studies in the Philosophy of Science* 2 (Minneapolis: University of Minnesota Press, 1958), reprinted in Sosa, Ernest (ed), *Causation and Conditionals* (Oxford: Oxford University Press, 1975).

Seward, Helen, *The Ontology of Mind* (Oxford: Oxford University Press, 1997).

Shavell, Steven, 'An analysis of causation and the scope of liability in the law of torts', Journal of Legal Studies 9 (1980), 463–503.

—— 'Strict liability versus negligence', Journal of Legal Studies 9 (1980), 1–25.

Simons, Kenneth, 'The hand formula in the draft restatement (third) of torts: Encompassing fairness as well as efficiency values', Vanderbilt Law Review 54 (2001), 901–40.

Simpson, Joe, *Touching the Void* (New York: Harper Collins, 1988).

Skyms, Brian, 'EPR: Lessons for metaphysics', in P French, T Uehling Jr, and H Wettstein (eds), *Midwest Studies in Philosophy Vol IX* (Minneapolis: University of Minnesota Press, 1984).

Smith, Adam, *The Theory of Moral Sentiments* (London: Printed for A Millar, and A Kincaid and J Bell, 1759).

Smith, Jeremiah, 'Legal cause in actions in tort', Harvard Law Review 25 (1911–12), 103–28, 223–52, 303–27.

Smith, KJM, *A Modern Treatise on the Law of Criminal Complicity* (Oxford: Clarendon Press, 1997).

Sosa, Ernest (ed), *Causation and Conditionals* (Oxford: Oxford University Press, 1975).

—— 'Varieties of causation', Grazer Philosophische Studien (1980) 99–100, reprinted in Ernest Sosa and Michael Tooley, *Causation* (Oxford: Oxford University Press, 1993).

Sosa, Ernest and Tooley, Michael (eds), *Causation* (Oxford: Oxford University Press, 1993).

Spencer, 'Trying to help another person commit a crime', in P Smith (ed), *Criminal Law: Essays in honour of JC Smith* (1987).

Stalnaker, Robert, 'A theory of conditionals', in N Rescher (ed), *Studies in Logical Theory* (Oxford: Blackwell, 1968), reprinted in Ernest Sosa (ed), *Causation and Conditionals* (Oxford: Oxford University Press, 1975).

Stapleton, Jane, 'Perspectives on causation', in Jeremy Horder (ed), *Oxford Essays in Jurisprudence, Fourth series* (Oxford: Oxford University Press, 2000).

—— 'Legal cause: Cause-in-fact and the scope of liability for consequences', Vanderbilt Law Review 54 (2001), 941–1009.

—— 'Choosing what we mean by "causation" in the law', Missouri Law Review 73 (2008), 433–80, reprinted in condensed form in Helen Beebee, Peter Menzies, and Chris Hitchcock (eds), *Oxford Handbook in Causation* (Oxford: Oxford University Press, 2008).

Stevenson, William, *A Man Called Intrepid: The secret war* (New York: The Lyons Press, 1976).

Stone, Alan, 'Legal education on the couch', Harvard Law Review 85 (1971), 392–411

Strawson, Galen, *The Secret Connexion: Causation, realism, and David Hume* (Oxford: Clarendon Press, 1989).

Strawson, PF, *Individuals* (London: Methuen, 1959).

Stroud, Barry, *Hume* (London: Routledge and Kegan Paul, 1977).

Suppes, Patrick, *A Probabilistic Theory of Causality* (Amsterdam: North Holland, 1970).

Sussman, David, 'What is wrong with torture?', Philosophy and Public Affairs 33 (2005), 1–33.

Taylor, Richard, *Action and Purpose* (Englewood Cliffs: Prentice Hall, 1965).

Terry, Henry T, 'Proximate consequences in the law of torts', Harvard Law Review 28 (1914), 10–33.

—— 'Negligence', Harvard Law Review 29 (1915), 40–54.

Thalberg, Irving, Jr, *Perception, Emotion and Action: A component approach* (New Haven: Yale University Press, 1977).

Thode, Wayne, 'A reply to the defense of the use of the hypothetical case to resolve the causation issue', Texas Law Review 47 (1969), 1344–58.

Thomson, Judith, 'Self-defense and rights', Lindley Lecture, University of Kansas, 1976.

—— 'A defense of abortion', Philosophy and Public Affairs 1 (1971), 47–66.

—— *Acts and Other Events* (Ithaca: Cornell University Press, 1977).

—— 'Causation and rights: Some preliminaries', Chicago-Kent Law Review 63 (1987), 471–96.

—— 'The Trolley problem', Yale Law Journal 94 (1985), 1395–415.

Tooley, Michael, *Causation: A realist approach* (Oxford: Oxford University Press, 1987).

—— 'The nature of causation: A singularist account', in David Copp (ed), *Causation Philosophers: Celebrating twenty years of the CJP,* Canadian Journal of Philosophy Supp 16 (1990).

Turley, Jonathan, 'Alleged torture in terror war imperils US standards of humanity', Los Angeles Times, 6 March 2003, Part 2, 17.

Urmson, JO, 'Some questions concerning validity', in Antony Flew (ed), *Essays in Conceptual Analysis* (New York: St Martin's Press, 1956).

Vendler, Zeno, 'Facts and events', in his *Linguistics in Philosophy* (Ithaca: Cornell University Press, 1967).

—— 'Agency and causation', Midwest Studies in Philosophy 9 (1984), 371–84.

Von Wright, GH, *Logical Studies* (London: Routledge and Kegan Paul, 1957).

Watling, John, 'Are causes events or facts?', Proceedings of the Australian Society 80 (1980), 168–70.

Weinrib, Ernest, 'The passing of Palsgraf', Vanderbilt Law Review 54 (2001), 807–11.

Westen, Peter, 'Why criminal harms matter: Plato's abiding insight in the *Laws*', Criminal Law and Philosophy 1 (2007), 307–26.

Williams, Bernard, 'A critique of utilitarianism', in JJC Smart and B Williams, *Utilitarianism: For and against* (Cambridge: Cambridge University Press, 1973).

—— 'Moral luck', Proceedings of the Aristotolean Society (Supp) 50 (1976), reprinted in his *Moral Luck* (Cambridge: Cambridge University Press, 1981).

Williams, Donald, 'On the elements of being: I', Review of Metaphysics 7 (1953), 3–18.

—— 'On the elements of being: II', Review of Metaphysics 7 (1953), 71–92.

—— 'Universals and existents', Australian Journal of Philosophy 64 (1986), 1–14.

Williams, Glanville, 'Causation in the law,' Cambridge Law Journal (1961), 62–85.

—— *Criminal Law: The general part* (2nd edn, London: Stephens and Sons, 1961).

—— 'The risk principle', Law Quarterly Review 77 (1961), 179–212.

—— 'The problem of reckless attempts', Criminal Law Review (1983), 365–75.

—— 'Finis for novus actus?', Cambridge Law Journal 48 (1989), 391–416.

Wilson, George, *The Intentionality of Human Action* (2nd edn Stanford: Stanford University Press, 1989).

Wilson, Jessica, 'Resemblance-based resources for reductive singularism', The Monist 91(4) (2008).

Bibliography

Wilson, Neil, *The Concept of Language* (Toronto: University of Toronto Press, 1959).

Winch, Peter, *The Idea of a Social Science* (London: Routledge and Kegan Paul, 1958).

Wittgenstein, Ludwig, *Philosophical Investigations*, tr GEM Anscombe (3rd edn, Oxford: Blackwell, 1958).

Wolf, Susan, 'The moral of moral luck', Philosophical Exchange 31 (2000), 5–19.

Woods, Michael, *Conditionals* (Oxford: Clarendon Press, 1997).

Woodward, Bob, and Bernstein, Carl, *The Brethren* (New York: Simon and Schuster, 1979).

Woodward, James, 'A theory of singular causal explanation', Erkenntnis 212 (1984), 231–62.

Wright, Richard W, 'Causation in tort law', California Law Review 73 (1985), 1735–828.

—— 'Actual causation vs. Probabilistic linkage: The bane of economic analysis', Journal of Legal Studies 14 (1985), 435–56.

—— 'The efficiency theory of causation and responsibility: Unscientific formalism and false semantics', Chicago-Kent Law Review 63 (1987), 553–78.

—— 'Causation, responsibility, risk, probability, naked statistics, and proof: Pruning the bramble bush by clarifying the concepts', Iowa Law Review 73 (1988), 1001–77.

—— 'Once more into the bramble bush: Duty, causal contribution, and the extent of legal responsibility', Vanderbilt Law Review 54 (2001), 1071–132.

Yaeger, Daniel 'Helping, doing, and the grammar of complicity', Criminal Justice Ethics 15 (1996), 25–35.

Yagisawa, T, 'Counterfactual analysis of causation and Kim's examples', Analysis 39 (1979), 100–5.

Zimmerman, Michael, 'Taking moral luck seriously', Journal of Philosophy 99 (2002), 553–76.

Zipursky, Benjamin, 'Rights, wrongs, and recourse in the law of torts', Vanderbilt Law Review 51 (1998), 553–76.

Index